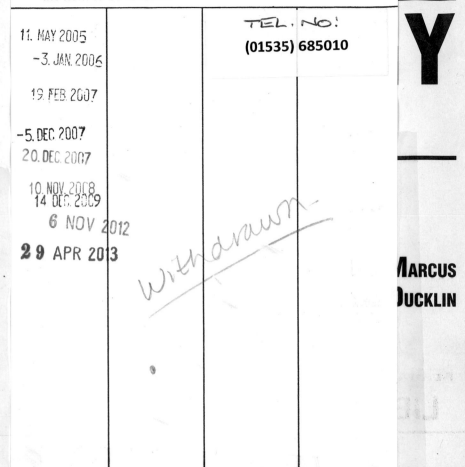

MARCUS

DUCKLIN

Dedication

To the two Lindas, without whom nothing would be possible, and to all the staff at the Transplant Centre, Churchill Hospital, Oxford

To pupils, students and colleagues, who have made sociology so worthwhile.

Martin Marcus, 1997

Success Studybooks

Advertising and Promotion
Book-keeping and Accounts
Business Calculations
Chemistry
Commerce
Commerce: West African Edition
Communication
Electronics
European History 1815–1941
Information Processing
Insurance
Investment

Law
Managing People
Marketing
Politics
Principles of Accounting
Principles of Accounting: Answer Book
Psychology
Sociology
Statistics
Twentieth Century World Affairs
World History since 1945

© Martin Marcus and Alan Ducklin 1998

First published in 1998
by John Murray (Publishers) Ltd
50 Albemarle Street
London W1X 4BD

Layouts by Eric Drewery
Artwork by Phil Ford and Linden Artists

Typeset in 10.5/12pt Sabon by Wearset, Boldon, Tyne and Wear.
Printed in Great Britain by the Bath Press, Avon

A CIP catalogue record for this book is available from the British Library

ISBN 0 7195 5370 9

Contents

Acknowledgements

The authors would like to thank the following people for their assistance:
Janet Pickett, Christine Suff and Lesley Spencer, who typed the majority of the text.
Peter Joslin, Head of Sociology, The Emmbrook School, Wokingham, Berkshire.
David Gaskin, who provided valuable advice on the use of the computer and the Internet.

While every effort has been made to trace copyright holders, the publishers apologise for any inadvertent omissions. The publishers would like to thank the following sources for permission to reproduce material.

Photographs
p.68 Peter Joslin; p.70 E.Gottman/AKG London; p.111 © Peter Correz/Tony Stone Worldwide; p.116 Peter Joslin; p.117 Colin McPherson/Sygma; p.133 John Townson/Creation; p.156 © Peter Correz/Tony Stone Worldwide; p.162 Margaret Wilson; p.173 *left* © Hulton Getty, *right* Zoom/Rex Features Ltd; p.185 Peter Joslin; p.213 reproduced with permission of Punch Ltd; p.246 Raissa Page/Format Photographers; p.275 The Herald; p.293 Sporting Pictures (UK) Ltd; p.304 *top left* John Townson/Creation, *rest* © Wales News & Pictures; p.329 Rex Features Ltd; p.337 Ulrike Preuss/Format Photographers; p.352 Pam Isherwood/Format Photographers; p.384 Brenda Prince/Format Photographers; p.415 *left* Peter Joslin, *right* The Independent/Glynn Griffiths; p.423 Frank Field; p.442 Rex Features Ltd; p.459 Rex Features Ltd; p.599 Francesco Guidicini/Rex Features Ltd; p.620 Talya Baker; p.643 Peter Joslin.

Written material
Association of Chief Police Officers 541
The Big Issue in Scotland Ltd 275
Cambridge University Press 194
Causeway Press Ltd 38, 241, 325, 333, 434
Christian Research/Paternoster Publishing 641
Daily Mail 140, 558
Daily Telegraph 149, 192 (© Tim King), 201, 409, 626, 649
Martyn Denscombe/Sociology Update 96, 155, 208, 286, 308
Evening Standard 656
Fourth Estate Ltd (© 1997 Guardian News Service and Steve Peak) 287
Glasgow University Media Group 294, 295
Guardian 104, 146, 153, 181, 182, 202, 224, 232, 242, 243, 246, 248, 254, 275, 278, 304, 322, 329, 358, 381, 384, 407, 531, 545, 548, 587, 658

Crown copyright, reproduced with the permission of the Controller of Her Majesty's Stationery Office 83, 166, 353, 355, 386, 532, 534, 536, 537
Independent 173, 203, 414–15, 599–600
Kelvin Mackenzie 297
Macmillan Ltd 41–5, 98, 303, 526, 607
Mail on Sunday 117
Thomas Nelson & Sons Ltd 96
New Internationalist 72, 257, 489
New Statesman & Society 55, 63, 542–3
Observer 101–2
Office for National Statistics, Crown Copyright 1998 79, 93, 113, 114, 115, 140, 142, 143, 145, 148, 167, 172, 180, 197, 207, 215, 216, 219, 220, 223, 237, 238, 239, 240, 244, 245, 251, 255, 274, 277, 282, 283, 284, 311, 312, 313, 314, 361, 370, 371, 416, 417, 418, 419, 514, 535, 538, 539, 542, 544, 547, 549, 553, 557, 560, 640, 643
Penguin Ltd 38, 399
Philip Allan Publishing Ltd 37, 52, 104, 155, 271, 276, 421, 648
Polity Press 184, 277, 453, 454, 517, 523
Routledge 285, 305, 323–4, 354, 369, 495, 654
Sage Publications, Inc. 302, 306
The Scotsman 221
The Sunday Times STYLE 88
The Times 103, 165, 423, 529, 642, 644
The Times Educational Supplement 160, 196, 197, 204, 207 (© Gaby Weiner)
Dr Paul R. Trowler 433
Weidenfeld & Nicolson 605

Tributes to Martin Marcus

To Martin

Soon after completing work on this book Martin Marcus, my co-author, sadly died. As co-writer and co-examiner at GCSE and A level with Martin for over ten years, I find the loss of someone with so much to offer, tragic. His friendship, support, mischievous humour and commitment to a high quality (and quantity!) of work despite crippling medical conditions, stand testimony to his fortitude. This book offers a fitting tribute to Martin's skills as an educator, as a teacher and as a committed sociologist. It will also serve as a personal reminder to all who knew him. He will be sorely missed.

Alan Ducklin, January 1998

The publishers would like to pay tribute to Martin Marcus, the leading author of this text, who very sadly died before he could see it published. He had continued – and completed – work on this project, as in several other areas, with unwavering enthusiasm and a courageous disregard for his failing health. His personal contribution to the field of sociology extends well beyond that represented in this book – he will be missed by many.

Studying sociology

Success in Sociology is an up-to-date and lively advanced level text on sociological ideas and debates. It does not assume any prior knowledge of the subject, only that you are interested in sociological issues and ideas. The authors have included many recent examples from familiar, current sources, including the media and everyday life, to give relevance to the theory and history of sociological thought. It is hoped that this will make *Success in Sociology* both interesting and easy to use, while also covering all the key syllabus areas, some of which represent new areas of study for Sociology at advanced level.

How to use this book

Success in Sociology is divided into units to provide a manageable and, it is hoped, logical coverage of all the topic areas of advanced courses in sociology. Each unit seeks to offer comprehensive coverage of its area. It is also intended that the breakdown of material will work equally well for those following a 'terminal' exam route and those taking a modular route to A level and similar courses.

However, there is a danger in seeing sociology as a discipline divided into separate units: major issues such as stratification cut right across all areas of study within sociology. Questions and assignments you will tackle during your course or in your exam will require responses which touch on more than one topic area or unit of this book. For example, subcultural youth groups may be linked to deviance and control or to mass media and popular culture. You should therefore be prepared to make use of the units in a flexible manner, and be aware of the need to apply your knowledge and understanding appropriately to the issues raised. Many of the *Think about it* suggestions, which appear in all units, will remind and prompt you to make links between related areas of sociology

References to other studies and sources

It is not possible or practical to include in this book detailed accounts of all the sociological studies and sources relevant to the themes of the units. Key studies are covered in some detail, and mention is made of many others. Full reference details are given in the selected reading lists at the end of each unit and in the bibliography at the end of the book. This will enable you to find and investigate those studies which relate to the area you want to pursue, perhaps for coursework purposes.

Study skills, coursework and exams

Pages 7–17 provide practical help on tackling learning, revision, coursework and exams. There are also opportunities to practise typical exam questions, with examples and advice given, at the end of each unit. Coursework suggestions for each unit theme are also provided at the end of each unit.

Success in Sociology *and your syllabus*

Success in Sociology is intended for students on a wide range of advanced courses in sociology, particularly at GCE A and AS levels, and also for Access to Higher Education. It is also relevant for students of GNVQ Health and Social Care at Intermediate or Advanced level (Applied A level), and in Scotland for the Higher Still Sociology course and SCOTVEC 'People in Society' modular programmes. Details on how the book covers the different course requirements are given on pages 3–6.

The authors' motivation for writing this book has been based on their commitment to sociology as a discipline, and their wish to provide assistance to teachers and students at a time when considerable developments have been taking place in terms of the delivery and assessment of sociology. In particular, changes have been introduced by the public exam boards, such as the development of the Interboard A/AS level syllabus and extensive revisions to all advanced syllabuses including the introduction of modular schemes (dividing subjects into examinable chunks) throughout the United Kingdom.

These developments were followed by complete revisions of all advanced syllabuses, which altered the relationship between AS level and the 'full' A level.

This book aims to prepare you for the variety of exam requirements, including stimulus response, data response and structured (or subsectioned) questions as well as more traditional essay writing; and to help you become more involved in your own learning processes via other forms of assessment such as extended essays, personal studies and projects. Accompanying such innovations have been the ongoing national curriculum changes, and the development of the vocational education route via GNVQs.

Make sure you have a copy of, or access to, the syllabus or specifications for the course you are following. You should study this carefully to ensure you are aware of the specific skills and knowledge which you will be required to show as evidence for assessment purposes.

The following tables show how the units of *Success in Sociology* cover the topic/module areas in the A/AS level syllabuses. These tables are followed by information on Access courses and the relevance of this book for GNVQ courses.

Using this book for AS
or A level

AEB topic area/module	*Success in Sociology* unit	
Theory and methods (AS/A)	Unit 1	What do sociologists do? An explanation of theory and method in sociology
Family (AS/A)	Unit 3	Households and families
Education (AS/A)	Unit 4	Education and training
Work, organisations and leisure (AS/A)	Unit 5	Work and organisations; non-work and leisure
Stratification and differentiation (AS/A)	Unit 2	Different groups in society: social differentiation, power and stratification
Culture and identity (AS/A)	Unit 6 (Unit 4 (Unit 9	Mass media and popular culture Education and training) Community, nation and development)
Crime and deviance (A)	Unit 10	Crime, deviance and control
Health (A)	Unit 7	The sociology of health and medicine
World sociology (A)	Unit 9	Community, nation and development
Wealth, poverty and welfare (A)	Unit 8 (Unit 2	Poverty and welfare Different groups in society: social differentiation, power and stratification)
Mass media (A)	Unit 6	Mass media and popular culture
Sociology of locality (A)	Unit 9 Unit 2	Community, nation and development Different groups in society: social differentiation, power and stratification
Power and politics (A)	Unit 11	Power and politics
Religion (A)	Unit 12	Religion and ideology

Interboard topic area/module	Success in Sociology unit	
The sociological approach – theory and method (AS/A)	Unit 1	What do sociologists do? An explanation of theory and method in sociology
Social differentiation and stratification (AS/A)	Unit 2	Different groups in society: social differentiation, power and stratification
Households and family forms (AS/A)	Unit 3	Households and families
Mass media and popular culture (AS/A)	Unit 6	Mass media and popular culture
Community and nation (AS/A)	Unit 9	Community, nation and development
Health (AS/A)	Unit 7	The sociology of health and medicine
Welfare and social policy (AS/A)	Unit 8	Poverty and welfare
Education and training (A)	Unit 4	Education and training
Religion and ideology (A)	Unit 12	Religion and ideology
Work and economic life (A)	Unit 5	Work and organisations; non-work and leisure
Power and politics (A)	Unit 11	Power and politics
Deviance and control (A)	Unit 10	Crime, deviance and control

NEAB module	Success in Sociology unit	
Theoretical perspectives in sociology (AS/A)	Unit 1	What do sociologists do? An explanation of theory and method in sociology
Social differentiation, power and stratification (AS/A)	Unit 2	Different groups in society: social differentiation, power and stratification
	Unit 11	Power and politics
Methods of sociological enquiry (AS/A)	Unit 1	What do sociologists do? An explanation of theory and method in sociology
Social change (A)	Unit 2	Different groups in society: social differentiation, power and stratification
	Unit 5	Work and organisations; non-work and leisure
	Unit 8	Poverty and welfare
	Unit 6	Mass media and popular culture
	Unit 9	Community, nation and development
	Unit 11	Power and politics
Social control and deviance (A)	Unit 10	Crime, deviance and control
Debates and issues in sociology (A)	Unit 1	What do sociologists do? An explanation of theory and method in sociology
	Unit 3	Households and families
	Unit 4	Education and training

Access to Higher Education

Access courses have flourished as an alternative route to a degree or a profession for mature students over the age of 21. There are no official qualification requirements for entry to these courses. They have become increasingly available at local adult and further education colleges, and also via more flexible open and distance learning schemes. The most common schemes operate as daytime (or evening) one-year full-time (or two-year part-time) programmes. Access programmes are usually modular: subjects may be chosen from an increasingly wide range of options. Sociology has become a popular choice among Access students; a typical syllabus summary is provided below.

Sociology Access to Higher Education: syllabus summary

Aim
The aim is to enable students to understand and apply a range of sociological approaches through the study of selected topics.

Objectives
- to use evidence critically;
- to interpret and evaluate a range of information and evidence;
- to recognise that there are different ways of studying and interpreting social phenomena;
- to appreciate the difficulties involved in conducting social research;
- to select and use relevant examples to support arguments.

Content
Knowledge
Students will study:

- different sociological perspectives and methods;
- two compulsory topics: 'Households and family forms' and 'Education and training';
- two option topics, e.g. 'Deviance and control' and 'Mass media'.

Skills
Students will practise and achieve competence in:

- note-taking and note-making;
- essay writing;
- independent use of learning resources;
- research methods;
- evaluation of material;
- revision and exam techniques.

Assignments
Students are required to submit the following for assessment:

- two essays of approximately 1000 words (weighting 12.5% each);
- one extended essay of approximately 2000 words (weighting 25%);
- one data response/stimulus question (weighting 10%);
- a mini project or case study of approximately 2500 words (weighting 40%).

Exam
At the end of the course there is a 3-hour exam, consisting of two papers:

- Paper 1 ($1\frac{1}{2}$ hours) – seen essay paper on the option topics and theory and methods (weighting 50%);
- Paper 2 ($1\frac{1}{2}$ hours) – unseen data response/short answer paper on the compulsory topics (weighting 50%).

GNVQ Health and Social Care

Success in Sociology will be a useful source of information and ideas for students following intermediate or advanced Health and Social Care courses. Among the mandatory units, it will be particularly relevant for the following.

<u>Intermediate units</u>
2. Influences on health and well-being
3. Health and social care services

<u>Advanced units</u>
1. Equal opportunities and individuals' rights
4. Psycho-social aspects of health and social well-being
5. Structure and development of health and social care services
8. Research perspectives in health and social care

■ STUDY SKILLS

Note-taking

Note-taking is an extremely important skill for advanced level students, and one that will be useful for life, but it needs to be undertaken efficiently. The first point to remember is that note-taking is not the same as essay writing! Long, detailed notes are rarely useful for revision purposes and are virtually impossible to remember. When you take notes from a book, article, class talk or lecture, you are trying to make an *accurate summary* of what you are reading or hearing. You should tailor your notes for an immediate task (for example writing an essay) and also to be of use to you later (perhaps for revision).

To help you develop the skill of note-taking, a list of DOs and DON'Ts is provided below.

Do	Don't
Aim to sort out the **main points** of a lecture or a written source. **Ignore what is irrelevant.**	Don't attempt to write virtually everything down without thinking about it and its possible future use.
Listen or look for **key words**, **concepts** and **short phrases** which can be efficiently and swiftly recorded.	Don't make notes in sentences or as slightly reduced versions of the original, e.g. copying long phrases.
Adopt a system of **abbreviations** (see below).	Don't write long words in full, unless these are new key words or concepts.
Leave space between points (and across the notepad for future additions, references, etc.).	Don't clutter the notepad or jumble your notes, making them difficult to understand (or add to later).
Use **numbers**, **letters**, etc. during or after note-taking to sequence and provide a structure to your notes. Develop a logical, simple system for identifying key items, for example underline, CAPITALS, circle, box.	Don't rely on memory or a rambling set of notes.
Make a record of all your **sources**.	Don't mix up different sources without identifying them.

You may find the following list of common abbreviations useful for note-taking.

∴	therefore
∵	because
...	implies, it follows from this
>	greater than
<	less than
=	equals, is the same as
≠	does not equal, is not the same as
"	ditto
@	at
e.g.	for example

c.f.   compare/cross reference
N.B.   note
i.e.   that is
wd   would
cd   could
shd   should
b4   before
c.   about, approximately
v   versus
+   also, in addition to
→   leads to, led to, causes
←   is caused by, depends on

Always keep your notes carefully – perhaps file them with your class notes. Organise your file well, using file-dividers. Reorganise it regularly.

Essay writing

Answer the question!

Relevance is vital. No matter how interesting or well-written your essay is, you will not be given credit unless you answer the specific question that has been set. Make sure you understand what the question is asking and what you are required to do before you begin to write.

Provide a clear structure

Your essay should follow a carefully thought-out plan. The points made should be logical, you should make clear the relations between issues and you should state directly the connection between what you are writing and the question set.

Essay plan		
Remember: you may wish to use the last sentence to link into the next paragraph. Paragraphs should not be too long; you may get lost in your argument and the reader will find it difficult to follow what you are writing.	INTRODUCTION (1–2 paragraphs)	• Interpret the question. • Introduce key words/concepts, and main issues, debates. • Indicate what is to follow, i.e. 'set the scene' for the essay.
	MAIN BODY (5–6 paragraphs)	• Deal with one major point per paragraph. • Give supportive evidence but not a 'shopping list'. • Consider criticism of above point(s), mention opposing point(s).
	CONCLUSION (1 paragraph)	• Weigh up the evidence based on points provided. • Show how appropriately you have covered the question. • Draw conclusion(s) even if these are tentative. Remember: try not to end your essay abruptly as this may give the impression that you have run out of ideas. A good conclusion should refer back to the introduction.

Watch out for **legibility**, **grammar**, **punctuation** and **spelling**. If possible, allow time to check back through your work for these points.

In exams, it makes sense to write on alternate lines (there will always be plenty of paper) so that you can go back and make additions or corrections clearly if you need to later. Try to develop this habit from the beginning of your course.

Data response and structured questions

Data response questions

These questions contain an item or items of data which may be written, pictorial, numerical or diagrammatic and may be from a sociological or a non-sociological source. Questions based on the data are divided into subquestions or subsections; most require you to refer to the data in your answer. Mark allocations for the various parts are shown. These are important as they give you an indication of the length of time and depth required for the responses. Data response questions are sometimes referred to as stimulus response questions.

Structured questions

Stimulus material, as above, may be written, pictorial, numerical or diagrammatic and may be from a sociological or a non-sociological source.

Common mistakes in answering data response and structured questions

Problem	Solution
Failing to read fully and carefully the material provided before attempting the response.	Read and study carefully the data or stimulus material given and its questions (*at least twice*).
Badly planned, disorganised responses.	Underline or make jottings on the material given on the exam paper, and make further rough notes in your exam answer booklet in preparation for your response.
Subquestions not separated and labelled.	Most questions are divided into several parts, as subquestions. Answer them as separate questions, and write clearly in the left-hand margin the letter or number of each subsection.
Ignoring the mark weightings allocated to each subquestion, and giving a lengthy response to a subquestion which carries just a few marks; paying too little consideration to the timing of each subquestion in relation to the mark weighting, and to the total time which should be allowed for the whole question.	• Pay careful attention to the marks available for each subquestion: responses for 2 marks will often require just two points (not even in sentences). • Get your timings right: for example, if the total question response time is one hour and the total possible marks are 25 marks, a question giving 2 marks requires no more than five minutes.
Failing to prepare for the paper in advance despite the availability of past papers and a range of practice books.	Remember, the aim of such questions is to examine your ability to use and evaluate the material, not merely to reproduce sociological knowledge or rehearsed answers.
Not sticking to the actual subquestion set, in each answer.	Pay careful attention to the wording of each subquestion and make sure you do what the subquestion asks, rather than what you might have preferred to have been asked.

However, some structured questions do not contain any data or stimulus materials. Questions are divided into subquestions or subsections to provide a logical sequence for the development of the response. Mark allocations for the various parts are shown and, as indicated above, are very important in answering the questions.

Sample data response question

The example below is taken from an Interboard specimen paper. It is followed by a reproduction of the guidelines supplied by the examining board to its examiners, for use when marking this question. These are included here to give you an idea of what is expected and how marks are allocated.

INTERBOARD SYLLABUS

General Certificate of Education

Advanced Level

Specimen Paper

Read the newspaper article reprinted here, and answer the questions that follow.

OXBRIDGE GENERATION STILL FINDS ROOM AT THE TOP

There may be room at the top in the 1990s for a working class, state-educated lad like John Major, but Britain's power-brokers are still drawn from the public school and Oxbridge elite, according to a new survey.

The educational and social backgrounds of the top 100 people reveals little has changed in the past 20 years, despite the **so-called meritocratic revolution of the Thatcher years** and the current Prime Minister's "classless society".

Two-thirds of the country's great and good – selected by the Economist magazine – have had a private education, and more than half went to Oxford or Cambridge universities.

In 1972, 52 per cent of the top 100 went to one or the other. That has risen to 54 per cent this year.

Twenty-five years after the feminist movement established itself, Britain's movers and shakers are overwhelmingly male – only four women make the magazine's list, up from two in 1972.

The Queen is joined this year by Commons speaker Betty Boothroyd, the head of MI5 Stella Rimington and the Director of Public Prosecutions, Barbara Mills, QC.

The survey also reveals that the days of the state school pupil made good are on the way out. More than one in five of the 1972 elite succeeded without further education, compared with one in 10 this year.

"I regard myself as a product of the old-fashioned meritocracy of the fifties and sixties, based on the idea that people who got anywhere did so on their merits."

Ian Plaistowe insisted his exclusive education at Marlborough College and Queen's College, Cambridge, had little bearing on his progress to the Economist's top 100 and presidency of the Institute of Chartered Accountants.

"It made no difference to employers where I had been educated. I believe that in the 1960s, when I was being educated, people were taken on by employers for their ability rather than for the fact that they went to a particular educational establishment – that is still the case."

The Economist's top 100 lists people in politics, business, the arts and the City. It was an arbitrary choice, the magazine admitted, but it showed that Mr Major's social revolution had not even started – sentiments echoed by Graham Stringer, Manchester city council leader and product of the city's Moston Brook High School.

"We live in a society where the ability to buy yourself an education buys you a job. That will only get worse in the future. We are not living in a meritocracy but in a society where it matters who your parents are and how much money they have. If they are rich then you can make it."

The Queen, educated by a private tutor, also made the top 100 without a public school or Oxbridge education, a Buckingham Palace spokeswoman confirmed yesterday, adding: "But we never comment on the findings of any survey."

(Source: Adapted from Lawrence Donegan, *The Guardian*, 19 December 1992.)

(a) As a sociologist, how would you sum up the main conclusions to be drawn from the survey carried out by The Economist? [4]

(b) Explain the phrase 'the so-called meritocratic revolution of the Thatcher years'. [4]

(c) What does Ian Plaistowe believe is the reason for his success in life and how do sociologists analyse this type of belief? [6]

(d) Study the comments made by Graham Stringer. Does the evidence available to sociologists tend to support or to disprove this statement? [16]

Total: 30 marks

Source: Interboard Specimen Question Papers, GCE Advanced Level, Summer 1996

Examiner's marking scheme

(a) 3–4 <u>Analyses and interprets</u> data briefly in terms of sociological concepts, e.g. degree of openness/closedness, and refers to trends/continuities with particular reference to public school/Oxbridge education, etc. Not all of these points or concepts are required for 4 marks.

1–2 <u>Identifies one or two key points</u> but these may simply be referred to with little or no reference to sociological ideas on mobility; may refer to conclusions with regard to access to top positions today as distinct from noting the continuity over two decades.

4 marks

(b) 3–4 <u>Shows understanding of the concept of meritocracy</u> as it relates to the claim that the 1980s saw a dramatic expansion in opportunities to "get on" or move up from below, <u>and</u> also indicates some scepticism about this claim, sees it perhaps in terms of ideology as well as reality. Not all points required for 4 marks.

1–2 <u>Shows some understanding of the phrase</u> but may focus on just one feature e.g. definition of meritocracy or make rather simple connections between the 1980s and the importance of merit.

4 marks

(c) 4–6 <u>Refers to the belief as meritocratic</u> and relates this to sociological notions of legitimacy or ideology or the sociology of knowledge.

1–3 <u>Identifies the belief as meritocratic</u> and makes some basic attempt to relate beliefs to social situations or backgrounds.

6 marks

(d) 3–4 <u>Shows knowledge</u> of the degree of homogeneity (sameness) or heterogeneity (differences) of background of people in the highest levels of the occupational hierarchy, particularly key elites.

1–2 <u>Shows a little knowledge</u> of the social background of people in high social positions.

plus

6–8 <u>Demonstrates an ability to evaluate Stringer's argument</u> by reference to how the data on social background are interpreted, such as the relative importance of focusing on origins or destinations and/or the difference between absolute and relative mobility and possibly to the 'left'–'right' split on this, with the issue of bias being looked at here. It is the use of the evidence rather than the mere citing of the evidence that is crucial.

3–5 <u>Some attempt to evaluate the argument</u> by reference to the material on social background, such as its diversity, the way it's interpreted or the issue of bias.

1–2 <u>Some simple attempt at evaluation</u> is made, perhaps by referring to conflicting evidence, or even just some examples that challenge Stringer's argument, or to problems with the material (bias, method of interpretation or whatever).

plus

3–4 <u>The argument will be logical and coherent</u> in the way that it links material cited (empirical, theoretical, conceptual) to the evaluation of Stringer's argument and reaches some conclusions, even though no definite agreement or disagreement with Stringer may be present.

1–2 <u>The answer will be logical in places</u> and will usually focus on the question, but may do so only generally.

16 marks
TOTAL: 30 MARKS

Source: Interboard syllabus 1996

Personal studies and coursework projects

Personal studies and coursework projects are both forms of extended written assignment offered as an alternative to some of the timed exam papers. The student selects a topic of interest relating to an area of the syllabus being studied. Coursework is the usual form of work for Access courses, while specified forms of 'evidence' (not necessarily written) are required for GNVQ.

The aim of personal studies and coursework projects is to enable you to demonstrate your own, independent ability to produce relevant written work on a topic of your choosing, though of course you will receive some guidance from your tutor, teacher or lecturer. In your assignment, you should demonstrate:

• your understanding of the relationship between sociological theory and sociological methods in your selected area of investigation;
• your knowledge and understanding of the topic selected.

You should check your own syllabus for expected length of pieces of coursework or personal studies. They range from 2500 to 5000 words. However, *quality is more important than quantity*.

You will be assessed on your ability to:

- design a sociological investigation using primary and/or secondary data;
- try out this design by assembling a limited but illustrative amount of data;
- interpret quantitative and qualitative data;
- relate your knowledge of sociological theory and methods to the topic of interest selected;
- identify facts, opinions and value judgements;
- evaluate theories, arguments and evidence;
- analyse and evaluate the design of investigations and data collection;
- evaluate the outcome of the exercise in terms of the strengths and weaknesses of the research design and materials collected.

How to choose your topic

Your choice of topic may arise from a range of sources:

- the sociology course itself;
- discussions with your tutor;
- personal interest;
- the media;
- your own reading;
- personal experience.

Identify a topic area which:

- is relevant to the syllabus;
- is of particular interest to you, and therefore motivating;
- will assist in linking theory and methods;
- will develop knowledge which may also be useful for the written exam paper(s).

Ideas for written assignments may be taken or adapted from the exercises provided at the end of each unit in this book.

Warning points to consider when finalising your choice of topic:

- Is it too large and ambitious?
- Is it legal and ethical? Legal and ethical principles have become increasingly important in sociological research, as has political correctness (avoiding sexist language, etc.);
- Might you become *too* interested, *too* involved? Will this affect the results?
- Is there any existing sociological literature for you to refer to? If not, what sources exist to ensure that the sociological dimension is covered? What methods or sources of data can be used?

Check these factors using the chart 'How to choose a topic' on page 14.

How to choose a topic

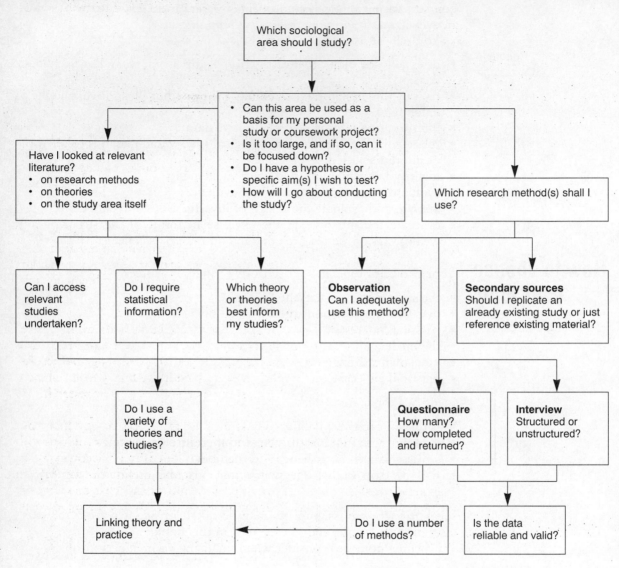

Source: Adapted from *A Level Sociology Coursework: Worked Exemplar Materials and Strategies*, A Ducklin (Richard Ball Publishing, 1993)

Presentation of your personal study or coursework

The way that you present the written assignment is very important and will affect the mark that you receive. Your assignment will need to have a clear layout and be either neatly handwritten or wordprocessed. Any charts or diagrams must be clearly set out and labelled.

Title and contents pages

Present these pages clearly and neatly. Include subtitles in each section. Use page numbers throughout.

Sections Each section needs to be separately labelled and listed on the contents page at the beginning. The sequence of sections should show a logical progression.

Rationale You need to give a clear reason or rationale for choosing your topic. This may include why you are interested in it, or why it is a central concern for sociology. You must also include your aims in researching the topic and/or the hypothesis that you have decided to test.

Context It is important to show the sociological context of your study. To do this, you need to present different sociological theories with regard to your topic area, showing evidence of your background reading (by making reference to articles or books). It is vital that you relate your own aims and research to this theoretical background.

Methodology Here you must describe the methodology that you have used and its theoretical background, including examples of other similar research that you have read about. Explain clearly the reasons for choosing particular methods and rejecting others. You should also outline problems associated with the method(s) of study.

Content In this section you must present your research and its findings. Include a copy of any questionnaire or interview schedule that you have used (this may be located in an appendix at the end). If you are presenting your results in the form of charts or graphs, then it is essential that you label each clearly and include a commentary to show its relevance to your research.

Evaluation and conclusion This should include firstly an assessment of the methodology that you have used – was it successful in meeting your aims? What problems did you face? Might another method have worked better? Secondly, you need to draw together the theoretical and methodological aspects of your personal study or coursework project and assess what conclusions you are able to make. Have your aims been met? Was your hypothesis supported by your findings, or flawed?

You will need to evaluate your assignment realistically, including its successes and its weaknesses. This is critically important and is usually reflected in higher marks.

Sources and bibliography List all the sources you have used, either section by section in the order used, or alphabetically by author in a bibliography at the end (this is more usual). State which of these two methods you are using. Do not forget to include any non-written sources, for example television programmes, computer-generated material (i.e. from the Internet), etc.

Appendices You may add as separate appendices a research diary (see below), examples of your questionnaire or interview schedule, and any information that is relevant but will not fit well into the main body of your study.

Some syllabuses require a **research diary** to be kept and submitted with the written assignment. This should include a record of all your research activities, with comments. Such a record is extremely useful and shows how the investigation developed and what you have gained from the experience.

Exam preparation and technique

Revision   Efficient exam preparation takes months and should certainly not be left until the evening (or even the fortnight!) before the exam.

- Use syllabus notes for guidance.
- Use past papers.
- Use your own coursework and notes.
- Do not rely upon certain questions being on the paper – there are no guarantees!
- Prepare more than the minimum necessary topic areas in case of difficult or unusual questions.
- Fix your material in your long-term memory, so that you can recall it days or weeks later.

Break it up   Break up your material into manageable chunks, keeping it in its proper context. For example, sex-role socialisation, unwaged domestic labour and gender identity are separate areas of study, even though each may be applied to several sociological spheres. Remember that you will have to be able to link these smaller chunks of material back together.

Reorganise   Re-reading is not memorising. Memorising is much more active – you need to seek out the meaning of what you are reading, think it through and structure it in the way you feel is most relevant. Once you have read a chapter:

- run it through your mind;
- write down the key points.

This reinforces the information and helps you to restructure it in your thoughts.

Space out learning   Start your revision several months in advance, reminding yourself regularly of the key factors. Every time you re-read material it will take less effort, and you will be storing the information in your long-term memory.

Beating boredom   The biggest obstacle to learning is boredom. Try to overcome it by asking challenging questions and disputing what the author has written. If you can find points of debate, the material will start to become more interesting. Vary the activity and the way you are trying to learn the material.

   You learn best when your mind is working on the material, transforming it in different ways. Visualisation is a very active and useful process – take notes in the form of illustrations, either diagrams, graphs or pattern notes as exemplified on the page opposite.

Know your paper

Before the exam make sure you know the number of questions to be answered, whether there are compulsory question sections and the time and length of the exam. Knowing how long to spend on each question is a crucial factor in your exam performance.

Pattern notes on
secularisation

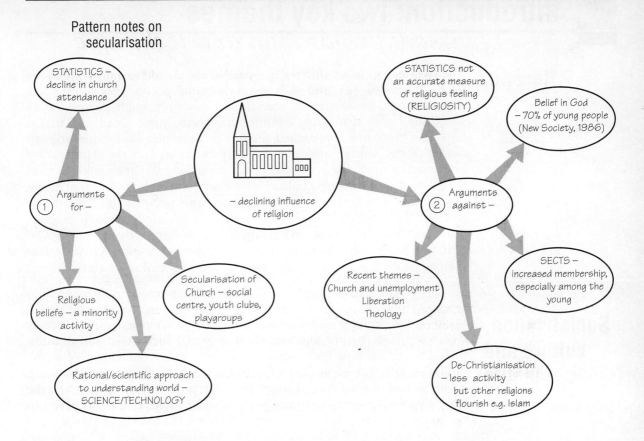

STATISTICS –
decline in church
attendance

STATISTICS not
an accurate measure
of religious feeling
(RELIGIOSITY)

Belief in God
– 70% of young people
(New Society, 1986)

1 Arguments
for –

– declining influence
of religion

2 Arguments
against –

Religious
beliefs – a minority
activity

Secularisation of
Church – social
centre, youth clubs,
playgroups

Recent themes –
Church and unemployment
Liberation
Theology

SECTS –
increased membership,
especially among the
young

Rational/scientific approach
to understanding world –
SCIENCE/TECHNOLOGY

De-Christianisation
– less activity
but other religions
flourish e.g. Islam

Exam technique

On receiving the exam paper, make sure the instructions are the same as those you expected. Check with the exam room invigilator if there are any issues that concern you.

Choice of questions

Tick (or question mark) specialist topic areas which you consider you could tackle in relation to the actual questions set. Cross through questions you cannot answer or do not fully understand. Look carefully at *all parts* of a question. Take your time in selecting questions to avoid 'missing' a potentially *good* question.

Planning your answer

- Jot down a concise list of relevant debates and issues; 'decode' the question, underlining key words, terms or phrases to be explained.
- Decide and note down what you intend to cover and in what order.
- Pay careful attention to time allocation – do not overplan and use up your writing time. If you have 45 minutes for each essay, allow about 30–35 minutes for writing, the rest for planning and checking.
- Remember to stick to the precise point of the question – don't scribble down everything you can think of in the general area to which the question relates. Similarly, do not 'pad out' answers – give only what is *relevant* to the question.
- When the time for a question is up, draw it to a conclusion and start another. Leave space on the page so that you can come back and improve your answer if time allows at the end of the exam.

Introduction: two key themes

The two themes below form a key part of the subject cores specified for GCE Advanced (A) and Advanced Subsidiary (AS) Sociology. The themes should be interpreted broadly as running through many areas of social life rather than being confined to specific topic areas, and that is how this book has approached them. For example, whilst questions of 'socialisation, culture and identity' may be located in the 'Households and families' unit, they can also be found in several other units such as 'Mass media and popular culture'. Similarly with 'social differentiation, power and stratification'; whilst a whole unit has this title, the theme can also be located in almost any aspect of sociology, though perhaps most obviously in power and politics; and welfare, poverty and social policy. This theme interacts with the other important cross-cutting themes which have become well established in sociology – class, ethnicity, gender and age.

Socialisation, culture and identity

Socialisation, culture and identity are interlinked sociological concepts which are basic to our understanding of social behaviour. **Socialisation** relates to the life-long processes involved in learning the culture of a particular society. Indeed, socialisation and culture may be seen as providing an individual identity for each member of society through family life, the education system, the workplace and the wider location. **Culture** refers to the main characteristics of a society which are shared via language (spoken and written), knowledge, skills, norms, values, beliefs, customs, etc: these combine to make up the 'way of life' of a society. Socialisation is necessary for the survival of culture. Therefore socialisation and culture work together so that individuals can find their identity through the shared ideas and traditions which are handed down from one generation to the next. '**Identity**' becomes framed from birth by sex, names, expectations, etc., adopted by a particular culture: this may vary between societies and across periods of time. However, an identity is not easily framed, cultures are not uniform and in the modern world individual identities may seem less fixed. Individuals, regardless of socialisation agents and within cultural expectations, are often able to form or even change their identity and to make their own decisions.

Social differentiation, power and stratification

Social differentiation, power and stratification refer to differences considered as important to the structure of society. Such differences can be attributed to the power held by an individual or group. **Stratification** refers to the way in which advantages or disadvantages are distributed systematically as structured inequalities; this is also described as **social differentiation**. The power and statification associated with systems of differentiation are discussed fully in this book. Structured inequalities exist in all societies regardless of the distribution of wealth or property: at a fundamental level inequalities may exist between men and women, the young and the elderly etc. While it may seem possible to differentiate or distinguish between individuals or groups according to their positions, some positions carry far more or far fewer benefits within and across societies. Trying to allocate positions or status, particularly in complex or changing societies, provides considerable challenge to sociologists.

This book focuses closely on the two key themes outlined above. Specific references are made to them throughout, and in the 'Think about it' sections which form integral parts of each unit of this book the reader is required to consider all relevant issues in the light of these themes.

What do sociologists do? An explanation of theory and methods in sociology

Introduction

Sociology is the study of how human society works. As such, it is a dynamic subject, constantly responding to new developments and finding new ways of discovering and understanding information. It is also a discipline, rooted in two key strengths:

- the range and depth of its **theories**;
- the constant striving for thoroughness and accuracy in **research methods**.

Sociology owes much to the works of three influential nineteenth-century thinkers: **Max Weber, Karl Marx** and **Emile Durkheim**. Many of the contemporary debates in sociology are in some way investigating or responding to the ideas first put forward by these writers. Only Durkheim claimed to be a sociologist first and foremost; Weber spanned the disciplines of politics and sociology and Marx addressed issues in political economy and revolutionary politics and philosophy.

This unit first looks at the development and nature of sociology, and then at traditions in sociological thought – in other words, how sociologists have sought to make sense of the world. It then comments briefly on the form and range of various sociological perspectives (from macro to micro), before looking at the research methods sociologists use to collect data, and some of the difficulties of researching human social behaviour. Finally, the unit refers to the development of **postmodernism**, illustrating the ever-changing nature of the study of society and social questions and concerning debates about the 'nature of social facts'. In particular, it looks briefly at the modernist–postmodernist debate, which is key to much of the recent sociological literature.

The development of sociology, the study of human behaviour

Is sociology objective or subjective?

The name 'sociology' was given to the scientific study of human behaviour in social situations by **Auguste Comte** in the early part of the nineteenth century. Comte believed that the problems faced by France in maintaining political stability and social harmony could be resolved once the laws ('the nature of social facts') that govern human behaviour were understood by scientists. The knowledge resulting from scientific understanding could then be used to end the social conflict and other social problems which existed in rapidly changing and industrialising societies.

This scientific approach became known as **positivist** and it remained dominant in sociology until the 1960s. It was based on **empirical** methods, which mean:

- collecting data via observation;
- developing theories from this data; and then
- testing and refining them through more observation.

The scientific or empirical approach has been widely used in sociological research throughout the latter part of the nineteenth century and during the twentieth century. Durkheim's classic study of suicide and the study of a group of schoolboys by D.J. West and his colleagues are two examples. Through such empirical studies, sociologists hope to arrive at **objective explanations** of deviant or anti-social behaviour; the ultimate aim being to remove or alter the factors causing such behaviour.

A significant alternative to the scientific or empirical approach has been **Marxism**, with its basic principle that it is *economic forces* that determine people's social, political and cultural attitudes.

A more direct challenge to Comte's scientific positivism, however, is a more **subjective** approach, based on intuition and empathy. This involves an attempt to interpret human behaviour by *identifying* with the individual or groups being studied, rather than standing apart and viewing from afar, in an objective way, as the scientific approach suggests. This approach, known as **interpretivist**, has grown in prominence in recent years.

Max Weber, at the turn of the twentieth century, tried to combine the merits of both approaches. One of the most influential sociological theorists, he sought the 'objective', **value-free** (i.e. unbiased) study of social structures; but he also emphasised the focus on interpreting the meaning of social action by individuals.

The nature of social facts

Is sociology a 'science'? If we made a list of the typical characteristics of a science it might include:

- laboratory **experimentation**, allowing us to control external factors and thus to test the particular variable under investigation;
- a step-by-step method of **observation**;

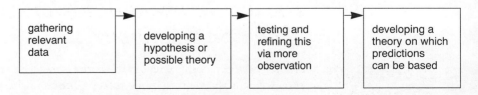

- researchers who behave in an objective or value-free way, not allowing their personal beliefs to influence their study;
- terminology and methods of measurement which are clear so that others can understand the study and the conclusions of the research;
- scientific research that is valid and reliable, providing true information which other researchers can use as a basis for further work.

With regard to sociology, important questions to ask are:

- can the empirical or scientific method really be used in studying social behaviour?
- if it can be used, is it in fact a suitable approach to the area of study?
- how far is it possible for sociologists to be value-free (objective) in their studies?

The response to such questions often depends upon the sociologist's **ideological position**. A Marxist sociologist, for example, begins from a **committed** position – seeking to expose the negative aspects of capitalist society – so certain beliefs affect his or her research from the outset. The fact that sociology involves humans studying other humans makes it very different from a study of rocks or metals: the sociologist can *relate* to what he or she is studying (people), and those people may behave differently if they are aware they are being investigated. Supporters of the scientific or empirical approach admit that there have been problems with previous research and methods. They continue to stress, however, the critical importance of objectivity; and argue that empirical study leads to reasoned debate which is preferable to the adoption of a particular ideological position.

■ SOCIOLOGICAL THEORY

Sociologists use a range of different types of theory to try and make sense of the social world. These may be loosely separated out into three basic forms:

- **formal** (or **foundational**) **theory**
- **substantive theory**
- **positivistic theory.**

Formal or foundational theory

This kind of theory, sometimes referred to as **grand theory**, seeks to identify a *set of basic principles* which underlie the form and direction of human life. The main types of formal or foundational theory are:

- **agency theory;**
- **structuralist theory;**
- **systems theory.**

The table on page 24 sets out the main influences on these theories.

Substantive theory

Unlike formal theory, substantive theories try to explain *general events*, such as:

- the stages through which human societies have developed;
- how powerful sections of society attempt to maintain their positions of dominance.

An example would be the question of why, in recent years, there has been less support for major political parties and more for 'social movements', for example disability rights or environmental groups. Major areas of substantive theory are:

- **cultural theory;**
- **critical structuralist theory;**
- **feminist theory;**
- **stratification theory.**

The table on page 25 sets out the main influences on these theories.

Formal or foundational theory – key influences

	Agency theory	Structuralist theory	Systems theory
What is it?	Studies the 'agent' (person who acts) and seeks to understand how people make sense of, and influence, the world around them.	Sees the individual as being influenced by factors outside themselves, e.g. parents, teachers, the economic and political system.	Studies the way in which individuals are born into an existing social system and are required to fit into it, i.e. to conform.
Influential theorists	M. Weber: stressing 'action'. G. Simmel	S. Freud: unconscious structures of the mind. K. Marx: material structures which underlie history. Levi-Strauss: analyses the structure of myth.	E. Durkheim: the system imposes requirements on social action. T. Parsons: refers to systems and sub-systems.
Other influences	G.H. Mead: symbolic interactionism. T. Schutz: 'Lifeworld'. Berger and Luckman H. Garfinkel T. Parsons/J. Habermas: see societal analysis beginning with agency but then being subordinate to structure. A. Giddens: views structure as the unintentional consequence of action.	L. Althusser: notes the existence of ideological and repressive state apparatuses. T. Parsons: society is determined by the overall needs of the system. A. Giddens: society is structured by the actions of human agents.	J. Habermas: refers to the need to develop 'communicative action'.

Substantive theory – key influences

	Cultural theory	Critical structuralist theory	Feminist theory	Stratification theory
What is it?	Suggests that culture is passed on from generation to generation, to ensure one group's dominance and/or to assist in maintaining social stability.	Suggests that power (social, economic, political, etc.) is the key factor influencing social relationships, with individuals or groups being able to control others.	Ranges from liberal feminist view (women's position in society can be improved by legislation) to radical feminist perspective (sees men as the 'problem' and tends to argue for women to be dominant).	Refers to the stratification or layering of society, with some groups or classes being wealthier or more dominant than others.
Influences	K. Marx: the material condition determines consciousness. M. Weber: culture and society exist in a complex relationship with neither necessarily dominant. A. Gramsci: bourgeois society held together by hegemonic control. G. Lukacs: any group may dominate in respect to power. Frankfurt School: a conspiracy exists to ensure the populace conform. Debate between Marxists and Postmodernists over the form and impact of culture.	K. Marx: power is a fundamental structural relationship. Society is organised in power terms. S. Lukes: refers to the power of some groups to prevent most people having access to political decision-making in the UK: 'the three dimensions of power'. J. Habermas: the state serves ruling class to ensure economic stability but this causes a legitimation crisis.	M. Barrett: women's oppression occurs mainly in the household, and this serves capitalism's needs. K. Millett: refers to 'patriarchy' as masculine system of political domination, operating in a variety of ways: • ideological; • biological; • sociological; • class-based; • economic; • educational; • psychological; • supported by force, by myth and by religion. S. Firestone: locates patriarchy in the system of biological reproduction, forcing women to be dependent and subordinate.	M. Weber: patriarchalism – based upon traditional domination. F. Engels: control of private property. Allows some men to control other men but also allows all men to control women. Women confined to the domestic sphere. T. Parsons: differentiation of gender roles within the family.

Positivistic theory

This group of theories tries to explain human behaviour and relationships by *collecting empirical data* (for example, from survey work and questionnaires) to test a hypothesis. Following the ideas of Auguste Comte, this approach seeks to develop and to use a 'science of the social'. It includes:

- social exchange theory;
- public choice theory;
- rational choice theory.

	Positivistic theory and key influences		
	Social exchange theory	**Public choice theory**	**Rational choice theory**
What is it?	Looks at the costs and benefits which people obtain in social interaction, including money, goods, status. Based on the principle that people always act to maximise benefit. However, to receive benefits, there must always be an exchange process with others.	Argues that collective organisations (e.g. political parties) act rationally to maximise their own benefits. Believes individual differences are best resolved by collective involvement within organisations. The role of the state is important in arbitrating between large-scale interests.	Assumes that individuals will operate in a rational way and will seek to benefit themselves in the life choices they make.
Key influences	M. Olsen K. Arrow	G.C. Homans P. Blau	J. Elster J. Roemer

■ PERSPECTIVES IN SOCIOLOGY

A perspective is a viewpoint which involves interpreting data in a certain way. Sociological perspectives are ways of looking at society, focusing on particular issues and types of questions.

For your study of sociology you will need to be able to use a number of distinct sociological perspectives, and to understand and be able to discuss the difference between positivist (scientific or **macro**) and interpretivist (phenomenological or **micro**) approaches to the subject.

Macro-sociology and positivism

Positivism envisages a world of impersonal laws that can be revealed by the scientific method of observation. It sees our behaviour as the product of social forces which are outside our control. The emphasis is on the way the whole of society is structured, rather than on a particular individual. This view is known as a **systems** or **holistic approach**. It uses methods of investigation which enable precise measurement, and it produces theories of behaviour which claim to predict what will happen in given situations. This large-scale study of sociology is also known as **macro-sociology**.

| Society | → | influences | → | the individual | → | who acts |

Micro-sociology and interpretivism

According to interpretivists, the objective nature of the world is seen in a subjective or personal light by the individual observer. It is, therefore, the task of the sociologist to try to identify with the individual's view of the world in order to understand and clarify the meaning of his or her actions (often by asking the actors themselves). The individual is seen as a thinking being whose ideas and actions are influenced by interaction with other people. The focus is on the individual or small group.

This approach is known as **micro-sociology** because of its focus upon the small-scale. It uses methods of investigation which provide *richness of detail* about particular individuals, leading to general propositions about human behaviour. It is also referred to as the **action** or **atomistic approach**.

| individual action | → | individual interpretation | → | individual action | → | individual interpretation | → | shared ways of making sense of the world |

Micro v. macro

While some writers take extreme positions in the micro/macro debate, many see the merits of both views: for example Howard Becker, whose work is referred to in Unit 10. Anthony Giddens has attempted to bring the two approaches together by arguing that 'men (sic) produce society but not under conditions of their own choosing'. Paul Willis used this combined approach in *Learning to Labour* (see Unit 4), where he studied a group of working-class boys in school and the way the choices they make in terms of attitudes and behaviour reinforce wider societal and structural constraints, for example the schools they go to, the work opportunities available.

What is sociology?

Macro-sociology (Positivism)	Micro-sociology (Interpretivism)
1. Emphasis on **social systems**, structures and institutions in society.	1. Emphasis on **social action** and interaction of human beings.
2. A **macro** (global) view of society in which systems and institutions are 'out there' and 'outside' the individual.	2. A **micro** (particularised) study of social action in which what happens is 'in here', 'inside' the heads of individuals.
3. Emphasises **society** in relation to wo/man.	3. Emphasises **wo/man** in relation to society.
4. Stress on **common value** systems and shared norms in society.	4. Interest in the ways in which wo/men **vary** in their interpretations of and reactions to society.
5. Concern about the problems of how society holds together and maintains social order.	5. Interest in how wo/men manage and gain control over social institutions.
6. Stress on **neutrality** and **objectivity** in approach.	6. Recognition of **subjectivity** in analysis and that the subjective interpretations of reality made by human beings are likely to be different. An interest in the interaction between different subjective realities.
7. A view of social order as something which is **given** or **inherited** from the past and which wo/men passively receive.	7. A view of wo/men actively and continually making and remaking the social order around them.
8. Empirical collection of evidence and data by surveys, questionnaires, statistical analysis, standardised tests and structured interviews. Emphasis on **objective facts** and **figures**.	8. Collection of data from participant-observation and open-ended interviews and discussions. Recognition of different subjectivities and emphasis on the **meanings** and **interpretations** made by wo/men in the process of social action.
9. Sociological theories which involve a systems analysis of society include **functionalism**, **positivism** and some varieties of **Marxist** sociology.	9. Sociological theories which involve an action analysis of society include **symbolic interactionism**, **phenomenology**, **ethnomethodology** and some varieties of **Marxist** sociology.
10. The 'founding father' most associated with a systems approach was **Emile Durkheim**.	10. The founding father most associated with an action approach was **Max Weber**.

A range of different perspectives

Alongside and intertwined with the debate on positivism (macro) as against interpretivism (micro), a number of other sociological perspectives have developed. They should not be regarded as totally separate from each other: it is possible, for example, to be both a feminist and a Marxist. Some perspectives, like functionalism, fall within the positivist approach, in that they focus on 'objective' data, while others, such as interactionism, are more associated with the interpretivist approach. The different perspectives are illustrated in the diagram below. It will be useful to refer back to this diagram as you learn about each perspective.

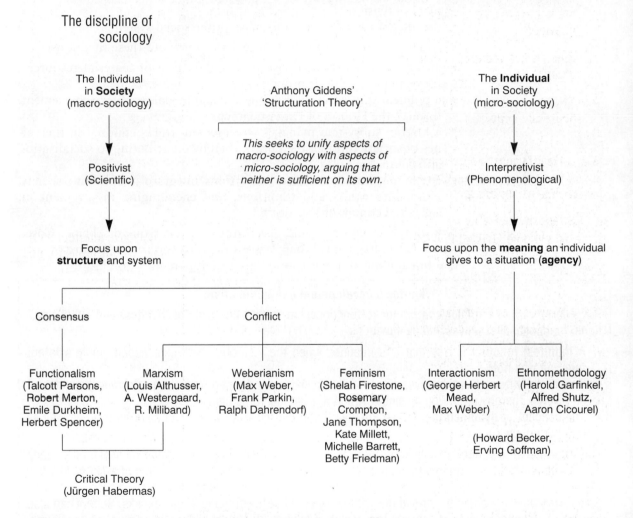

Functionalism

Functionalism views society as a living organism, and argues that to understand any particular aspect of that society, it is essential to *see* that aspect in its full social context. The family, the school, the trade union, or the workplace should be studied not in isolation but in terms of their contribution to the wider society and its functions within that society.

The origins of functionalism as a school of thought and method of approach lie in the nineteenth century with writers such as Spencer and Durkheim. However, in the twentieth century, **Talcott Parsons** (1902–79) is widely acknowledged as its key thinker. He held that **consensus,** or agreement on values, was central to a stable society, and laid down four basic functions which any society has to address:

- adaptation to the physical environment;
- agreement on goal attainment;
- the motivation of members to accept existing patterns and management of tensions;
- the integration of the various parts of the social system.

He suggested that various systems exist to carry out these functions:

- an economic subsystem ensures the allocation of material resources, for example wealth or property;
- a political subsystem determines goals and enables their achievement, through the Houses of Parliament, etc.;
- a kinship subsystem manages tensions and trains children in the values of society through the family, thereby contributing to socialisation and cultural continuity;
- community and cultural organisations integrate people into society, reinforcing values and traditions, and encouraging involvement in, e.g., local community projects.

Not all functionalists would accept the entire Parsonian scheme. Coser, for example, has argued that Parsons presents too rosy a picture of societal functioning and that **conflict** is often apparent.

Merton's development of functionalism

R.K. Merton, another major contributor to functionalism, raised the ideas of manifest and latent functions, functional alternatives and dysfunctions.

- A **manifest function** is one that was intended when the institution was established, while a **latent function** was not.
- **Functional alternatives** involves the idea that a particular function can be performed by different structures, thereby rendering no single structure essential for society.
- The concept of **dysfunction** involves the idea that a particular structure can have harmful as well as positive effects on society.

The example of a school will illustrate Merton's points. The *manifest functions* of a school include social, academic and vocational training, and perhaps discipline. A possible example of a *latent function* is that the school operates as a childminding agency, enabling parents to go to work. In terms of *functional alternatives*, it could be argued that the family could perform many of these tasks. School can also have *dysfunctional* aspects: it can lead to wastage of talent with some children being labelled as failures, and some writers have argued that school can inhibit self development by confusing teaching (and the power of teachers) with learning (and the needs of the learners).

By emphasising the relationships between the various elements of society, functionalism enables societies to be compared. For example, a contrast may be made between a modern industrial society in which there are specialised agencies to perform each necessary function, and pre-industrial society in which the family and community tended to perform all the functions.

Problems with functionalism

Functionalism can be criticised for not being value-free (despite its claims to be so); and for its conservative bias which often favours the status quo (although a stress on dysfunctional questions can also support social change). It also tends to assume that individuals have little free will, a view that is unacceptable to many.

Conflict theory

If functionalism views society as an integrated whole based on a harmony of values, the **conflict approach** or **theory** emphasises division, coercion and hostility. While stability and agreed norms are stressed in the Parsonian approach, conflict theory emphasises competing interests, deep social contradictions and the inevitability of change. Perhaps the most significant contribution to the conflict perspective has come from the writings and ideas of Marx and his followers, with their emphasis on the role of class interests in shaping society.

Marx's conflict theory

According to Marx, it is the relationship between the forces of production that determines patterns of economic development, the nature of the state and the political process, and the culture and beliefs of society.

Under capitalism, a ruling class (the **bourgeoisie**) owns the means of production (factories, land, machinery, etc.) and a much larger working class (the **proletariat**) owns only its own labour power which it has to sell to the bourgeoisie in order to raise the money to stay alive. The aim of the bourgeoisie is to increase profits, and this is done by employing workers and exploiting the value of their work. In Marx's view, the bourgeoisie will eventually be overthrown by the proletariat and a fundamental reordering of society on socialist and then communist lines becomes inevitable.

Marx's conflict theory and functionalism

The Marxist analysis comes close to functionalism in that various institutions are seen as socialising people to conform to the norms of society. Louis Althusser has distinguished in particular the family and the school as institutions performing this role. He sees the family as reproducing the labour power required by capitalism, both in breeding new generations of workers and also in satisfying the basic needs of the worker to enable him or her to return to the factory. The family instils values in the worker, through socialisation, that are family-centred rather than community-orientated and so helps to weaken 'class consciousness' (see Unit 2). The school is seen to create the skills necessary for the factories (or offices, shops, restaurants, etc.), and to spread ideas of competitiveness, selfishness, obedience to authority and so on, which enhance the position of the ruling group in society (see Unit 4). Functionalism would see similar processes taking place, but view them as positive for society as a whole rather than serving a particular set of class interests, or generating conflict.

Conflict theory is often limited in its coverage to Marx and his followers, but it does, in fact, embrace a whole range of writers who attempt fundamental criticisms of the Marxist model. Examples include Mosca and Pareto, who argue that whatever the outward aims of a state, it is inevitably ruled by a small elite that operates in its own interests; and Dahrendorf, who sees advanced industrial society as containing a wide variety of social relationships based on power and subordination (he argues, however, that as the same people will not be in subordinate positions in all their social relationships they will have no great desire to change the existing order, or status quo).

Conflict theory offers a useful contrast to the functionalist approach and it shows how the same social phenomena can be interpreted in contrasting ways. Since the 1970s many Marxist sociologists have undertaken relevant and detailed studies of aspects of contemporary British society. These include Murdock on the mass media, Westergaard on income and wealth, and Jock Young on crime and deviance.

Feminism

Feminist sociology focuses on the particular disadvantages, including oppression and exploitation, faced by women in society. In essence, it represents a strand of conflict theory, with some feminist writers seeing conflict between men and women as inevitable. Feminism is not a unified perspective; it ranges from **liberal feminism**, which recognises inequalities but believes that reform can take place without a fundamental restructuring of the social system, to **radical feminism**, which advocates the fundamental need for societal change.

Feminism, since the late 1960s, has created a heightened sociological awareness in respect to gender roles in society, the family, the educational system, and at work. It has raised important issues relating to masculine and feminine social roles and whether or not these reflect biological differences. An emphasis on social change to the benefit of women's position is a universal feature of feminist theory.

The table opposite sets out key points relating to three distinct strands of feminism.

The following two perspectives are located on the interpretivist or phenomenological side of the diagram on page 29.

Interactionism

Interactionism reflects a Liberal philosophy which believes in the importance of individual liberty. Its rise in popularity in the 1960s coincided with liberalising social and political movements in the USA and in Europe. Interaction theorists, as micro-sociologists, focus on the individual actor, believing that the self (who and what we are) is a complex phenomenon with many dimensions. The individual is viewed as a conscious being capable of considering the consequences of various alternative courses of action. Interactionism is associated with writers such as Howard Becker and Erving Goffman.

Goffman views the individual as a theatrical performer, acting out various roles and presenting different images, aware of the kinds of behaviour that will be approved or disapproved of by others in particular circumstances. Such awareness allows the actor to select the words, gestures and strategies of behaviour appropriate for given situations and contacts. For example, you are likely to behave differently when interacting with your close family than with friends.

For the sociologist, it is important to know which individuals are significant in the life of the person being studied, and how they view him or her. Interactionism sees the social world as a pattern of identity networks with a two-way flow of information serving to confirm or deny previously held assumptions. This helps us explain the differing ways in which people behave in different social situations. The interactionist suggests, for example, that it is wrong to label people as deviants when they exhibit what may be 'abnormal' aspects of personality – these

	Liberal feminism	Radical feminism	Marxist/Socialist feminism
Nature of the problem	• Sex discrimination and sex-biased laws seen as a product of: – irrational prejudice – stereotyping	• Patriarchy: men's control over women's reproduction and sexuality • Institutionalisation of sexism	• Patriarchy and capitalism
Suggested solutions	• Reform of sex-biased laws • Challenging sexist views and practices • Access to opportunities and rights	• Challenging male power • Relieving women of biological reproductive role • Separation • Connecting personal and political	• Fundamental change in relations between production (public) and reproduction (private) • Reorganisation of the sexual division of labour • End to divisions between paid and unpaid work
Strategy to be adopted	• Women into power • Removal of legislative discriminations • Using legislation to change attitudes • Providing alternative sex-roles and models • Provision of anti-sexist resources • Reversal of gender roles • Public education • Equal opportunities – access • Provision of resources to reduce effects of biological differences, e.g. childcare	• Establishing women's-only culture • Defining private space • Challenging (male) expertise • Reclaiming 'her' story • Pre-figurative working relationships	• Gendered class consciousness • Working within the State as focus for collective struggle • Connecting workplace with domestic issues • Increasing representation of women in political parties • Autonomous women's organisations • Pre-figurative politics
Influential writers	B. Friedan A. Rossi	S. Firestone K. Millett	I. Young M. McIntosh A. Oakley

aspects may be 'normal' amongst certain groups or in particular situations, and could be incorrectly interpreted by an observer who is not fully aware of group behaviour (norms). David Matza, for example, has argued that most criminals are really normal human beings who 'drift' into crime from time to time.

Howard Becker has argued that the sociologist must identify with one of the parties in the interaction being studied. He poses the question, 'Whose side are we on?' His own political ideology is revealed in his preference to side with the so-called deviant whose views of the world are as important as those of the agencies of social control (for example, the judicial system, the police). Prior to Becker's work, most studies focused on a view of deviants which was defined solely by these social control agents.

Interactionism has played a major role in questioning assumptions about the existence or possibility of obtaining objectivity in sociology, and has revealed the danger of falling back on the works of Weber, Durkheim, Marx, etc. to explain all aspects of contemporary behaviour. It is largely critical of attempts to formulate a 'scientific' sociology, and has contributed much to debates concerning the deprived, powerless or downtrodden in society. The film *Trainspotting* (1996) would be of particular interest to interactionists with its focus upon disadvantaged young people and their drug-related lifestyle, as would *The Full Monty* (1997), which focused on unemployed ex-steelworkers in Sheffield.

Ethno-methodology

Since the 1960s, **radical sociology**, which includes ethnomethodology, has contributed to our awareness of social behaviour, with the writings of **Alfred Schutz** being particularly influential.

The view here is that social groupings are based upon *the sharing of common-sense knowledge of taken-for-granted assumptions*, and that this basis is much more fragile than is commonly recognised. Once those things that have been taken for granted are questioned and normal behaviour patterns broken, then social groups would quickly cease to function. **Harold Garfinkel** illustrated this experimentally by seeking to disrupt the 'taken-for-granted' world of undergraduate students and their parents. He set up a situation where students returning home for the vacation behaved as though they were lodgers. They behaved politely, tidied up around the house and said 'please' and 'thank you' regularly. This caused their parents difficulty, as it was not 'normal', not what they expected. The researchers questioned the families in order to identify their 'taken-for-granted' expectations by comparing their actual behaviour with what the parents had expected as 'normal'. Such experiments allow the researcher to uncover the anticipated patterns of expectation, the 'rules' or assumptions which are understood to assist us in our everyday lives.

The phenomenological or interpretive perspective also takes account of how sociologists have their own background expectations which will lead them to research areas of interest to themselves. This will have a significant impact both on the focus and choice of the research and on the selection of methods.

Aaron Cicourel, an influential phenomenologist, sought to investigate the taken-for-granted assumptions of decision-makers such as the police, coroners and teachers. He did this using observation techniques, examining written records, and recording actual patterns of interaction on audio or video tape. Such studies have highlighted the process by which a decision-maker sifts the available material and attempts to make sense of it, and of how they have used their power to influence the outcome of events.

Garfinkel used ethnomethodology to study how ordinary people make sense of their social situation. For example, he recorded conversations in a jury-room in order to see how people made sense of their role as jurors. Harvey Sacks in the USA recorded telephone calls to a Suicide Prevention Centre in the USA to try to identify common-sense assumptions about the would-be suicide case.

Ethnomethodology uses experimentation in order to control and identify taken-for-granted assumptions governing social behaviour. This approach may be used unwittingly by many of us when we try to identify behavioural expectations in situations which are unfamiliar to us.

Think about it

- Try to picture how you behave when you go into new situations, what 'rules' you try to follow, and how easy it is to get these 'rules' wrong. Where do the rules come from? Why does it matter if you 'get it wrong'?

Summary of the discipline of sociology

- Positivist sociology seeks to apply scientific methods to the study of social behaviour.

- Macro-sociology attempts to discover the 'rules' of social behaviour and to offer predictions about future behaviour, often using survey techniques.

- Micro-sociology seeks to identify the 'taken-for-granted' rules of behaviour – the major research technique used here would be observation.

- The discipline of sociology contains within it a range of *perspectives*, or views of the world, and a number of different *theories*, ranging from those which emphasise *structure* (society, the macro) to those which emphasise *agency* (the individual, the micro).

- Different perspectives focus on *order* (functionalism), *conflict* (Marxism) and *patriarchy* (feminism).

- Attempts have been made to unify a number of perspectives and to seek a more detailed explanation of the social world, for example A. Giddens' *Structuration Theory*.

Influential writers and their major works

Biographical notes	Major works
Auguste Comte (French) 1798–1857	*Cours de Philosophie Positif*
Emile Durkheim (French) 1858–1917	*The Rules of Sociological Method* *Suicide*
Harold Garfinkel (American) b. 1917	*Studies in Ethnomethodology*
Anthony Giddens (British) b. 1938	*StructurationTheory*
Erving Goffman (American) b. 1928	*Asylums* *The Presentation of Self in Everyday Life* *Encounters* *Stigma*
Karl Marx (German) 1818–83	*Communist Manifesto* *Das Kapital*
George Herbert Mead (American) 1863–1931	*Mind, Self and Society*
Robert Merton (American) b. 1910	*Social Theory and Social Structure*
Talcott Parsons (American) 1902–79	*The Social System*
Alfred Schutz (Austrian) 1899–1959	*The Stranger* *The Homecomer* *The Well-Informed Citizen* *Don Quixote and the Problem of Reality*
Max Weber (German) 1864–1920	*The Protestant Ethic and the Spirit of Capitalism*

■ SOCIOLOGICAL METHODS

During sociology's relatively short history a wide variety of methods of data collection have been used. In the 1890s, for example, the use and collection of **statistics** was highly favoured by Durkheim in his study of suicide and by Rowntree and Booth in their studies of poverty in York and London respectively. **Participant observation** has also been regularly used, as in Erving Goffman's studies of mental hospitals and 'James Patrick's' study of a Glasgow street gang, where he assumed a false name in his writing for his own protection.

The wide range of possible research techniques has led to arguments as to their relative usefulness and validity. Choice of method often depends upon the sociological perspective adopted, the resources (for example money and time) available, and the nature of the subject under investigation, as shown in the following diagram.

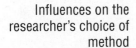

Influences on the researcher's choice of method

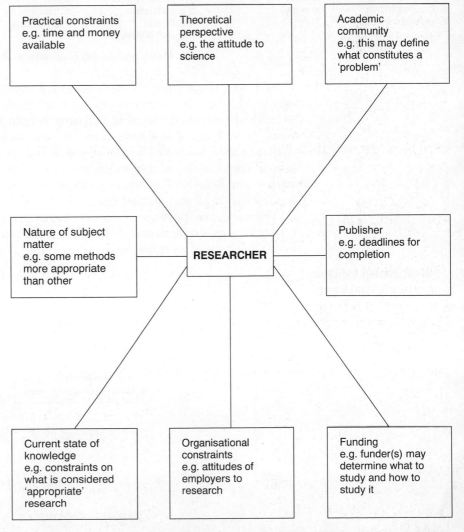

Source: T. Lawson, 'In the shadow of science', *Social Studies Review*, Vol. 2:2, November 1986

Sources of data and methods of collection

The key methods of collecting data, and sources of data are:

- survey methods;
- questionnaires;
- interviews;
- observation;
- longitudinal studies;
- official statistics.

A typical research
process

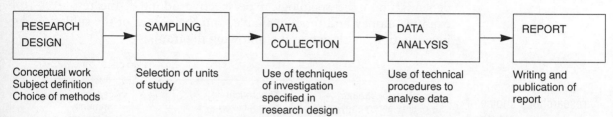

RESEARCH DESIGN	SAMPLING	DATA COLLECTION	DATA ANALYSIS	REPORT
Conceptual work Subject definition Choice of methods	Selection of units of study	Use of techniques of investigation specified in research design	Use of technical procedures to analyse data	Writing and publication of report

Source: Adapted from Burgess, *Developments in Sociology* (Causeway Press, 1985)

In addition, those who call for a more scientific approach within sociology would look to the **experiment** as a desirable form of research. However, the problems involved in isolating people in laboratory conditions from outside influences have generally led sociologists to abandon the experiment in favour of survey research. Experimental work also raises ethical considerations, and in an attempt to minimise difficulties of this nature, the British Sociological Association has produced a set of ethical guidelines for all sociological researchers to follow.

The range of primary research methods require differing levels of researcher involvement and differ also in the number of people who can be included as subjects, as the diagram below illustrates.

Relationship between
number of respondents
and degree of personal
involvement of
sociologist

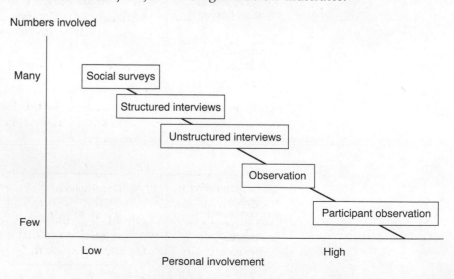

Source: Peter Worsley (ed.), *Introducing Sociology 2nd edn* (Penguin, 1977)

The survey

Surveys are a primary research method with the researcher aiming for:

- **reliability** – i.e. would other researchers repeating the research using the same method on the same sample obtain the same results?
- **validity** – does the data obtained give a true picture? Suicide statistics, for example, may not reflect the 'true' rate of suicide, as some unproven or unrecognised suicidal deaths are defined as accidental death.

Survey techniques

The survey is seen as a way of gathering hard data in an objective, scientific way. It has held a prominent position since Booth's nineteenth-century studies of poverty. Voting studies by Curtis, Heath and Jowell; Schofield on the sexual behaviour and attitudes of teenagers; and Marshall's work on the proletarianisation of clerical workers, all used survey techniques. However, as Moser and Kalton point out:

> 'Fact-collecting is no substitute for thought and desk research ... Sometimes good judgement requires the deliberate sacrifice of quantitative precision for the greater depth attainable by more intensive methods ...'
> Moser and Kalton, *Survey Methods in Social Investigation* (Heinemann, 1971)

Surveys are dependent on the judgement of the sociologist in the way they are devised and how the results are interpreted. They should not, therefore, be seen as totally reliable sources of scientific or useful information.

The government's ten-yearly census of the UK population is often seen as one of the most significant surveys undertaken and one which produces data on a wide range of matters of interest to sociologists. However, there are problems with the reliability of the data for several reasons:

- the census forms are not always easy to interpret, and so are sometimes filled in inaccurately or incompletely;
- some people are unwilling to fill in the forms, even though they are legally obliged to do so;
- some people are difficult to trace or unwilling to open the door to census enumerators.

One of the temporary staff employed on the 1991 census, writing in the *Guardian*, described his team's impression that interviewees' responses (or lack of response) demonstrated that:

> "In the past 10 years there has been a sea change in society. There is more suspicion and fear of authority, a growing distrust of statistics, a greater feeling of helplessness, a more widespread doubt about the ability of government or any other agency to meet people's needs as citizens – in short, a pervasive sense of disenfranchisement."

Such views could well influence the form and detail of responses.

Planning and carrying out a survey

It is essential that a survey be planned and carried out precisely and that the data be carefully analysed.

- The objectives of the study must be clearly set out.
- The resources available for the survey need careful consideration.
- The collection of data must be supervised by the researcher if assistants are being employed to conduct interviews, for example.
- Cross-checking should be carried out to eliminate errors in processing and analysis.

One of the most important considerations is to obtain a **representative sample** of the group or population to be studied. There are various ways of ensuring this.

1. **Random and systematic sample**   This involves the selection of names at regular intervals from a list prepared by someone else. Rosser and Harris, in their study of family patterns, used the electoral register of Swansea, selecting every fiftieth name. The list is known as the **sampling frame**, and the population from which the sample is to be obtained is known as the **survey population**. The closer the sampling frame is to equalling the survey population the better. This system is valuable in that it avoids interviewer bias in the selection of the sample, but it can be very time-consuming and may not be wholly representative of the population at large.

2. **Quota sample**   When the size of the sample has been determined, a number of important variables are taken into account so that the sample *reflects the whole group* in terms of these characteristics. This method is commonly adopted in public opinion polls, with factors such as age, sex, education, employment status and income being taken into account. A quota for each of these is set in advance to try and match the general population's characteristics. The more factors that are taken into account, the greater the accuracy of the sample, but the more time-consuming the study will be. The possibility of interviewer bias in the selection of people may distort the representative nature of the sample.

3. **Stratified random sample**   This combines some features of the random sample with some of the quota sample to obtain a more accurate cross-section of the population. If the population of a particular town is 70 per cent white and only 30 per cent black, then separate lists of whites and blacks are drawn up before names are taken at regular intervals from each. This gives an appropriate quota of white and black respondents, while avoiding interviewer choice over who is actually selected.

4. **Multi-stage sampling**   This involves the selection of a sample from an already existing sample. For example, at election times, key marginal constituencies are identified and chosen as the focus for study.

5. **Snowball sampling**   This method, as used in L. Taylor's work in London's criminal underworld, involves the use of 'informants' who will identify other key contacts; this then opens up further contacts. Although unlikely to give a representative sample, it overcomes the impossibility of getting professional criminals to fill out a questionnaire mailed to their address.

The questionnaire

About 90 per cent of social surveys involve the use of a questionnaire. Its construction can be a very difficult and time-consuming task; ideally a **pilot study** should be undertaken to test the appropriateness of the questions. Such a pilot study ought to be conducted in a similar area or among a similar group of people to that for which the final questionnaire is designed. A good example of this is the pilot study carried out by Hannah Gavron when studying housebound mothers as a way of developing questions for her work on her study reported in *The Captive Wife* in 1966.

Questionnaires can be useful in gaining some kinds of information: for example, information about the demographic characteristics of a group of people and their social environment can be obtained and checked. Information about activities and opinions can be less reliable, however. Michael Schofield, who has undertaken research into the sensitive subject of teenage sex, stresses the importance of building into the questionnaire, as a way of checking the honesty of replies, some questions whose answers are already known.

An example of a questionnaire

These questions are part of a questionnaire which was sent to all policewomen and also to a random, representative 10 per cent sample of all policemen in the 'Medshire' police force in 1983.

Please tick the appropriate boxes

1. Male ☐   Female ☐

2. Age
    18 to 24 ☐
    25 to 34 ☐   45 to 54 ☐
    35 to 44 ☐   55 and over ☐

3. Marital status
    Single ☐   Widowed ☐
    Married ☐   Divorced ☐

4. Number of children (if any) ----------------------------------

5. Rank --

6. Length of service
    Under 2 yrs ☐   15 to 20 yrs ☐
    2 to 5 yrs ☐   20 to 25 yrs ☐
    5 to 10 yrs ☐   Over 25 yrs ☐
    10 to 15 yrs ☐

7. Qualifications when you joined the police service:
    CSE/O-Levels ☐   How many? ☐
    A-Levels ☐   How many? ☐
    OND ☐   Degree ☐
    HND ☐   None ☐
    Other (please specify) ---

34. Compared with police officers of the opposite sex, how would you assess your own capability in each of the following situations? (tick the response which applies to you for each task)

	Better	Same	Worse
a. General purpose motor patrol			
b. Clerical work			
c. Child abuse cases			
d. Motoring offences			
e. Foot patrol			
f. Questioning victims of rape/or indecency offences			
g. Writing reports			
h. Traffic accidents			
i. Interviewing female suspects			
j. Observation work			
k. Domestic disputes			
l. Getting information at the scene of a crime			
m. Dealing with a crowd of 4–6 male drunks on the street			
n. Juvenile offenders			
o. Threatening situations where someone has a knife			
p. Interviewing male suspects			
q. Community liaison			

35. Which of the following definitions most closely describes the way in which you think policewomen should be employed in the police service:

Policewomen should take on all the same duties as policemen. ☐

Policewomen should take on similar duties to policemen except those where violence is anticipated. ☐

Policewomen should not do the same work as policemen, but should specialise in duties such as female offenders and victims, juveniles and children, and missing persons. ☐

38. Please indicate how far you agree or disagree with each of the following statements by ticking the appropriate box.

	Strongly agree	Agree	Neither agree nor disagree	Disagree	Strongly disagree	Don't know
Since integration there has been a serious loss of expertise in dealing with young people, female offenders and missing persons.						
Since integration women officers are involved in far more interesting work.						
Policemen find it difficult to accept that women should perform the same duties as they do.						
Policewomen do not have the physical strength that is required for police duties.						
Most policewomen leave the police service in order to get married and/or have a family.						

39. What proportion of your work would you estimate involves the possibility of physical violence:

Less than 10%   ☐
Up to a quarter   ☐
Up to a half   ☐
More than half   ☐

40. Please indicate whether you have ever been in any of the following situations during the course of your duties as a police officer:

Been threatened verbally   ☐
Struggled, unaided, with a violent person   ☐
Been threatened by someone with a knife, gun or other weapon. ☐
Been physically assaulted   ☐

If you have at some time been physically assaulted please answer the following questions:
How many times have you been physically assaulted?   Number ☐
Did any of these assaults result in you being injured?

Yes ☐
No   ☐

If yes, for each occasion please indicate whether your injuries were minor or serious.

	Minor	Serious		Minor	Serious
1.	☐	☐	4.	☐	☐
2.	☐	☐	5.	☐	☐
3.	☐	☐			

42. Has a member of the public ever made a complaint about the way you performed your police duties?

Yes ☐
No   ☐

If yes, did this complaint result in formal investigation under the complaints procedure?

Yes ☐
No   ☐

The following questions are for policewomen who joined the police service before integration (before 1975).

Policewomen only
If you joined the police service before integration (before 1975)
please answer the following questions

43. Listed below are some of the changes, resulting from integration, which are said to affect policewomen. Please indicate (by ticking the appropriate box) how far you agree or disagree that these have affected you.

	Strongly agree	Agree	Neither agree nor disagree	Disagree	Strongly disagree	Don't know
There is a greater variety of work.						
Shifts, night duty and irregular hours disrupt personal life.						
There is more chance to specialise, for example, in the CID.						
There is more exposure to danger and violence.						
Working relationships have improved.						
Policewomen have equal status with policemen.						

Source: Sandra Jones, *Policewomen and Equality* (Macmillan, 1986)

Criticisms of the questionnaire

- It can be very expensive – one of Schofield's studies involved asking 300 questions to 2000 teenagers, while Rosser and Harris had almost 2000 residents of Swansea complete their questionnaire on changing family patterns. The larger the study, the greater the expense of employing and training research assistants.
- The appearance of interviewers can distort results – for example, very different results were obtained on the subject of race relations when the interviewer was black compared to when the interviewer was white.
- Postal questionnaires often receive a poor and unrepresentative response, although in large-scale surveys this rate of non-return is taken into account. It is also difficult to know if the questions have been correctly understood or answered honestly.
- The results of questionnaires give a false impression of factual precision. When questions require Yes/No or Agree/Disagree answers, people might want to respond 'Yes, but . . .' or they may give a random answer without having understood a particular question. Cicourel has argued that **quantification** (stating how many people expressed a particular view) distorts behaviour or attitudes by linking together different responses as if they were identical. For example, in an opinion poll several people might express their intention to vote Liberal Democrat, but their degree of voting commitment to that party may not be at the same level.

The interview

This can range from the questionnaire (conducted in person), through open-ended questions to free-flowing discussion either with individuals or with **focus groups**. The latter can allow a deeper understanding of individual opinions and behaviour to develop, but loses the capacity to engage meaningfully with large numbers of people and makes statistical analysis problematic. The interviewer needs always to be aware of the possibility of interviewer bias.

The use of interviews can offer important insights into patterns of social behaviour. Elizabeth Bott (see Unit 3) studied changing family patterns on the basis of detailed interviews with only 20 families, and yet her findings on the role of close kinship connections affecting marital relationships have been regularly quoted in textbooks for their insightful understandings. Howard Becker is critical of the interviewers' role, suggesting that the requirement for them to be passive does not represent meaningful social interaction and that the data collected is likely to lack authenticity.

Perhaps the most valuable way to employ detailed interviews is in conjunction with other methods. Young and Willmott, in their study of Bethnal Green (see Unit 3), supplemented their questionnaire approach with detailed interviews and long-term observation, whilst Hollowells' study of lorry-drivers used interview and observational techniques.

Observation

Observation as a method of gathering data can be either **direct** (**overt**), referred to as **non-participant observation**, or **indirect** (**covert**), usually called **participant observation**. In the former, those observed know they are being studied; in the latter, the observer (researcher) behaves as one of the group.

Observational studies offer particular insights into social behaviour where a lengthy period of observation is possible: for example, working as a teacher and covertly observing staffroom culture. John Williams, and others, have used participant observation in looking at English football supporter behaviour at matches overseas. Generally, the increased use of participant methods mirrors an increased use of the interactionist perspective within sociology. Participant observation, although time-consuming, can be considerably cheaper and a potentially richer source of data than a survey approach; it may also 'get inside' the patterns of social behaviour in a way that other methods cannot.

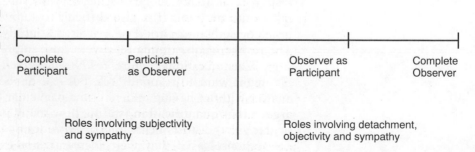

Ideal typical research roles in participant observation

Source: Adapted from Junker, *Fieldwork* (University of Chicago, 1960)

Criticisms of observational studies

- The findings of such studies are, it is argued, impressionistic rather than precise, and the sociologist loses objectivity when identifying with the people being studied.
- There are ethical concerns involved with studying people 'unawares'. They might behave more naturally, but information about them is being gathered without their permission. Laurie Taylor was taken to task by police officers for condoning criminal activity when, as an observer, he accompanied criminals who were engaging in criminal acts.
- The presence of the sociologist can distort behaviour, and a member of a group can easily become influential. Ned Polsky, in his 1967 study *Hustlers, Beats and Others*, has pointed out that non-criticism of an action acts as a reinforcement to the individual who commits it.

The longitudinal study

This involves the gathering of data on a particular group of people over a period of time. Information is gathered at the outset of the study and subsequent developments are traced in an attempt to isolate those social factors that affect a person's life chances or to monitor change in, for example, their voting behaviour. Davie's study of a group of children born in September 1958 through their life-span and life changes was represented in the TV documentary *35-UP* which reflected upon the sample's life situation up to the age of 35.

A longitudinal study enables a dynamic or changing picture to emerge, allowing a richness of detail to be gathered on the subject of the investigation. However, it is difficult to keep track of a large sample, and a small group does not allow satisfactory generalisations to be made. It is also difficult to keep track of external factors and experiences that can influence the results or behaviour patterns. Finally, it is a time-consuming method, and is very expensive.

Official statistics

Official statistics can be defined as statistics collected by the government and its agencies for purposes other than sociological research. They are attractive to sociologists because of their apparently factual nature, and because they offer a rich variety of otherwise inaccessible data. Also, their use frees the sociologist from the time-consuming work of collecting and publishing statistics, enabling him or her to concentrate on the interpretation of the data. The *Annual Abstract of Statistics* and *Social Trends* appear particularly valuable, with their wealth of detail on population trends and social behaviour.

Sociologists have made good use of official statistics in the past. Karl Marx used official economic statistics as his prime source of information for his study of capitalist society. In the 1890s Emile Durkheim undertook his classic study of the causes of suicide in Europe by comparing the official statistics of recorded suicides in the countries concerned. As a result he devised a **typology** of suicide and isolated a number of factors that seemed to determine a high suicide rate in particular countries. Shaw and McKay used official statistics to demonstrate that crime and delinquency can be associated with low income, while Sutherland indicated the extent of white-collar crime by using data supplied by various American government agencies.

Criticisms of the use of official statistics

However, in recent years sociologists have become increasingly critical of the use of official statistics. Barry Hindess, from a Marxist perspective, has raised numerous questions about the utility and accuracy of official statistics produced for and by the government. The methods of calculating UK unemployment statistics, for example, have been altered some 30 times since 1980. Similarly, an uncritical use of Inland Revenue statistics would not take account of the vested interests of people in making low declarations of their income and wealth ownership.

A more extreme view is put by Aaron Cicourel, who stresses that statistics that appear to be objective facts are simply the personal judgements of influential individuals. In his study of delinquency, Cicourel observed the way law officers used their own background assumptions in selecting data that indicated guilt on the part of those being tried or investigated. The resulting criminal statistics were therefore partly the result of prejudice and inference. Maxwell Atkinson has used the same argument to attack Durkheim's methods of suicide investigation. Atkinson studied the process by which coroners registered particular deaths as suicide and found that a wealth of personal judgements were involved.

The above criticisms do not, however, totally deny the value of official statistics to sociologists. Statistics on certain subjects have been shown to be virtually unusable (for example, suicide, vandalism and crime – 'the dark figure'), while others have to be treated a great deal more carefully than they have been in the past. It is important to take account of who compiled particular statistics and whether that person or group had a vested interest in a particular finding.

The usefulness of official statistics

Some statistics may be assumed to be accurate, such as those relating to birth, marriage and divorce in Britain. Useful sources of such data can be found in *Social Trends*, *Regional Trends* and the *Annual Abstract of Statistics*. Rosser and Harris used census findings to check the accuracy of their random sample of Swansea, and Julienne Ford used statistics on income and occupation to find a set of comparable schools in the London area. Other statistics, however, such as those relating to social class on the Registrar General's scale, are not very useful because the definitions employed differ from the requirements of the sociologist.

As one of several resources and a potential source of interesting hypotheses, official statistics do remain of some value to sociologists.

Think about it

- What do you consider to be the main advantages and disadvantages of using official statistics?
- What examples of official statistics can you think of other than those referred to above?
- Can you think of examples of research in which you might feel
  i) quite confident
  ii) rather wary
  of the use of official statistics?

Other secondary sources

While official statistics are the most common examples of secondary data used by sociologists, various others have also proved to be of value. Newspapers, academic journals, government reports and published books are all useful sources of information, although they do need to be used very carefully. In some instances personal diaries and letters may also prove helpful in sociological enquiry.

Ethnography

This involves the researcher in describing the way of life of a group of people, using participant observation over a time period. It owes its origins to anthropology and the studies of pre-industrial communities, but has been adapted to investigate industrial/post-industrial societies in recent times. The intention of the researcher using this approach is 'to tell it as it is'. This requires that the researcher gains access to the group and that group members are willing to share their thoughts and ideas. Eileen Barker's study of the Moonies would fit this approach well, as would a number of studies of work organisations from the perspective of an employee, such as S. Kamata's 1983 study of a Japanese car factory entitled *Diary of a Human Robot*.

KEY RESEARCH TERMS

sample	a group selected for study, representative of the people the researcher wishes to study.
sampling population	the people the researcher is interested in studying and who could therefore be included in the survey.
sampling frame	the people the sample is actually taken from, e.g. list of names. It is essential that the sampling frame accurately represents the overall population.
primary data	information obtained personally by a researcher, e.g. surveys, participant observation.
secondary data	information that is already available from another source, e.g. official statistics, diaries, autobiographies.
quantitative data	is presented in statistical form, e.g. graphs, charts.
qualitative data	is presented in written form, e.g. accounts of discussions recorded in participant observation studies, and usually attempts to understand the world from the point of view of the people being studied.
experiment	a method of testing a hypothesis in a carefully controlled manner.
structured interview	the exact wording of the questions and the order of asking are worked out beforehand and are the same for all respondents.
unstructured interview	similar to a discussion, where the interviewer directs the discussion as appropriate and dependent on the respondent's previous answers.
interviewer bias	the effect the appearance, personality and behaviour of the interviewer has on a respondent's answers.
participant observation	a method of research in which the observer joins the group being studied and participates in their activities.

■ EVALUATING RESEARCH METHODS

Within the past few years there has been vigorous debate about whether sociologists should stick to using research methods which 'match' their theoretical perspective. A positivist stance was assumed to lead to the use of survey methods, allowing **quantitative data** to be collected, whilst an interactionist approach would favour the collection of **qualitative data**. In Ray Pawson's view (1989), such distinctions are unhelpful; he proposes that a more appropriate approach would be to use a variety of research methods (**triangulation**) to obtain richer data and findings. If observation, questionnaire and interview, for example, were used alongside each other, then, providing their respective results were consistent, the researcher would feel more confident that the findings really did offer a reflection of the life experiences of those being studied.

A number of factors can influence the selection of methods to be used in a particular study. These include the following:

<u>Appropriateness of method</u>   Certain methods are always more suitable than others for particular pieces of research. Official statistics are hazardous when studying crime, while participant observation would be unsatisfactory for studying voting behaviour. However, as each method has its drawbacks, sociologists will select different combinations of methods when studying a particular institution or behaviour pattern.

<u>Sociological perspectives</u>   People in the positivist (scientific) tradition of Auguste Comte tend to select the questionnaire, while social interactionists generally prefer participant observation. Some Marxists have tended to theorise rather than engage in empirical research; whilst others such as Westergaard and Murdock have undertaken empirical study. Cicourel and the phenomenologists have concentrated on tape recording conversations to determine how meanings are negotiated by the participants in the discussion.

<u>Support for research</u>   Certain methods require considerable resources of time and/or money, which may put them beyond the reach of the sociologist. The source of funding – a government agency, a university or private industry – might also influence the form, extent and outcomes of a piece of research. This is particularly so at present with primary emphasis on sociological research being used in considerations of social policy. Access to a computer, a tape-recorder and research assistants may be needed and can be costly.

In summary, sociologists have used many different methods of data collection, each of which is open to some criticism as being imperfect. This leaves sociologists free to be selective; their own perspectives, the subject under investigation and the resources at their disposal are all influential, to differing degrees, in their choice of research method(s).

Application and appropriateness of research methods

The application of research methods and their appropriateness need to be assessed according to practical, ethical and theoretical criteria. A key point for consideration is likely to be the debate between positivist and interpretivist sociology in terms of the choice of methods.

As we have seen, positivists aim to be scientific and seek to obtain factual data that can easily be quantified and used to support or question a theory of behaviour. For them the study must be capable of validation by another researcher who is able to repeat the study and produce the same findings. It must also be accurate in terms of the group being studied, which must reflect the wider population under investigation. Ideally, therefore, large numbers should be studied and precise sampling techniques used to ensure representativeness.

Interpretivist sociologists, on the other hand, seek richness of detail about a small group in order to understand the meanings they give to their behaviour and to the world around them. The aim is to relate to their subjects in order to understand their world view. They believe that people have the ability to produce and negotiate their own meanings for

Summary of approaches to sociological theory and methods	
Positivist (macro-sociologists and some micro-sociologists)	**Interpretivist (micro-sociologists)**
Whilst social phenomena are different from natural phenomena, they can be studied using the 'scientific method' to identify general theories. Need to have precise definitions of concepts used, clear indications of method, minimal amount of subjective influence, and to aim for value-freedom and objectivity. Seeks to use a quantitative approach to data collection, seeking numerical data analysis.	Social phenomena are substantially distinctive from natural phenomena; our understandings of the world derive from the ('social') interpretations we make of it. Given that each individual will have different 'understandings', it is not possible to develop generalised theories of the human world. The methods used are more likely to be qualitative rather than quantitative, seeking out the richness of people's own interpretations.
Most likely to use data collection techniques of social surveys, incorporating structured questionnaires and interviews. Validity is achieved through the use of precisely defined concepts, operationalised in a measurable way, with data collected by standardised means.	The preferred forms of data collection are most likely to be unstructured interviews and observation (both direct and participant).
Claims reliability and representativeness through compiling techniques such as stratified random sampling.	Validity is viewed as being achieved through the use of techniques which allow 'reality' to be uncovered with little or no interference from the researcher – a form of 'naturalistic validity'.

their behaviour and that it is vital for the sociologist to see people on their own terms and not impose meanings on them. Creating the opportunity for the respondents' 'own voices' to be heard rather than imposing the researcher's agenda (by questionnaires, etc.), is considered very important to the interpretivist sociologist.

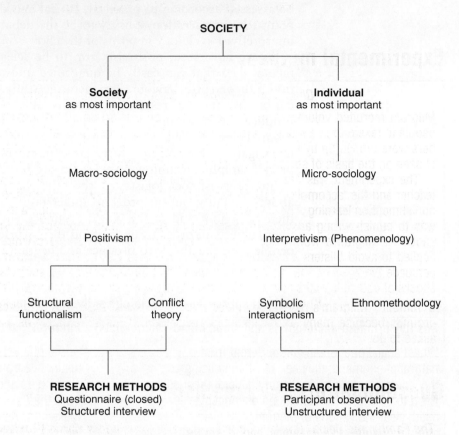

A number of studies have sought to utilise mixed methods of research. There is evidence to suggest that this strategy is becoming more widely used in contemporary sociological research, and enriching the quality of the research.

The relationship between theory and method						
Forms of data	Positivism					Anti-positivism
Secondary	Birth and Death Statistics	Suicide Statistics	Official Records	Newspaper Reports	Diaries Letters	Novels
Primary	Experiments Structured Questionnaires		Formal/ Informal Interviews	Observation	Participant Observation	Unobtrusive Measures

← More standardised, generalisable, objective, reliable?   More insightful, valid, interpretive, → subjective?

Source: T. Lawson, 'In the Shadow of Science', *Social Studies Review*, Vol. 2:2, November 1986

Using research methods in sociological studies: three case studies

Three case studies help to show how and why particular methods are used by researchers. Note that the first example was a social psychology rather than exclusively sociological study.

Experimental method

Obedience to Authority, Stanley Milgram (Tavistock, 1974)

Milgram recruited volunteers for his experiment by placing an advertisement in a local newspaper for people to take part in a study of memory and learning. Almost 300 replies were received, and then numbers were topped up by names taken from the New Haven telephone directory. Specific volunteers were chosen on the basis of sex and occupation, and they were asked to appear at Yale University.

The experiment was set up so that the volunteer (the 'experimenter') was always given the role of teacher and the 'accomplice' that of learner or victim in what was supposed to be a test of the effects of punishment on learning. The learner was strapped to an electric chair apparatus and the task of the teacher was to punish wrong answers to questions by administering progressively increasing levels of electric shock. In Milgram's words, 'An electrode was attached to the learner's wrist, and electrode paste was applied to avoid blisters and burns.' In reality no shock was given, but circumstances were designed to persuade the 'teacher' that it was. It was found that 60 per cent of the subjects would have administered shocks of 450 volts to the learner. This differed little whether the teacher was male or female, young or old.

Comment Milgram's research required much in terms of resources, and it can be criticised on ethical grounds because many of the volunteers experienced mental anguish as a result of what they were asked to do.

Questionnaire/survey method

The Family and Social Change, Colin Rosser and Christopher Harris (Routledge & Kegan Paul, 1965)

The main element of Rosser and Harris's research was a questionnaire on family patterns based on a random starting point in the Electoral Register, after which every fiftieth name was taken. They employed 21 temporary interviewers and interviewed almost 2000 people – 87 per cent of the initial sample. In addition, they interviewed a number of people from both within and outside the basic sample on an open-ended basis, who seemed willing and able to produce rich details about family life. Finally, they claim that a year's residence in Swansea enabled them to gain the insights offered by participant observation as a method.

Rosser and Harris admitted with hindsight that the schedule of questions asked was unsatisfactory, with important questions being omitted.

Comment This study is in the long-standing British **empirical** tradition of gaining information via a social survey. The method was time-consuming and potentially expensive, and it is possible to doubt the accuracy and honesty of some answers produced by it. On the other hand, their mixture of methods displays flexibility, and their willingness to accept the limitations of their study is positive. A pilot study, in which questions could have been tested, would have been of value. (John Rex and Robert Moore, in their study of race relations in Birmingham, undertook a pilot study in the ethnically similar area of Balsall Heath before they studied attitudes in Sparkbrook. Moore claims that the use of the questionnaire provided a broader picture of the structure and opinions of the population than interviews with officials of various organisations ever would.)

Participant observation method

A Glasgow Gang Observed, 'James Patrick' (Eyre Methuen, 1973)

'Patrick' had been working part time in an approved school for two years, before obtaining a full-time post in 1966. He befriended one inmate and decided to join a street gang in order to understand why the boys became involved in further trouble when released.

'Patrick' identified several important problems with his research. He was afraid that his presence in the gang would lead to incidents being staged for his benefit, with the behaviour of his 'friend' being particularly affected. He was also concerned with the extent to which he should participate in gang activities, eventually deciding to remain as passive a participant as possible. Finally, he found it very difficult 'being a middle-class teacher during the week and a member of a juvenile gang at the weekend'.

Comment 'Patrick's' relative youth and his knowledge of the teenagers he was studying enabled him to gain access to and acceptance by the group. Such means of entry are not always available to sociologists and this can create a serious practical problem. Ned Polsky was also fortunate in having the skill to play billiards which thereby enabled him to study the activities and attitudes of over 50 pool-room hustlers. Both 'Patrick' and Polsky rejected the use of cameras or tape-recorders because they place a barrier between the investigator and the investigated. Unlike 'Patrick', however, Polsky believed it important that people should be aware of his role, and he attempted to gain the confidence of his subjects before combining participant observation with informal interviews.

The major ethical criticism of the use of participant observation was made by Kai T. Erikson in 1967 in *A Comment on Disguised Observation in Sociology*. Erikson argued that covert research could harm the subjects of investigation in unexpected ways, and that it was therefore wrong to study people without their prior approval. He also argued that the reputation of sociology could be affected and avenues of research consequently closed, and that it was particularly unethical to involve graduate students in a research situation which could pose both personal problems and stress for them. Finally, from a theoretical point of view, he argued that the method was bad science, since no one could be certain as to the level of success of the sociologist in becoming a full participant accepted by the whole group.

Studies using mixed methods

SOCIETY TODAY

Researching child abuse

PAT McNEILL talks to **STEVE TAYLOR** of the London School of Economics about the qualitative methods he uses to research child abuse. This is part of an occasional series of such interviews.

PAT McNEILL: What is the subject of your research?

STEVE TAYLOR: I'm researching child abuse, and in particular how various experts, such as social workers and doctors, come to "recognise" that a child has been abused or is "at risk."

PM: Is your work intended to guide social policy in this area?

ST: As a sociologist, what concerns me is that most people researching this area oversimplify the problem. They assume that there is a thing called child abuse which is relatively easy to define, that it happens, and that it is easy to identify who is being abused. For them, the only questions are about why it happens.

I think the sociologist has to say: "Before we get into those questions we must see what we mean by child abuse, what officials mean by child abuse and how we respond to what we perceive to be child abuse." Then you can say to social workers, doctors and others: "These are the theories you are implicitly working with when you define one case as child abuse and another as normal parenting. What do you think of these theories? Do you want to go back and re-examine them? Do you think you should be doing any-

thing differently?" This type of research can help practitioners to clarify their thinking and improve the quality of their work.

PM: What research methods are you using?

ST: First, we did formal interviews with the various professional groups involved. We asked them how they defined child abuse, and how they recognised something as a case of child abuse. But sociologists should not just reproduce what people say, and you cannot conduct research purely on interviews. So, having identified some of the things professionals saw as problematic about child abuse, we did some participant observation. This meant going out with social workers on visits, going to case conferences and to court in order to see their ideas in action.

At the same time, we were able to put further questions; for example, asking social workers to explain particular decisions. We also used documentary data, such as social work files and case conference minutes.

We formed the impression during the research that social services felt under such pressure from the media, from policy guidelines and from lack of resources that they were being more defensive and were bringing more cases to court than they really wished to, or would have done a few years earlier. Official figures show that the proportion of children coming into care compulsorily has increased

in the last few years. Some people suggest that this is because abuse is on the increase. Our data suggests that it can be explained by our changing response to children at risk.

At one point I played the role of a trainee social worker. The advantage of this was that I could be more sure that people weren't being extra efficient and careful for my benefit. The disadvantage was that I couldn't stop people and ask them research questions. It's not a question of a right or wrong method. You pick your method to suit the nature of the problem, and you look for interplay between methods.

PM: Is it difficult to keep your own personal values distinct from the research you are doing?

ST: If we let our personal values predominate, then we cease to be sociologists. Just recently, every politician and pundit has suddenly become an expert on child abuse. If you are on the political right, it's because of the decline in family values. If you are left of centre, it's because of bad housing, stress, and the deprivations of capitalism. If you are into feminism, it's just another example of male power.

All these views are immediate political responses, and there is an important distinction between politics and sociology. Politicians only look for evidence to confirm a pre-conceived view. Sociology, on the other hand, is about discovery. The sociologist may have pre-conceived views, but research must be structured so that there is always the chance of discovering the unexpected.

You must also keep your emotions as well as your values out of research. As a citizen, child abuse alarms me. As a social scientist, it is behaviour to be observed and analysed.

Source: *New Society*, 15 January 1988

Think about it

• Evaluate the appropriateness of the methods chosen by the researchers in each of the three studies.
• Analyse the role of the values of the researcher in these studies.

■ MODERNISM AND POSTMODERNISM

In this unit we have looked at a range of sociological theories, which owe their development to the so-called 'founding fathers' of sociology, and the debates which these theories have generated. Towards the end of the twentieth century, these theories have come under prolonged attack. The ideas generated by structural functionalism, Marxism and Weberianism, were classified as **modernist theory**. Modernist theory refers to a particular way of thinking about the world, a way of thinking which developed in the seventeenth-century and eighteenth-century Enlightenment and is, therefore (over a 300-year period), modern. These theories held in common a clear set of ideas:

- It is possible to produce objective and valid knowledge of the world and this is desirable.
- Such knowledge is based upon evidence obtained through rigorous and systematic research methods used by objective researchers (positivism).
- Such knowledge can be applied to social situations to enhance the quality of life, for example, through their effect on social policy (see Unit 11).
- Such knowledge can be applied to whole societies or cultures and to the elements (for example, institutions) which make up the societies, upon which generalisations can be made.

This modernist agenda contains reference to a number of elements of theory and methods already referred to in this unit. For example:

- scientific study – positivism;
- objectivity;
- value-freedom;
- use of research methods such as interview, questionnaire, observation;
- major 'traditions' of sociology – Marxism, functionalism and interactionism.

All of these elements are seen to contribute to attempts by sociologists to seek out the 'truth' relating to particular aspects of human behaviour in large- or small-scale social situations. In addition, such attempts to uncover the 'truth' are usually concerned to seek to improve the social and/or material conditions where people live, to improve 'the lot' of the population.

Modernist theory

Focus	Focus upon the individual in *society*		Focus upon the *individual* in society	
Macro sociology	Positive 'science'	Emphasis upon 'structure'	Micro sociology	Emphasis upon 'agency' (the individual's interpretations and actions)
Schools of thought	Functionalism	Marxism	Interactionism	Ethnomethodology

A. Giddens' 'Structuration Theory' seeks to draw from both traditions

Modernism

Modernism is generally used to refer to the modern age in terms of the scientific and rational ideas which have developed since the Middle Ages and the Renaissance in the fourteenth and fifteenth centuries. A cluster of interlinked institutions developed, including capitalism, industrialisation and the military.

To gain a broader view of modernism specific aspects are worthy of note:

- The need for raw materials and labour for capitalist production involved countries well beyond Europe and this formed an important part of modernity. Ethnic relations developed, based on imperialism and colonialism, which have determined many forms of social interaction across the globe.
- The Industrial Revolution in the eighteenth and nineteenth centuries brought about considerable changes, for example in the relations between the sexes. Women's sphere became domestic, while men's became public, which reinforced the existing patterns of domination.
- From the nineteenth century, a major development was in the economy, with monetary exchanges and complex capitalist relations. In political terms, new laws began to shape people's lives in modern industrial societies. The boundaries for such societies became represented as 'nation states'; national common cultures developed, identified by flags, anthems and a wide range of cultural symbols.
- During the twentieth century, a mass society developed with shared interlinked institutions such as schools, public limited companies, government departments, which socialised its members to identify with its norms and values. After World War II, modernism could be associated with settled class relations, clear party political loyalties and recognisable status groups, particularly in relation to consumption patterns. By the 1960s in the UK, state policy had established the provision of social welfare in health, education, housing, etc., and class differences – some claimed – were decreasing. The nation seemed to be moving towards a wealthy mass society with widespread leisure activities.

Modernist ideas have been dominant in the social sciences, and certainly in sociology, throughout the twentieth century and still retain much of their influence over sociological thinking. However, a number of significant events have brought into question the earlier certainties of a modernist view of the world. Such events might include:

- the collapse of the Soviet Union and with it the dream that Marxist explanations can assist world change and freedom from capitalism;
- the dominance of capitalism and the market on a global scale;
- the impact of 'globalisation', with multinational companies dominating the world economy;
- the rapid expansion of technology and its impact upon societies in terms of jobs, pay rates, etc.;
- the continuing inequalities within and between societies.

Postmodernism

As a consequence of the inadequacies of modernist theory to account for the kinds of changes noted above, some theorists have begun to develop their ideas under the heading of **postmodernism**.

Major criticisms of modernism by postmodernists are that:

- it is not possible to study society and develop unified conclusions; and
- human behaviour is more likely to be characterised by differences (**heterogeneity**) than by similarities (**homogeneity**). Whereas Marxists attempt to base their theories on social class, postmodernists see little relevance in looking at class for explanations of individual behaviour in contemporary society.

Postmodernism suggests a change in the way people relate to or experience modern ideas, social, economic or political conditions, as well as forms of social life. It looks at changes in culture, communications, technology, economic production, politics and social relationships. For some theorists, postmodernism represented a period of time from the mid-1970s to the late-1980s when theorists sought to understand why the ideas of modernist theory appeared to offer so little in explaining the social, political and economic changes which were taking place in Britain and elsewhere. For Giddens, writing in 1990, postmodernity appeared to offer the prospect of societies which were becoming more prosperous; which involved more levels of democratic participation; which were demilitarised; and which had developed positive links between the use of technology and human labour (for example robots taking over boring jobs).

C. Wright Mills (1970) had already noted that the 'modern' traditions of liberalism and socialism were no longer 'adequate explanations of the world and of ourselves'. Fourteen years later, Lyotard noted the end of 'grand narratives' (suggesting that modernist explanations were no longer able to offer relevant or sufficient explanations of a rapidly changing world), to be replaced by 'little narratives' which were closer to people's lives and experience.

For Hollinger, writing in the 1990s, postmodernism creates clear opportunities for social scientists to rethink the ideas which have dominated modernist thought and to develop more relevant theories of our social world by looking again at a range of key social scientific concepts such as self, society, community, reason and values which are firmly located in modernist theorists. Indeed, the major contribution of postmodern thought might have been to create opportunities for women, ethnic minorities, disabled groups and a whole range of previously ignored or unrepresented sections of society to have a 'voice' in sociology for the first time.

Paolo Portaghesi (1992) links his ideas on postmodernism to 'the age of information', made possible by 'the new electronic technology', whilst others look to culture, architecture, art or changes in the composition of economic, political and social structures. Postmodern societies, it is argued, are becoming increasingly fragmented, containing ever greater numbers of differing groups (plurality) and a tendency towards **individualism** – as opposed to **collectivism** – on the part of the citizens. Such a view is reflected in the debates between **Fordist** and **Post-Fordist** theories which look at the organisation of work (see Unit 5). In addition, this view can be noted in debates between the influence of **locality**, the **'nation' state** and **global change** (see Unit 9). Here, for example, political parties give way to 'new social movements' based upon gender, race or sexuality and the 'collective identities' of class (see Unit 2) are reduced or removed from people's living experiences. This leads to, for example, the decline of trade unions or the growth of 'New Labour' – without socialism (see Unit 11).

Fordism v. postmodernism

Fordist production, based on the production of Ford motor cars in the USA, was typically characterised by the following:

- standardised products;
- specialised machinery allowing mass production;
- jobs that can be standardised and broken down into their key elements to ensure efficiency;
- automated production lines allowing the product to move and the worker to stay put;
- production geared to meet a 'mass market' of buyers.

During the 1980s these production techniques began to disappear, to be replaced by post-Fordism or postmodernism. This is characterised by:

- rapid production;
- rapid delivery;
- rapid consumption of products;
- production intended to meet affluent and small 'specialist markets' rather than 'mass markets'.

Sainsbury's supermarket chain, for example, studied by Murray in 1989, uses computers to monitor and record customer purchase and to reorder instantly, with next day restocking of shelves. The emphasis is clearly on consumption, whereas in Fordism it is on production.

Individuals in the world of Fordism may have had to work hard in boring jobs, to be convinced that they needed to wear similar clothes to everyone else, to eat the same food and to enjoy holidays in the UK. In the shopping situation, postmodernism would see different individuals: at work they hold more responsibility and act on their own initiative; when shopping they can express their individuality by buying fashionable clothes with their Switch or Mastercard.

The universality of the Body Shop, of Macdonalds, even the Metrocentre in Gateshead, are seen as illustrative of postmodernism – they could be found virtually anywhere in the world from Beijing and St Petersburg to Manchester or Oslo.

Think about it

Postmodernism has sought to question the value of modernist – i.e. Marxist, Durkheimian and Weberian – views, that social theory can offer general and inclusive views of the social world.
- Do you think that it is no longer possible to construct general sociological perspectives of the social world?
- Why should some postmodernists believe that there is now more freedom for the individual to create his or her own identity?

■ SOCIOLOGY AND SOCIAL POLICY

The relationship between sociology and **social policy** has become closer in recent years. This is because major funding for research has been increasingly directed to the identification and resolution of specific social problems, such as crime, drug abuse and social disorder. Research in the sociology of education, for example, has helped policy makers to look carefully at the place of the school in the community, at the issue of parental choice, at the interaction between teacher and pupils, and at the influence of peer groups in addressing the issue of bullying in schools. Whilst sociologists do not make social policy, their work contributes to the debates that take place around issues of policy, although ultimately the government's political agenda may override the findings of research. The sociologist Sir David Marsland, for example, was an adviser to Margaret Thatcher's Family Policy Unit and as such was influential in the changes to the Welfare State which took place in the 1980s.

Sociology has also contributed to the development of social policy in the area of health and illness (see Unit 7). Through research, sociologists have shown how socio-economic factors (for example social class, occupation, unemployment) and cultural factors (for example religion, region) can and do influence health. They have also shown how the dominant medical model of health (see Unit 7, page 338) has shaped our view of health and illness. By placing the analysis of this research very firmly in the wider arena of the politics of welfare, sociologists have ensured that the debates on health in the UK are conducted at the highest levels of the government's social policy.

Selected reading list

A Glasgow Gang Observed, 'James Patrick' (Eyre Methuen, 1973)
The Outsiders, H.S. Becker (The Free Press, New York, 1963)
The Rules of Sociological Method, Emile Durkheim (The Free Press, New York, 1938)
Social Structure, G.P. Murdock (Macmillan, New York, 1949)
The Social System, Talcott Parsons (The Free Press, New York, 1951)
Social Theory and Social Structure, Robert Merton (The Free Press, New York, 1968)
The Sociological Imagination, C. Wright Mills (Penguin, 1970)
Stigma, Erving Goffman (Prentice Hall Inc., Englewood Cliffs, 1964)
'Structuration theory: past, present and future', Anthony Giddens in *Giddens' Theory of Structuration: A Critical Appreciation*, C. Bryant and D. Jary (eds) (Routledge, 1991)
Studies in Ethnomethodology, Harold Garfinkel (Prentice Hall Inc., Englewood Cliffs, 1967)
Suicide: A Study in Sociology, Emile Durkheim (1897) (Routledge & Kegan Paul, 1970)

2 Different groups in society: social differentiation, power and stratification

Introduction

The cartoon illustrates how we commonly make snap judgements about people based on what they look like, how they behave, and how they live. We then make assumptions about what 'sort' of people they are and what **social class** they might belong to. The concepts of social **differentiation** and **stratification** are rooted in this idea of how people become ranked or graded in a system of unequal social groups with different degrees of **social power**.

Think about it

- What do you think of at the mention of **social class**? You might focus on different occupations or jobs, higher or lower incomes. Differentiation takes many forms.
- What about **ethnicity**? Are white skin and the values associated with 'white culture' seen by some as superior to dark skin and 'black culture'? Why might this be the case?
- **Gender** differentiation is another form of ranking or stratification. Why, in many spheres, are males ranked more highly than females?
- Consider **age**. Why are the very young and the very old given lower social rankings?
- How do these four forms of differentiation – class, ethnicity, gender and age – interrelate?
- What do you think is meant by **social power**?

The word 'stratification' gives us an image of 'layering'. It makes us think of societies as ordered, relatively permanent hierarchies of different social groups, one above the other with the more powerful on top. However, sociologists reject the idea of the existence of some innate or God-given order or grouping among people. They consider that social differentiation, power and stratification are human creations and relate to people's values, which vary across place and time dimensions. Sociologists use the terms 'social differentiation', 'power' and 'stratification' to describe social *processes* concerned with **structured social inequality**:

- **structured** because sociology attempts to identify structures and systems of inequality rather than isolated cases of injustice;
- **social** because inequality is related to social groups and their social differences;
- **inequality** because the focal interest for sociologists is the differences between social groups, especially in terms of access to advantages such as power and wealth.

In this unit we will look at:

- examples of stratification and power systems such as caste, slavery and feudalism;
- the nature of social class, with reference to Marx, Weber and contemporary theories of the working, middle and upper classes;
- social class and social mobility in contemporary society;
- inequalities in wealth, income and life chances in relation to the effects of stratification by class, gender, age and ethnicity.

What is stratification?

Stratification, as stated above, is the division of society into 'layers' on the basis of difference or inequality. Every society has some form of stratification. Very often it is on the basis of wealth, inherited and accumulated from previous generations, for example land, property and personal possessions. But even in the simplest of societies where wealth may be virtually non-existent, some social groups will be distinct (and superior to others) on the basis of particular skills or strengths.

Power in sociological terms is the extent to which some social groups or individuals are able to exercise their will over others regardless of the consent of the others. Often they use such power to further their own political, economic or social advantage.

Stratification and power structures affect every aspect of human life, every individual, group and organisation, whether people realise it or not. In the UK, for example, opportunities for health, wealth and employment are unequally distributed, as the article opposite illustrates.

An important feature of stratification is that such inequality is not random: it is *systematically distributed* according to the basis on which the stratification occurs. We must try to understand not only what factors may cause stratification but how these factors affect the life opportunities of individuals in different **strata**. Members of each group (or **stratum**) tend to share certain features which separate them from other groups; features which are often the cause of further inequality, and which often may be passed on to their children. The concept of stratification usually implies that this structure can persist across generations.

Sink or swim Britain

Let's start with teeth. Half of all unskilled manual workers between the ages of 55 and 64 have no teeth left at all. Yet only 7 per cent of professionals in the same age bracket are similarly deprived.

Did someone mention social inequality? Disparities in income, in diet, in access to health care? All elementary stuff, and after a decade and a half of a "sink or swim" culture, measuring the gaps between rich and poor has almost lost the power to shame. The principle that inequality is wrong, and should be combated, has been subtly eroded by a Conservative Party that values differentials as an index of success.

Imagine going back to basics, and teaching school-children about social inequality. Repeat after me, Samantha, that 10 per cent of the population owns 50 per cent of the wealth, a figure unchanged since 1976. If you exclude wealth tied up in houses, that's just 5 per cent of the population owning 50 per cent of the wealth.

Next, income. If you take the poorest fifth of the population, their share of the total income cake has fallen, from 10 per cent in 1979 to 7 per cent in 1991. The richest fifth have actually increased their share, from 35 per cent to 41 per cent of the total.

Meanwhile, a canter round the country suggests that we should all migrate to East Anglia without delay. Unemployment is lowest there (it's highest in Northern Ireland, the West Midlands, and the North). What's more, men there are safe and sober, unlike their dangerous counterparts in the north and north-west, a third of whom drink more than the recommended limits for "sensible" alcohol intake.

Speaking of regional divides, it will not amaze anyone to hear that the highest average weekly disposable income is in Greater London, where households wield £156 a week. The lowest is in Northern Ireland, at £116 a week.

What *Social Trends* reveals is a Britain divided not just by region but by race. Over half of the ethnic minority population lives in the south-east, with 20 per cent of Londoners belonging to an ethnic minority group. They, however, have not seen much of the fabled prosperity of the south-east. Unemployment is 30 per cent among blacks and 28 per cent among Pakistanis and Bangladeshis, compared with less than 10 per cent among whites. One in five Pakistani and Bangladeshi families live in housing classified as "unsatisfactory".

British parents are not getting the time to *be* parents. In particular, fathers are not getting the time to be fathers. British men continue to work the longest hours in the European Community, an average of 43.5 a week. Only one in 15 men who are working has a part-time job, compared with one in two women. If there's to be a reorganisation of work and gender roles to create a more child-centred society, we have a long way to go.

Source: Adapted from *New Statesman and Society*, 28 January 1994

Stratification and the concepts of advantage and power

Although different societies produce different patterns of inequality, or stratification, sociologists have noticed that they all tend to include one or more forms of **advantage** or greater social power:

- **life chance** – material advantages which improve the quality of life of the person who receives them. In the UK this includes not only wealth and income, but also health and security;
- **social status** – prestige or high standing in the eyes of other members of the society, and the social preferment that goes with it;
- **political influence** – when a group is able to dominate other groups, to have a major influence on decision-making, or to benefit from decision-making.

It is important to note that some advantages (or indicators) are subjective (i.e. constructed by members of society), while others are objective (i.e. factual, describing actual material benefits).

- **Objective indicators** consist of certain characteristics which can be used to represent abstract ideas. For example, in defining social class, occupations tend to be the most commonly used indicators.
- **Subjective indicators** may describe political, material or even sexual prowess. Our own feelings about stratification can also be seen as subjective – we all have some awareness of class differences in our views and behaviour at an entirely personal level.

Examples of stratification systems

It is helpful to look at different kinds of power and stratification systems to see that this general idea of 'inequality' can be evidenced by different societies in different ways. Three of the most commonly quoted forms of stratification are **caste**, **slavery** and **feudalism**.

Caste

The classic example is the traditional Hindu caste system in India which has existed for over 3000 years. The main features are:

- a very formal and ritualistic system, with a religious routine based on Hinduism;

The five main castes, or *varna*, of traditional Hindu India		
Each caste is subdivided into thousands of *jatis* (subcastes), each with its own rituals.	1. Brahmins, e.g. priests and teachers	There is no mobility between castes. According to *kharma* (Hindu belief in reincarnation), those who obey their caste's code (*dharma*) will be reborn into a higher caste; those who do not obey will be reborn into a lower caste.
	2. Kshatriyas, e.g. warriors, landlords	
	3. Vaishyas, e.g. merchants, farmers	
	4. Sudras, e.g. servants, manual workers, artisans	
Out-'castes', segregated to prevent pollution of higher castes.	5. Harijans ('untouchables'), e.g. leatherworkers, roadsweepers	Although higher castes are often richer than lower, this is not necessarily so. The purest Brahmins may reject all possessions, a Harijan leatherworker may become rich.

- a system of **ascribed** (rather than **achieved**) status, since individuals are born into and remain in a particular caste;
- a **closed** (or hereditary) system of social differentiation and stratification with no movement between castes.

Slavery This represents the most extreme form of stratification, since some human beings are regarded as chattels, or items of property, belonging to other more powerful individuals or social groups.

Slavery has taken different forms, depending in part on the economic use to which slaves were put. In the ancient world, slaves were acquired through conquest and trade, and were seen as an investment for wealthy citizens. In North America, where the enslavement of Africans and their descendants continued until the late nineteenth century, slavery formed a highly profitable system of exploitation.

Slavery was 'justified' by beliefs about racial inferiority, and was supported by the following structures:

- The legal system: slaves in North America lacked power as they had few civil or property rights; strict laws regulated slave behaviour, restricting the slave's right to travel or seek defence against attacks by whites; penalties for breaking the regulations included beatings and death.
- The perpetual nature of slavery: because they were the property of their owner, slaves, and their children, were destined to occupy this status throughout their lives.
- Slaves, as property, were under the absolute power of their owners. They could be bought, sold or traded at the whim of the master.

Feudalism This was the system of social stratification in Medieval Europe. It also existed in many other parts of the world, including West Africa, and even survived in Russia and Japan until the twentieth century.

It was a system based on land ownership, land being the chief source of power and wealth in agricultural societies. To ensure the agricultural system worked and to try and keep some form of law and order in the era of constant wars, societies were organised into a hierarchy of authority, rights and power from the highest, the king, to the lowest, the peasants or serfs. Everyone 'knew their place', and was kept in it.

In Medieval England the feudal hierarchy consisted of royalty, nobility, lesser gentry, free tenants, villeins and serfs. The nobility swore allegiance to the king, in return for certain territories. This land was subdivided and distributed down the pyramid in smaller and smaller portions, always in return for allegiance: military service, money or produce from the land.

The rigid hierarchy was reinforced by the power of the Church, one of the most wealthy of landowners, which would use its powers of excommunication (excluding someone from contact with the Church) against those who rebelled against the king. The excommunicated were believed to be condemned to hell.

The feudal system is often referred to as the **estates system,** with the nobility and clergy forming the first two 'layers' or estates. The nobility provided the soldiers, administrators and magistrates; the clergy provided for the people's spiritual and moral welfare.

The feudal or estates system

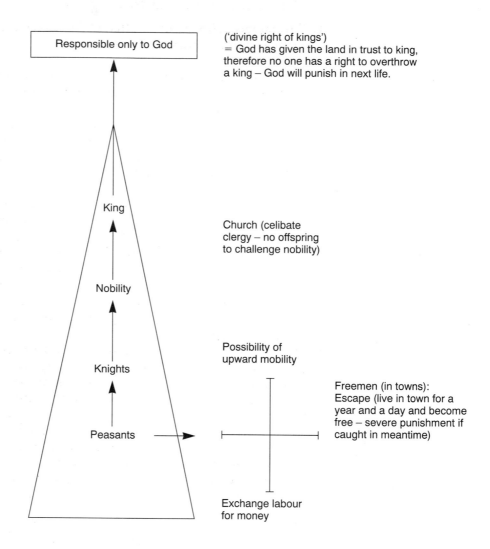

Industrialisation and the growth of towns, together with increasing money circulation, the rise of the professional classes, political centralisation and the development of professional courts, led to the decline of feudalism in Britain. It was gradually replaced by a system based on occupation, skills and business wealth: the present class system of middle and working class. Yet even today there are remnants of feudalism in modern Britain – the monarchy and the House of Lords, for example. The film *Braveheart*, starring Mel Gibson, illustrated how the English feudal system affected the Scottish people, often to their detriment, for example by removing many crofters from their land during the Highland Clearances.

The nature of social class

The principle of social class, of people being ranked socially, is not part of some natural or unchangeable scheme. It is influenced by historical developments. It is important to note the following points.

1. **Natural inequality** is quite different from **social rank**. This was commented upon centuries ago by Rousseau:

   > 'I conceive that there are two kinds of inequality among the human species; one, which I call natural or physical, because it is established by nature, and consists in a difference of age, health, bodily strength, and the qualities of the mind or of the soul, and another, which may be called moral or political inequality, because it depends on a kind of convention, and is established, or at least authorised, by the consent of men. This latter consists of the different privileges, which some men enjoy to the prejudice of others; such as that of being more rich, more honoured, more powerful, or even in a position to exert obedience.'
   >
   > Jean-Jacques Rousseau, *A Dissertation on the Origin and Foundation of the Inequality of Mankind* (1755)

2. Modern social class, in contrast to the caste system or the feudal or estates system, is defined less by religion or landownership and more by economic factors.
3. Boundaries are less rigidly defined in modern societies, although the principal class groups, such as landowners and the working class, may be identifiable in most societies. Intermediate strata, often conveniently referred to as the **middle class** have proved difficult to define (see pages 77–9).
4. Membership of a modern social class is usually less stable and more 'open' than in the old hierarchial systems. There are fewer restrictions on movement between classes. Even within one generation an individual, family or group may rise or fall in the social hierarchy of the class system. This is referred to as **social mobility**, which may be:

- *inter*generational – when someone is in a different class from their parents (perhaps because of success in education); or
- *intra*generational – when a person changes social class within their own working life (for example through promotion or business success).

Think about it
- Identify:
  - at least one person who is an example of intergenerational social mobility;
  - at least one person who is an example of intragenerational social mobility.

  It may be a real-life example, or one you have observed in a fictional setting, for example a TV soap opera or a novel.

Theories of social class

Karl Marx

Marx was one of the most influential writers in terms of sociological analysis of social class. His writings formed the basis for a significant perspective in sociology (see Unit 1) and for an ongoing political debate. Sociologists owe a fundamental debt to Marx for starting the discussion about the class system and the class analysis of society (see page 31 and below).

At the heart of Marx's writings is the concept of class. Almost the first statement of his famous work *The Communist Manifesto* (1848) declares:

> *'The history of all hitherto existing societies is the history of class struggle.'*

Karl Heinrich Marx (1818–83) was born in Trier, in the Rhineland, son of a German lawyer and a Dutch mother. Originally from distinguished Jewish families of rabbis, the father converted to Christianity in order to hold public office. Karl Marx studied law and philosophy at the Universities of Bonn and Berlin. In 1843 he married Jenny von Westphalen and soon after met Friedrich Engels, his life-long friend and co-writer of over 50 books. Marx lived the last 25 years of his life in London and is buried in Highgate Cemetery.

Karl Marx

Marx describes history as a series of conflicts between the two main classes in different forms of society. One class (the **proletariat**, the exploited majority) does the productive work, whilst the **bourgeoisie** (the minority class) dominates them and seizes all the profits. He argues that each society's particular form of class exploitation depends on the form of economic relationships or **mode of production** that society employs.

The **capitalist** mode of production, for example, began in England before the Industrial Revolution. Rural workers lost their land-use rights and were forced to become landless proletarians. The only way they could survive was to sell their labour to the landowners, who paid them less than the value of their labour. The landowners (the bourgeoisie) became more wealthy on the profit, which Marx termed **surplus value**, that they had gained.

Later, in the craft and cottage industries, new machinery and new technologies encouraged people to move to urban areas to sell their labour in factories and offices. Again, Marx saw that it was the bourgeoisie who owned the factories and other **means of production** and who were able to employ the wage-earning proletariat.

As well as the workers and the landowners, there were also groups of professional workers such as doctors and lawyers, shopkeepers and clerks. These people made up what Marx called the **petit-bourgeoisie** or intermediate strata.

Conflicts of interest between the two main groups were exacerbated in times of economic recession. Fierce competition between capitalistic enterprises meant that the strong would overcome the weak using their power over resources and knowledge. According to Marx, profits, or surplus value, and power tended to become concentrated in the hands of a smaller and smaller group of increasingly powerful and exploitative people (the ruling classes), with adverse consequences for wage levels and the standard of living of wage-labourers. Wage-labourers would become increasingly aware that they were being exploited and would come to realise that with a different distribution their living conditions need not be so bad. This **class consciousness** is a critical point for Marx: the point at which the proletariat turns from being a class-*in*-itself to a class-*for*-itself.

Marx's conception of class is, then, a **dichotomous** one: in any class system there exist two main classes which are interdependent and, because one exploits the other, antagonistic. This antagonism in a capitalist society provides the driving force for revolutionary social change and the transformation of capitalism into socialism or communism.

To what extent did Marx get it right?

In some ways it may be argued that most of Marx's ideas and predictions have been disproved by events.

- The polarisation of the bourgeoisie and proletariat has been blurred by the expansion of a 'new middle class' and the relative affluence of the working class.
- Marx's expectations of the growth of class-consciousness and the political movement towards communism have not been realised.

However, these criticisms do not invalidate Marxist philosophy.

- The crucial contribution of Marx, to make the essential connection between stratification and the mode of production, is still valid; even in modern, Western 'mixed economies', where the state is involved in economic activity.
- The worker still tends to occupy a minor role in the workplace. Workers' incomes are very low in comparison with the income or wealth of those who control them and who have power over them.

Conclusions on Marx

An important issue for the Marxist analysis of class is the link between the facts and conditions of class and the consciousness people have of their class position. What is it that makes someone think of themselves as belonging to a particular class and become willing to take action (strike, vote or revolt, for example) that reflects the interests of that class? For Marx the answers were a combination of:

- objective factors, such as economic conditions;
- social and organisational factors, for example trade unionism;
- ideological factors, such as the writings of theorists like Marx himself.

Marx never really developed a theory of the middle class, and this has remained a central problem for his followers. However, there are three characteristics of Marx's approach to class which are still important in the study of stratification:

1. the emphasis on the concept of class rooted in the **economic relationships** of production, especially the ownership or non-ownership of the means of production;
2. the inevitability of **class conflict** – the idea that class difference is not an unfortunate side-effect of social processes but basic to the nature of society;
3. the **bi-polar model** of class – stressing the development of the two opposing camps of the bourgeoisie and the proletariat. (In this sense Marx's theory can be seen as a theory of non-stratification, in that it rejects the idea of layering in favour of the image of a battlefield on which two armies are drawn up against each other.)

These themes in Marx's work are taken up by later writers both within and outside the Marxist tradition.

Think about it

- Do you think that Marx offers a useful portrayal of social class? Is his analysis valid in Britain today?
- How aware are you of people's social class and socio-economic background in relation, for example, to education or employment?
- To what extent do you think ideological factors have had and continue to have a major impact on society?

Max Weber

Max Weber (1864–1920) was born in Erfurt, Prussia, the son of a lawyer and liberal politician. He studied a range of subjects at Heidelberg, Berlin and Gottingen Universities. In 1892 he became lecturer in law at Berlin University and soon moved to professorships in political economy. In 1898 he suffered a nervous breakdown, brought on by a row with his father who died shortly after. After travelling across Europe and America he turned to sociology. In 1902 he founded the German Sociological Association. He died unexpectedly of pneumonia in 1920.

Max Weber

There is much in Marx's analysis that Weber would agree with, but crucial differences exist in relation to two issues:

- the idea of different dimensions of stratification; and
- the central importance of the middle class or middle classes.

These issues form much of the modern debate on stratification.

Weber's analysis of class begins by accepting the heart of Marx's view that class relates to the ownership of property, but he expands the idea of property to include both goods and services. People could offer either what they owned (goods or commodities, land or capital) or their services, in order to make a living. What individuals received for their goods or services was determined by supply and demand in the market. The rewards for their goods and services determined what Weber called the **life chances** of the group – its opportunities, health, welfare, etc.

This gives Weber a basis for dividing up Marx's proletariat into different groups and to develop a theory of stratification based on market position, status and party:

- **Market position** for their services, rather than property, determined people's market value. Independent professionals, civil servants, paid managers, etc., made up different classes for Weber because they enjoyed higher levels of reward and better life chances as a result of their superior position in the market for occupational skills. Unlike Marx, who believed the proletariat had an identity of interest, and who urged the 'workers of the world [to] unite', Weber argued that the working class was never likely to unite. Those who enjoyed a relatively privileged lifestyle simply had too much to lose.
- **Status** was important in Weber's idea of stratification. Groups who are given high levels of social 'honour' or prestige by the rest of society have high status. This may be because of their lifestyle, their education or their family. Whatever its source, sharing a similar status makes a group a separate 'stratum' regardless of its economic or market position. An example of such a group is the Hindu Brahmin caste, who are allocated the highest status within the traditional Hindu caste society despite their supposed dedication to lifelong poverty as priests (see page 64).
- **Party** defined a group of individuals who worked together because of their common backgrounds or interests. Examples of parties include political parties, trade unions and other interest and pressure groups such as the Automobile Association and Greenpeace. Party formation was an important aspect of power for Weber, and could influence stratification independently of class and status.

Conclusions on Weber Weber's contribution to the concept of stratification was enormous. By stressing the idea of class as reflecting the market position of different occupational groups, he established the mainstream tradition of class analysis within sociology where class is seen as concerned with different hierarchies of occupational groups. By opposing Marx's emphasis on polarisation, he initiated a concern with the growing middle class and the analysis of class 'fragmentation'. His development of status and, to a lesser extent, power as different dimensions of stratification was taken up by later sociologists.

Functionalism and stratification

The **functionalist** view of sociology, as we saw in Unit 1, was developed by Talcott Parsons and his followers in the USA in the 1930s (see pages 29–30). It made little comment on the stratification theories developed by Marx and Weber, and was more concerned with social **consensus** (or agreement) and stability. Part of the American dream was the model of an open society, free from the class barriers which had characterised traditional European society.

INTERVIEW WITH STUDS TERKEL **THE ANCIENT MARINER**

STUDS TERKEL, now well into his eighties, has broadcast *The Studs Terkel Show*, a daily one-hour radio talk show in Chicago, for more than 40 years, and produced 10 classic books of oral history, including *Race*, for which he won a Pulitzer Prize. David Ransom spoke to him.

DR: I suppose people around the world still look to America as a kind of model; we have this idea of a go-getting, 'open' sort of a place with no class system, where anyone can make it if they just try hard enough.

ST: The United States never was a classless society, you know. It was a myth to begin with. For example, we never use the word 'working class'. Here's a case in point: a young girl whose father is a garbage collector, a sanitation man. I say to her: 'Your father is doing very important work. He's stopping plagues taking place, stopping diseases, terribly important work. Martin Luther King died for the garbage men of Memphis, you know.[1] You are a working-class family.'
   She says to me: '*I beg* your pardon! We're middle class.'

DR: Why are Americans so anxious to think they're all 'middle class'?

ST: I guess we're told that. At the end of World War Two the veterans that came back got a GI Bill of Rights. It gave them the right to buy a home or go to school, and for the first time millions went to college. But something new happened. The suburbs came into being, suburbs of GIs. They were given money to start homes. Before the War — and certainly before the Great Depression — the suburbs were where the rich people lived. Then along came a new kind of suburb, a blue-collar suburb. Now there are as many blue-collar suburbs in America as there are middle-class ones. So the young GI of working-class family starts thinking he's middle class. He's told that. And he buys things. He owns a home of his own, and people think as he does. And he's away from *them* — the blacks of course ... The young, the new crop of Americans, have no sense of past. They've been deprived of it, and many are anti-union.

DR: How did that come about?

ST: Well, because of the elimination of history. So now the young pick up a newspaper, and there is no labor section. There's a business section, a sports section, an entertainment section — no-one thinks about labor, except when a picket takes a swing at a scab, when it's a news item. And so how would they know? They've been deprived of labor history. They don't know how the eight-hour day came into being.
   I tell this tale of a young, up-scale couple waiting for a bus in Chicago, at the same place I do. We're there every day, and I can't get into conversation with them.
   One day I say: 'Labor Day is coming up!' I knew that was the right thing to get them. They just turned away from me.
   And I say: 'On Labor Day we march down the main streets of Chicago with banners flying, singing songs . . .'
   And they say: 'We *loathe* the unions!'
   Well, that was all I needed. I've become the Ancient Mariner now, you know, with a 'glittering eye', and I've got them pinned against the mail box, they can't get away.
   And I ask him: 'How many hours a day do you work?'
   He says: 'Eight.' He's caught unaware.
   And I say: 'How come you don't work *eighteen* hours a day?'
   And he's looking for escape and thinking this guy's nuts or something, and the girl is trembling, you know.
   And I say: 'You know why you work eight hours instead of eighteen hours a day, as your great-grandparents did? Because some guys got hanged for you!' And I tell them about the Uprising, something that happened in 1886.[2]
   And the bus is coming and I'm giving him this lecture. Finally he hops on the bus and gets away with this girl, and I never see them again. And to this day I think, in the mornings they look down at the bus stop from that very posh high-rise building, and he says to her: 'Is that old *nut* still down there?'
   Well, it's a comic tale but it's basically true. How would this couple know about the eight-hour day? No-one's told them about it. There's no labor history they were ever taught. So they wouldn't know. All they do is read the business section of *The Wall Street Journal*, and they've become part of it.

1 Martin Luther King had gone to Memphis to lead a garbage-collectors' strike when he was assassinated in April 1968.
2 On 1 May 1886 there were strikes across the US for an eight-hour working day. On 5 May an 'anarchist' bomb killed seven people in Chicago. The perpetrator was never found, but seven men were arrested and sentenced to death for 'incitement': one committed suicide, four were executed and the other two had their sentences commuted. These events were formative in marking 1st May as Labor Day around the world.

Source: *New Internationalist*, July 1996

Think about it

- In relation to your knowledge of the USA, perhaps through acquaintances, books or films, do you think that America provides a model for an open and classless society?
- Why, in your opinion, might so many Americans think of themselves as middle class, regardless of their occupational backgrounds?
- Do you think New Labour would find it easier to introduce a minimum wage if it did not have to consider the history of labour and the trade union movement in the UK?

A major contribution to debates about stratification came from an article written by two of Parsons's disciples, **Kingsley Davis** and **Wilbert E. Moore,** in 'Some Principles of Stratification' (1945). It attempted to set out a model of stratification which:

- starts from the assumption that a modern industrial society has a range of *occupational positions* requiring different types and levels of skill for their effective performance;
- sees some positions as *functionally more important* than others. The ability to fill these positions is not evenly spread across the population. Even people with the ability require considerable investment of time and effort in training and education;
- attaches *extra rewards and benefits* to functionally important positions, to ensure a sufficient supply of people willing to occupy responsible and vital roles;
- maintains that any society with a complex division of labour *needs* stratification to ensure that roles are allocated to maximise efficiency and the most important jobs are done by those most able to do them.

Summary of major theories of social class

	Marxist (Karl Marx)	Weberian (Max Weber)	Functionalist (Kingsley Davis and Wilbert E. Moore)
Defines class as ...	those who own (bourgeoisie) and those who do not own (proletariat) the means of production.	the market situation based on property ownership, market position for services, status, etc.	functionally important to ensure roles are allocated and appropriately rewarded to meet society's needs.
Relationship depends on ...	exploitation and conflict.	market position of different occupational groups.	cooperation and consensus.
Number of classes	mainly two – bourgeoisie and proletariat.	many separate class groups according to their market position.	many separate class groups according to their occupational ranks.
Viewed by society as ...	fair, in short term, because of 'false class consciousness' until the realisation of 'true class consciousness', i.e. exploitation of proletariat.	fair, based on market value of occupational skills.	fair – because regardless of inequalities the system fits the advanced needs of societies.
In the future	a social revolution to overthrow class inequality and unfair distribution of wealth.	class inequality to continue, with increasing fragmentation within classes.	class inequality to continue in relation to the functional importance of occupations.

Criticisms of Davis and Moore

- By implying that functional importance is related to responsibility and managerial authority, they ignore the vital role of, for example, nurses or public health inspectors.
- They assume that the only possible source of motivation is financial or material possessions.
- Their ideas are based on Parsons's model of an advanced industrial society built on achievement and meritocracy. If, as is argued in Unit 4, education in societies such as the UK and the USA is characterised by barriers and inequalities, then the stratification system will not succeed in matching the most able with the most important jobs.
- By seeing stratification as functional, Davis and Moore were 'writing a blank cheque' for inequality. They seemed to be saying that inequalities, however large, must be acceptable because they 'fit' the needs of advanced industrial societies.

Think about it

- Do you think that some forms of paid employment are more functionally important than others? Which do you consider (a) particularly important and (b) less important? Why?
- What about unpaid work, such as caring for children and the elderly? How important are these in terms of the needs of contemporary society?

The embourgeoisement theory

The word 'embourgeoisement' (becoming bourgeois) was used to describe the process in which manual workers became as well off as their middle-class counterparts (the lower middle class rather than the bourgeoisie in Marx's sense). F. Zweig, along with other sociologists writing in the 1950s and 1960s, developed the **embourgeoisement theory**. In *The Worker in an Affluent Society* (1961), Zweig argued that affluent workers were becoming like the middle class not only on account of their increased earnings but also in their lifestyles, values and political allegiance. This thesis had a major impact, especially in terms of its political implications. Traditionally, manual workers had been seen as the basis for support for parties of the Left (for example, the Labour Party in the UK), while the middle class had traditionally supported parties of the Right (for example, the Conservative Party).

The embourgeoisement theory was, however, challenged in the late 1960s by John Goldthorpe's **The Affluent Worker Study** (see page 75).

The affluent workers seemed happy with their lot and certainly showed no signs of becoming militant class warriors despite their stated lack of job satisfaction. Nevertheless, other sociologists pointed to radical changes which could take place if wages or work conditions worsened: indeed there was a strike at Vauxhall car works soon after the study was completed.

Following on from the work of Goldthorpe and his team in challenging the embourgoisement theory, other sociologists spoke out in its support. M. Young and P. Wilmott, in their study *The Symmetrical Family* (1975), introduced the idea of 'embourgeoisement with a time lag', arguing that what the middle classes have now the working classes will eventually seek also. R.E. Pahl, in *Divisions of Labour* (1984), saw the emergence of a 'middle mass' with less clear-cut boundaries, developing from the middle class and the skilled manual class.

The Affluent Worker Study

The 'Affluent Worker' writings of John Goldthorpe, David Lockwood, Frank Bechhofer and Jennifer Platt, published in stages during the late 1960s, set out to test the embourgeoisement theory. Luton was chosen as the location of the study. A large percentage of people living in Luton had moved there from other parts of Britain attracted by the relatively high wages paid by 'new' industries such as motor cars, light engineering and chemicals. The team felt that if anyone in the UK were undergoing embourgeoisement, surely it would be these mobile, well paid, 'modern' workers.

- The study interviewed a sample of 229 married men aged between 21 and 46 who lived in or close to Luton and who were 'affluent'. Interviewees were selected from three firms, Vauxhall Motors, Skefko Ball Bearing Company and Laporte Chemicals, to reflect a range of types of work and technology.
- Two sets of interviews were carried out – one at work concentrating on employment-related questions and the second in the interviewees' homes concentrating on family, social and political issues.

Findings of the Affluent Worker Study
- The people interviewed in the sample did not expect work to give them a sense of personal fulfilment, nor did they see work as a focus for social activities.
- Very few carried on social relationships with workmates in their non-work time. Work was seen as merely a means of earning wages, to improve their living standards. They continued to accept their position as manual wage-earners.
- The key motivation in wanting to keep their present job was the rate of pay rather than the job satisfaction or career prospects of their white-collar counterparts. Loyalty scarcely featured.
- Most workers interviewed (87 per cent) belonged to unions, but only 20 per cent gave their reason for joining as a 'belief in unionism in principle or in a worker's duty to join'; 79 per cent attended branch meetings 'rarely or never'. Union membership was seen in terms of self interest, as a means of increasing wages and improving living standards at home.
- This 'privatised' or 'home-centred' view (affluent workers remained close to their families and neighbours, along traditional working-class lines) extended to political allegiance. They saw the Labour Party as the party most likely to create conditions in which working people could 'get a better deal' from the existing system, rather than as representing the working class in some kind of generalised class struggle.

What the findings suggest is that the embourgeoisement thesis as crudely stated is not valid. Affluent workers are just that – workers who have become affluent. They remain a part of the working class despite increased affluence and improved living standards.

Criticisms of The Affluent Worker Study
- Do the findings of the study actually support the theory of embourgeoisement? The study found, for example, that 52 per cent of the sample thought that 'Unions should just be concerned with getting higher pay and better conditions.' Yet 40 per cent agreed that 'They should also try to get workers a say in the running of the plant.' It could be argued that this is quite a high commitment to a union role going beyond immediate income rewards.
- The sample was based on a group of mobile workers, moving to Luton in search of high wages. It is hardly surprising that the findings should reveal the workers to have weak community roots and to prioritise their wage packets!

Think about it

- What might be the advantages of attempting to carry out interviews in workplaces, followed up at the interviewees' homes?
- What problems do you consider might be associated with the research methods adopted to study affluent workers? Why?
- Do you think the affluent worker studies have made an important contribution to sociology? Explain your reasons.

The 'New Right' and stratification

A similar viewpoint to that of Davis and Moore is put forward by those of the **'New Right'** – also referred to as **neo-conservatives** and **market liberals** – who maintain that capitalism is capable of providing wealth and happiness for all through the market system. This is apparent in the political arguments developed by the economist **Friedrich Hayek** in *Road to Serfdom* (1944), a book which had a major influence on the governments of Reagan in the USA and Thatcher in the UK in the 1980s.

Hayek claimed that totalitarian societies, whether fascist or communist, are unequal and 'unfree'; they are also inefficient and stifle creativity and growth. State interference in the distribution of rewards, because it interferes with the driving force of change – the incentives of the market place – makes for a less efficient economy in which everyone is less well off. Hayek saw the free market as the sole determinant of the allocation of rewards.

Hayek's argument suffers from some of the problems of functionalism:

- It assumes that the only possible incentives for people are economic rewards.
- It assumes also that people don't strive for community motives.
- It downplays what may be seen as the 'dysfunctions' of inequality (i.e. the argument that disparity of rewards may create dissatisfaction and resentment which can lead to deviance and social disorder).
- It offers the same 'blank cheque' as functionalism, in that it suggests no ceiling to the amount of inequality of rewards it is acceptable to allow free markets to generate.

Peter Saunders, in *Social Class and Stratification* (1990), points out that the economic growth resulting from such market liberalism has the effect of improving the standard of living of *all* members of society. Inequality is the price to be paid for society as a whole becoming more prosperous; unequal societies come in different forms, but a society based on market inequalities at least has economic growth and expansion to offer.

Social class in contemporary society

The working class

The Labour Party's election victory in the UK in 1997 was a reversal of what had been, in the 1980s, a pattern of electoral defeat for what was claimed to be, traditionally, the party of the working class. Attempts to explain those defeats often returned to the embourgeoisement debate.

- The 'privatised' affluent worker with an instrumental (self-interested or image-based) view of work and politics had always been only loosely attached to traditional working-class loyalties; it was argued that the success of the Conservatives was built on appealing to this self interestedness. The 1980s represented a political and social shift of emphasis from the worker as a producer to the worker as a consumer, especially in respect to housing – for example the buying of council houses.
- Workers saw themselves as split and sectionalised by their different lifestyles and patterns of spending outside the workplace.

- The defeat of the national miners' strike in 1984/5 was seen by many as a last gasp of a traditional proletarian view of society. The coal miners, with a class-based view of social conflict (at least as expressed by their leadership), lost a struggle which was, at heart, concerned with defending a sense of working-class community and solidarity.
- Several writers expressed views that the working class had changed. André Gorz, from a French Marxist tradition, in *Farewell to the Working Class* (1982), argued that the changes in modern industrial societies had produced a split between, on the one hand, a skilled, organised group of manual workers, relatively affluent with stable employment and high levels of security and, on the other hand, a sub-group of casual workers, temporary, part-time employees, unorganised, untrained and constantly threatened with and frequently experiencing unemployment. In contrast, Goldthorpe, in *The Current Inflation – A Sociological Account* (1978), argued that the key trend in class structure had been the emergence of a tighter, more mature, slimmed-down but homogenous working class, equipped to get a better deal from society in material rewards, particularly in competition with a new, immature, middle class whose identity was less clear.

The middle class

The middle class covers a range of non-manual occupations which have grown dramatically in the last hundred years. It is commonly argued that this growth has produced a number of strata within the non-manual sector of employment, and that it might be more appropriate to speak of the 'middle classes' rather than of a single middle class.

Who are the middle class?

As with the working class, attempts to define the middle class raise the issues of changing structure, formation and consciousness. The confusion rests on the debate within stratification theory over whether some 'occupational' positions (often associated with middle-class status) might belong at the top of the non-manual occupational layer, while others belong in an upper class. Can we identify the relatively small group who really are 'in the middle', in that they are neither propertyless proletarians, forced to sell their labour in routinised, closely supervised jobs, nor higher managers whose role and conditions of life make them similar to the upper class they live alongside?

The 'new' middle class

The classic Marxist model of the traditional petit-bourgeoisie may be linked to the self employed, or to small employers such as shopkeepers. This group formally belong to the propertied ruling class in that they are independent and their returns are in the form of profits not wages. Nevertheless, they are likely to share many of the conditions and circumstances of the waged and salaried groups around them.

F. Bechhofer and B. Elliott's study, 'The Market Situation of Small Shopkeepers' in the *European Journal of Sociology*, 9:2 (1968), found that small shopkeepers were generally financially less well off than many of their manual worker customers and that even this low standard of living was at the expense of long hours of work. A newsagent, for example, might work from very early in the mornings and across weekends. It makes little sense to identify this group with the ruling class, although being in business for themselves and therefore not subject to the supervision and control characteristic of manual work makes it hard to see them as working class. They seem a classic example of what the American Marxist writer Erik Olin Wright calls a 'contradictory class location'. This traditional petit-bourgeoisie then makes up one section of what could be seen as the 'real' middle class.

The other section of the middle part of the diagram on page 77 is the group of middle management and lower professionals, covering such jobs as departmental managers, college lecturers and social workers. These workers are employees in that they are paid wages and salaries by their organisations, but they have characteristics which separate them from the working class – high levels of independence, for example, based on their expertise and their role in the organisation. The significant characteristic of this group is that it is trusted to supervise and control subordinates: it is given a stake in the rewards of that supervision. Because of this 'sharing in the role of capital', middle management and lower professionals cannot be seen as working class and because they are involved only in day-to-day control of production within a framework of 'strategic control' laid down by their superiors, they cannot be seen as upper class.

This 'new' middle class is often considered crucial to the analysis of occupational change in modern society. It is this group that most closely fits Weber's emphasis on the expansion of the middle class as a stabilising force. Their privilege and status comes from organisational position. A large percentage of this group are upwardly socially mobile, i.e. recruited from the working class. Unlike the ruling class proper, inheritance plays only a small role in their class trajectory.

Proletarianisation At the other end of the non-manual sector a debate has centred on the experience of routine clerical workers and the claim that they can be seen as being or becoming part of the working class – a process, perhaps misnamed, of **proletarianisation**.

For Marx, all those forced to sell their labour power on the market to survive were part of the proletariat. While he did not foresee the enormous growth in size of the routine white-collar sector, on the basis of Marxist analysis, these workers would have been proletarians.

Within the Weberian tradition of stratification analysis, however, with stress laid on status, the traditional distinctions between blue and white collar, office and shop-floor workers and staff, form the basis for identifying a significant division between skilled manual and routine non-manual workers. Indeed this is the basis for the division in the Registrar General's class 3 into 3M and 3N (see page 80). From this point of view, changes in the occupational structure, the system of rewards or the nature of work which make white-collar workers more like the working class are of interest.

David Lockwood, in his early study *The Blackcoated Worker* (1958), developed Weber's ideas on class. He suggested that the class position of a group can be understood in terms of three different aspects:

- Market situation: the position the group is in in relation to supply and demand for its skills, its rewards, terms of pay, perks, etc. Clerical workers are among the lowest paid groups in the occupational hierarchy, but the immediate rate of pay is not the only factor in determining the market position of a job.
- Work situation: the way occupations fit into organisations, relationships with superiors and subordinates, closeness of supervision, relation to technology, etc.
- Status situation: the prestige or honour which attaches to occupations, their social standing. Status is a significant difference between manual and non-manual work.

The upper class

The idea of an upper class is a difficult one for stratification theory. The tendency of stratification to identify class by occupation risks overlooking the importance of a group whose power is based not on occupation but on wealth and property. **Wealth** is what people own; it is a 'stock' that is held by the person in the form of land, buildings, shares, savings, etc. By contrast, anything which flows from one person to another, for example wages, profits, interest or rent, is a form of **income**. The distinction between wealth and income is not clear-cut, however: a 'private income', usually considered a characteristic of the wealthy, can be gained from profit, shares, interest on capital, or rent.

Much wealth is 'inert' in the sense that it is hard to identify and often only comes to the attention of government statistics when wealth holders die. It is suggested that tax avoidance and evasion are often ignored, with the richest few using sophisticated techniques like special family trusts to disguise the true extent of their holdings.

Wealth is highly concentrated in British society, with the richest 1 per cent of the population owning approximately 17 per cent of all marketable wealth, as shown in the table below.

Marketable wealth		1981 (%)	1986 (%)	1991 (%)	1993 (%)
Percentage of wealth owned by:	Most wealthy 1%	18	18	17	17
	Most wealthy 5%	36	36	35	36
	Most wealthy 10%	50	50	47	48
	Most wealthy 25%	73	73	71	72
	Most wealthy 50%	92	90	92	92
	Total marketable wealth (£ billion)	565	955	1711	1809

Source: *Social Trends*, 1997

J. Scott, in *The British Upper Class* (1985), argues that at the heart of this wealthy 1 per cent, a tiny core (at the most 5000 people or about 0.1 per cent of the population) exercises control over the major units of capital.

Occupation and social class

A major factor in emphasising the importance of occupation in terms of class inequality is related to the collection of official statistics. For their own purposes, governments and official bodies within industrial societies collect data on paid work and employment status. This data is often organised into hierarchies of occupational groups which reflect differences in status or reward. In the UK this process has produced what is known as the **Registrar General's Classification of Occupations**. (It should be stressed, however, that this is not officially seen as a recognition of the existence of class differences.)

The Registrar General's classification

This system groups occupations, not individuals. Within each category, occupations are further graded in accordance with their 'employment status', for example foremen or forewomen, managers, self employed, etc.

Typical occupations by social class	
Social class	**Examples of occupations**
1 Professional	Accountant, architect, chemist, clergyman, doctor, lawyer, surveyor, university teacher
2 Intermediate	Aircraft pilot, farmer, manager, Member of Parliament, nurse, police officer, fire fighter, schoolteacher
3N Non-manual skilled	Clerical worker, cashier, sales representative, secretary, shop assistant, telephone supervisor
3M Manual skilled	Bus driver, butcher, bricklayer, carpenter, cook, electrician, miner, railway guard, upholsterer
4 Partly skilled	Agricultural worker, barperson, bus conductor, fisherman, machine sewer, packer, post deliverer, telephone operator
5 Unskilled	Kitchen hand, labourer, messenger, office cleaner, railway porter, car park attendant, window cleaner

Source: Registrar General's Classification of Occupations, 1980

For various reasons a line is drawn through social class 3, to identify a non-manual class above the line (although many jobs in social class 2 might be seen as manual) and a manual class below. Class 3N can then be identified as middle class and class 3M as working class. The Registrar General seems to suggest a two class model. Not surprisingly, it has been seen as convenient to use for research and marketing purposes.

Problems with the Registrar General's classification

- It is not based on any sociological theory of inequality or stratification, so it is not clear what the criteria for ranking are.
- From 1921 to 1971 the ranking was supposed to be based on the different occupational groups' 'standing within the community', but this was based not on opinion poll findings or on public images of different jobs but on judgements made by the Registrar General's own staff.

- In 1980 the criteria for allocating occupations to categories changed to 'occupational skill'. (This new system of coding only altered the position of 7 per cent of cases.)
- Changes introduced over the years make historical comparisons difficult, thus compromising the main advantage of the Registrar General's scheme: its ability to get a consistent view across different sets of data and time periods.

The Hall–Jones scale

Many sociologists have attempted to construct alternative ways of classifying occupations, based on a firmer idea of what class means. The **Hall–Jones scale** for example, developed in the 1940s, was based on the social standing of occupation as assessed by surveys of public attitudes.

Hall–Jones' seven classifications

Social class	Example of occupation
1 Professional and high administrative	Company director of large firm
2 Managerial and executive	Civil servant
3 Inspectional, supervisory and other non-manual, higher grade	Teacher
4 Inspectional, supervisory and other non-manual, lower grade	Insurance agent
5 Skilled manual and routine grades of non-manual	Clerk
6 Semi-skilled manual	Agricultural worker
7 Unskilled	Barperson

Source: John Hall and D. Carog Jones, 'The Social Grading of Occupations', *British Journal of Sociology* (1950)

The Hall–Jones scale follows a more logical approach than that of the Registrar General but it suffers from similar problems.

- Would people rank occupations in the same way if the questions were phrased differently, asked by different people, etc.?
- How can categorisation systems like this cope with changes over time in public attitudes to occupations, either long term or short term?

The Hope–Goldthorpe scale

Virtually all the systems for categorising occupations outside a Marxist analysis make use of some element of **subjective ranking**. K. Hope and J.H. Goldthorpe also produced a seven-point scale. They condensed their categories from a scale of 124 into a 'collapsed' version of 36, which were combined again to form the seven classes.

This scale was taken from 223 unit groups used by the Office of Population Censuses and Surveys and put into a rank order according to a series of exercises which classified the 'social standing' of occupations. It has been used as a research tool in a number of important surveys on social mobility and voting behaviour.

Hope–Goldthorpe classification	
Social class	**Descriptive definitions**
1	All higher grade professionals – self employed or salaried, higher grade administrators/officials in central/local government and public/private enterprises (including company directors), managers in large industrial establishments
2	Lower grade professionals/administrators/officials, higher grade technicians, managers in small business/industrial/service establishments, supervisors of non-manual workers
3	Routine non-manual, mainly clerical, sales and rank-and-file employees in services
4	Small proprietors, including farmers/smallholders/self-employed artisans/own-account workers other than professional
5	Lower grade technicians (whose work is to some extent manual), supervisors of manual workers
6	Skilled manual wage workers, all industries
7	All manual wage-workers in semi- and unskilled grades, agricultural workers.

Source: J H. Goldthorpe and K. Hope, *The Social Grading of Occupations: a New Approach and Scale* (Clarendon Press, 1974)

Why use occupation as a basis for categorising social class?

One major reason is simply that a vast amount of official data is classified according to occupational categories. This applies to areas such as market research, for example, where analysis of consumer groups, newspaper readership, etc., is classified in terms of categories closely modelled on the Registrar General's system.

Market research socio-economic categories

Who's who of AB, C1, C2 and DE

Market researchers divide people into six socio-economic categories – according to the occupation of the head of household – but usually reduce them to four: AB, C1, C2 and DE.

• A, professional grade (3 per cent): surgeons, consultants, bank managers, head-teachers of larger schools, solicitors who are partners, and managing directors of firms with more than 25 employees.

• B, managerial grade (15 per cent): dentists, ordinary solicitors, nursing sisters, and senior planners.

• C1, white collar grade (23 per cent): bank clerks, junior doctors, police constables, computer programmers, editors, primary school teachers – and also cricketers.

• C2, skilled manual workers who have done an apprenticeship (28 per cent): plumbers, electricians, HGV or train drivers, stevedores, technicians and foremen.

• D, semi or unskilled manual workers (18 per cent): packers, porters, craftsmen's mates, van drivers and milkmen.

• E without income (14 per cent): the unemployed, state pensioners without other income and those otherwise dependent on benefits.

Source: *Sociology Stratification* (Further Education National Consortium, 1994)

There are, however, problems with equating class and occupation and reducing the analysis of stratification to differences in lifestyle or life chances between different groups based on the job they do.

- Not everyone has an occupation, and not everyone is in paid employment. The very young, the retired, the unemployed and – most controversially – 'housewives' (adult women engaged in work in the home) do not have an obvious occupational category.
- Many families have more than one member who has an occupation. Should each individual be allocated their own class or should the basic unit of analysis be the family? If the family is being categorised, then what should be done with 'cross-class families', where different members' occupations would put them in different social classes?
- The issue of property also raises questions. Ownership and non-ownership of property were basic to Marx's approach to class and also played a major role in Weber's theory. However, in models of stratification based on occupation, property loses significance as people are ranked on their status or rewards from work.
- A graduated hierarchy of occupational groups may well be valuable as a way of classifying data on lifestyles and rewards, but it misses important points about modern capitalist societies. Power remains mainly with those who own capital, and any class analysis which 'ignores the capitalists' ignores the real division of interests between the ruling class and the proletariat.
- An extreme Marxist view would argue that occupational systems of classification are not class systems at all but just different ways of ranking and grading the proletariat. This diverts attention from the really important conflict between the working class and the capitalist.

The class boundary problem

As we have seen, defining the boundaries between different classes in modern society is a complex issue. Modern Marxist writers in particular have been concerned with what Nicos Poulantzas calls the **boundary problem**. Workers in the managerial and professional categories, although selling their labour-power (the Marxist's traditional definition of working class), are the people who manage industry, operate systems of control and discipline and make decisions about wage rates, lay-offs, etc. When class conflict happens the chances are that the people on the other side of the negotiating table are not capitalists in the literal sense of 'owners of the business', but managers who are themselves employees. Can these people also be seen as proletarians with a distorted class consciousness? Surely their real interests are different from those of the workers they manage?

Erik Olin Wright, from a Marxist perspective, described these ambiguous class locations as 'contradictory'. In *Class, Crisis and the State* (1978), he produced a 12-class model. This is simplified in the following chart.

Wright's 12 class categories		
1 Bourgeoisie	2 Small employers	3 Petit-bourgeoisie
4 Expert managers	5 Expert supervisors	6 Expert non-managers
7 Semi-credentialled managers	8 Semi-credentialled supervisors	9 Semi-credentialled workers
10 Uncredentialled managers	11 Uncredentialled supervisors	12 Uncredentialled workers

The bourgeoisie and the proletariat are shown at opposite ends of a left–right diagonal, while the 'contradictory class locations' are organised on the basis of 'organisation assets' (top to bottom) and 'skill/qualifications assets' (left to right).

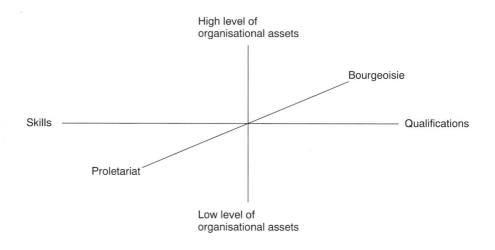

Think about it

- What counts as skill in relation to a job? Jobs are sometimes performed by people who are overqualified for the tasks involved, if their qualifications reflect the job's **status** rather than the real **skill** demands of doing the job. Why might this occur?
- How much control over other workers makes you a supervisor?

Changes in occupational structure

The pattern of occupations within a rapidly changing society presents a dynamic shifting picture with some occupations growing in number and others declining. The critical issue for the analysis of stratification is to consider the extent to which occupational change alters opportunities between different groups. It is more than a century since Marx died; Weber's major work was completed before World War I. Although it says a great deal for the power of their theories that their models still provoke much debate, it is inevitable that the picture of class and occupation in modern societies is different from what Marx and Weber witnessed.

Changes in the distribution of jobs across different sectors influence the nature of the stratification system, especially if occupation is used as the basis of that system.

- A decline in manufacturing occupations, as in the UK in the later part of the twentieth century, would result in a dwindling proletariat, in contrast to Marx's vision of a class which would come to stand for the whole of humanity (see also Unit 5).
- Some changes are short term and perhaps associated with specific economic problems, while other influences are long term and follow from technological changes (see also Unit 5).

In terms of social differentiation, the most important occupational change relates to the distribution of the labour force into different occupational categories. How have the relative sizes of the different class categories changed over time?

Changes in class distribution

In the UK, an undeniable change in the distribution of the population between different occupational groupings is the huge rise in non-manual work, both in terms of job numbers and in the size of non-manual categories relative to manual ones. This has been caused by:

- the dramatic growth in employment in 'clerical' occupations;
- the growth of the public sector as an employer. Public sector employment in the UK rose from less than 6 per cent of the workforce in 1901 to nearly 30 per cent in 1978. In 1997 it was around 27%. A large percentage of these employees are in clerical and administrative jobs (now generally classified as public services, since few are actually employed by the state).
- the growth of professions, particularly the emergence and expansion of the so-called 'new' professions based on scientific and technical expertise;
- the growth of the administrative function in all organisations, reflecting the growth of bureaucratic styles of management.

Changes have affected men and women in different ways. Although women account for a larger percentage of white collar than of manual occupations, within both categories they tend to be concentrated in the 'less skilled' sector – routine white-collar jobs, semi- and unskilled manual work, for example. This tendency has become more not less marked in recent times. (See also unit 5 pages 222–5 and 240–1.)

Social mobility in the UK

In 1949, David Glass and a team of sociologists based at the London School of Economics carried out a major study: 'Social Mobility in Britain'. This study, contrary to what might have been expected from functionalist assumptions about an advanced industrial society, produced the following findings.

1. Despite considerable movement up and down the social ladder, long-range mobility, for example from unskilled manual to higher management, was rare.
2. There was a large amount of elite self-recruitment: social classes 1 and 2 were relatively successful in gaining high status for their children.
3. This pattern of differential mobility was stable in the long term: it had not dramatically changed over the first half of the twentieth century.

Criticisms of the study included its static view of the occupational structure and its apparent failure to recognise that large parts of the managerial and professional groups in the UK are of working-class origin. Indeed the very process of long-range mobility (and the associated problems of adjustment and rootlessness), not considered important by Glass, has dominated much of post-war British literature – the works of John Osborne and John Braine, for example, and Dennis Potter's television plays.

In the 1970s, the Nuffield Study threw new light on the issue of social mobility in the UK.

The Nuffield Social Mobility Study

This study, carried out in 1972 by a team led by John Goldthorpe, was based on a survey of 10,000 men between the ages of 20 and 64. The men were asked for details of both their own and their fathers' lives and careers; and to tell their class history as a pathway through the occupational structure. This fits Goldthorpe's central claim that it is most useful to see class as experienced by people – not as a stratified layer cake (or a series of class pigeonholes) but as a *process* through which different people find their own routes of change. Goldthorpe maintains that this is vital for understanding the nature of class.

The sample were also asked to compare their own social class, as viewed when they were 14 years old, with that of their fathers. This gave a picture of the lifetime mobility of the individual from a base line of their class situation in childhood.

The findings of the Nuffield Study

- The shift in the occupational structure from manual to non-manual work, accompanied by steady or falling birth rates among higher groups, meant that to fill high status jobs there needed to be recruitment from below.
- The chances of reaching a high status position are better for those born into a higher class than for those aiming to rise from below. (The study included the calculation of 'odds ratios', i.e. the probabilities of reaching a particular class for people of different class origin. The results suggest that the chance of ending up in a **service class** job is 15 times greater for someone born in the service class (class 1 or 2) than for someone born in the working class (class 6 or 7).)

- The occupational structure is not rigid and there are high levels of movement, mostly up the social scale.
- There is no 'logic of industrialism', which maintains that in the long term all societies develop along a similar path and that this tends to equalise the chances of mobility. Different classes have different chances – the social 'dice' are loaded.
- The experiences of mobility and occupational change influence the way classes come to be and to see themselves (**class formation**). In Britain the service class is a 'class in the making': it has yet to make its mark on society.
- The working class by contrast is mature – the oldest industrial working class in the world; it is homogeneous and tied in with its representative institutions. It is in a powerful position to pursue its own interests within society, albeit within the limits of a capitalist market-based system.

From the Nuffield Study, and earlier studies on social mobility such as David Glass's, Goldthorpe concludes that while the total amount of mobility has increased, the relative chances of different groups have not shown a tendency to equal out during the twentieth century. What Goldthorpe calls 'social fluidity', or the pattern of relative chances, stays fairly constant despite the influence of state education or the Welfare State, for example. Indeed, using data from the 1983 General Election Study, Goldthorpe later extends this general point about the stability of relative chances.

Criticisms of the Nuffield Study

Criticisms of the Nuffield research concentrate on its theoretical basis, its model of stratification and its image of society.

- All the objections to an occupational model of class, based on a Weberian concept of status (see page 83), apply to this research and its findings about mobility within the class model.
- Marxists would attack Goldthorpe's inclusion of all high-grade professionals whose power is based on property ownership or control factors in the same class (i.e. class 1). This, they would argue, disguises the real nature of the capitalist ruling class. Goldthorpe argues in reply that the lifestyle, attitudes, etc. of top managers are indistinguishable from those of large capitalists. Furthermore a valid propertied ruling class in Marx's sense would be so small as to make survey-type research on it impractical.
- The Nuffield Study's decision to study only men misses the critical point that the experience of mobility for women is different from that for men. In relation to routine clerical workers it is suggested that while male members of this class are commonly 'on the way up', women are more often 'stuck'.
- It seems unduly pessimistic then to work with a picture of the class structure based purely on statistical calculations. The data could just as easily be used to show what a mobile society, 'open to talent', the UK really is.
- It takes no account of the class position of women.

Class of '94 from a 3-D perspective

Are you on the way up the social order? A new book helps you plot your course.
RACHEL COOKE reports

It's all downhill from here. I have just worked out my social standing according to the definition of a new book, Class: Where Do You Stand? Try as I might, it seems I am just not destined to become one of Britain's new elite.

According to the book's authors, Greg Hadfield, formerly of The Sunday Times, and Mark Skipworth, still with this paper, the old definitions of class are too one-dimensional: they may say where you stand in the system, but do not take into account your lifetime passage through — up and down — society. Their definition is *three*-dimensional. Readers of the book can fill out an exhaustive questionnaire and discover their past, present and future class expressed alphabetically — A signifies the top of the pile, Z the bottom. For example, you might be P-J-L — starting off as a modest P, rising to J status in your current situation, but looking likely to slip back to L in the future.

To test this tantalising theory, we asked four "new" professionals — a hairstylist, a top chef, an actor and an acupuncturist — plus one young bank manager, to complete the 60 questions. Me? I turned out to be G-N-M — middle-class, downwardly mobile.

The chef: Mark Holmes, 25, is head chef at the Lexington in Soho, London. The son of a builder and a florist, he was educated at a comprehensive school in Nantwich, Cheshire, before attending catering college in Crewe. He began his career at the Mayfair Intercontinental in London.

Mark's class position is Q-Q-A.

Although he is currently maintaining what he set out in life with, the future is bright. Mark is set to become one of Britain's new elite — reflecting, of course, the incredible rise of the celebrity chef; never before has what you eat and where you eat it been so important in the eyes of society.

Mark's reaction: "I'm well chuffed."

The hairstylist: Mark Hayes, 33, is the art director responsible for all Vidal Sassoon salons and schools in the United Kingdom. The son of a businessman, Mark was educated at a state grammar school in Romford, Essex, and joined Vidal Sassoon after he left art school in 1977.

By all accounts Mark, class position G-O-I, had a good start in life; but, seemingly, he has not made the most of it. Still, all is not yet lost. His downward mobility is not inexorable, as his last letter shows.

Mark's reaction: "I feel my life and career are going in the right direction; that's all that matters."

The acupuncturist: Juliette Lowe, 32, works as an acupuncturist in general practice, in hospitals, and in private practice. The daughter of the director of an English language school and a teacher, she was educated at a state grammar school in Camden, London, and at Edinburgh University, before beginning her training at the London School of Acupuncture.

Juliette is an F-O-K; this means she too is not quite making the most of her start in life — although in the future, she will move back up above the all-important halfway mark, M.

Juliette's reaction: "My mark doesn't mean much to me. I have never been materialistic or particularly motivated by money."

The actor: Helen Masters, 31, is currently starring in ITV's detective series, Wycliffe. The daughter of the managing director of a chain of hairdressing salons, she was educated at an independent school in Leamington Spa and the Webber Douglas Academy for Dramatic Arts in London.

Helen is an O-P-H — a position which, as Hadfield and Skipworth put it, lacks dynamism; she has moved only slightly down from where she started, and will move up only a few notches in the future.

Helen's reaction: "This means very little to me — an actor can't afford to be interested in money."

The bank manager: Tony Brown, 33, is a corporate account executive in NatWest's City Corporate Banking Unit. The son of a North Yorkshire farmer, he was educated at a comprehensive school in Settle. He joined NatWest straight from school at 18.

Like Mark Holmes, Tony, class position Q-J-B, is heading straight for the top of society. This reflects the many perks — including subsidised mortgages — now offered to career bankers who are willing to learn new skills and work their way up the company ladder.

Tony's reaction: "My parents taught me to strive to achieve the best standards possible; the results of the class quiz accord with my aspirations."

Source: *The Sunday Times*, 21 August 1994

Think about it

- How would you describe your own past, present and future social class position on the alphabetical scale referred to in this article?
- What sociological issues need to be considered when attempting to measure or analyse social mobility?

Differentiation, stratification and inequality of social power

Stratification by gender

Sociological approaches to the analysis of class have looked towards the resources of the household and the family, reflecting the idea that it is the male 'breadwinner' upon whom the household and family are dependent. The term 'family' has been used as the main unit of stratification because it is seen, by most researchers, as the basis of the household; within the household there is the sharing and dividing of resources between male and female partners. The household's financial and cultural resources determine educational achievements and occupational opportunities, particularly for their children. Such thinking about the family has led to:

- classes being seen as consisting of intermarried families with the members of each family having similar life chances. This enables researchers to allocate individuals to class positions;
- the head of the family household, often the adult male, being taken as an indicator of the resources and life chances of those living within that household; married women and children become allocated to classes on the basis of the adult male occupation.

Problems with the traditional family-based approach include the following:

- Many members of society (currently about 30 per cent of all households) do not live in conventional nuclear family households, for example single parents, retired couples and individuals living alone.
- Married and single women are categorised differently. A single woman living on her own would be classified by her occupation, whilst a married woman doing the same job would be classified according to her husband's occupation.
- It is not necessarily the male who is the head of the household, even within a nuclear family, as the sole breadwinner may well be female.

Can gender-based stratification problems be overcome?

Suggestions on how to overcome these problems, debated particularly by feminists, include the following:

- Females should be allocated to classes according to their own occupations and not those of their partners.
- Housework should be regarded as an occupation. Full-time and unpaid domestic labour should receive serious economic consideration.
- The French feminist Christine Delphy, in *Women in Stratification Studies* (1977), argued that married women are involved in distinct relations of production – a 'domestic mode of production' structured by patriarchal relations – and comprise a separate, distinct class.

- The English feminist Michelle Stanworth, in *Women and Class Analysis* (1984), maintained that women occupy a different class position from the family they are part of because they are women and are 'proletarianised' by their experience inside the family and in the labour market. Only by seeing them in a separate class position can it be recognised that occupational definitions of class have subordinated women. This reflects the more general 'invisible woman' approach criticised by feminists throughout sociology.

Think about it

- How have women's movements challenged the often traditionally-based cultural identities of women?
- Should women be paid for housework? Can it be regarded as an occupation? (see also Unit 5, pages 257–8)
- How might women be more accurately placed into a stratification system? What factors might need to be taken into consideration?
- Do you think that such issues of gender-based stratification will become outdated as women improve their position in terms of educational achievement and occupational advancement?
- Is a woman's identity seen negatively by society because she may be a housewife and mother?

Class, gender and life chances

People can be grouped into different social classes but this does not tell us very much about their lives. What needs to be added is an understanding of the implications of social differences. The most obvious cause of differences in life chances is the distribution of income and wealth.

Distribution of wealth

In the 1980s, thanks to well-publicised 'privatisations' such as British Telecom and British Gas, the number of shareholders as a percentage of the adult population in the UK rose from 6 per cent in 1981 to 20 per cent in 1989. Recent building society flotations in the 1990s (for example the Halifax in 1997) further increased share ownership, at least temporarily. However, this did not have an enormous impact on the concentration of wealth, since individual holdings were small and often rapidly sold to larger, established shareholders to realise a profit. While there have been significant changes in the nature and form of wealth-holding in the UK, and a certain amount of redistribution, wealth remains highly concentrated in the hands of a relatively small proportion of the population.

Distribution of income

Since income, for example wages, interest and rent, is of concern to the Inland Revenue, data is easier to come by than for wealth. Although such data is not collected in order to illustrate arguments about patterns of inequality, Inland Revenue figures do show some comparison of earnings for manual and non-manual occupations, and for men and women workers.

Average total income per week, 1995		
Occupations	Females	Males
Full-time	£270	£375
Full-time manual	£188	£291
Full-time non-manual	£288	£493
Part-time	£102	£126

Source: *New Earnings Survey*, 1996

There are consistent patterns of earnings between men of different social classes and between male and female workers, as shown in the table below.

Social class (Reg. Gen. adapted)	Men's average pay (as %age of all men's)	Women's average pay (as %age of men's)
1a High Professional	159	81
1b Lower Professional	104	72
2 Employers/Proprietors	154	63
3 Clerical workers	71	74
4 Foremen/Supervisors/Inspectors	90	69
5 Skilled manual	83	52
6 Semi-skilled	73	62
7 Unskilled	65	67
All	100	65

Source: Adapted from Ivan Reid, *Social Class Differences in Britain* (Fontana Press, 1989)

The table also shows that male managers and administrators (class 2) earned more than lower professionals and that male clerical workers earned less than any other male category apart from the unskilled.

Women's earnings are consistently less than men's in the same occupational categories, and overall only about three-fifths of male average earnings; there are also differences in hours worked, access to overtime, etc.

The effects of taxation The table is based on gross earnings – no account is taken of taxation. Final income, the amount people actually live on, would be lower after tax but may be increased after the payment of benefits such as child benefit, housing benefit or income support.

- The effect of changes in taxation and national insurance in the 1980s was to widen differences in take-home pay rather than to narrow them.
- Tax avoidance and fringe benefits are not reflected very accurately in official data.

- Tax evasion and avoidance are much more significant in determining final spending power for those in self employment than for employed earners. Generally, the higher people's income the better able they are to make use of and pay for sophisticated advice on managing their assets so as to avoid tax.
- Fringe benefits play a greater part in the reward structure of the better paid and, while governments attempt to identify and tax them, it is generally thought that their full value is not subject to taxation. The value of company cars, insurance, telephone allowances, low-interest loans, share deals, private school fees, etc. is likely to be under-represented in official data.

In summary, it is clear that there are major inequalities in income distribution and that despite some changes these have proved remarkably stable. Non-manual occupations are better paid than manual ones, while men are better paid than women. These patterns of difference are softened but not dramatically altered by the impact of taxation and welfare benefits.

Life chances at work – inequalities of class and gender

We have seen that the rewards from work go beyond the straightforward wage packet or salary. Fringe benefits, such as sick-pay arrangements, pension schemes, etc. play an important part in determining the overall attractiveness of a job, and are more likely to be attached to higher paid occupations. Conditions of work, too, are not evenly distributed. Routine manual workers are more likely to be regulated as far as lateness, absence from work and required notice of dismissal are concerned. Similarly, non-manual workers continue to receive longer paid holidays than manual workers, and men receive longer holiday entitlements than women. Pension schemes are also unevenly distributed between different occupational levels.

Gender and white-collar work

Studies of routine white-collar workers suggest that the experience of male and female clerks is different.

- One of the critical features of white-collar work identified by Lockwood is promotion prospects: male clerical workers in the routine grade are far more likely to be there as a stepping stone on their way up the stratification order, while women clerical workers are more likely to stay at that level.
- Some writers, such as A. Heath and N. Britten in *Women's Jobs Do Make a Difference* (1984), argue that the notion of proletarianisation makes sense for women clerical workers but does not fit the situation of men at the same level.
- However, G. Marshall et al. in *Social Class in Modern Britain* (1988) suggest that while relative chances for women are less good than those for men, a large proportion of women do attain upward mobility during their careers.

Unemployment

There is also a consistent pattern of differentiation by class and gender in unemployment.

- Statistics suggest that men are more likely to become unemployed than women (although this may simply reflect different patterns of registration) (see also Unit 5, pages 238–41).

Unemployment rates by sex and age					
		1986 (%)	1991 (%)	1992 (%)	1996 (%)
Males	16–19	21.8	16.5	18.7	20.6
	20–29	15.7	12.3	15.3	16.2
	30–39	9.4	7.8	10.4	8.7
	40–49	7.8	5.8	7.8	6.4
	50–64	9.3	8.4	10.4	8.9
	65 and over	9.3	5.9	4.9	4.1
	All males aged 16 and over	11.7	9.2	11.5	9.7
Females	16–19	19.8	13.2	13.8	14.6
	20–29	14.4	9.4	9.4	8.9
	30–39	10.1	6.9	7.2	6.3
	40–49	6.7	4.9	5.0	4.1
	50–59	6.1	5.1	5.0	4.2
	60 and over	5.1	4.4	3.1	3.9
	All females aged 16 and over	10.7	7.2	7.2	6.3

Source: *Social Trends*, 1997

The unemployed by sex and previous occupational group, 1992			
Percentage of the unemployed in each occupation group	Males 1992 (%)	Females 1992 (%)	All 1992 (%)
Managers and administrators	6.9	4.8	6.2
Professional occupations	2.5	2.0	2.3
Associate professional and technical	4.1	2.9	3.8
Clerical and secretarial	5.2	16.7	8.9
Craft and related	23.5	4.2	17.3
Personal and protective services	4.7	10.2	6.5
Sales	3.7	9.7	5.7
Plant and machine operatives	13.9	8.0	12.0
Other occupations	12.2	8.0	10.9
All non-manual	20.5	37.3	26.0
All manual	56.1	29.3	47.4
Total unemployed (= 100%) (thousands)	1,846	886	2,732

Source: *Social Trends*, 1994

- Different occupational groups have different patterns of experience of unemployment. The data on page 93 indicates that not only are manual workers, especially men, disproportionately likely to be unemployed, but they also have less chance of securing another job than non-manual workers.

Generally, then, conditions of life and benefits related to work follow much the same pattern of class inequality as that apparent in the distribution of income and wealth.

Life chances, health and mortality

Patterns of class and gender inequalities are even more apparent when we look at the areas of health and mortality. Perhaps the most dramatic indicator of differences in conditions are the literal 'life chances' reflected in the official data.

- Stillbirth rates for mothers in the Registrar General's social class 1 are only 56 per cent of those for mothers in social class 5. Infant deaths (between birth and one year) are 7.0 per 1000 for social class 1 as against 11.4 per 1000 for social class 5. Similar class differences operate for chances of death in childhood and for childhood illnesses.
- Mortality rates rise as we move from class 1 to class 5 for virtually every significant cause of death. This includes deaths from heart disease and ulcers which, though often viewed as afflicting the 'stressed executive', are in fact far more likely to affect unskilled manual workers (see also Unit 7).

Housing type, tenure and quality

Housing is often seen as a major factor in health and well-being, as well as for some a source of wealth and security. While all types of housing are lived in by all social classes, social class 1 households are more likely to live in detached houses, and class 5 in flats, tenements and maisonettes. Manual worker families are more likely to rent accommodation from local councils.

Significantly more people have become home owners since the 1980s. According to analyses of the 1991 census, two out of every three households owned or were buying their own house. Owner-occupiers, as this group are known, accounted for 14.5 million out of a total of nearly 22 million private households.

Class differences are also marked in the chances of households living in accommodation which may be seen as overcrowded. **Overcrowding** is measured in relation to what is called the 'bedroom standard', which attempts to identify adequate amounts of accommodation for households of different sizes. I. Reid, in *Social Class Differences in Britain* (1989), noted that four times as many households in class 5 are below this 'bedroom standard' as in class 1.

Similarly, social classes 4 and 5 are more likely to live in accommodation without central heating, or without sole use of a bath or an inside lavatory.

Class, gender and control of cultural resources

Concerns about the relationships between class, gender and the control of cultural resources first emerged in the 1960s with the development of the modern feminist movement (see Unit 1, pages 32–3). Betty Friedan's *The Feminine Mystique* (1963) and Germaine Greer's *The Female Eunuch* (1971) showed how cultural resources are often linked to financial resources and are subject to the same dangers of exploitation and inequality along gender and social class lines. An example of such exploitation is described in Unit 6 (see pages 328–9). In this example, males in powerful social class positions use the mass media to culturally manipulate females by portraying extremely slim models in designer clothes as 'ideal' images and associating these with consumer and culturally 'desirable' resources.

The American feminist writer Sherry B. Ortner, in *Is Female to Male as Nature is to Culture?* (1974), maintains that women have been oppressed universally not only in terms of their class position in capitalist societies but also in terms of cultural expectations. Ortner argues that biological differences between men and women are linked to cultural differences: early man's cultural resources included weapons and hunting techniques which became associated with religion and ceremonies over which men had control – an influence which has persisted.

Stratification by age

The term 'ageism', often used in the context of age 'cut-off points' in the labour market, carries negative connotations of people being less able or less important. Age inequality takes a variety of complex forms.

Age sets

In age-set societies, a whole age group passes through successive rituals, which may include physical marking. Thus status changes with age and is institutionalised. In tribal societies, such as the Panyako in Central Africa, age sets form the basis of warrior social organisation: the age set of the warrior age is responsible for defence, while the elder age set carries out important tasks befitting their age, experience and wisdom.

Childhood

In most advanced Western societies childhood is viewed by sociologists as a social construction rather than simply a period of biological immaturity. However, children are rarely questioned in sociological surveys – perhaps because they are not considered capable of making rational responses.

The way in which childhood is experienced varies considerably between social groups and also between cultures. Contrast white middle-class children in the UK with either street children in Brazil who survive in gangs by stealing and trading, or with the nearly 4 million disadvantaged children in the UK living in poverty, about half of whom live with lone parents.

Number of children in UK families which are either dependent on income support or have incomes below this level

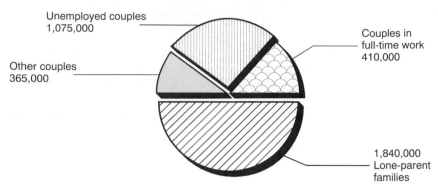

Unemployed couples 1,075,000

Other couples 365,000

Couples in full-time work 410,000

1,840,000 Lone-parent families

Source: M. Denscombe, *Sociology Update* (Olympus Books, 1996)

Age divisions

In the UK, as in most advanced Western societies, age divisions tend to be formally and legally established. Age 18, for example, marks an important age division because it allows voting at elections, drinking alcohol in pubs, etc.

Those aged under 16 and those aged over 65 may be seen as socially differentiated with less power than other members of society. Both groups are categorised as 'economically inactive'.

Social structuring of age

Although age sets and age divisions vary, in most advanced societies there exists some structuring of age identities, as shown in the following table.

Age division	Structure	Contemporary issue
Childhood	Parents State (law)	Pre-school (nursery) provision Neglect/abuse ('home alone'/Childline, etc.) Poverty
Youth	Parents Education/training Peers: relationships/sex Work/non-work	Authority Control Commitment (Dis)order
Young adulthood	Committed relationship? Children? Career development	Cohabitation/marriage/divorce Responsibility/stability Equality (gender/ethnicity)
Middle age	Continued parental role but commitments/responsibilities reducing and stability increasing	
Early old age	Retirement 'Leisure'	Irrelevance Wealth (or not) Gender
Late old age	Retirement Single living	Community Care Cost factors

Source: Adapted from M. O'Donnell, *A New Introduction to Sociology 2nd edn* (1992)

Think about it

- How would you construct age divisions? Would you have fewer or more divisions than those shown in the table? What identity would you suggest for each age division?
- Look at the structure and contemporary issues columns in the table. What additions or changes would you make to these lists?
- What are the specific inequalities associated with various age divisions? Are there any possible ways of overcoming such inequalities?

Biological factors

Biological differences in relation to age can become inequalities within stratification systems. Such inequalities seem to relate to allocating unequal rewards, based on age. So in societies such as the UK, laws dictate, for example, the age when people may drink alcohol, marry, vote, etc. Also, retirement often brings with it negative labelling or identity – as if certain people had passed their 'sell-by' date; this contrasts sharply with less 'advanced' societies such as the Australian aborigines referred to below.

Both age and sex, as biological factors, account for the age grades among Australian aborigines. Aborigines move through age grades, similar to age sets, which emphasise differentiation between age groups and also the sexes. Aborigine males become initiated, often in the age set of 13 to 16 years, and pass through a series of age grades from hunter to warrior to becoming an elder. In such a society, stratification constitutes a **gerontocracy**: the older men, by virtue of their biological age and sex, hold the most respect and authority.

Categorising the elderly

The elderly are not a single homogeneous group with a single identity. The living standards of the elderly vary considerably according to social class, gender, disability and ethnicity factors: some may experience higher living standards based on their occupational financial benefits, accumulated savings, private pensions, etc.

Attitudes and old age

In contrast to the high status accorded to elderly men in Aborigine society, in many advanced Western societies the elderly often carry negative labels such as 'wrinklies', 'crumblies' and 'seniles', which indicate a general disrespect for this age group. Even when the elderly are referred to as 'senior citizens', there still prevail attitudes associated with lower status. Terms such as being 'pensioned off' and being 'put out to grass', are further evidence of attitudes which see the elderly in contemporary Western societies not just as lacking in power, but as worthless.

Disengagement

Disengagement by the elderly, as put forward originally by E. Cumming and W. Henry in *Growing Old* (1961), suggests that ageing has certain fixed effects such as physically slowing down, psychologically losing concentration and socially disengaging or withdrawing from the world. However, critics of disengagement, such as M. Johnson in *That Was Your Life* (1978), argue that the attitudes of the elderly themselves vary considerably, with some preferring to mix with other age groups. A Eurobarometer survey from the Centre for Policy on Ageing, in 1994, states that about two-thirds of the elderly people studied led active lives, with many seeing or looking after family or relatives, going out shopping and exercising regularly.

Inequality and ethnicity

Ethnic inequalities are those situations which disadvantage people of ethnic origin – most often black people – as compared with white people in British society. This led some writers to develop the idea of an **underclass** as a way of relating racial disadvantage to broader class issues. The term has since come to be applied, however, to a much wider range of social groups, as shown in the following definition.

A definition of 'underclass'

'Underclass' is a term which has been applied to disadvantaged groups who have fallen to the bottom 'rung' of society. It is also used to refer to those with the least desirable jobs and who are denied the basic legal, political and social rights of the rest of the labour force. The term is sometimes extended to cover most of those in the 'second sector' of a dual labour market (see Unit 5, page 217). Alternatively, it may refer to specific groups whose poverty is based on social, economic and political inequalities: the long-term unemployed, single-parent families, the elderly. Membership of these groups tends to be ascribed to those of black or brown skin, females and the elderly but it represents a group which is constantly changing.

Source: Adapted from M. Mann, *Student Encyclopaedia of Sociology* (Macmillan, 1983)

Put simply, the argument is that black people in Britain constitute a separate layer beneath the rest of the stratification system and are excluded from participation in the normal institutionalised processes of white society. Rex and Tomlinson, who conducted an important study *Colonial Immigrants in a British City* in Handsworth, Birmingham, in 1979, argue that immigrant workers fail to share in the 'Welfare State' contract which white workers have 'negotiated' with the system.

The underclass theory differs from the one that traditional Marxists would suggest. Instead of a working class sharing the same economic and social disadvantages and needing only to overcome the false consciousness of racial difference to be united, the theory of an underclass argues that:

- there are real tangible differences in class position and class interest between white and black workers;
- the rational pursuit of their own best interests would lead black workers to join together on the basis of a shared racial identity, based on links with Third World liberation movements.

R. Miles, in *Racism* (1989), analyses the position of black people in the UK in terms of Marxist class categories, pointing out that people of Asian and Caribbean origin in the mid-1980s 'occupied all the main economic sites in the relations of production'. Most Asian and Caribbean men and women are described by Miles as 'proletarian', i.e. of working age and in paid employment, while a substantial proportion are part of the 'relative surplus population', in other words unemployed. A small but increasing proportion belong to the 'petit-bourgeoisie'. About a quarter of men of East African Asian origin are self employed, along with 15.4 per cent of women. The proportions for Indian and Pakistani/Bangladeshi men and women are 21.2 per cent and 16.6 per cent respectively, and among those of Caribbean origin 7.5 per cent of men and 1.5 per cent of women are self employed (see also Unit 5, pages 243–5).

Miles also points to the existence of a small Asian bourgeoisie, composed of people who migrated to the UK with significant capital, and to petit-bourgeois Asians who have accumulated capital to become employers of significant amounts of wage labour.

Miles does not deny that black people suffer disadvantages in society and that those disadvantages help to determine their class position. He points out that within each class location, Asians and Caribbeans occupy a less advantaged position. He argues that it is wrong to see black people in the UK as occupying a 'unitary class position', rather that they are spread across the class structure, with the positions they occupy being determined by different factors such as levels of skill or capital as well as the effects of racism.

Racial and ethnic categories

Extract from
1991 census

11	**Ethnic group**		
	Please tick the appropriate box.	White	□ 0
		Black-Caribbean	□ 1
		Black-African	□ 2
		Black-Other	□
		please describe	
		Indian	□ 3
		Pakistani	□ 4
		Bangladeshi	□ 5
		Chinese	□ 6
		Any other ethnic group	□
	If the person is descended from more than one ethnic or racial group, please tick the group to which the person considers he/she belongs, or tick the 'Any other ethnic group' box and describe the person's ancestry in the space provided.	*please describe*	

The 1991 census shows that the process of allocating people to particular ethnic groups for classification purposes is inevitably sensitive. Various complex issues arise.

1. The category *'West Indian'* (or 'Black Caribbean'), widely used in the collection of statistics on race in Britain, contains a range of assumptions and inconsistencies.

   - If used to describe people born in Britain, it assumes that 'West Indian' and 'of West Indian descent' are the same.
   - The West Indies is not an identifiable nation state; it is made up of a range of separate countries, all British colonies until the 1950s and 1960s, in and around the Caribbean.
   - There are many other islands in the Caribbean, the largest being Cuba, whose people are not referred to as West Indians because they were previously part of the Spanish Empire.
   - Guyana, by contrast, is frequently linked with the West Indies in these categories yet is a country on the South American mainland between Brazil and Surinam. (Guyanese people are rarely identified as South Americans because they share their colonial past with islands like Jamaica and Barbados.)

2. Classification systems often identify people in terms of their colonial and racial past. A description such as *'Afro-Caribbean'* breaks with this tradition to some extent:

   - It identifies people's 'descent', i.e. from slaves imported to the Caribbean from Africa, and it identifies the geographical location of parents or grandparents.
   - It does not build in assumptions about colonial history, first language, and so on. Therefore, a person from Cuba or Martinique would also belong to this category.

3. Many 'West Indians' are descendants of labourers from other parts of the British Empire, particularly India, rather than African slaves; the term 'West Indian' does not acknowledge the enormous cultural diversity in terms of religion, lifestyle, etc.

4. In discussing race and ethnicity, language cannot be separated from history. Attempts to change the words that are used have powerful implications for the way people are demanding to be treated. While arguments about language may appear petty, they often carry messages of political sensitivity important to the people concerned.

Age, ethnicity and the distribution of resources

Stats, lies and stereotypes

The 1991 census is advertisers' latest crib for targeting consumer groups. **Alexander Garrett** reports

This month, the 1991 census results are dispatched to market analysis firms – companies that process the raw data on our sex, incomes, occupations and method of commuting to work, and then put a label on the neighbourhood where we live.

Already some statistics have been publicised. Cleveland and Bedfordshire, for example, have most children in percentage terms, while Sussex and the Isle of Wight have most pensioners. Wiltshire has the most employment while Surrey has most cars.

The census included new questions on ethnic background and long-term illness. So we now know that Leicestershire has the most Indians, West Yorkshire the most Pakistanis and inner London the most Caribbeans. West Glamorgan, on the other hand, has the greatest incidence of people with long-term ailments. The first of these will certainly be a boon to those in the fledgling ethnic marketing business, which sells products such as hair and skin treatments to the nation's black consumers.

Marketing people of every persuasion will be less interested in headline statistics, however, than the practical business of allocating resources for maximum effect.

Census data has traditionally been used to select recipients in direct mail campaigns, to identify the best locations for stores and to find the optimum sites for advertising posters. The uses are becoming increasingly sophisticated. 'For retailers, it is not just a question of where to site stores. I might want to have a different product mix in each store, according to the make-up of the local population.'

A less positive use of 'geodemographics' (matching addresses to lifestyles and social ambition) is the way banks, building societies and retailers identify those branches they should close down.

One new area where the census will be deployed is in buying television airtime for advertisers. Agencies have depended on information from BARB — the Broadcasters Audience Research Board — which has a panel of 4,500 couch potatoes recording every zap of their viewing habits in special diaries. The results — as well as providing weekly television ratings — give some insight into who watches what.

But a new system called Viewpoint, developed by Pinpoint in conjunction with BARB, links the BARB panel directly with the census results, via the postcodes of the panelists. Advertisers will now be able to buy a commercial in a particular programme knowing precisely the households that will be watching.

For example, analysis of a typical Wednesday evening in August shows that among Type A households — farmers

TYPE A
"Rural". Very high proportion of the population employed in agriculture. Tendency towards large houses. Many non-working women; high multiple car ownership (necessary in rural areas). Relatively few children.

TYPE B
"Armed forces". Predominantly members of H.M. armed forces. Large numbers of young children and adults 20–34. Many housewives at home, high incidence of families moved within the previous year.

TYPE C
"Upwardly mobile young families". Clear age profile of adults aged 25–44 years with children 0–15 years. Many women work, more full-time than part-time. Predominantly owner occupiers in fairly large houses (5/6 rooms).

TYPE D
"Affluent households". Older profile than type C; adults 35–54 with older children, mainly teenage. Mostly owner occupied houses with six, seven or more rooms. Multiple car ownership. Mainly employed in finance, services and public admin.

TYPE E
"Older people in small houses". One quarter are over 65. Council housing, few cars, most dwellings are small. Those inhabitants who do work tend to travel to work by bus or on foot.

TYPE F
"Suburban middle-aged or older". Not quite as old a profile as type E, but nearly half are over 45. Predominantly owner occupied, in contrast to type E, and houses are larger (4–7+ rooms).

TYPE G
"Working people with families". Predominantly middle-aged parents with teenaged children, many housewives working part-time. Mix of council tenants and owner occupiers.

and other rural dwellers — *Home and Away* was easily the most popular programme on ITV, outdoing even *News at Ten*. Quite why this tale of 'everyday' life in suburban Australia should appeal to the country set is a mystery; but for purveyors of fertilisers, Range Rovers and Barbour jackets, it is clearly the place to book airtime. Type Cs — 'upwardly mobile young families' — showed a distinct indisposition to watch anything on ITV on the evening in question — maybe because they were all washing nappies — but did tune in to *Brookside* on Channel 4.

Type Ds — 'affluent households' — shot through the roof when superchef Anton Mosimann came on, while Type Es — 'older people in small houses' — watched lots but showed a curious ambivalence towards the *Golden Girls*.

The advantage of this to advertisers is that the census-based 'neighbourhood types' are a more useful barometer than the more straightforward 'social class'. 'For example,' he points out, 'a C2 often has more disposable income than a C1.' Another potential benefit is that consumers can be reached initially through television, then followed up with direct mail or leaflet drops — all based on neighbourhood definitions.

But how accurate are these methods? After all, even the basic census data is in some doubt, with claims at one stage that the Office of Population Censuses and Surveys 'lost' up to 800,000 people, possibly because of non-registration for poll tax. And the BARB panel seems a small sample from which to predict the viewing habits of 56 million people. 'It's as accurate as the rest of the BARB figures,' argues Ford. 'This data doesn't necessarily say anything about you as an individual, but it does say that in your neighbourhood there is a high proportion of people with particular traits. If an advertiser wants to reach those people, he is going to get more of them in one programme than in another.'

The greatest danger — perhaps outweighing privacy considerations — for the householder is that their choice of consumer goodies will be restricted because they live in too poor an area. But who knows? By 2001, perhaps enough citizens will be sufficiently clued-up to exaggerate on their census form and get that new Harrods food hall built down the road after all.

TYPE H

"Poor urban areas". Many young adults, plus some retired people, some children – thus rather a mixed age profile. Some incidence of people born in the Indian sub-continent. High owner occupation.

TYPE I

"Low status areas with flats". Many young adults, many immigrants, high unemployment. High incidence of students, full-time working women, house-moving. Poor amenities.

TYPE J

"Inner city bedsits". Many young adults, few children. Volatile in terms of house-moving. Many students (relatively) and many full-time working women. High incidence of single people living alone.

TYPE K

"Poor multi-ethnic areas". Many children and young adults. Very high incidence of immigrants, predominantly from the Indian sub-continent. High unemployment; mixed housing tenure.

TYPE L

"Crowded council neighbourhoods." Many children, equally spread by age band. High unemployment. Overcrowding, few cars. Mainly council housing, typically 2–4 rooms. Employed in utilities, manufacturing, construction.

Source: Adapted from the *Observer*, 13 December 1992

Think about it

- What is the relationship between age and cultural resources indicated by the information in this *Observer* article? How would you present your findings about such a relationship?
- Why, in your opinion, did the 1991 census require information about ethnic background (see the extract from the census on page 99)? How might such information be 'a boon to those in the fledgling ethnic marketing business'?
- What possible uses, positive and negative, would you associate with matching geographical areas to lifestyles and cultural resources?
- How useful do you think sociologists might find the concept of 'neighbourhood types' based on census data, when compared with their more traditional ways of studying and measuring social class?

Stratification and lifestyle

Stand up and be counted

Some 30 years ago, Britain's class structure was still firmly in place. From a person's occupation, you could deduce most things about a person's life — where they went to school, where they lived, what they ate and drank, where they went on holiday, the car they drove and their leisure pursuits. In the early 1960s, a Coventry carworker (invariably male) in his mid-twenties had been to a secondary modern school, rarely if ever ate out, went to the pub, drank beer, drove a second-hand Standard Ten, watched football, went to a large English or Welsh seaside resort, voted Labour and was a member of a trade union.

Society consisted of great social boulders. It was marked by uniformity and homogeneity. What you did determined who you were. The structure was held together by an enormous sense of discipline. You acted according to who you were: "people like us" was the motto. It dictated behaviour, habit and association. It also proscribed certain activities: "people like us don't." Our carworker of fond memory did not drink wine, eat at French restaurants, drive a foreign car or holiday in Tuscany.

This mentality started to break down in the 1960s. The revolution began among the young, it always does. As people became more prosperous and consumption more important, occupation became a less reliable indicator of the rest of one's life. The pattern of work began to change, with the decline of manufacturing and blue-collar jobs. The entry of women into the workforce and the disruption of the old sexual division of labour was a further spanner in the works. Homogeneity slowly gave way to diversity, the old block mentalities — "people like us don't" — were undermined.

Society has increasingly come to resemble a patchwork quilt. You may think you know what your electrician is like, but in fact he proves to be very knowledgeable about wine, speaks German, and is a keen golfer. There is no longer any easy fit between work and lifestyle. The old collectivist disciplines have given way to a more individualist ethos: "make yourself." Class never told us everything, but it used to tell us a great deal. Now it tells us rather little. That is why advertising executives and market researchers have invented a plethora of lifestyle categories, from yuppies and dinkies to ewes and yaks.

Class, of course, still matters. It remains the most accurate single guide to a person's health, for example. Nor does the new social mosaic suggest that inequalities have been abolished; on the contrary, the bottom fifth have got relatively poorer over the past 15 years. But class no longer dominates our culture, as it once did. The ways of living, the range of lifestyles, the pathways through life, have become infinitely more varied.

Source: *The Times*, 21 August 1994

As this article demonstrates, social differentiation and stratification have tended to be used by journalists as well as sociologists in a generalised manner in attempts to describe the processes concerned with structured social inequality. The treatment of such important concepts and their related issues has varied considerably from the highly theoretical approaches adopted by Karl Marx and Max Weber to contemporary debates between and amongst competing perspectives including the academic researches of John Goldthorpe and others. This unit has attempted to provide some insight into the wide areas covered by sociologists concerning issues of social differentiation, power and stratification which have widespread implications for us all.

Think about it

- What other examples can you think of which might back up the 'what you did determined who you were' view of social class in the 1960s?
- What do you think have been the advantages and disadvantages of viewing the British class structure as being 'marked by uniformity and homogeneity'?
- Why might occupations have become less reliable indicators of social class since the 1960s?
- In what ways do you consider that social class still matters, for example in terms of lifestyles and differing cultures?

Revision and practice tasks

Data response question

SOCIAL CLASS FACTORS

ITEM A
Women to take half of all jobs 'by 2000'

Women are expected to make up more than half Britain's work-force by the turn of the century, according to a survey by the influential Henley Centre. At present, women account for more than one in three jobs, but their changing role in society, together with the restructuring of the family, means that there will be more female employees than male by the year 2000. Three-quarters of all jobs created during the 1990s are expected to be filled by women. The proportion of women in full-time professional occupations or senior management will increase from its present 5 per cent.

The forecasting centre attributes the rise in female employment to the importance women now place on careers as well as the much larger numbers who delay having children or who return to work before their offspring reach school age. Leading corporations, such as the High Street banks, are trying to make it easier for women to return to work after having children, and to encourage older women to work. "Pressure is on single-parent women to work to provide for their family. Furthermore, divorce and illegitimate births are also set to rise significantly, adding still further to the disruption of the traditional family base," the report says.

Source: Adapted from the *Guardian*, August 1989

ITEM B

The extent to which an ethnic minority culture is absorbed into the majority culture can be presented in the form of a model as follows:

Extent of ethnic minority absorption into the majority culture:

Total absorption   No absorption

← ── →

Assimilation   Integration   Pluralism   Separatism

Ethnic assimilation occurs when an ethnic group becomes fully absorbed into the majority culture. An example of assimilation is the case of the French Huguenots whose descendants today appear to have little or no ethnic identity other than perhaps some memories of their forebears.

Ethnic integration occurs when an ethnic group retains its own identity and practices but also fully participates in the 'mainstream' life of a society. The Jews are a good example of a group which has adapted this way. Many continue to practise their characteristic religious and cultural rituals and behaviours whilst also working and socialising with non-Jews.

Ethnic pluralism occurs when an ethnic group retains a high degree of separate identity and lifestyle from the majority culture. Certain groups of Asian origin tend to fit this pattern. Thus, a large number of British-Bangladeshis – notably in the Tower Hamlets area of London – do not speak much English and participate relatively little in life outside their own families and ethnic community.

Total **ethnic separation** within a majority culture is virtually impossible (though it is sometimes put forward as a goal). In Britain, some Rastafarians argue that a return to Africa is the only way blacks will ever achieve social justice.

Source: Adapted from M. O'Donnell, 'Culture and Identity in Multi-ethnic Britain' in *Social Studies Review*, vol. 5:3, January 1990

ITEM C
A Definition of Underclass
Underclass: A term sometimes used for the poor who are also denied full participation in their societies. It may refer to employed workers who do the least desirable jobs and are also denied the basic legal, political and social rights of the rest of the labour force. Illegal migrant labourers are the most cited example, but the term is sometimes extended to cover all or most of those in the 'second sector' of a 'dual' labour market. Alternatively, it may refer to particular groups whose poverty derives from their non-employment: the long-term unemployed, single-parent families, the elderly. Membership of these is often ascriptive: black or brown skin, females, the elderly.

Source: M. Mann, *Student Encyclopedia of Sociology* (Macmillan)

(a) Provide **one** reason to explain why it is virtually impossible for ethnic minority groups to remain separate from the majority culture. **(1 mark)**

(b) Using the information in **ITEM A,** show what measures large-scale employers might introduce to encourage more women back into the workplace. **(2 marks)**

(c) Look at **ITEM A** and assess how the information contained there would be of interest to sociologists studying Britain's class structure. **(6 marks)**

(d) Find evidence in **ITEM B** to show how sociological research has contributed to the debate on the 'absorption' of ethnic minorities into mainstream culture. **(8 marks)**

(e) To what extent is the idea of an 'underclass' helpful in looking at women's position in British society? **(8 marks)**

Total: 25 marks

Sample answer to data response question

(a) Complete ethnic separation within a majority culture seems virtually impossible, since contact between the groups is inevitable, involving both national and local governmental agencies and the more mundane, routine activities such as shopping, children's schooling, etc.

(b) Large firms might make it easier for women to return to work by clearly allowing for defined maternity leave and contract safeguards. A second way to facilitate this may be in the form of childcare arrangements, by providing either financial assistance for childminding or on-site crèches and nurseries.

(c) In some ways, the sociological views of class structure ignore females in employment, who do in fact make up virtually half of the labour force. The social stratification system of the Registrar General, for example, uses the occupation of the male in the household to determine the social class of the family. Although, in many cases, because of the lower wages paid to women, the man is the main breadwinner, this will probably change, as indicated by Item A. Increasingly, it may be the woman who supports the family, either as a single parent, or because she brings in a higher wage than the man.

Item A implies that over the next few years an extensive change concerning women's role in the labour market will occur. More women will occupy professional and management positions, and males will be a minority in the workforce. This will need serious changes in the way we think about both women, sometimes seen as an 'underclass', and social class, which in terms of traditional thinking has been seen as a patriarchal or male-dominated system of stratification.

(d) The extent to which ethnic minorities in Britain are absorbed into the majority culture may be higher, as indicated by Item B, when assimilation takes place historically. The case of the Jews escaping the Russian pogroms at the turn of this century and settling in East London and elsewhere is an example of quite high assimilation. In the case of Irish navvies, a marginalised group of labourers, the degree of absorption was not so high, and they may be seen as being integrated rather than totally assimilated. Clearly such divisions cannot be firmly fixed, but form a useful continuum as indicated by the diagram in Item B.

Assimilationists consider that immigrant ethnic minorities should conform in most public areas of established British mainstream culture or way of life. This approach is particularly associated with the New Right, who have argued that the main purpose of education in Britain is to facilitate the participation of the individual in British culture and that 'there can be no real argument for a "multicultural" curriculum'. Similarly, assimilationists do not consider that other institutional areas of British society should adapt to minority groups, but argue that the latter should do the adapting. However, perhaps few would insist on assimilation in the area of private life and personal taste. Norman Tebbitt is an exception. His 'cricket test' was that a true English person would support the English cricket team rather than, say, the West Indies.

Pluralists consider that a variety of cultural groups can and do exist in Britain within a common legal and democratic framework. This view can be illustrated in the area of education, where pluralists argue that the curriculum ought to reflect the multicultural nature of contemporary Britain whilst also teaching basic skills and fundamental values. Pluralists maintain that in other institutional areas of British life, such as the Welfare State, awareness of specific cultural needs is also desirable.

Therefore, Item B provides a model for different levels and views of the absorption of ethnic groups. The broad spectrum which the model provides serves to highlight many of the controversies which surround issues of race, ethnicity and nationality.

(e) The concept of an 'underclass', as defined in Item C, refers to a group of people who are considered to be below the 'normal' level of competence and quality of work.

J. Rex and S. Tomlinson, in *Colonial Immigrants in a British City* (1979), used the term 'underclass' to indicate the existence of a disadvantaged group which does not possess the material or other benefits which are available to the white working class. Life experiences, including educational, housing and employment opportunities, are differentially accessed by the (white) majority and, in this respect, ethnic and gender-based minorities may not be seen as a part of the working class at all. When the existence of social discrimination and the group closure of working-class white communities (e.g. trade unions) are added to the equation, the underclass is forced to lead a marginalised existence.

Generally the term 'underclass' is used to refer to the poor and unemployed, or illegal migrant labourers, but the idea can also be used to describe the position of women.

In society, and especially in the labour market, women have often been looked upon as 'second-class citizens', whose abilities were best used in terms of the functionalist 'expressive' roles in housekeeping and child rearing. In this respect, women have been seen as having little effect on their social class, and the class structure as a whole. Item C states that the underclass must carry out 'the least desirable jobs', and are denied full participation in their societies. This is a traditionally founded description of women's place in society, where the most highly paid and highest status jobs are occupied by men; and where women have difficulty being taken seriously in areas such as politics, business and sport – all male-dominated spheres.

The idea of an 'underclass' helps us to explain women's lack of standing in society. Their opinions may not be treated with respect or seriousness by some men, who may see females as the mindless and inferior sex who are often considered as better off in the home and are encouraged to remain there.

Whether the increased awareness of female liberation and opportunities, as exemplified by Mrs Margaret Thatcher and others, serves to offer more potential for women, or whether it merely provides an illusion for the majority of women represented in the underclass, only time will tell.

Task: stimulus response question

Read the following data carefully and then answer the questions that follow.

ITEM A: Case Studies

Case A

Vanessa and Simon Waring (aged 35 and 42) live in a leafy suburb of Newcastle-on-Tyne and have two children, Thomas aged nine and Emma aged five. Simon is a solicitor and partner in a very successful firm, founded by his grandfather, which specialises in tax advice to companies but also has a good reputation for work in divorce cases. Vanessa is about to give up her job as secretary to a consultant at the hospital because she is expecting their third child. Simon drives a BMW supplied by the firm and Vanessa has a Volkswagen Polo.

Case B

John Rawlins (37) and Pat Mitchell (33) have lived together in Longbridge, Birmingham for twelve years, though Pat is still married to her former partner, an unemployed sales manager. John, whose parents came to England from Jamaica, has a semi-skilled job assembling brake-linings, and Pat is a part-time cleaner at the same factory. They have three children, Tracey (7), Danielle (5) and Dean (3). Pat is expecting their fourth child. They live in a former council house which they are now in the process of buying with the help of a mortgage. The children attend the local primary school. John has been told that he will be made redundant in two months' time.

Case C

Jack Harris (72) is a retired bricklayer, financially dependent on his state pension and on Income Support. His health broke down in his early sixties and, since his wife died five years ago, he has lived in a local authority residential home for the elderly. He stayed on in the Army for a few years after the War, and then worked full-time through the nineteen-fifties and sixties, making very good money, enjoying expensive holidays and regular new cars, and even running his own business for a while, but he saved nothing and never bought a house.

Case D

Mary Marks is the 32-year-old daughter of one of England's oldest and wealthiest noble families. She achieved just one O-level pass while at school and then worked part-time in a private kindergarten. She married, aged 20, the son of a very wealthy family and they had two sons. After twelve years, the couple separated. Mary now lives in a large house with an income which is partly from her own family's wealth and partly from her estranged husband's. She does a great deal of voluntary work. The children attend a private school whose fees are paid by Mary's husband.

ITEM B: The Registrar-General's Scale of Social Classes

1. Professional, etc.

2. Intermediate Occupations.

3N. Skilled Occupations, non-manual.

3M. Skilled Occupations, manual.

4. Partly skilled Occupations.

5. Unskilled Occupations.

[6. Armed Forces.]

(a) Identify one classification other than the Registrar-General's that is used by sociologists to measure social class, and briefly contrast it with the Registrar-General's. [4]

(b) Explain how you would set about using the Registrar-General's classification to place those mentioned in Cases A to D in their appropriate category. Outline any problems you may face. [16]

(c) Assess the value and limitations for sociologists of scales of social class, drawing on Items A and B for illustrative examples where appropriate. [10]

[Total: 30 marks]

Source: Interboard Specimen Paper 2, 1994

Ideas for coursework and personal studies

1. **Social class and family background**   How may these be seen or how may they have changed for a particular sample of people? Focus on one or two important factors, such as age transition, gender expectations or ethnic background.

2. **Changes in social class experience**   Consider the conclusion to this unit: how people view social class in terms of the stereotypes of the 1960s and changing patterns of social class in contemporary society.

3. **Social mobility**   Consider the article on pages 87–8 of this unit and how it might apply to a wider cross-section of society. How comfortable might your sample feel about the concept of upward/downward mobility? How useful do you consider the approach to be in relation to other sociological means of stratification and differentiation?

4. **Social class and leisure activities**   Consider the differences in how the various social class groups use their leisure time. This could be based on different types of family and household (see Unit 3) or alternatively by carrying out research at two or three different leisure venues.

Selected reading list

The Affluent Worker in the Class Structure, J. Goldthorpe et al. (Cambridge University Press, 1969)

The Blackcoated Worker, David Lockwood (Allen & Unwin, 1958)

'The British upper class', J. Scott in *A Socialist Anatomy of Britain*, D. Coates et al. (Polity Press, 1985)

Class, Crisis and the State, Erik Olin Wright (New Left Books, 1978)

The Communist Manifesto, Karl Marx and Friedrich Engels (1848) in *Karl Marx, Selected Writings*, D. McLellan (ed.) (Oxford University Press, 1977)

Social Class and Stratification, Peter Saunders (Routledge, 1990)

Social Class Differences in Modern Britain, 3rd edn, I. Reid (Fontana Press, 1989)

Social Class in Modern Britain, G. Marshall et al. (Unwin Hyman, 1988)

'Some principles of stratification', Kingsley Davis and Wilbert E. Moore in *Class, Status and Power*, R. Bendix and S. Lipset (eds) (Routledge & Kegan Paul, 1966). Originally published in *American Sociological Review* 10 (1945)

Social Mobility and Class Structure in Modern Britain (The Nuffield Social Mobility Study), J. Goldthorpe (Clarendon Press, 1980)

3 Households and families

"If you two don't stop this fighting and get a divorce – we're going to leave you!"

Introduction

The image of the family as a married couple with their dependent children forms a common model of a 'normal' family. From birth, for most of us, there exists some kind of family group or relations who are very important in our early stages of development. Often, especially during the early years, we tend to accept our own family experience as 'normal'. However, as the cartoon suggests, there seems to be a decrease in people's expectation of the unconditional pattern of marriage. UK rates of cohabitation (couples living together), single parenthood and divorce have all risen during the last 25 years, and it is becoming increasingly inappropriate to make assumptions about what a 'normal' family or household pattern might be.

Sociological interest in the family, shared also by historians and politicians, may be related to its key role in social life; family life may provide markers or offer signs of the quality and stability of society itself. Newspapers, magazines, television and films put forward ideas about – an implied 'ideology' of – the family in various forms, looking at its continuity and change; television soap operas, which seem to thrive on family relationships – especially on tensions and conflicts within and beyond the family – enjoy continued popularity. Religious groups often focus on the family, sometimes issuing judgements about behaviour towards and within the family. Although no political party has yet appointed a minister for the family, there are frequent celebrations of the family; wives and husbands of political leaders hug and warmly support their spouses. Politicians who violate this ideology of the family may suffer short political careers, especially in the higher ranks of government. So, whilst the family may be seen as a personal and private institution, the concept or ideology of family has a high public profile. Despite the controversy surrounding 'alternative' forms of family life, for example single or gay parenting, advertisers' images of happy families tend to support traditional family values or the ideology of the family.

An advertiser's image of
the happy family

This unit will look at the following issues:

- definitions and theories of households and family forms;
- the ideology of the family in terms of socialisation, identity and culture;
- family and household diversity, including changes over time in relation to such variables as social class, ethnicity and age;
- couples and children, conjugal (or 'marital' relationship) roles, cohabitation and divorce, including the position of children and gender socialisation;
- the family and wider society, including family functions and the relationship between family and state (for example in relation to community care).

Definitions of the family and the household

This section will look at the distinction which has been drawn by sociologists between households and families; and at the differences which exist between the wide variety of family forms, including nuclear and extended families.

Households or families?

Definitions of the household are more straightforward than those of the family. **Households** consist either of people living alone or of groups of people in a given dwelling place at any particular point of time. The **family** may be considered the most basic unit of human social life.

In the decades following World War II, households were seen to be based around families. **George Peter Murdock,** in his classic text *Social Structure* (1949) – which was based on his studies of 250 societies, varying from basic tribal groupings to complex industrialised societies – claimed that family forms existed in all societies and that the family was a universal social institution. The extent to which Murdock's claim holds true depends on how 'family' is defined. This remains problematic, as illustrated by the three definitions discussed in the following extract.

Definitions of family

Definition 1

Murdock's definition: The family is a social group characterised by common residence, economic co-operation and reproduction. It includes adults of both sexes, at least two of whom maintain a socially approved sexual relationship, and one or more children, own or adopted, of the sexually cohabiting adults.

Problems of this definition
It does not allow the use of the term 'family' about:
(a) Those headed by one parent.
(b) Those in which a couple have no children.
(c) Parents who live in a commune (such as a kibbutz) where the children grow up separately from them.

Comment   Whether or not the family is a universal institution depends to some extent on the definition that is used. If 'a family' is defined in a specific way, then there will be examples drawn from cross-cultural studies to indicate that it is not a universal institution. If it is defined more broadly, then it is harder to find exceptions.

Definition 2
A family is a social unit made up of people related to each other by blood, birth or marriage.

Problems of this definition   It allows a married couple without children to be described as a family, but not an unmarried couple who are living with each other in a permanent union.

Comment   This wider definition does meet the problems arising from Murdock's description.

Definition 3
A family is a social unit made up of people who support each other in one or several ways; for example, socially, economically or psychologically (in providing care, love, affection, etc.) or whose members identify with each other in a supportive unit.

Problems of this definition   It is now so broad that it is difficult to conceive of exceptions to the existence of some form of family in every society.

Comment   This wider definition would allow the term 'family' to be applied to:
(a) A cohabiting couple of the same sex.
(b) Unrelated members of a cohabiting group, such as a children's home, commune, etc., whose members regard themselves as 'a family'.

Source: P. Selfe, *Work Out Sociology* (Macmillan, 1993)

Households, family structure, marital status and age

The number of households in the UK has increased considerably since World War II, partly because households contain fewer people.

Households by size					
	1961 (%)	1971 (%)	1981 (%)	1991 (%)	1995–96 (%)
One person	14	18	22	27	28
Two people	30	32	32	34	35
Three people	23	19	17	16	16
Four people	18	17	18	16	15
Five people	9	8	7	5	5
Six or more people	7	6	4	2	2
All households (= 100%) (millions)	16.2	18.2	19.5	22.4	23.5

Source: *Social Trends*, 1997

The table shows that there were over 23 million households in the UK in 1996; this number has risen steadily since 1961. Single-person households and those consisting of just two people make up almost two-thirds of all households. Such a figure will help us to understand why sociologists have turned towards considering households rather than families, despite the latter providing the heading in many sociological textbooks and elsewhere.

Another interesting development is the significant rise in the number of people living alone: well over a quarter of all households in 1996 were one-person households. This was the largest percentage increase in terms of households by size for the period 1961–96, an increase of 100%.

One-person households

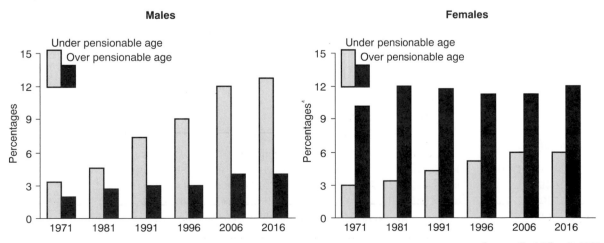

Source: *Social Trends*, 1995

Within one-person households, as illustrated in the bar graphs on page 113, there has been an increase in the number of households consisting of women under pensionable age. This may reflect the growing independence of women through participation in higher education and in professional occupations such as medicine and law. The bar graphs also show that by 2016 it is estimated that 13 per cent of households will consist of a man under pensionable age living alone compared with only 3 per cent in 1971. The growth in the percentage of those living alone, especially at a younger age, may be due to various factors such as the rise in divorce and the increased tendency for younger people to set up independent households.

Households: type of household and family		1961 (%)	1971 (%)	1981 (%)	1991 (%)	1995–96 (%)
One person	Under pensionable age	4	6	8	11	13
	Over pensionable age	7	12	14	16	15
Two or more unrelated adults		5	4	5	3	2
One family	Married couple, no children	26	27	26	28	29
	1–2 dependent children	30	26	25	20	19
	3 or more dependent children	8	9	6	5	4
	Lone parent, dependent children	2	3	5	6	7
Two or more families		3	1	1	1	1
All households (millions)		16.2	18.2	19.5	22.4	23.5

Source: *Social Trends*, 1997

The two tables on household and family type show some interesting trends:

- The percentage of 'traditional', one-family households with children has been falling – from 38 per cent of all households in 1961 to 23 per cent by the mid-1990s.
- The percentage of lone parents with dependent children, although a relatively small proportion of all **households,** has been steadily growing since the 1960s; this has become a topic of social and political debate.

Think about it

- How would you go about studying families in the UK and elsewhere in the world to see whether particular family forms were still evident? How might developments in modern technology, for example home and library computers, CD-Roms, the Internet, etc., assist this research?
- What do you consider has happened in many contemporary societies to give rise to the term 'household'?

People in households: by gender, age and family type, Spring 1996						
United Kingdom						Percentages
		Couple		Lone parent		
	One person	No children	With children	Dependent children	Non-dependent children only	All people (=100%) (millions)
Males						
Under 16	0	–	78	22	–	6.2
16–24	15	7	64	8	7	3.3
25–34	21	22	51	1	5	4.7
35–44	14	12	69	2	3	4.0
45–54	12	27	57	1	3	3.7
55–64	16	57	25	–	2	2.8
65–74	21	68	9	–	2	2.3
75 and over	34	59	4	–	3	1.4
Females						
Under 16	0	–	78	22	–	5.9
16–24	14	11	55	14	5	3.2
25–34	12	20	51	15	2	4.6
35–44	7	11	67	13	2	4.0
45–54	11	32	47	4	5	3.8
55–64	21	58	15	1	5	2.9
65–74	40	50	5	–	4	2.7
75 and over	68	25	1	–	5	2.4

Source: *Social Trends*, 1997

Types of family

Sociologists tend to refer to two main types of family: **nuclear** and **extended**.

- Nuclear families form the smallest of family units. They consist of two generations, with parents and their children – whether natural or adopted – sharing the same home.
- Extended families are extensions of nuclear families with at least one additional relative living in the same home. There may be vertical extension by the addition of a third generation, for example grandparent(s), or horizontal extension by the addition of members of the same generation as the parents, for example their brother(s) or sister(s).

A typical Victorian
extended family

Variations of these types of family, as well as alternative family forms, may serve to challenge Murdock's view that the family is a universal social institution to be found in all societies. These types and alternatives are listed below.

Extended kinship groups   These consist of groups of nuclear families living close to their relatives and having close kinship ties. 'Kinship' refers to a limited set of close relatives, covering relationships based on real (or consanguine) or assumed (such as adopted) ties.

Reconstituted (or re-ordered) families   A relatively new term, this describes nuclear families in which one or both parents have had children from previous relationships who become part of 'renewed' families. This type of family will typically include step-parents.

Single-parent families   These are households where one or more children live with only one parent. Debate has arisen as to whether lone parents are a discrete type of family or an incomplete nuclear family. (See pages 148–50 for more on lone parents.)

Clan groups   A clan is a group of members who consider themselves to be descended and linked through common ancestors going back several centuries, for example Scottish clans and some gypsy groups. Clan groups are large kinship groups extending beyond family relations.

Communes   Probably the most familiar family alternative, communes consist of groups of individuals living together and perhaps sharing community duties and tasks. Over 25,000 agricultural communes were established in China during the period of Mao Tse-Tung's Great Leap Forward (1958–60). In the 1960s in the USA and the UK communes became quite commonplace as alternative forms of living together, although they were often short-lived. More recently various peace and religious movements, even large-scale open-air concerts lasting several days, may be included as examples. Groups of New Age Travellers may also be viewed as communes.

Kibbutzim   In Israel kibbutzim consist of communes based on collective farms and industrial settlements. The land is owned by the Jewish National Fund and is rented at a small fee. Farming and other work is communal; collective living is the rule for children, who live in 'children's houses', although adults have their private dwellings. Children visit their parents regularly, for example during the Jewish Sabbath and other religious festivals. There are 240 kibbutzim totalling some 100,000 members; with each kibbutz varying in size from about 50 to 2000 members. However, only about 5 per cent of Israel's population live on kibbutzim. The main distinction between kibbutzim and communes is that the former does more than merely provide the basis for collective living: it is essentially a unit of agricultural or industrial production.

<u>Gay-parent families</u>   This remains a somewhat stigmatised term – indicating social disapproval – despite the many homosexual male and female couples living in stable open relationships with dependent children. However, there has developed a more tolerant attitude towards such couples in the courts in both the USA and the UK. Child welfare agencies now seem more prepared to accept gay parents, particularly female couples, receiving custody of children. The first adoption of its kind, in England and Wales, was approved in April 1997, of an 11-year-old girl living with a female couple, when a High Court judge overruled objections from the girl's natural mother.

DADDY AND POPPY BRAZENLY SHOW OFF THEIR 'DAUGHTER'

Two gay men and a surrogate baby

By Clare Henderson

WITH unabashed pride, Daddy and Poppy gaze into the face of 'their daughter', Sarah Clare.

US-born academic William Zachs and his gay Scottish lover, social worker Martin Adam, agreed to pose with the baby they bought from a surrogate mother in America for around £15,000 – but they remain tight-lipped about the storm the deal has caused.

The arrangement has been widely criticised by MPs and church leaders, and social workers have launched an investigation. But since the matter was exposed earlier this month the shutters and curtains have remained closed at the couple's £190,000 Georgian townhouse in Edinburgh while the morality issue is debated.

Dr Zachs, who came to Britain 12 years ago from the New York area, spent thousands of pounds on three attempts to have surrogate mother Andrea Gibson artificially inseminated with his sperm.

Mrs Gibson, 27, lives in an Illinois caravan park with her seven-year-old son and her ex-boyfriend's two young sons.

Support

In the final weeks of her pregnancy, she moved into a New York apartment paid for by Dr Zachs until she gave birth to Sarah Clare on July 22.

Both Mr Adam, who is originally from Irvine, Ayrshire, and Dr Zachs are listed as the fathers on the baby's birth certificate. The child will call one Daddy and the other Poppy.

Friends and family reportedly support the arrangement, saying Sarah Clare will be brought up in a loving and good environment.

But MPs and church leaders have called into question child protection laws and whether the arrangement constitutes 'baby-selling'.

The couple, who met through the Gay Society at Edinburgh University where both studied, have lived together for seven years.

Dr Zachs is a widely respected academic who spends his time between Edinburgh and New York, where he is helping to edit the papers of James Boswell, Dr Samuel Johnson's biographer.

His grandmother, Louise Zachs, who lives in Connecticut, said the baby was the result of 'long-term planning' and that her grandson 'had always wanted a child'.

Source: *Mail on Sunday*, 22 September 1996

Matrifocal families   An example of the matrifocal, or female-led, family is found amongst the Nayar, a warrior caste who lived in south-west India in the late eighteenth century. The women had no husbands, just *sandbanham*, i.e. temporary, visiting men, who were more like lovers. The women were officially married at puberty to another male of the kinship group, but the marriages were merely social arrangements and in no way permanent. When the marriages were dissolved, the Nayar women were free to take as many as 20 *sandbanham*; who had no duties or obligations towards their women or offspring. The only duty of wives to their official husbands was to mourn their warrior deaths.

A similar matrifocal arrangement has existed among the Ashanti people of Ghana, where the husband lives with his mother and visits his wife only occasionally: their children are not his, in social terms, but hers.

The Nayar and the Ashanti also illustrate the difficulties in defining the concepts of family and marriage. Some sociologists have provided definitions of the family as units established around mothers and their children:

> '*The basic unit is the mother and her child, however the mothers come to be impregnated. Whether or not a male becomes attached to the mother on some more or less permanent basis is a variable matter.*'
>
> Robin Fox, *Kinship and Marriage* (Penguin, 1967)

New black families   Contemporary cross-cultural studies, particularly in low-income black communities in the West Indies and Guyana, for example, have found households headed by women with no stable male/father figure. The family unit consists of a woman and her children, sometimes with the addition of the woman's mother. It is interesting that over 50 per cent of West Indian mothers living in the UK are lone parents – a statistic rarely quoted perhaps because of its racist undertones.

Think about it

- Which of the types of 'family' groups described above should be considered, in your opinion, as a family and which should not? Provide reasons for the decisions you have reached.
- Having read about households and families, how would you now attempt to provide basic definitions of these concepts? Give examples, from this unit and from your own sources, to accompany your definitions.
- What problems occur in discussions on households and families? Refer to your own experience and the information given so far in this unit.

Theories and ideologies of the family

Functionalist theories

Functionalist theories tend to be based on the view that society consists of a system of interrelated, supportive parts which adapt to each other in order for society to remain in a state of harmony and equilibrium. These parts perform **functions** which contribute to the maintenance, continuation and integration of society. Within the functionalist perspective there are different interpretations of the functions carried out by the family.

G. P. Murdock

For Murdock (see also page 111), the universal functions of the family are as follows:

- Sexual: the family provides control and expression of sexual drives which helps to anchor society and prevent conflict within it.
- Reproductive: society needs to reproduce itself in order to survive. The family is seen as a culturally acceptable unit in which to have and rear children.
- Economic: if there is economic cooperation within the family, division of labour thrives and specialised tasks can be carried out to the advantage of family members and for society as a whole.
- Educational: knowledge and skills are passed down through generations and the family teaches expected patterns of behaviour and the shared attitudes and values of society.

Criticisms of G. P. Murdock

- He sees the multi-functional family as the necessary, all-purpose basic unit of society: both universal and inevitable.
- He fails to consider whether his listed functions could be undertaken by other social institutions.
- The happy haven of the family he pictures is too good to be true.

> 'Murdock's nuclear family is a remarkably harmonious institution. Husband and wife have an integrated division of labour and have a good time in bed!'
> D.H.J. Morgan, *Social Theory and the Family* (Routledge & Kegan Paul, 1975)

Talcott Parsons

Parsons and his co-authors, in *Family Socialisation and Interaction Process* (1955), relating to contemporary American society, claim the family has two 'basic and irreducible functions'.

- Primary socialisation of children: during the early years of childhood, within the family, the culture of a society is learned and *internalised*, so that shared social norms and values become accepted from a young age.
- Structuring of the personality: the family holds a structuring role to offset the psychological pressures of everyday life that might disturb the adult personality.

In addition to these two 'basic and irreducible' functions, Talcott Parsons maintains that:

- the family is functional only when its members fulfil their allocated roles;
- women naturally possess an **expressive** role in the family: they are subservient to men and look after men, children and the home; they are sensitive, patient and kind by nature;
- men naturally possess an **instrumental** role in the family as its breadwinner; they are leaders, dominant and aggressive by nature.
- the subordinate position of women in capitalist society is functionally necessary in order to maintain family cohesion and the class structure. The maintenance of the class structure is necessary in order to secure the harmony and equilibrium of society.

Criticisms of Talcott Parsons

- He adopts a conservative stance and does not allow for the likelihood of a wide variety of, and alternatives to, the nuclear family.
- His traditional functionalist ideas on the 'natural' role of women are challenged by cross-cultural studies and feminist views.

Functional or dysfunctional families?

Both Murdock and Parsons assume that the family has a positive functional position in society. However, some sociologists have suggested **dysfunctional** influences. Contemporary functionalists, such as Norman Bell and Ezra Vogel in *A Modern Introduction to the Family* (1968), and radical phenomenologists, such as M. Voysey in *A Constant Burden* (1975), have pointed towards the chilling and sometimes painful tensions which can exist between members of the modern family. More recently Brigitte and Peter Berger, in *The War Over the Family* (1983), have aimed to 'capture the middle ground' in the debate over the family: whilst accepting the modern family has its problems, they claim that there is hardly a viable alternative to meet the needs of individuals and wider society, thereby harking back to many of the implications of the ideas of Murdock and Parsons.

Think about it

- How important do you consider Murdock's four key functions of the family are to the sociology of the family today?
- Would you agree that in order for the young to be adequately socialised into the shared norms and values of society, punishments – including physical punishments – may be justified?
- Can the domestic roles of many women, and their often inferior position in society, still be seen as functionally necessary for family life?

Critical theories

Critical theories of the family are associated with a group of 'radical psychologists', whose main theme is that family life can harm individual development. The principal contributors to critical theories have been **Ronald David Laing** (a Scottish psychiatrist and cult figure in the 1960s), **David Cooper** and an anthropologist, **Sir Edmund Leach**.

R.D. Laing R.D. Laing considered that there was a dark, unhappy, dysfunctional side to the family. His works include an account of his clinical experience, as a psychiatrist, of schizophrenia within the family and a study of family interaction and dynamics (see Bibliography). Some of his main points are as follows.

- The family is capable of damaging individual development by providing a limiting environment. More significantly, confusion about family relationships can combine with anger, jealousy and guilt between spouses. Such confusion can get passed on to offspring with damaging results.
- The family group, which Laing terms **nexus**, can become an emotional, exploitative battleground with the offspring suffering in terms of developing an identity which may have been thrust upon them. He refers to 'reciprocal interiorisation'; by this he means that individuals within a family become almost a part of each other, and charged emotions are shared and exchanged. This can be psychologically damaging and hinder self development.
- Although parents want to see their offspring grow, they often seek to prolong the dependence of their children; this can lead to forms of physical violence, or even to the label of 'madness'. Mental disturbances such as schizophrenia may be seen as an escape route from the children's experience and stresses of family life.
- Mental illness may be best understood as an individual experience with a social, particularly family, setting, and intervention treatment could help the mentally ill to grow and develop through their illness.

Criticisms of R.D. Laing

- His emphasis on the 'dark side' of the family, based mainly on clinical studies rather than on detailed fieldwork, seems to lack balance, especially in relation to the support often given to and by family members.
- His view of the parent–child relationship as the key factor in socialisation processes assumes that such processes flow from parent to child. However, children do not passively receive: they also learn how to resist and even exploit differences between their parents.
- He sees parents as having complete power and overlooks the roles played by siblings, peers, teachers, the media etc. as agents of socialisation in a complex social structure.
- He does not place the family into a social context and fails to discuss how childrearing practices are redefined by the links between the family and the world outside which form the social system.

D. Cooper D. Cooper, also a psychiatrist, worked with R.D. Laing and expresses similar ideas. For Cooper, the family destroys the inner life of people by obstructing the development of the 'self'. In *The Death of the Family* (1971), he argued that:

- family relationships form a 'love trap' which prevents self realisation. We are not able to be ourselves since, as children, we are taught and develop self–other roles and dependencies rather than thinking for ourselves;

- although family members have a need for love and security, family relationships can contain within them the very ingredients which produce stress, guilt and even violence;
- the family serves as an ideological conditioning device in an exploitative society, whether slave society, feudal society or capitalist society.

Criticisms of Cooper

- Like R.D. Laing, D. Cooper did not carry out detailed fieldwork but relied on his case studies of those labelled as schizophrenic.
- He makes no mention of class structure/its relationship to family life.
- Both D. Cooper and R.D. Laing look only at Western families, and have worked only from a specialised psychological perspective.

E. Leach Leach caused a major stir in the annual Reith Lecture in 1967, with his attack on what he coined 'the cereal packet norm family' and his support of 'radical psychology'. In his study, *A Runaway World* (1967), he makes the following claims:

- In the modern, isolated, nuclear family there is an intensity of emotional relationships between spouses, and between spouses and their offspring; this makes family members become inward looking and expect too much of each other.
- The increased expectations and demands of family members lead to friction and conflict inside the family and fear of the outside world.

> *'The strain is greater than most can bear. Far from being the basis of the good society, the family with all its tawdry secrets is the source of all our discontents.'*
> Sir Edmund Leach, *A Runaway World* (1967)

Criticisms of Leach

- Whilst offering a radical alternative view to functionalist and other approaches, he has not carried out detailed fieldwork to support his claim, although his anthropological studies did involve family and kinship groups in small-scale non-Western society.
- To some extent he presents a view of society which has got out of control, virtually gone mad. Such a view may be criticised as being unbalanced and extreme. In 1992 he reinforced his extreme views when he wrote that the present-day family leads to:

> *'claustrophobia for all . . . the English continue to rear their children cooped up in boxes like battery hens.'*
> Sir Edmund Leach (1992)

Think about it

- Do you think that family life may be seen as a 'safe haven' or as an 'emotional battleground'? What do you think are the key points of each of these opposing views of family life?
- Why might it still seem quite common for parents to cling on to the dependence of their offspring? In what ways does this seem to operate? How do you think independence may be achieved by children in contemporary society?

Marxist theories

Whereas functionalists consider the family as a universal, static social institution, Marxists – such as Engels and Eli Zaretsky – put it into the context of the evolution of capitalist society and, in particular, the class nature of that society.

Engels on the family

Friedrich Engels (1820–1885), the German socialist, linked the family to the evolution of classes, property and the state. His most influential writing on the family was *The Origin of the Family, Private Property and the State* (1884), which is still a basic source for Marxists. It was also one of the few nineteenth-century texts to consider the position of women and the existence of gender inequality in capitalist society. Engels maintained the following:

- The nuclear family and male domination developed through history. In the nomadic stage of human evolution there was a large degree of sexual equality; there was no restrictive sexual possessiveness nor private property; much was held in common even though mothers had considerable attachment to their offspring.
- As the male role started developing into more specialised activities, for example hunting and later mining and trade, men gained more control over wealth and property, which was inherited by their sons.
- Free sexual relations within the tribe had to give way to a monogamy and inheritance system formed by blood ties. This became the basis of a male-dominated society.
- Men were supported via the legal system to gain control over the family, women and private property; and so the development of private property, patriarchy and male domination of society and state evolved.

Doubt has been expressed about the accuracy of Engels's historical analysis of the origins of the family. More recent findings have challenged some of his ideas about the evolution of the family and marriage (for example, monogamy has been found in gathering and hunting tribes in Africa and South America). However, his writings throw light on the social construction of patriarchy via marriage.

Marxists claim that the family is the result of class conflict which has maintained the family (and the associated tradition of inheritance) so that economic wealth stays with the capitalists. Hence the family perpetuates the reproduction of capitalism by the following processes:

- Ideological production and conditioning within the family ensures that capitalist values are passed down through successive generations.

> *'[the family] with its authoritarian ideology is designed to teach passivity, not rebellion.'*
> Diane Feeley, 'The Family' in L. Jenness (ed.), *Feminism and Socialism* (Pathfinder Press, 1972)

Usually it is the mother who serves as the major force of such ideological production and conditioning.
- Physical reproduction or the production of the labour force serves as a stabilising force which maintains (and exploits) the family unit as dependent on the male wage.
- Financial commitment by workers to the family discourages them from withholding their labour. The family therefore bears the brunt of workers' frustrations and alienation in the capitalist labour market so that anger is vented upon family members rather than capitalism itself.

- By purchasing ever-increasing amounts of consumer durables from televisions to telephones, from cars to computers, the family supports the maintenance and perpetuation of the capitalist market economy.

Criticisms of Marxists
- There is a tendency to be negative about the family, seeing it solely as an exploitative social structure within capitalist society.
- Marxists tend to overlook the similarities in family forms in capitalist and socialist societies, with divorce, prostitution and sexual abuse occurring in both systems.
- The family seems to be viewed as a natural social institution for the reproduction of the workforce but as having no influence on what, for Marx, was the key process: the means of production.

> *'As a consequence [Marx] treated the family as peripheral and of marginal interest in the analysis of social life.'*
> Faith Robertson Elliot, *The Family: Change or Continuity?*
> (Macmillan, 1986)

- The argument that social problems arise from the negative aspects of the family in its contribution and service to capitalism represents a very narrow analysis of these problems.

Think about it

- Do you think that the family bears the brunt of workers' frustrations and alienation in a capitalist labour market?
- To what extent do you consider it to be true that the family openly supports capitalism by purchasing cars, houses and a wide range of consumer durables?
- How do Marxist views of the family differ from functionalist and critical theories?

Feminist theories

Feminist theories often overlap and extend other theories, particularly critical and Marxist theories. Whilst Marxist theories view the family as being exploited by the capitalist system, feminists have drawn attention to the specific exploitation of women.

Most feminists agree on the need to understand female subservience, and to free females, but they lack agreement on the causes of such subservience and on how freedom might be achieved.

As we saw in Unit 1, there are four types of feminist theory:

- liberal (or reformist) feminism;
- radical (or revolutionary) feminism;
- Marxist feminism;
- socialist feminism.

An excellent analysis of these feminist approaches is given by Pamela Abbott and Claire Wallace in their book *Introduction to Sociology 2nd edn.* (1997). They put forward two linked structures of subordination of females in the family:

1. women's position as wives and mothers; and
2. socialisation processes in the family, whereby the young internalise the male and female attitudes they observe in their parents.

Whilst Marxist feminists emphasise that women's exploitation in the family serves the interest of capitalism, radical or revolutionary feminists stress that it serves the interests of men, who gain from the unpaid labour of women. All feminists argue that women's subordinate position in the family as wives/mothers is partly due to economic dependency, but also due to shared ideologies of the family.

Barrie Thorne, in *Feminist Rethinking of the Family: an overview* (1982), puts forward four themes as key to the feminist attack on traditional notions.

1. Traditional assumptions of the structure and function of the family view the nuclear family, with its gender divisions, as the only natural and legitimate form of the family. Feminists challenge the idea that any family form is natural, i.e. based on biological differences.
2. Feminists claim that family forms are based on social organisation and beliefs about people's roles held by the members of a given society. There is no biological reason why men cannot do housework, for example; only that people in society believe that it is not right for them to do it. Feminists claim the family as an area for analysis and, in doing so, counter the gender-based categories of analysis of what they term '**malestream**' sociology.
3. Feminists argue that different family members experience family life in different ways. They argue that women's experiences of motherhood and family life have shown that families carry power relationships that can and do result in conflict and violence.
4. Feminists challenge the notion that the family should be a private sphere. The form that the family takes is influenced by economic and social policies. Feminists maintain that common beliefs about the nature of the family deny women the opportunity to participate in the wider society and achieve equality with men. This may also explain female inequalities in the labour market, youth cultures, political life and other areas of social life.

Criticisms of feminist theories

- Feminists have generally put forward a view of the family as oppressive. Any attraction of marriage, motherhood and family life for women becomes ignored. Historical achievements by the suffragettes and other female freedom and resistance movements also seem to be overlooked.
- Feminists, while drawing attention to the variety of family forms and gender relationships, have challenged claims to the notion of the Western family's advantages (improved social, economic and legal status).
- There are some sociologists who question the link between the family and the sexual division of labour.

> '*What is impressive about views supporting the conventional division of labour between men and women within the household is both their relative stability over time and the wide range of people who share these views.*'
> David H. J. Morgan, 'The Family' in M. Haralambos (ed.), *Developments in Sociology*, vol. 7, 1990

Furthermore, the continued traditional division of labour in communes and in cohabiting couples suggests that the variety does not seem to have led to any major reforms of the sexual division of labour. Both marriage and cohabitation continue to satisfy many individuals and serve as a goal for many adolescents. A major task for feminists, therefore, is to account for the breadth and depth of pro-family sentiments.

Think about it

- Do you agree with the feminist viewpoint that the family oppresses women?
- To what extent is it true, as feminists maintain, that common beliefs about the nature of the family deny women the opportunity to participate in the wider society and achieve equality with men?

New Right theories

The New Right embraces a range of ideologies associated with a less centrally controlled free-market economy and a more socially dictated authoritarian attitude. Free enterprise and the rolling back of the state, it is argued, could increase market efficiency and wealth creation.

The New Right shares the functionalist view that the stability of the family is important for the harmony of society. It supports clear-cut roles: females as wives, with the caring responsibility for their husbands and children, and their spouses as the stalwart patriarchal breadwinners. The New Right in both the UK and the USA has criticised the welfare and benefits systems. It sees the family as crumbling under the steady impact of changes in society – increased sexual permissiveness, cohabitation, etc. – changes that, in turn, destabilise society itself, bringing about unwanted social change.

Paul Johnson

Paul Johnson, the British journalist and author of *Wake Up Britain* (1994), writes in alarmist terms of 'the malaise that is afflicting British life'. One of the case studies he refers to concerns a mother of 11 children, nine of whom were illegitimate by the same father. Neither adult had ever been in paid employment. This case caused public outcry as the 'family' had jumped the council housing queue and received three council houses knocked into one. The council had had to carry out its legal duties at a public cost of £196,580, which has been calculated as the equivalent of the total taxes paid by 60 working people in that tax year (1994).

Charles Murray

Charles Murray, Fellow at the American Institute of Washington DC and author of *Losing Ground* (1984), popularised the idea of an underclass (see also Unit 2, page 98), whose abuses of the welfare system were, in his view, becoming a menace to American society. His New Right views have received support from both right- and left-wing American politicians.

Murray visited the UK in 1989, referring to himself as 'a visitor from a plague area come to see if the disease is spreading'. He prophesied that the ills of American society and 'the deplorable behaviour' – notably never-married parents, rising crime rates and the unemployed living well on benefits – would soon produce a similar scenario in the UK.

During Murray's second visit to the UK, in 1994, he identified two distinct groups whom he termed the 'New Rabble' and the 'New Victorians'.

New Rabble
- Low-skilled working class, poorly educated
- Single-parent families are the norm
- Largely dependent on welfare and the black economy
- High levels of criminality, child neglect and abuse, and drug use
- Impervious to social welfare policies that seek to change their behaviour
- Will not enter legitimate labour force when times are good, and will recruit more working class young people when times are bad
- Children attend school irregularly and pose discipline problems
- Large and lucrative market for violent and pornographic films, television and music

New Victorians
- Educated, in professional occupations
- Incomes above level at which tax or benefit changes determine whether they have children
- Less mesmerised by careers than in the past; more concerned about children and community
- Free sexual expression less of a priority
- Revived interest in religion and spiritual matters
- Renewed concern for concepts such as fidelity, courage, loyalty, self-restraint and moderation
- Less inclined to divorce

Murray's concerns focus on a vigorous debate about how a civil, free society can sustain itself and about the role that the family plays in that process. Murray adds 'a few cautionary notes and general thoughts' on the following subjects:

- Aiming for full employment: Murray views full employment as part of the solution to high levels of illegitimacy.
- Stopping the penalties of marriage: the benefits system favours single mothers over married mothers so, Murray suggests, benefit levels should be changed to ensure that marriage is not financially damaging.
- Facing up to hard choices: Murray suggests that benefits for unmarried mothers be removed from all but those currently receiving them. He contends that the benefits structure should be reduced to the much more limited form that it took in 1960, when the welfare system seemed more workable and beneficial to society as a whole; the state should stop intervening and should let the natural economic penalties occur.

Criticisms of the New Right
- The New Right have been accused of blaming the most unfortunate members of the 'underclass', in particular unmarried mothers and the long-term unemployed.
- Terms such as the 'New Victorians' and 'New Rabble' are emotive and lack credibility.

- Murray's degrading of the 'underclass' has been criticised for representing a flimsy cultural rather than structural analysis of poverty. It does not address stratification theory whereby structuralists who are concerned with the unequal structure of society would tend to view the underclass as victims rather than as perpetrators of poverty and inequality.
- It has been argued that if a dependency culture exists it has been created by 'targeted' means-tested benefits received only by the poorest groups; the welfare system is far from generous and universal provisions which afforded all members of society an acceptable living standard would be preferable.
- The New Right have proposed extreme measures and attracted the attention of many governments grappling with similar social problems. However, in both the USA and the UK, attempts to make natural fathers contribute financially towards their offspring (e.g. the Child Support Agency) and their former partners, if not living together, have proved problematic, as have attempts to provide financial benefit to two-parent patriarchal-styled families.

Think about it

- In what ways may there be support for, or challenges to, the New Right view that family life has begun to crumble because of increased sexual permissiveness and high levels of illegitimacy?
- Do you consider that it would be in the interests of society for the state to give one year's warning of no new provision of financial and welfare benefits to unmarried mothers? What problems might this create?
- What are the problems for sociologists when a New Right theorist such as Charles Murray labels social groups as the 'New Rabble' or the 'New Victorians'?

The family and social policies

Welfare State policies

The **Beveridge Report** (fully titled the 1942 Report on Social Insurance and Allied Services) introduced the concept of a Welfare State, in which the state provided universal (i.e. for all citizens) rights to its members and held greater control over their lives. Beveridge's aim was to abolish what he termed the 'five giant evils' of want, disease, ignorance, squalor and idleness by the introduction of a comprehensive national insurance scheme and a range of social services and welfare benefits. In terms of changes in family life, the post-war period brought:

- a lessening of family poverty caused by unemployment and sickness;
- financial allowances for the family, including maternity grants, pensions for the elderly and even payments at death – a 'cradle to grave' or 'womb to tomb' support system;
- universal access to free health care and education, plus the greater availability of rented accommodation through local authorities.

These policies were introduced by the Labour government of 1945–51. The state was to maintain full employment and economic growth in order to avoid the problems associated with the mass unemployment of the 1930s. State intervention was seen as a way of protecting and supporting family life, which in turn protected and supported the interests of society as a whole.

Summary of main theories and ideologies of the family

Criteria	Functionalism (George Peter Murdock Talcott Parsons)	Critical (Ronald David Laing David Cooper Edmund Leach)	Marxism (Friedrich Engels Karl Marx Eli Zaretsky)	Feminism (Pamela Abbott Claire Wallace Ann Oakley)	New Right (Roger Scruton Paul Johnson Charles Murray)
Overviews family . . .	as necessary for smooth running and continuation of an integrated society.	in radical terms, draws attention to stressful and damaging effects of family life.	in structural terms, in relation to the evolution of class-based capitalist society.	as a gender-based analysis of 'malestream' sociology in relation to female subservience within the family and society.	as important in terms of its stability for the harmony and efficiency of society but with minimal state intervention.
Main role seen as . . .	performing universal functions, notably sexual, reproductive, economic, educational.	teaching role behaviour which produces some conformity in an exchange of charged emotions.	perpetuating the reproduction of capitalism by teaching passivity not rebellion, and by purchasing its products.	socialisation by females of the young to internalise male and female attitudes to maintain male domination and female subordination.	promoting 'normal' heterosexual family life with clear-cut gender roles, rather than promiscuity, divorce and lone parenting.
Advantages for . . .	family members and society as a whole.	capitalist society with family a psycho-sociological ideological conditioning device.	capitalist society by ideological production and conditioning passed down through successive generations.	capitalist society and men, who gain by the unpaid domestic labour of women.	family and state in terms of stable personal relationships and less welfare benefit expenditure.
Disadvantages for . . .	no one, except those who act dysfunctionally and do not fulfil their allocated roles.	family members by the development of 'love traps' which prevent development of the 'self'.	family members, in particular women, who become exploited in order to maintain the capitalist market economy.	women, who become exploited because of their economic dependency and ideologies of the family.	short-term and transient relationships reliant upon welfare provisions in a private wealth-producing economy.
Criticisms include . . .	a conservative view with the nuclear family as best basic unit of society but wider varieties and alternative forms not considered. Ignores negative aspects, e.g. domestic violence.	the 'dark side' of (unhappy) families based on a relatively small number of clinical studies which lack balance and overlook the support families can provide.	the tendency to remain negative about the family and its members and treat the family narrowly as of marginal interest in the analysis of social life as an aspect of capitalist society.	an oppressive view of the family with any attraction of cohabitation, marriage, motherhood or family life for women ignored. Diverse elements which do not yet have a unified approach.	'victim-blaming' of divorced partners, long-term unemployed, etc. Represents a flimsy cultural and right-wing political approach rather than structural analysis of the family and society.

However, in the 1960s problems began to develop.

- The increase in welfare expenditure by the state to finance its policies, although sustainable during the post-war growth period, began to pose problems.
- During the 1970s, because of Welfare State funding problems and the need to save money, there was a move towards a more selective targeting of the most needy rather than the provision of universal benefits. This led later to the freezing and cutting back of a range of benefits.

In spite of these problems, the major political parties remained committed to the Welfare State.

New Right policies Since the 1980s there has been a tendency for the state to turn back towards viewing the family and family relationships as basic and essential sources of welfare, in the interests of both the individual and society. Governments in the UK, the USA, New Zealand and Germany have embarked upon a series of measures to reduce welfare expenditure. Their reasons include the following.

- Ideological views: the state should concern itself with moral issues even to the cost of individual freedom. Roger Scruton, a right-wing philosopher, in *Sexual Desires: A Philosophical Investigation* (1986), maintained that support for the 'normal' heterosexual family should be the pillar of state involvement in social policy. It was the state's failure to give such support, he claimed, that had led to increased promiscuity, high divorce rates and increasing numbers of single parents.
- Welfare State reconsiderations: reductions in government revenue and worldwide recession meant increased demands on Welfare State provisions. Public spending began to be seen as parasitic on the private wealth-producing economy: growing social welfare provisions damage reward incentives.
- State/family relationships: the family was held to operate better with minimum state involvement. It was argued that parents should take responsibility for the young, infirm and elderly, with the support of voluntary or community care provisions (see also Unit 7).

The hidden agenda behind these policies seems to be to cut public expenditure. In spite of supposed support for the traditional nuclear family, successive Conservative government ministers in the UK failed to introduce any policies for benefits or taxation in favour of, for example, mothers in their home-life and childcare roles (there has been no increase in Child Benefit). If anything, the family has become more financially burdened by measures such as the curbing of unemployment benefits for school-leavers, the freezing of student grants and the introduction of loans, and the placing of care for the infirm and the elderly back into the family and out of the more costly state institutions.

Think about it

- What do you know about current state policies on matters relating to the family? Choose one policy area and find out what it offers the family.
- Why do you think that lone-parent families lost £11.50 per week family support in New Labour's first budget in November 1997?

Household and family diversity

The effects of industrialisation

From the Middle Ages to about the eighteenth century, most goods and services were produced in households involving the cooperation of parents, children and other members. Some households provided board and lodging for relatives in return for labour, others hired servants. From 1574 to 1821, about 60 per cent of the population in England aged 15 to 24 were servants, and 46 per cent of farmers' households contained one or two servants. Such household units produced goods and services for their own survival (with any surplus goods being stored or sold at local markets): they could be seen as independent commodity- or service-producing units – in other words, units of production.

During the eighteenth century changes, particularly the 'separation of home and workplace', began to occur. **Industrialisation** – the advent of mechanised production processes associated with the mass production of goods and services – developed right across Europe, changing family life and increasing household diversity. The effects of industrialisation included:

- industrial work in factories, mills and workshops using powered machinery. Goods became cheaper and more plentiful than those produced in families and household units;
- the moving of the workforce from the countryside, with its agricultural production and small-scale cottage industries, to urban industrialised areas;
- increased **urbanisation** (population growth becoming more concentrated in towns and cities), accompanied by higher fertility and lower death rates (see Unit 5, page 229).

Parsons and the development of the nuclear family

For Talcott Parsons, there was a direct link between industrialisation and the development of the nuclear family as an isolated unit. According to him, the family became:

- 'structurally isolated', because it no longer formed an integral aspect of kinship relationships: although such relationships may continue to exist they had become less obligatory;
- 'structurally differentiated', since other institutions with more specialised and fewer functions, for example schools, hospitals, police and Church, began to develop;
- more geographically mobile, with the nuclear family moving to find work without being burdened by kinship ties and obligations;
- based on achieved rather than ascribed status. Individuals could achieve status on their merit in industrialised societies, rather than having to follow in the family's occupational footsteps.

Criticisms of Talcott Parsons

Parsons's idea of a 'fit' between industrialisation and the development of the isolated nuclear family has been criticised for the following reasons:

- It is not clear that industrial economies need greater geographical mobility than other types of society. It may be that urbanisation *lessens* the need for geographical mobility, by making available a range of jobs in the locality.

- The growth of mass communications and transport systems which often accompanies industrialisation enables more people to work away from their homes and to keep close contact with kin who are geographically spread further away.
- It may be claimed that modern social mobility has been exaggerated. Short-range social mobility may have been common in pre-industrial societies, and there are more hurdles to social mobility in modern industrial societies than some would have us believe.

Post-war research on the family and industrialisation

Although early research on the family and industrialisation is both interesting and useful, more recent material has flourished. A selection of such material follows.

- **Eugene Litwak**, in *Geographical Mobility and Extended Family Cohesion* (1960), maintains that the concept of 'modified extended family' may help to clear up some of the problems associated with the 'isolated nuclear family'. For Litwak, in modern industrial society, nuclear families exchange important services in times of need or for important family events, regardless of geographical distances.
- **Colin Rosser** and **Christopher Harris**, in *The Family and Social Change* (1965), favoured Litwak's concept of 'modified extended family' from their study in Swansea. They found that the nuclear family formed the centre of family life but that the extended family retained a modified – but still significant – supportive role, with letters, telephones and cars making contact easier than in previous historical periods.
- **Colin Bell**, in *Middle Class Families* (1968), also carried out research in Swansea and showed how middle-class families gave financial assistance to help the independence of their offspring. He identified two types of family:
  (a) 'burgesses', who stayed in their home locality establishing their careers and creating a local network of contacts including both relatives and friends; and
  (b) 'spiralists', who were geographically and socially more mobile, often drawing themselves away from their kin and thereby promoting greater sharing of domestic roles.
- **Graham Allan**, in *Family Life: Domestic Roles and Social Organisation* (1985), also accepts Litwak's concept but prefers the term 'modified elementary family' in his research in a commuter village in East Anglia. For Allan, non-nuclear kin do not usually rely upon one another and have few exchanges of goods and services. Nevertheless, family members do feel obliged to maintain contact and support each other particularly at times of difficulty. He sees the 'modified elementary family' as a more appropriate concept, since it is confined to the elementary family of husband and wife (or partner), their parents, their siblings and their children.

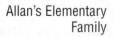

Allan's Elementary Family

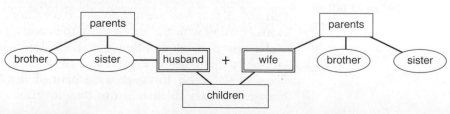

Young and Willmott's research on family life

The British sociologists **Michael Young** and **Peter Willmott** are among the most notable commentators on family life. Their early classic study, *Family and Kinship in East London* (1957), looked at the impact of the post-war housing relocation programme on working-class families from Bethnal Green in East London to Greenleigh, a new housing estate about 30 miles away in Essex.

In the first part of their study, in Bethnal Green, strong extended family networks played an important part in mutual help, particularly between mothers and daughters. Many daughters made frequent visits to their mothers for advice, help with children and to keep in touch with other members of the family and kinship group.

Front cover of *Family and Kinship in East London*, 1957

However, in Greenleigh, the family took on a nuclear-family form and 'privatisation' occurred: the family became a more private, isolated, inward-looking and home-centred unit. Wives no longer had regular contact with their mothers and relied more on their husbands for support. Husbands no longer visited pubs with kin and workmates and became more involved in home-based activities such as gardening and DIY.

A second study by Young and Willmott, *Family and Class in a London Suburb* (1960), attempted to find out whether a middle-class London suburb, Woodford, had a different pattern of family life from that of a new working-class suburb such as Greenleigh. In Woodford, middle-class couples were able to overcome the effects of distance from family and kin as they had greater access to telephones and cars, and more spacious housing which allowed them to accommodate visiting relatives.

The third study by Young and Willmott, *The Symmetrical Family* (1975), puts forward a theory, building on their previous studies, to describe the stages in the development of family life from pre-industrial to contemporary Britain. In this they identify four stages:

1. The pre-industrial family: the family acts as a unit of production, with the husband, wife and unmarried children working as a team involved in agriculture and small-scale cottage industries. Some examples of this type of family persist in contemporary Britain, for example farming families.

2. The early industrial family: with the advent of the Industrial Revolution, individual family members were employed mainly as wage earners. The family, especially the least successful struggling against unemployment and poverty, became a support unit rather than a unit of production. Among the poor in urban areas the extended family again became an important structure, and remained so until the development of the Welfare State brought improvements in living standards.

3. The symmetrical family: based on a survey of about 2000 people in and around London in the 1970s, the nuclear family was seen to have emerged from stage 2 to become the main family type. In the symmetrical family, husbands and wives take an equal share in domestic life. Young and Willmott were careful to point out that they saw this as a coming, rather than an existing, family form, originating in the emerging middle class.

4. A possible stage 4 family is asymmetrical. Young and Willmott's 1970 survey found that the attitude of managing directors towards work was that it is a central life interest. These values are likely to filter through society, so that families will become less privatised as husbands become more committed to their jobs and the domestic role returns to being the responsibility of their wives: couples spend less time in joint activities.

The principle of stratified diffusion

This describes a process whereby the norms of those at the top of the social hierarchy gradually influence those at lower levels of society. New ideas of family life, for example, filter down from higher social classes to become accepted by lower social classes.

Criticisms of Young and Willmott

- Their 'march of progress' theory, in which family life develops and improves, has been criticised by Marxists and feminists for neglecting the negative aspects of family life.

- The principle of stratified diffusion has been challenged, since research such as the Affluent Worker study (see Unit 2, page 75) do not show that the working class automatically accepts and follows norms set by the middle class.

- Feminists have attacked the notion of the symmetrical family.

> *'As long as the blame is laid on the woman's head for a dirty house it is not meaningful to talk about marriage as a "joint" or "equal" partnership. The same holds of parenthood. So long as mothers and not fathers are judged by their children's appearance . . . symmetry remains a myth!'*
> Ann Oakley, *The Sociology of Housework* (1974)

- The extended family may be more significant than is indicated by Young and Willmott, who also tend to overlook a widely divergent variety of households and family forms.

Social class and family patterns

Does social class affect family patterns? David Eversley and Lucy Bonnerjea, in *Social Change and Indicators of Diversity* (1982), stated that manual workers tend to marry and have children earlier than non-manual workers. J. Haskey, in *Social Class and Socio-economic Differentials in Divorce in England and Wales* (1994), showed a relationship between husbands' occupations and divorce rates: the three highest divorce rates are unskilled manual workers, the unemployed and the armed forces, whilst the three lowest are for professional, intermediate and skilled manual groups.

Whether or not it is possible to talk about such class characteristics is debatable, but it is quite straightforward to demonstrate that factors such as wealth, income and employment do affect living patterns within the family. The role of the family in class terms becomes more important if we look at relationships between family members, especially across generations. Here the issues of inheritance and the way class inequalities are reproduced over time are significant. Cycles of advantage benefit the wealthy, especially the property-owning classes, whilst cycles of disadvantage adversely affect the poorer sections of society. It should also be noted that the processes of inheritance are often formed on gender grounds so that boys and girls do not necessarily inherit identical resources from their parents, as pointed out by Christine Delphy and Diana Leonard in *Class Analysis, Gender Analysis and Family* (1986).

Charles Murray's New Right views, described earlier in the unit, (pages 126–8) have focused also on social class and the family, as illustrated in the two scenarios depicted below.

BRITAIN TOMORROW: THE TWO VIEWS

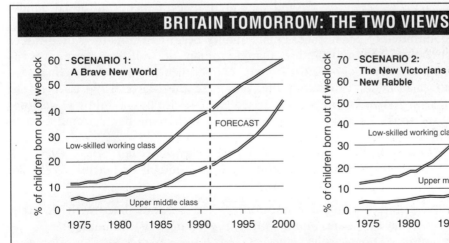

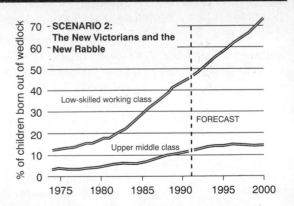

Class I families were having only about 11% of their children out of wedlock as of 1991, compared with 45% among the daughters of Class V families.

A distinctive feature of the second scenario is that I show illegitimacy levelling off, and even declining, among the upper middle class. This is why I talk about the "New Victorians" and the "New Rabble", meaning that one part of society — the affluent, well-educated part — will edge back towards traditional morality while a large portion of what used to be the British working class goes the way of the American underclass.

Source: The *Sunday Times*, 22 May 1994

The family and gender roles

Talcott Parsons, the American functionalist, referred to the natural 'expressive' role of women (see page 120), since they provide warmth, security and emotional support which is essential for the socialisation of children and the structuring of personality and identity, in contrast to the 'instrumental' role of men as breadwinners. This view that there is a biological explanation for behavioural differences between the sexes has been challenged, particularly by feminists who argue that gender roles are culturally rather than biologically determined.

Culture and identity: gender socialisation and gender roles

Ann Oakley, the Marxist feminist, has outlined key factors which account for gender socialisation in modern industrial society:

- 'manipulation' of the self concept of the young, for example mothers taking more care over their daughters' hair and feminine appearance;
- 'canalisation' or directing the young to different objects, for example girls to toy dolls and ovens, boys to toy guns and bricks;
- 'verbal appellations' or the language used by parents, for example 'sweet girl' as opposed to 'tomboy';
- 'different activities' in relation to domestic tasks, for example cooking with mother, DIY with father.

Oakley argues that gender socialisation reinforces and maintains culturally constructed domestic roles which serve the interests of males rather than females in capitalist society.

Research by Catherine Hakim at the London School of Economics, published in early 1996, found that only between a quarter and a third of females seek careers, and that many accept their traditional gender roles in the home-based domestic sphere. Feminists, for Hakim, seem committed to promoting sexual equality because it suits their own career interests. She argues that many women do not see themselves as exploited in poorly paid part-time employment, because what they care most about is their family life. However, the March 1996 issue of the *British Journal of Sociology* carried two articles by a total of 11 sociologists attacking Hakim's views and stating that she had selected data to support her case.

Elizabeth Bott, in her classic study *Family and Social Network* (1957), produced an interesting view of conjugal or marital roles. She identified and termed such roles as:

- **segregated conjugal roles:** couples led separate lives with different tasks in the home. Mainly found in working-class families;
- **joint conjugal roles:** couples led more shared lives in domestic responsibilities and leisure activities. Mainly found in middle-class families.

However, when Bott found joint conjugal roles being carried out also in working-class families, she suggested that it was not social class so much as the social networks brought by each partner to the marriage (i.e. the number of people with whom interaction took place regularly) that mattered.

- Close-knit social network (for example, traditional working-class communities): husbands and wives from such a background tended to be less dependent on each other and to adopt segregated conjugal roles. Each partner would have their own well-established network of kin and friends.
- Loose-knit social network (for example, newer housing estates): husbands and wives from such a background tended to adopt joint conjugal roles. They would be less likely to have a close circle of kin and friends and would need to provide more support and time for each other.

Criticisms of Elizabeth Bott

Her methods of measurement as well as some uncertainty about the nature of conjugal roles and social networks have caused concern.

- In conducting her research into conjugal roles, she failed to distinguish between 'role' as an expectation and 'role performance' (i.e. what actually happens).
- The survey has not stood the test of time. Contemporary research suggests that the relationship between role segregation and network connectedness is less regular than Bott maintained. Young and Willmott, for example considered that the modern privatised family had become more isolated from social networks and that conjugal roles had become more joint and symmetrical (see pages 133–4).

Power to make decisions and set agendas

Stephen Edgell, in *Middle Class Couples* (1980), challenged notions of symmetry in his survey of 38 professional couples. He found little evidence for the existence of the symmetrical family with equal sharing of household tasks, although about 45 per cent of his sample shared some childrearing responsibilities.

Earlier studies had not linked decision-making within families in terms of how frequently such decisions were taken or of their importance. Edgell found that women exercised decision-making in certain areas, for example food shopping and children's clothes, but men controlled important decisions such as moving house and car purchase and possessed overall control of financial resources. Husbands set the agenda on most issues of marriage and family life: wives lacked power to change or even affect decision-making. Indeed, Edgell found that about half of the husbands and two-thirds of the wives did not view sexual equality favourably.

Mary Boulton, in *On Being a Mother* (1983), studied 50 young married mothers, none of whom was in full-time waged employment. She found that whilst husbands might help with certain tasks or play with their children, it was the wives who had major responsibility for the children. This vital role dominated the wives' lives both within and outside the home and curtailed their leisure activities.

Inequalities of power and ideology

Power to make decisions, as indicated by Edgell's study, can be considered in relation to who controls family finances.

Jan Pahl, in *Money and Marriage* (1989), interviewed 102 couples, all of whom had at least one child under 16, and found four ways in which these families organised their money.

1. 'Husband-controlled pooling': couples had a joint account; the husband controlled household finances and paid the bills. This was most common at higher-income levels especially when the wife was not in employment (39 couples).

2. 'Wife-controlled pooling': couples had a joint account; the wife controlled the money and paid the bills. This was most common at middle-income levels with both partners in employment (27 couples).

3. 'Husband controlled': couples did not have a joint bank account; the husband paid bills from his sole bank account and gave his wife a set sum each week or month for housekeeping. This was most common when the husband was the main earner; if the wife worked, her earnings went into her housekeeping money (22 couples).

4. 'Wife controlled': couples did not have bank accounts at all; the wife managed cash payments of bills and family finances. This was most common in low-income, unqualified, working-class households (14 couples).

Pahl, then, found a link between how a couple organised their money and socio-economic factors such as their total income, educational qualifications, etc. He also found that the way in which a couple controlled their finances reflected the happiness or quality of the relationship:

Marital happiness by control of finances		
Marriage described as:	Happy/ Very happy	Average/ Unhappy
1. Husband-controlled pooling	37 (35)	2 (4)
2. Wife-controlled pooling	23 (25)	4 (2)
3. Husband controlled	13 (16)	9 (6)
4. Wife controlled	13 (13)	1 (1)

Wives' answers (husbands' answers in brackets)   Source: Adapted from Jan Pahl, *Money and Marriage* (1989)

For Pahl, an ideology which underlines the sharing of resources 'helps to conceal the structurally weak position of those who do not earn', whilst 'an ideology of separateness of financial matters strengthens the position of those who earn compared with those who do not'. Hence, although there might exist a variety of ways in which families organise their money, in most cases it is the men who derive greatest benefit.

Families and localities

The region in which sociological studies on the family have been under-taken needs to be taken into account as it has been shown that locality may affect households and family forms. E. Eversley and L. Bonnerjea have identified six kinds of areas associated with specific types of house-hold family forms.

1. 'Sun belt': the more affluent, higher social class, owner-occupied housing areas of south and south-east England and 'Silicon Glen' in Scotland with many two-parent households.

2. 'Geriatric wards': the coastal areas of England and Wales occupied by the elderly living in one- or two-person households often away from family and kin.

3. Older declining industrial areas: with older populations located around traditional industries such as iron and steel and coalmining, and maintaining well-established, stable, patriarchal family struc-tures.

4. Newer declining industrial areas: located mainly in the Midlands, with high rates of unemployment among older workers and with younger members moving away, providing little support for extended kinship networks.

5. Rural areas: farming and business tend to remain important, with many two-parent families and single elderly households (though with the influx of commuters and others in predominantly agricultural regions few of the truly rural areas still exist except in the outlying parts of Wales and Scotland).

6. Inner cities: including areas of economic and social deprivation, with a high ratio of immigrants, single parents, subdivided (or multi-let) households and the homeless. There tends to be isolation from extended and, in some cases, nuclear family forms.

There has been very little sociological research in relation to patterns of contemporary families and households and their regional locations (see also Unit 9).

Think about it

- How might geographical locality influence the households and family forms within it?
- What research methods might be suitable for investigating the relationships between a geographical area of the UK and the types of households and family forms who live in that area?
- How appropriate are such terms as 'sun belt' and 'geriatric wards'? What other terms can you devise to accompany the six kinds of areas identified by Eversley and Bonnerjea?

Changes and trends in family and household patterns

Marriage

In the UK, during the last quarter of the twentieth century, the total number of marriages has fallen by about 20 per cent. The graph below shows the decline in first marriages, in particular since the 1970s. More than one-third of an overall total of nearly 300,000 marriages in 1993 were remarriages. Nevertheless, remarriage rates seem to be levelling off. Divorce levels show a fluctuating but increasing trend, although there was a slight fall in 1994.

Marriage and divorce in the UK

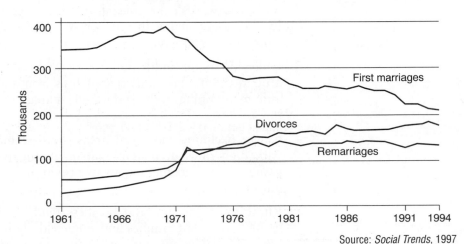

Source: *Social Trends*, 1997

Couples wed later but are quicker to divorce

MARRIAGE continues to lose out to divorce, according to the latest official figures.

The number of weddings in England and Wales fell to 299,000 in 1993, the lowest for 50 years.

At the same time, the number of divorce decrees made absolute rose to 165,000, the highest number on record and 3 per cent more than the previous peak of 160,000 in 1992.

Couples spent less time together before splitting up, and the main ground given for divorce was the husband's unreasonable behaviour.

The figures, from the Office of Population Censuses and Surveys, also reveal that the trend towards putting off marriage continued.

The average age of men marrying for the first time was 28.2 while brides were 26.2. In 1992, the ages were 27.9 and 25.9 respectively and in 1983 they were 25.7 and 23.4.

Among those born in 1961, 62 per cent of the men and 74 per cent of the women had married before they were 30 — for those born a decade earlier, the figures were 78 and 88 per cent.

Of those who married in 1993, 51 per cent did so in a register office and only 49 per cent chose a church.

In all, marriage rates were 37.3 per 1,000 men and 32.4 per 1,000 women. In the previous year the figures were 38.6 and 33.5 respectively, while in 1983 they were 51.2 and 41.8.

Marriages which ended in divorce had lasted an average of 9.8 years, compared to 10.1 in 1983.

Children were more likely to be affected. The number of divorces among parents with children under 16 rose to 95,000 — 58 per cent of all couples divorcing — compared with 91,000 in 1992 and 87,000 in 1983.

Wives initiated 72 per cent of divorces, a proportion that has remained constant for several years. The main reason they gave — in 54 per cent of all cases — was unreasonable behaviour, followed by adultery in a further 23 per cent.

For divorces granted to husbands, 39 per cent were because of the wife's adultery and 23 per cent for her unreasonable behaviour.

Average ages at divorce were 37 for husbands and 35 for wives — about one year older than their counterparts in 1983.

Though England and Wales already have the highest divorce rate in Europe, the Church of England was optimistic about the latest figures. 'The good news is that the rate of increase of divorces is slowing down,' a spokesman said. 'You would not expect the trend to change direction immediately.'

Source: The *Daily Mail*, 23 August 1995

Figures from the Office of Population Censuses and Surveys show that 1993 was the first time since 1943 (when the number was affected by World War II) that fewer than 300,000 couples had married. However, some surveys have challenged the notion that marriage has become a declining social institution, as exemplified below.

Putting off the big day

THE death of the institution of marriage has been greatly exaggerated, according to a survey today which shows couples in Britain are postponing, rather than abandoning, the decision to marry.

A Gallup survey, commissioned for ITV's documentary *World In Action*, tonight found people still want to get married, but only when it suits them.

More than half of the unmarried couples questioned — 52 per cent — said they would "definitely"

get married in the future while a further 28 per cent said they probably would.

The most popular reason for getting married was love. More than three-quarters cited it as their reason, while having children was second on the list at 13 per cent.

However, the stigma of having children outside marriage appears to have all but disappeared, with 72 per cent claiming it was socially acceptable.

Think about it

- To what extent do you consider it reasonable to suggest that marriage, and in particular 'white weddings', are going out of fashion?
- What sociological factors do you think might influence whether a couple cohabit or marry?
- How do you think the role of values in relation to marriage has changed between your parents' and your own generation?

The European scene Trends in the UK have been reflected across Europe, where there has also been considerable social change in terms of attitudes towards marriage.

- Couples are choosing to cohabit before marriage, as a 'trial' marriage or perhaps instead of marriage.
- Changes in attitudes have tended to reduce marriage rates and to increase the age at first marriage.
- Couples appear to be placing less emphasis on the unconditional commitment of marriage and to consider divorce more readily than in previous decades. Most men and women do eventually marry, however.
- There is less variation in marriage and divorce rates across Europe in the 1990s than there was in the 1980s. Variations can be attributed to the effects of religion, cultural and social differences, and legal requirements. The divorce rates are very low in Italy, Greece and Spain and are highest in the UK.

Marriage and divorce rates: EU comparison, 1994

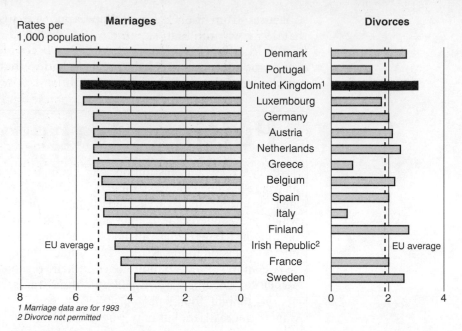

1 Marriage data are for 1993
2 Divorce not permitted

Source: *Eurostat*

- European marriage and divorce data indicate that the number of marriages per thousand population has fallen in most countries, while the number of divorces has generally risen. There are some exceptions. In Denmark and Luxembourg, marriage rates were low in 1981, but they had increased in 1992; the Netherlands and Spain show slight increases. In Denmark and Germany, divorce rates fell between 1981 and 1992, but from a relatively high level.

Cohabitation

Until recently, cohabitation was considered of quite minor importance in compiling statistics of household composition and marriage. By 1992, however, some 18 per cent of unmarried men and women aged 16 to 59 were living together, if we take an average from the General Household Survey, 1995:

Cohabitation as a percentage of the unmarried population by sex and age, Great Britain, 1992

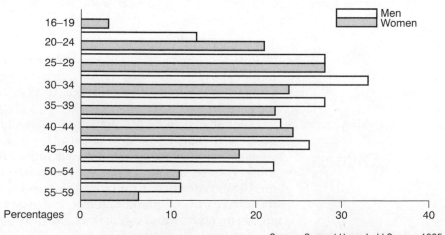

Source: General Household Survey, 1995

Cohabitation is usually seen as a prelude to marriage rather than a substitute for it, with people being more likely to live together before their second marriage than before their first. Nevertheless, if these trends continue, the meanings of both marriage and divorce will have undergone important shifts. Joan Chandler, in *Women Without Husbands* (1991), views the increase in cohabitation as important, since it seems to be becoming a long-term alternative to marriage rather than merely a short-term trial period. However, she also points out that this is not new – research has shown that as many as one-third of couples in eighteenth-century Britain lived in consensual unions rather than formal marriage.

Divorced women are more likely to cohabit than single women who have never married, as illustrated by the table below. This may be due to an inability or unwillingness to remarry, perhaps because of previous experience of marriage and divorce.

Women cohabiting: by age, Great Britain, 1991–92					
	Single (%)	Separated (%)	Divorced (%)	Widowed (%)	All non-married women (%)
16–24	14	3	–	–	12
25–34	30	11	29	–	11
35–49	17	15	29	4	5
50–59	4	12	14	4	2
All aged 16 to 59	18	12	26	4	7

Source: Office of Population Censuses and Surveys

- The table shows that the percentage of single women cohabiting varies in relation to age. In 1991–2, 30 per cent of those aged 25 to 34 were cohabiting, compared with just 4 per cent of those aged 50 to 59.
- There is some evidence that divorced men and women who cohabit tend to have been cohabiting for longer periods than their younger, single counterparts.
- A British Household Panel Survey, 1995, suggested that, on average, half of those who cohabit do so for two years or less: the main reason for this is that the partners marry.

Divorce

Changing expectations of marriage, it is claimed, have tended to make marriages more fragile. Partners have very high expectations of each other; when romantic ratings of love and marriage fade, there may remain little to hold partners together. However, this is not to say that couples enter into marriage lightly because they know they can easily escape.

Changing attitudes of women

Most divorces are initiated by women. More than two and a half times as many divorces were granted to women as to men in England and Wales in 1995. This might be due to increasing female participation in the labour force and greater economic independence. Increased self confidence and belief in their own rights may have given women the opportunity to divorce if they see it as being desirable to do so.

Women have gained a range of rights in terms of property, the vote, employment and education, and rising divorce rates may be seen as one aspect of this shift in the position of women within society. Women now seem less willing to accept an unsatisfactory marriage, and are more able to lead independent lives outside marriage. Men, on the other hand, seem to get more out of marriage, and are less likely to initiate divorce. Hence they may be more anxious to remarry following divorce.

Nicky Hart, writing from a Marxist perspective in *When Marriage Fails* (1976), suggests that despite the increasing participation of women in the labour force they still seem expected, by many men, to accept responsibility for childcare and domestic chores. This may cause conflict between couples which, with women's changing position, can affect their attitudes towards both marriage and divorce.

Causes of rising divorce rates

The 'cause' of divorce could refer to the formal 'grounds', recognised in the legal process, or to the 'reasons' that partners provide for their divorce. It is the larger causes found in major shifts or trends in the wider social structure that are of most interest to the sociologist in looking at the reasons for rising divorce rates. These are difficult to assess and are often influenced by moral or political considerations.

<u>Legal changes</u>   The definition of divorce is usually a legal one, and divorce rates are affected by legal changes. Since the Matrimonial Causes Act first made divorce available in the courts in 1857, six further Acts of Parliament continued to broaden the grounds and means for divorce, until the Family Law Act of 1996 attempted to set down some conditions that would slow the rise in divorce rates. Couples may take advantage of opportunities formerly denied to them, but legal changes themselves are not the sole cause of higher rates of marital breakdown.

<u>Moral and social shifts</u>   These have given rise to the legal changes favouring easier and generally quicker divorce and may be seen in some sections of society as evidence of a wider moral and social breakdown. It may be that people are becoming more individualistic or more selfish and focusing less on their family life.

<u>Loss of informal controls</u>   In traditional societies there were networks of kin relationships and community with informal controls over behaviour. Individuals who stepped out of line, for example adulterers, would be informally punished by gossip or ostracism. Contemporary society, with its increased geographical mobility, the break between home and work and the weakening of institutions such as the Church, has fewer informal controls over individuals. This has been a popular area of investigation, with many sociologists seeing divorce rates as an indicator of a weakening of wider social controls and linked to the 'breakdown of community'.

Socio-economic causes   Until quite recently formal legal divorce was available only to the upper- or upper-middle classes, i.e. those who could afford the costly and complex procedures. That does not mean that marriages in the lower classes were happier or more stable; indeed informal methods of 'divorce' or separation may have been important. However, the effect of changes in the divorce laws has been a greater rate of increase in divorce in the lower socio-economic groups than in the higher ones. Among the main high-risk groups are teenage brides, couples who start their childbearing earlier, and couples with relatively low incomes. These factors tend to be associated together:

> *'If one is going to focus on a single factor that can help to explain the association between young marriage, social class and divorce, then the financial condition of the marriage appears to be a strong contender.'*
>
> Colin Gibson, *Dissolving Wedlock* (1993)

Democratisation of divorce   Divorce rates have increased in all social groups, but more so in the lower socio-economic groups. However, we do not know how many people might have divorced in the past, had it been more accessible.

Consequences of rising divorce rates

Emotional cost   Concern for rising divorce rates has centred not only on the rates but also on the apparent consequences in terms of emotional cost. Simpler procedures and the decreased stigma attached to divorce have not necessarily reduced the associated emotional cost and pain. These are incurred as much during the events leading up to the divorce, for example violence or infidelity or the process of drifting apart while sharing the same roof, as at the moment of divorce itself.

Economic hardship   Women are more likely than men to experience economic hardship as a consequence of divorce. They are more likely to receive custody of the children, they may have difficulties in obtaining financial support for the children from their ex-husbands and they are in a less favourable position in gaining employment. Husbands seem more able to find employment; they are also more likely to remarry, as shown in the graphs below.

Marriages and remarriages by sex, Great Britain

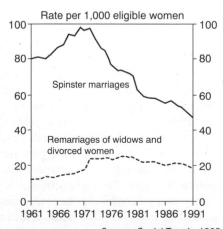

Source: *Social Trends*, 1995

Effects of divorce on children There have been challenges to the conventional wisdom that children's interests were better served by divorce than by feuding parents living together. Two studies are considered below.

Studies on the effects of divorce on children In 1994, Dr John Tripp and Monica Cockett of the Department of Child Health at Exeter University studied 152 Exeter children from 're-ordered' families, i.e. families who had broken up and remarried. Such children, they found, experienced a series of disruptions and changes more likely to lead to health, educational and social problems. The findings of their research are described below.

'Feuding parents better for children than separation'

David Brindle
Social Services Correspondent

RESEARCH published today will be used to lend weight to the argument that feuding couples should try to stay together for the sake of their children.

A study of 152 children in Exeter found that those being brought up by both parents experienced fewer health, school and social problems than those whose parents had split up.

Children of parents whose relationship was in difficulties, but were still together, fared worse than those whose parents' relationship was good. But they fared much better than children whose parents had parted.

The findings will fuel the debate over parental responsibility and lone parenthood and will give valuable ammunition to the pro-family lobby, which has been relying on dated and contentious research.

The 152 Exeter children, aged 9–10 and 13–14, were selected from 620 families and were paired so that 76 came from intact, two-parent households and 76 from "re-ordered" families. Pairings were based on factors including age, mother's education, and their social class as measured by occupation.

Of the 76 children not living with both parents, 31 were in lone-parent households, 26 had become part of a stepfamily and 19 had experienced multiple family disruption through at least three different homes.

Researchers Monica Cockett and Dr John Tripp, of Exeter University's department of child health, found marked differences. The children from re-ordered families were at least twice as likely to have problems of health, behaviour, school work and social life and to have a low opinion of themselves.

Health problems reported by these children included stomach aches, nausea and bed-wetting, as well as illnesses thought to be psychosomatic.

The 19 children who had experienced multiple family disruption emerged sharply different on all counts. They were eight times more likely than those from intact families to report health problems, eight times more likely to need extra help with school work and 10 times more likely to think badly of themselves.

The re-ordered families as a whole were more likely to be living on social security, less likely to have a car and had typically moved house more often — factors which would probably have added to the strain on children.

However, Dr Tripp says the research shows clearly that the loss of a parent is the critical factor. Its importance overshadows other factors such as conflict between parents still living together.

"We know conflict is damaging in that it undermines children's well-being and makes them feel less good about themselves," Dr Tripp says. "But our data suggests that is really a very minor effect compared to the effects that we see when a parent leaves home."

The research, sponsored by the Joseph Rowntree Foundation, also found that only a third of the children had frequent, regular contact with a parent who had left the family home.

Source: The *Guardian*, 7 February 1994

There are dangers of generalising on the rights and wrongs of divorce based on such small-scale surveys, especially when, as in this case, there is a large amount of media attention.

Another study, also in 1994, was carried out by Dr Martin Richards and his colleagues at the Centre for Family Research at Cambridge University. They consider that although harmful effects of divorce are apparent across all social classes, children from middle-class parents, aged under 16 before their parents' divorce, seemed most harmed. They were:

- twice as likely to leave school without any qualifications (boys and girls);
- a third more likely not to have a full-time job at age 23 (boys) – (girls were two-thirds more likely);
- two-thirds more likely to be a regular smoker by age 23 (boys) – (girls were one-third more likely).

Taking children of middle- and working-class parents together, children of divorced parents were:

- twice as likely to have a child before age 20;
- twice as likely to be married or living with someone before age 20.

The research by Dr Richards found also that children whose parents had divorced were on average less emotionally stable, left home earlier, and divorced or separated more frequently. They showed more behavioural problems in school, were more likely to be unhappy and worried, and were poorer at reading and arithmetic.

Most children of divorced parents end up living with their mothers, but if their mothers remarry the children tend to show more problems than those whose mothers stay single. Adolescents find it difficult to come to terms with a parent dating again.

Dr Richards argues that good and regular contact with the absent father can reduce some of the ill-effects of separation, even though this may be at the expense of increased conflict between the parents. Half of all divorced fathers lose contact with their children within two years.

<u>Criticisms of the Cambridge Study</u>

- The study was based on the 17,000 children from the National Child Development Survey who were born between 3 and 9 March 1958 and followed up at the ages of seven, 11, 16 and 23. As with other large-scale longitudinal surveys, there is 'sample attrition': by 1981, because of factors such as participation refusal, emigration, even death, research was only available on 12,500 of the original children. The reduced sample size can make the sample less representative.
- More specifically, it is difficult to know how many parents suffered rather than chose divorce. Conversely, parents may seek to avoid divorce, remaining with a violent spouse rather than becoming pilloried in public for having 'terminally damaged' their children.
- Whilst children of divorced couples may be more likely to suffer from health, educational and social problems, such problems also exist in a wide range of relationships and families and are related to the socio-economic circumstances of those families.

Lone or single parents

About 20 per cent of families (not of households) in the UK consist of single parents, as shown by the figures below. These families take a wide variety of forms.

Families with dependent children by family type: 1971 to 1995

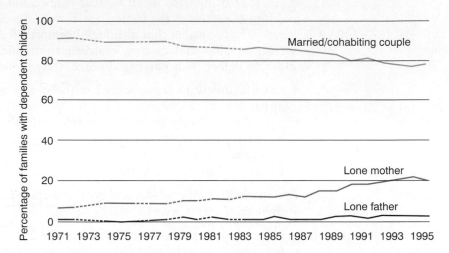

Source: General Household Survey, 1995

Patterns of lone parenting

- Children who live with just one of their natural parents are more likely to live with their natural mother than with their natural father. Less than 3 per cent of children living with a single parent live with their natural father. Children living with only their mother are likely to be in a one-parent family, whilst those living with only their natural father are likely to be stepchildren in a 're-ordered' family.

- Just over 1 million (8 per cent of dependent children) lived in step-families in the UK in 1991. If current divorce and remarriage rates continue, at least one-third of all children will experience divorce in their family by the age of 16. This is an international pattern, not limited to the UK.

- The percentage of lone mothers increased gradually until 1987, and then grew swiftly from 1990 to 1993, reaching a level where one in five mothers with dependent children was a lone mother. Since 1993 the level has not altered greatly.

- Since the mid-1980s, the percentage of divorced lone mothers has remained static, but the proportion of single never-married mothers has more than doubled. Despite this, marital breakdown is still the most common reason for a lone-parent family.

With increasing levels of cohabitation, the terms 'single' and 'lone' are becoming more difficult to define. They may form part of a continuum ranging from parents who are single for long periods (for example, husbands in the Armed Forces and away from home) to households which are led by a single parent with irregular or no contact with the former spouse or partner.

Causes of lone parenthood

Precise causes of lone parenthood are difficult to identify but there are a variety of routes by which parents become or cease to become lone parents.

Routes into lone parenthood	Routes out of lone parenthood
For married or cohabiting couple with dependent children:	1. Marriage or re-marriage
1. Separation, with or without divorce	2. Cohabitation or recommencement of former cohabitation
2. Death of one partner	3. Children no longer dependent or leave home
For non-cohabiting, single woman:	4. Death of lone parent
1. Birth of child	

Source: Adapted from John Haskey, *Lone Parenthood and Demographic Change* (1991)

Political concern about lone parents has tended to focus on lone mothers who are so by choice. To choose to have a child outside a marriage has been viewed as 'irresponsible', challenging the traditional ideas of the nuclear family and ideas of paternal power or authority. However, the notion of choice is a complex one, and it is not easy to divide single mothers into those who become so by choice and those who become so for other reasons.

Furthermore, the image of children in lone-parent families being born largely to unmarried, irresponsible or feckless teenage mums is not supported by research data. The article below reveals that about half of single parents are divorced and only one-third have never married. It is interesting to note that only one in six lone-parent families arises as a result of a woman without a partner giving birth to a baby.

Report 'ends myth of lone parents as scroungers'

By David Fletcher, Health Services Correspondent

MOST single parents are recently separated mothers who remain on their own for less than five years, research commissioned by the Department of Social Security said yesterday.

On average, only one in six lone parent families arises from a birth to a woman without a partner and more than four out of 10 have jobs.

The report, drawn up by the Right-of-centre Policy Studies Institute, gives the lie to the widespread belief that single mothers are feckless young women without partners, living off benefits.

It said: "Lone parenthood is a transitory state experienced by families for an average of less than five years, typically three to four.

"The majority are recently separated mothers who see their main role for the moment in the support of their children at home, even if this means accepting a lowered standard of living."

It said most single mothers had their first child while part of a couple and four in 10 said their child was planned. Only 13 per cent of "never-partnered" lone parents said they had planned their first child.

The report said: "More lone parents work than is commonly realised. Their problem is finding sufficient hours at reasonable rates. A total of 42 per cent had paid jobs by 1993, up from 38 per cent in 1991."

However, it added that debt problems were "endemic" among Britain's 1.4 million lone parents, with nearly half "coping poorly" with debt.

Most hoped to work but chose for the time being to stay with their children. About a third said difficulties with child care or its cost were the main barrier to work.

Source: The *Daily Telegraph*, 28 September 1995

Consequences of the rise in lone parenthood

The New Right views of Charles Murray on lone parents, whereby they become part of an underclass – or, in Murray's terminology, a 'new rabble' (see page 127) – have been widely challenged by many sociologists.

- Single-parent status is generally linked to poorer economic conditions, with single mothers lacking the support of a partner and with a limited position in the labour market. Such mothers have three potential sources of financial support: their former partner, the state and employment. In Britain, much of the support comes from the state, followed by employment, with relatively little coming from former partners.
- Support through social security payments has been the focus of considerable controversy in recent years, both in relation to levels of public expenditure and also through moral concerns about the extent to which non-traditional family forms should be supported from the public purse.
- Concerns have focused also on the long-term consequences of the absence of the second adult, usually the father. This may be linked to behavioural problems and educational difficulties on the part of the children, perhaps leading to the creation of further lone-parent households in the future.

Conclusion

While it may seem that children brought up in two-parent households do better than those brought up in single-parent households, we do not know enough about the causes of the differences. Research might be better directed at exploring what makes for more effective parenting in all kinds of household, whether single-parent or two-parent.

Think about it

- Summarise the opinions expressed above about single parents.
- What do you think research might reveal in terms of effective parenting in all kinds of households?
- How do you consider that value judgements about single-parent and two-parent households might be avoided in sociological research?

Domestic violence

The largest single study of domestic violence was undertaken by Rebecca and Russell Dobash. In *Violence Against Wives* (1980), they made the following claims:

- Violence against women represents a deep-rooted social problem. It stems from the patriarchal structure of households in which male authority creates a power relationship, with wives and mothers occupying subordinate positions.
- Men are more powerful politically and physically than women; they exploit the labour of women, who are expected to provide a range of domestic services for the men. A main cause of male violence towards their partners is when such males do not feel that domestic duties are being carried out satisfactorily.
- The police are often reluctant to intervene in domestic disputes, despite such disputes accounting for about 25 per cent of all serious assaults.

Statistics may well underestimate the full extent of domestic violence, since many incidents may go unrecorded. Before 1993, records were not routinely kept by British police forces of complaints about or incidents of domestic violence. Only in the last 25 years has the extent of domestic violence, particularly assaults on wives and also child sexual abuse, become more evident due, in part, to studies such as those undertaken by Dobash and Dobash into domestic violence. Women have been more prepared to report men who have become violent. There was delight among feminists when, in a marital rape judgement in March 1991, the appeal of a husband convicted of raping his wife a few days after she left him was dismissed, thereby recognising rape within marriage. However, feminists and other lobbyists maintain that the criminal justice system remains reluctant to accept the extent of domestic violence and to deal with male offenders.

The relationship between family and state

The family may be considered as a source of concern or challenge for the state or, alternatively, as a major social institution which, to the best of its ability, goes along with and supports state policies regardless of whose interests such policies may serve. Functionalists and right-wing politicians referred to earlier in this unit have tended to view the family as basic and necessary both for its members and for the state.

The family as a challenge to the state

Families may be considered to perform best when the state has least to do with them: parents, it is argued, should take responsibility for their children, the infirm and elderly, in both emotional and cash terms. Community care, for example, has involved a shift of responsibility from state institutions to the private sphere of family life (see Unit 7, pages 382–8). In the face of increasing public expenditure, the state sees rising family costs as a challenge. The dependent elderly and, in particular, single never-married mothers have been targeted by right-wing politicians.

From a Marxist and left-wing viewpoint, the state acts as an agent of social control, preventing any family form – especially working-class families with their proletariat tradition – from challenging capitalist society and patriarchy. There is the perceived need to dismantle the solidarity of working-class communities and instil (socialise) into them individualistic rather than collective values by providing such 'opportunities' as home and share ownership. The mutual support system and local loyalties associated with traditional working-class communities represent a challenge to the state because of their 'them and us' suspicions of the state and higher classes.

The family in support of the state

Liberal and social democratic thinkers tend to put forward the idea of a partnership between the family and the state. The family is seen as a key social institution. However, due to historical and social factors the family cannot function on its own. Community and voluntary care, along with other informal social networks, may be important but cannot meet the diverse family needs in relation to the pace of change in society.

There is now a geographically mobile workforce and increased female participation in the labour market in a highly technological society. This causes stresses and strains which have impacted on family life, for example the need for nursery provision and care for the elderly which require the mutual support of both family and state.

In another form of functionalism – not the right-wing variety – the family may be seen as in harmony with the state. Family 'values', as supporting consensus and averting conflict, tend to receive wide support from the state, but this is focused on traditional family forms, based on monogamous nuclear households led by male breadwinners, by taxation measures and welfare benefits. However, in reality, whilst paying lip-service to the ideology of the family, the state has done very little to promote it. State policies have always tended to reinforce patriarchy. The notion of the supportive relationship between family and state may be viewed as reflecting the mythical relationship between husbands and wives in which power inequalities are covered up. In fact many family inequalities continue to exist for a considerable number of households and family forms in contemporary society, despite the changes which have taken place.

Revision and practice tasks

Before attempting Task 1 on page 155, read the following worked example of a data response question. The question is followed by an example of a satisfactory answer.

Data response question

ITEM A

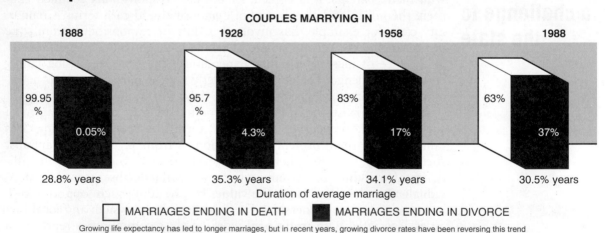

COUPLES MARRYING IN

Growing life expectancy has led to longer marriages, but in recent years, growing divorce rates have been reversing this trend

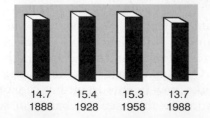

MARRIAGE RATE PER 1,000 POPULATION

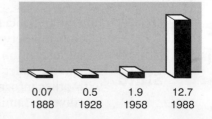

DIVORCE RATE PER 1,000 MARRIED COUPLES

ITEM B

One of the major changes in family life over the last century or so has been in the relationships between parents and children. The way that society has perceived childhood has altered, as the economic circumstances of families have changed. The emergence of a distinctive 'teenage' period, which has become longer and longer, is a more recent occurrence, sustained and developed by youth unemployment. Similarly, as people have experienced greater life expectancy, the role of old people has also undergone significant changes. In particular, many of the elderly have been side-lined by the development of modern computer technology, so that they are no longer the source of wisdom.

ITEM C

Resisting the pressure on people to become parents at any cost was the reason the British Organisation of Non-Parents was formed in 1983. The media constantly portray perfect mothers and babies, and depict childless adults as miserable and unfulfilled. No wonder people have children for all the wrong reasons without thinking it through. People often have the worst possible motives for parenthood, in Bennett's opinion. "Maybe there is a maternal instinct, but I don't think it exists in everyone. Many people have children to keep a bad relationship together, to persuade their partner to marry them, to prove they are real women or men or to 'keep trying until they get a boy'. What's more we have no right to count on our children for automatic care when we reach the other end of the age spectrum. One woman told us how foolish it was for couples to stay childless because everyone has to think ahead. 'Who's going to look after the elderly?' she asked me. I didn't say anything, but I do remember thinking, 'Probably not their children.'"

(Items adapted from *Modern Lovers: Childless by Choice*, Helen Chappell, The *Guardian*, May 1990)

(a) Look at **ITEM A** and identify **one** suggested reason for:

    (i) shorter marriages

    (ii) longer marriages.   **(2 marks)**

(b) What changes in marriage and divorce rates are shown in **ITEM A**?   **(2 marks)**

(c) Explain what is meant by 'serial monogamy'.   **(2 marks)**

(d) In what ways have sociologists enhanced our understanding of parent and child relationships? (**ITEM B**)   **(9 marks)**

(e) It is suggested in **ITEMS B and C** that the position of elderly people in British society has changed. What sociological evidence is there for this view?**(10 marks)**

Total: 25 marks

Sample answer to data response question

(a) With reference to Item A, a longer lasting marriage may be associated with the shorter life expectancy earlier this century, which meant that married couples spent relatively fewer years together before one partner, usually the husband, died.

One factor which may make for shorter marriages may relate to increasing life expectancy – life-long monogamy is likely to mean a marriage of 50 years or more. Another factor may be the increased means of divorce, particularly since the Divorce Reform Bill 1969 which took effect in 1971.

(b) The crude marriage rate, or the number of marriages taking place per 1000 of the population, fluctuated between 1888 and 1988, with a downward trend in the post-war period. The divorce rate increased during the 1970s, with a large rise from 1.9 divorces per 1000 married couples in 1958 to 12.7 per 1000 in 1988.

(c) Monogamy is a marital arrangement consisting of only one partner of each sex. Serial monogamy occurs when both partners have systematic divorces and remarriage(s) during their lifetimes, i.e. the couple divorces and one or both partners go on to become remarried.

(d) Sociologists maintain that childhood has been a 'social invention' since the sixteenth century when it became separated from adulthood.

The rise of the isolated nuclear family in the post World War II period created a division between the sons and daughters with families and contact with their parents. Traditionally, if a son was produced it was seen as a type of investment, as it still is in modern China, or as insurance for care in old age and financial support. The principle still remains in the relationship between parents and children, with many parents supporting their children financially until the age of 23 or more when the child/adult finally leaves education; in return for such financial investment, the parents might expect to be cared for later in life.

Item B's reference to a 'teenage period' highlights the point about the educational system, where people can spend up to one-third of their lives in education. However, many more young adults seek independence from parents and move away from home at, or soon after, age 16.

Other factors relevant to an assessment of the changing relationship between parents and children would include high levels of youth unemployment during economic recession, and also the varied forms of family life. Children as 'units of consumption' need to be placed within the wider scenario of over a million children with single parents, many of whom experience considerable relative poverty. Also the high divorce rates may have effects on children. Whereas the conventional wisdom was that divorce between embattled parents was in the children's interests, this has been challenged by recent research – *Children Living in Re-ordered Families* (1994) by Monica Cockett and Dr John Tripp – which seems in line with New Right views and their support for the 'back-to-basics' traditional, heterosexual, nuclear family relationships.

(e) Functionalist 'fit' theory held that, up to the industrial revolution, the most common family form was the extended family. Some sociologists have challenged this theory and believed that the nuclear family form as a traditional family unit had existed well before this time. However, in the UK today the nuclear family accounts for only a minority of all households, so the relevance of such discussions and statistics would apply more to the question of whether Britain has reverted more to extended families with close-knit kinship networks – or has recent diversification of the family meant greater isolation for the elderly?

P. Willmott and M. Young, as functionalists, identified the stage 2 'early industrial' family in the low-income area of Bethnal Green, East London. From their survey of these often matrifocal families, two out of three married people had parents living a short distance from their residence; also, over 80 per cent of women had seen their mothers in the previous week. The constant exchange of obligatory familial services, such as babysitting, cooking and shopping, led Willmott and Young to conclude that elder family members still had important roles within close-knit extended families. Willmott and Young also identified the more affluent stage 3 'symmetrical family', in which the roles of the elderly were greatly reversed. For example, the nuclear family unit of two adults and their children moved away from the areas where they were raised, thus reducing contact with grandparents, etc. Increased economic independence led to less need for contact with kinship networks, with the elderly less in demand.

G. Allan believes that kin outside the nuclear family remain important to family members. Allan's study of an East Anglian community demonstrated a familial obligation for nuclear families to keep in touch with the elder mothers and fathers, especially in times of crisis or difficulty. Although his small study could be criticised for being unrepresentative, many similar studies have agreed with Allan's conclusions. E. Litwak presented the 'modified extended family', which also maintained contact with elderly relatives and which extended his theory to uncles, aunts and cousins.

Task 1: data response question

ITEM A

Functionalists would interpret male superiority in terms of the more significant roles males play in the fulfilment of certain societal needs: their greater role in war, in government, in the economy and in ceremonials that promote social solidarity and cohesiveness. They believe that the higher the skill and responsibility of the man in extra-familial roles, the greater is the effective superiority of the husband in family decision-making.

According to the Marxist model, male superiority arises from, and is related to, control of private property by males. Frederick Engels traced an evolutionary pattern in husband–wife relationships that corresponded to stages of economic development. The earliest stages, where property was communal, were characterised by the relatively unstable matings of group marriage and temporary pairings. Women's status was not only high, it was 'supreme', because the biological fathers of offspring could not be identified and because in the communistic household, the administration of the household was seen as a socially necessary industry.

Source: Adapted from B. Yoburg, *Families & Societies* (Columbia University Press)

ITEM B

There has been a growing acceptance amongst sociologists that childhood, like so many other vitally important aspects of social life – gender, health, youth and so on – was socially constructed. It was, in other words, what members of particular societies, at particular times and in particular places, said it was. This has two implications:

(1)   Childhood is a social construction. It isn't natural and should be distinguished from biological immaturity.

(2)   Childhood varies, both in relation to class, gender and ethnicity and across national cultures. There is no single universal childhood.

Source: Adapted from Stephen Wagg, '"I blame the parents": childhood and politics in modern Britain', *Sociology Review* (Vol. 1:4, April 1992)

ITEM C

As many as one in five families with dependent children are now headed by a lone parent. This covers about 1.3 million parents living with 2.1 million children. Two per cent of all households in Britain are headed by a lone father, a figure which has been fairly stable in recent years. Lone mothers head 18 per cent of all households, but here there has been a marked increase over the last few years. Jo Roll argues that whereas the growth in lone-parent families over the last decade could be attributed to rising divorce and separation rates, "In Britain in the late 80s there also seems to have been an increase in the number of younger unmarried women deciding to have children and living alone without their partners".

Source: Adapted from M. Denscombe, *Sociology Update* (Olympus Books, 1993)

ITEM D

Social Security Secretary, Peter Lilley wrote: "We have produced a generation of fatherless children. No father to support them, discipline them and set them an example." He claimed that the rise in violent crime since 1950 was largely caused by the increasing absence of fathers in families. He is wrong. The overwhelming scientific evidence shows that neither illegitimacy nor the absence of fathers causes these children to grow up more violent than those raised by couples, married or otherwise.

Source: Adapted from Oliver J. Vicious, *Outcome of the poverty trap*, The Observer 23 May 1993

(a) From **ITEM C** identify the percentage of families headed by a lone parent.

(1 mark)

(b) 'Male superiority' is noted in **ITEM A** as being a feature of capitalist society. Provide **two** criticisms of the reasons for this given by

    (i) Marxists

    (ii) Functionalists. **(4 marks)**

(c) Offer a feminist view of 'male superiority'. **(5 marks)**

(d) How have sociologists demonstrated that childhood is socially constructed?

(7 marks)

(e) Using information from **ITEMS C, D** and elsewhere, outline the key features of sociological research on lone parents. **(8 marks)**

Total: 25 marks

Structured question

Read the following example of a structured question and the advice on how it should be tackled.

Households and Family Forms

Consider the stimulus material below and answer the questions which follow:

(a) What is the difference between a 'family' and a 'household'? [4]

(b) Why is it always important to make this distinction between 'family' and 'household' when carrying out research into the extended family? [4]

(c) A growing percentage of the population lives alone. What changes in family, household or other social patterns explain this? [7]

(d) Assess the view that images used by the advertising industry, such as the one above, support and sustain a particular model of family life. [10]

Total: 25 marks

Advice for a response to the structured question

(a) You need to demonstrate knowledge and understanding of the difference between the concepts of 'household' and 'family'. A household may be seen as a single, lone-parent or shared place of residence, whereas a family may be seen as a basic unit of social life and more closely linked to kinship relationships, etc.

Note: this carries only 4 marks, so there is no need for lengthy debate or discussion about these concepts.

(b) A demonstration of your understanding of the concept of the extended family, possibly with reference to horizontal and vertical (or modified) forms, would be a useful starting point. This subquestion also carries only 4 marks, and requires you to apply understanding of the concepts to the research issue. Try to keep your answer clear and concise and keep to the basic points.

(c) Here 7 marks are available, so more coverage is required than for subquestions (a) and (b), although no assessment or evaluation of the issues is asked for. You need to relate evidence, such as divorce rate increases and greater life expectancies (particularly among women), to explanations of social change. You can make reference to changes in social attitudes and divorce laws, in relation to living alone, and also refer to increased female career opportunities, independence sought by the young, lone parents, etc.

(d) This is the major subquestion, carrying 10 marks. It requires you to assess the image of a 'particular model of family life' which clearly reflects the 'cereal packet' idea of a 'normal' (assumed) married couple with son and daughter accompanying the 'appropriate' parents in 'appropriate' gender poses.

How do such above statements interestingly sum up the pictorial image provided?

In your response, you need to show your ability to select, apply and assess (this is important) relevant theory and evidence in relation to family ideologies, for example functionalist, Marxist, feminist, to the representation of the 'family' in advertisements (see the Introduction to this unit).

You can refer to domestic roles and the division of labour, to two- versus one-parent families, but do not overlap with subquestion (a), etc. Your response may also include 'invisible' families, for example inner-city/flat dwellers, ethnic minority groups, the poor, etc., in contrast to the heterosexual, nuclear privatised model of family life.

Task 2: structured question

Bearing in mind the advice provided for the questions above, now write your own response to the following questions, which are based on the same stimulus and photograph.

(a) Briefly explain what sociologists mean by a 'nuclear family' and how it differs from a 'household'. (4)

(b) Describe any TWO aspects of contemporary society which may be affecting family relationships. (4)

(c) Outline evidence for the view that relationships within family forms have become less patriarchal and more democratic. (7)

(d) Evaluate the contributions made by critical theories to our understanding of the family. (10)

Total: 25 marks

Essay questions

1. To what extent does the wide variation of household structures in contemporary Britain mean that the concept of family has virtually lost its meaning?

2. Examine the view that the development of isolated nuclear families has been at the expense of extended families and kinship networks.

3. Do increased levels of cohabitation and high divorce rates suggest that marriage has lost its importance in contemporary society?

4. Discuss whether contemporary households and family forms may be seen as developing into more democratic social institutions.

5. How successful have been attempts to establish alternative types of family life in contemporary society?

6. Evaluate the view that the isolated nuclear family, and similar family arrangements, best suits the needs of industrial and post-industrial societies.

7. Assess the contributions made by critical thinkers to the sociology of the family.

8. How have feminists contributed to our understanding of relationships within the family?

9. Discuss whether the views of the New Right on the family have affected state policy and social opinions.

10. Have the contributions provided by functionalists stood up to those who have adopted more critical attitudes towards the family?

Sample plan for essay question 10

Have the contributions provided by functionalists stood up to those who have adopted more critical attitudes towards the family?

Essay plan

Introduction: Functionalism – functions of family in relation to whole social system, e.g. Murdock, Parsons, versus critical theories of radical psychiatrists, e.g. Laing, Cooper, and feminists, e.g. Oakley, Delphy, etc.

Paragraph 1: In more specialised family unit, essential functions, e.g. Murdock – sexual, reproductive, economic and educational; Parsons – socialisation and structuring of personality, male 'instrumental' / female 'expressive' roles.

Paragraph 2: Criticise Parsons, e.g. Morgan. Static and rigid sex roles – ignores potential for change (e.g. dual-career families). Fails to consider causes and effects of change and diversity of family forms.

Paragraph 3: Contradictions, stresses, disparities, class differences and other important power aspects, e.g. patriarchy.

Paragraph 4: Laing – families as repressive and limiting individuality, parent–child relationships, power aspect (world view); Cooper – family as a psychological prison.

Paragraph 5: Contradictions, Laing and Cooper, unbalanced view, children not passive recipients; family not a social vacuum. Also reflect differences in approaches between mainly American social theorists and British clinical psychologists.

Paragraph 6: Contemporary involvement of feminists, women oppressed, repressed in family, male dominant, power – domestic violence, e.g. Dobash and Dobash.

Conclusion: Sum up by selecting a few of the major issues discussed, e.g. positive and negative diversity and commitment, loss of freedom, etc. Also diversity of family life in contemporary society, rapid change, political debates, etc.

Ideas for coursework and personal studies

1. A study of the changing concept of family, based on a sample of diverse family forms or households contrasted with traditional sociological definitions of the family.
2. Feedback on attitudes towards marriage, including 'white weddings', from a sample of cohabiting partners and newly wed couples.
3. Children's or young people's views on cohabitation, marriage or divorce in relation to their own experience and its effects on their attitudes and future expectations.
4. Research into male and female domestic roles in households in which both partners are in paid employment and/or where there is the need to consider responsibilities for childcare.
5. Research into the views of the elderly towards the implications – emotional, family, financial, etc. – of their anticipated future in society.

Selected reading list

The Death of the Family, David Cooper (Penguin, 1971)

Family and Kinship in East London, Michael Young and Peter Willmott (Penguin, 1962)

The Family and Social Change, Colin Rosser and Christopher Harris (Routledge & Kegan Paul, 1965)

Family and Social Network, Elizabeth Bott (Tavistock, 1957)

The Family: Change or Continuity?, Faith Robertson Elliot (Macmillan, 1986)

Family Socialisation and Interaction Process, Talcott Parsons and R.F. Bales (The Free Press, New York, 1955)

The Politics of the Family, R.D. Laing (Penguin, 1976)

'Social change and indicators of diversity', David Eversley and Lucy Bonnerjea in *Families in Britain*, R.N. Rapoport et al. (Routledge & Kegan Paul, 1982)

Social Structure, George Peter Murdock (Macmillan, New York, 1949)

The Symmetrical Family, Michael Young and Peter Willmott (Penguin, 1975)

When Marriage Fails, Nicky Hart (Tavistock, 1976)

4 Education and training

Introduction

Education consists of more than life at school, college or university. Throughout our lives we are learning: the life-long processes of education take place in the family, at schools and other institutions, at places of work and through a wide range of activities, events and experiences which are important in equipping and preparing us for society. The role of education, in terms of socialisation, is well noted in the literature, be that in primary, secondary, further or higher education, albeit for different purposes at different stages.

Think about it

- What type of schools have you attended? How do you consider that your schooling has affected your life? Do you feel that more has been learnt by you inside or outside school?

State education in the UK developed only towards the end of the nineteenth century, when a belief was expressed by some – although not shared by all, as illustrated in the following extracts – that every young person should learn to read, to write and to do arithmetic (the 'three Rs'). This was seen to be particularly important in the context of growing developments in science and technology.

> '... poor boys sent into the world, without fixed principles, may in consequence of having been taught to read and write become very dangerous members of society.'
> Sarah Trimmer, writing in the eighteenth century

'. . . however spacious in theory the project might be of giving education to the labouring classes of the poor, it would teach them to despise their lot in life, instead of making them good servants in agriculture and other laborious employments.

Instead of teaching them subordination, it would enable them to read seditious pamphlets, vicious books, and publications against Christianity: it would render them insolent to their superiors; and in a few years the legislature would find it necessary to direct the strong arm of power towards them.'

The debate on Samuel Whitbread's Bill, 1807

'. . . I doubt whether it would be desirable, with a view to the real interests of the peasant boy, to keep him in school till he is 14 or 15 years of age. But it is not possible. We must make up our minds to see the last of him . . . at 10 or 11 . . . It is quite possible to teach a child . . . all that is necessary for him to possess . . . by the time he is 10 years old . . . He will be able to spell correctly all the words that he will ordinarily have to use . . . If gone to live at a distance from home, he shall write to his mother a letter that shall be both legible and intelligible . . . He has acquaintance enough with the Holy Scriptures to follow . . . the arguments of a plain sermon to know what duties are required of him . . .'

Evidence given by the Reverend James Fraser to the Newcastle Commission (1861)

'. . . in a manufacturing country, when so much of excellence in our productions depends on a clear understanding, and some degree of mathematical and mechanical knowledge which it is impossible to obtain without first receiving the rudiments (the three Rs), the superiority of workmen with some education over those who had none will be sensibly felt by manufacturers in the country.'

Speech by Lord Stanhope in the House of Lords (1807)

Universal education (i.e. education for everyone) and training have since been deemed necessary and will remain so; they seem likely to continue to be increasingly designed to serve the world of work. This unit will cover a wide range of issues in relation to education and training, including:

- informal and formal education;
- state, private and alternative forms of education;
- educational policies and the role of the state;
- schools and their organisation, structures and processes;
- patterns, differences and inequalities in educational achievement.

Informal and formal education

'Education', in broad terms, refers to a wide range of experiences in relation to skills, knowledge and values which allow each of us to take part in everyday life. It involves life-long processes of **socialisation** and learning, including the development of skills, knowledge and values passed on from one generation to the next. It takes place in both informal and formal settings, with many links between both settings. For example, a process such as the sending of greetings cards involves social, cultural and written skills which are learned both in the home and at school.

Informal education and socialisation

Even in advanced, industrial societies with well-developed systems of education, **informal education** – the constant absorption of information and values from those who surround us – is an important learning influence and is part of a complex process of socialisation, integrating individuals into their society. In pre-literate societies with no formal education, where people do not learn to read or write, informal education (through socialisation) is the crucial means by which the young are taught what they need to know in order to take their place in a society. Informal learning processes in such societies can be complex, since specific skill requirements may be taught by the family, the kinship group and also by religious leaders. The **oral tradition** (or word-of-mouth) has been important, for centuries, in the passing on of skills, knowledge and values.

The Baaka

One such pre-literate group is a nomadic tribe of African Baaka pygmies. The Baaka are believed to be the original inhabitants of the Central African tropical rainforests. The earliest documented recordings are Egyptian inscriptions, dating back more than 4000 years, referring to them as 'dwarfs, dancers of God' who live in the 'land of the spirits'. Today there are only 250,000 members of this race, well known for their short size – about 4 feet tall. They believe in, and teach their children, ancestral worship: the spirits of ancestors gave them life and protect them from evil, meeting their needs by providing game, berries and fruit in return for their trust and worship.

For the Baaka, the forest has always been a living, conscious being both natural and supernatural and to be relied upon, respected and loved: this has formed the basis of the education and training for the African Baaka pygmies for thousands of years.

Informal education among the Baaka pygmies

In almost any society the first stage of learning is mainly home based, within the family. The family is therefore described as an agent of **primary socialisation**, since it forms the earliest stage of informal education and training.

Formal education

Formal education provides what may be termed as **secondary socialisation**; it consists of the teaching received in an organised, often time-regulated, educational institution. Such a broad division between primary and secondary socialisation, and between formal and informal education, however, needs to be treated with some caution. Until about the 1970s, starting school at the age of five seemed to produce a neat, dividing line; a **rite of passage** from home to school, from child to pupil. This boundary is no longer so clear cut, with the increasing provision of childminders, creches, playgroups, nurseries and pre-school groups. Furthermore, relatively formal learning can take place at home when children are taught hygiene, table etiquette and domestic routines; while informal education continues alongside formal education in peer/friendship groups, teacher–pupil relationships and by other informal agents such as the mass media, particularly television.

Sociological theories of education

Two major sociological perspectives, functionalist and Marxist, have contrasting theories about education.

Functionalist theories of education

Theorists such as the American Talcott Parsons have focused on how education helps to maintain society, and its smooth-running, as an important part of the social system. For functionalists, key elements of the education system consist of:

- **culture transmission**, since it holds a socialisation function which maintains and promotes society's norms and values between generations. Particularly in advanced and complex societies, schools ensure continued harmony and equilibrium by transmitting the society's culture and core values from one generation to the next;
- **social control**, based on the need for each society to regulate the actions of its members. Schools produce rules and regulations so that students can learn what is expected of them within, and also outside and beyond, schools. Such a social control also passes on acceptance of the society's legal and political practices;
- **social selection**, which places the academically more able students into more complex occupations, such as law and medicine. The education system sifts and grades students in relation to their abilities so that individuals and society may take maximum advantage of the talents available;
- **economic training**, which refers to meeting the economic needs of a society to ensure its survival and well-being. The education system needs to provide skills training, ranging from those involved in caring services to those involved in high technology, and to match the wide-ranging and often changing needs of society.

Criticisms of functionalist theories	• It seems unlikely that a society may have a major, single set of norms and values to transmit. Many contemporary societies are multicultural and contain a variety of often conflicting norms and values.
	• Functionalists imply that the education system operates to the benefit of all students and that it serves to develop their skills and talents. This has been challenged by many sociologists, in particular Marxists, as we shall see below.

Marxist views on functionalist education theories

Educational issues	Functionalist views of education	Marxist views on functionalist perspective of education
Main concerns	• transmission of culture • social control • social selection • economic training to meet the needs of the capitalist economy	• transmission of capitalist culture • serving the interests of the rich and powerful • an illusion of equality of opportunity
Main assumptions	• society needs shared values and beliefs • acceptance of the political and legal system • education provides adequate supply of a trained labour force • the 'right' people are allocated the 'right' jobs	• capitalism shapes the nature of the education system • working-class pupils are taught obedience and are monitored closely by the system • inequality is justified by a 'fair' achievement-based education system • pupils often follow their class background in employment
Major criticisms	• assumes single culture of norms and values (transmitted by bourgeoisie) • 'overeducation' results in the 'qualified' doing jobs which could be carried out by the 'unqualified' (see page 165) • unemployment – a major problem for the poorly qualified – is overlooked	• reinforces predetermined economic division, i.e. bourgeoisie (minority) governs proletarian masses (majority) • personalises failure and poverty for the working class • mundane work needs to be carried out, with low status and poor pay.
Sociologists include	E. Durkheim T. Parsons K. Davis and W.E. Moore	K. Marx S. Bowles and H. Gintis P. Bourdieu

Problems with both functionalist and Marxist views on education include the following:

- Functionalists take '**macro**' (or large-scale), broad-sweeping views of the part played by education in the much wider social system and take little account of what actually happens within education, particularly classrooms (unlike many valuable interactionist and '**micro**' (or small-scale) approaches such as that of Paul Willis, outlined on page 188).
- They both depict individuals as mere creatures of the social system who may be manipulated and treated like 'puppets on a string'. In reality subcultures and forms of opposition exist in virtually all systems of education.

A major criticism of the functionalist view of education relates to the 'overeducation' problem explained in the following article.

Half of graduates feel underused and underpaid

By David Charter, education correspondent

MORE than half of graduates consider themselves to be underpaid and underused at work three years after leaving university, according to research published today.

Student numbers have doubled since the start of the decade but many will end up frustrated in jobs previously held by school leavers, the report concluded.

Nearly three quarters of graduates had permanent jobs three years on, with half earning less than £14,000. One in ten was paid £20,000 or more. The study of 1,000 graduates from Sussex University found it was taking them longer to find a permanent job than their predecessors and that traditional graduate training courses were disappearing.

Richard Pearson, director of the Institute for Employment Studies, which carried out the research, said the mass higher education system was turning out graduates who felt underemployed. This was due mainly to a lack of intellectual challenge.

"The labour market is becoming more complex, and graduates are moving into new areas of employment," he said. "In some cases they are displacing less-qualified candidates and adding new value to these jobs. In other cases they are frustrated." The study tracked graduates from 1991, 1992 and 1993. Those who held what they considered a graduate-level job fell from 84 per cent of the 1991 university leavers to 73 per cent of the 1993 group.

One in ten said they were in a job they knew had previously been done by a school leaver. However, even those who followed traditional career paths complained they were not being stretched at work.

Helen Connor, one of the authors of the report, said: "The main problem area identified was the lack of job opportunities."

The job most commonly taken was teaching, followed by clerical work, journalism or writing, computer analysis and software engineering. Two thirds took extra studies after their degrees to help to enhance career prospects and 15 per cent were still studying three years after their degree.

Unpaid work was increasingly being taken by graduates to help get "a foot in the door", the survey said. Fewer were taking time off for travel or other reasons before beginning their careers.

Male graduates were being paid £14,477 on average compared with £13,502 for females. The top earners had studied mathematical sciences (average salaries £15,787).

Source: *The Times*, 18 July 1996

What are schools for?

The following table suggests some purposes of schools, together with some comments and basic evaluations.

Purposes of schools	Comments
The main tasks of schools are:	*Schools do other things too. They:*
• to transmit knowledge and skills;	• enable pupils to meet; make friends and form wide social groups;
• to educate pupils for their life-time experiences.	• provide a custodial function by looking after children while parents work.
Schools also serve to:	*They also serve to:*
• preserve our culture and social heritage;	• preserve intellectual order and the hierarchy of existing knowledge;
• prepare pupils for occupations via relevant education;	• socialise pupils to fill occupational roles;
• provide vocational skills and self discipline;	• prepare pupils (particularly in private education) for leadership roles.
• provide equality of opportunity, with access to 'neutral' or rational knowledge for those who seek it.	• Inequality of opportunity remains: some kinds of knowledge have higher status than others.
• Schools are well-run organisations whose main function is to educate pupils.	• The school is an organisation with professional and managerial ideologies which impose authority and control.

The development of maintained and independent schooling

In the UK today, formal education is legally compulsory for all children between the ages of five and 16. As schooling has developed, its organisation has grown complex, and age-related stages have been established for the different ages of pupils. The usual division is into primary (age 5–11), secondary (age 11–16) and tertiary (age 16 and over). The tertiary stage includes sixth-form colleges, colleges of further education and universities.

In the UK, 93 per cent of schooling is provided by the state, sometimes in cooperation with other, notably religious, bodies. There are about 30,000 schools in the UK, with a total of 9.3 million pupils.

School pupils, by type of school, in the UK

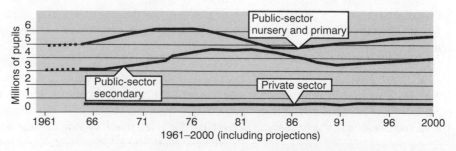

1961–2000 (including projections)

Source: Education Statistics for the UK, 1994–5, DfEE

			1994–5
Schools	maintained	primary	24,000
	maintained	secondary	4,000
	independent schools	primary and secondary	2,000
Pupils	maintained	primary	5,062,000
	maintained	secondary	3,651,000
	independent schools	primary and secondary	591,000

Source: Adapted from *Social Trends*, 1993

State education

Historically, the Church played a leading role in setting up schooling (or formal education) in the UK. During the twelfth century, many cathedrals established schools, staffed entirely by clergy, which taught boys Latin grammar, the language of the Church. Gradually these grammar schools became less religion based, and other types of schools, such as guilds for merchants and craftsmen, were founded. Schooling remained limited, particularly for the poor, until the late nineteenth century.

The Elementary Education Act 1870

Forster's Education Act in 1870 provided a national system of elementary education for every child. It took the form of a basic network of state-supported primary schools, with voluntary attendance, and was introduced for the following reasons:

- to meet the needs of industry: the UK was falling behind its competitors, particularly Germany and the USA, in terms of industrial development;
- to meet the need for an educated workforce: there was a lack of literate and numerate workers for the industrial and commercial developments linked to the new technology of the time;
- to provide a custodial function, and prevent child labour exploitation: working parents required schools for the safe-keeping of their children. The factory system often required the labour of both parents. Reformers, for example Lord Shaftesbury, were responsible for the Factory Acts which restricted the general employment of young children.

Elementary education, based on reading, writing and arithmetic/numeracy (the 'three Rs'), was made compulsory in England and Wales in 1880. This was the beginning of **state education** for all, although such education was not provided free in most schools until 1891.

Think about it

- What purposes do you think were served by the introduction of elementary education and the 'three Rs'? How important do you think they are today?
- What else might have been useful for children to learn in the early days of state education?
- What do you think might be the problems arising from placing a custodial function upon schools?

The Education Act 1944   This major Act, introduced by **Rab Butler,** implemented the findings of several reports on education, for example Hadow (1926), Spens (1938) and Norwood (1943). The Act introduced the concept of **meritocracy,** or education based on individual achievement rather than on ascribed (or inherited) factors such as wealth, sex or age. This meant that a child would receive an education according to his or her ability rather than to the parents' ability to pay. The main features of the Act are outlined below.

Butler's Education Act, 1944

The Education Act, 1944
Summary of main provisions

- **Appointment of a Minister for Education**
  This improved the status of the political head of the education service. He or she now had a place in the Cabinet as of right.

- **All pupils to be educated according to 'age, ability and aptitude'**
  This did not necessarily involve selection for different types of secondary school, although that was the way in which Local Education Authorities interpreted the Act in the post-war years.
     Pupils were supposed to be educated according to their parents' wishes. However, there were often clashes between teachers' estimates of pupils' abilities and parents' preferences.

- **Education to be in three stages: primary, secondary and further**
  Prior to 1944, the term 'secondary school' applied only to a limited number of selective schools whose pupils either paid fees or won a free place by means of a scholarship. But in future there would be 'free secondary education for all'.

- **'Collective worship' and compulsory religious instruction in state schools**

- **Local Education Authorities to make arrangements for regular medical and dental inspections**
  Parents could be prosecuted if they refused to allow their children to be examined.

- **Local Education Authorities to make provision for the education of the blind, deaf and physically handicapped**
  Previously this had often been left to voluntary bodies.

- **Local Education Authorities to provide milk and meals**
  Milk was originally provided free and meals at a reduced price. Since 1980, schools no longer have to provide milk, and the control over the price of meals has been removed.

- **Action to be taken to raise the school leaving age to fifteen, and then to sixteen as soon as circumstances permit**
  The leaving age was raised to fifteen in 1947, but it did not become sixteen until the school year 1972–3.

- **Ministry of Education to set standards of new school building**
  This was partly to try to achieve 'parity of esteem' in secondary education. All types of secondary school could be built to similar standards.

- **The Minister to have powers to overrule any Local Education Authority judged to have acted 'unreasonably', and to take over the powers of a Local Authority if it defaults on its responsibilities**
  This showed clearly where ultimate power lay.

Butler's Education Act also introduced three types of secondary education – a **tripartite system**:

- **grammar schools** for the academically able;
- **technical schools** for training in practical skills, for technical and skilled jobs (but few were actually built);
- **secondary modern schools** for most pupils, offering a non-academic, general education.

Independent schools (fee-paying) might also exist, and administrative mechanisms would be set up for their control and inspection. There would be three ways of deciding the educational institution attended:

- age: 11-year-olds would take the '11-plus' examination;
- aptitude: those with talent for working with their hands might go to technical schools;
- ability: the most academically able, who passed the 11-plus examination, would go to grammar schools.

Criticism of the tripartite system

The 1944 Act attempted to ensure 'equality of opportunity' for all pupils to have a fair chance to develop their potential in a free system. However, mounting criticisms, in particular of selection by the 11-plus examination, led, by the 1960s, to criticisms of the entire tripartite system. The criticisms were as follows:

- Intelligence, and its measurement, was assumed to be innate (set at birth) and static. At the age of 11, children sat tests of intelligence based on questions in English, mathematics and general knowledge. There were few opportunities for late-developers to transfer to grammar schools; there were also geographical differences in the number of grammar school places available. Middle-class children were thought to have the advantage over working-class children because of factors such as parental encouragement, home background, etc. Grammar schools became mainly middle-class institutions, while secondary modern schools catered mainly for the working classes. The higher classes used the independent schools.
- 'Parity of esteem', or the equal status of all secondary schools referred to in the 1944 Act, was soon eroded, as grammar schools received higher status, more qualified staff and better resources. Furthermore, as GCE O and A level examinations were only taken in grammar schools, most secondary modern pupils became stigmatised as 'failures' at 11 and left school with no qualifications. The introduction of CSE examinations in 1965 partly offset this imbalance. Nevertheless, the tripartite system was condemned by its critics as being socially divisive, inefficient and wasteful.

Think about it

- What do you think are the benefits and the drawbacks associated with testing pupils aged 11?
- Is it possible to overcome the problems which arise from the geographical location of schools and the social class backgrounds of children?
- In what ways, other than by lack of educational achievement, can pupils become stigmatised?
- Should grammar schools be reintroduced throughout the UK?

The development of comprehensive schools	Criticisms of the tripartite system led to the growth of the **comprehensive system**, although some Local Education Authorities (LEAs) resisted this change and the tripartite system has survived in several areas. **Circular 10/65** was issued in 1965 by the Labour government to all LEAs to plan for the reorganisation. By the mid-1980s, the secondary education system comprised:

- over 3 million pupils in nearly 4000 comprehensive schools;
- about 170,000 pupils in 285 secondary modern schools;
- about 120,000 pupils in 175 grammar schools.

The shift towards comprehensive schools aimed to put all children, regardless of ability, into neighbourhood schools based on three main advantages:

- Economic: one large neighbourhood comprehensive school was considered cheaper than several smaller schools; economies of scale allowed for a greater range of subjects and better facilities, for example purpose-built faculty or department blocks, drama studios, sports centres, etc.
- Educational: no longer based on selection or divisions at a particular age, the comprehensive system could provide greater opportunities to all pupils to fulfil their educational potential both in traditional subjects and in developing curriculum areas such as social sciences and technology.
- Social: the comprehensive system would break down class divisions perpetuated by the tripartite system and allow the mixing of social classes, both teachers and pupils, in one school setting.

Criticisms of the comprehensive system

- Size and anonymity: in their earliest forms, many comprehensive schools contained 2000 or more pupils, often with 12 classes of 30 pupils in each year group. It was feared that individual pupils would become 'lost' in the system, with many teachers not knowing their own colleagues, let alone the pupils. Anonymity, it was argued, for example by the **Hillgate Group** led by Baroness Cox and Dr John Marks in 'The Black Paper', led to a lack of corporate identity, poor discipline and weak academic results.
- The demise of the grammar school was seen by some as the loss of a 'fine academic' school tradition. Many grammar schools were well established, even before the 1944 Act, and, it was argued, had become the bastions of scholarly learning. They met fully the needs of academically talented pupils and prepared them for higher education. Some parents felt that comprehensive schools did not and could not 'push' or 'stretch' bright pupils, especially when taught in mixed-ability groups.
- Loss of an upward mobility route: many notable figures, for example Margaret Thatcher, have achieved upward social mobility, from lower middle-class backgrounds, via the grammar school route. The grammar school tradition enabled a small proportion of 'bright' working- or lower middle-class pupils to go on to universities, especially with the availability of scholarships to cover their costs.

Sponsored mobility and contest mobility

Sponsored and contest mobility are forms of social mobility based on the education system. R.H. Turner, in an article entitled 'Sponsored and Contest Mobility and the School System' (published in *American Sociological Review*, vol. 25, 1960), compared the British and American educational systems in relation to upward social mobility. In Britain, R.H. Turner claimed, the selective system of education represented **sponsored mobility**. Such sponsorship was associated also with parental influence, including financial and other resources. By contrast, in the USA, pupils engaged in **contest mobility** – a more continuous and open competition for educational and socio-economic advantages. This is strongly denied by S. Bowles and H. Gintis in *Schooling in Capitalist America* (1976), see page 187, who maintain that the American system provides less of an open contest than is claimed by R.H. Turner.

While the Americans tend to believe that their education system allows for upward social mobility 'from log cabin to White House', the claims made in the UK by John Major, on taking office as Prime Minister in 1990, of creating a more open, meritocratic and classless society, have been seen by many to have had little impact.

Think about it

- To what extent do you think that the criticisms of the comprehensive system offset the original reasons for its development?
- Do you think that the decrease in provision of grammar schools contributed to a loss of opportunity for upward mobility?
- Why do you think some sociologists might not take too seriously John Major's claims of creating a society based on merit rather than class?

More recent developments in state education, and in particular the Education Reform Act (ERA) of 1988, are covered in the section on educational policy, pages 177–9.

Private education

The independent education sector consists of all **private schools** and colleges, and also the University of Buckingham, which charge fees. Included within this sector are **public schools** – the higher status, most expensive educational institutions such as Eton and Harrow. Traditionally, public schools have catered mainly for boys (they are now increasingly coeducational) from the upper and middle classes; they form the most prestigious and well-established schools in the independent sector. The usual definition of a public school is by its membership of the Headmasters' Conference (HMC). The HMC was formed in 1871; its initial membership was limited to 50 but gradually increased to 233.

There has been little sociological research on girls' independent schools. The Girls' School Association (GSA) and the related Governing Bodies of Girls' Schools Association (GBGSA) with 257 members approximate to the HMC, although they tend to be wider in terms of school size, geographical location and religious affiliation. The percentage of girls receiving independent education has increased rapidly to almost 50 per cent of the independent sector. Some of this growth has been taken up by a number of HMC schools becoming coeducational, particularly post-16.

Pupils in independent schools as a proportion of all school pupils: by sex and age		1976 (%)	1981 (%)	1986 (%)	1991 (%)
Boys aged:	Under 11	4	4	5	5
	11–15	7	6	7	8
	16 and over	16	17	19	20
	All ages	6	6	6	7
Girls aged:	Under 11	4	4	5	5
	11–15	6	6	6	8
	16 and over	13	12	14	15
	All ages	5	5	6	7
All pupils		5	5	6	7

Source: *Social Trends*, 1993

As shown in the above table, only 7 per cent of pupils attend independent schools; 93 per cent, the vast majority, remain within the state education system. However, this percentage increases with age: by age 16, 20 per cent of boys and 15 per cent of girls attend independent schools. Growth in the independent sector seems to be in the form of 'exiles' from the state sector rather than from the continued support of families traditionally associated with private schools. In 1991, there were 2287 independent schools educating about 565,800 pupils. However, the Independent Schools Information Service (ISIS), which represents 80 per cent of the independent schools, reported in 1994 that for the second consecutive year numbers attending these schools had fallen back to the percentage figures of the 1980s. The ISIS report referred to the effects of the continued economic recession. There also seems to be the issue of parents' long-term commitment to independent education.

Support for independent education is often based on these claims:

- It is every parent's right to choose their children's education, and such freedom of choice includes the right to pay for independent education if money is available. (Parents actually pay twice over for their children's private education, through taxation which contributes towards state education as well as through private school fees.)
- Over the centuries, the independent sector has developed and become part of British heritage and culture. The public schools often have excellent facilities, small teaching groups and high standards of academic and sporting distinction. Hence public schools such as Rugby have achieved a worldwide status, with termly boarding fees (in 1996) of £4090.
- Through independent education children make social contacts which serve them throughout their careers. In 1992, eight of the 12 largest government departments were run by permanent secretaries, all men, educated at independent schools (and all but one had attended Oxford or Cambridge University). An official survey by the House of

Commons select committee, published in June 1996, found that 80 per cent of judges went to public schools and to Oxford or Cambridge University. This phenomenon has been referred to as the **'Oxbridge'** connection, and forms part of what is termed the **'old boy network'** which retains many of the elite occupational positions of top jobs for ex-public schoolboys.

Today, establishment figures sending their sons to Eton are expected to mix not only with the likes of Prince William but also with 'new toffs' such as Mick Jagger and his son James.

Everyone wants to be a 'tit'

Why do all the 'new toffs' seek places at Eton for their sons, asks **Rebecca Fowler**

For the once dissatisfied young man who sang one of the greatest anthems to disaffected youth, Eton seems an unlikely choice of school for his 11-year-old son. But Mick Jagger appears determined that Master James should concentrate his own voice on the Boating Song as part of the new hierarchy of British Toffery, where pop stars are the modern equivalent of dukes, and everyone still wants to be a tit.

The money may have changed hands, as dusty aristocrats fight to keep up their crumbling country seats while pop stars, lawyers, accountants and dentists buy them up. But a tit in the family – Etonspeak for a new boy – remains the surest sign of all of being part of the social élite of the day, the new hybrid of pop heirs, aspiring multi-millionaires and financially embarrassed viscounts.

At Eton, like nowhere else in the world, tits can still rub shoulders with royal tits, rich tits, clever tits and the tits of the future who will be leaders in their various fields. It is a start in life without comparison, and according to former pupils only the most sanctimonious or stupid could emerge without an inflated sense of their own superiority. At £12,500

a year, it is still a mere snip for most toffs, old and new.

So last week Mr Jagger, a Dartford grammar school boy and son of a PE instructor, and Mrs Jagger, the Texan model Jerry Hall, joined a select group of parents to be taken on a tour of the Berkshire school, with a view to James taking one of 200 places. Here he would don the famous frock coat, leave the bottom button of his waistcoat undone, sit at a desk where Shelley, George Orwell, Ian Fleming and 18 prime ministers once sat, and learn to walk to the left of the statue of Henry VI, the founder, ready to draw a sword in his protection.

Mr Jagger is not alone in seeking to educate his son among the élite of the day, although pop stars appear to be divided down the line on where they send their children to school.

David Bowie sent his son Zowie to Gordonstoun where the Prince of Wales had such a famously miserable time. Paul McCartney sent all his children to local state schools in East Sussex, although they received private tuition when they travelled abroad with their parents.

But what must James do to secure his place? Eton, founded in 1440, remains the largest public school in the land, and most parents scramble to add their sons to the

Toffs old and new: James Jagger, son of Mick and Jerry, may join the Eton elite

waiting list even before the umbilical cord has been cut. Eleven years later the boys must then sit a common entrance exam, and perform to an increasingly high level.

Since the current generation of hopefuls was spawned during the Thatcher years, a time of particularly acute aspiration and social climbing, competition is likely to be especially fierce. Among Prince William's class of 13-year-olds are the sons of lawyers, merchant bankers, civil servants, a landscape gardener, a dentist and a news presenter. While a number had fathers and grandfathers at Eton, many are first-generation.

Their attitudes to the school vary: "My father thinks it's the best school, but you are made to look down on other people," said William

Bland, who wants to be a poet or a criminal barrister. "My sisters say I'll become snobbish and arrogant, but I don't have to become a snob," said Tom Ehrman who wants to be a soldier. "Some people say it's stuffy, but dad says it'll look right on my CV," said Nigel De Grey, who is third-generation Eton.

How right Mr De Grey is. For this generation, when their time comes, they will still be part of the "best club in the world". The make-up of the Establishment may have changed, with music studios and dental surgeries now part of the backdrop. But the benefits will be the same, as they bump into each other through the rest of their lives, bonded by the old school tie, just as they have for five centuries.

Source: Adapted from the *Independent*, 18 June 1996

Criticisms of independent education

- It is mainly the most affluent who can afford to send their children to public schools. The independent sector is therefore highly divisive and maintains social class divisions and barriers.
- The powerful and rich decisions-makers of society have been drawn from and send their own children to independent schools. Those who govern and decide educational policy have relatively little contact with state schools, which are attended, and for the most part supported, by the majority.
- Public school pupils occupy a large number of university places, often because of close connections between public schools and universities. This is particularly the case for the Universities of Oxford and Cambridge, where about 50 per cent of their undergraduates come from public schools. Thus the 'old boy network' and the 'Oxbridge' connection referred to above are perpetuated. However, research evidence in June 1997 pointed to university admissions officers preferring state school applicants with, often, lower A level/Higher level grades.

Think about it

- How important are top public schools in producing the leaders of society?
- How might sociologists view the educational placement of a future monarch alongside 'new toffs' and pop heirs?

Alternatives to state and private education

Traditionally it has been assumed that teachers, by virtue of their education and training, are best able to educate and train pupils, and that this is best carried out in a well-organised institutional setting through a broad, balanced and relevant range of subjects which make up the school curriculum. However, there are educationalists who have advocated alternatives. **Freeschoolers** and **deschoolers** are probably the most important groups.

Freeschoolers

Freeschoolers have set up free schools in an attempt to modify schooling and its curriculum. They seek to make education more relevant to children and offer more freedom within schools by:

- supporting more democratic rather than hierarchical decision-making processes in the running of such schools;
- not insisting on compulsory attendance at lessons, which are based on the perceived needs and interests of pupils.

The famous free school, **Summerhill**, was started by **A.S. Neill** in 1921. He argued that it was futile to force pupils into learning an irrelevant range of traditional subjects within classroom situations, and that schools ought to teach pupils what they actually feel they need to know. Summerhill has always been a 'free school', with voluntary lessons and pupil self-government. There are regular meetings, which all school members attend, and a tribunal system to deal with disputes, though the school's director, Zoe Redhead (Neill's daughter), reserves the right to make important decisions including staff appointments. In 1997, after several years of criticism from official inspectors, the school was threatened with closure unless it 'improved'; Redhead's response was that closure would be preferable to conformity on key points such as making lessons compulsory.

IMAGINE A SCHOOL . . .

... where children only attend the lessons that interest them.

... where climbing trees and building dens are considered as important as decimal fractions.

... with small informal classes, allowing every child to progress at their own rate.

... where living away from home is a positive, enriching experience.

... where children learn lessons for life; self-confidence, tolerance and consideration for others.

... where the whole school deals democratically with issues such as bullying and racism, with each individual having an equal right to be heard.

... where creativity is not stifled by pressure and self-expression is not curtailed by conformity.

... which produces young people who, having lived life fully as children, go on to be contented, self-assured adults.

Imagine such a school!

A.S. NEILL'S

SUMMERHILL

GIVING CHILDREN BACK THEIR CHILDHOOD

**Summerhill School, Leiston, Suffolk, England.
IP16 4HY. Tel/Fax: 01728 830540**

Deschoolers

Deschoolers are more extreme and radical than freeschoolers and seek to abolish schools entirely. For deschoolers, schools are places where students are forced to learn subjects and values so as to become docile workers rather than thinking human beings. Deschoolers argue that:

- compulsory schooling does not promote equality or the development of individual talents;
- compulsory schooling should cease and deschooling should provide access to available resources to all those who want to learn at any time of their lives;
- a deschooled society would consist of an 'educational framework' of learning opportunities and resources, including materials and human skills made readily available via 'communication networks'.

These ideas originated from Ivan Illich's *Deschooling Society* (1971), which argued that the institutionalisation of education and its compulsory nature hinders learning processes. A deschooling movement arose during the 1970s, supported by writers such as Everett Reimer and Paul Goodman. More recently the American Lewis Perelman, in *School's Out . . .* (1992), has attempted to relaunch the case for deschooling.

Home-based education

Probably the most unusual arrangement for education in the UK is that of the education of children at home. This is more accurately seen as **home-based learning**, because the majority of families use the home as a springboard into a range of community-based activities. Most people wrongly believe that attendance at school is compulsory. The law in fact states that:

> *'It shall be the duty of the parent of every child of compulsory school age to cause him to receive efficient full-time education suitable to his age, aptitude and ability, either by regular attendance at school or otherwise.'*
> Section 36 of the Education Act (England and Wales) 1944

The law is clear: education is compulsory, schooling is not. In 1976, a self-help and mutual support organisation – Education Otherwise – was set up for parents who chose to educate their children at home. Over 2000 families involved in home-based education are associated with Education Otherwise, and there are many more who are not. A reasonable estimate of the total number of families with home-based educational programmes is about 5000.

Criticisms of alternative forms of education

Critics of freeschoolers, deschoolers and home-based education have put forward the following arguments:

- Such alternatives focus on the problems of education systems, in particular schooling, and seem to offer idealistic solutions without considering other important socio-economic factors, for example wealth, class, gender issues.
- Deschooling just would not work. Extreme problems could arise in any society without schools or social order, which are required for the workforce and very survival of society.
- Pupils generally learn best in an organised, disciplined, classroom-styled atmosphere; children do not necessarily know what may be in their long-term interests.

Educational policy and the role of the state

Until quite recently very little had been written on educational politics and educational policy-making from a sociological viewpoint. Recent texts, such as *Education and Training 14–19: Chaos or Coherence?* by R. Halsall and M. Cockett (1996), review state educational initiatives and their contribution to the thinking that might influence future educational policy. Key issues to consider include who is involved in educational policy-making, why and how they participate, and with what aims.

The 'Great Debate'

In 1976, at Ruskin College, Oxford, the Labour Prime Minister, James Callaghan, started what has become termed the **Great Debate** on education. During his brief premiership, James Callaghan's main concerns were:

- the education and attainment standards of pupils receiving state education;
- the relationship between education and industry.

The New Right movement

In 1979, Margaret Thatcher succeeded James Callaghan as Prime Minister and her Conservative government set out to tackle the concerns of her predecessor. Conservative educational policy was influenced by the New Right movement. Also termed **modern market liberals**, New Right thinkers held firm views about the nature and scope of the Welfare State, including its educational ideals. They maintained that:

- state involvement and support should not be monopolistic, since this was wasteful, unfair and inefficient;
- more competition was required in both the state and private sectors;
- public spending should be minimal; so too should taxation, so that incentives could be created for people to start new enterprises and people would have more choice on how to spend their money.

Previous emphasis on equality of educational opportunity and the development of individuals' potential talents was, according to the New Right, reducing educational standards; furthermore, they believed that the school curriculum was not meeting the skills required by employers. The government introduced sweeping changes in educational policy; the Educational Reform Act (ERA) of 1988 (see below) has become recognised as the most important state educational legislation since the Butler Education Act of 1944.

The Education Reform Act 1988

The main features of the Education Reform Act (ERA) include:

- the establishment of a **national curriculum** for England and Wales, consisting of three **core subjects** (English, mathematics and science) and seven compulsory **foundation subjects** (history, geography, technology, music, art, PE and, at secondary level, a modern European language) for all pupils aged five to 16. (Scotland's education system is separate from that of England and Wales and went through its own reform process in the 1980s and 90s);

- the introduction of **national standardised tests**, with assessment of the core and foundation subjects at four **key stages**: at the ages of seven, 11, 14 and 16;
- **local management of schools (LMS)**, giving headteachers and governors greater control over their finances;
- **open enrolment**, intended to allow parents to send children to the school of their choice. This gives schools the incentive to compete for pupils and expand their intake;
- **opting out**, which refers to schools, rather than local education authorities (LEAs), having control of their own affairs, including the hiring and firing of teachers and other school services. Such schools receive independent, grant maintained status, and are funded directly by central government.

The 'slimline' national curriculum, 1994

Sir Ron Dearing, Chairman of the School Curriculum and Assessment Authority (SCAA), attempted in 1994 to simplify the national curriculum. The aim was to make it more manageable, particularly in terms of teaching and assessment. By 1996 only six subjects were compulsory for key stage 4: English, mathematics, science, design and technology, a foreign language and information technology. However, wider options, in particular vocational routes, were introduced at key stage 4.

The Education Reform Act 1988 and the 'free market'

The implications of the Education Reform Act were far-reaching.

- LMS (local management of schools) and open enrolment offered schools more freedom from LEAs, especially in terms of finance. Opting out went even further and allowed schools to apply to the Minister of Education for permission to leave LEA control altogether and to be maintained by central government grants. LMS removes power from the LEAs and gives it directly to individual schools.
- LEAs, it has been argued, can plan efficiently and effectively on the basis of needs and can deal with wider concerns than can individual schools, who may lack the expertise in important educational issues. For example, it has been the responsibility of LEAs to reach decisions on pupils with special needs, welfare services, etc. How will such decisions be reached within opted-out schools?
- LEAs have been responsible for introducing and managing local comprehensive systems aimed at increasing equality of opportunity from a sound, educational basis. Opting out, along with LMS and open enrolment, could foster self interest based on 'free-market' strategies: who knows what kind of an educational system this might produce by the next century?

The ERA, in sociological terms, seems in accord with functionalist views of education, as outlined on page 163, in its move towards the provision of a trained labour force.

A return to grammar schools?

Grant maintained status (GMS) schools are those schools which 'opted out' of the control of local education authorities under the terms of the 1988 Education Reform Act. They gained independence from the politics of their LEA and exchanged local financing for centralised, government funding. There has been intense political debate over whether the

GMS option has created a new two-tier system. Despite financial incentives from the government to encourage schools to 'opt out', however, only 1000 of the 28,000 schools in England and Wales had opted out by the mid-1990s and only one secondary and two primary schools in Scotland by mid-1997.

In June 1996, the Conservative government White Paper, entitled 'Self Government for Schools', brought the selection of pupils for secondary education back into the debate; thereby reinforcing the views expressed almost two decades previously by the modern market liberals or New Right thinkers (see page 177). However, the Labour Manifesto published prior to its election success in May 1997 announced its rejection of either a return to the 11-plus and grammar schools or homogeneous comprehensive schools taking no account of differing abilities. They favoured all-in schooling identifying individual pupils' abilities. A planned reorganisation of schools set out in the new government's White Paper in July 1997 included most of the 1000 GMS schools opting to become foundation schools.

Think about it

- Do you think that there should be a reintroduction of selective schools in areas dominated by comprehensives? What, in your opinion, might be the advantages and disadvantages of selecting pupils according to their ability?
- Do you consider that more diversity and choice should be made available in the current system of education and training?
- How do you consider a fair admissions system for secondary school education might be achieved?
- What values, if any, do you think should be put across to students in primary, secondary and further education? What social policies may need to be adopted to reinforce any such values?
- Do you consider that formal education still acts effectively as a form of social control?

The transition from school to work

'New Vocationalism' in the 1980s

The New Right have argued that education and training should be concerned with promoting economic growth by providing the basic skills required by the workforce. Hence there developed a 'New Vocationalism', which included the following measures:

- The **Technical and Vocational Education Initiative (TVEI)** was launched as a pilot scheme in 1983, in 14 LEAs, and became extended nationally for 14- to 18-year-olds. It accompanied and often broadened the curriculum and ensured work experience.
- The **Certificate of Pre-vocational Education (CPVE)**, launched in 1985/6, emphasised preparation for the workforce. It taught practical skills, which could be combined with examination subjects, and ensured work experience.
- **National Vocational Qualifications (NVQs)** and **General National Vocational Qualifications (GNVQs)** are new vocationally-related qualifications. The former are specific to a particular working skill while the latter cover broader areas of study such as 'Business' or 'Hospitality and Catering'.

Other developments, furthering the aims of 'New Vocationalism', include:

- **City Technology Colleges (CTCs)** to provide a science and technology based curriculum, ideally set up with industrial sponsorship, at the same time extending the range of secondary schools in inner cities;
- **City Technology Colleges of the Arts** to specialise in arts technology, film, music, etc., providing training in a range of skills that support the arts industry;
- **records of achievement (RoAs)** for all pupils leaving secondary schools, covering all accomplishments from practical and social skills to academic qualifications.

Issues related to 'New Vocationalism'

- The degree to which education and training should provide vocational preparation is open to debate. The development of 'New Vocationalism' in the UK may be seen as much in terms of political direction as economic needs.
- Considerations of vocational education and training have often focused on the relatively low percentage of 16- to 18-year-olds who remain in the education system (see below) by comparison with the UK's economic competitors.

Participation of 16- to 18-year-olds in education and training (per cent)		16 years			16 to 18 years		
	Minimum leaving age (years)	**Full-time (%)**	**Part-time (%)**	**All (%)**	**Full-time (%)**	**Part-time (%)**	**All (%)**
Germany (Fed. Rep.)	15	99	0	99	89	0	89
Netherlands	16	93	5	98	77	10	87
Belgium	14	92	4	96	82	4	87
France	16	90	0	90	82	0	82
USA	16–18	96	0	96	81	1	82
Denmark	16	92	0	92	79	0	79
Japan	15	93	1	94	76	3	79
Canada	16–17	100	0	100	78	0	78
Sweden	16	83	0	83	73	0	73
United Kingdom	16	57	37	94	40	31	71
Australia	15–16	76	12	88	52	17	69
Italy	14	54	15	69	47	18	65
Spain	16	71	0	71	61	0	61

Source: *Social Trends*, 1994

- Key questions include not only how best to prepare young people for the world of work but also the quality and appropriateness of such education and training. This directly affects the competitiveness of the UK in the world market, as illustrated in the following diagrams.

Education and training
in which the UK trails
behind its competitors

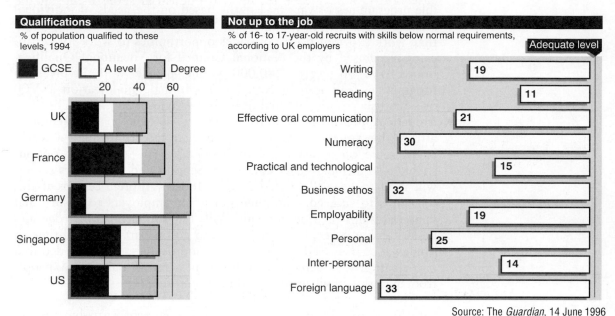

Qualifications

% of population qualified to these levels, 1994

■ GCSE ☐ A level ▨ Degree

20   40   60

UK

France

Germany

Singapore

US

Not up to the job

% of 16- to 17-year-old recruits with skills below normal requirements, according to UK employers

Adequate level

Skill	%
Writing	19
Reading	11
Effective oral communication	21
Numeracy	30
Practical and technological	15
Business ethos	32
Employability	19
Personal	25
Inter-personal	14
Foreign language	33

Source: The *Guardian*, 14 June 1996

Skills training in the 1990s

The figures given in the diagram above show evidence of what may be termed a 'skills crisis'. Employers in the UK claim that they cannot recruit people with the skills they require. During the 1980s and 1990s, the Conservative government's measures to address the 'skills crisis' involved privatising and localising the provision for training by the establishment of the following organisations and initiatives.

- **Training and Enterprise Councils (TECs)**, launched in April 1990 in England and Wales, and **LECs (Local Enterprise Companies)** in Scotland, receive 80 per cent of the money available for skills training. TECs are led by local businessmen who assess the skills needed by the local labour market and develop training and enterprise strategies to meet local needs. TECs have attempted to bridge the skills gap identified as a major cause of the UK's economic decline. However, a report by a team led by Professor Bob Bennett of the London School of Economics in 1994 concluded that the TECs had been manipulated by successive employment ministers and that their impact had been lessened by their programmes being pitched too low and including elements irrelevant to the world of work; this had cost £250 million during the three-year period studied, according to the report.
- **Employment Training (ET)**, launched in September 1988, aimed at providing high-quality training directed at individual employment needs. It is intended mainly for the long-term unemployed but relates also to women returning to work, those made redundant and those in particular areas of skills shortages. However, during its first two years, ET failed to attract the numbers anticipated, suffered from a high drop-out rate and did not receive full support from local employers.

- **Youth Training (YT)**, launched in June 1990, replaced the **Youth Training Scheme (YTS)** designed for school leavers. YT moved away from a national scheme of one- to two-year programmes to more flexible programmes of varying lengths based on the needs of individual school leavers and local employers. YT is employment training rather than work experience, and provides opportunities to work for certificates recognised by the **National Council for Vocational Qualifications**. By 1996 nearly 280,000 young people were involved in programmes leading to a National Vocational Qualification (NVQ) or a Scottish Vocational Qualification (SVQ) level 2.
- **Modern Apprenticeships** were introduced in 1995 in an attempt to attract able young people to develop their careers through a work-based route on a fast track to NVQ level 3. Subsequent options should also include higher education. Schools and the careers service will need to be well briefed about Modern Apprenticeships if this scheme is to succeed. The intention is for employers to ensure that apprenticeships provide not only skills but sufficient knowledge and understanding to enable participants to go on part-time, full-time or sandwich courses leading to diplomas and degrees. It is intended that participation and achievement for males and females, and people from minority ethnic groups, will be monitored.

Adult education and training in the 1990s

Adult education and training is a growth area, currently involving 6 million people, mostly aged over 25, every week. However, it is claimed that millions more could become involved if it were not for financial arrangements, weak legislation and an education and training system aimed mainly at young people in which 'school' and 'education' are seen as almost the same thing.

Adult learners

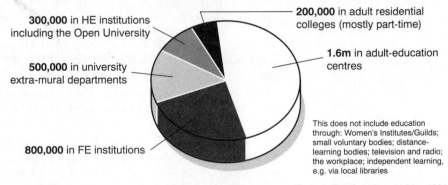

300,000 in HE institutions including the Open University

500,000 in university extra-mural departments

800,000 in FE institutions

200,000 in adult residential colleges (mostly part-time)

1.6m in adult-education centres

This does not include education through: Women's Institutes/Guilds; small voluntary bodies; distance-learning bodies; television and radio; the workplace; independent learning, e.g. via local libraries

Source: The *Guardian*, 11 May 1993

Think about it

- The above information on adult learners refers to the formal sector of adult learning. How much room do you think there is for development of less formal adult learning, such as the forms listed on the right of the pie chart?
- Apart from being in a rapidly changing technological society, what socio-economic factors do you think might account for the increasing number of adult learners?
- How might more relevant and worthwhile training be achieved among the workforce?

The economic case for adult learning is clear: a rapidly changing technological society requires higher skill levels. Adults need to be encouraged to invest in acquiring skills for an information-rich economy, in which the traditional skilled jobs are rapidly disappearing.

Over 80 per cent of the UK workforce for the year 2000 is already at work; more than half have had no training in the last five years (if at all). Furthermore, the likelihood of an increasingly mobile, skilled workforce in the European Union, not to mention the poor competitiveness of the UK, underlies the need to create a learning culture in which education and training are seen as life-long processes – a need which, since the mid-1990s, is becoming recognised by policy-makers.

Schools: organisation, structure and institutional processes

School organisation and structure

Schools are complex organisations to study. Even school brochures, a legal requirement for all state schools, rarely reflect fully the organisation, structure and, in particular, the institutional processes (for example the ways pupils are placed into various subject groupings or the extent of tutor support) of the school. Schools vary greatly in their organisation and structure, as well as in their size, geographical location, intake of pupils, etc. However, the school hierarchy (or ladder of power and seniority) in its internal organisation may be seen to reflect the wider hierarchical structure of society, as illustrated in the diagram below.

Organisation of a typical secondary school

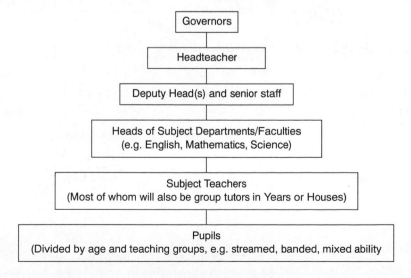

- The school hierarchy usually consists of governors (led by a chairperson), headteacher, with a senior management team of deputies and senior staff, heads of subject departments (sometimes grouped into faculties, for example Humanities), subject teachers and, at the bottom rung of this ladder of power and seniority, the pupils.
- The headteacher holds the key role in guiding the decisions of governors who, since the Education Reform Act of 1988, run the school.

What is not reflected in the diagram is the pastoral system, which meets the caring needs of pupils. Most subject teachers are also group tutors either in a horizontally organised year-group system or a vertically organised house system (a tradition from public schools). Indeed, some subject teachers may also be a Head of Year (or House), with responsibility for ensuring that group tutors maintain registers, pupils' profiles and records of achievement.

Restructuring in many schools, in line with developments evolving from national curriculum requirements, may serve to overcome subject and pastoral divisions by the appointment of Key Stage Coordinators.

The social construction of knowledge

Within the organisational hierarchy of schools and colleges there is also a hierarchy of knowledge. Knowledge is what is defined, categorised and controlled as such by powerful people and institutions, for example headteachers and universities. It tends to be based on status, with certain forms of knowledge having higher status, so it is not neutral or value-free. For example, schools classify theoretical knowledge as having higher status than practical knowledge. The diagram below shows a simple classification of knowledge.

A simple classification of knowledge

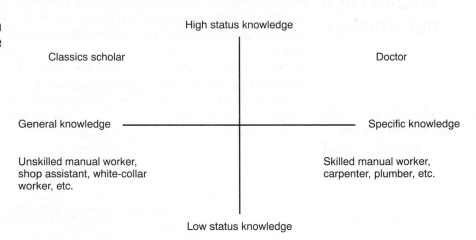

Source: Adapted from M. Joseph, *Sociology for Everyone 2nd edn* (Polity Press, 1990)

School knowledge

The publication of the book *Knowledge and Control* in 1971 by **M. Young** and others marked a turning point in what has become labelled as a 'New Sociology of Education'. The writers became concerned at the ways in which some forms of knowledge were supported and delivered by schools while other forms of knowledge became excluded. Their starting point was that there was nothing superior about school knowledge over other forms of knowledge. For Young, knowledge was a social construction based on political and social values.

According to Young, the controlling tendency has been for schools to teach the 'curriculum-as-fact', so that knowledge is treated as fixed and unchangeable rather than as a social construction. He contrasts this with 'curriculum-as-practice', which he sees in terms of what actually happens in classrooms which adds a social and political value to school knowledge.

School knowledge and the national curriculum

A major feature of the Education Reform Act of 1988, as noted on page 177, has been the introduction of a statutory national curriculum. This means that the nature and form of the curriculum is determined by law. The national curriculum applies to all pupils in England and Wales aged five to 16 years, except those in private education. There is no *overt* national curriculum in Scotland. The aims of the national curriculum are asserted to incorporate both the needs of individual pupils and the needs of society. A. Hartnell and M. Naish, in *The Sleep of Reason Breeds Monsters: The Birth of a Statutory Curriculum in England and Wales* (1990), have argued that the national curriculum provides a definition of what is to count as knowledge. The importance of such school knowledge is underlined politically by the establishment of a system of assessment at the end of each of the four key stages at the ages of seven, 11, 14 and 16.

The hidden curriculum

The **hidden curriculum** consists of the set of values, attitudes or principles delivered to pupils, as opposed to the **open curriculum** which is the formal, knowledge-based, taught curriculum of timetabled lessons. An example of the effect of the hidden curriculum is the way in which girls have traditionally been encouraged in subjects considered more appropriate for them, for example home economics and biology, whereas boys have been directed towards mathematics and physics. Similarly, teachers and parents may adopt expectations about particular gendered patterns of behaviour: girls may be expected to be neater and quieter than boys, for example.

The hidden curriculum: expectations and values

Expectations and values associated with the hidden curriculum, but not gender-specific, include the following:

• Social control: in school and society, social control is promoted by the hidden curriculum by educating and training people to conform to, obey and respect society.

The hidden curriculum in the early twentieth century

- Attendance, punctuality and cooperation: pupils are expected to attend school, arrive at registration and lessons on time, to 'fit in' and to 'get on' with others.
- Obedience and the value of hard work: pupils are expected to do what they are told and are often rewarded and regularly reminded of the importance of hard work.

The hidden curriculum and gender-role socialisation

In general the hidden curriculum involves a number of important aspects of school life which socialise girls into accepting an ideal of femininity: feminine meaning 'soft', docile, and 'sugar and spice and all things nice'.

<u>Patriarchy</u>   As a result of the hidden curriculum, schools, according to Dale Spender in *Invisible Women: The Schooling Scandal* (1983), are patriarchal, male-dominated institutions in which boys do well. She argues that the ideas taught are male, as is the world-view presented, and that this contributes to a limited and limiting experience for girls. Spender also notes how the school structure is part of the hidden curriculum; the longer girls stay in education the more males they will encounter in positions of power and authority and the fewer positive female role models there will be.

<u>School knowledge</u>   Dale Spender claims that the knowledge taught in schools is male-orientated and the subject matter directed at boys. Boys, she concludes from her studies, make twice as many demands on the teacher and ask twice as many questions: this is expected. If the subject matter in lessons is directed specifically at girls, boys exhibit behavioural problems and disrupt the class. Spender maintains that the classroom experience becomes a male experience.

<u>Teacher expectations</u>   These are one of the most integral parts of the hidden curriculum, contributing to the negative experience of education for girls. Michelle Stanworth, in *Gender and Schooling* (1983), claims that teachers view different futures for boys and girls, and as a result direct them towards different programmes of study; for girls, this means they are directed back towards the home. Stanworth argues that girls accept these expectations and begin to see the home and the mother/housewife role as the only possibility open to them.

Two contrasting extracts from Ladybird readers, showing how portrayal of gender roles changed between the 1960s and 1990s

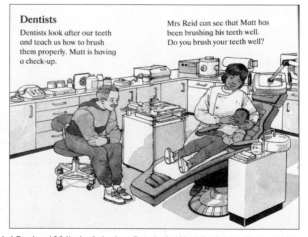

Source: *Boys and Girls*, Book 3b (Ladybird Books, 1964); *Let's look at People At Work* (Ladybird Books, 1995)

Gender portrayal in school reading schemes

Glenys Lobban, in a famous article in *The Times Educational Supplement* (1 March 1974) entitled 'Data Report of British Reading Schemes', revealed that in 179 stories from six reading schemes, she found only 35 stories with heroines, whilst 71 stories had heroes. This supported how the hidden curriculum operates through textbooks. In her study of early reading primers, there were rarely examples of working women and few of women carrying out a dual role in the home and the workforce. Women were portrayed as merely carrying out the stereotypical mother/housewife role. This bias has since become much less common.

Think about it

Choose a few of your textbooks that include illustrations.

- To what extent do you think they show evidence of bias towards any particular group (gender? ethnic? class?)?
- Look at the publication dates of the editions you have and see if you can detect any trends.
- How do you consider that values and opinions may differ from facts in any aspect of the hidden curriculum? What examples can you provide of facts, values and opinions in one of these books?

A Marxist perspective on the hidden curriculum

Samuel Bowles and Herbert Gintis, in *Schooling in Capitalist America* (1976), argue from a Marxist perspective that schools in the USA and all other capitalist societies have an important role in teaching the qualities required by the workforce in capitalist society: punctuality, cooperation, hard work, etc. They note that creative or free-thinking pupils do relatively poorly compared with conformists who comply with the hidden curriculum; which also *reinforces class divisions* within gender divisions.

Bowles and Gintis contend also that working-class attempts to change the education system have failed. They claim that the working class is likely to remain content with the system because it promotes the attitudes and values appropriate for work in a capitalist society. By *legitimating inequality*, the hidden curriculum serves to prevent the working class seeing further than their everyday needs and own life experience. According to Bowles and Gintis, exploited groups are not encouraged to develop ideas about how to change the education system, within a capitalist economy, to serve working-class interests.

Criticisms of the hidden curriculum

- The taught school subjects, i.e. the open curriculum, are seen as of lesser importance than the messages of the hidden curriculum.
- The **correspondence principle**, which refers to the correspondence between social interaction in the workplace and social relationships developed in the education system, has also been criticised. Many pupils are not socialised to become disciplined workers; this is evidenced by industrial sabotage, spying, conflict, disputes and employee resistance to management control.
- Resistance to the hidden curriculum, in the form of pupil subcultures which reject authority and school values, occurs within schools. Sociological studies such as those by Paul Willis have identified these mainly among the academically less successful.

Learning to Labour: a study by Paul Willis

Paul Willis's *Learning to Labour* (1977) represents a classic study. Like Bowles and Gintis (see page 187), Willis discusses the way in which education prepares pupils for work, but he rejects the notion that education is necessarily an effective agent of socialisation. Instead, Willis maintains that education can have unforeseen consequences, not entirely beneficial to capitalism.

Using observation techniques, Willis studied a small group of working-class boys in a secondary school in the Midlands in the 1970s. The 'lads' saw the school as an alien institution but one which they could manipulate to suit them. In resisting the school's attempts to control their activities, the 'lads' perfected techniques for 'having a laff', for evading rules and for maintaining group solidarity. The 'lads' referred to their conformist peers, who accepted the values of the school system, as 'the ear-'oles' or 'lobes'. The 'lads'' disaffection with school and their resistance to the school ethos, Willis maintained, was not just a reaction to academic failure and economic forces beyond their control.

Willis suggests that schools are not entirely dependent on economic forces and do not merely reproduce the social relation of capitalism. The 'lads' receive insights into the operation of the capitalist system, which Willis terms 'penetrations'. Hence the 'lads' find enjoyment in school, which they see as an oppressive institution, preparing pupils for boring, dead-end jobs.

Willis concludes that there does occur, within schools, resistance, rejection, innovation and change. Pupils are not simply shaped by the education system; quite often they are occupied in rejecting and reshaping it.

Think about it

- Were/are you aware of the hidden curriculum at school or college?
- From your own experience, do you think that pupils who comply with the hidden curriculum gain greater academic success than others?

Structures, processes and pupil-groupings

Sociologists are interested in the factors, both external and internal to schools, which may affect pupils' groupings within schools and encourage or discourage pupils' studies and educational attainment. Examples of external factors include intelligence and home background; while the school ethos and the 'sifting and sorting' processes for pupil-groupings are examples of internal factors.

Intelligence

IQ (intelligence quotient) tests have been widely used in the UK and the USA as attempts to measure intelligence. IQ tests are used:

- to provide objective, unbiased, accurate assessments of an individual's intelligence for placement within the education system or employment market;
- to allocate generations of pupils to different types of schools, as with the 11-plus system, or within schools into academic groups;
- to support the view put forward by Sir Cyril Burt and Hans Eysenck that intelligence is largely innate (or genetically determined) and inherited from parents.

Criticisms include the following:

- Whilst some mental capacity, along with physical characteristics, may be inherited from parents, cultural factors associated with parental upbringing and quality of home life cannot be dismissed. (Sometimes this is referred to as the 'nature v. nurture' debate.)

- Definitions of intelligence, and intelligence tests themselves (which are often designed to measure abstract reasoning ability), may vary between cultures within a society, from one society to another, and over different age and time periods.
- IQ tests may merely measure an individual's skill on such tests and, as with jigsaw and crossword puzzles, may be of limited value and application.

Home background   In the 1920s and 1930s, the home background and material deprivation associated with working-class families became a major concern for sociologists interested in differential factors in educational attainment. The effects of poverty – poor, overcrowded, insanitary housing, poor health and malnutrition – were seen to have direct or indirect consequences for educational attainment.

After World War II and the establishment of the Welfare State in the late 1940s, changes in living standards made sociologists reconsider whether poverty, and its effects, could remain a key factor in determining educational attainment, and in particular working-class underachievement. Sociological focus began to turn towards social class differences and pupils' school performance.

J.W.B. Douglas and his colleagues, in *The Home and the School* (1964), carried out a nationwide survey of 5362 British children born in the first week of March 1946. This longitudinal study, using social class groupings, questionnaires and tests, followed the majority of these children through to the age of 16; the results were published in *All Our Future* (1971). Douglas's main concern was the wastage of talent caused by inequalities in the education system. His analysis revealed a high correlation between middle-class children and grammar school placement, with most grammar schools located in private rather than council estate housing. Educational attainment, according to Douglas, was influenced by the following factors:

- the social class background of students and their parents;
- family size and the position of the child in the family;
- the level of parental interest and encouragement, for example frequent visits to the school to discuss their children's progress.

The results of the study led Douglas to conclude that:

- good primary education could not compensate for material deficiencies in the home or lack of parental involvement;
- streaming reinforces the process of social selection, with middle-class children found in higher streams (see page 193).

Factors internal to the school   The role of the school itself has increasingly become the focus of sociological attention as a source of influence on pupils' educational attainment. Several internal factors may be considered to be influential.

<u>School ethos</u>   This refers to the direction and organisation offered by a school, often centred on teachers creating and maintaining a positive atmosphere of care and cooperation with pupils. A good school ethos, with a consistent set of values and with teachers acting as role models for pupils in terms of, for example, punctuality and involvement in extra-curricular activities can, it has been claimed, influence pupils' achievement.

Michael Rutter, and his team of psychologists, studied school ethos in *Fifteen Thousand Hours…* (1979). This is the approximate number of hours required for school attendance for pupils from five to 16 years. Rutter's group gathered data from about 2000 pupils in 12 Inner London secondary schools over a period of six years; data covered attendance, behaviour in school, delinquency outside school and academic achievement. Their findings concluded that:

- school ethos (rather than home background – see J.W.B. Douglas, page 189) had a considerable effect on educational achievement;
- the quality of teacher–pupil interaction and well-organised course preparation affected the quality of the learning environment, regardless of size of school, material resources and condition of building.

Criticisms of Rutter et al. have included the vagueness of definitions and measurement of factors in relation to 'school ethos', 'good schools' and 'good behaviour'. There seemed to be an underestimation of social class background and an overemphasis on schools as influential factors on pupils' achievements. Gender and ethnic considerations were also neglected.

Labelling   This refers to categorising pupils into broad groups and then treating the groups according to that categorisation, for example 'labelled bright/dim/lazy' etc., with its consequences for pupils in terms of academic performance. If a teacher labels a pupil 'a nuisance', this will affect the way the teacher may act towards and treat that pupil, thereby discouraging and hindering his or her academic progress. The importance of teachers' labelling of pupils has been emphasised particularly by interactionist sociologists.

One such interactionist, David Hargreaves, in *Social Relations in the Secondary School* (1967), found that teachers disliked teaching lower-stream pupils and expressed this clearly. The boys reacted to the teachers' labelling them as nuisances or unpleasant to teach by deliberately causing trouble in school.

Interactionists view the education system in terms of human behaviour, with the **self concept** of the pupil (how he/she sees himself/herself) influenced by interaction with other pupils and teachers. The self concept may be changed if others regularly contradict it, especially in relation to academic performance.

Other important interactionist concepts are **social roles** and **pupil subcultures**. Social roles are the norms which direct and guide expectations of pupils' behaviour. However, they are not fixed around the 'ideal pupil'. Pupils may modify their behaviour patterns to create pupil subcultures and peer-group loyalties. 'Subcultures' are small groups of like-minded pupils who do not share the same views about education as the majority; they attach different, sometimes negative, meanings to their experiences of education. They may be labelled and treated differently by teachers.

Further studies were carried out by Hargreaves, in association with S. Hester and F.J. Mellor, and were published in *Deviance in Classrooms* (1975). Using classroom observation techniques and unstructured interviews with teachers in two secondary schools, they examined the ways in which teachers got to know new pupils entering the first year and the processes or stages which evolved during that year. Hargreaves refers to these processes as **typing** or ways in which pupils become typed or classified to form teachers' general pictures during an academic year.

We can identify three stages of typing or classifying:

1. Speculation: teachers guess the types of pupils they are dealing with.
2. Elaboration: teachers' judgements are confirmed or contradicted, typing is refined.
3. Stabilisation: teachers know and understand their pupils, and their actions are evaluated according to the type of pupil, for example deviant.

Typing leads to labels being attached to pupils. In itself, it may not seem to be important but sociologists maintain that typing or labelling does have considerable consequences for pupils' progress.

The 'self-fulfilling prophecy' The concept of the self-fulfilling prophecy is linked with typing and labelling. It occurs when teachers make predictions about the academic future of their pupils, which leads to the pupils' self image being shaped by the labelling process. The classic piece of research on the self-fulfilling prophecy was done by Robert Rosenthal and Leonara Jacobson in *Pygmalion in the Classroom* (1968). They selected a random sample of 20 per cent of the pupils in a Chicago elementary school, informing their teachers that such pupils could be expected to show swift intellectual development. Rosenthal and Jacobson carried out IQ tests at the beginning and end of their one-year research period and found that the sample showed greater increases in IQ than others. Hence they concluded that 'teachers' expectations can significantly affect their pupils' performance'. Rosenthal and Jacobson maintained that teachers' facial expressions, body language, degree of friendliness and encouragement all contribute to the self-fulfilling prophecy.

Criticisms of such research have been based on doubts about the validity of IQ tests, the use of statistical data rather than observation of classroom interaction, and the ethical issues involved in conducting research or experiments on pupils. Nevertheless, despite such criticism, other commentators, such as C. Rogers in *The Social Psychology of Schooling* (1982), consider that the self-fulfilling prophecy does indeed occur widely within the education system.

West Indians 'fail because teachers expect them to'

By Tim King

CHILDREN from a West Indian background are doing less well than other ethnic groups in Britain's schools, partly because teachers expect them to do badly.

A report from the Office for Standards in Education shows that Indian students achieve better examination results at the age of 16 than any other ethnic group including whites, while blacks fall further behind.

Ofsted warns that a disproportionately high number of black children have been expelled from school and says schools with so-called "colour-blind" policies are only allowing inequality of opportunity to persist.

The report warns of "a considerable gulf between the daily reality experienced by many black pupils and the stated goal of equal opportunities for all".

The authors say teachers often view Asian pupils as better behaved, more highly motivated and more able than black children.

By contrast, black pupils' experience of school is less positive than other groups, "regardless of ability and gender".

There was often conflict between black pupils and white teachers. Teachers may, the report says, play "an active (though unintended) part" in creating conflict with West Indian pupils, "thereby reducing black young people's opportunity to achieve".

Social class remains more important than ethnic background in determining children's achievements, and gender is also important.

The report's authors, David Gillborn and Caroline Gipps from London University's Institute of Education, complain of a shortage of reliable data that also takes into account children's ethnic, gender and social background. They had to go back to 1985 for such data based on a nationally representative sample.

They conclude that West Indian children, of both sexes, "achieved below the level attained by the other groups. Asian pupils did as well or better than whites of the same class and gender".

The pattern of girls out-performing boys was true only for white pupils.

For information on the past decade, the report extrapolates from a series of local studies and its own interrogation of local education authorities with significant populations of schoolchildren from ethnic minorities.

In Brent, which has the largest proportion of ethnic-minority pupils, Asians improved on scores attributed for GCSE grades from 30 to 38 points between 1991 and 1993. White pupils improved from 26.9 to 32.3 points and West Indians from 19.1 to 25.6. All groups did better but the gap between Asians and West Indians widened.

One in two Asian and white girls achieved five or more GCSE passes at grade C or better, compared with less than one in four West Indian girls. For boys, the figures were one in three Asian and one in four whites compared with one in six West Indians.

But almost one in 10 white boys left without any GCSE passes, compared with one in 25 West Indians and one in 200 Asians.

HM Inspector of Schools, Chris Woodhead, said Ofsted would consider asking inspectors to collect more evidence about ethnic under-achievement.

"Schools can and do make a difference. But it would be blinkered to pretend that family background and social class and ethnic origin are not also important," he said.

Cheryl Gillan, education minister, said the report's findings were a "real cause for concern".

She said the department would be improving arrangements for gathering information on the performance of ethnic minorities.

Source: The *Daily Telegraph*, 6 September 1996

Think about it

- To what extent do teachers' expectations affect pupils' performance?
- What factors might affect the way in which pupils seem to acquire – as individuals or as groups – positive or negative images?
- Think of some ethical issues which might be raised in conducting research on pupils and pupil–teacher relationships.

'Sifting and sorting' processes for pupil-groupings

- **Streaming** is the division of pupils into teaching groups according to their measured ability, often based on IQ or other intelligence tests.
- **Banding** has taken various forms. Pupils may be divided into wide ability groups and then divided again into random teaching groups or sets.
- **Setting** is sometimes also used, whereby pupils are divided into sets according to their ability in some subjects only – mathematics and French, for example.

Nell Keddie, in *Classroom Knowledge* (1973), studied the introduction of a new, unstreamed humanities course in a large, socially mixed, London comprehensive school. She was interested in the processes involved in creating academic 'failures'. Keddie also investigated the ways in which teachers categorised and evaluated classroom knowledge. The knowledge which teachers made available to pupils relied upon the assessment of the pupils' ability to cope with it. Hence pupils categorised as 'bright' were given greater access to 'superior' knowledge of an abstract form. Although it was adamantly denied by the teachers in Keddie's study, they categorised pupils in the classroom according to social background. Despite absence of streaming, pupils were thought of as 'A streamers' or 'C streamers' and were treated accordingly. In other subjects, pupils were streamed into three groups in terms of ability. Pupils from higher social class backgrounds tended to be placed into the 'A stream', whilst those from unskilled manual backgrounds occupied the 'C stream'.

Keddie maintained that pupils labelled as 'bright' were those who submitted, without challenge, to their teachers' authority; and that pupils were differentiated by teachers as in a streaming system, thus limiting the academic achievement of working-class pupils.

Beachside Comprehensive

Stephen J. Ball, in *Beachside Comprehensive* (1981), examined banding introduced for first-year pupils at a comprehensive school. Pupils were placed into one of three bands based on information from primary schools: the top band contained the most able, and the bottom band the least able pupils.

Like Nell Keddie, Stephen Ball found that academic groupings reflected social class backgrounds and contributed to pupil subcultures opposed to the ethos of the school. Ball noted how early keenness and conformity on entry to Beachside began to alter, as band identities began to affect both pupils and teachers in a stereotypical manner: the top band became seen as well-behaved and hard-working but the bottom band became seen as troublesome and with learning difficulties (see table on page 194). Teachers found the middle band most difficult to teach, which was evidenced by their behaviour and attendance. Because of teachers' expectations, different bands were taught in different ways and with different expectations – a finding similar to Nell Keddie's. However, Ball noted that although not all middle-band pupils became 'failures', there was a high correlation between banding, social class background and educational performance.

When Beachside Comprehensive abolished banding and moved to mixed-ability groups, many behavioural concerns previously associated with middle-band pupils ceased. The differentiation of pupils did not disappear, however. Teachers continued to distinguish between 'bright' and 'dull' pupils and to encourage the former and write off the latter. For Ball, the stratification of pupils produced through the bands was condensed and reproduced within each mixed-ability group.

Like Beachside Comprehensive, many comprehensive schools adopted unstreamed, mixed-ability groups in order to overcome the problems caused by streaming. By not streaming, schools would avoid creating and maintaining divisions between pupils on the basis of social class background. The move to mixed-ability teaching was, however, viewed with caution by some headteachers and parents, who believed that more able pupils would be held back in mixed-ability groups. This probably accounts for the present compromise of banding or setting arrangements.

Different bands, different worlds?		
	Top band	**Middle band**
Teachers' stereotype of each band	Academic potential Neat workers Bright, alert and enthusiastic Want to get on Rewarding	Not up to much Rowdy and lazy Cannot take part in discussions Not interested Unrewarding
Proportion of pupils from working-class homes	36%	78%
Proportion of teachers' time in class devoted to maintaining order	1.5%	12.5%
Average number of detentions, per pupil per year	0.4	3.8
Average number of absences per pupil in term 1	8.1	12.6
Average number of minutes spent on homework per pupil	47	16
Proportion of end-of-year subject tests graded at 50% or higher	58%	11%
Number of extra-curricular activities or club memberships, per class	43	10
Proportion of pupils who dislike school	13%	48%
Views held about each band by pupils in the other band	Brainy/Unfriendly/Stuck-up/Arrogant	Thick/Rough/Boring/Simple

Source: Adapted from Stephen J. Ball, *Beachside Comprehensive* (CUP, 1981)

Think about it

- Have you experienced any types of streaming or banding? What are your opinions on such systems of grouping pupils?
- What other stereotypes of pupils placed into bands might be added to the list provided for Beachside Comprehensive?

Patterns, differences and inequalities in educational achievement

Education and social class

Comprehensive education was introduced to improve educational opportunities, particularly for pupils from working-class backgrounds. Such pupils have received considerable attention from sociologists, who have drawn comparisons between middle-class advantages and working-class deprivation in relation to academic achievement.

Working-class deprivation, along with material disadvantages, seems to be linked to the following factors:

- Family size: working-class families tend to be larger, with less to spend on food per child, lack of space and quiet for homework, etc.
- Poor health: studies show that children in the lower working class (social classes 4 and 5) have poor diets, receive less medical attention (from doctors and dentists) and have higher absentee rates from school, which disrupts academic progress.
- Geographical location: children from poor backgrounds and inner city areas suffer **material deprivation**, which disadvantages them throughout the education system. The local environment tends to be important in relation to educational success and failure. Many sociologists consider that working-class areas may seem to be in conflict with the middle-class culture and values of school.

Generally, working-class children receive far less parental support and encouragement in the pursuit of long-term academic qualifications. This suggests immediate gratification, i.e. shorter term gains (leaving school early to start earning), rather than the deferred gratification, i.e. longer term rewards, seen in middle-class families where education and training are seen as an investment with advantages to be gained in the future.

Language patterns

Middle-class children tend to develop speaking and writing skills to a higher standard at an earlier age than working-class children. B. Bernstein's writings on language codes and social class draw distinctions between the **'elaborated' linguistic code** expressed in middle-class families and the limitations of the **'restricted' linguistic code** associated with working-class families.

- The elaborated code is context-free and has what Bernstein terms universalistic 'codes of meaning'. It is used when someone wants to offer full details of what he or she has to say, including explanations and details, so that those who share this code can also share the experience(s) being communicated.
- The restricted code is context-bound and is used when someone wants to say something to a group who already share his or her basic knowledge. To the outsider it may seem vague and difficult to understand: for example, when family or friends meet and talk to each other using minimal words, part sentences, gestures, slang and inarticulate grunts.

Harold Rosen, in *Language and Class* (1974), criticised Bernstein for implying that working-class, restricted codes were inferior. Rosen claims that so-called restricted code is strong in many ways and is not 'deformed or under-powered'. William Labov, in *The Logic of Non-Standard English* (1973), also criticised Bernstein, stating that there was nothing restricted about the speech patterns of the group he studied and that the group had the same ability for conceptual learning.

Bernstein, however, maintained that formal education is based on an elaborated code. Teachers use this code and reward pupils who use it. Therefore, children who are accustomed to using the elaborated code and the cultural assumptions inherent in it, namely middle-class pupils, find school a familiar and positive experience and are advantaged over working-class pupils.

Deficit or **cultural deprivation** is based on the lack of appropriate forms of language and knowledge needed to obtain success in the educational system. It has been used to explain the achievement limitations of working-class children and those from ethnic minority groups. Such a deficit theory of educational failure has been criticised for suggesting personal inadequacy rather than cultural differences.

The relationship between social class background and educational experience gained is illustrated in the articles and data below.

The gap is growing all the time

An indicator of poverty is the gap between rich and poor. In *Poverty and Inequality in the UK: The Effects on Children*, Vinod Kumar cites 1993 statistics to show that the real income of the bottom 10 per cent of the population declined by 14 per cent from 1979 to 1991. "This contrasts with the growth in the average real income of the general population of 36 per cent in the same period," he says. "The rise in the income of the top 20 per cent of the population in the same period was 40 per cent."

The increase in child poverty stems from the effects of rising unemployment, the increase in single-parent families, benefits falling behind average earnings and, in the words of Lisa Harker of the Child Poverty Action Group, "the Government's failure to provide affordable childcare services that would allow parents to go out to work".

The impact of poverty on children's educational performance is most clearly illustrated in GCSE results. While results overall have increased in the past eight years, children in the impoverished inner cities, with some notable exceptions, have been left behind.

As Professor Michael Barber pointed out in his 1993 report for the National Commission on Education, "Social class appears to be the single most important influence on educational achievement."

A study published in *Urban Trends* in 1992 looked at examination results between 1979–80 and 1989–90. It shows a widening gap between deprived and better-off areas. The proportion of pupils in deprived LEAs leaving school with no graded GCSEs was, in the main, more than 50 per cent above the national average.

Jesson and Gray's 1991 Nottinghamshire study further underlines the link between poverty and poor educational outcome, showing that half of pupils receiving free school meals had low GCSE scores (below 15 points when A=7pts, B=6pts, etc) as opposed to one-sixth of pupils who did not qualify for free school meals.

Source: The *Times Educational Supplement*, 31 January 1997

Social class linked to results

Research fuels debate over relationship of poverty and pupil performance. **Clare Dean** reports

Social class is one of the key factors that determine whether a child does well or badly at primary school, according to new research.

The study, by Ian McCallum, the former principal research officer at the London Research Centre, compares last month's key stage 2 league table results with the information on social class taken from the 1991 census. It shows that local education authorities with the lowest proportion of household heads in partly skilled or unskilled occupations are those with the best key stage 2 skills.

The research fuels the debate over the extent to which poverty and social background excuse poor school results.

Dr McCallum said his research should be studied carefully by politicians of all parties.

He said the census data provided important additional indicators of factors likely to be associated with the ways in which parents are able to provide their children with educational support. No account was taken in Dr McCallum's research of the percentage of children with English as a second language. But he claimed that just 20 per cent of differences in pupil performance in London LEAs could be attributed to other variables, which were independent of social class.

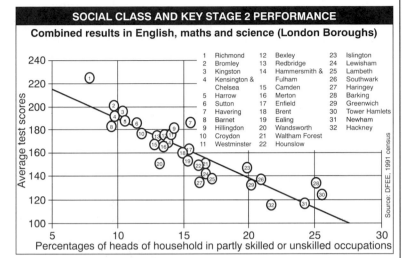

SOCIAL CLASS AND KEY STAGE 2 PERFORMANCE

Combined results in English, maths and science (London Boroughs)

1	Richmond	12	Bexley	23	Islington
2	Bromley	13	Redbridge	24	Lewisham
3	Kingston	14	Hammersmith &	25	Lambeth
4	Kensington &		Fulham	26	Southwark
	Chelsea	15	Camden	27	Haringey
5	Harrow	16	Merton	28	Barking
6	Sutton	17	Enfield	29	Greenwich
7	Havering	18	Brent	30	Tower Hamlets
8	Barnet	19	Ealing	31	Newham
9	Hillingdon	20	Wandsworth	32	Hackney
10	Croydon	21	Waltham Forest		
11	Westminster	22	Hounslow		

Source: DFEE, 1991 census

How to read the table

The scattergram shows primary school test scores for each of London's 32 education authorities. It shows what proportion of children in each borough come from unskilled or semi-skilled families. The line drawn through the middle plots the average test score achieved at each point on the horizontal scale.

The overall picture is of the boroughs with the highest proportion of unskilled families, ranged on the right, doing less well in the tests than those with the lowest proportion, on the left.

The graph, however, also shows variations between boroughs with similar occupational characteristics, lending support to politicians' claims and other research that social class is not the only important factor.

Source: The *Times Educational Supplement*, 18 April 1997

Highest qualification held by socio-economic group, Great Britain 1992–93

	Degree	Higher education	GCE A level	GCSE, grades A–C	GCSE, grades D–G	No qualifications
Professional (%)	61	16	7	7	1	3
Employers and managers (%)	19	19	16	21	7	15
Intermediate non-manual (%)	21	29	12	20	5	10
Junior non-manual (%)	3	6	13	35	16	24
Skilled manual and own account non-professional (%)	2	9	14	23	15	36
Semi-skilled manual and personal service (%)	1	4	7	21	12	51
Unskilled manual (%)	–	2	3	12	10	70
All persons (%)	12	13	12	22	10	28

Source: *Social Trends*, 1995

Culture, identity and education

In debates concerning the relationship between culture and education, ideas about cultural deprivation have been criticised for assuming that middle-class culture is superior to working-class culture, with the implication that working-class parents are to be blamed for their children's failure in the education system. Here we will look at other views on the relationship between culture and education.

'Cultural reproduction': education as social control

For Pierre Bourdieu and his French neo-Marxist colleagues, cultural reproduction is the process whereby the function of the education system is to reproduce the culture of the dominant classes. The dominant classes possess the power and wealth to impose their meanings and to define their culture as worthy or superior. In *Cultural Reproduction and Social Reproduction* (1973), Pierre Bourdieu uses the term **cultural capital** to refer to the power and wealth unevenly distributed between classes and largely accounting for class differences in educational attainment. This concept of 'cultural capital' extends the Marxist idea of economic capital; it provides power over other groups, and the use of that power to obtain high occupational positions. Pupils from higher class backgrounds, according to Bourdieu, are socialised into the dominant culture and therefore achieve more academic success than those from working-class backgrounds: middle-class subculture is closer to the dominant culture and its values. The language, values and models of success and failure within schools represent the dominant culture; the rewarding of pupils' ability to absorb this culture by, for example, certificates, validates and legitimates the existing social order.

Habitus, another concept used by Bourdieu, forms the basis of cultural meaning which, through socialisation, shapes thought, taste, appreciation, etc. The dominant class has the power to impose its own framework of meaning on to the lower classes (and on schools) as the only legitimate culture. So, for Bourdieu, habitus, established by historical and social conditions, is more fundamental than consciousness or language, because it imposes ways of seeing the world which support the interests of the dominant classes.

Symbolic violence is the means by which working-class pupils are ideologically persuaded to fit into their unrewarding roles. Through symbolic violence, the dominant class defines the school curriculum and what is to be regarded as an 'intelligent' or 'knowledgeable' activity. Although Bourdieu presents the education system as neutral, based on equality of opportunity and meritocratic principles, he considers that a major role of the system is the 'social function of elimination'. Through examination, failure and self elimination, the working class are more likely to fail at school and are less likely to go on to higher education.

Primary and secondary effects of stratification

For Raymond Boudon, also a French neo-Marxist, there are two key factors involved in educational inequality, or what he terms as a 'two-component process'.

- The **primary effects of socialisation** involve the subcultural processes between social classes as outlined by the work of Pierre Bourdieu, above.

- The **secondary effects of socialisation**, or **positional theory**, stems from a person's position in the class structure. Boudon states that even if there were no subcultural differences between classes, educational inequality would still exist because individuals start at different positions in the stratification system.

Boudon speaks of **cost benefit analysis**, referring to the encouragement given by upper- and middle-class parents to their children to opt for courses leading to professional qualifications. By contrast, working-class parents, who may not have sufficient money for their children to remain in the education system, are more likely to settle for skilled manual or clerical jobs for their children. According to Boudon, levels of ambition, like levels of parental encouragement, may reflect not only cultural values but the material circumstances in which people live.

Cultural and material factors associated with Boudon's 'primary effects of education' were studied by A.H. Halsey, A. Heath and J.M. Ridge in *Origins and Destinations* (1980), using data spanning the years from 1913 to 1972. They found that:

- **cultural factors**, or family climate, including attitudes, norms and values measured according to parents' education and their attitude towards education, were important in determining the secondary schools attended by children;
- **material circumstances**, based on family income, standard of housing, food, clothes, etc. were major factors in relation to school leaving age.

Although their study showed an increased tendency for children to improve on the formal educational attainment of their parents, they found little evidence to suggest an increasingly meritocratic society.

The data on which their study was based, however, did not take account of more recent changes in the education system, and failed to consider inequalities based on gender or ethnicity.

Education and race

Educational inequality

Various factors have become associated with the disadvantages experienced by ethnic minority groups:

- Racism based on skin colour: blacks and others experiencing racism tend to lose trust and confidence in schools, teachers and education and training in general. West Indian pupils, for example, tend to be seen by teachers as being less able and more disruptive than their white counterparts.
- Culture: it is difficult to know how cultural differences in the lifestyles of ethnic minority groups affect educational achievement. Asian pupils, for example, tend to keep a lower profile and accept the ethic of hard work, which may give them an *advantage* over other groups.
- Poverty: in terms of income and wealth, certain ethnic groups, for example Bangladeshis, tend to form part of a disadvantaged 'underclass' stratum.

Race and intelligence

Much sociological debate has arisen from studies in the USA in the 1960s linking race and intelligence. A. Jensen's famous article 'How Can We Boost IQ and Scholastic Achievement?' (1969) claimed a 12 to 15 point difference in general intelligence test scores between blacks and whites, thereby assuming blacks to be less intelligent. This led to:

- innate intelligence being seen as a cause of black underachievement;
- deficient culture, and even a pathological family life, being 'identified' amongst black groups.

Challengers to A. Jensen, disturbed by the implications of his case, argued that:

- black experience in the USA had been rooted in extreme poverty, which had developed over a long, downtrodden historical period;
- there were innumerable cases of discrimination, at all levels and in all social institutions, mainly by whites;
- blacks had traditionally received a substandard education, and a high percentage were labelled as 'mentally retarded';
- comparisons of black and white performances on IQ tests (constructed by white, middle-class academics) contained cultural and racial biases and could not be considered valid.

Sources of racial inequality

Teachers and schools in the UK have been seen as sources of racial inequality in terms of:

- negative stereotyping: whereby, for example, West Indian boys were diverted away from academic courses to 'ethnic pursuits' in sports and music;
- low teacher expectations: whereby teachers' 'hidden prejudices', taking a variety of forms, particularly in classroom interaction, affected pupils' academic achievement, as referred to by M. MacAnGhail in *Young, Gifted and Black* (1988);
- institutional racism: occurring when rules or organisations act in a racist manner. Such racism may be intentional or unintentional. The British educational system has been viewed as institutionally racist: C. Mullard, for example, has argued that there are relatively few black headteachers and a relatively high number of Afro-Caribbean children in lower streams and labelled as educationally subnormal, in a racially biased curriculum in a structurally racist British education system.

The Swann Report 1985

The Swann Report aimed to change attitudes and behaviour in order to promote a multicultural multi-racial education system. Its findings included the following:

- Racial discrimination and social deprivation were more important than IQ in the underachievement of West Indian pupils.
- Asian pupils of Indian origin seemed to do at least as well as white children, despite any deprivation factors. The following article, based on more recent data, confirms this pattern.
- Ethnic minority children, in comparison with white children, tended to come from homes which suffered more in terms of economic and social deprivation.
- Racism and racial prejudice did not have the same effects on all ethnic minority groups, and the attitudes of whites varied towards the different groups.

ACHIEVERS AND UNDER-ACHIEVERS

■ Indian pupils: Achieve better on average than any other ethnic group, including the white population, research in London suggests.

■ Pakistanis: In Bradford, Pakistani pupils achieved a better average examination score than Bangladeshi pupils but below Indians, whites and blacks, in that order.

■ Bangladeshis: Often less fluent in English than other ethnic minorities. In the London borough of Camden they were below blacks and well below whites but in the London borough of Tower Hamlets, which has almost a quarter of all Bangladeshi children aged 5–15 in England, Bangladeshis have higher average examination scores than both white and Caribbean pupils.

■ West Indian and African: Less successful than their Asian and white peers. Pupils of black African background often achieve relatively higher results than those of black Caribbean background. On average, Caribbean young men achieve significantly below their potential.

EXAM RESULTS AND EXCLUSIONS

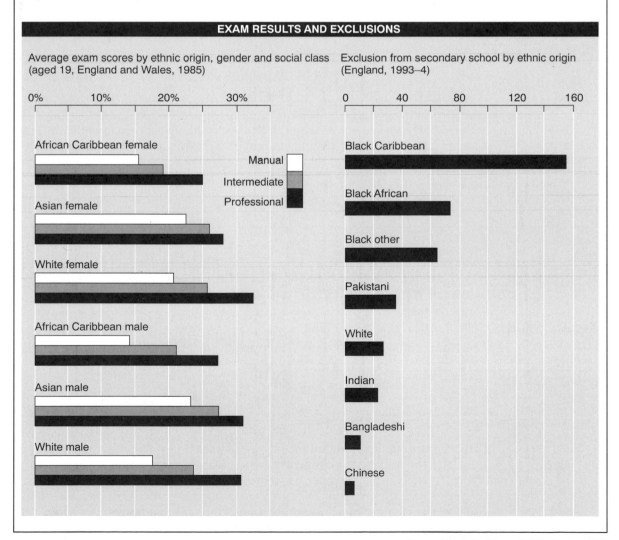

Average exam scores by ethnic origin, gender and social class (aged 19, England and Wales, 1985)

Exclusion from secondary school by ethnic origin (England, 1993–4)

Source: The *Daily Telegraph*, 6 September 1996

Ethnic minority children 'still suffer racism daily'

Stuart Millar

ETHNIC minority youngsters are still suffering blatant racial harassment on a daily basis, according to a report published by the charity ChildLine yesterday.

Despite years of progress in race relations the lives of many young people were being blighted by unrelenting bullying and abuse, it said.

Researchers analysed the case records of more than 1,600 callers to the charity's helpline who had experienced racism in the year to March 1995. Although they formed a tiny percentage of the 90,000 callers in the period, ChildLine insisted that the findings were significant.

Callers came from backgrounds including African, Afro-Caribbean, Asian, Jewish and Irish. Most described themselves as British.

In many cases, the perpetrators were other young people. One in four callers said they had suffered racist bullying. Many were afraid to discuss it with their families or teachers.

'They call me black bitch'

"I'm coloured. They call me nigger and black bitch. I just want to be respected." – *Mandy, aged 14*
"I am being bullied by girls at school because I'm slightly tanned. It's being going on for five years. My mum says ignore it, but I can't." – *Simone, 12*
"I'm half-caste. I've been bullied about it for 10 years. I feel like killing myself sometimes."
– *Jason, 16*
"Mum has left because dad was hitting her. Now he's hitting me and calling me 'half-breed' and 'nigger' because my mum is black." – *Lesley, 12*

A girl aged 13 said she had been attacked after school by three boys who poured petrol over her and called her names. She was now terrified of walking to school.

Ethnic minority children in predominantly white schools were most at risk of harassment, the report concludes. Around 75 per cent of those bullied described themselves either as the only one in their class or school or as one of very few similar children.

More than one in eight had experienced racism in the home – usually those who were in relationships their parents found unacceptable. Around half described their families as racist. Some had come to resent their parents. One caller told the counsellor: "I hate myself, I hate my father. He made me black."

Valerie Howarth, ChildLine's chief executive, said: "These are not isolated incidents. For many young people these are a way of life."

Herman Ouseley, chairman of the Commission for Racial Equality, which is supporting ChildLine's campaign, along with Mizz magazine and Crime Concern, said the findings reminded him of his experiences as a child in the 1950s. "For too many young people, growing up in Britain today means facing racially motivated violence and persistent racial discrimination."

Source: The *Guardian*, 23 July 1996

The Swann Report demonstrated evidence of racism and prejudice experienced by ethnic minority groups in education and training, but considered there was no simple, single explanation for unequal educational performance. Over a decade later, evidence of racism and prejudice is still being produced to show how Afro-Caribbean boys continue to perform badly in terms of academic achievement.

Think about it

Look back at the text about the self-fulfilling prophecy and the related article on page 192, before going on to read the articles on pages 203 and 204. Then consider the following issues.

- What sociological explanations might be put forward for the underachievement of Afro-Caribbean boys?
- Why do you think there has been such a marked improvement in the academic achievement of Bangladeshi pupils?
- How might it be made possible to carry out more accurate monitoring of ethnic minority pupils in schools with 'colour-blind' policies?

Black pupils 'held back by prejudice'

JUDITH JUDD
Education Editor

Black boys do badly at school because teachers believe they are disruptive and unacademic, leaders of the Commission for Racial Equality said yesterday.

Twenty years after an official report accused schools of stereotyping Afro-Caribbean males, nothing has changed, the commission said.

One explanation may be that teachers are frightened by the sheer size of the boys and find their physical presence threatening, said Herman Ouseley, the commission's chair.

A report to be published shortly by the Office for Standards in Education is expected to underline the poor performance of black Caribbean boys in exams. Recent research shows that Afro-Caribbean boys lag far behind other ethnic minority groups in maths and science. They even do worse than white working class boys, whose underachievement was highlighted earlier this year by school inspectors.

The commission has written to the Secretary of State for Education, demanding national ethnic monitoring of pupils' achievement.

Mr Ouseley said Afro-Caribbean boys found it much harder than whites to secure training or jobs. "They are hooked into a cycle of failure."

In London, 62 per cent of those aged between 16 and 24 are unemployed.

How the races fare

Birmingham analysis based on 1995 GCSE results.

Percentage of boys getting grades A to C in maths:

Afro-Caribbean	8.6
Black African	14.3
Indian	34.2
White	32.2

Percentage of boys getting grades A to C in science:

Afro-Caribbean	12.4
Black African	28.6
Indian	44.1
White	36.9

Mr Ouseley said: "We see a crisis developing in education with regard to children from particular ethnic backgrounds.

"A feature in all of this is that the black male is seen as a problem within schools. Undoubtedly teachers have said that and employers are saying it."

Philip Barnett, the commission's principal officer, said: "Teachers' attitudes and stereotyping have been on the agenda since the Swann report identified them in 1985."

A recent study by the Association of Metropolitan Authorities and the National Foundation for Educational Research which analysed the 1994 GCSE results in 14 authorities showed that most ethnic groups – black African, Indian, Pakistani, Bangladeshi and Chinese – make more progress at school than whites.

Only black Caribbean pupils fared worse, particularly in maths and science, where they scored an average one third of a grade below their white counterparts in maths and more than half a grade below them in science.

A Birmingham local authority study found that Afro-Caribbean boys did better than their white counterparts at primary school but fell behind at secondary school.

Around four times as many black Caribbeans as whites are excluded from school.

The commission says the Government should set national improvement targets for those ethnic groups that are failing and that a working party should be set up to investigate ways of reducing the number of Afro-Caribbean exclusions.

Local authorities should do more to support supplementary Saturday schools set up by Afro-Caribbean communities who are unhappy with their children's progress in mainstream schools, the commission believes. They should also do more to ensure that there are more well-qualified teachers from ethnic minorities.

Mr Ouseley said: "If we continue to overlook these problems, they are going to get worse and they will have dire consequences for our society.

"It is a waste of human resources. The state is picking up the tag. And there is a danger that these young people will be lured into unlawful activity."

Source: The *Independent*, 10 May 1996

Black sociologist attacks race 'doom and gloom'

by Nicholas Pyke

Commentators who blame racism for black under-achievement at school are harming pupils' chances of success, according to a prominent black sociologist.

Dr Heidi Mirza, head of sociology at South Bank University, told a conference of the Association of Teachers of Social Science last week that "doom and gloom" headlines about black education demoralise families and underplay much valuable progress.

She criticised last week's report from the Office for Standards in Education, which said that schools should introduce anti-racist and multi-cultural education policies. It said that black pupils, particularly boys, are continuing to fall behind.

"For the teachers and students going back to school this week, the timing of the report can only serve to undermine everyone's morale," she said.

Good jobs and structured careers are more important than multi-cultural programmes and are a key to the comparative success of young black women, said Dr Mirza.

The 1993 Labour Force Survey showed that 61 per cent of black women aged 16 to 59 had higher and other qualifications. Figures for 1995 showed 52 per cent of black women aged 16 to 24 in full-time education, compared with 28 per cent of white women in the same age range. The equivalent figures for men show that a greater proportion of black men (36 per cent) are in full-time education than their white counterparts (31 per cent).

"We found that girls were able to take advantage of education because of the opportunities that the labour market threw out for them," said Dr Mirza this

week. "Boys don't have those labour market opportunities."

Girls have been able to look to traditionally female jobs such as nursing which not only provide stable employment, but offer educational opportunities.

"People are quite rational. If there's nothing for them, they're not going to invest. It isn't that girls are genetically cleverer than boys."

"We always compare black girls to black boys. But very rarely do we contrast black girls with working-class white girls. The black girls do better. They just expect to work."

Dr Mirza said that the common picture of black failure to get involved with the education system was wrong. "I live among black people and education is all anybody talks about. I see so much personal investment."

Source: The *Times Educational Supplement*, 13 September 1996

Education and gender

Gender inequalities have attracted considerable attention from both within and outside the education system. Early studies, particularly from psychologists, concentrated on biological and psychological differences between the sexes. However, in more recent years, sociologists have tended to focus upon socialisation processes as a key factor in determining differences between girls and boys in the education system.

Biological and sociological factors

Some early accounts of gender inequalities assumed that biological and genetic differences provided a major explanation. Later research, however, has found no reliable evidence to establish such differences in relation to self esteem, intelligence or analytical abilities between men and women. There have even been suggestions, for example by H. Goldstein in *Gender Bias and Test Norms in Education Selection* (1987), that girls performed better than boys on the 11-plus examinations and have a higher innate ability.

<u>Socialisation processes</u>   These start at birth and take effect before children enter formal education. Ann Oakley, in *Sex, Gender and Society* (1975), stated that babies are treated differently at birth according to their sex despite the lack of evidence to support genetic differences other than those relating to the reproductive organs. Thus, sex is a biological concept based on reproductive biological characteristics, whilst gender is a social expectation reflecting the way people are expected to behave from birth.

<u>Sex role ideology</u>   The belief system which stems from the socialisation processes held responsible for gender identities is based on the social expectations and the characteristics of a particular sex: hence the ideologies of femininity and masculinity.

- Gender roles are the roles people play in accordance with social norms, values and expectations. M. Eichler, in *The Double Standard: A Feminist Critique of Feminist Social Science* (1980), states that such roles include girls being expected to be quiet, gentle, caring and non-aggressive, whereas boys are expected to be much the reverse.
- Reinforcement of gender roles occurs during childhood through early learning and imitation of behaviour observed by, and expected of, children.
- F. Norman et al., in *Just a Bunch of Girls* (1988), maintain that children's play and toys establish their attitudes and future aspirations, which reinforce women's traditional stereotypical role as wife/mother/home-carer. This tends to be further reinforced by comics, magazines, advertising, television 'soaps', etc.

<u>Schooling</u>   Schools, in their hidden curriculum (see page 185), serve as further reinforcement of gender roles. Indeed, feminists generally maintain that the development of the British education system has been characterised by sex role ideology. M. Scott, in *Teach Her a Lesson ...* (1980), suggests the following assumptions are influential in girls' education:

- The main priority in girls' lives (particularly those of low academic ability) is to marry, have children and care for the family.
- Paid work tends to be seen as a non-essential part of their adult lives.

- They will enter paid work only in limited areas of employment.
- The work carried out in employment is not that important to their family or society and their pay serves as 'pin money'.

It has been claimed that classroom interaction works to the detriment of girls, and that the curriculum is structured according to boys' interests. Women's contribution to history and literature is all but 'invisible' in the curriculum, and the language used in the classroom often also renders women and girls 'invisible': the 'man in the street', for example.

<u>School and subject choice</u>   The effects of sex role ideology are also shown in the choice of school subjects. Alison Kelly, in *The Missing Half: Girls and Science Education* (1981), examined reasons why science is seen as masculine, and considered factors such as the image of science subjects, the sex of the science teacher, the type of teaching and assessment carried out and the career prospects associated with science to be of importance. She demonstrated that girls do not study the sciences because they cannot associate them with something girls do: boys dominate science lessons, apparatus, questions and answers. As a result, girls tend to lack self confidence and to blame themselves for their failure.

Observational research by B.G. Licht and C.S. Dweck, in *Sex Differences in Achievement Orientations* (1983), produced similar findings. Girls explained their success as luck, convinced themselves that they were incapable of succeeding and avoided academic challenges. Boys explained away their failure in terms of external factors such as behaviour, which they could modify in order to succeed in academic challenges.

Criticisms of sex role ideology   Socialisation theories, it is claimed, fail to explain gender inequalities for the following reasons:

- Socialisation theories do not provide adequate explanations of the diversity of experience between girls of different social class backgrounds and ethnic groups.
- The ideology and its analysis seem to be based on the assumption that there is a single, unified ideology of femininity, rather than complex and sometimes contradictory processes.
- Sex role ideology theorists have assumed that each agent of socialisation transmits the same ideology, regardless of whether this agent is the family, the school, the peer-group or the media.

Gender, academic achievement and the world of work   These issues have attracted considerable attention, especially in relation to the effects of schooling on gender relationships in the world of work. An interesting summary of much of the research referred to above in relation to inequality between the sexes in schools is provided in the article below. It makes the suggestion that research can itself be of influence within the education system.

Creation of an equality ethos

GENDER

Gaby Weiner,
South Bank University

In the 1970s and 1980s, it was girls' underachievement rather than boys' to which educational researchers drew attention. So perhaps the recent panic about boys' underachievement is testimony to the success of researchers who highlighted unequal gender patterns earlier – and to teachers who drew on this work to persuade colleagues of the need for change.

Several studies proved influential: Alison Kelly's work on the masculine nature of school science and Leone Burton's challenge to the male-dominated mathematics curriculum in the 1980s both had a major impact on teachers and LEAs. Dale Spender's work on gender and language identified the ways in which aspects of the language used in schools (in speech and in textbooks) disadvantaged girls. John Pratt's study of sex-stereotyping in subject choices of secondary pupils underpinned Kenneth Baker's claim that a national curriculum would result in more girls studying physics.

Other research was equally influential: Katherine Clarricoates showed how the hidden or informal curriculum mitigated against the progress of girls in primary schools. Sue Lees described graphically what girls in secondary schools felt about the sexual harassment and verbal abuse they received from the boys. Research by Rehana Minhas, Avtar Brah and Heide Mirza illustrated and explained the discriminatory experiences of black schoolgirls and how they negotiated them. Rosemary Deem and Madeleine Ariiot drew attention to the academic benefits of single-sex education for girls, and Valerie Walkerdine and Miriam David explored the impact of different family forms and values on the schooling of girls (and boys).

The outcome of this and other educational research on gender has been that the gap between girls' and boys' performance has closed dramatically for most subjects at GCSE, though less so post-16. Also, according to a recent Equal Opportunities Commission study, the ethos of schools has become more gender-fair and comfortable for both sexes. Quite an achievement for research, I would think.

Source: The *Times Educational Supplement*, 28 June 1996

During the last 20 years, there has been a dramatic increase in the percentage of pupils leaving school with qualifications. Between 1970 and 1990, the proportion of boys with at least one GCSE or its equivalent (grades A to C) rose from 40 per cent to 60 per cent, while for girls it rose to an even higher 70 per cent.

Female students on full-time degree courses increased in all subjects in the decade up to 1994, to a total of nearly 50 per cent, although they were unevenly distributed, as shown by the table below.

Enrolments in Higher Education by subject and gender, 1993/4					
	Full time		Part time		All enrolments (000s)
Higher education	Males (000s)	Females (000s)	Males (000s)	Females (000s)	
Combined and general	61	74	8	11	154
Languages/humanities	66	96	10	14	186
Business and finance	77	76	67	64	284
Engineering and technology	124	23	70	8	225
Sciences	145	121	40	111	417
Education	21	58	15	35	129
Social sciences	57	66	15	21	159
All enrolments	551	514	282	319	1,664

Source: *Social Trends*, 1996

However, despite the marked increases in females gaining academic qualifications throughout the education system, the world of work does not reflect such improved achievement.

In 1995, the number of females in the UK workforce totalled 12.12 million, an increase of 34 per cent since 1975 according to figures published by the Department for Education and Employment. However, men still tend to dominate the professional occupations, as illustrated in the table below.

Men and women in professional occupations, 1990		
	Males (%)	Females (%)
Engineers	99.5	0.5
Solicitors	78.6	21.4
Surveyors	94.3	5.7
Barristers	78.8	21.2
Surgeons	96.8	3.2
General practitioners	77.6	22.4
Architects	92.2	7.8
Dentists	76.8	23.2

Source: Adapted from M. Denscombe, *Sociology Update* (Olympus Books, 1991)

Even though within the professions overall females now comprise about half of those newly *recruited*, only a small percentage manage to reach the most senior positions. This is demonstrated by the following data.

Percentage of females in top positions and one tier below, 1991							
Judiciary (%)		Civil Service (%)		Trade Unions (%)		Companies (%)	
House of Lords' judges	0.0	Permanent secretaries	2.9	General secretaries	2.7	Chief executives	0.5
All judges	4.0	Under-secretary and above	6.6	National Executive	20.0	Board members	0.5

Source: Adapted from M. Denscombe, *Sociology Update* (Olympus Books, 1993)

Women are, however, making breakthroughs in some areas of employment: cracks are appearing in the so-called 'glass ceiling'. According to official statistics, there are now more female than male solicitors under the age of 30. The first female bomber pilot, Flight Lieutenant Jo Salter, became 'combat ready' in 1995. That same year saw the appointment in Lancashire of Pauline Clare as the first female Chief Constable; in view of the alleged sexism within the police force this may be seen as a significant breakthrough.

We shall take a more detailed look at gender and work in Unit 5 (see especially pages 240–3).

Reasons for gender differences: the political economy perspective

The **political economy perspective** attempts to explain why gender differences exist. It does not merely describe the processes involved in the reproduction of such inequalities; more importantly, it seeks out the origins and reasons for gender differences. The benefits of this approach may be summarised in terms of its ability to view critically:

- the development of state education policies in relation to social class, race and gender issues;
- the school and other educational institutions and their products in relation to the structure of the workforce and domestic life;
- the powerful forces and structures outside the school.

Elements of this viewpoint may be seen in the discussion of the hidden curriculum (see page 185) or in the Marxist concerns of Pierre Bourdieu (see page 198). According to the neo-Marxist writer L. Althusser, the political economy is served by education in the form of an **ideological state apparatus** (ISA), which reproduces and reinforces inequality and gender inequality along with other supportive ISAs such as the family, religion and the mass media. Feminist versions of this viewpoint point to the sex role ideology (see page 205) in capitalist social organisation: they, like the patriarchy theorists, assume that capitalism has 'needs' reliant upon the sexual division of labour in the household, in education, in the workforce and right across the political economy.

Revision and practice tasks

Data response question

Reread the study skills section relating to data response questions on pages 9–12. Then study the example below and the notes which follow on the first three sub-questions.

ITEM A

The role of the teacher as an agent of social control is extremely important in assessing the role of the hidden curriculum in maintaining gender inequality. Obviously, teachers' attitudes towards the role of education for women and men will influence their relationship with students. Spender found that in mixed classrooms, boys received two-thirds of the teacher time, benefiting from the teacher's attention and distracting from the amount of time spent with the girls . . .

Just as the attitudes of teachers can play a role in reinforcing gender inequalities through the hidden curriculum so can the attitudes and behaviour of the students. Jones highlights the high level of sexual violence initiated by boys in mixed schools against females, both students and teachers. Jones argues that school is a system for legitimating male violence against women and for making this violence seem part of everyday life.

(*Feminist Thinking on Education*,
Kate Reynolds (Social Studies Review Vol 6, No. 4))

ITEM B
Schools can make a difference
Although most people remain in the class they were born in, about one in three working-class children move up the social scale and about the same proportion of middle and lower-middle move down. Individual intelligence is one reason that partly explains upward movement, and going to a good school is another. But what is a good school?

Michael Rutter's study *Fifteen Thousand Hours* examined this problem. Rutter and his team looked at only twelve Inner London secondary schools so it is important not to over-generalise their findings. Rutter's research is summarised below:

Factors measured	Teacher's qualities linked with success in these four areas

Attendance
Academic achievement
Behaviour in school
Rate of delinquency outside school
	Teachers who are:
	    Punctual
	    Well organised
	    Patient
	    Encouraging
	    Inspiring
	    Willing to share extra-curricular activities
	        with pupils
	    Consistent

(*Sociology in Practice*,
M. O'Donnell and J. Garrod (Nelson))

ITEM C
The Self-fulfilling Prophecy
When pupils come into a school, teachers make judgements on their ability, based on many different things. These labels are, for example, 'bright', 'able', 'thick', 'less able', 'practical', 'academic', etc. However, these labels are not neutral, nor do they describe the real possibilities of students, but are based on commonsense knowledge of what type of student is 'good' and which 'bad'. Thus, it has been shown that teachers have stereotypes linked to class ('from broken homes'), gender ('she's just a girl'), race ('West Indians are noisy') and even physical attractiveness ('snotty-nosed kid'). Teachers then act towards students on the basis of such stereotypes – for example, those students who are labelled 'bright' are given more time to answer questions than those who are seen as unlikely to know the answer anyway.

(Adapted from *Sociology: A Conceptual Approach*,
Tony Lawson (Checkmate))

(a) Referring to **ITEM A,** state how schools help to 'legitimise male violence'.

(1 mark)

(b) How, according to **ITEM B**, can upward social mobility be explained?   **(1 mark)**

(c) Note **three** criticisms of the concept of 'self-fulfilling' prophecy as described in **ITEM C.**   **(3 marks)**

(d) Explain how the 'hidden curriculum' affects female pupils.   **(10 marks)**

(e) To what extent might exclusive focus upon schools and schooling contribute to an explanation of differential social class attainment?   **(10 marks)**

Total: 25 marks

Advice on answering the data response question

- Items A, B and C in the above question are relatively brief. Note their sources and, in the case of Items B and C, their titles: these provide useful keys for the response.
- When reference is made to an item as, for example, in questions (a) and (b), the information may be given in the stimulus material.
  (a) The hidden curriculum and the attitudes of teachers and students both serve to legitimate male violence as it is seen as a part of everyday life.

(b) Individual intelligence (or each person's innate ability) and going to 'a good school' (or attending a well-organised school which has a sound, purposeful ethos).

A full sentence reworded from the stimulus material, as in (a), or the identification of the two factors, as in (b), is all that is needed. Any further writing (such as the parts in brackets in the answer to (b) above!) will not gain additional marks, and will take up valuable time.

- Timing is extremely important. The total time allocation for the question is one hour, and there is a total of 25 marks. Question (a) (1 mark) should therefore require no more than two minutes; question (c) requires about two minutes for *each* criticism, making a total of six minutes.
- Criticisms identified for question (c) should include:
  1. Doubts about the validity of IQ tests.
  2. Doubts about the use of statistics rather than observation, in the research.
  3. The ethical issues involved in conducting 'experiments' in this area.

Task 1

Now write a response for sub-questions (d) and (e) above.

Task 2: structured question

Male graduates tended to find jobs in industry and commerce whereas female ones were much more likely to find jobs in public service or education. This difference is, however, largely explained by the different subjects that were studied by men and women.

The type of work which graduates found was also different. Men were predominant in scientific, engineering, financial and legal work and in management services. Women outnumbered men in personnel, medical and social jobs, and in teaching and lecturing. (. . .) The differences are largely explained by the different subjects studied by men and women.

Statistical Bulletin on Women in Post-Compulsory Education, DFE, Dec. 1993

(a) Briefly outline the relationship between gender and employment among graduates. (4)
(b) Explain, with examples, how the different subjects studied by males and females can affect the jobs which they find. (4)
(c) Why are sociologists interested in the subjects studied by males and females? (7)
(d) Evaluate the view that recent changes in educational policy may help to reduce gender differences in education and employment. (10)

(Total: 25 marks)

Source: *Interboard Specimen Examination Papers, Summer 1996*

Essay questions

1. Evaluate the extent to which the 'hidden curriculum' disadvantages girls.
2. Critically assess whether class differences in educational achievement may be adequately explained by using the concept of 'cultural capital'.
3. Assess the view that what happens to children inside school is more important than what happens outside in determining their level of educational achievement.
4. What have sociologists learnt from studies of interaction in schools and classrooms?
5. Assess the view that teacher expectations play a major role in creating educational inequalities.
6. Examine the relationship between educational achievement and social mobility in modern society.
7. 'Sociological discussions of education have been too much preoccupied with class differences.' Explain and discuss.

8. How far can the educational system ensure equality of opportunity between the sexes?
9. How important is the study of what happens inside classrooms for an understanding of the educational experience of either girls or pupils from ethnic minorities?
10. Critically evaluate the view that recent changes in education have been designed to better fit school leavers to the needs of the economy.

Ideas for coursework and personal studies

1. A study of changes in state policies in relation to education and training in the 1980s and 1990s, and how these have influenced the curriculum and/or structural organisation of two contrasting educational institutions.
2. Research into how educational statistics are used, for example, to collate school league tables, and whether/how this influences the schools' image within a geographical locality.
3. A consideration of changes in children's reading schemes in terms of gender/race/class representation, making use of content analysis, questionnaires and/or interviews.
4. A study of the hidden curriculum and its influence in an educational institution, based on secondary sources and observation techniques.
5. A survey of parental interest in education with reference to attendance at parents' evenings, homework checking, purchasing of equipment and other factors which may relate to social class or ethnic minority backgrounds.

Selected reading list

Beachside Comprehensive: A Case Study of Secondary Schooling, Stephen J. Ball (Cambridge University Press, 1981)

Fifteen Thousand Hours: Secondary Schools and the Effects on Children, Michael Rutter et al. (Open Books, 1979)

The Home and the School, J.W.B. Douglas (MacGibbon and Kee, 1964)

Invisible Women: The Schooling Scandal, Dale Spender (Women's Press, 1983)

Learning to Labour, Paul Willis (Saxon House, 1977)

Pygmalion in the Classroom, Robert Rosenthal and Leonara Jacobson (Holt, Rinehart and Winston, Inc, 1968)

Schooling in Capitalist America, Samuel Bowles and Herbert Gintis (Routledge & Kegan Paul, 1976)

Social Relations in the Secondary School, David Hargreaves (Routledge & Kegan Paul, 1967)

Young, Gifted and Black, M. MacAnGhail (Open University Press, 1988)

5 Work and organisations; non-work and leisure

"I'm afraid he still hasn't quite mastered the new technology."

Introduction

This unit aims to cover the following key aspects of the sociology of work:

- What constitutes work? How do we define work, and what forms does it take? What forms of work are likely in the future?
- What occupational trends can be identified? What changes are there in the labour market and production? How do these trends relate to issues of gender, ethnicity, age and class?
- What is the location of work within the wider social structure and what is its positive or negative impact on people's experience?
- What is meant by 'non-work'? What are the implications of unemployment for social groups and individuals? What is leisure and how do leisure and work relate to each other?
- How can we attempt to understand the form and development of organisations in the UK and their economic and social impact?

Definitions and forms of work

'Work' is not easy to define. Can the form of work be defined, for example by its **location**: 'real' work is that which takes place outside the home, whilst domestic labour – i.e. washing and ironing – may be considered not to be 'real work'? Generally, definitions of work tend to focus on **paid work** or **wage labour**, but there is no obvious or clear-cut definition; indeed a range of definitions are used in sociology and these definitions are not consistent. Keith Grint, in his 1991 study, *The Sociology of Work*, points out that work is socially defined; in other words, any definition will be related to a particular society at a specific point in time.

Reasons for working

One way to try to understand what is meant by 'work' is to look at people's reasons for working. Sociology identifies **intrinsic** and **extrinsic** reasons; the latter applies to a person working in order to be paid, earning a wage or a salary, while intrinsic reasons include not merely the desire to earn money but rather (or as well as) the interest or enjoyment derived from work. In both instances work will have a social aspect. In the intrinsic situation this may be the primary reason for undertaking the work in the first place.

Reasons for working	
Necessity	to earn a living
Social	to have contact with others
Paternal	to assist others
Escape	to get away from, for example, restrictive domestic circumstances
Identity	giving a person an identifiable role
Status	giving a person a relative position in an occupational structure

M. Argyle, in *The Social Psychology of Work* (1974), lists the main motives for working as:

- economic;
- social;
- satisfaction.

Another study of almost 4000 15–19-year-olds in Ipswich in 1984 found that six out of ten young people would prefer to work rather than be on benefit, even if the money were the same. This outcome implies that the activity of work itself possesses a quality which cannot be assessed only in terms of money. This attitude was expressed by between two-thirds and three-quarters of employees questioned for a British Social Attitudes Survey in 1994, as the table opposite shows.

Employees' views on work commitment: by age, 1994						
	18–24 (%)	25–34 (%)	35–44 (%)	45–54 (%)	55–59 (%)	All aged 16 and over (%)
Would still work if no financial need	76	73	70	60	64	69
Job is much more than just earning a living	54	61	67	64	58	62
Do the best I can, even if it sometimes interferes with my life	30	45	49	53	49	46

Source: *British Social Attitudes Survey, Social & Community Planning Research. Social Trends,* 1996

The organisation of work as we understand it in our society does not necessarily apply to other cultures. Sahlins, who looked at hunter-gatherer societies, showed in his study *Stone Age Economics* (1972) that the wish to fill time with productive activities such as work is a distinctly Western idea. Among the hunter-gatherers, when the food has been gathered no 'work' is undertaken until it is necessary to eat again.

The place of work within the economy

There are four types of economy in which work takes place:

- The **formal economy** is recognised by the government; it is based on paid employment and is subject to regulation, taxation and rigorous statistical recording by officials.
- The **informal economy**, often known as the 'black economy', is not officially recorded. For example, in the construction industry in the 1950s and 1960s many workers in Britain had no legal status: they received cash-in-hand, did not pay tax and were not entitled to health service facilities as they paid no national insurance. A more common contemporary example might be a motor mechanic using his or her skills to repair cars from home, at weekends, and not declaring the earnings.
- The **household** or **domestic economy** involves work undertaken within households offering services to family or household members, such as washing dishes or caring for young children. Most of this form of work, in the majority of households, will be undertaken by women. A number of feminist writers refer to it as domestic labour. For example, Ann Oakley's book *The Sociology of Housework* (1974) looks at this aspect of the household activity. Home-based DIY work, a major growth industry, can also be located within the household economy.
- The **communal economy** includes unpaid activity or work undertaken outside the household and outside the employed workforce. In the early 1980s Margaret Thatcher, as Prime Minister, sought to engage more women (particularly middle-class women) in voluntarism, working in an unpaid capacity for charitable organisations such as Cancer Relief or Christian Aid.

Types of employment

The formal economy of the UK is divided into three key sectors. Within each sector are the forms of work (occupation roles, jobs) that people undertake. The three key sectors are:

- the **primary (extractive) sector**, where the jobs largely relate to the extraction of natural products from the land or sea. Examples include deep-sea trawling, coalmining, quarrying, North Sea Oil production;
- the **secondary (manufacturing) sector**, where a raw material such as metal or clay is shaped or constructed in order to produce a particular manufactured product. Examples include the manufacture of motor cars, cups and saucers, electric kettles;
- the **tertiary (services) sector**, where products and services are provided to the public. Examples include insurance, banking, retailing, restaurants, garages, supermarkets.

Table A, below, gives the percentage of people employed in a range of industries and shows the composition of employment by gender. Table B shows the percentages of males and females employed in particular types of jobs.

Table A:
People in employment:
by gender and industry,
Spring 1995

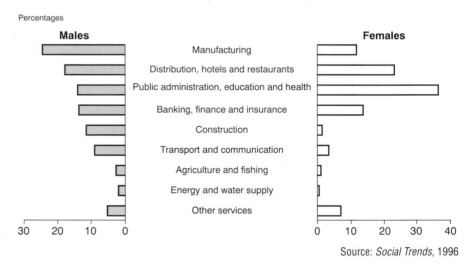

Source: *Social Trends*, 1996

Table B:
Employees: by gender
and occupation, Spring
1995

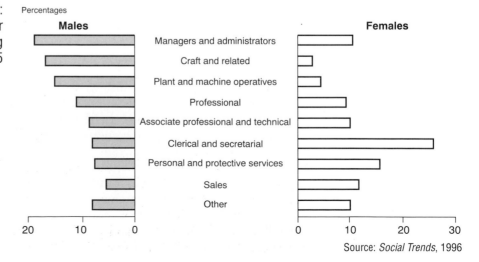

Source: *Social Trends*, 1996

The Central Statistical Office categorises employment into the following occupational groups:

- employers and managers;
- professional;
- intermediate non-manual;
- junior non-manual;
- manual (foreman, supervisor and skilled and own-account (self employed));
- personal service and semi-skilled manual;
- unskilled.

Think about it

Where would you place the following jobs into the categories of employment listed by the Central Statistical Office?

- a building site labourer
- a coal mine manager
- the owner of a small company
- the Prime Minister
- a doctor
- the chairperson of a professional football team
- a supervisor in Marks and Spencer's food hall
- a plumber
- a waitress
- a bar worker

- the manager of a restaurant
- a machine operator with little training
- a nurse
- a bus driver
- the owner of a large company
- a newsagent
- an insurance salesperson
- a self-employed accountant
- a self-employed decorator

Dual/ segregated labour markets

Several economists and sociologists argue that there are at least two labour markets in the UK. The division in the **dual labour market** lies between:

- employment in the **primary labour market,** which provides security, high wages, career prospects and job enhancement. Senior company executives or computer software development workers, and employees with a high level of technological expertise can be found here; and
- employment in the **secondary** (or **segmented**) **labour market,** which is insecure, has low wages and few promotional opportunities. Clerical jobs, or jobs in semi-skilled or unskilled work in electronics plants with hand-assembly tasks are typically found here.

Women and ethnic minorities tend to form a higher proportion of the secondary labour market than they do of the primary market; they consequently have less secure work, poorer employment conditions and lower wages, on the whole, than their male, or white, counterparts.

The effects of the different forms of work

Any work has an effect on a whole range of life experiences. Access to income from paid work (employment), for example, can affect the opportunity for house purchase, credit, personal wealth and also health and length of life. Work also can be linked to the process of **socialisation** (see Unit 3, pages 119 and 136, and Unit 4, pages 161–2 and 198–9), and affects the role or identity of the worker, their expectations and their social status. Indeed, as we saw in Unit 2, a person's social class is primarily based on their occupation, particularly on the separation of manual from non-manual work (see page 80), according to the Registrar General's classification.

There is a range of social and economic consequences that may derive from the form of work which an individual undertakes. These include:

- **status:** senior civil servants, for example, enjoy a higher status than clerical assistants;
- **finance:** a director of a large company will be better off financially than a farm labourer, for example;
- **security:** a teacher or lecturer on a permanent employment contract will have greater security than a temporary secretary, for example;
- **career opportunities:** a newly appointed hospital doctor will have more such opportunities than a nursing auxiliary.

The criteria used to distinguish between **non-manual** and **manual** workers usually include:

- conditions of work;
- employment security;
- levels of pay.

However, changes in the employment structure have meant that some elements of the non-manual sector are now more vulnerable to insecurity of employment, part-time working and poorer relative pay. This process of **occupational change** was noted as long ago as the 1950s; for example by David Lockwood in his study of clerical workers, *The Blackcoated Worker* (1958). During the 1980s and 1990s, employment conditions and circumstances in the manufacturing and primary sectors have deteriorated, as they have in the service (tertiary) sector in spite of a substantial growth in the total numbers of workers employed in that sector.

Occupational patterns: work and stratification

As we saw in tables A and B on page 216, there are clear differences between men and women in terms of the industries in which they are employed and the role they play at work. About 28 per cent of males are employed in manufacturing, compared with only 12 per cent of females; public administration, education and health, however, employ 37 per cent of women compared with under 20 per cent of men. About 20 per cent of male employees are managers and administrators, compared to 12 per cent of females, while clerical and secretarial employees include 27 per cent of females and 8 per cent of males.

The table on page 219 shows that, in spring 1995, 62 per cent of males and 54 per cent of females worked under 20 hours per week, whilst 33 per cent of males and 56 per cent of females in full-time employment worked 35–40 hours, with 13 per cent of males and 4 per cent of females working over 60 hours per week.

Total usual hours worked by people in full-time and part-time employment: by gender, Spring 1995						
	Males		Females		All persons	
	Full time (%)	Part time (%)	Full time (%)	Part time (%)	Full time (%)	Part time (%)
Under 20	–	62	–	54	–	55
20–24	–	17	1	23	–	22
25–30	1	14	3	17	2	16
31–34	1	2	3	4	2	3
35–40	33	1	56	2	41	3
41–44	15	–	14	–	14	–
45–48	16	–	10	–	14	–
49–59	20	–	8	–	16	–
60 and over	13	–	4	–	10	–
All persons (=100%) (thousands)	13,136	1,082	6,391	5,115	19,527	6,196

Source: Labour Force Survey, Central Statistical Office, in *Social Trends*, 1996

The graph below indicates that the average number of full-time hours worked in a week by both male and female workers was higher in the UK than in the other 11 European Union countries. Part-time workers, however, worked fewer average hours in the UK than elsewhere: only Denmark (for men) and Spain (for women) showed lower average hours worked.

Average hours usually worked per week: by gender, EC comparison, 1994

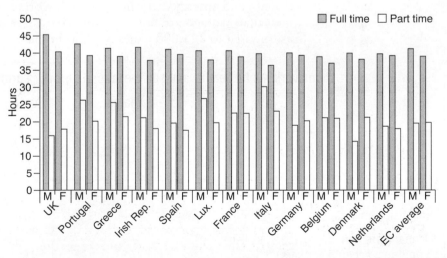

Source: Eurostat

Among part-time and full-time workers an increasing trend in Britain during and since the 1980s has been a growth of temporary employment. In spring 1995, 720,000 males and 827,000 females were employed in temporary jobs. The chart on page 220 indicates the reasons for this form of employment.

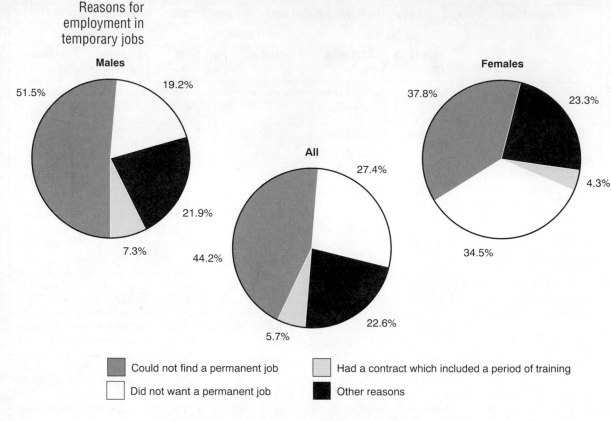

Reasons for employment in temporary jobs

Males
51.5% 19.2% 21.9% 7.3%

All
27.4% 22.6% 5.7% 44.2%

Females
37.8% 23.3% 4.3% 34.5%

■ Could not find a permanent job □ Had a contract which included a period of training
□ Did not want a permanent job ■ Other reasons

The table below deals specifically with work undertaken from the worker's home. It indicates that among employers and managers, professionals and intermediate non-manual workers a higher proportion of men than women are homeworkers. However, overall, 473,000 females as opposed to 225,000 males work at home.

Homeworking: by gender and socio-economic group, Spring 1995			
	Males (%)	Females (%)	All persons (%)
Employers and managers	22	14	16
Professional	20	3	8
Intermediate non-manual	25	17	20
Junior non-manual	–	18	12
Manual (foremen, supervisors, skilled and own account workers)	28	41	37
Personal service and semi-skilled manual	–	6	5
Unskilled	–	–	–
All homeworkers (=100%) (thousands)	225	473	697

Source: *Social Trends*, 1996

Survey: *The stresses of putting in longer hours at work*

Hidden costs

WENDY ROBERTSON

BRITONS who are working more hours than their counterparts in any other European country are damaging their health and family life, according to a new survey.

Experts fear a culture of long hours is becoming an industrial epidemic, which could undermine the economic recovery.

The survey by the recruitment and communications organisation, Austin Knight, discloses that two-thirds of workers do more than a 40-hour week, while 25 per cent put in more than 50 hours.

Three out of four people say working long hours affects them physically, causing them to take time off work, and costs industry millions of pounds. The Health and Safety Executive has estimated that 20 per cent of all days lost through sickness last year were due to occupational stress – at a cost of £2 billion.

Dr Eamon Shanley, a senior lecturer in Nursing Studies at Glasgow University, has a particular interest in occupational stress. He said the practice of wringing longer hours out of staff was a false economy.

"Stress at work is caused by the feeling of not being in control and not feeling valued, and the initial response is to put in a lot more hours. Then people become more tired, then less efficient and so make more mistakes.

"They keep going until something happens such as feelings of dread when they have to go to work one day and they go to see their doctor."

Working around the clock

The number of people in thousands who worked more than 48 hours a week in 1984 and 1994.

Area	1984	1994	Increase
North/North west	483	600	24%
Yorks/Humberside	262	357	36%
West/East Midlands	542	685	26%
South West	258	327	27%
East Anglia	121	177	46%
South East	1,195	1,450	21%
Wales	97	167	72%
Scotland	288	348	21%

The cost in terms of relationships cannot be under-estimated, said Dr Shanley. The tendency to become cynical, blame others and distance oneself from the people around is damaging.

"If your work requires you to deal with a lot of people all day – as does nursing or journalism – you go home after an extremely long day and you don't want to see or talk to anybody, which can be detrimental to relationships."

To overcome work-related stress, Dr Shanley suggested people try to manage their time more effectively, distract themselves through leisure activities like sports, keep everything in perspective and not let "molehills become mountains".

A conference in Edinburgh next month will examine the changes to the law which can be made to ease the pressures of work on family life. The forum is being organised jointly by BT and Children in Scotland.

"Lengthy working hours impact so much on children and families because the balance between home life and work life is lost," said Celia Carson, early years development officer at Children in Scotland. "We have to try to introduce family-friendly policies such as special leave for when children fall sick and for responsibilities such as taking a child to medical appointments."

Other priorities would be paternity leave and the equivalent of maternity leave for couples who adopt children, job-sharing, flexitime and properly paid part-time work.

Of those questioned in the survey, a minority saw positive aspects to working long hours in terms of business performance, including improved competitive edge and an enhanced image among customers as having the ability to deliver.

Others, such as Donald Hardie, director of the Scottish division of the Institute of Directors, disputed the survey's findings. "It is ridiculous to say we work more hours. We have a more successful economy and the number of hours worked depends on the individual's ambition to climb the ladder or to make more money.

"I don't think it [the survey] is worth the paper it's written on. So what if we work more hours?"

Source: The *Scotsman*, 27 January 1996

Think about it

- Identify those points in the article which demonstrate the social consequences of long hours and stress at work. List them under the headings: Family, Health, Community. Under each heading, add at least one idea or example that you have researched yourself.

Changes in and at work

A number of significant changes have had a marked impact on the work people do, its availability and form. Key factors are outlined below.

The move to non-manual work

In the early part of the twentieth century, 20 per cent of the working population of the UK were non-manual workers; today the figure is over 50 per cent. Major reasons for this change include the following:

- Many more women than men have taken up non-manual employment, so that two out of every three female workers are in non-manual work, compared with less than half of men. This has been accompanied by an increase in the numbers of women working (see page 223).
- The biggest growth in employment has been of professional and technical staff which has more than doubled since the mid-1960s.

Since the mid-1960s there has been a 50 per cent reduction in the number of jobs in agriculture, and a loss of more than 3 million jobs in manufacturing. In the service industries over the same time period more than 3 million jobs (many part-time) have been created. Manufacturing – which in 1971 held 41 per cent of all male jobs – by 1994 accounted for only 28 per cent, whilst services – which collectively had 43 per cent of all jobs in 1971 – had increased to 63 per cent in 1994. Female employment in manufacturing, which was at 29 per cent in 1971, fell to 12 per cent in 1994; whilst in the service sector it increased from 68 per cent in 1971 to 85 per cent in 1994. Since 1980, however, the increase in service jobs has slowed down and in many regions of the UK there is currently little or no increase.

The growth of the service sector

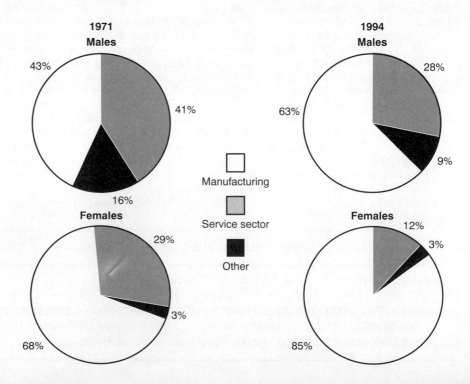

The move to part-time employment

In 1984, male employment included 13,240,000 full-time and 570,000 part-time jobs; in 1994, the figures were 12,875,000 full-time and 998,000 part-time positions. For women, there was a substantial increase in both full- and part-time employment: from 5,422,000 to 6,131,000 full-time jobs and from 4,342,000 to 5,252,000 part-time jobs. In proportionate terms, over the ten-year period, part-time work for both males and females increased significantly.

The change in the numbers of people in both full-time and part-time work in the United Kingdom is shown in the graph below. Since 1987 part-time working has become more common for both men and women. Between 1987 and 1995 the number of women in part-time employment increased by 12 per cent to 5.2 million; among men the number increased by more than half over the same period, but only to 1.2 million. However, women's increased economic activity is not just confined to part-time work.

Full-time and part-time[1] employment[2] by gender

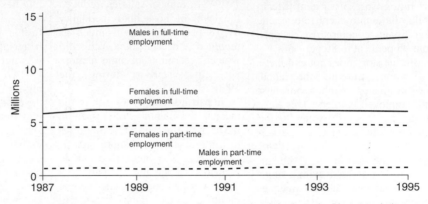

1 Full/part time is based on respondents' self-assessment. It excludes those who did not state whether they were working full or part time
2 In Spring each year. Includes employees, self-employed, those on government training schemes and unpaid family workers

Source: *Social Trends*, 1996

Hours worked in employment

As the figures in the graph on page 219 indicate, males in full-time employment in the UK work longer hours, on average, than their counterparts in other European countries; the same does not apply to females, but this might be partially explained by the high number of women working part-time in the UK.

More women in the labour force

In 1971 there were 8,224,000 women employees in the UK; by 1994 this had increased to 10,363,000. Over the same period, the number of males in employment declined from 13,425,000 to 10,539,000.

Think about it

The following article describes the impact of women's working (and their pay) on families and households, and raises a number of interesting issues.
- What is the impact of female earnings on income inequality?
- Why do you think there has been an increase in the number of married or cohabiting women working?
- What could explain the lower levels of non-work amongst the poorer as opposed to the richer households?
- What trends does the article illustrate over time, in women's employment?

Working women nail the pin-money myth

Briefing

Richard Thomas

Women now make up half of the workforce, up from a third in 1950, and will soon overtake men. While male employment rates have been declining, the proportion of women in paid work has shot up. In the late 1970s, some 60 per cent of women aged 24 to 55 had a job. By 1991 this figure was 75 per cent. Meanwhile, the employment rate among their male counterparts dropped from 95 per cent to 86 per cent.

But the story does not end there. The women entering the labour force in greatest numbers are those with employed partners. This trend has driven a wedge between "work-rich" households with two earners and "work-poor" families with none. At the start of the 1980s, the number of households with a single male breadwinner almost matched those with two earners. By the close of the decade, the dual-income families outnumbered those with a traditional set-up by three to one.

On the face of it, the conclusions seem clear: the increase in employment of women is damaging male job prospects, and in the process exacerbating the gap between rich and poor households.

But new research challenges this conventional wisdom. Susan Harkness and colleagues at the London School of Economics have used data from the General Household Survey to estimate income inequality with and without women's wages. Their findings show that women's earnings *reduce* rather than widen the gap between affluent and poorer couples.

The LSE research shows that if women did not work at all, the level of inequality between couples of "prime working age" (24 to 55) would have been 34 per cent higher in 1989–91.

Why? The explanation given is that female incomes are distributed more equally than men's — while rich women are clearly better off than their more ordinary sisters, the gap is nowhere near as big as that for men. So female wages go some way towards offsetting the huge difference between male pay packets.

But the most interesting aspect is the change in the impact of women's earnings over time. In 1979–81, female salaries reduced the level of household inequality by 18 per cent, half as much as recorded a decade later. Why did women's earnings become a more powerful equaliser during the 1980s?

In part it is simply a result of the increase in the number of women on the payroll. But the LSE team points to a more subtle and more significant factor. The biggest change in women's labour market participation was among middle-income families, as the graph shows. By going out to work, the wives of Middle England have ensured their families did not fall even further behind the affluent Joneses.

An unpublished regional analysis by Ms Harkness supports this conclusion. She found that the areas with the lowest proportion of women in employment were the richest, such as East Anglia and the South-east, and the poorest — including Wales. The highest rates were recorded in middle-income areas like the East Midlands and North-west.

If more women in lower-income families brought home some wages, inequality could be reduced further. If four out of five wives in better-off households are at work, why not in all?

Two of the main barriers to taking up work specific to women are the cost of child care and low earnings potential. These are the problems policy-makers must tackle. Policies to boost women's employment and wages could provide a positive and sustainable way of reducing the gap between affluent and poor in our society.

Evaluating the Pin Money Hypothesis, by Susan Harkness, Stephen Machin and Jane Waldfogel, London School of Economics

Women at work

Percentage of females in employment, married or cohabiting, aged 24–55 years

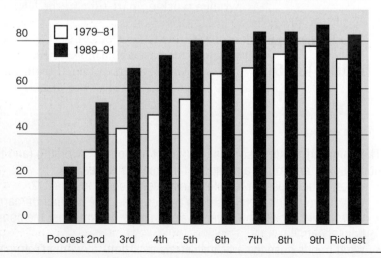

Source: Adapted from the *Guardian*, 10 March 1996

Flexible working patterns

In 1995, 9.5 per cent of male and 14.7 per cent of female employees worked flexible hours, whilst, for part-time workers, the figures were 6.9 per cent and 8.8 per cent respectively. If other flexible patterns, such as job sharing and sessional working, are taken into account, 16,734,000 full-time and 5,451,000 part-time workers were engaged in some form of flexible working pattern in 1995.

Trends to early retirement

In the two decades between 1975 and 1995, there was a decline in full-time employment for males aged 50–65. This might, in part, be explained by the increase in female employment, as well as by the major shift in industrial composition from manufacturing to service sector jobs. Changing attitudes towards early retirement may also play a part. According to figures in the 1995 General Household Survey, only half of all men between 60 and 65 consider themselves still 'economically active' in the sense of having a job or seeking work.

The figures reflect the fact that men in their 50s and 60s are finding it increasingly difficult to secure re-employment once a job finishes and are opting for – or are resigned to – early retirement.

In 1975, 94 per cent of men aged 55–59 and 84 per cent aged 60–64 were classified by the survey as economically active: either in work, or unemployed but having looked for work in the previous four weeks and available to start a job within a fortnight. In 1995, however, only 73 per cent of men aged 55–59 and 50 per cent aged 60–64 were economically active.

The trend among women is quite the opposite, and points towards a future scenario in which the number of women in jobs will outstrip the number of men.

In 1995, 60 per cent of married women and 46 per cent of those unmarried were classified as economically active. In 1975 the proportions were respectively 51 and 42 per cent.

The pattern has been linked to the rise in part-time service sector jobs, many of which are taken by women, and the decline of full-time manufacturing employment traditionally a male sphere of work. However, it has become more socially acceptable for men to retire in effect in their 50s.

Growth in unemployment

Since the late 1970s, unemployment has increased significantly in the UK, peaking in 1986 at about 3.1 million claiming benefits, whilst at the end of 1997 the official figure was 1.8 million. As noted in Unit 1 (pages 47–8), the construction of these official statistics – i.e. what 'counts' and what is left out – is often seen by sociologists as problematic. In this instance, school leavers and those over the age of 55 are no longer included in the unemployment statistics.

Changing technology

Increases in the use of robots to manufacture cars, for example, or of computers in offices have led to radical shifts in working practices and levels of employment. This issue is taken up in more detail on pages 231–6.

Development of core and periphery employment

Given the statistics noted above on the increases in part-time and flexible working, it is possible to develop a view that there are now two forms of jobs available in the economy: **core** jobs in the primary market (see page 217), which are secure, full-time and highly skilled, and

periphery jobs (including those in the secondary market), which are part-time, flexible and insecure. The growth in service industry employment is seen as increasing the number of jobs which are peripheral, whilst there appears to be a decline in the number of core jobs.

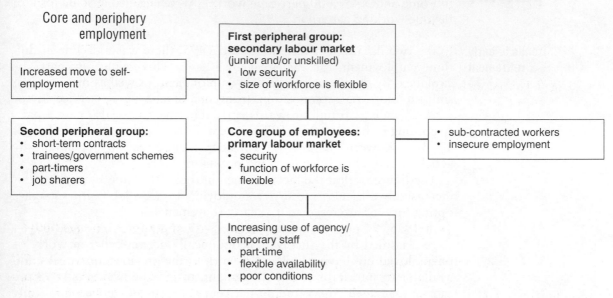

Source: Adapted from G.C. Mangum, 'Temporary work: "The flipside of job security"', *International Journal of Manpower*, vol. 17, no. 1, 1986

The impact of Europe on British working practices

The 1989 EC **Social Charter** provided a basis for the protection of workers under the EC **Social Chapter**, which was agreed by member states in 1991 but which the British government of the time rejected. The key aims of the Social Charter and the Social Chapter are to extend workers' rights and improve conditions at work, but the British government and some major employers had misgivings about the long-term effects on employment, arguing that implementing the Social Chapter would increase employers' costs and, therefore, increase unemployment.

- Employers expressed fears that one of the Directives of the Social Chapter could restrict their right to manage: The Works Councils Directive requires all companies employing more than 1000 people to set up a 'democratic forum for consultation'.
- Employers were also concerned about the requirements regarding maternity/paternity leave. Employers in those countries subscribing to the Social Chapter are required to give three months' unpaid leave to new parents – fathers as well as mothers.
- The Social Chapter includes clauses intended to prevent discrimination by race or gender; politicians and employers felt that this was adequately dealt with already by national law.
- The Working Time Directive of the Chapter sets limits on the number of hours that may be worked in a week. In Britain there is no statutory limit on this, but in most other European countries the national law is already more strict than the Working Time Directive:
  Maximum working week of 40 hours: Belgium, Finland, France, Luxembourg, Portugal, Spain, Sweden.
  Maximum working week of 48 hours: Italy, Ireland, Greece and Germany (but in Germany most contracts are set at under 40 hours).
  Maximum working week of 45–48 hours: The Netherlands.
  'Agreed norm' of 37 hours: Denmark.
  Paid holiday entitlement also varies within the EU, from 30 to 15 days per annum.

The Labour government declared on its election to office, in May 1997, that Britain would sign the Social Chapter as a framework under which legislative measures could be agreed. Labour maintained that the Social Chapter could not be used to force joint social security or tax changes but rather to promote employability and flexibility without high social costs.

Think about it

- What differences might the adoption of the Social Chapter make to workers in Britain?
- What are the implications for workers of a shift from 'core' to 'periphery' employment?

Sociological ideas on the nature of work

Marx, Durkheim and Weber

Debates concerning the sociology of work reflect the important influences of Marx, Weber and Durkheim, as do so many aspects of contemporary sociological inquiry and theoretical investigation. In Britain, and most of Western Europe, the process of **industrialisation** and its changing patterns of employment occurred within a system of capitalism; this system has had a profound effect on the form and conditions of work. In turn, the organisation of work has been linked to **social stratification**.

Karl Marx: the division of labour and the concept of 'alienation'

For Marx, capitalism occurs when the productive system (land and capital) is privately owned: controlled by only a few capitalists and organised in such a way as to maximise profit. Along with industrialisation came the factory system, a new emphasis on technology and the beginnings of the **division of labour**, identified by Adam Smith in his *Wealth of Nations* (1786). Factory production, and the working methods associated with advancing technology and the division of labour, were to have significant implications for the experience of work for individual workers. Such work organisation would, in Marx's view, increase the **exploitation** of workers by their employers and lead to the **alienation** (or separation) of workers from the fruits of their labour.

The division of labour refers to the splitting up of work into a number of different occupations in which people specialise. In pre-industrial societies, people were employed either in agriculture or in craft-based work, for example gun-making, where a lengthy apprenticeship would be served and the worker would make the gun from start to finish. With the rise of industrial production, however, workers began to specialise in a particular part of the manufacturing process. A joiner, for example, working in a factory, might only inspect and repair items of wood, or might engage with only one or two tasks in the manufacture of a piece of furniture. On a wider scale, this industrial division of labour has been influenced by the ideas of **Taylorism** and **Fordism**, which we shall look at later in this unit.

Emile Durkheim   In *The Division of Labour* (1933), Durkheim introduced the idea of **anomie**, relating to the meaninglessness of work. He described anomie as a social situation in which individuals lack any clear guidelines about how to behave in relation to each other; in a work context, this would be when the work itself does not allow people to develop a sense of social solidarity but rather only to be viewed, and to view themselves, as isolated individuals.

Durkheim identified a tendency, in the late nineteenth century, for the developing factory system to encourage a **de-skilling** of the workforce (see also page 235). However, he did not see developments within the workplace necessarily moving towards anomie. They could, in fact, lead to more meaningful and fulfilling opportunities. This would happen, he contended, as **corporations** and **occupational associations** assisted trade unions and employers to work together in common cause. The closest contemporary equivalent of such mediating organisations might be ACAS, the Arbitration and Conciliation Service. Meaningless work and unjustifiable inequalities at work may, according to Durkheim, lead to major difficulties and should therefore be avoided. He favoured a consensus-based interpretation over the conflict-based Marxist view.

P. Holmos, in *The Personal Service Society* (1970), noted the growth of the 'personal service professions'. The growth of the Welfare State (see Unit 7) has seen the expansion of a wide range of service professionals such as community educators, youth workers, social workers, health workers and teachers. This 'caring professional industry' does not, on the face of it, appear to fit the patterns of either alienation or anomie.

Max Weber   As we saw in Unit 2, Max Weber accepted that property, in the form of goods and services, was central to the development and perpetuation of capitalism. Deriving either through inheritance or through occupational position, it was a basic element in determining a person's social class position. Those without work, and hence without income – the unemployed, slaves and people undertaking unpaid domestic work – did not 'fit' into this analysis of social class. Weber used the term 'status' (see page 70) as a way of indicating the diversity of social relations and as a counter to Marx's 'two-class model' which sees conflict as inevitable. For Weber, unlike for Marx, there is little prospect of collective class action against capitalism, as workers are more likely to be in conflict with each other (for example, trade union **demarcation disputes** over who is responsible for what) than they are with the capitalist class. Many interactionist studies on the workplace have been influenced by Weber's work.

Work in modern industrial societies

In the seventeenth century, Britain had a population of about 3 million. By the start of the nineteenth century it had grown to 6 million and, in 1991, to 56 million. Such a startling growth took place alongside the expansion of industrial production, which included the division of labour and the growth of **urbanisation**. The population growth was sustained by **capitalist social relations** which, according to Abercrombie and Warde in *Contemporary British Society* (1995), mean:

- private ownership of the means of production (land, property, machinery);
- economic activity which seeks to generate profits;
- profits going directly to the owners of the means of production;
- workers receiving payment for their labour and not owning productive property;
- the sale of goods produced and services provided being organised into **markets**, where everything is **commodified** (i.e. viewed as a commodity whose worth is determined by the market).

There are three types of economy evident in industrial societies: **capitalist** (or **decentralised**), **socialist** (or **centralised**) and **mixed**.

<u>Capitalist economy</u>   In a capitalist economy, goods and services are produced and provided in order to ensure a profit for the producers. In a truly capitalist economy, all activity resides in the 'private sector', with no provision of 'public services' provided by the government or paid for by taxpayers. There is no central regulation of the market, and both producers and consumers will seek to maximise their benefit in any transaction.

<u>Socialist economy</u>   By contrast, a socialist economy is one which is publicly owned, one where the state centrally plans and organises all aspects of the supply and delivery of goods and services. The collapse of the Soviet Union and its satellite economies in the late 1980s and the early 1990s effectively marked the end of such centrally controlled economies in the West, but in China and Cuba the essential elements are still evident. China's reincorporation of Hong Kong, from Britain, in 1997 allows a socialist economy to operate in a capitalist economic system, 'One Country, Two Systems'.

<u>Mixed economy</u>   Within a mixed economy, a substantial 'private' or capitalist sector and a large 'public' or state sector work in parallel. Often the public sector includes state-run welfare services, schools, hospitals and so on, as well as public utilities such as water, gas and electricity. In Britain, privatisation of the utilities, plus large companies such as British Airways and British Telecom, has greatly reduced the state's role in industrial enterprises. Rail privatisation in 1996 marked a further shift from public to private ownership.

Employment in the UK economy

The British economy (and hence employment opportunities) has declined faster than most other economies since the 1970s, despite increasing levels of productivity in the 1980s and 1990s. Two issues are of particular interest in relation to this decline: the ownership and control of industry, and the implications of technology for the economy of the future.

Ownership and control of industry

The growth of business enterprise, with its emphasis on shareholders and key decisions being taken by directors, began to emerge in the 1870s. It was perceived that this would lead to a 'managerial revolution', in which managers in the industrial enterprise would take over power from the capitalists. In fact, the trend since the 1980s towards substantial shareholdings being held by financial companies suggests a rather different view of ownership than the managerialist one: in the Anglo-American countries at least it is possible to identify an increasing tendency towards **financial hegemony**, with banks, insurance companies and pension funds holding vast numbers of shares in many major companies. (See Unit 11, pages 606–7 for a definition of hegemony.) It has been argued that the globalised interests of these major owners has had a detrimental effect on the UK economy, since international considerations are given priority over those of the UK.

Also during the 1980s, British business underwent a 'merger boom'; in the 1990s, this is affecting the recently privatised utilities such as the electricity and water industries. In the media and communications industry, newspaper owners such as Rupert Murdoch have begun to accumulate interests in television, cable, satellite and telecommunications, leading to massive concentrations of power in a few corporate hands.

Government policy of selling off publicly owned service and utility industries, such as telecommunications, railways and water, in the 1980s and 1990s attracted criticisms, including the accusation that these assets had been sold too cheaply.

The convergence thesis

This theory claims that industrialisation, in its creation of the division of labour and the factory system, brings about similarities in the occupational structures of different countries: managers in Britain or America, for example, will operate in increasingly similar ways, industries will possess similar structures and societies will show equivalent social class hierarchies.

The notion of convergence applies to some extent to the economies of the West but there are still significant contrasts. Comparisons between the economies of Britain, Sweden and Japan indicate substantial differences in organisation, ownership, concentration, profitability and growth. Fulcher and Gould, in their attempts to compare Britain and Sweden (*Sociology Review*, April 1993), noted that there has indeed been convergence, reflected largely in economic crises affecting Sweden. These crises have resulted in government action to increase employer power and to introduce the kinds of neo-liberal policies evident in many major economies, including Britain. Such governmental policies have sought to deliver a 'managed capitalism', which regulates employment, protects and assists industries, and seeks to ensure the effective operation of the market economy. Global capital, according to the convergence thesis, has become ever more concentrated in multinational enterprises, forcing individual countries to compete for their 'patronage' or investment. One example of the problems this can cause occurred when the car manufacturer Peugeot, having received large UK government grants to set up operations in Britain, then pulled out in order to benefit from even more lucrative grants from the Spanish government. Similarly, movement of car production by Ford from Halewood in Liverpool to Germany was announced in January 1997, as shown in the following Ceefax extract.

'The car giant said it had to cut the workforce at its Merseyside plant as Escort production would switch abroad [to Spain and Germany] after the year 2000 ... TGWU (Transport and General Workers' Union) spokesman Tony Woodley said, "The decision is an opportunity to cut costs at the expense of British jobs."'

Source: BBC Ceefax, 16 January 1997

Think about it

- In sociological terms, think of at least two advantages and at least two disadvantages for:

  (a) private ownership of railway, electricity, gas, water and coal industries;
  (b) public ownership of these industries.

The development of new technologies and globalisation

Both Fordist and post-industrial analyses (see below) stress the importance of new technologies, particularly in the fields of information, communication (for example the Internet) and knowledge as crucial agents of change.

From Fordism to global post-Fordism	
Fordism	**Global post-Fordism**
• Mass production of standardised products • Strong, centralised control over labour • Assembly-line system • Mass production for mass consumption • Geared to meet 'first world' markets such as UK, USA.	• Rapid modification of products for new markets • Identification of specific target groups for products • Specialisation in specific product areas • Flexibility of assembly-type production system • Global orientation

Source: adapted from T. Bilton et al., *Introductory Sociology* (1996)

Post-Fordism seeks to organise production in a flexible and responsive way so that constantly altering consumer demands can be met swiftly. Under Fordism, the choice available to the consumer was limited by what came off the assembly line – to quote Henry Ford himself, 'consumers can have any colour of Ford so long as it is black'. The post-Fordist approach would be to find out what the consumer wanted and then to supply it.

It is likely that a number of 'lead industries', based on micro-technology and information technology leading to the applications of **nano-technology** (i.e. the ability of miniaturised machines to build more machines), will dominate in the early twenty-first century. This represents a new form of industry and clearly has implications for work and workers. Such technological developments can create major problems for the UK where ownership and control of the technology industry is not UK-based, since multinational companies are likely to make global, corporate decisions, not based solely on interests within the UK.

The emphasis on a higher level of skills brings education firmly into the arena of competing for employers' investment and therefore jobs.

Comparatively high levels of educational qualifications will be a significant factor in the location of new jobs, so there is some cause for concern for UK governments in figures such as those revealed by the graphs below.

How the UK compares in terms of educational qualifications

On the level
Percentage of total adult population qualified to level 3 (A level and equivalent) or above

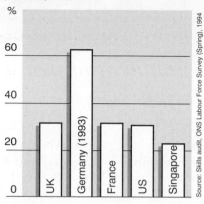

Source: Skills audit, ONS Labour Force Survey (Spring), 1994

Falling behind
Percentage of young people qualifying at level 3 (A level and equivalent) in 1994

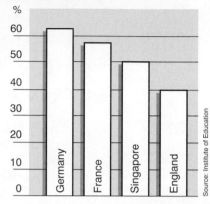

Source: Institute of Education

Source: The *Guardian*, 1 July 1996

Perceptions of the qualifications needed for particular job roles differ from one culture to another, and this too is likely to become an important consideration in a scenario where the employment market is international. The following case study illustrates this in the context of the car industry.

Case study: flexible skill strategies

This example concerns the German and British subsidiaries of a multinational car manufacturer. The company-wide job structure was based on a three-tier system of grades: A, B and C. A-graded jobs were purely for new entrants; B-grade jobs were for workers who had acquired the necessary speed and skills to perform a job on the line; and C-grade jobs were for multi-skilled workers who could perform several different types of assembly work, and tasks like basic maintenance and quality control.

Although this wage/skill structure was identical in both plants, the distribution of skills was very different. In the British plant the vast majority of manual employees were on the B grade and were regarded simply as normal line workers. Workers on the highest grade, the so-called C-men, were in a minority of around 10 per cent and were used as a labour pool. In cases of absenteeism, particularly on difficult or critical jobs, production foremen tended to request a C-man.

In the German plant, however, a far higher proportion of employees, between 60 per cent and 70 per cent, were C-graded. The grading system was seen as a kind of career structure for labour. Workers were encouraged to acquire skills and to move through the grades, and job rotation and training were provided to help them do this.

Significant points about this case include the difference in managerial attitudes. This was a company with a very strong corporate policy for uniform production operations across all plants, irrespective of national differences. Despite this the German management had secured the resources needed to maintain a high-skill workforce. The British attitude was to use skilled labour only selectively. Also important is the fact that the case is from mass production. This was a typical Fordist industry associated with de-skilling. But the German management still succeeded in upskilling workers.

Social consequences of the globalised employment market

Globalised competition for the provision and location of work which may move from, say Britain, to other developing countries, creates a pressure on employers to adopt working conditions which might be associated with third-world economies: a marked increase in average hours worked by those employed, a comparative reduction in wages and conditions at work, less employment protection for workers, and fewer industrial stoppages.

TOP EUROPEAN EARNERS		
Country	Income per head	Hours worked
1. Luxembourg	£19,791	37
2. Belgium	£13,971	35
3. Denmark	£13,869	36
4. Austria	£13,794	n/a
5. France	£13,573	37
6. Germany	£13,331	35
7. Holland	£12,696	37
8. Italy	£12,634	36
9. **UK**	**£12,236**	**41**
10. Sweden	£12,137	n/a
11. Finland	£11,200	n/a
12. Ireland	£9,985	39
13. Spain	£9,599	37
14. Portugal	£8,513	39
15. Greece	£7,784	38

Source: The *People*, 17 November 1996

Unless Britain can compete efficiently and effectively with its competitors then multinational companies will move elsewhere. Many long-established manufacturers (for example Dunlop and Peugeot) have moved their factories out of the UK, whilst American and Japanese firms (e.g. IBM and Motorola, Nissan and Honda) have moved in. It has been estimated that in Scotland over 50 per cent of the large-scale industrial companies are owned by non-UK companies or groups, whilst the ownership of over 80 per cent of companies making electronics and computers is non-UK.

Think about it

- Do you think that increased opportunities for locating work in developing countries could affect social structure in any British working communities?
- What factors do you consider might attract multinational companies to the UK? What social and, in particular, cultural changes could such multinationals bring with them?

Positive aspects of the increase of technology

Daniel Bell, in *The Coming of Post-Industrial Society* (1973), said that a process of de-industrialisation can offer positive consequences. He envisaged the following benefits:

- work becoming more pleasant as manual work is replaced by professional occupations, with more emphasis on thinking skills;
- the general growth of a vibrant services sector;
- companies becoming smaller;
- skills being more widely shared than in the past.

Skills, technology and work satisfaction

The term 'work satisfaction' clearly involves value judgements in its interpretation: it can be equated to work enjoyment and feelings of accomplishment, or it can be limited to a toleration of working conditions resulting from the level of financial rewards. Such ambiguity makes it difficult to study work satisfaction. An interviewer can be misled by the over-simplifications contained in a straightforward answer to a question involving an assessment of attitudes to work. Participant observation may offer better opportunities for insight, but it too contains dangers: the researcher's values and occupational views may bias their interpretation of what is considered to be boring or rewarding work.

Think about it

- Would a Marxist sociologist obtain different findings from participant observation of people at work than, say, a functionalist (see Unit 1)?
- If so, explain why this might be the case.

Satisfaction at work	
Work which gives intrinsic satisfaction	**Work which gives extrinsic satisfaction**
• The work is enjoyable in itself • The work provides a challenge • The individual develops and finds work fulfilling • The meaning of work is expressive	• The work itself gives no satisfaction • The work is only a means to an end • Satisfaction and fulfilment are found outside work • The meaning of work is instrumental

Source: Adapted from T.J. Watson, *Sociology, Work and Industry* (1980)

A number of sociologists have stressed the positive aspects of technological advancement. It is contended that society has seen a rise in its overall living standards as wealth has increased. Lenski, for example, saw the resulting labour specialisation as contributing to a narrowing of the gap between the wealthy and the poor, while Daniel Bell saw an end to the divisive ideology of 'Them and Us'. Certainly, the use of new technology can make many forms of work less exhausting, and more fruitful leisure time can be created. Workers may, however, be dissatisfied that their training and ability are not fully utilised; and recent developments in micro-technology have shown that technological innovation at a time of economic recession can result in higher levels of unemployment or short-term, insecure employment rather than a shorter working week and greater leisure time.

What is sometimes ignored is the ability of the individual to cope with what may outwardly appear to be monotonous and boring work. Baldamus has developed the concept of **traction**, by which he means that people adapt to tedious work by allowing themselves to be pulled along with a sensation of reduced effort, from which they gain relative relief from a fundamentally disliked situation. It is common for people to reduce tension and frustration by a variety of techniques, including simply letting one's mind wander to other things. Laurie Taylor and Paul Walton quote the more unusual example of disgruntled workers in a Blackpool Rock factory, who inserted four-letter words instead of the customary greetings in a half-mile length of rock.

The de-skilling debate

As we have seen, a person's job (their occupation) often determines their social class and perhaps also their social status. Within work, it is possible to talk about a hierarchy in terms of the level of skill required; for example, in manual work sociologists refer to skilled, semi-skilled and unskilled work. It has been argued, for example by Harry Braverman, that the development of industrial work in capitalist societies will gradually **de-skill** people's jobs. Braverman's view is that the skill level required of all employee groups (both office and factory workers) would be reduced, in order to keep wages low and profits high, but also as a way of controlling workers. The computerisation of supermarket tills, with bar-coded pricing and stocktaking, and the use of wordprocessors in place of typewriters can be seen as examples of de-skilling.

Criticisms of this theory of the 'degradation' of work include the following:

- It ignores the fact that new skills and specialisations emerge.
- It ignores the fact that some worker groups have organised themselves in protection against the danger of de-skilling.
- It overstates the resources, knowledge and intention of capitalists to apply such an approach.

The effects of technological change

It has been suggested that new computer technology may have a major impact on the social environment and on employment opportunities. Technological change will enable people to:

- shop from home using computer keyboards and adapted television sets;
- receive all the latest entertainment directly into our homes at the touch of a button;
- work from home, setting up electronic cottage industries;
- access the Internet from home-based connections;
- E-mail friends and colleagues anywhere in the world instantly and receive a reply in seconds;
- receive education at home rather than at school;
- access fax machines and teleconferencing facilities from home, allowing communicators to see each other from anywhere in the world.

Such a scenario appears to offer many potential advantages for those who can afford to gain access to the information. It is also possible, however, to see potential dangers:

- problems of political or ideological control;
- inequality of access to further advantage some at the expense of others;
- a temptation to assume that such technological development is 'rational' and 'neutral' when it may well not be.

G. Salaman, in *Social Studies Review* (1987), points out some potential consequences of the growth of **information technology** (IT) and the introduction of ever more sophisticated technology. He sees two key theoretical perspectives on the introduction of information technology. The first advocates development of technology as a logical progression which will significantly benefit the world of work and the wider society. The second view, a Marxist perspective, argues that information technology serves to benefit certain interests at the expense of the majority and that it is being used, and will continue to be used, to serve the interests, beliefs and values of capitalism. This fits the views expressed earlier by Braverman and others as evidence of a loss of jobs and an increase in profits accruing throughout industry and commerce. On this view, information technology will be directly used to increase profitability, increase managerial control and cut costs and jobs.

However, as noted in the criticisms on page 235, not all jobs are necessarily lost with the introduction of information technology: new jobs are created and different skills are developed.

Work in the future

Daniel Bell (see page 233) suggested that we are living in a post-industrial society dominated by scientific, service and professional work. Such an idea has been reinforced by the significant changes brought about by the growth of information technology, with writers such as Gorz noting the development of an information society developing out of post-industrialism. In Gorz's view, work as we have come to know it will be replaced and the manual working class (the proletariat) will be of little significance. In *Farewell to the Working Class* (1982), he envisages a society in which leisure will be available to all as a result of changing work commitments. Some, however, suggest that post-industrialism has not arrived and that the decline in manufacturing in Britain is more than compensated for by its growth in developing countries.

Postmodernism, in ways very similar to those noted by Bell above, suggests that we live in a time of fundamental change in work, leisure and consumption. Such change will affect the social structure and the nature and form of social relationships which shape our lives. Alongside the decreasing relevance of industrial work is the growth of the leisure and service industries. The emphasis is less on work and more on consumption.

In the UK, the idea of a 'leisure society' or of 'work being shared out' appears to be a very long way off, with official unemployment standing at 1.8 million (December 1997) and the government attempting to reduce benefit to the long-term unemployed.

Differentiation in patterns of employment

Employment opportunities – and the risk of unemployment – are subject to many 'outside' economic forces such as competition, globalisation, and the development of technology, as seen already in this unit. From the point of view of a particular individual or social group, a number of other factors also come into play, affecting their life chances in the arena of employment. Unemployment affects some sections of the population more than others; in particular, differences can be seen in terms of social class, region, age, disability, gender and ethnicity.

Social class A person's social class – usually defined in terms of their occupation, as we saw in Unit 2 – can be seen to have an impact on the likelihood of their being unemployed. Those whose occupations fall into the categories of unskilled or semi-skilled manual work form a much larger proportion of the unemployed than those in management and other professions. For example, in 1994, only 4.2 per cent of the unemployed were from professional occupations, whilst over 13 per cent were former plant or machine operators. (See also Unit 2, page 93.)

Region Where you live in the UK is also significant, as can be seen from the following sample of unemployment rates from 1994, the data on regional disparities in earnings, and the map showing variations in unemployment rates throughout the UK in 1995.

Unemployment rates[1] by county[2]

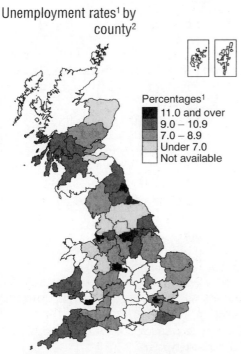

Percentages[1]
- 11.0 and over
- 9.0 – 10.9
- 7.0 – 8.9
- Under 7.0
- Not available

[1] Unemployment based on the ILO definition as a percentage of those economically active. See Appendix, Part 4: Unemployment – ILO definition.
[2] Regions in Scotland.

Source: *Social Trends*, 1996

REGIONAL UNEMPLOYMENT (1994)	
Northern Ireland	11.5%
North of England	11.7%
East Anglia	7.4%

Source: *Social Trends*, 1996

TOP UK EARNERS	
1. G. London	£17,812
2. South East	£14,364
3. East Anglia	£12,487
4. Scotland	£12,026
5. South West	£11,642
6. E. Midlands	£11,471
7. Yorks & Humberside	£11,240
8. W. Midlands	£11,234
9. North West	£11,042
10. North	£10,979
11. Wales	£10,358
12. Northern Ireland	£9,777

Source: *The People*, 17 November 1996

Think about it

- Look at the map on page 237 and identify the unemployment rates for your own county and one contrasting county. Identify possible reasons for, and sociological consequences of, the differences.

Age The General Household Survey noted in 1995 that age and unemployment are related. As many as 37 per cent of unemployed men over the age of 55, with up to ten years' potential working life left, had given up looking for future employment. Similar disadvantages also seem to appear at the other end of the scale: ICO/EUROSTAT figures reveal that in the period 1992/3 Britain had the highest increase in young jobless in the European Union: 37 per cent of under-25-year-olds were unemployed. The following table from *Social Trends* 1996 shows this pattern among the younger age group appearing fairly consistently over the first half of the 1990s, though the rise in unemployment rates after the age of 55 is more consistent among men than among women.

Unemployment rates[1]: by gender and age in the United Kingdom		1991 (%)	1992 (%)	1993 (%)	1994 (%)	1995 (%)	1996 (%)
Males	16–19	16.4	18.6	22.0	20.9	19.6	20.6
	20–24	15.2	18.9	20.3	18.3	17.0	16.2
	25–44	8.0	10.5	10.9	10.2	9.0	8.7
	45–54	6.3	8.4	9.4	8.6	7.4	6.4
	55–59	8.4	11.2	12.3	11.6	10.2	9.9
	60–64	9.9	10.2	14.2	11.6	9.9	8.9
	65 and over	5.9	4.9	4.6	3.7	–	4.1
	All males aged 16 and over	9.2	11.5	12.4	11.4	10.1	9.7
Females	16–19	12.7	13.6	15.9	16.0	14.8	14.6
	20–24	10.1	10.2	11.8	10.7	10.6	8.9
	25–44	7.1	7.3	7.3	7.0	6.7	6.3
	45–54	4.6	5.0	5.0	5.0	4.5	4.1
	55–59	5.5	4.5	6.0	6.5	4.7	4.2
	60 and over	4.4	3.1	3.9	2.9	–	–
	All females aged 16 and over	7.2	7.3	7.6	7.3	6.8	6.3

1 At Spring each year. Unemployment based on the ILO definition as a percentage of all economically active.

Source: Labour Force Survey

The table on page 239 shows that among men and women, long-term unemployment (three years or more) is highest in the older age group.

Duration of unemployment[1]: by gender and age, Spring 1995

	Less than three months (%)	Three months but less than six months (%)	Six months but less than one year (%)	One year but less than two years (%)	Two years but less than three years (%)	Three years or more (%)	All durations[2] (=100%) (thousands)
Males							
16–19	39.9	19.4	22.4	13.5	–	–	164
20–29	18.6	16.4	19.9	18.7	9.3	17.0	541
30–39	14.2	15.7	14.7	17.6	13.6	24.1	345
40–49	14.8	11.9	13.5	15.3	14.3	30.1	256
50–64	15.6	11.2	12.5	18.4	13.7	28.3	293
All aged 16 and over[3]	18.7	14.9	16.6	17.3	11.3	21.0	1,607
Females							
16–19	40.7	22.5	21.1	11.1	–	–	114
20–29	32.8	18.9	18.8	14.6	6.2	8.7	273
30–39	33.8	17.6	16.4	15.1	6.8	10.4	202
40–49	26.9	15.1	17.9	15.2	9.8	14.9	154
50–64	22.3	11.3	16.8	18.2	10.8	20.2	100
All aged 16 and over[3]	31.7	17.4	18.2	14.8	7.2	10.6	846

1 Unemployment based on the ILO definition.
2 Includes those who did not state their duration.
3 Includes males aged 65 and over and females aged 60 and over who were unemployed.

Source: Labour Force Survey, in Social Trends, 1996

Finally, the table showing Britain's workforce by age provides a different slant: people in the 16–24 age group form a relatively small proportion of the workforce, partly due to the fact that many are still involved in full-time education or training. The 60–64 age group is by far the smallest, with the exception of those above the official retirement age of 65. It is not clear how many of those aged 60–64 who have stopped working are included in the number officially registered as unemployed.

Labour force: by age		16–24 (000s)	25–44 (000s)	45–59 (000s)	60–64 (000s)	65 and over (000s)	All aged 16 and over (000s)
Estimates	1984	6,214	12,201	7,077	1,252	429	27,172
	1986	6,326	12,788	6,968	1,083	402	27,566
	1991	5,684	14,256	7,311	1,102	462	28,815
	1992	5,224	14,192	7,596	1,069	501	28,582
	1993	4,941	14,258	7,742	1,070	443	28,454
	1994	4,710	14,301	7,922	1,051	437	28,421
Projections	1996	4,404	14,609	8,227	1,049	429	28,717
	2001	4,313	14,893	8,748	1,105	409	29,469
	2006	4,519	14,609	9,252	1,295	416	30,092

Source: Labour Force Survey, in *Social Trends*, 1996

The pattern of low employment rates for the older section of the population (those aged 55–64) is common to the major industrialised countries. In 1994 the highest 'economic activity' rate for older men was in Japan – 85 per cent – while the USA had the highest rate for older women – 49 per cent.

Gender and employment

Female workers tend to be concentrated in a narrow range of occupations: clerical work, personal services, and professional occupations such as education, welfare and health. The notion of **horizontal gender segregation** is used by sociologists to describe a situation where women and men work in very different employment areas. In addition, women experience **vertical gender segregation** – in other words, they form a large proportion of lower-grade workers and a small proportion of senior workers. In 1993 only 3 per cent of company directors were women, only five women were High Court Judges (there are 91 in total) and only 28 Circuit Judges out of a total of 496 were women. Women comprised 32 per cent of managers and administrators and 40 per cent of professionals as a whole, but are particularly scarce in certain professions: for example, only 5 per cent of engineers and technologists being women. In terms of income, as the following table illustrates, women's vertical segregation is reflected in the fact that their earnings are generally lower than men's.

Average weekly income for manual and non-manual and male and female workers, 1974–1994				
Full-time male employees		**1974**	**1984**	**1994**
	manual	£42.30	£152.70	£280.70
	non-manual	£54.10	£209.00	£428.20
	manual worker's income as percentage of non-manual	78%	73%	65%
Full-time female employees		**1974**	**1984**	**1994**
	manual	£22.80	£93.50	£181.90
	non-manual	£28.30	£124.30	£278.40
	manual worker's income as percentage of non-manual	80%	66%	65%
	female earnings as percentage of male	57%	66%	72%

Source: K. Mann, 'Work, Dependency and the Underclass', *Developments in Sociology* vol. 11

The unemployment picture also differs according to gender. Since the early 1970s there has been a significant increase in the numbers of women (particularly married women) in the workforce, with a tendency for them to be employed largely in insecure, poorly paid, part-time and unprotected jobs. Whilst many women with children may find the flexibility of part-time work crucial if they hold primary responsibility for their dependants, this effectively means that they have a 'dual career' in the home and the workplace. In Britain, 45 per cent of women workers are part-time, and for those who have children there is almost always a career break – of variable length. For those in full-time employment, the majority are at the lower end of the pay scale: in 1994, over half of women in full-time employment earned poverty-level wages (then defined at under £170 per week). The increase in the number of part-time jobs accounts partly for the fact that while, for men, the overall rate of unemployment in the UK has been steadily rising in the 1990s, for women it has been falling, as can be seen from the table showing unemployment rates by gender and age, on page 238. The fact that women are having fewer children, or having their children later, or being more likely to return to work after having a child also influences these figures.

The extracts on page 242 provide further details relating to women and employment in various parts of the world, whilst the article on page 243 gives a more personalised picture of women's employment in Britain.

Women at work: average percentage of total labour force who are women

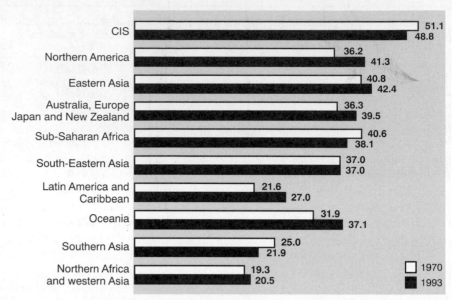

Region	1970	1993
CIS	51.1	48.8
Northern America	36.2	41.3
Eastern Asia	40.8	42.4
Australia, Europe Japan and New Zealand	36.3	39.5
Sub-Saharan Africa	40.6	38.1
South-Eastern Asia	37.0	37.0
Latin America and Caribbean	21.6	27.0
Oceania	31.9	37.1
Southern Asia	25.0	21.9
Northern Africa and western Asia	19.3	20.5

☐ 1970
■ 1993

Source: The *Guardian*, 30 May 1995

A woman's lot

Women contribute 66 per cent of the hours worked in the world, earn about 10 per cent of the world's income and own only 1 per cent of the world's property.

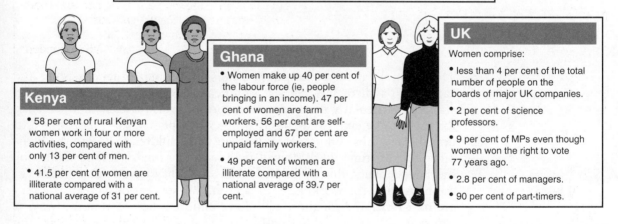

Kenya

- 58 per cent of rural Kenyan women work in four or more activities, compared with only 13 per cent of men.

- 41.5 per cent of women are illiterate compared with a national average of 31 per cent.

Ghana

- Women make up 40 per cent of the labour force (ie, people bringing in an income). 47 per cent of women are farm workers, 56 per cent are self-employed and 67 per cent are unpaid family workers.

- 49 per cent of women are illiterate compared with a national average of 39.7 per cent.

UK

Women comprise:

- less than 4 per cent of the total number of people on the boards of major UK companies.

- 2 per cent of science professors.

- 9 per cent of MPs even though women won the right to vote 77 years ago.

- 2.8 per cent of managers.

- 90 per cent of part-timers.

Source: The *Guardian*, 30 May 1995

Think about it

Read the case study on the next page and then consider the following questions, bearing in mind the information provided above.

- Identify those points in the case study which you feel reflect changes in the social values attached to the employment of women.
- Identify those points which you feel represent any improvements in the work prospects of women, compared with the situation of the two previous generations.
- What do you think might be the effects on women's work prospects of the changes in
  - maternity leave provision
  - the age at which women have their children?

Women in Britain

ABIGAIL GREEN comes from a long line of active women. Her mother is a psychologist and ice dance teacher; her grandmother went to Newnham College, Cambridge. "My grandmother trained as a doctor in the 1930s but when she got married, fellow students accused her of letting the side down. People thought she should be fulfilling the feminist work ethic. Having a career and getting married were two different lives then, almost impossible to combine."

Two generations down the line, giving up her career is not an option that Green — who is doing a PhD in German history at Cambridge — is ever likely to consider: "Most of my friends have just happened on things," she says, "but I have always loved studying history. I like to be by myself in the peace and quiet of the library, running my own projects."

Academic life, at least in the early stages, is no money-spinner. Green manages on a grant of £5,000 per year. While her friends are busy arranging their mortgages, she lives alone in a room full of institutional furniture. "Of course I would like to have money," she explains, "but I would hate to do something else."

Independence has always been "a bit of a theme" for Green. "I guess there is a conflict between working and having a family, but having a working mother never bothered me when I was growing up. It helps you to stand on your own two feet," she says. "If I gave up work, I'd be bored. I want a house-husband to look after the kids because I'm not a very maternal person. I don't know if I want to have children at all. I would be horrified if I found out tomorrow that I was pregnant. But maybe that will change when I'm 35. It would be quite interesting to give birth."

Marriage is "not on the agenda". She has been in a relationship with Wayne, a musician, for four years. They did cohabit, but more recently it has become a "weekend thing".

Does Green feel that feminism remains as important to her generation as it was to the Newnham undergraduates of the 1930s? "When I edited a feminist magazine at university, my grandmother asked: 'Is this still really necessary? Surely we have achieved everything we want?' Instinctively I feel things are still hard for British women — especially with childcare — though I haven't found them particularly hard myself.

"I think every woman I know is a feminist, whether or not they admit it. They have just taken the assumptions of feminism for granted."

Average age at marriage: 25.6
Percentage who marry: 52% of women are single
Divorce rate: 41% of 18–49-year-olds
Average number of children: 1.75
Single mothers: 20% of families with dependent children
Maternity leave: 90% of earnings for first six weeks, then statutory pay of £52.50 per week for 12 weeks
Work: 20% work full-time
Average wage: a third of women earn £190 gross per week
Breast cancer: 5.5 per cent of women screened
Average life-expectancy: 79
Women MPs: 63[1]

[1]After the May 1997 general election, this number increased to 120.

Source: The *Guardian*, 1 July 1996

Employment and ethnicity

In spring 1994, about 15 per cent of Pakistani/Bangladeshi members of the UK population were long-term unemployed, as opposed to about 4 per cent of the white population. The definition of 'long-term unemployment' in these statistics was taken to mean that the person had been out of work for at least 52 weeks.

The information in the table on page 244 suggests that ethnic minorities, particularly people of Pakistani or Bangladeshi origin, have a higher rate of economic inactivity (non-employment) than any other ethnic category in the UK. The table also shows that the white population has the highest percentage in full-time work and the lowest rate of unemployment. There is a good deal of evidence to suggest that employment discrimination takes place and this operates in a variety of ways:

- offering higher quality training and promotion prospects to certain ethnic groups;
- limiting access to certain types of job, e.g. law and the other professions;
- offering jobs to some ethnic groups rather than others.

Economic status of people of working age: by gender and ethnic group, Spring 1995		White (%)	Black[1] (%)	Indian (%)	Pakistani/ Bangladeshi (%)	Other[2] (%)	All ethnic groups[3] (%)
Males	Working full time	72	49	65	41	51	71
	Working part time	5	8	7	8	8	5
	Unemployed	8	21	10	18	12	9
	Inactive	15	22	18	33	29	15
	All (=100%) (thousands)	16,993	273	306	216	224	18,017
Females	Working full time	38	37	36	12	30	38
	Working part time	29	15	19	6	16	28
	Unemployed	5	14	7	7	8	5
	Inactive	28	34	38	75	46	29
	All (=100%) (thousands)	15,420	296	279	191	238	16,428

1 Includes Caribbean, African and other Black people of non-mixed origin.
2 Includes Chinese, other ethnic minority groups of non-mixed origin and people of mixed origin.
3 Includes ethnic group not stated.

Source: Labour Force Survey, *Social Trends*, 1996

The Department for Education and Employment's *Labour market and skill trends 1996–97* shows the following picture (for the end of 1995) in relation to ethnic minorities:

- They have lower levels of economic activity (i.e. work) rates for both males and females, than the white population, for example:

Economic activity	Male (%)	Female (%)
White	85	72
Black	78	66
Indian	82	62

- They do different jobs – in other words, there is horizontal segregation in employment between ethnic groups, as there is between the genders:
  - the Bangladeshi/Pakistani group has the highest level (49 per cent) of employment in manual work, with the proportion for Black and Indian populations being 45 per cent and 38 per cent respectively;
  - they are under-represented in both craft and skilled occupations, clerical, secretarial, administrative and managerial positions.
- They are less well qualified – 21 per cent of ethnic minorities have no qualifications.

Unemployment rates in different ethnic groups	
	Unemployment rate (%)
White	8.3
All ethnic minority groups	19.3
Black	24.7
Indian	11.9
Bangladeshi/Pakistani	29.8

Source: Labour Force Survey No. 14, December 1995

- The disparity between white and non-white unemployment is wider for women than for men. In 1995, three-quarters of women of Bangladeshi and Pakistani origin were economically inactive, nearly three times as many as the proportion for women of white ethnic origin.

In 1974 a PEP (Political and Economic Planning – a research organisation) study used 'situation tests' where actors from different ethnic backgrounds applied for a range of occupations whilst pretending to have very similar qualifications and experience. The findings revealed that black applicants were discriminated against by employers in 20 per cent of the vacancies for skilled manual jobs, 30 per cent of non-manual jobs, and 37 per cent of semi- and unskilled jobs. A 1984 study, 'Black and White Britain: The Third PSI (Policy Studies Institute) Survey', interviewed 5000 black and 2305 white adults. The findings revealed that the percentage of men with jobs in the 16–24 age group was 61 per cent for whites, 48 per cent for Asians, and 42 per cent for West Indians.

Think about it

- Read the article on pages 246–247, 'Surely you can't be the barrister?'. Which commonly recognised *disadvantages* for would-be black professionals does the article mention?
- Identify situations and developments which are a positive influence for the improvement of employment prospects among West Indians. Are there other problems which are as yet not being addressed, according to what you can interpret from this article?
- Can you think of reasons other than discrimination for why 'economic activity' rates in the UK are exceptionally low among women of Bangladeshi/Pakistani origin?

Surely you can't be the barrister?

Educational achievement is rising rapidly among black people in Britain. So where are the jobs to reflect this?
Melanie Phillips reports

THE GROWING young black professional class may be taking it on the chin these days but they're still taking it. "You go to court and find that court staff assume you're the defendant or the defendant's sister," a black woman barrister says. "The last thing anyone assumes you are is the barrister."

A black journalist says: "A stallholder said to me 'This is a good orange; you should know, where *you* come from.' I said 'What, *east London?*' You expect it from someone like that but you get it in liberal society too. That makes me so angry and that's another reason I don't think about it because once I start thinking about it I feel very radical and it's almost as if when the next person comes up I want to smack them. And I'm tough. I can take it," she says.

The good news is that self-confidence and achievement are rising fast among young black people. The bad news is that they're still being knocked back by racism.

Progress *has* been made in race relations in the last few years and there are many optimistic signs. There's a growing young, articulate, black middle class. Black Britons born here have a confidence that their parents never possessed. Their educational achievements are beginning to foster a benign cycle of upward mobility. "There's a revolution taking place in the educational achievement of ethnic minorities," David Smith, a senior fellow of the Policy Studies Institute, says. "In 20 years' time, they will be better educated than white people." Black children fall behind at primary school, he says, but they catch up in secondary school, particularly in English where black children now gain more passes than white children, although they do less well in maths. "Subsequently, they are much more likely to go on to further education colleges and to tertiary education."

It's the employment picture, however, that's still depressing. According to the Government's Labour Force Survey, while unemployment among white people is running at eight per cent, among ethnic minorities it's 15 per cent — and, worse still, as high as 25 per cent among Pakistani and Bangladeshi people. Education may be looking up, but the crunch comes when black people try to get a job. "More black children than white always stayed on at school because they couldn't get jobs," Carlton Duncan, headmaster of George Dixon school in Birmingham, says. "But sooner or later they have to face the working world and that's where the problems remain."

Over to the New Empire hotel in Tottenham Court Road where a Renaissance event is in full swing. Renaissance is a black marketing agency that holds regular seminars for young black professionals. This one is devoted to the phenomenon of the glass ceiling, the invisible barriers to progress through a management hierarchy. On stage Keith Kerr, a senior manager with British Airways, is wowing the audience. They are young, middle-class, mainly Afro-Caribbean. They are eager to learn how to overcome prejudice and discrimination and get on and up. "In British Airways," Keith Kerr says, "99 per cent of senior management is white." There is a quiet hiss from the audience; or it could be a sigh. "0.2 per cent is Afro Caribbean. That's me." Cheers and whoops of delight from the audience. Out of 487 senior managers at BA, he says, only three are not white; out of 1,028 middle managers, only 36. The company has now changed its employment practices under his prompting and introduced an equal opportunities programme. But, he says, black people have to have a strategy if they are to succeed. It's all very well, a member of the audience says, but I've got a degree too and I just can't make it up that ladder; so what made *you* so special? The answer seems to be, simply, Keith Kerr's apparently boundless self-confidence and faith in himself. "Sure you've got to compromise," he says, "but that doesn't mean you stop being proud to be black."

Charlotte Fadipe works as a producer with the BBC World Service and also runs her own PR business. There has been much superficial improvement for black people, she says, but the changes have not kept pace with their rising expectations. "People don't say it to your face but they're saying unofficially, we've got 10 black people here and one or two black managers and that's enough. That's why there are so many black people now who are starting up their own businesses." Yet here, too, black people come up against barriers. "If you're black and you want to start a business in catering or something domestic, that's fine; but if you want to go into PR or engineering or law forget it. You go to the bank with your business plans, the details of all the Tec schemes and everything, and it's still not quite right; you ask them to explain why and they say, it's just too much of a risk."

THERE is much concern about the lack of role models for black youngsters. The African, Caribbean and Asian Lawyers' Group tours schools to show such youngsters that it is possible to be a successful black lawyer. Initiatives like this, thinks David Edwards, the group's publicity co-ordinator, have contributed to the burgeoning applications by black folk to become lawyers. But they still come up against prejudice, despite the ostensible commitment by official legal bodies to equal opportunities. David Edwards, the son of West Indian immigrants, a solicitor specialising in commercial work for a big City firm, says the new entry qualifications requiring candidates to have articles fixed up before they can take their qualifying exams discriminates against black applicants who are less likely to have got the articles in advance; they may be considered to have come from the wrong school, or polytechnics rather than universities; their ethnically distinctive names or, even worse, the photograph they may be asked to supply all enable prejudiced employers to reject them out of hand.

Elpha Lecointe, a barrister, says: "We're getting there slowly but more through cajoling and embarrassment. It's a painfully slow process. People won't say it now to your face but you may have to fight for work, particularly in commercial law where solicitors are still unhappy about briefing a black barrister although they say it's their clients who are unhappy."

There are now many disparate black communities and like the wider society that surrounds them, they are becoming more and more fragmented and isolated from each other. Some find this dismaying. "When we came here 80 per cent of us were working class," A. Sivanandan, director of the Institute of Race Relations, says. "We've lost the Third World perspective we had, the consciousness of a land base. It was something metaphysical." The new assertiveness of black people, he says, is being channelled into dangerous and divisive nationalisms and fundamentalism. Thus Islamic schools are the wrong response to a set of prejudices no longer perceived as a common problem. "Fundamentalism is a sign of the oppressed," he says.

Ranjit Sondhi agrees. The labour market, he says, is promoting individualism among black people. "They are becoming a service class, not working class, expected to set up their own businesses as window cleaners, gardeners. It has its good side but it also destroys the identity between people subject to discrimination. It used to allow them to act in concert, but that kind of political identity has been undermined by a misplaced ethnic pride."

Source: Adapted from the *Guardian*, 1 July 1992

Employment and disability

As noted in the article below, the government introduced legislation, in place from 1997, which sought to ensure that opportunities were available for disabled people to obtain employment and to prevent employers discriminating against someone purely on the grounds of disability which would not prevent them from undertaking a particular job. The author notes, however, that there is still a long way to go!

Society

Fear of the fall-out factor

Jeanne Braybon, former chair of the Disablement Income Group, gives a cautious welcome to the changes

WILL December 2, 1996, be remembered as the beginning of a change of attitude towards disabled people and greater awareness of the problems that we encounter in our daily lives? I wonder.

As a disabled person who has worked with chronically-sick and disabled people in a voluntary capacity for many years, I see weaknesses in several parts of the Act – although I do welcome the progress towards equal rights that it represents.

There are far too many exemptions and exclusions, making it very easy for large numbers of employers, providers of goods and services and landlords to avoid doing anything at all. And the National Disability Council, set up to advise the Government, has no enforcement powers. It may become a mere talking shop.

The act exempts all employers with fewer than 20 employees. This means that about 85 per cent of businesses, employing 40 per cent of the total labour force, fall outside the provisions.

What guarantee is there, anyway, that larger employers will even invite a disabled person for interview if they have no wish to make premises accessible? It will be only too easy for them to say they have better-qualified applicants. It will be many years, it appears, before there is any real improvement in the prospects of the many disabled people who aspire to employment.

The musts and the maybes

What changes next week

■ Unlawful for an employer to treat disabled people less favourably, unless there is "good reason".

■ Employers must consider reasonable adjustments to workplace to help disabled people.

■ Companies with fewer than 20 staff are exempt, but encouraged to follow good practice. Armed forces, police, prisons, ships and planes also exempt.

■ Unlawful to refuse goods, facilities or services to disabled people, or to offer inferior provision, except on health and safety grounds.

What changes eventually

■ Unlawful to make it impossible or unreasonably difficult for disabled people to access goods or services.

■ Suppliers of goods or services must provide equipment or aids to help disabled people where reasonable.

■ Suppliers must remove physical obstructions, or provide alternative access, at no extra cost.

■ Minimum standards for new taxis, trains, buses and coaches to ensure disabled people can use them.

One of the most glaring failings of the act is its lack of priority for accessible transport for disabled people — one of our greatest concerns and one of the big holes exposed by the community care system.

In Bognor Regis, where I live, plans are afoot to make another large part of the town centre a no-go area for motorists. In future, orange badge holders are to be allowed in before 11am and after 4.30pm. The same "concession" already applies to most of the town centre. The result: disabled people go to other towns for their shopping.

If public transport were made accessible to all, many orange badge holders would no longer have to take their cars into the town centre.

Finally, disabled people are still likely to face discrimination in insurance services. Where a person has a life-threatening disease, or a degenerative condition, one can understand the problem that insurers have in setting premiums. Many disabled people, however, have functional limitations but are as healthy as anybody else. They should not have premiums loaded against them.

There is a pressing need to define the difference between disability and disease — particularly as, it seems, people are increasingly to be expected to cover their health and long-term care needs through private insurance.

Source: The *Guardian*, 27 November 1996

Think about it

- To what extent do you think changes in employment law can bring about changes in employers' – and employees' – attitudes? Try to support your answer with examples.
- Why are smaller companies exempt from the provisions of the new Act, and what sociological message could this give?
- Some companies operate on a quota basis when recruiting, stipulating that disabled people should make up a certain percentage of their workforce. What do you think might be the sociological consequences of
    - operating this kind of positive discrimination policy in favour of disabled people?
    - *not* operating such a policy?

Non-work, unemployment and leisure

This section looks at two key areas of contemporary life:

- the consequences of unemployment, both for those directly affected and in terms of the impact that large-scale unemployment may have on wider social and economic circumstances;
- the provision and experience of leisure, and its relationship to work.

Non-work, while clearly incorporating leisure, also includes situations such as unemployment or enforced convalescence to do with illness, or circumstances associated with disability which may make work – or leisure – impossible. There is also the question of whether housework, where it is not classified as work, could be construed as non-work – the idea that it could be construed as leisure is patently flawed. Within the realms of leisure, factors such as gender, age, ethnicity, family and education, along with occupation, personal preference, time and money may all affect both opportunity and level of involvement.

Unemployment

Unemployment statistics

We have already noted that the official rates of unemployment peaked in 1986 when 3.1 million people were entitled to claim benefit. This figure does not include those who chose not to claim; nor does it reflect the downward effects on the figures of changes in the way unemployment is calculated. As we saw in Unit 1 (page 48), by 1996 there had been over 30 alterations to the calculations since 1980, only one of which was constructed in such a way as to make the numbers of unemployed look higher. The Unemployment Unit, an independent research body, claim that in the late 1990s there are more than 4 million people unemployed, with over 1 million not included in the official statistics; the difference is partly accounted for by the fact that men over the age of 55 who do not work are not included in the official statistics. The percentage of unemployment amongst this group has increased significantly since 1975.

Types of unemployment

Unemployment is often considered under five key categories, as follows:

- **Frictional unemployment** This relates to the time when workers change employment, when they have left one job but not yet taken up another. Frictional unemployment is considered to be inevitable in an economy in change.
- **Structural unemployment** This is where industries close down in large numbers and the workers are unable to take up the jobs which are available elsewhere. This type of unemployment can be either **sectoral**, where workers are insufficiently trained and lack the necessary skills, or **regional**, where there are vacancies available, for example, in the south-east but workers are only available in the north.
- **Cyclical unemployment** This is where the number of unemployed people exceeds the number of job vacancies, in a fluctuating pattern according to the booms and slumps of the economy. Generally there are high levels of unemployment in economic slumps and low levels of unemployment when the economy is booming. According to a number of writers, however, economic booms will not necessarily lead to greatly reduced levels of unemployment in the economy of the future.

- **Related to technological change** The introduction of micro-technology, increased computer use, the 'global village' and 'home-working' using communications technology all serve to reduce employment – a view offered by Hawkins in his book *Unemployment* (1984).
- **De-industrialisation** and **globalisation** The decline in the manufacturing industry and a move to smaller-size factories, combined with globalisation, have, it is argued, greatly contributed to lower levels of employment, while increased foreign competition places traditional British markets under pressure from other developed and developing economies. The demise of the British motorcycle industry is an example, where market domination by the Japanese in the 1980s and 1990s has replaced British domination in the 1950s.

The table below shows overall figures for unemployment in the G7 countries (i.e. the world's seven leading economies) in the period 1989–1994.

Unemployment rates adjusted to SOEC concepts*: G7 comparison						
	1989 (%)	1990 (%)	1991 (%)	1992 (%)	1993 (%)	1994 (%)
France	..	..	9.5	10.4	11.7	12.3
Italy	10.0	9.1	8.8	9.0	10.3	11.4
Canada	7.5	8.1	10.3	11.3	11.2	10.3
United Kingdom	7.3	7.0	8.8	10.1	10.4	9.6
Germany	..	..	5.6	6.6	7.9	8.4
United States	5.3	5.5	6.7	7.4	6.8	6.1
Japan	2.3	2.1	2.1	2.2	2.5	2.9

* Except Canada which is based on OECD concepts.

Source: SOEC, OECD in *Social Trends*, 1996

Researched effects of unemployment

The group of people labelled 'unemployed' are in fact very diverse: they have little in common other than their unemployment. Unemployment is primarily an individual experience, with its effects varying from person to person. Nevertheless, sociological and psychological studies of unemployment have found various general effects. Fagan and Little (1984) noted four stages in the typical reaction to unemployment:

1. Shock – inability to accept job loss.
2. Denial and optimism – many job applications.
3. Anxiety and distress – concern about the future, increasing the longer the time of unemployment.
4. Resignation and adjustment – acceptance of unemployment, with a tendency to become lethargic and apathetic.

Other generally recognised effects of unemployment include:

- loss of social contacts, leading to social isolation;
- leisure time often unstructured and purposeless;
- precarious financial situation, with the long-term unemployed prone to poverty;
- negative effects on family life, relationship difficulties;
- possible adverse effects upon health;
- increased potential for anti-social behaviour, with unemployment being linked to crime, drug abuse, drink abuse and suicide.
- reduced contact with both the world of work and with informal networks which might have provided contacts leading to work possibilities. In Young and Willmott's study of Bethnal Green in the 1950s, for example, such networks were seen to open up opportunities for employment, access to housing and so on. If the unemployed have fewer contacts with people in work they will also have lower chances of hearing about prospective job vacancies, except via the Job Centre.

Jan Pahl, in *Divisions of Labour* (1984), and Harris et al., in *Redundancy and Recession in South Wales* (1987), noted evidence of social polarisation, which showed a concentration of work opportunities for some households and the total absence of these opportunities for others. They noted a tendency for the married population to divide into two-worker and no-worker homes, with the former increasing by 14 per cent between 1973 and 1987 and the latter by 7 per cent. In addition, whilst 69 per cent of married men in employment had wives who were also employed, only 27 per cent of unemployed married men had wives in employment.

The financial consequences of unemployment can be devastating and in some instances (for example where rent or mortgage arrears result in eviction or house repossession), can result in suicide. The long-term unemployed are most vulnerable, with changes to benefits or mortgage support often adding to the psychological and financial pressure. On the whole, unemployed people of all ages are relatively inactive, with leisure activities the first casualties of a tight budget.

Paul Willis has carried out research to support his theory that many young unemployed people live in a kind of suspended animation because they have never experienced full-time work. The lack of a wage means that they cannot obtain a home, which many see as the main embodiment of the worker's freedom and independence: its promise of warmth and safety more than offsets the risk and coldness of work. Willis particularly stressed the feelings of dependency on the State and family of the young, working-class unemployed. A sense of liberation afforded by the ability to earn a weekly wage is replaced by a feeling of dependency that results from being on a training scheme or on limited welfare benefit.

The gap between those who have and those who have not has increased since 1979; this applies to income and wealth (see Unit 2), and also to employment and unemployment. The ideas of Charles Murray, (see page 413) in *The Emerging British Underclass* (1990), can be seen to apply to the 'have nots'. Sociologists such as Robinson and Gregson, in *The 'Underclass': A Class Apart?* (1992), see the term 'underclass' as targeting the poor in a way which allows the development of a **moral panic** (see page 301) and the political targeting of benefits evident in the Budgets of November 1995, 1996 and 1997.

Approaches to unemployment – policy directions

J. Owens identified a number of possible responses to the problem of unemployment:

- the full employment welfare state which ensures that everyone who wishes to work has the chance to do so;
- a strong state allied to the free market: the state invests in some employment but employment levels are determined largely by industry and the market (the cost of wage labour, etc.);
- greater state investment in employment initiatives and the retraining of the unemployed, with particular emphasis on new technology.

All political parties aspire to the eradication of unemployment or at least to what is termed 'Keynesian full employment' (which means unemployment rates of about 2.5 per cent). The Conservative Budget of 1995 attempted to ensure that a section of the long-term unemployed were 'encouraged', through the benefits system, actively to seek employment or lose their benefit entitlement. In the USA, in August 1996, legislation was passed which limits a person's benefit entitlement to a maximum of five years over the course of their life. The newly elected Labour government (1997) intends to limit benefit entitlement.

Leisure

What is leisure? Definitions may include some of the following:

- lack of contractual obligations;
- choice of available activity;
- emphasis on personal satisfaction;
- little restriction in terms of role imposition;
- no or limited financial commitment (although some leisure pursuits, for example skiing, can be very expensive);
- experience which allows subjective attachment to the activity itself.

This short list, however, cannot take account of the class and gender base of many leisure activities. Whilst, for some, leisure can become a central life interest and generate an opportunity for self expression and personal freedom, for others it may be unavailable. This may be due to an inability to afford it; a lack of access to it (needing a car); its social exclusiveness (needing to meet social criteria of acceptability); or, if it is competitive, the need to be good enough in order to gain admittance.

Leisure activities – who does what?

The following graph indicates that whilst the 25–44 age group has the least leisure time, after the age of 44 leisure time appears to increase with age. However, there is concern about the ability of those in the older age groups to afford to make the most of their leisure time. In addition, women appear to have less leisure time than their equivalent male age group.

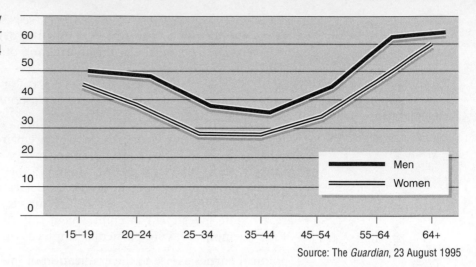

Average leisure time by age group, hours per week, 1994

Source: The *Guardian*, 23 August 1995

Leisure and social differentiation

Looking at another question, the table opposite offers some insight into the leisure activities of different social classes. For the selected activities, the percentage of the professional classes engaging in them is much greater than that of the intermediate and junior non-manual class, and very significantly more than that of the unskilled manual class. This provides limited but compelling evidence of the class-based nature of many leisure activities.

The social class grouping of football fans has been analysed in terms of income and education, based on data collected in the Premier League Survey, as shown below.

A Football fans' education
B Football fans' incomes

A

Season ticket holders who go now or who did go to University or Polytechnic, %.

Wimbledon	38.6
Manchester Utd	36.8
Leeds Utd	34.6
Queens Park Rangers	34.4
Bolton Wanderers	34.2
Middlesbrough	33.8
Nottingham Forest	33.0
Manchester City	32.8
Liverpool	32.2
Sheffield Wednesday	31.4
Tottenham Hotspur	30.8
Blackburn Rovers	30.5
Newcastle Utd	30.0
Arsenal	29.1
Chelsea	28.6
Southampton	28.1
Everton	26.9
Aston Villa	26.0
West Ham Utd	25.2
Coventry City	24.9

B

How important would you say this club is in your life right now? % by salary.

☐ One of the most important things in my life
▨ Just one of the things I do

	One of the most important things	Just one of the things I do
£10,000 or less	34.5	9.9
£10,001 – £15,000	31.0	9.1
£15,001 – £20,000	27.6	10.1
£20,001 – £25,000	22.9	11.9
£25,001 – £30,000	19.8	12.3
Over £30,000	17.5	18.6

Source: Premier League Survey, 1995/96

The table below shows a range of leisure activities, and the percentage of each social class who participate in each activity.

	Social class (Registrar General's scale)				
	AB (%)	C1 (%)	C2 (%)	DE (%)	All (mean average) (%)
Pub	67	70	65	59	65
Meal in restaurant (not fast food)	81	74	56	44	61
Drive for pleasure	50	53	45	39	46
Meal in fast food restaurant	48	49	39	37	42
Library	57	46	32	31	39
Cinema	46	39	29	24	33
Short break holiday	41	34	28	19	29
Disco or nightclub	21	25	25	28	25
Historic building	41	29	19	12	23
Spectator sport event	25	24	23	18	22
Theatre	33	24	16	10	19
Museum or art gallery	34	23	14	10	19
Fun fair	12	13	15	16	14
Exhibition	24	17	10	8	14
Theme park	12	10	12	9	11
Bingo	3	6	11	17	10
Betting shop	5	8	13	11	10
Camping or caravanning	9	9	10	7	9
Pop or rock concert	8	9	8	6	8
Classical concert or opera	15	9	3	3	7
Evening class	11	6	4	4	6
Circus	1	1	3	4	2

Source: Adapted from *Social Trends*, 1994

Further data relating to leisure activities is provided in Unit 6. See, for example, page 283 for data on levels of participation in various home-based leisure activities by men and women; and page 313 for data relating to the use of free time amongst different age groups.

Think about it

Study the figures on the preceding two pages and then do the following:

- Identify the most popular leisure activity for each social class, and offer an explanation of why these differ from one class to another.
- Explain why some activities have a significantly higher percentage participation rate for classes A, B and C1 than for other classes.
- Why might social classes D and E have the highest participation level for bingo?

Women and leisure

Until the early 1980s, the sociological focus on leisure was dominated by concerns about class differences, and studies concentrated largely on male leisure pursuits.

Rosemary Deem, however, in a study published in *Social Studies Review* in 1990, looked at gender divisions in the context of leisure. She observed that the gendered nature of responsibilities for:

- housework;
- childcare; and
- care for elderly or disabled dependants

had a significant impact on the differing leisure patterns for men and women. The time-consuming nature of this kind of home-based activity restricts many women's opportunities for a range of leisure pursuits. A major focal point for female leisure is provided among women themselves through socialising in each other's homes, shared leisure activities, or task sharing (baby-sitting/childminding) to create time for each other's leisure activities. However, in *All Work and No Play* (1986), Deem noted that the concept of 'free time' meant very little to most women. 'Leisure' was restricted to the home and consisted often of watching TV, reading and knitting – activities which 'fitted in' with other domestic tasks.

Deem identified a number of factors which make it easier for women to engage in purposeful leisure activities:

- lack of family commitments;
- a social support network;
- a positive view of self;
- a belief in the importance of and need for leisure;
- an independent source of money;
- a means of transport;
- some form of work.

Linked with the tradition of gendered home-based responsibilities are social expectations about women's participation in certain forms of leisure, where they remain in a small minority (as participants or spectators, in the case of sports). These expectations also contribute to the difference between male and female leisure patterns. The only sports in which women participate more than men are: indoor swimming, keep fit and yoga, and netball, according to the General Household Survey in 1990. The most common leisure activities for women are watching television or visiting friends, but the number gardening or carrying out DIY has increased since 1983, while those doing needle work and knitting has declined.

In terms of who does what at home, there is still a gender gap, though it is less wide than it was.

Division of household tasks, %	Actual allocation of tasks			Respondents' views on how tasks should be shared		
	Mainly women	Mainly men	Shared equally	Mainly women	Mainly men	Shared equally
Household shopping	45	8	47	22	1	76
Making evening meal	70	9	20	39	1	57
Doing evening dishes	33	28	37	11	11	75
Doing household cleaning	68	4	27	36	1	62
Doing washing and ironing	84	3	12	58	–	40
Repairing household equipment	6	82	10	1	66	31
Organising household money and bills	40	31	28	14	17	66

Housework myths

Labour-saving devices save time

In the 1920s women in the US spent an average of 60 hours a week doing housework. By the 1970s housework was taking up even *more* time: an average of 70 hours a week[1]. In 1925, when most clothes were washed by hand, women spent 5.5 hours a week doing the laundry. After the invention of the washing-machine the time had gone *up* to 6.25 hours[2]. By 1982 80 per cent of UK households owned a washing machine and 95 per cent had a vacuum cleaner, but women are doing more housework than ever[3]. This is because families change their clothes more often, expect a cleaner house and a more varied diet – and because today's mother gets practically no help from the rest of the household.

Housewives have lots of free time

Men have an average of 33.5 hours of free time per week, compared with 24.6 hours for women[4]. Even at weekends, while men and children relax, housewives work an average of six hours each day[2].

Housework is natural for women

Hunting is no more natural to men than housework is to women. In one study of 224 different traditional cultures, there were 13 in which women hunted and 60 in which they fished. Housebuilding was an exclusively female occupation in 36 cultures, while there were five in which men did all the cooking and a further 38 in which cooking was routinely done by either sex[5]. In parts of Indonesia and Zaire it is the father who is expected to care for his infant child[6].

Men are beginning to help

Married men in the US now do *six* per cent more housework than 20 years ago[7]. Only 55% of UK men in one survey had washed the dishes at all in the previous week[8]. One in four women in another UK survey said their husbands were more of a hindrance than a help[9]. No reliable study has ever estimated men's share of the housework at anything more than 1.5 hours a day[10].

1 B Ehrenreich and D English, *For Her Own Good*, Pluto, UK, 1979. 2 J Vanek, *Time Spent in Housework*, Scientific American, November 1974. 3 W Faulkner and E Arnold, *Smothered by Invention*, Pluto, UK, 1985. 4 HMSO *Social Trends* 1987. 5 G P Murdock, *Comparative Data on the Division of Labour by Sex*, Social Forces, 1937. 6 A Oakley, *Housewife*, Penguin, 1976. 7 S A Hewlett, *A Lesser Life: The Myth of Women's Liberation*, Michael Joseph, London, 1987. 8 The Association of Market Survey Organizations, UK, *Men and Domestic Work*. 9 *The 1,001 Dirt Report*. 10 R Cowan, *More Work for Mother*.

Source: Adapted from *New Internationalist*, March 1988

Think about it

• The cartoons on page 257 date from 1988. Do you think the image they portray is still accurate? If changes have occurred, what are they, and what has helped to bring them about? Refer to the article 'Housework myths' in your answer but also supply your own examples.

Leisure and ethnicity

There has been relatively little sociological study of leisure and ethnicity. S. Scraton, writing in *Developments in Sociology* (Vol. 8), noted how little research had been carried out into the leisure activities of ethnic minorities. One aspect which has been investigated, however, is in connection with the sociology of sport. Issues of race were addressed through a study of the low rates of participation in some sports by, for example, Afro-Caribbean young people.

E. Green, whose study *Women's Leisure – what leisure?* was published in 1990, looked in particular at the leisure patterns of women from ethnic minorities. Green found that such women are often 'subjected to social oppression in the form of institutionalised discrimination as well as random interpersonal acts of harassment and racial attack' which limited their likelihood of going out. In addition, the study observed that among Asian families, the traditional patterns of expectation would require women to look after the household unit exclusively and to adhere to the wishes of the eldest male. It is suggested by Green that Afro-Caribbean women are far less restricted in their leisure activities. However, economic issues of unemployment and low incomes, and the geographical problem of access to leisure pursuits, also impose limitations on leisure pursuits for many from ethnic backgrounds, of either gender.

In the 1990s, postmodern theory has challenged the idea that leisure activities are determined mainly by social group, whether it is class, gender or ethnicity, emphasising instead the individual's choice and a fragmented pattern of leisure activity, rather than a collective one.

The growth of leisure

The 1980s witnessed a significant expansion in leisure provision with the arrival of theme parks, health centres and entertainment centres. Behind these developments lie sets of assumptions about consumerism and the universality of leisure provision which sociologists are interested to investigate.

Clarke and Critcher, in *The Devil Makes Work* (1985), argued that changes in employment and the collapse of manufacturing industry have not 'liberated' people from demeaning work: there are more non-manual jobs, but these are often part-time, poorly paid and insecure. In such a situation, the idea that leisure holds out opportunities for fulfilment holds little relevance.

Whilst leisure 'appears' to be more available, offering wider opportunities for personal choice, it often represents simply a new form of consumerism. It is linked more closely to the consumption of goods than to the potentially positive virtues of a true 'leisure society', offering choice, activity and fulfilment.

Leisure is seen as an extension to paid work on the part of a core workforce offering opportunities for recuperation, escape, or the pursuit of hobbies.

The relationship between work and leisure

Work can be interpreted as physical/mental effort or as a duty imposed by a paid job. However, in the former definition it would be difficult to distinguish between work and active leisure; while the latter definition would be unacceptable to feminists such as Ann Oakley (see Unit 3) who saw housework as comparable in all respects except pay to the labour of a factory worker. It is therefore more useful to take work to mean a person's main employment (whether paid or unpaid) and the duties resulting from it. Leisure, too, can be difficult to define, with some writers stressing the role of positive or productive activities. It is probably most useful to think of leisure as that which is left after work obligations are completed.

Many sociologists have noted the effect that work can have on leisure:

- The income from work extends or restricts the range of leisure options: the higher a person's earnings, the greater the range available and vice versa.
- Working hours can have a significant effect on leisure activities and familial relationships. The Newsons' Nottingham study revealed that men on shift-work were unable to play a very active part in the socialisation of their children:

> 'Of particular importance in its impact on family life and routine is shift-working, since it makes a good deal of difference to the amount of time the father spends at home while his children are up and about the house ... some factories (in Nottingham) work three shifts from, normally, 6.00am to 2.00pm; 2.00pm to 10.00pm and 10.00pm to 6.00am. Workers may take one shift and stick to it, so that the father is "on nights" or "on afternoons", or they may alternate.'
> John and Elizabeth Newson, *Patterns of Infant Care* (1963)

The afternoon shift of 2.00pm to 10.00pm is particularly unsociable in that it excludes most normal recreational options.
- Work companionship can influence attitudes to work through the sharing of out-of-work activities, whether drinking or bungee-jumping.
- Work skills can be carried over into leisure as a way of saving or earning money, for example when a motor mechanic maintains his own car, or repairs friends' cars in exchange for other favours or a small payment.
- Work skills can equally be carried over into leisure as a matter of personal interest, for example when the motor mechanic rebuilds or restores a car for pleasure. Gerstl refers to other examples of this: university professors reading in their leisure time and advertising professionals writing and drawing.
- Job status may limit leisure options amongst particular occupational groups: some forms of leisure, such as pigeon-fancying, might be considered below the dignity of professionals, for example; whilst others, such as croquet or polo might be seen as above the status position of some groups of workers.
- The type of job, the location of work, and the amount of time and energy available after work, also contribute to the extent to which work may affect leisure.

Stanley Parker, a sociologist who has made a specialist study of work and leisure, outlined three relationships between the two:

- leisure as an extension of work;
- leisure as a complement to work;
- leisure in opposition to work.

Extension   Parker found that childcare officers and youth employment officers regarded leisure as an extension of work. This is echoed by the findings of Child and Macmillan in 1972: the dominant attitude of American managers was that work was central to their lives and that leisure was a refreshment process enabling work to be performed more efficiently. Various forms of leisure activity can be viewed in this way: studying for vocational qualifications in evening classes, or businessmen playing golf with prospective customers to generate business, are two examples.

Complement   Parker found that bank employees tended to segment their lives, with a complete separation between work and leisure. This seems to be a common reaction of people in jobs which, though neither dangerous nor unpleasant, are routine and boring: office work and conveyor-belt type production, for example.

Opposition   People in dangerous and unpleasant jobs may use leisure time to forget work. In their study of Yorkshire coalminers in the 1950s, Dennis and others found strong communal ties and a high alcohol intake to be reactions to the dangerous and physically demanding work; whilst Turnstall's study of Hull fishermen a decade later found them adopting fatalistic attitudes and spending much of their leisure time drinking together.

There is, however, a danger of overstressing the impact of work on a person's leisure. Factors such as shorter working hours, technological change reducing heavy manual labour, and people living at greater distances from work may have reduced the potential direct effects of work on leisure.

Many factors, other than work, affect leisure time and the selection of leisure activities. Attitudes are passed down from parents, peer groups and the community in various ways that are independent from work, and these influence people's outlook on life and their choice of interests. Age often acts as a limit on the choice of leisure patterns; Abrams has developed a model of leisure based on age that makes no reference to type of work. Other factors include the region you live in (access to leisure activities, for example, may be affected by whether you live in an urban or a rural area), and your personality.

Think about it

- In what ways might work and leisure be related to a) social class position, b) gender, c) age, d) ethnicity?
- With changes in patterns of work anticipated in the future, what might be the effects upon use of leisure time for a) workers, b) those over 50 not in employment?

Organisations and bureaucracy

What are organisations?

An organisation is a form of collective, set up to achieve certain specific aims or goals. Organisations are characterised by:

- a formal structure of rules;
- authority relations;
- a division of labour;
- limited membership or admission.

One of the major differences between modern industrial and pre-industrial society lies in the number and significance of organisations. If we take an organisation to be an institution or social structure designed to achieve specific goals, then organisations did exist in pre-industrial society. The modernisation of society, however, has been closely associated with an increase in specialised organisations such as the school, the trade union and the government department.

Organisations are approached in contrasting ways by different sociologists. In *The Theory of Organisations* (1970), David Silverman outlines the vast array of approaches: sociologists from a **systems perspective** (macro) see organisations in terms of their goals or inevitable patterns of **conflict**; whilst others look at organisations from an **agency perspective** (micro), examining the role of individual actors within an organisation and seeking to get the workers to define the reality as they see it. It is important to understand these conflicting approaches, to be able to identify the ideological assumptions behind them, and to evaluate their worth in describing and explaining the nature of human behaviour in organisations.

Large-scale or complex organisations are found in all aspects of life: for example, business corporations, schools, hospitals, prisons, the military, political parties, trade unions, churches and so on. Such organisations tend to be structured along formal lines, so that the collective purpose is carried out by a recognised hierarchy of decision-makers and implementers. J. Beardman and D. Palfreman, in *The Organisation in its Environment* (1984) put forward the following breakdown of organisations into three types.

Formal/Informal	
Formal	**Informal**
These organisations have been established for the specific purpose of achieving certain goals or objectives, and they possess a set of rules to assist in their attempt to achieve the objectives.	In these organisations activities are carried on usually without the existence of clearly defined goals or rules, for example friendship networks.

Productive/Non-productive	
Productive	**Non-productive**
These organisations are concerned with the production of goods (e.g. cars) or services (e.g. restaurants, banks).	These organisations include, for example, legal institutions, such as courts of law or trade unions, and exist to serve the interests of the state or their members.

Public sector/Private sector	
Public sector	**Private sector**
These organisations are owned and directed by government or their appointed agents (e.g. the armed forces).	These organisations are owned and controlled by shareholders or individuals, often taking the form of PLCs (public limited companies).

Most forms of organisations tend to affect only parts of a person's life, although some 'total institutions', such as monasteries, prisons, military bases, merchant ships, can be almost all-embracing (see references to Goffman's classic study, page 264).

Organisational culture Organisations (particularly the large-scale or complex ones) tend to develop a culture of their own: they tend to influence the behaviour of employees or members in particular ways through the process of socialisation, thus developing their own culture and shaping members'/employees' own identity. During the 1980s, in British commercial and industrial organisations, this became an important area for study, prompted by three key issues:

- the challenge of Japanese competition;
- concern over the need to ensure economic recovery in British industry;
- the apparent failure to organise efficiently and effectively since 1945.

One area that has attracted considerable attention is the role of managerial control and power in the shaping of organisational culture. During the 1980s, particularly in the NHS and in newly privatised companies, a high priority was placed on the need for effective management. Charles Handy, in *Understanding Organisations* (1989), considered a number of different types of organisational cultures. He looked at how the strength or weakness of an organisation was linked to its managers' power, role and personal qualities. In this view managers can shape the culture of an organisation and, in so doing, create either a positive or negative environment in which to work and enable the organisation to attain its key goals.

Formal and informal structures of control

Max Weber (see below), in looking at bureaucracy or the administration of organisations, identified the **legal-rational** form as the most effective system of administration. He believed that its operation should be based on well-defined rules laid down by the government which, in turn, was democratically elected. Gouldner, writing in the 1950s, suggested that rather than **punishment-centred bureaucracy** based on strict application of rules, the most effective form of administration was one based on **representation** – that is, one which took account of the needs and preferences of both the organisation's employees and its clients, whilst still retaining a formal structure. Interactionist sociologists' accounts of organisations have focused attention on the informal processes at work in all organisations, and on the significant impact which small groups of workers can have on the wider organisation's aims.

Weber's concept of bureaucracy

When Weber was writing, the nation states of Western Europe were becoming increasingly involved in the mobilisation of resources and they required state employees to make rapid, effective and acceptable decisions on a whole range of subjects. Weber saw the development of bureaucracy, with the following characteristics, as the essential means of enabling this transition to take place:

- a staff with *distinct roles* to perform. Each member should have a fixed area of jurisdiction and the specialised knowledge to deal with it;
- a *hierarchy of authority*, each individual within it knowing their own decision-making capacity and that of others in the structure;
- *impersonality*, with consistent rules being followed in the making of any decision. Personal emotions or obligations should not interfere with this rational allocation process, and members of the bureaucracy should deal with each other in terms of their organisational role, not on a personal basis;
- all members selected on the basis of *merit* via examinations, qualifications and experience, and employed on a fixed salary on a free, contractual basis, involving a career-structure with promotion prospects.

Weber saw this **bureaucratic model** as suitable for the whole range of profit-making, military, political and religious organisations. He was aware of the potential dangers of the consolidation of power and the effects of impersonality on the individual, and he stressed the need for close 'parliamentary' (i.e. representative) control; but nevertheless he saw the development of bureaucracy as essential.

The limitations of bureaucracy

The functionalist argument claims that elements of bureaucracy can be **dysfunctional** for the organisation or society in general. Robert Merton argued that prescribed rules might not cover every situation; conformity to regulations can become an end in itself instead of a means of ensuring efficiency; and an overemphasis on formality can cause friction with the public. A rigid hierarchy of authority and impersonality can create feelings of tension and insecurity. In the most extreme examples of bureaucratic dysfunction, employees apply rules rigidly and may not achieve the aims of the organisation. Some critics of the Benefits Agency and the Child Support Agency note how impersonal and inflexible these organisations have been in dealing with clients.

Goffman's concept of 'total institutions'

As a result of observational studies in asylums (psychiatric hospitals) in the 1960s, **Erving Goffman** isolated certain qualities which would justify the description of **total institution** being applied to organisations such as prisons, army barracks, merchant ships, hospitals, monasteries and boarding schools. These qualities include the following:

- 'Inmates' sleep, work and take their leisure time in the same environment, under the same authority.
- All 'inmates' are treated alike, and activity is in the company of a large number of others.
- There is a tightly scheduled, daily routine for activities.
- There is a large managed group, with a small supervisory staff. Great social distance exists between the two groups.

Goffman saw the total institution as a social hybrid, part residential community, part formal organisation. He identified the following organisations, based on their aims, as being the purest examples of the total institution:

- those caring for the incapable and the harmless, for example geriatric hospitals;
- those for people who pose an unintended threat to the community, for example quarantine clinics;
- those for people who pose an intentional threat, for example high security prisons;
- those where efficiency is paramount, for example military establishments;
- those that act as retreats from society, for example monasteries.

For Goffman, the value of studying such institutions is that they are the forcing houses for changing persons; inmates are forced to adapt to the pressure being placed upon them. Goffman isolated five modes of adaptation:

- situational withdrawal: the inmate minimises interaction with others;
- the intransigent line: non-cooperation with the authorities;
- colonisation: the institutionalisation of the inmate;
- conversion: the inmate submits to the pressures and becomes the perfect or model inmate;
- playing it cool: by far the most common reaction – the inmate avoids conflict with the authorities while trying to minimise the effects of the formal rules and restrictions.

Goffman's concept of the total institution is valuable in the following ways:

- It reveals how such institutions can have effects that are far from those intended. If we accept, for example, that a major function of a prison is to rehabilitate the inmates, then, it can be argued, the modes of adaptation rarely coincide with that aim.
- By focusing on groups that are isolated from society, it may be possible to identify behaviour patterns that are normally taken for granted. This may increase our ability to see everyday life as being built on 'taken for granted' patterns of expectation.
- Goffman has demonstrated that to understand an organisation it is insufficient to analyse it on the basis of its declared aims.

Goffman's work has been extremely influential. His ideas come through clearly, for example, in *Escape Attempts*, a study by Stan Cohen and Laurie Taylor of the inmates of Durham prison, published in 1971. Despite his influence, Goffman's idea of the total institution gives rise to several questions:

- How far are the apparent similarities between total institutions overridden by important differences between them, such as who commits the person to the institution and how long their stay is?
- To what extent is the inmate isolated (for example, soldiers with evening passes, republican or loyalist prisoners released on parole over Christmas)?

Think about it

- Why do you think society provides 'total institutions', e.g. prisons and psychiatric hospitals?
- To what extent do such 'total institutions' meet the needs of the 'inmates'?

An increasing number of organisations in business seem to be moving away from the traditional patterns of bureaucracy, if these are defined as:

- sharp divisions of labour and hierarchies;
- highly formalised behaviour on the part of officials;
- standardisation of procedures;
- centralised authority;
- central planning and control.

Many companies are **decentralising** their decision-making and communications: decision-making is devolved to ever smaller units or subcontracted out to other firms. The idea of a large-scale bureaucracy in the business context – if not in public or national institutions – has become less prevalent than in the past.

Whereas, for Weber, rules are at the heart of bureaucratic organisations and are necessary to ensure that officials are working in the same way to common organisational objectives, recent studies of a number of companies note a clear intention to keep rules to the minimum and, in flatter organisational hierarchies, to use face-to-face (or computer-to-computer) communication to develop agreed rules between work groups.

However, claims that bureaucracy has little relevance in contemporary organisations can be readily challenged: we need look only at the structures that are in place in hospitals, schools, colleges, government departments, the Church, the military or even a large supermarket chain.

Think about it

- Outline the organisational structure of your school/college/workplace.
- Give some examples of private companies which have **decentralised**.
- What do you understand by a 'flatter' organisational structure? How might a school look different if it was less hierarchical?

Organisations and goals

A functionalist approach to organisations sees them as having particular goals or functions to perform for society. The table below gives examples.

Organisation	Examples of functions
school	educate pupils; deliver the curriculum
private firm	maximise long-term profitability; increase market share
political party	unite the electorate in the community; compete for political power
pressure group	protect and expand the interests of members by putting pressure on those with power in society

A basic logical flaw in this approach is that it attributes thought and action to inanimate objects. As Silverman points out in *The Theory of Organisations*:

- It would be possible to focus on members of the organisation having goals, but the organisation itself can only have goals insofar as they are written into it and adhered to by its members.
- The original goals of an organisation's founders may be forgotten or displaced. For example, the Peace Movement in Northern Ireland, in its later stages, tried to establish a form of community politics and a new political structure.
- There may be no agreement over the purpose of the organisation, with conflict between workers and managers, or divisions within political parties. For example, the Scottish National Party and Plaid Cymru have both been divided between those who see them as the means of gaining political independence and those who see them as pressure groups for cultural, social and economic interests, looking for a devolution of power but not separation.
- Leaders may be dishonest in their statement of goals, using them to gain power and status rather than having a true commitment to them.

In sociological thinking on goals and organisations, there are a number of views, of which four of the most significant are outlined below.

Four sociological views of organisations and their goals

1. T. Parsons (1960) looked at organisations' goals in terms of different intended outputs to the wider social system. These were defined as follows:
   - those oriented to economic production (e.g. British Aerospace)
   - those oriented to political goals (e.g. the NHS)
   - those oriented to the cultural and educational (e.g. universities, art galleries)
   - those oriented to the legal sphere (e.g. police, courts).

2. Blau and Scott (1963) were interested in identifying who benefits from the organisation and identified four groups of potential beneficiaries:
   - members – mutual benefit organisations such as trade unions
   - owners/managers – business enterprises
   - clients – service organisations such as hospitals
   - public – 'commonweal' organisations such as the ambulance or fire services.

3. Etzioni placed his emphasis on the structures of compliance – in other words, how do the organisations' leaders secure the members'/workers' support? He suggested three forms:
   - order goals – coercive structures such as prisons
   - economic goals – e.g. workplaces
   - cultural goals – e.g. political parties.

Each of the above writers sought to develop an understanding of how organisations are affected by, and try to bring about, their goals.

4. A conflict approach to organisations and their goals perceives them as being divisive, as being used to exploit the workforce and, in a capitalist society, to operate in order to maximise profits for owners or shareholders.

Theories of management

Taylorism

F.W. Taylor began to introduce incentive schemes to the workplace in the latter part of the nineteenth century with the development of his **scientific management** theories. Taylor sought out agreement in companies for management to decide how work was to be performed and to ensure that workers operated in the most efficient, effective and productive way possible. This was to be done by including systems of incentives or rewards for work and by specifying precisely how the work would be carried out. Many firms now include bonus and incentive schemes in their work practices, including piece-work bonuses, productivity awards and the existence of 'time and motion' techniques to assess workers' performance before setting a standard time allocation for a piece of work. Taylorism has had a marked impact on the organisation of production and the application of technology.

However, Japanese companies, using work teams and work groups, lacking precise job divisions and offering great job flexibility, represent a radical move away from the very prescriptive ideas of F.W. Taylor.

Fordism

As we saw in Unit 1 (page 59), this is the name given to the system of mass production evident in industries such as car manufacture, particularly since the 1920s. The development of a moving assembly line, with workers undertaking small repetitive tasks, contributed to high levels of production but also to a high level of labour turnover. According to Sabel in *Work and Politics* (1982), the 'high point' of Fordism as a productive technique affecting worker performance and task is over. This has opened up a key debate about the relationship between the organisation of production, the use of technology and the implications for work and worker – summarised in the table below:

	Fordist	Post-Fordist
Technology	Fixed, dedicated machines Vertically integrated operation Mass production	Micro-electronically controlled, multi-purpose machines Subcontracting Batch production
Products	For a mass consumer market Relatively cheap	Diverse, specialised products High quality
Labour process	Fragmented Few tasks Little worker discretion Hierarchical authority and technical control	Many tasks for versatile workers Some autonomy Group control
Contracts	Collectively negotiated rate for the job Relatively secure	Payment by individual performance Dual market: secure core, highly insecure periphery

Source: Adapted from Alan Warde, 'Fordism and Post-Fordism', *Social Studies Review*, September 1989

C. Smith, in *Work, Employment and Society* (1989) argues that 'flexible production' is becoming the norm for large-scale producers where it might be necessary to switch production quickly. This process has been hastened by automation, computer-aided design and the use (as in the Japanese example above) of a variety of job rotation, collaborative or group production teams which cut across the rigid hierarchies of Taylorist or Fordist work organisational principles.

Mike Reed, in 1989, identified three key perspectives that have shaped sociological research and analysis of management, all of which have been developed since 1900. These are the technical, political and critical perspectives, outlined below.

The technical perspective

Management is seen to be concerned with the means rather than the ends of an organisation's operation, seeking to ensure that the formal structure is in place to maintain day-to-day efficiency and effectiveness. The works of Amitai Etzioni (1975), Thompson (1967), Laurence and Lorsed (1967) and Pugh and Hickson (1976) have contributed to this approach. It assumes that:

• organisational structures are formal;
• these structures are likely to persist over time;
• organisational change is not itself to be managed;
• managers' role in change is therefore limited.

The political perspective

This sees the role of management as being to minimise conflict between different groups within the organisation. It sees management itself as consisting of a **plurality** (variety) of competing groups or coalitions of interest, which come into conflict over a range of day-to-day or longer-term policy issues. There is a key emphasis here on the power issue of management, of the 'right' to manage and the power which is exerted in doing so. Influential theorists associated with this model include Selznick (1949), Gouldner (1954), Peter Blau (1955) and Burns and Stalker (1961).

The critical perspective

This sees management as representative of the interests of the capitalist class or owners. The political and economic interests of this group will be advanced and protected by the managers who are employed for this purpose. Managers need to achieve a degree of control over the workers, sufficient to ensure that production is profitable and that workers produce the necessary 'surplus value'. Both managers and the organisations which they manage (but do not own) are direct products of the socio-economic (capitalist) system in which they function. Contributors to this largely Marxist perspective include Zimblast (1979), Wood (1982) and Knights and Willmott (1986).

Summary of management theories

	Underlying analysis	Sociological theory	Policy
Technical	Rationally designed to ensure that management meets particular objectives	Systems theory	Improved effectiveness for policy application
Political	Negotiated social process for the regulation of interest-group conflict	Action or agency theory	Improved negotiation skills for managers
Critical	Managers are required to maximise profit through 'surplus value' production	Marxist theory	Downsizing, maximisation of worker productivity

Problems with management theories

Mike Reed identifies a number of problems with the theories described above, including:

- a failure to give full consideration to managerial behaviour, organisational structures and institutional settings;
- a tendency to emphasise the *structure* of the organisation as determining management policies;
- a primary focus on managers as being either *reactive* to or the mere *transmitters* of wider social forces (owners, profits, etc.), rather than autonomous decision-makers;
- a failure to recognise the unavoidable conflicts of managerial practice, in that choices may be forced by cost-cutting, redundancies, etc.

The practice perspective

Reed suggests a fourth possible model as the basis for future theoretical analysis, which he calls the **practice perspective**. In this perspective, management is seen as a process or an activity which is based on the attempt by managers to coordinate and integrate the social interaction of workers. Work organisations tend to be seen as constantly changing (not static) forms of social contract, which share an essential function or functions. Management, therefore, seeks to ensure the efficient operation of administrative tasks. This work has been developed by writers such as Burns (1977) and Tomlinson (1982).

Professionals and management: what is the role of the professional?

A number of writers, such as Peter Blau and Amitai Etzioni, have stressed the problems that can be faced by professionals who are employed in bureaucratic organisations. For Max Weber, as we have seen, such organisations imply a hierarchy of authority, a division of labour, the presence of rules and procedural specifications, and impersonality.

The main issue here is the distinction between bureaucratic authority and professional authority. Max Weber saw no problem in this: a person's position in the hierarchy is determined by technical expertise. However, this is not necessarily the case. In many organisations the most highly qualified individuals are found in the middle of the hierarchy; Burns and Stalker carried out a study (published in 1961) which showed that this can lead to conflict, with experts challenging the legitimacy of the hierarchy. They noted that some managers feared their authority was being undermined and the chain of command blurred. Amitai Etzioni, writing more recently, argues that administrative decisions, based on the organisation's rules and regulations, can conflict with professional decisions based on personal expertise. This can place the professional in a dilemma: as a member of the organisation they should obey a superior, while as a professional they may wish to follow their own judgement.

Empirical studies have provided evidence in support of Etzioni's approach. In Lane's study of the publishing industry in the 1980s and 1990s, a situation of role conflict arose between professional commitment and the profit-making motivation of the industry; while Salaman found similar problems among architects in the 1970s.

Negotiation can reduce these patterns of conflict. Peter Blau studied a number of employment agencies and finance departments and found that decentralisation of authority to specialists could result in administrative efficiency so long as sufficient communication channels were made available. Blau and Schoenherr have also shown that it is possible to motivate professional commitment towards the organisation by giving professionals freedom to operate on a day-to-day basis, while the organisation maintains checks through recruitment and promotion policies.

Definition of a professional

A professional:

- uses the profession as a major reference group (both formal and informal);
- has a belief in its indispensability to the public;
- has a belief in self regulation, with only a fellow professional being able to pass judgement;
- has a sense of vocation and dedication; and
- believes in the existence of personal autonomy to make his or her own decisions.

Source: Adapted from Richard Hall, *Professionalism and Bureaucratisation*, 1968

Think about it

- In what ways might the managers of an organisation wish to direct a group of specialists/professionals to undertake tasks that conflict with professional values?

Postmodernism and organisations

For many postmodernists (Foucault, Lyotard, Derrida, for example), organisations threaten humanity with a form of total control which removes individuality and the human spirit. The essence of organisations ensures control of ideas through ideology and control of human aspiration with an emphasis on materialism, whilst claiming to act in a legitimate way. In addition, and in contrast to modernist organisational theorists such as Silverman and Pahl, postmodernists see organisations as fostering instability, uncertainty and dissension, as no one is deemed to be in 'control'.

Characteristics of modern and postmodern organisations

Modern organisations	Postmodern organisations
• rigid • mechanistic • mass production and consumption • production methods dictated by technology • high division of labour specialisation and demarcation of jobs	• flexible • organic • production for specialised 'niches' • new technology developed to allow flexibility and choice • overlap between areas of work • breakdown of demarcation, multi-skilled workers, use of subcontracting and networking

Source: Adapted from S. Clegg, 'Modern and Postmodern Organisations', *Sociology Review*, April 1992

Globalisation

As already noted, many studies have suggested that organisations are becoming increasingly global; large firms are being seen as transnational companies characterised by:

- their control of economic activities in a number of countries;
- their ability to maximise geographical, economic, social and political differences between countries;
- their flexibility to move resources, operations and personnel between countries.

The trend towards globalisation should not be taken to mean that a country's government, or its workers, are unable to challenge such transnational companies, merely that these companies are no longer constrained by territorial boundaries when seeking to undertake their business.

Industrial relations

It has often been contended, at least in the tabloid press, that during the 1960s and 1970s the balance in the relationship between employers and employees (collectively in the form of **trade unions**, with 12–13 million members) fell in favour of the employees. British industry, according to such views, was regularly shut down because of **industrial action** or strikes, a message which was widely believed in other European countries and in America. The view was also expressed that 'workers were holding the country to ransom', with high pay demands. In 1973, the then prime minister, Edward Heath (reported on the front page of the *Daily Mail*), posed the question 'Who runs Britain?' Over the period 1978–87, however, as the table on page 272 shows, trade union membership declined, real earnings tended to rise (except in 1981), the numbers of strikes and days lost due to strikes declined, and unemployment rose (peaking in early 1986).

	Union membership (000s)	Change in real earnings (%)	Number of strikes	Strike days lost (000s)	Registered unemployed (%)
1978	13,112	+4.6	2,498	9,405	5.7
1979	13,289	+2.0	2,125	29,474	5.3
1980	12,947	+3.8	1,348	11,964	6.8
1981	12,106	−0.7	1,344	4,266	10.4
1982	11,593	+2.3	1,538	5,313	12.1
1983	11,236	+2.5	1,364	3,754	12.9
1984	10,994	+1.9	1,221	27,135	13.1
1985	10,716	+3.0	903	6,402	13.5
1986	10,333	+3.4	1,074	1,920	11.7
1987	10,200	+4.8	1,016	3,546	10.7

Conflict and consensus Some writers have viewed the development of trade unions as a process of integrating the working class into the values and structures of capitalist society. Miliband, for example, has stressed that trade union leaders are pressured into accepting the capitalist logic of a national interest and that incorporation into the governmental process has reduced their ability to stress their members' interests. For Louis Althusser, trade unions are examples of **ideological state apparatuses** (see Unit 11 page 575) that reinforce capitalist society by appealing to selfish motivation, while accepting the rules of negotiation and arbitration. By institutionalising industrial conflict, it becomes moderated and manageable, and the success of the strategy is reflected by the lack of violence and by the conduct of both negotiation and strike action in terms of the rules of a game, thus removing potential conflict and replacing it with consensus.

Such an approach contrasts with the **pluralist view** of society, which sees the trade unions voicing the interests of their members in opposition to a wide range of groups that make up modern industrial society. Ralf Dahrendorf, for example, sees trade unions as having equal power to employers' associations in their ability to influence government policy; while Robert Dahl, in his study of New Haven, claimed that trade unions, businesses and educational establishments all had some impact in decisions made about improvements in the urban environment.

Much media coverage of industrial relations stresses the role of the **strike**. Kerr and Siegel found that certain groups of workers (such as miners, dockers and seamen) had the highest strike records and that this was related to their closely knit, local, occupationally-based communities. Whilst media coverage might stress the anti-social nature of a strike, a closely integrated striking community can maintain its own value-system in the face of such pressure. This was well evidenced during the 1984/85 Miners' Strike in the response of mining communities in Yorkshire and elsewhere to the anti-strike media reporting (see Glasgow University Media Group studies, pages 294–5). The analysis of the nature of strikes depends on the perspective adopted: an interactionist would analyse them in terms of interpersonal relations; a functionalist would see them as a reflection of the malfunctioning of a society that required a reinforcement of consensus; whilst a Marxist would see them as the inevitable consequence of the conflicting class interests within capitalism.

Industrial action may be the end-product of the failure of established union–employer negotiating procedure, with strike action being a reflection of the lack of power to influence negotiations in the desired direction. This point was emphasised in the case study *A Strike at Pilkingtons* by Lane and Roberts. Huw Beynon and others have shown that strikes can vary in their prime objective: from a weapon designed to beat down management to a form of workers' action to show discontent at the industry's techniques of decision-making.

However, industrial relations involve more than the study of strikes. While strikes receive a great deal of media publicity, much more significant – in terms of both cost and for an understanding of the nature and problems of industrial relations – may be **absenteeism**, a worker technique called **working to rule** and **industrial sabotage**, each of which may have complex causes. Taylor and Walton, for example, in their study *Industrial Sabotage: Motives and Meanings*, suggest that the aim of industrial sabotage may be to relieve the tension and frustration experienced by workers with boring or monotonous jobs, or, alternatively, there may be a more political aim of the workers asserting control over the work process.

Trade unions in the 1980s and 1990s

Since 1979, the power of the trade unions, as employee organisations, has been considerably reduced by a series of Acts of Parliament, although one third of employees were still union members in 1994. In contrast, the same legislation has also been designed to ensure that employers' rights are strengthened. This, coupled with increased unemployment, has allowed employers to impose their policies more forcefully on issues such as pay, conditions, flexible working patterns, fixed-term contracts and a shift from full-time to part-time employment. The following table indicates employees' ideas of what the functions of trade unions are in the 1990s, and how priority has moved away from pay and towards job protection, since 1989.

Employees'[1] views of what trade unions should try to do, 1989 and 1994		
	1989 (%)	1994 (%)
Protect existing jobs	28	37
Improve working conditions	21	20
Improve pay	28	15
Have more say over management's long term plans	6	14
Have more say over how work is done day to day	3	5
Reduce pay differences at the workplace	6	4
Work for equal opportunities for women	3	2

1 Employees with a recognised trade union or staff association at the workplace were given a list of things trade unions do and asked 'What, if any, is the most important thing they should try to do at your workplace?'

Source: British Social Attitudes Survey, Social & Community Planning Research, *Social Trends*, 1996

An increasing number of major employers have adopted alternative methods of handling employer–employee relations, with more emphasis on North American practices and 'human resource management'. Rather than creating industrial relations conflict, the focus here is on employers seeking to obtain employee loyalty. In many service and financial sector industries, this has meant the exclusion of trade unions – or at least a lessening of trade union influence.

Edwards and Scullion, in 1982, conducted research into why a variety of forms of conflict, ranging from absenteeism to sabotage and bargaining disputes, existed in some employer–employee settings and not in others. They concluded that the differences lay in the patterns of control exerted by both management and workers.

It is possible to argue that the pattern of employer–employee relations is now less conflict-based than it was in the 1970s, and that a consensus-based interpretation offers a more useful explanatory model, with an emphasis on social order rather than social control being in the ascendancy.

Marxists, however, would point to the continuing spate of strikes in the mid- to late 1990s (Post Office employees, railworkers, Liverpool dockers, etc.) as evidence of underlying conflict. In addition, they might see the conflict between a number of groups of professionals (for example doctors with the National Health Trusts; judges with the Home Office; social workers with the Social Services Department) as representing an ongoing dispute between the employer and the employee.

Sacked workers send New Year talks plea to factory bosses

by Lindsay McGarvie

WORKERS occupying a Glasgow factory have delivered a New Year plea to bosses calling on them to open negotiations to bring their long-running sit-in to an end.

Staff at Polmadie's Glacier RPB engineering factory have branded managers "callous bullies" after leaving 103 sacked employees penniless over the festive season, including one man suffering from a brain tumour.

The sacked workers, dubbed the Polmadie 103, are now in the eighth week of their sit-in after management dismissed Amalgamated Engineering and Electrical Union (AEEU) members for refusing to accept new working conditions.

Protesters claim they suffered a catalogue of injustices. The man suffering from a brain tumour received his P45 through the post while recovering from surgery.

Sit-in organiser, Peter Little, said factory manager Ted Milligan had acted "heartlessly".

Little claimed: "There is no humanity to management tactics. Their refusal to enter into negotiations is proof of their contempt for us."

He said the sit-in workers were keeping the factory in good working order, and ready to go back to work immediately if management opened negotiations.

The dispute started when a turning machine operator refused to take part in additional machine duties, which his fellow employees claimed were dangerous and could lead to poor quality work.

AEEU members refused to accept a new manage-

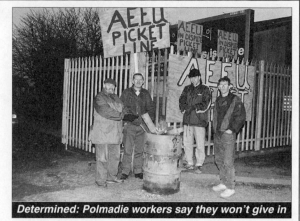

Determined: Polmadie workers say they won't give in

ment 15 point non-negotiable plan. Milligan then told the massed workforce that they were dismissed.

Little said: "Milligan is more interested in penny-pinching schemes rather than using the skills of the workforce to keep the factory a profit-making concern."

The 15 new working conditions to be imposed included: selective overtime at management's request, an end to productivity bonuses, and cuts in sick pay.

Campbell Scott, a sacked engineering inspector, said: "This isn't a militant workforce. We just want to work. Christmas has been cancelled for us, through no fault of our own."

The workers' campaign has the support of Scottish celebrities including author William McIlvanney and comedian Elaine C Smith, the local community and other unions including UNISON and the TGWU.

A major rally is planned for January 21 to back the sacked staff.

Glacier RPB declined to comment.

Source: *The Big Issue*, 28 December 1996–8 January 1997

Trade unions

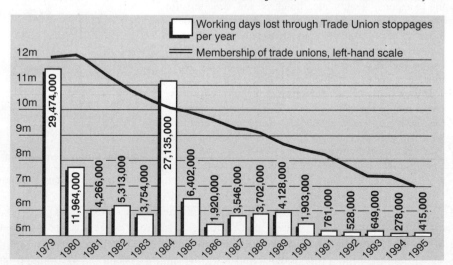

Working days lost through Trade Union stoppages per year

Membership of trade unions, left-hand scale

Source: The *Guardian*, 9 September 1996

IN FOCUS

WORK AND THE TRADE UNIONS

MOST RECENT discussions about unions and the workplace have concerned strikes and the minimum wage, but wider questions on the future role of trade unions are also coming to the fore. The TUC's call for a minimum wage is resisted by critics because it will, it is alleged, 'cost jobs', though recent research by Cambridge academics suggests that it is lack of manufacturing investment in Britain which is most closely associated in a causal way with rising unemployment (Figure 1).

The British trade unions still have strong links with the Labour Party, of course, but their influence in this quarter may be in long-term decline as party funds are increasingly drawn in from elsewhere (Figure 2). Only 31% of British workers are now unionised (down from 59%) and, critically, the figure for workers under 25 is just 7%. With the shrinking of the manufacturing base, government attacks on unionisation, and the rise of short-term and part-time work, the traditional image of large, 'blue-collar', male unions in Britain seems to have given way to a smaller 'white-collar' and more 'feminised' membership profile for the 1990s (Figure 3).

The TUC general secretary, John Monks, recently claimed that 5 million non-unionised workers in Britain would like unions to represent them, many of them women working in small firms in the private sector. A major incentive here may be a possible reduction in the long hours worked by UK workers for low pay.

Geoff Mulgan from the left-of-centre 'think-tank' Demos believes, however, that unions will have to change radically what they do, if they are to get membership up. He has called for unions to become Employee Mutuals, doing usual union tasks and managing pensions, health-care, holidays and time off for workers. They might also organise and 'sell' labour to prospective employers. This management of 'human capital' would strengthen and extend the role of the unions and help them to 'modernise' and regain public trust, he argues.

How, exactly, will the unions respond to recent shifts? One thing seems sure: they will have to demonstrate their worth to workers who need their support at a time when flexibility in the workplace and in training seems ever more the watchword.

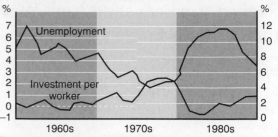

Figure 1 Investment and unemployment

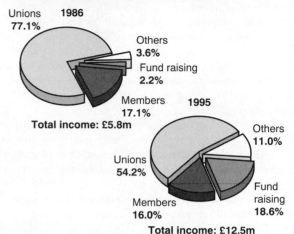

Figure 2 Labour Party income by source, %

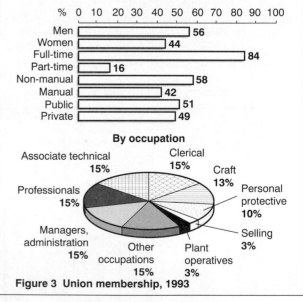

Figure 3 Union membership, 1993

Source: J. Williams, *Sociology Review*, Vol. 6:3, February 1997

Think about it

- To what extent does evidence support the view that trade unions have little influence in the 1990s?
- Show how both a functionalist and a Marxist might explain the existence of strikes in Britain.

Revision and practice tasks

Task 1: data response question

ITEM A

In the 1980s the emphases on 'paper-free' offices and 'worker-free' factories came together to provide a powerful account of the way changes in the workplace were having an impact on society. The movement from manufacturing to service employment was explained as an historical shift from industrial to post-industrial society. Equally, the changes in the organisation of work and employment were variously interpreted as a move from Fordist to post-Fordist practices. Critical traditions which once emphasised the damaging effects of work upon workers gave way to those which celebrated the enriching aspects of employment. These were regularly contrasted with the damaging experiences of unemployment. In this way, the major division within society became understood as that between those with and those without work.

Source: Adapted from H. Beynon in N. Abercrombie and A. Warde, *Social Change in Contemporary Britain* (Polity Press) 1992

ITEM B

Full and Part-time Employment in the UK: By Sex

	Males (000s)		Females (000s)	
	Full-time	Part-time	Full-time	Part-time
1984	13,240	570	5,422	4,343
1985	13,336	575	5,503	4,457
1986	13,430	647	5,662	4,566
1987	13,472	750	5,795	4,698
1988	13,881	801	6,069	4,808
1989	14,071	734	6,336	4,907
1990	14,109	789	6,479	4,928
1991	13,686	799	6,350	4,933
1992	13,141	885	6,244	5,081
1993	12,769	886	6,165	5,045

Source: Adapted from *Social Trends*, 1994

ITEM C

Quite often today we hear of politicians and economists talking about leisure replacing work as a central life interest, if not as the central life interest. In this type of analysis, economic, technological and workplace changes are seen as setting the agenda of change. We are constantly told that, for example, 'we can't expect to have the same job for life', or that we should expect to be periodically re-trained for new jobs and/or that unemployment is becoming a permanent reality. On the other side of the same argument, it is also stressed that, possibly because we have more time on our hands, this 'time-vacuum' can or should be filled with leisure activities. A related part of this argument points to the opportunities that such a 'leisure society' offers to us, for example, in participating in personal or mass leisure activities, we can achieve the fulfilment that we are denied in highly-structured work regimes. Sociological evidence, however, indicates that the impact of the spread of leisure in society is very uneven.

(a) Look at **ITEM B**. How many more full-time male workers than full-time female workers were there in 1993? **(1 mark)**

(b) What, according to **ITEM A**, is:

(i) Fordism

(ii) Post-Fordism? **(4 marks)**

(c) Explain the decline in full-time male employment, referring to **ITEM B** and other evidence. **(4 marks)**

(d) **ITEM A** states that unemployment is 'damaging'. What do sociologists consider this damage to consist of? **(6 marks)**

(e) Evaluate the contention in **ITEM C** that leisure, not work, is now central to many people's lives. **(10 marks)**

Total: 25 marks

Task 2: structured question

ITEM A

Charles Handy, an industrialist turned academic, suggests several scenarios of the future effects of new technology. Underlying his predictions is a pessimistic view of the economy's ability to create jobs at a fast enough rate to match the growth in productivity brought about by the new technology. The Unemployment Society is what will come about, he suggests, if we merely follow present trends and if we persist, as a society, with our present views about what constitutes a full-time permanent job. In this scenario, present employment and income patterns continue, but at a higher level of unemployment. Those in employment earn a relatively high income but those out of work will continue to exist at rather low levels of unemployment benefit. We would be even more of a country of two societies than is already the case, with the divide between the employed haves and the unemployed have-nots.

Source: Adapted from *New Technology at Work*, A. Francis (Open University Press)

ITEM B

No official statistic will ever escape criticism, least of all one of the most politically sensitive such as the unemployment count. But the present authorities have come under more seathing criticisms about the register of jobless in the UK than any other government in history, partly because they have redefined "unemployment" over 30 times since assuming office in 1979 ... and, bar once, each new definition has seen the count shrink in size. This makes any comparison of joblessness in the 1990s with unemployment in previous decades perilous – because official figures cannot catch the effects of tightening eligibility rules – and although the data provide us with an indication of the trend movements in unemployment, precise interpretation of the figures is fraught with difficulty.

The central feature of the new statistics is that they only record the number of people out of work and receiving unemployment benefit. They do not include all those who are ineligible for benefit, even though they may be actively seeking work.

Source: Ruth Kelly, 'Interpreting the unemployment figures is fraught with difficulty', the *Guardian*, 10 August 1992

ITEM C
The Experience of Unemployment

Of all the reactions to being out of work for the first time, surprise is the most common. This point has emerged in every study of unemployment, certainly since the war, that I have ever read. It indicates the lack of awareness about the problems of being out of work among the rest of the population and may help to account for the generally unsympathetic and often suspicious attitude towards the unemployed. As one apprenticed tradesman in his early twenties commented in 1979: 'It's changed my attitudes to the unemployed. I used to think they were just skivers and was quite a lot against them, but now I've experienced it, it's no joke, man'. Another in North

Tyneside said, 'once you've been on the dole yourself, you begin to think differently about the other people there. You can't help it, and you realise that perhaps they can't either'. It was the actual experience of unemployment that led these workers to alter their own opinions of what it was like to be out of work and so to start breaking down their own stereotypes of the unemployed.

Source: Craig R. Littler, *The Experience of Work* (Gower)

(a) Look at **ITEM A**. What key change can be noted? **(1 mark)**

(b) **ITEM B** suggests that certain groups of people are not eligible for benefit and yet are available for work. Name **three** such groups. **(3 marks)**

(c) How valuable are official statistics of unemployment to sociologists? **(6 marks)**

(d) To what extent have sociological studies of unemployment enhanced our understanding of the experience? **(7 marks)**

(e) Increased unemployment may result from the introduction of new technology, according to **ITEM A**. To what extent does the sociological literature support this view? **(10 marks)**

Total: 25 marks

Ideas for coursework and personal studies

1. Choose two sporting or leisure activities – at least one of which should be an outdoor group activity – which you know are reasonably easily accessible in your area. Conduct a survey to find out levels of participation in each sport, and reasons for greater/lesser participation by each person you include in your survey. Analyse your results in terms of:
   - gender;
   - ethnicity;
   - social class;
   - age.

2. Survey a small sample of those whom you consider to have high and low status occupations. Are pay and working conditions their main differences? What other differences can you find out, perhaps in relation to their values and their attitudes to work?

3. Interview a group of workers whose jobs may be described as boring and repetitive. Enquire as to whether they enjoy any aspects of their work, and find out whether they refer to social contacts and friendships within and beyond the workplace.

Selected reading list

All Work and No Play, Rosemary Deem (Oxford University Press, 1986)
Contemporary British Society, N. Abercrombie and A. Warde (Polity Press, 1995)
Divisions of Labour, Jan Pahl (Blackwell, 1984)
The Forsaken Families, L. Fagin and M. Little (Penguin, 1984)
The Postmodern Condition, J.F. Lyotard (Manchester University Press, 1984)
The Social Organisation of Industrial Conflict. Control and Resistance in the Workplace, P.K. Edwards and H. Scullion (Blackwell, 1982)
The Social Psychology of Work, M. Argyle (Penguin, 1974)
The Sociology of Management, Mike Reed (Harvester Wheatsheaf, 1989)
Understanding Organisations, Charles Handy (Penguin, 1989)
Writers on Organisations, D.S. Pugh and D. J. Hickson (Penguin, 1995)

6 Mass media and popular culture

Introduction

The term 'mass media' is used to refer to all the forms of communication by which opinions, ideas, information, knowledge and entertainment are transmitted to large numbers of people at the same time. Scientific and technological developments, particularly since the nineteenth century, have made possible the huge expansion of the mass media. It is maintained by some that this has led to traditional forms of culture being replaced by more popular forms which reflect the interests of the majority.

This unit will cover the following issues concerning mass media and popular culture:

- the nature and forms of the mass media;
- organisation, ownership and control of the mass media, including technological developments;
- the relationship between the mass media, popular culture and ideology;
- media content and news reporting, including the representation of specific groups with reference to stereotypes, moral panics and ideologies;
- media audiences and the problems of researching the effects and uses of the mass media;
- definitions and themes associated with popular culture, including youth culture, folk culture, consumer culture, modernism and post-modernism.

The forms of the mass media

Films, television, radio, books, newspapers, magazines and records, tapes and CDs are the major forms of media produced for masses of people. Each method of transmission or distribution is known as a **medium**. Mass media are characterised by the following:

- Ideas and opinions, as well as information and knowledge, are broadcast to large numbers of people across a widely diverse population and to geographically dispersed audiences.
- Whilst audiences may be extremely large – for example, television coverage of sporting events and TV soap operas – the number of 'deliverers' is comparatively small.
- Communication is mostly – with exceptions such as the Internet – one-way, with audiences receiving few if any opportunities to join in or 'feed back' their views.

In relation to the last point, 'phone-ins' to television or radio programmes, dedicated feedback programmes such as the BBC's *Points of View*, and letters to newspapers and magazines, have increased audience participation in recent decades, but such interaction may be subjected to filtering and editing processes. Nevertheless, those who own and control the mass media cannot afford to ignore their audiences; they need large numbers of customers to survive commercially.

Printing

The first medium of mass communication arose with the invention of movable type. Johann Gutenberg (*c.* 1397–1468), a German printer, is believed to have been the first European to print with movable type. Johann Fust, using Gutenberg's press, printed the first European book, a *Book of Psalms*, in 1457.

The early hand press, in which ink was rolled over the raised surfaces of handset letters pressed against paper, remained in use until the early nineteenth century. As the nineteenth century progressed, so did the quality of printing. However, high costs and low literacy levels kept readership small, until the end of the 1800s when technology and marketing techniques developed.

Newspapers

Newspapers have been read on a daily basis since around the turn of the twentieth century. They were an important development in the history of the mass media since they packaged a variety of information within a limited and easily reproduced format. Cheap daily newspapers started in the USA, with the first one-cent daily paper being established in New York. By the early twentieth century, the two main status newspapers were the *New York Times* and *The Times* (of London). These served as models for the development of newspapers around the world.

Newspapers became a major way of conveying information swiftly to the general public, although with the development of radio and cinema, and more importantly television, their influence may be considered to have decreased. Nevertheless, despite an apparent decline, in 1995, an average of over 27 million people in the UK read at least one daily newspaper. The most popular is the *Sun*, read by over 10 million people – nearly one in four adults – as shown by the following table. It is the most widely read daily paper among all social groups except for classes A and B.

National newspaper readership 1995					
	Males (%)	Females (%)	All adults (%)	Readership (millions)	Readers per copy (numbers)
The Sun	26	19	22	10.1	2.5
Daily Mirror	16	13	14	6.5	2.6
Daily Mail	11	10	10	4.4	2.5
Daily Express	7	6	7	3.2	2.5
The Daily Telegraph	6	5	6	2.8	2.7
Daily Star	6	3	4	2.0	2.8
The Times	4	3	4	1.7	2.7
The Guardian	3	2	3	1.3	3.5
The Independent	2	1	2	0.9	3.3
Financial Times	2	1	2	0.7	4.3
Any national daily newspaper	62	54	60	27.2	

Source: *Social Trends*, 1997

Think about it

- Why do you think fewer women than men read daily newspapers?
- What may be the reasons for the *Sun* being the most popular daily newspaper?

The difference in style between the **tabloids** (or picture-based press) and the **broadsheets** (or quality press) has become less extreme. Alan Rusbridger, the editor of the *Guardian*, coined the word 'broadloid', referring to the traditional broadsheet newspapers running picture-based showbiz and royal gossip alongside their coverage of politics and economics. An example is the space given to the discovery of the film star Hugh Grant's encounter with a prostitute in July 1995. Judged in terms of column inches, this story got the 'broadloid' coverage:

	Column inches		Column inches
The Guardian	505	Sunday Telegraph	180
The Daily Telegraph	482	The Observer	42
Sunday Times	247	Independent on Sunday	37
The Times	229	Financial Times	1
The Independent	210		

Broadcasting: television and radio

Undoubtedly one of the most important developments in the mass media since World War II has been that of television. Watching television has become the most popular home-based leisure activity, as illustrated by the table below.

Participation in home-based leisure activities: by gender					
Great Britain					Percentages
	1977	1980	1986	1990–91	1993–94
Males Watching TV	97	97	98	99	99
Visiting/entertaining friends or relations	89	90	92	95	95
Listening to radio	87	88	87	91	91
Listening to records/tapes	64	66	69	78	79
Reading books	52	52	52	56	59
DIY	51	53	54	58	57
Gardening	49	49	47	52	51
Dressmaking/needlework/ knitting	2	2	3	3	3
Females Watching TV	97	98	98	99	99
Visiting/entertaining friends or relations	93	93	95	97	96
Listening to radio	87	88	85	87	88
Listening to records/tapes	60	62	65	74	75
Reading books	57	61	64	68	71
DIY	22	23	27	29	30
Gardening	35	38	39	44	45
Dressmaking/needlework/ knitting	51	51	48	41	38

Source: General Household Survey, Office for National Statistics, in *Social Trends*, 1997

According to official statistics, people watched more television in 1992 than in each of the previous five years – about $26\frac{3}{4}$ hours per week; although this varied between social classes, with those in the lower social groups watching more television than those in the higher.

Television viewing, by social class			
Social class	1986 (hrs per week)	1991 (hrs per week)	1992 (hrs per week)
AB	19:50	18:51	19:56
C1	23:05	23:56	25:08
C2	26:00	26:57	27:30
DE	33:35	31:56	31:54
All persons	26:32	26:04	26:44

Source: *Social Trends*, 1994

Think about it

Study the data above and on page 283 on participation in home-based leisure activity in Britain and television viewing by social class.

- Why do you think watching television seems to be the most popular home-based leisure activity? What do you think needs to be taken into consideration when interpreting the data provided? For whom might listening to the radio be more popular than watching television?
- According to the figures given, television viewing hours are higher for the lower social classes. What reasons can you suggest for this?
- How do you think the development of television technology might have influenced the data above?

Trends in the organisation of the mass media

New printing technology

Advanced computer systems have cut production costs of newspapers. A 'single keying' system allows journalists to insert copy (or text) directly into a computer terminal, and then transfer it electronically into columns of type.

News International publishes three daily and two Sunday papers at its London Docklands headquarters. It has more than 500 computer terminals, one of the largest systems installed in the world. The *Financial Times'* printing plant in Docklands has about 170 production workers, compared with the 600 employed at its former London base. A trend has arisen in regional and local press to close ageing press plants and contract out the printing of their weekly newspapers to larger groups. Many of these groups have invested in state-of-the-art full colour printing to meet both their own needs and those of their growing number of customers.

New broadcasting technology

As far as television and radio are concerned, **digital broadcasting** seems to hold the future. It involves a technique that converts sound and pictures into computer digits which can be transmitted in compressed form. This opens the way for wide-screen TVs, CD-quality sound, and many new TV channels and radio stations to be created, following the first digital broadcasting licence being advertised early in 1997.

Technology and ownership

A wide range of changes have taken place in television broadcasting in the 1990s. The Broadcasting Act 1990 was concerned with the reorganisation of the independent broadcasting network: independent television franchises were granted after a process of competitive tendering (or, as termed by some, an 'auction' process). Three companies – Thames Television, Television South and Television South West – lost their franchises and were replaced in 1993 by Carlton, Meridian and West Country TV. The breakfast television company TV-AM lost out to GMTV.

By 1994, **terrestrial** (or earth-based) **television** received increased competition from celestial or **satellite television,** with a further nine TV channels being broadcast from the Astra satellite. There are now hundreds of channels being beamed down from satellites based above Europe: the three main television satellites are Astra, Eutelsat and Intelsat.

BSkyB

Satellite television first 'took off' with Sky TV in 1989. It was financed with profits from the newspapers owned by Rupert Murdoch's News Corporation. Within a year, Sky TV had absorbed BSB (British Satellite Broadcasting), its only real rival, to become BSkyB. By the mid-1990s, BSkyB was making profits of over £50 million and repaying the original investment by covering the losses accrued during a period of competitive newspaper price-cutting. There are 3 million satellite-dish owners in the UK (4 per cent of the TV audience), attracted largely by BSkyB's sports coverage. BSkyB has sought to shrug off a reputation for junk TV by becoming a significant news provider. In February 1995, it announced a deal with Reuters to manage a round-the-clock news channel. The partnership challenged both Channel 3's Independent Television News (ITN) and the BBC Worldwide satellite channel, announced just a month earlier.

Concerns about new broadcasting technology

Developments in satellite and cable television seem to be challenging the power and control previously held by traditional terrestrial broadcasting companies. Such developments seem to pose problems for governments, who may seek to exercise control over broadcasting.

Electronic forms of media broadcasting, in particular the **Internet,** have brought with them the problems of pornographic and paedophiliac broadcasting. Video games have caused concern too. Eugene Provenzo, in *Video Kids: Making sense of Nintendo* (1991), maintains that such games form a key part of the culture and experience of the young. In the USA, there are about 19 million Nintendo games alone, mostly operated by young people.

Video games and the characters and storylines linked to television and films, etc. have also been shown to influence social codes and behaviour:

> '. . . *virtual reality computer graphics can allow people to experience various forms of reality at second hand. These surface simulations can therefore potentially replace their real-life counterparts.*'

Dominic Strinati, *Popular Culture* (1995)

The scale of developments in broadcasting technology is unprecedented: the BBC has estimated that, by 2005, over 50 per cent of British households will be linked to multichannel broadcasting via a digital superhighway. Virtual reality studios with programmes needing one person instead of huge crews also carry implications for the changing labour market.

The increasing use of subscription and pay-as-you-view systems could become socially divisive in terms of the socio-economic groups who might be able to afford the required equipment and regular subscription fees – particularly for the more technical and commercial multi-media, computer-based services. However, evidence to date seems to suggest that subscription to cable and satellite television seems to be more in line with social class television viewing patterns, as suggested by the graph below.

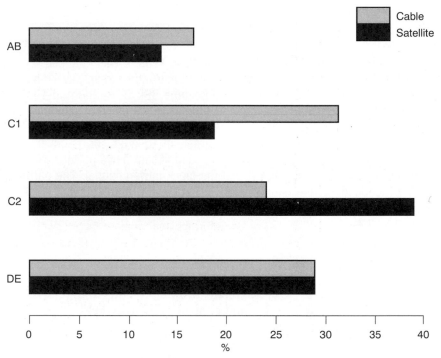

Percentage of households who have subscribed to cable/satellite TV by social class

Source: M. Denscombe, *Sociology Update* (Olympus Books, 1995)

Think about it

- Why, in your opinion, do about one in five households in the UK subscribe to satellite television?
- In sociological terms, what do you consider to be the main advantages and disadvantages of celestial (i.e. satellite-based, as opposed to terrestrial or land-based) broadcasting?
- Do you think that the Internet, video games and recent developments in subscription cable and digital television have come to form a key part of our cultural experience? Does your answer vary according to the age group you are considering and, if so, how?
- Virtual reality games and programmes claim to allow users to experience various forms of reality at second hand. What might be some of the social consequences of the development of virtual reality technology?

Ownership and control patterns and the influence of the state

During the twentieth century, especially since World War II, there has been a trend, via mergers and take-overs, towards the formation of large-scale corporations and multinational media companies. This has led to the ownership of the mass media becoming highly concentrated, as shown below. It is interesting to note the diverse activities of the media owners; it can also be seen that where media forms appear to compete with one another, there is an element of overlap and interrelationship. The top five national newspaper owners account for 85 per cent of the sales of national papers.

Media ownership and market share of national newspapers

News International – 35 per cent

Dominated by Rupert Murdoch, News International owns *The Sun*, *The Times*, *Today*, *News of the World* and *Sunday Times*. Also owned is 40 per cent of the satellite company BSkyB. Murdoch is the big baron in the new global village and his UK interests are a mere fiefdom.
America: Fox TV network, Fox film studio, *The New York Post*, *TV Guide*.
Asia: Star TV (by satellite to 54 countries) covering India, China, Japan, the Philippines, Thailand and Hong Kong.
Australia: Numerous print groups and newspapers (half the newspapers sold) and stakes in TV stations.

Mirror Group – 26 per cent

Owns the *Daily Mirror*, *Sunday Mirror*, *Daily Record* and the *People*. The group has a 43 per cent stake in Newspaper Publishing, the company which runs the *Independent* and the *Independent on Sunday*. It also has a 40 per cent share in Scottish Television and owns Live TV and Wire TV.

United News and Media – 13 per cent

It owns the *Daily Express* and *Sunday Express*, and also publishes over 80 local newspapers and Miller Freeman magazines.

Daily Mail and General Trust – 12 per cent

It owns the *Daily Mail* and *Mail on Sunday*. The trust is the second largest regional paper owner via the Northcliffe Newspapers Group and has shareholdings in Teletext, local radio (especially the GWR Group), Reuters, 20 per cent of West Country TV and 100 per cent of Channel One.

The Telegraph – 7 per cent

Owns the *Daily Telegraph* and *Sunday Telegraph*. Controlled by Conrad Black, via the Canadian company Hollinger.

Guardian Media Group – 3 per cent

Publishers of the *Guardian* and *Observer*, the Group also publishes some 50 local papers and several magazines, and owns 15 per cent of GMTV. The parent of the group is the Scott Trust, whose main object is the continuation of the *Guardian*.

Pearson – 1 per cent

Owners of the *Financial Times*, Pearson is a diverse company which spreads into most parts of the media. It owns the local newspaper group Westminster Press, Longman and HarperCollins book publishers, and Future Publishing magazines.

Source: Adapted from S. Peak and P. Fisher (eds.), *The Media Guide* (1998)

The politics of the mass media

The contribution which the mass media make to the political climate is determined by the influences which weigh most heavily on them. Such influences, listed below, all work in the same conservative and conformist direction.

1. The ownership and control of the **means of mental production**: except for state ownership of radio, television and other means of communication, the mass media are overwhelmingly in the private domain. Those who own and control the capitalist mass media are most likely to be men whose **ideological dispositions** run from conservative to reactionary. In many instances, most notably in the case of newspapers, the impact of their views and prejudices is immediate and direct: newspaper proprietors often not only own their newspapers but also closely control their editorial and political line, turning them, by daily intervention, into vehicles of their personal views.

   However, it is not always the case that those who own or control the mass media seek to exercise a direct influence on their output. Often editors and journalists are given considerable independence. Even so, ideas tend to 'seep downwards' and provide an ideological framework whose existence cannot be ignored by those who work for the commercial media. They may not be required to take tender care of the '**sacred cows**' found in the conservative stable, but it is at least expected that they will spare the sensitivities of the men whose employees they are, and that they will take a proper attitude to free enterprise, conflicts between capital and labour, trade unions, left-wing parties and movements, revolutionary movements and much else. The existence of this framework does not require total conformity: general conformity will do, sometimes even allowing for a generous seasoning of disagreement.

2. Pressures exercised, directly or indirectly, by capitalist interests, not by owners but by advertisers: the political influence of large advertisers on the commercial media need not be exaggerated. It is only occasionally that such advertisers are able, or probably even try, to dictate the contents and policies of the media of which they are the customers. But their custom is, nevertheless, of importance to the financial existence of newspapers, magazines, commercial radio and television, and this may be enough to affect the attitude of these media to show exceptional care in dealing with such powerful and valuable interests.

3. Pressure, often indirect, from the government and other parts of the state system: governments, ministries and other official agencies now make it their business to supply newspapers, radio and television with explanations of official policy. The State goes in more and more for 'news management', particularly in times of crisis (which, for most leading capitalist countries, means almost permanently); and the greater the crisis, the more purposeful the management, the half-truths and the plain lies.

   Many people working in and for the mass media suffer various degrees of political frustration, and seek – sometimes successfully, often not – to break through the **frontiers of orthodoxy**. But there is little to suggest that they constitute more than a minority of the 'cultural workmen' employed by the mass media. The cultural and political **hegemony** of the dominant classes could not be so prominent if this was not the case.

Source: Adapted from R. Miliband, 'The State in Capitalist Society' (1973) in P. Trowler, *Active Sociology* (1987)

Meaning of terms
- **means of mental production:** techniques used to affect the way people think about things and the subjects they think about;
- **ideological dispositions:** sets of beliefs which are firmly held;
- **frontiers of orthodoxy:** the limits of what is considered normal;
- **hegemony:** the dominance of a particular set of ideas.

> *Think about it*
>
> Ideas 'seep downwards' from the owners and the controllers of the mass media to the journalists and editors. Miliband describes these ideas as the '**sacred cows**', and gives some examples of the kind of topics these cover: free enterprise, conflicts between capital and labour, etc.
>
> - Suggest some other media 'sacred cows' and their treatment by the mass media.
> - To what extent do you think that the media can assist in social control and reinforce social order?
> - Does the media operate as a socialisation agency? If so, what values does it transmit to the public?

Some concerns about concentration of media ownership

Many corporations have adopted a policy of **diversification**. Their business interests have expanded into various fields to compensate for potential losses in any one particular field. It could be argued that this cross-media ownership affects editorial policy: commercial interests may take over editorial interests. Indeed, it would be surprising if media conglomerates did not censor media output that was detrimental to their diverse financial concerns.

Media commentators have accused press owners of putting their own interests before the public interest and of being more concerned with profit than with producing quality newspapers. Proprietors have also been accused of political bias, promoting their own political ideology at the expense of democracy. If this is true, then it is a very serious case indeed as newspaper ownership in Britain is more concentrated than anywhere else in the Western world.

Concentration of ownership within the media field means that the owners wield an enormous amount of economic power. This situation is unacceptable to many.

- Marxists see it as part of the polarisation process between the ruling elite and the proletariat, with the mass media being used as instruments for controlling the masses and forcefully sustaining dominant interests (see L. Althusser, *ideological state apparatuses*, Unit 5, page 272 and Unit 11, page 575).
- Pluralists hold that media power is shared between competing groups, defending the autonomy of media institutions. They maintain that free-market competition within the media field is healthy. They quote, for example, the Broadcasting Act 1990 which granted licences to TV companies based on an 'auction' system (see page 285), thus ensuring that franchises were gained by those able to pay the most money or meet the criteria laid down, often regardless of quality of programming. (The market, however, is not quite as 'free' as it may seem due to the high costs of buying a newspaper or television franchise.)
- Robert Maxwell (1923–1991), one-time owner of the *Mirror* and the *People*, did little to provide support for the pluralist perspective. His foothold in Fleet Street was established after Rupert Murdoch's, but he displayed the same ruthless business techniques and editorial interference. In 1949, he bought the Pergamon Press, and six years later the Department of Trade and Industry deemed it necessary to investigate the company. The Department's inspectors concluded that Maxwell was '... not a person who can be relied upon to exercise proper stewardship of a publicly quoted company.'

- Rupert Murdoch, who controls the *Sun*, *The Times* and *News of the World*, is renowned for editorial interference and using his papers for his own political purposes. Following the example of Lord Beaverbrook, he made it clear that he had no intention of leaving his newspapers to run themselves: 'I did not come all this way not to interfere.'

Up to 1996, the Broadcasting Act (1990) stated that newspaper groups could not have more than a 20 per cent share in terrestrial television companies. The intention was to prevent any media giant swallowing up its competitors and thereby being able to dictate the information received by the public. However, such restriction on cross-media ownership could apply only to UK broadcasting. Rupert Murdoch's News International was able to gain a 40 per cent stake in BSkyB's initial five satellite channels (broadcasting from outside the UK) in spite of Murdoch's ownership of five British newspapers. Such cross-media ownership is seen by other British newspaper and media groups as monopolistic and unfair, since they are legally held back in their activities. This situation gave rise to the following developments:

- The British Media Consortium Group (BMCG) was formed in 1993 to lobby on behalf of those losing out. They argue that technological and commercial considerations require changes in the law. Convergence between media telecommunications and computer industries was taking place, alongside the globalisation of the media industry which makes demands on the financing and the organisation of companies. The BMCG seeks to increase the permitted level of cross-media ownership.
- The government, perhaps in response to the BMCG, published *Media Ownership: The Government's Proposals* in 1995. These proposals include the suggestion that the newspaper groups (not just individual newspapers) below a certain circulation (expected to be 20 per cent of the total market) will be able to control up to 15 per cent of television plus a national radio station.
- There was a political shift in 1996 by Rupert Murdoch, head of News International, from Conservative to Labour. Suspicions have been voiced that this was to protect his own interests, as in the late stages of the Conservative government in the mid-1990s there seemed to be a general shift towards the Labour Party by the electorate, a view reinforced by the General Election result on 1 May 1997.

Think about it

- How do different sociological perspectives view the power base of the mass media? Which social groups seem to hold or lack such power?
- Do you think that cross-media ownership such as that held by Rupert Murdoch affects the policies of his media editors and producers? Can you provide examples to support your views on this?
- What do you consider to be the reasons for and problems with government attempts to control or regulate media broadcasting? Offer a couple of examples.

The relationship between the mass media, popular culture and ideology

The creation of 'artefacts of meaning'

The term **artefacts of meaning** is used to refer to the way in which material objects develop cultural and social significance. Because we associate certain objects with certain ideas, they have a meaning beyond that of their everyday use or function. When particular objects become valued in this way they can become status symbols, and their ownership can provide – or reinforce – cultural or social superiority; it can represent financial advantage too, since such objects' commercial value is inflated by their marketable prestige. The recognition of certain objects as 'art' and the debate over what is meant by art is an example of the role of artefacts of meaning and the conferring of 'cult' status on certain objects.

In the early twentieth century, Marcel Duchamp, a French painter, presented ready-made commonplace objects as works of art; his work drew attention to how artefacts of meaning are created. For example, when a urinal entitled 'Fountain', which he signed as R. Mutt, was exhibited in Paris in 1917, Duchamp argued that this was an art form and that there could be no 'sacred' category of objects which were 'art' with a value superior to that of other artefacts.

Control over what becomes an artefact of meaning, and over the image associated with these artefacts, may have a powerful influence on our perception of the social status of individuals or groups. Who decides what is to be labelled as 'popular culture' or 'highbrow' – what is the role of the ruling ideology and/or the media (in its various forms) in these developments?

Karl Marx, in *The German Ideology*, stated that those who owned the means of production also controlled the production and distribution of ideas. In other words, the ruling class can rule not only by economic force but also through ideas. Clearly, the mass media can serve to promote a ruling ideology. Marxists would argue that popular culture satisfies the needs of the proletarian masses and promotes a 'false consciousness' or a kind of 'feel good' factor which enables them to develop their own sense of well being within a capitalist market economy. Ideology thus allows the masses to make sense of their world so that class domination and exploitation become submerged in their everyday lives. Neo-Marxists have maintained that all consciousness reflects ideology, since language itself, as the basic medium of communication, can never be neutral: in its meanings and interpretations, language supports the interests of capitalism.

In the twentieth century, particularly in the 1960s, the post-World War II period of stability was challenged. Across Europe students and workers held demonstrations and strikes; while the USA experienced widespread race riots. In this atmosphere of conflict, a more critical academic approach to the role of the mass media developed among sociologists, particularly among Neo-Marxists. Mass media researchers started to look at media representations in terms of their ideological content and power base. This study focus continued to develop and has been widely debated, as the mass media have become a major cultural institution in which ideas and images are created both within and across classes, cultures and societies.

Globalisation of the mass media

When sales of music albums by bands such as Oasis reach 9 million, it is clear that the mass media is international in scale. In this situation it is possible for multinational media owners such as Rupert Murdoch to become 'big barons in the new global village'. Apart from Murdoch's large media interest in the UK, his global estate includes Twentieth Century Fox Films in the USA, Vox Satellite and television channels in Germany, and 99 per cent of Star TV covering Japan, India, China and Hong Kong. Furthermore, artefacts of meaning are shared across the globe, rather than their significance being confined to a national or even local level, for example Americanisation via Hollywood (and McDonalds).

Advertising on a global scale

Significant links have developed, on a global basis, between popular music and advertising, particularly in relation to the large-scale corporations and multinational media companies (see page 287). In 1986, Levi's hit upon the idea of having a male model stripping in a launderette to the sound of Marvin Gaye's 'I Heard it Through The Grapevine'. There followed a popchart flow of ad-linked rock and soul hits, including the Hollies' 'He Ain't Heavy, He's My Brother' (for Miller Lite), Free's 'Alright Now' (for Wrigley's chewing gum) and the Bluebells' 'Young At Heart' (for Volkswagen), all of which re-entered the pop charts in several countries after their use in advertising campaigns.

Criticism has been expressed from a variety of sources of the links established across media forms. Even within the pop industry, for example, Paul McCartney fell out with Michael Jackson who, as owner of the Beatles' publishing rights, sold them to Sony Music. McCartney claimed that their songs have been cheapened by being used for advertising purposes, while fellow ex-Beatle George Harrison commented:

> '*Unless we do something about it every Beatles song is going to end up advertising Bass and pork pies!*'

The global marketing of products seems to be taking an increasingly firm grip on artefacts of meaning in both the mass media and popular culture, whether we look at Disney or McDonalds, whose founder Ray Kroc swore he could see universal beauty in a hamburger bun.

Think about it

- What might sociologists of different perspectives say about a male model stripping in a launderette as part of a global advertising campaign to market a brand of jeans? How might different cultures be affected by such campaigns? Discuss this and other examples of global marketing of, for example, drinks or foodstuffs.
- How do you think that changes in popular music might reflect wider social changes?

Think about it

- To what extent can the mass media *create* popular culture via artefacts of meaning, rather than merely *reflect* it? Use your own examples to illustrate your comments.

Sponsorship

As a relatively recent development, television programmes in the UK are now sponsored by industries such as newspapers, chocolate makers, brewers and soft drink producers. Cigarette companies, while excluded from TV sponsorship, have become major sponsors of sporting events such as Formula 1 motor racing teams, with a very high global presence. In 1997 there was widespread criticism of the new Labour government's failure to ban tobacco companies' sponsorship of Formula 1 racing despite manifesto promises.

Even cricket – the traditional bastion of sporting values – has given way to globalised marketing as demonstrated in the 1996 World Cup, sponsored by Tetley brewery. This prompted Andrew Sweeting to suggest:

> '*A multi-billion dollar deal with Nike, share options in a friendly privatised water company and a spin-off album of easy-listening snippets of patriotic music might be what we need to attract players of the right calibre.*'
> 'The whole world's gone logo', the *Guardian*, 8 April 1996

Formula 1 teams make lucrative contracts with tobacco companies

Media content from a sociological viewpoint

The making and reporting of news

Those who make and report the news would like us to believe that their reportage deals with 'facts' and as such is 'objective'. However, a sociological response is that the need to put the day's events on to a television screen for a set number of minutes (sometimes 15 minutes or less) or into a set number of pages of a newspaper challenges such ideas of objectivity. Since the news must be *selected* from a potentially enormous range of events, newsmakers need to *choose* those they decide are *newsworthy items* and reject others. This need to choose significant items for inclusion sets up criteria (or main principles) for selection.

Defining news

Several sociologists have pointed to newsmakers' difficulties in defining news. Since reporters wish to believe that news items are 'facts' which they report objectively to their audiences, they tend to overlook that news may be something which they helped to form. News is supposedly what happens out there in the world, and which appears on screen and page undisturbed by human intervention. The idea of *making* the news/'facts' seems like distortion or making things up. However, it is precisely this which many sociologists maintain: that news is a **social construct**; it is a *manufactured* process. A significant contribution to the debate was made by the Glasgow University Media Group studies.

Coding television news
The Glasgow University Media Group

Television is an especially important source of information and seems to have more credibility than the press: many people seem to regard television news as more 'objective', 'reliable', and so on. It is therefore not surprising that a debate developed when the Glasgow University Media Group, in its examination of television news, produced a series of studies which maintained that:

> *'The news is not a neutral and natural phenomenon: it is rather the manufactured production of ideology.'*
> Glasgow University Media Group, *More Bad News* (1980)

The Glasgow University Media Group stated that values are evident in television news through:

- time allocations: the longer the story, the more important it is portrayed to be. This impression of importance is also reinforced by the type of coverage – film clips, live reports, for example;
- order of placement: the hierarchical order of television news serves as an index of its value, the first item being the most important, going down to the relatively trivial;
- categorisation of items: newsmakers need to categorise items, for example political issues, foreign news, etc., to make the news manageable and to achieve a smooth flow. However, categorisation becomes important in terms of values when differing issues become linked. This is illustrated in the diagram opposite.

The Glasgow University Media Group analysed and decoded television news

> *'. . . to reveal the structures of the cultural framework which underpins the production of apparently neutral news.'*
> Glasgow University Media Group, *Bad News* (1976)

They maintained that:

- the structuring of TV news – what gets most coverage and whose views are given most attention – contributes to news which lays the 'blame for society's industrial and economic problems at the door of the workforce';
- the news is socially constructed and cannot be 'objective' and 'impartial'; it is systematically biased against working-class people (see the illustration opposite and consider the language used to refer to labour, and then management, issues).

Criticisms
The Group was challenged by Martin Harrison in *Television News: Whose Bias?* (1985). At the suggestion of Independent Television News, Martin Harrison carried out a review of the Group's data and conclusions; as ITN had not retained tapes of the original programmes, Harrison's data was based on scripts of the broadcasts. From such data he argued:

- that the Glasgow Group had misrepresented the nature of television news reviews;
- that the Glasgow studies were not only 'imprecise, . . . inaccurate, selective and unrepresentative' but also 'shoddy', 'as firm as a wet blancmange'.

Replies to criticisms
The leading members of the Glasgow Group maintained that Harrison was himself 'no stranger to inaccuracy and misrepresentation' and they pointed to the following flaws in his work:

- It was based not on actual broadcasts but on printed scripts: conclusions drawn from the latter are of little relevance to the former. Harrison made no attempt to find out whether the Glasgow Group would make copies of the broadcasts available to him, and he did not reply to a letter offering to let him see the tapes.

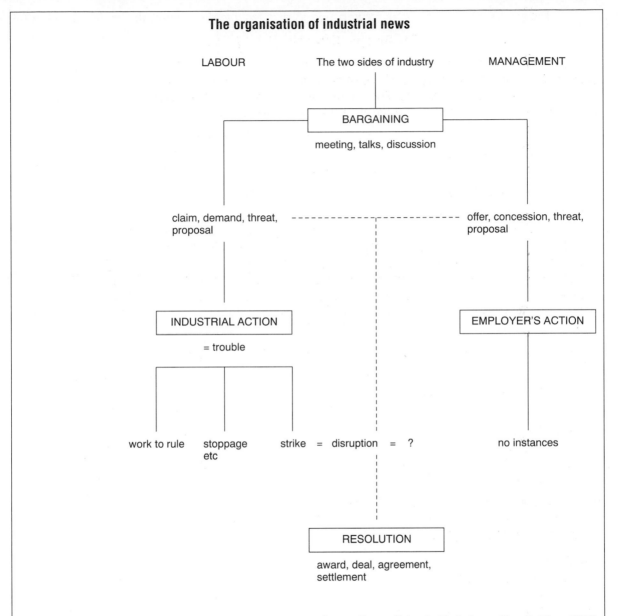

The organisation of industrial news

LABOUR · The two sides of industry · MANAGEMENT

BARGAINING
meeting, talks, discussion

claim, demand, threat, proposal — offer, concession, threat, proposal

INDUSTRIAL ACTION
= trouble

EMPLOYER'S ACTION

work to rule · stoppage etc · strike = disruption = ? · no instances

RESOLUTION
award, deal, agreement, settlement

Source: Glasgow University Media Group, *More Bad News* (1980)

- Harrison examined only ITN coverage and not BBC coverage which was included in the original study.
- Large sections of broadcasts, such as Conservative MP James Prior's attack on British Leyland workers, were not included in the transcripts.
- Some passages contained in the printed transcripts were not actually broadcast, for example statements about the causes of disputes and union procedures.

They argued that if the Glasgow research is indeed misleading, then the necessary research to establish this has not been carried out.

The gatekeeper   How is 'newsworthiness' decided by the newsmakers? Media sociologists use the concept of **gatekeeper**, coined by D.M. White in *The Gatekeeper: A Case Study in the Selection of News* (1950). The gatekeeper is the newsmaker who acts as a filter between events in the world and the news article or programme; certain items pass through, while others are blocked. The main gatekeepers are **editors, reporters** and **sources of news**; though there are others in various forms.

Early studies of gatekeeping tended to focus on the editorial process. They observed the choices made in press and television offices from news items flowing in from agencies, reporters, etc., and looked for evidence of patterns of selection or rejection. From such analysis of news content, conclusions might be made about the values behind definitions of newsworthiness. For example, it might be found that some newsmakers' religious commitment led them to accept or reject items on divorce or abortion; others' preference for 'real-life' stories might lead them to favour unusual incidents over, for example, dull reports from government departments; while others might be guided by political outlook, or the views of the proprietor.

A problem with the gatekeeper concept is that it assumes that news-making is a passive process – that news items arrive ready-made in the newsroom, some to be chosen, the rest to be rejected. Later studies of gatekeeping have emphasised that it is a more active process of news creation. Steve Chibnall, in *Law-and-Order News* (1977), showed the importance of sources for gatekeepers in creating news. In his account of crime reporters, he emphasised the role of journalists cultivating contacts in the police and courts as sources of stories, as well as the role of official sources that are routinely checked by journalists.

Organisational factors   Chibnall's emphasis on the role of sources in newsmaking reminds us of the importance of organisational factors in manufacturing the news. A basic look at the news may show it as events 'out there' which, because they 'happen', get into the media; a second look, however, may make us realise the extent to which newsmakers must *organise* their affairs to ensure the survival of the newspaper or television news. Since TV news is produced at a given time for a given period every day and a newspaper is of a given length each day, reporters must *plan* for a *smooth flow*.

This organisational factor goes against any notion that news is simply 'a window on the world'. If newsmakers set up routines and work in institutions based on the idea that enough (and not too much) news will be created each day, then these organisational factors are active ingredients of news construction. For example, all news agencies use 'diaries' to plan for 'significant events' – political, sporting, etc. – and 'do the rounds' of organisations such as the Conservative and the Labour parties with the expectation that these will be newsworthy. In this process, what is newsworthy is decided in advance, even if it produces boring news: as argued in the article opposite.

The nine o'clock snooze

Why should all television news be the same?
Kelvin MacKenzie, former editor of the *Sun* and now head of Live TV, says it's time to scrap the regulatory straitjacket

Forty years ago news-readers wore dinner jackets. They don't any more, but the network news shows are all still forced to wear the same mental uniform. Television news bulletins are dull and regimented, in a way newspapers don't need to be. Whatever the channel, they are clones of each other, driven to work to an agenda which is light years away from the interests of great swathes of the population.

The problem is regulation. When the Independent Television Commission advertised Channel 5, it made it clear what sort of news service it — as the all-powerful regulator — expected and which anyone applying for the franchise would ignore at their peril. And what did it want? Yet another prime-time news programme with what it described as high-quality national and international coverage.

In other words, more of what the viewer already has plenty of. There's a long and boring show on Channel 4 at seven o'clock; there's a pretty dull half-hour on BBC1 at nine o'clock; there's yet more on ITV at 10 o'clock. Why are they so afraid to let the public have something different to choose?

We're already able to get our news in different shapes and sizes from cable and satellite — Sky and CNN offer the ability to access hard news round the clock. I can see no reason in trying to keep news on other channels in one particular format.

We are going to have to abandon a lot of the assumptions we have made about television news. In particular, there is an underlying paradox about the different roles of television and print which will need to be faced. In newspapers and print, we all think that democracy is best served by freedom of speech and opinion. But the rules for broadcasting have been framed on the assumption that democracy is best served not by freedom of speech, but by requiring impartiality.

No one is suggesting that this familiar rule should be chucked out tomorrow, merely on the promise of a more relaxed, multi-channel future. Nor should we delude ourselves into thinking that British broadcasting has achieved some unbiased state of grace. It hasn't. It can't. Your neutrality is my bias.

And even if we could find an agreed degree of impartiality, it would be so dull that I'm not sure what good it would do for the viewing public. They're not fools. They know that TV drama has been taking sides for years — don't tell me that *Casualty* is politically balanced.

Television news and current affairs will follow drama in the end. My own guess is that in as little as 20 years from now people will look back and see the impartiality requirements on broadcasting as quaint pieces of history, like censorship of the theatre and newspapers in the 18th century.

If you think that is fanciful, just look at what is going on even now. Soon computers and television sets will be available in the same box in the home. Is it a computer or is it a telly? It's both, and it begins to blur the easy distinctions we're used to. Several British national newspapers are already available on-line. Should home viewers of these services be "protected" from the sponsoring paper's editorial line? Of course not.

By the time new digital services are on offer, British viewers will potentially have access to dozens if not hundreds of channels. It can't make sense for all of them to be stifled by regulations designed for a two-channel environment.

If the BBC continues to be paid for by the licence fee, by all means let's keep it subject to the impartiality rules. We will all know what we're getting from it, just as we know what we get from the *Mirror* or the *Telegraph*. But in the long term, impartial news is no more real than impartial drama.

In the shorter term, we really must be more relaxed about different styles of news programming. For choice to be real, the differences of approach need to be real. Live TV's News Bunny may not be your cup of tea and you may prefer Trevor McDonald to rolling news on cable or satellite, but they aren't mutually exclusive propositions.

I'm not arguing for an "anything goes" approach which would sanction pornography and worse. Newspapers are subject to the laws of the land on obscenity and defamation, and television should be on the same footing. What I find impossible to defend is a position in which the great and the good tell us that the news can come in one form only. Yes, television has a greater impact than a paper. Yes, there must be proper consideration for children. But we don't make all swimming-pools two inches deep because some people can't swim.

Source: *The Daily Telegraph*, 27 February 1996

Think about it

- Do you think attempts to remain neutral have led to boring and dull news coverage? Give reasons for your answer.
- What do you think are the best and worst features of some of the wide range of media news coverage available to the public?
- In what sense is the organisation of news reporting likely to focus attention on the existence of social conflict and the need for social order?

Philip Schlesinger, in his study *Putting Reality Together: BBC News* (1985), shows how important organisation is for defining 'news'. He writes:

> 'The routines of [news] production have definite consequences in structuring news. . . The news we receive on any given day is not as unpredictable as much journalistic mythology would have us believe. Rather, the doings of the world are tamed to meet the needs of a production system in many respects bureaucratically organised.'

He describes ways in which TV news is planned, noting the use of an 'advance diary' by news editors, which arranges the schedules of reporters and recorded materials. Schlesinger stated that some 70 per cent of such diary fixtures are used for news bulletins, and considers 'most news is not spontaneous'.

Agenda setting

Agenda setting puts forward the idea that individuals are not free to make use of, and construct, the media as they may wish. It is the media, rather than individuals, which provide the framework for defining issues and events. Within the concept of agenda setting is the idea that the media operate in the interests of dominant and powerful groups: through the media are transmitted messages which reinforce dominant ideology. The groups limit the way in which individuals see issues and events by setting a restricted agenda. Stuart Hall et al., in *Policing the Crisis* (1978), introduced into media sociology important concepts associated with agenda setting:

- **Pyramid of access to the media:** Access depends on your standing in the social ladder: society may be seen as a pyramid in relation to your chances of getting access to the media. For example, the monarchy, MPs and judges are high in the pyramid, while clerical workers are relatively low. Position in the pyramid of access to the media shapes a person's ability to be a primary or secondary definer (see below) of what forms news.
- **Primary definers** include, for example, a judge who has high access and who comments that violent crime is soaring in the inner city. He (or she) can thus become the primary definer of news. A headline like VIOLENT CRIME SOARS IN INNER CITY will set the agenda for the news: the judge's remarks are the primary definition.
- **Secondary definers** may be illustrated in relation to the above example. Other people, such as police and politicians, may be asked for their views because 'balance' is important to media professionals and also because statements from 'sources' make news items more 'factual'. These people may disagree with the primary definer's views and their ideas will get an airing, but it is important to note that they will be in response to the original definer's agenda. To this extent they may be termed secondary definers: they carry less weight since often they are responding to an agenda which they would not have chosen in the first place.

These concepts imply that newsmakers routinely go to 'accredited sources' for news stories.

Professional ethics

Journalistic practice is controlled to a certain extent by professional codes which contain the profession's own group culture. The interpretation of these codes varies, and journalists range from the tabloid 'hack' or 'cheque-book journalist' to the investigative journalist on a quality newspaper. However, codes are important both in the selection of news and for the ways in which issues are treated.

The **ethos of objectivity** stresses the importance of the journalist dealing in 'facts'. Newsmakers usually link 'objectivity' with 'facts' but, as already noted, selection of 'facts' about an issue or person can often reflect the values of a journalist. For example, the fact that a politician is divorced can be introduced into a news item in order to devalue that person and hence their party's right to take a particular position in a debate concerning, for example, the 'back to basics' and 'family values' issues (see Unit 3).

News values determine what becomes news and how it is covered. The influence of news values in the newsmaking process is shown in the diagram below.

News values

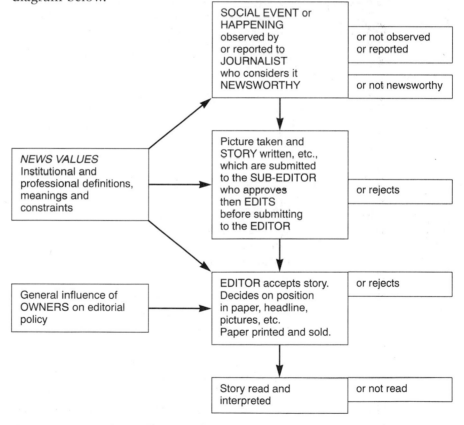

An important news value is **ethnocentrism**, a term used to describe the way in which British news stories feature more prominently in the British media than foreign ones. This value prioritises, say, '1 killed in London' over '6 killed in Paris' over '1000 killed in Iraqi Kurdestan'; it indicates the limitations of the belief that news is just 'what happens'. It is a professional requirement, and has been referred to as the **threshold of importance**, in which national (or local) news is judged as more important than faraway news. Steve Chibnall (see page 296) provides a description of this and other professional requirements which guide the construction of news stories. The following six are the most widespread:

1. **Immediacy**   News is about what is new, what has happened. This means that it is concerned with the present rather than the past and with immediate events rather than long-term processes. The Cambridge sociologist, John Thompson, refers to this as the 'struggle for visibility'.

2. **Dramatisation**   There is an emphasis on the dramatic. News is commercial knowledge, designed in a competitive market with profit in mind. To give greater impact, concrete happenings are shown rather than background causes. This is essential to the understanding of how, for example, political criticism is reported. News coverage tends to concentrate on the *form* of opposition rather than the reasons, as was the case with the Greenham Common Peace Movement in the 1980s.

3. **Personalisation** stresses people rather than events. The emphasis on personalities and celebrities is important for the news media, and was clearly illustrated by the coverage of the trial of the US basketball player O.J. Simpson, charged with the murder of his ex-wife, in 1996. The more that news enters the market place of entertainment the more it is obliged to recognise and promote the cult of the star. The consequence of this is not merely that newspaper front pages are occupied by the famous, but that issues are increasingly defined and presented in terms of personalities.

4. **Simplification**   A tendency to simplify news coverage is bound up with practical elements and professional competence. The popular news story must be put together quickly. Also, it must be easily understood by readers of widely differing intellectual abilities: it is claimed that the *Sun* requires a reading age of 8 years. For the 'popular' journalist, then, good reporting involves 'pruning down' the reality of the situation: the simpler the better.

5. **Titillation**   Advertisers have long realised that, carefully handled, sexual titillation can sell anything from cars to chocolate. In the form of tasteful nudes and scandalous news, it also sells newspapers.

6. **Novelty**   The above professional requirements which guide the construction of news stories both support and demonstrate newspaper ideology. However, one more requirement brings an element of randomness into newspaper stories, even if it too may use ideological interpretations and stereotypes. This demands that stories be 'kept alive' by the search for fresh 'news angles', the 'unexpected' or 'elements of surprise' – often in the form of speculation supported by only slender evidence. In some cases, when deadlines become very close, it seems that almost any story may do, almost any fresh twist of interpretation may become acceptable, even as a front-page leader.

Think about it

- Monitor news items over a seven-day period on radio or TV or in the newspapers, or any combination of these, and collect examples of stories which have been chosen and presented on the basis of each of the six categories of journalistic professional requirements listed above.
- Which of the above could be applied to media coverage of the death, in August 1997, of Diana, Princess of Wales?

Moral panics

The concept of 'moral panics' (see also Unit 10, pages 522–4) was identified by Stan Cohen in his classic study of Mods and Rockers, mid-1960s' youth movements: *Folk Devils and Moral Panics* (1972). He coined the term 'moral panic' to describe the combined reaction of the media and society to acts of deviance – such as teenage pregnancies or the use of recreational drugs such as Ecstasy – which challenge perceived social values. Cohen noted that people high in the pyramid of access to the media (see page 298) and those directly involved in the media, alert for sensational(ised) stories, pick up on these events and use them to express fears for social order. This creates a rolling process:

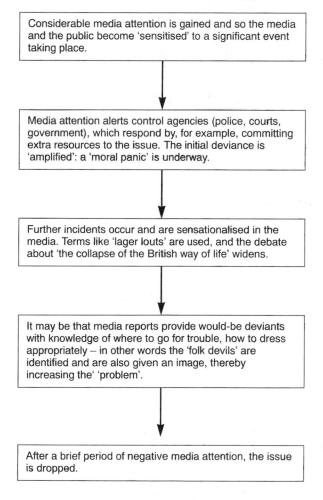

Considerable media attention is gained and so the media and the public become 'sensitised' to a significant event taking place.

Media attention alerts control agencies (police, courts, government), which respond by, for example, committing extra resources to the issue. The initial deviance is 'amplified': a 'moral panic' is underway.

Further incidents occur and are sensationalised in the media. Terms like 'lager louts' are used, and the debate about 'the collapse of the British way of life' widens.

It may be that media reports provide would-be deviants with knowledge of where to go for trouble, how to dress appropriately – in other words the 'folk devils' are identified and are also given an image, thereby increasing the' 'problem'.

After a brief period of negative media attention, the issue is dropped.

The concept of 'moral panic' suggests reasons as to why and how certain groups and actions are treated in the news media. It has been suggested that the media may aggravate problems which, if left alone, would be relatively trivial.

Content analysis

Content analysis is a research technique involving the in-depth study of samples of media. It is the method most commonly used to show that news is a social construction: news is examined, patterns of content are noted and analysed. Content analysis is also used as a way of measuring the amount of coverage of a particular issue (domestic violence, for example) in some form of communication – newspapers, comics, sit-coms, soap operas, etc. The advantages and disadvantages of content analysis are outlined below.

Advantages of content analysis	Disadvantages of content analysis
• It is relatively inexpensive to carry out by individuals and groups.	• It is hard to be certain whether the sample studied is representative.
• It is usually easy to get material in written or video form.	• It is often difficult to obtain a sound working definition of the topic being studied (for example, what is violence?).
• It is unobtrusive and as such does not influence the people or factor being researched.	• It is not easy to find a measurable unit, such as frames in a video recording.
• It provides a rich source of data that can be quantified.	• It is not possible to prove that conclusions drawn from content analysis have been accurate – theoretically, in the social world, everything depends on *interpretation*.
• It can deal with current events or past events, or both.	

Source: Adapted from A.A. Berger, *Media Analysis Techniques* (Sage, 1982)

Wider issues associated with content analysis

Content analysis requires hard work and demands high-quality skills. Samples of media must be thoroughly studied and carefully examined for representativeness. A major problem for content analysis lies in its **construction of categories** for analysis. To what extent are these categories adequate? Do they exclude certain types of reportage? Or do they force news items into categories which they do not easily fit?

Associated with this, and noted in the above table, is the key question of whether the findings are 'scientific' and a true representation of what is in the media. When analysts identify, for example, patriarchal ideology in newspapers or racist stereotypes in the reporting of crime, there is the need to ask to what extent these findings are a consequence of the interpretation of the analyst rather than the 'reality' of the media.

Think about it

• Consider the pros and cons of content analysis and discuss why results produced by this method of analysing the media may be misleading.
• Carry out some content analysis yourself. Assess images of gender in the media by analysing a month's issues of a teenage magazine. How does it present its readers with an ideology of adolescent femininity or masculinity?

Semiology

Semiology began as a way of studying language. The term was first used by the linguist Ferdinand de Saussure in his *Course in General Linguistics* (first compiled 1916). More recently it has gone further than language to include films, advertising, television, photography, etc. It has been defined as 'a science which studies the life of signs within society'. Of interest to semiologists, and sociologists, is how signs as well as words or images help us to make sense of our world.

SEMIOLOGY applies to all sign systems including direct communication (such as semaphore and language), ambiguous communication (such as literature) and conventions (such as ritual, etiquette and fashion). Semiologists argue that signs get their meaning from the system in which they are located. All signs are made up of a *signifier* (that is, the sound or visible object, such as the letters DOG) and a *signified* (that is, what is represented by the signifier, such as 'a hairy animal that barks'). The sign is the coming together of the signifier and the signified. Signs thus *denote* something, the word 'dog' denotes an animal.

However, a sign may *connote* something else, for example in a discussion about controlling dogs, such as pit bull terriers, the word 'dog' connotes 'danger' or 'viciousness'.

Social semiologists thus argue that the meaning of a sign is dependent on its context. Signs do not have a single straightforward meaning. In some contexts, for example, the sign 'rose' means a flower, in others it means passion and in others it means the British Labour Party. Signs often connote something other than their obvious meaning and this depends on the taken-for-granted view of the sign reader. So when looking at the media, social semiologists attempt to reveal the taken-for-granteds that are implied by the use of certain language and to expose the ideology underlying media content.

Source: L. Harvey and M. MacDonald, *Doing Sociology* (Macmillan, 1993)

The extract quoted above suggests that communication is structured around rules which are understood within a particular context. Whilst content analysis often uses typical sociological methods such as data collecting or surveys, semiologists prefer in-depth observation. The main focus of semiological analysis is the sign which, as explained in the extract, has two parts: the **signifier** and the **signified**.

Roland Barthes, a French semiologist, distinguished between the way signs denote and connote meaning:

- **denotation:** the simple meaning of a sign. For example, a sign on supermarket doors showing a crossed out dog denotes no entry for a dog (unless it is accompanying a blind person);
- **connotation:** the cultural meaning of a sign which is not fixed and is open to interpretation. (A dog may be interpreted as a pet or as a danger.)

Barthes also used the term **myth** to refer to a chain of ideas linked to a sign. By myth, he did not mean that the ideas are false, but that they form cultural ways of making sense of the world. For example, an image of a white man wearing a white coat in front of a statistical diagram symbolises science as factual (and white/masculine) knowledge; hence its frequent use in advertising. These are cultural codes which we use to give meaning to the world.

As a means of studying mass media, semiology can be applied to words, pictures and sounds. It looks at the sign systems or audio-visual codes contained in media 'texts' and **decodes** them to reveal the underlying ideology. When certain codes become popularly recognised they are referred to as **genres** or particular types, such as 'musicals', 'gangster movies' or 'western' films. Westerns become recognised by visual signs such as the cowboy clothes and the landscape, and by narrative themes of the hunt for the outlaw, civilising the West. Brian Dutton, in *The Media* (1986), referred to the western's ideological messages in relation to American history as tending to show Indians as aggressive savages civilised by law and order. Thus he has written:

> *'Genres then may carry certain messages which limit how a given text can be interpreted.'*
> Brian Dutton, *The Media* (1986)

Posters and other public signs can form an interesting genre in terms of interpretation, as illustrated below.

'Grim': the official sign

Give way to pogo stick pensioners

By Sarah Schaefer

RESIDENTS at an old people's home, irritated by road signs depicting a stooping couple with a walking stick, have put up their own speed warnings showing elderly people unicycling with a zimmer frame and doing "wheelies" in a wheelchair.

"We are not as doddery as the official signs make us out to be," said resident Eddie Tovey, 83.

"We keep fit and active and these signs show the younger generation how very original and young-at-heart we are at this home."

The signs, which cost £200 each, were put up to stop visitors speeding on the mile-long private road to the Ysguborwen home in Aberdare, Mid Glamorgan.

Other designs show an old woman skateboarding and an elderly man bouncing on a pogo stick.

The administrator of the home, Jacqui Coombes, said the

residents hoped that other homes would follow their example.

"We had these signs made with the help of professional road sign designers," she added.

"We needed warnings to make delivery vans and visitors slow down because they were endangering residents having a stroll. But the Department of Transport ones were quite grim.

"We are sure that our fun signs will be more effective because at least now drivers are likely to look twice before they speed down to the home. It would be fantastic to have other homes following our lead."

Nellie Thomas, 80, said: "We are very proud of the signs. We hope they will be a talking point among visitors and residents alike and make everyone smile."

Danger: unicycling OAPs

Stop: pogoing pensioners

Slow: skating grannies

Source: The *Guardian*, 22 August 1996

Semiology should not be seen as a replacement for content analysis. The two approaches may, and have been, used together. The Glasgow University Media Group, for example, attempted some decoding of television signs (see page 294).

Roland Barthes, in *Mythologies* (1973), refers to '**anchorage**' on an image which is more 'open' than words to an alternative interpretation. Thus the media may attempt to 'fix' an interpretation by the use of pictures, banner or slogan headlines or photo captions, which make a more dramatic, and arguably a more lasting, impact, than a piece of text.

Judith Williamson, in *Decoding Advertisements* (1978), maintained that in many advertisements people become closely identified with products. People become encouraged to identify with others in terms of what they drink, what they wear, how they think, how they behave, etc., almost regardless of the product. Marxist observers argue that if, as a result of advertising, people identify strongly with particular clothes, cars, high technology developments etc. and if this encourages a 'feel-good' factor within capitalism, then it is not merely products which are being sold but the ideology of capitalism itself.

Evaluating semiology   Semiology has been widely criticised.

- It does not form a systematic approach to media interpretation. It is extremely wide-ranging and, in terms of the elements of the media on which semiologists focus, may be considered as subjective and unrepresentative.
- The decoding of texts by semiologists may not provide the same meanings as those identified by audiences. How can semiologists maintain that their understanding of popular culture signs is adequate if it ignores groups who consume such signs?
- Cultural codes are constantly changing and therefore require renegotiation.
- Although Barthes has referred to texts as 'polysemic', i.e. open to different interpretations, this has not deflected criticisms such as the following:

> '*What validity does Barthes's interpretation of a particular cultural item possess? He does not attempt to indicate why his interpretation is to be preferred to others. For example, he suggests that roses signify passion. But how can he validate this conclusion, and say they should be understood in this way, and not as a way of signifying a joke, a farewell, or a platonic thank you? How do we discriminate between these interpretations? What evidence could a semiologist call upon to back up Barthes's interpretation? Similarly, semiologists are fond of referring to the codes which lie behind, or are embodied in, a particular sign or myth, but rarely if ever produce evidence of this code independently of the sign or myth under consideration.*'

Dominic Strinati, *Popular Culture* (Routledge, 1995)

Media stereotyping and stratification

The media have been considered to produce a range of stereotypes, particularly around gender, ethnicity, age and class.

The media and gender

Considerable research has been carried out into the representations of men and women in the media. Much of this research has been based on content analysis. Gaye Tuchman reviewed content analysis across the media in *Hearth and Home: Images of Women in the Media* (1978). Her survey of relevant literature offered the following findings:

- Women were portrayed in two significant roles – the domestic and the sexual (including romantic).
- By contrast, males appeared mainly in spheres of employment, politics, sport and other areas of social life.
- An earlier study by Tuchman, *The Symbolic Annihilation of Women in the Media* (1977), found that men outnumbered women on television by three to one.
- Women counted for only 26 per cent of characters in all TV soap operas, serials and dramas. Game shows and quizzes were, almost without exception, presented by men.
- In so-called 'serious programmes', the picture was a little better. However, discussion programmes such as *Question Time* typically featured four males and no females.

Teenage magazines

Feminist studies have drawn attention to a patriarchal ideology in the media. This ideology is seen to limit the spheres of activity for women and to represent gender roles – where man is seen as the economic provider and woman as the emotional provider in the home – as 'natural' and inevitable. This is exemplified in Angela McRobbie's study of the teenage magazine *Jackie*:

1. [Jackie] sets up, defines and focuses exclusively on 'the personal', locating, as the areas of main importance to teenagers, romance problems, fashion, beauty and pop, and marks out the limits of girls' concerns.
2. It presents 'romantic individualism' as a guiding principle for the teenage girl. The 'Jackie' girl is alone in her quest for love; she refers back to her female peers for advice and reassurance only when she has problems in fulfilling this aim.
3. To receive self-respect, the girl has to escape the 'bitchy', 'catty' atmosphere of female company and find a boyfriend fast. She has not only to be individualistic in outlook, she has to be prepared to fight ruthlessly by plotting. However, this independent-mindedness is short-lived.
4. As soon as she finds a 'steady', the girl must give in to his demands, acknowledge his domination and resign herself to her subordination.

Source: Based on Angela McRobbie, *Jackie, an ideology of adolescent femininity* (1981)

Into the 1990s there is still a wide range of teenage magazines which seem to carry similar messages to those identified by Angela McRobbie over a decade earlier – as exemplified by newer, glossy magazines such as *MIZZ*.

Things have certainly changed since Tuchman's studies, but not dramatically. It has been suggested by writers that women's views of themselves and their position in society have been moulded and reinforced by such representations. This process is ideological in the sense that it supports powerful vested interests in society – those of men – and so helps to maintain the subordination of women.

Think about it

- What effects might reading *MIZZ* have on teenage girls? It may well be claimed that we do not really know; and research does not tell us. Perhaps girls read it to relax or just to laugh at it? Do the heroines of such magazines offer role models which may be consciously or unconsciously imitated?

Women's magazines

Women's magazines have been widely researched. A brief glance at the range of women's magazines will tend to show that women are portrayed mainly in terms of domestic role (as homemaker, wife or mother) and their sexuality; whereas magazines aimed at men cover a whole range of leisure interests, from sailing and motor racing to computing and photography. The exception to this 'rule' are the newer men's magazines with small circulations. In addition, we must acknowledge that research indicates that about 13 per cent of British men regularly look at a women's weekly.

Magazines aimed at women tend to take one of two forms:

1. those that focus on fashion, beauty and 'getting a man';
2. those that deal with the 'three deadly Cs' – cooking, cleaning and caring.

These forms of magazines stand almost in opposition. On the one hand they address women's interests, for example providing information and advice, while on the other hand they seem to reinforce narrow feminine roles.

Marjorie Fergusson, in *Forever Feminine* (1983), provides a full account of women's magazines. She argued that they celebrate being a woman and promote the ideal of the outstanding woman. This is a sacred ideal (rather than a religion), with its own beliefs and rituals 'attached to beautification, childrearing, housework and cooking'. Fergusson termed this the **cult of femininity**. She also recognised that:

- women's magazines are both a social and economic phenomenon: the increased sense of female solidarity they promote is part of a profit-making exercise;
- they share values which underpin the cult of femininity (as shown by her analysis of the three bestselling women's magazines in Britain between 1949 and 1974: *Woman*, *Woman's Own* and *Woman's Weekly*);
- a number of different types of items, for example fiction, problem pages, features and beauty columns, are constructed around 11 main themes, which include: the importance of emotional expression in women's lives, rather than logical thought; feminine unpredictability and mysteriousness. Two themes turned out to be dominant:
  (a) the theme of love and marriage: 'getting and keeping your man'; and
  (b) the theme of self improvement, leading to individual achievement.

In a follow-up study (1979–80), these dominant themes were reversed, with the theme of self improvement becoming the main message associated with the cult of femininity.

Gender representation on television

Whatever the nature of women's magazines, they are less important now as a source of gender representations than in the past. Expanding electronic media, especially television, has meant a fall in total circulation. However, gender representation on television, in soap operas and elsewhere has also been widely researched. Entertainment and comedy in Britain is predominantly male in tone and content, and also in terms of who creates the programmes – the vast majority of television executives and producers being men.

Advertising and gender

Sex-role stereotyping in television advertising was investigated in the 1980s by the Broadcasting Standards Council. Their report in 1990 was based on a survey of more than 500 peak-time TV advertisements over several months. The title of the report, 'Sexual Stereotyping in Advertising', gives the clue to its findings, which include the following:

- TV commercials in Britain are male dominated and tend to be based on sex-role stereotyping. Though most of the products are bought by women, advertisers use men to sell their products and services.
- Two-thirds of all people seen in advertisements are men. When 'voice-overs' are used, 90 per cent of advertisements rely on men's voices. (The voice-over spells out the message when there is no actor speaking the words on the screen.)
- The appearance of men and women in advertisements generally conforms with the classic images of masculinity and femininity. Men are nearly always well built, smooth and dark haired. Only one in ten men has fair hair: advertisers feel fair hair is more in keeping with a female image.
- The image of 'dependency' of women is further reinforced by the fact that they are frequently shown with male partners, such as husband or boyfriend. Women appearing on their own in an advertisement is the rare exception.

The Prudential Assurance Company's 'I want to be ...' pension advertisement attracts comment in the report as an example of sex-role stereotyping. The young girl says, 'I want to be like mummy'; the young boy says, 'I want to be a slug'.

Source: Adapted from M. Denscombe, *Sociology Update* (Olympus Books, 1991)

The media and ethnicity

Stereotyped images are our generalised, labelled views of certain groups within our social world, often portraying, for example, women and black ethnic minorities in an inferior position in society. Such stereotypes are powerful vehicles for ideology, a source of support for ideas which legitimate powerful vested interests, such as the social advantages enjoyed by whites at the expense of blacks. Four important studies of race relations coverage by the media are outlined opposite.

1. P. Hartmann and C. Husband, in *Racism and the Mass Media* (1974), found that the media tended to focus on issues of racial conflict whilst failing to refer adequately to issues of poverty and housing disadvantage. In a content analysis of race-related stories in the main British daily newspapers, they found evidence of negative stereotyped image. They concluded that the effects of such media coverage were to draw public attention to the following issues:
   (a) the numbers of black immigrants in Britain;
   (b) hostility and discrimination between black people and white people;
   (c) laws to control immigration and discrimination;
   (d) the views of the politician Enoch Powell.
   In 1968, Enoch Powell gave a speech, in Birmingham, which received wide media coverage. In it he spoke of the growth of the non-white population:

   'Like the Romans, I seem to see "the River Tiber flowing with much blood".'

   A Gallup poll found that 75 per cent of interviewees broadly favoured Powell's views.
2. B. Troyna, in his 1981 study of the local and national press and local radio, *Public Awareness and the Media: A Study of Reporting Race*, noted that coverage of black people was largely based on the notion of blacks being 'outsiders' who were living in Britain. Whilst editorials often stressed the need for tolerance, many papers also featured stories highlighting a different and more conflict-orientated view.
3. S. Hall et al., in *Policing the Crisis* (1978) (see also page 298), looked at the role of the media in promoting ideological representations of law and order, as well as the development of images of black muggers. This work drew on the Marxist ideas of A. Gramsci and used the idea of hegemony to emphasise the view that the ruling class does not merely rule, it also dominates, using its power to persuade other classes to accept their ideas. Mugging was one of the key themes by which the state sought to deflect attention from the economic difficulties faced by capitalism. After media coverage of mugging peaked in October 1972, it was reworked in 1975 with a specific focus on the involvement of West Indian youth as 'representative' of mugging. Given that inner-city crime rates were high, and racial discrimination and urban deprivation in evidence, the media began to foster an image of mugging as a black, urban, male crime, an image which influenced senior police officers and politicians as well as, ultimately, social policy.
4. Angela Barry, in *Black Mythologies* (1989), has also shown how black people are represented in television images, being portrayed as trouble-makers, dependants or sports figures. Black people are often treated by the press as problems; there is much emphasis on portrayals of their cultural or religious difference, in terms of criminality or involvement in racial conflict.

Explanation for the particular image of race portrayed in the media depends very much on the perspective adopted:

- Pluralists see the poor media representation of ethnic minorities as reflecting the position of these groups in society. Media reporting of race issues and, consequently, the portrayal of race express what the public are perceived to want, with news value enhanced by reference to conflict.
- Marxists and Neo-Marxists, however, do not accept the validity of the pluralist interpretation. In their view, the role of the media is to shape the views of the white majority, encouraging them to focus the blame for economic or social problems on black immigrants, which evokes conflict. As such, the images of black people contained in the media are invariably negative. These perceptions reflect the racist attitudes of the dominant group who, in their turn, affect media representations.

Age stereotyping in the media

In Unit 2 we looked at the significance of age in the stratification of society into different groups. Basically, those under 16 and those over 60 tend to be socially differentiated in the sense that they are perceived as unequal compared to other age groups (the 'working' population). The media plays an important role in influencing this perception – sometimes reinforcing it, sometimes questioning it. On the whole, despite media products such as films about precocious youth (for example *Home Alone*) or *Cocoon*, which portrayed the rejuvenation of the elderly, little has changed about the presentations of such age groups. Even more notable films such as *On Golden Pond* or *Driving Miss Daisy* generally depict the sadness, even when accompanied by the wisdom, of growing old.

Another aspect of the relationship between the media and the over 60s in the UK is the amount of time that this age group spends watching TV or listening to the radio – these two activities occupy half the leisure time of the over 60s, according to the data provided later in this unit, far in excess of time spent visiting friends, for example, or reading. This seems to point to the idea of **disengagement** (see Unit 2 page 97) – a process whereby ageing has been associated with withdrawal from society. However, critics of this idea point to the wide range of attitudes and activities within this growing and varied group (over 20 per cent of the UK population in the late 1990s).

Think about it

- What does the above indicate about the relationship between the media and their portrayal of (a) the elderly? (b) ethnic minorities?
- What media images of the elderly can you think of? (Consider soap operas, press reports, advertising.)
- Do you think that your age and sex affect what you read, listen to or watch in the mass media? Are you conscious of social groupings being reinforced by 'targeted' media items?
- How do you consider that social class background might have affected your own attitudes towards the mass media and popular culture?

Media audiences: social patterns in viewing, listening and reading

An overview of patterns in viewing, listening and reading is given in the table below. Watching television was the most popular – but not the only – media-related activity for both men and women at home. Across all ages, women were more likely to spend time reading than men. Participation in some activities varied more with age than others; for example, older people were less likely to listen to records or tapes. Overall, if other leisure activities such as sports or eating and drinking out are included, watching television and listening to the radio were still the most popular (see Unit 5, page 255).

Participation in selected, media-related, home-based activities, 1993–4								
	Age:	16–19 (%)	20–24 (%)	25–29 (%)	30–44 (%)	45–59 (%)	60–69 (%)	70 and over (%)
Males	Watching TV	99	100	99	99	99	99	97
	Listening to radio	93	95	95	94	91	86	83
	Listening to records/tapes	96	96	93	86	76	66	50
	Reading books	55	58	56	60	61	59	58
Females	Watching TV	99	99	99	99	99	99	98
	Listening to radio	97	95	92	91	88	84	77
	Listening to records/tapes	97	96	92	88	75	62	42
	Reading books	75	70	70	71	71	74	67

Source: Adapted from *Social Trends*, 1997

Music CDs are bought right across all the age ranges, by men and women equally; tapes are more likely to be bought by women, while the vinyl format (often a collectors' item purchase) is more likely to be bought by men. 'Pop' continues to be the most common type of music by buyers of albums, with 'rock' the next most common.

The most popular music magazine is *Smash Hits*, which had average sales of 325 thousand per issue in 1994. Its popularity is amongst females, as shown by the table on page 312.

The most popular magazines and newspapers among young people, by age and gender, 1995					
		Aged 7–10 (%)			Aged 11–14 (%)
Males	Beano	28	**Males**	The Sun	22
	Match	25		Match	18
	Shoot!	22		Shoot!	18
	Sonic the Comic	18		News of the World	17
	Dandy	17		Beano	15
Females	Smash Hits	16	**Females**	Just Seventeen	41
	Barbie	13		Sugar	39
	Girl talk	13		Big!	34
	Beano	12		It's Bliss	34
	Live and Kicking	12		Smash Hits	32

Source: *Social Trends*, 1996

The top five magazines for boys aged 7–10 are divided between comics and football magazines, with 28 per cent reading the *Beano*; for girls in the same age group music magazines are the most popular. The proportion of girls who read *Smash Hits* in the 11–14 age group is double that for those aged between seven and ten, but much more popular among the older girls is *Just Seventeen*. *The Sun* is the most commonly read newspaper or magazine among 11–14-year-old boys, followed by two football magazines, *Match* and *Shoot!*

The table opposite shows not only how people in different age groups choose to spend their leisure time but also how more time is spent on watching television or listening to the radio than on any other of the activities listed.

Use of free time					
Age:	16–24 years (hrs per week)	25–34 years (hrs per week)	35–44 years (hrs per week)	45–59 years (hrs per week)	60+ years (hrs per week)
Television or radio	14	15	13	17	26
Visiting friends	7	5	4	4	4
Reading	1	1	2	3	6
Talking, socialising and phoning friends	3	3	3	4	4
Eating/drinking out	6	4	4	4	2
Hobbies, games and computing	2	2	1	3	3
Walks and other recreation	2	2	1	2	3
Doing nothing (may include illness)	1	1	1	2	2
Sports participation	3	1	1	1	1
Religious, political and other meetings	–	1	1	–	1
Concerts, theatre, cinema and sports spectating	1	1	–	–	–
Other	1	–	–	–	–
All free time	40	37	33	40	52

Source: *Social Trends*, 1996

In terms of the number of hours spent each week on various activities, those aged 60 and over spend more time television viewing and radio listening than younger groups in the table above. Not shown, however, are four- to five-year-olds, who watch on average 18 hours of television per week. Furthermore, recent alternatives to the four main terrestrial or earth-based channels have extended the scope of television viewing. The number of children aged four and over who watch cable and satellite television has doubled during the 1990s from about 5 million in 1990 to over 10 million in 1996. Seventy per cent of children continue watching television beyond the 9 p.m. adult watershed, and 66 per cent have a television set in their own rooms.

In terms of social class, as noted on pages 283–4, television tends to be watched more by lower social classes, particularly among those in the skilled manual (CI) and unskilled manual (C2 and DE) class.

Social class differences are also apparent in relation to reading habits, as shown in the table on page 314. It may seem surprising that a larger percentage of social group AB read the *Daily Mail* than *The Times*, whilst *Sky TV Guide* has its highest percentage of readers from social class C2.

Daily newspaper and general magazine readership, by social class, 1994–5		AB (%)	C1 (%)	C2 (%)	DE (%)
Daily newspapers	The Sun	7	18	29	30
	Daily Mirror	7	13	22	20
	Daily Mail	14	13	8	6
	Daily Express	9	10	8	5
	The Daily Telegraph	6	6	2	1
	Daily Star	1	4	7	7
	The Guardian	8	3	1	1
	The Times	8	3	1	1
	The Independent	6	3	1	1
	Financial Times	5	2	–	–
General magazines	Reader's Digest	15	14	12	9
	Radio Times	17	13	8	6
	Sky TV Guide	9	11	13	9
	TV Times	7	9	10	11
	AA Magazine	16	10	8	4
	What's on TV	5	8	9	11
	Viz	6	8	7	5

Source: Adapted from *Social Trends*, 1996

Think about it

- What reasons can you suggest for the fact that women, across all age groups, spend more time reading than men do?
- Why do younger age groups spend more time than their elders listening to records and tapes?
- The data indicates that females aged 11–14 years choose magazines such as *Just Seventeen* whilst their male contemporaries prefer the *Sun* – can you suggest why this is so?
- What issues might be raised by sociologists in relation to the high percentage of children who watch television after the 9 p.m. adult 'watershed'?

The social impact of the media

Sociologists have encountered many complex questions in studying the effects and the impact of the media upon audiences. Two things seem apparent:

1. The audience are not one mass of passive receivers.
2. Research has shown that it is very difficult to measure the impact of a media form upon its audience.

The media and violence

Perhaps the most commonly asked question on the subject of the social impact of the media is whether the portrayal of violence in the media is a cause of increased violence in society. This was the issue which gave rise to an emotional outburst from actor Dustin Hoffman at the Cannes Film Festival in May 1996:

> *'Look at this global community we live in and what happens in Tasmania and what happens in Scotland. Are you saying it doesn't have anything to do with it?'*
>
> Dustin Hoffman, May 1996

Neither sociological research, nor the findings of other experts, can tell us for certain to what extent or in what way radio, television, video or screen violence might be connected to actual violence. The evidence, such as it is, would suggest that it is unusual for anyone to imitate things they see in the various media forms. Only occasionally has a direct link been identified between media and real-life violence. Two examples in the USA, in 1993, led to new calls for legislation to curb the excesses of Hollywood. One involved the death of a teenager who copied a scene from a Disney film about college football, in which a drunk football player plays 'chicken' by lying down in the middle of a busy road. The other concerned a five-year-old boy in Ohio who set light to his house, causing the death of his two-year-old sister, after watching *Beavis and Butthead*, a television cartoon series in which the heroes struck matches and proclaimed that 'fire is good'. The US government threatened censorship, but all that happened was that the 'chicken' scene was cut from the Disney film and *Beavis and Butthead* was moved from an early evening slot.

It was hard to see if any lessons could be drawn from these incidents. While the deaths of the teenager and the two-year-old girl were tragic, it would seem absurd to declare that no television programme or film in future should contain daredevil scenes and that no cartoon characters should again play with fire. The whole issue of the effects of the media, and in particular television violence, has been and undoubtedly will continue to be hotly debated via articles such as the one on page 316.

Television: a channel for aggression

Amanda Hemingway

IT HAS become dangerously fashionable to blame television for the level of violence in society. Politicians from both right and left can hold forth on this subject without offending their leaders, sure of a sympathetic ear from a largely peaceable electorate. The most outspoken intellectual will not say a word in dissent. The issue is safe, the arguments supposedly incontrovertible. Scarcely a voice is raised to point out that they are all talking rubbish.

Statistics offer no support to media pacifists. Japan, for example, has one of the highest levels of screen violence, while street violence is exceptionally low. Television became generally accessible after the War, yet history has been riddled with murder and mayhem since the first caveman hit out with his first hand-axe.

Viking Berserkers did not psych themselves up by watching *The A-Team*; Genghis Khan's Assassins could hardly take *The Professionals* as role models: more recently, consider Adolf Hitler's taste for revolting saccharine Hollywood musicals. Since television invaded our lives there has been no major war, and visual contact with the remoter parts of the globe has heightened our understanding of and sympathy for other peoples. So much for political humbuggery.

With every mass murder, the tabloid press, hot on a popular scent, manages to discover that the unhappy psychopath worshipped such idols as Rambo or Clint Eastwood. These allegations are often disproved later, but that is irrelevant. A psychopath is always a psychopath: he will find his idols where he may. In the past, those murderously inclined have taken their bloodlust to the altars of Kali and Hecate, Ashtaroth and Baal — all without the help of the modern media.

If we wish to 'cure' violence, we might look for other causes of the problem, if only to prove the idiocy of such theorising. Soccer hooliganism, for instance, is basically gang warfare — and what is gang warfare but an extreme version of team games played in schools? The primitive concept of team spirit crushes individuality and teaches unquestioning obedience to the captain's orders.

Play up, play up, and play the game, says the poet: but what is the game? On the soccer pitch, teams kick balls. Off it they kick each other. Yet no one suggests banning soccer, rugger, basketball, hockey or even cricket from either schools or screens.

Violence is the product of energy — it is drive, conflict, competition, ambition. It can also be cruelty and brutality, if misdirected. But it is always there. It cannot be denied. It is no accident that Man is more given to needless violence than any other species. This same striving, thrusting, savage force brought us from naked ape to our relatively civilised state in a fraction of the lifetime of our planet.

Now, some of us are afraid it has outworn its usefulness. They are wrong. The energy of violence will urge us to combat pollution, to fight injustice, to campaign for democracy and human rights. It is in our nature, an essential ingredient of survival. Without it, we would degenerate into semi-vegetables, lotus-eating our way to extinction.

Violence must be accepted and challenged. The real trouble is that for too many of us, particularly in the West, existence has become a safe and comfortable affair, over-protected, over-insured, cosy, dreary, banal. The natural man is shut in a padded cell with a beautiful view, pounding in vain against the cushions of the wall. Here, television violence is not the problem, but it could be a part of the solution.

The ancient Romans offered the populace bread and circuses to keep it quiet. The masses crammed the amphitheatres to watch lions eating Christians and gladiators hacking each other to pieces, then went away sated and less likely to rise in rebellion. It may have been barbaric, but the basic principle was sound. Spectator violence is cathartic. Tripping over corpses with Miss Marple, karate-kicking with Bruce Lee, gazing down a gun-barrel with Bond — these things provide excitement and release.

In addition, we know the dead bodies are not actually dead, the bullets and the blood are equally unreal. Mankind has progressed since ancient Rome. We should be able to revel in such scenes, free from guilt. The duller our daily routines, the deeper our need.

The clerk who dreams of murdering his boss goes home to Miami Vice — to grunts, flying fists, car chases, the scrunch of sugar glass and the crack of balsawood. He is involved, exhilarated, purged. He sleeps soundly. Without this release, he might well kick his dog or cut up his wife with a chainsaw. Too much sweetness and light on television would be a recipe for increased domestic brutality, vandalism and general thuggery.

Perhaps what we need is not less television violence, but more.

Source: The *Sunday Correspondent*, 4 February 1990

Think about it

- Can you think of other incidents which have been linked to screen violence?
- Do you agree or disagree with Dustin Hoffman's views (see page 315), given above, on cinema screen violence? Do you think that screen violence has a greater impact on its audiences than other forms of media representation of violence?
- Can media violence produce any positive and useful attitudes and values in contemporary society?
- What do you consider to be the main problems associated with quantitative and with qualitative research on media violence?

The media and politics

The relationship between politics and the mass media in the UK is the subject of a debate which is of great interest to sociologists. How do politicians influence the media – and vice versa? There seems little doubt that until the mid-1990s most UK national newspapers supported conservative politics. However, a Mori poll in 1992 indicated that it might be unwise to equate the politics of a national newspaper with the voting intentions of its readers. Individuals may not share the political views of the editors whose newspaper they read; they may also choose a newspaper for reasons other than its political leaning – for its entertainment or sports coverage, for example. The following three issues should also be borne in mind.

1. Politics is not what the majority of the British general public actually want to read about; sex, sport and the lives of the famous are the main centres of interest.
2. The reportage of political issues may be a low priority for readers but the personal lives of public figures is not. Sexual and financial scandal attracts prolonged and extensive coverage.
3. Whilst the tabloids claim to reflect the demands of their readers, their political influence cannot be dismissed and is in fact acknowledged by them. The *Sun*, for example, claimed credit for the defeat of Neil Kinnock's Labour Party in the 1992 general election.

Conflicting theories

Sociologists have come up with a range of explanations concerning the influence of the mass media – or at least a range of 'models' or theories showing how they believe such influences take effect. The most significant of these models are outlined below.

The hypodermic syringe model

The dominant theory until the late 1950s, which still influences 'uninformed' commentators of media effects, was the **hypodermic syringe model** (or psychologically based, 'stimulus response' model), which assumed that audiences were one homogeneous mass of impartial receivers who absorbed everything that was 'injected' into them.

This model goes back to the nineteenth century, when cheap shows and theatres were considered to corrupt the young and lead to juvenile delinquency. The development of cinema, and later television and video, increased support for the hypodermic syringe theory, but studies have not shown a direct causal link between film-watching and delinquency.

Moral campaigners, such as Mary Whitehouse, are strong supporters of this theory, and are keen to identify links between television and real-life violence to justify **censorship** of 'offensive' programmes. For example, in the moral panic over 'video nasties', moral campaigners have argued that they produce deviant behaviour of the type involving the murder of two-year-old Jamie Bulger, whose ten-year-old killers were allegedly influenced by a 'horror' film (see also Unit 10, page 546). However, not all individuals react in the same way to films. The hypodermic syringe model could be seen as **overdeterministic** in assuming that all viewers are vulnerable to media output.

Much psychological research has been carried out to assess the influence of television violence on behaviour. Two such studies are outlined on the next page.

The classic 'Bobo doll' experiments were undertaken by the American psychologists Albert Bandura, Ross and Ross and published in *Imitation of Film Mediated Aggressive Models* (1963). In one experiment, children were shown one of three television sequences:

- In one sequence a self-righting doll was subjected to various kinds of violence; the person (an adult dressed as a cat) who had inflicted the violence was then punished.
- In the second sequence the aggressor was rewarded.
- In the third, the aggressor was neither rewarded nor punished.

The children were then allowed to play with the doll.

Those children who had seen the aggressor rewarded tended to imitate the violent behaviour they had seen. So did the children who had seen the sequence where the aggressor was neither rewarded nor punished. The children who saw the aggressor punished did not imitate the violent behaviour. This led the Bandura team to argue that a causal relationship existed between watching violence on television and violent behaviour. However, this and other similar small-scale experiments raise problems. It is difficult to assess the attitudes of the subjects prior to the experiment. Also, since such experiments are so unreal, how can they demonstrate real-life situations?

The study *Television Violence and the Adolescent Boy* (1972), by W. Belson et al, attempted to test the hypothesis that 'high exposure to TV violence increases the degree to which boys engage in violent acts'. They investigated the viewing habits of 1565 London boys from mainly working-class backgrounds. Using a 'panel of judges', television programmes were given a 'violence rating'. Perhaps inevitably, Belson found that boys who had been exposed to high levels of violence on TV admitted having been involved in considerably more violent acts than others.

Criticisms of Belson's findings include the following:

- He was commissioned by a film company to prove a hypothesis: this is unsociological and in no way objective.
- His methodology relied on self-report data and memory – both unreliable sources.
- What was defined as constituting a 'high violence rating' is questionable, since the 'panels of judges' consisted of middle-class adults defining what they perceived to be screen violence, compared with the survey's sample of mostly working-class boys.

The two-step flow model

In the post-war period, the **two-step flow model** became influential in explaining the effects of the media. It was defined by E. Katz and P.F. Lazarsfeld in *Personal Influence* (1955). Using a study of the 1940 American presidential campaign, Lazarsfeld found that the impact of the media on voting behaviour was far less than 'hypodermic theorists' suggested. The theory of the two-step flow model was that:

- audiences were made up of groups of people, with 'opinion leaders' forwarding ideas;
- through 'opinion leaders', the effects of the mass media were transmitted to other members of society, thus creating 'molecular schools of thought';
- thus, the media was important in forming the opinions of the opinion leaders (first step) and, from them, in passing on ideas to others (second step).

D. Howitt, in *Mass Media and Social Problems* (1982), has criticised the two-step flow model. He argued that audiences could not be categorised into 'active' opinion leaders and 'passive' group members. Indeed, why stop at two steps? Why not three, four or five steps? Also, the model may be seen as untestable: opinion leaders may change and their relationship with others may be quite difficult to assess.

The uses and gratification model

This model suggests that different people use and enjoy the media in different ways. It offers a functionalist approach to the impact of the media and, unlike the two-step flow model, it concentrates on differentiated audiences who use and are 'gratified' by television. The **uses and gratification model** is based on the following:

- It recognises the social needs of a modern audience, acknowledging how people use television selectively, sometimes for companionship, or as a source of information or even as a background effect.
- 'Soap wars', for example between *EastEnders* (BBC) and *Coronation Street* (ITV), demonstrate the extent to which an audience can be gratified by a television programme; certainly there are people who feel they 'know' the characters in the TV soap operas.
- A potentially dangerous situation exists, where illusion is defined as reality, which places media producers in powerful positions of influence over vulnerable members of their audience.

This model would conclude that TV soap operas based on everyday life provide social companionship for some people; certain elements of the media satisfy different needs for a range of people; social prestige may be gained from reading a particular newspaper, entertainment may be gained from a music programme, or knowledge may be found in a documentary.

Criticisms include the danger of overemphasising the psychological influences of the media, and overlooking the social context in which people experience the mass media.

The cultural effects model

This model maintains that the media produce long-term build-up effects on audiences, often reinforcing cultural stereotypes (see pages 306–10). Images are received by different groups of people, so media effects are related to the social situation within which they are encountered. The **cultural effects model** links the media to the general culture of society. The long-term effect, it is argued, is to translate attitudes portrayed by the media into reality; this then provides the basis for further media portrayal.

Inherent in the cultural effects model is a view of audience susceptibility and vulnerability which assumes that there is no intervention between the communication of the media message and the way in which it is decoded by the audience. It is perhaps for this reason that the cultural effects model, like the hypodermic syringe model, is favoured by moral campaigners who believe that censorship would be 'beneficial' for the audience.

A criticism of this model is that it cannot be tested; although it seems to make sense, there are problems in providing evidence for it, as demonstrated in the research of the Glasgow University Media Group (see page 294).

David Morley's related research includes *The Nationwide Audience* (1982), which emphasises that the power which a media message or form possesses will come from the social context in which it is received. The social class, level of social deprivation, economic circumstances and culture of the viewer must be taken into consideration. Morley's approach to audience research differs from previous research in the following ways:

- It attempts to study both how television is used within the context of the family and also how its output is interpreted by the audience. Prior to this study, these two factors were seen in isolation from each other.
- It examines the role of the media within its social context, provides some insights into the use of the media as a social entity and claims that television performs various functions within the viewing context. It can be used, for example, as a mediator, a scapegoat, a reward or punishment, or to schedule other activities.
- It suggests that the impact of television cannot be assessed from a purely media-orientated study, because of the influential factors within the social viewing context.

Conclusions on the impact of the media

A shift from media-based research to audience-based research has given rise to specific problems for sociologists in assessing the impact of the media on audiences.

A. Giddens, in *Sociology 2nd edn* (1993), draws attention to a study which attempted to analyse the influence of television viewing on daily life. The researchers concluded that:

> '. . . television has had a larger impact on daily life than any other technical innovation outside the sphere of paid employment.'

The researchers gauged this 'impact' on the amount of time television viewers and non-viewers spent on leisure activities over a 24-hour period. However, whilst this study tells us something about the impact of television, it tells us little about the impact of television programmes.

The question of how the audience 'interprets' media output is an issue which has continued to pose problems for sociologists in assessing the impact of television programmes. Whilst it may be possible to identify short-term changes, it is virtually impossible to identify any long-term changes as the media and the wider society are so closely interlinked; causes cannot easily be isolated and identified.

In assessing the effects of the media, the nature and structure of the media audience need careful consideration. It cannot be assumed that the audience is a homogeneous mass and that all members of that audience will respond in the same way. Rather, the audience must be considered as heterogeneous – a highly differentiated group of individuals who will respond in a variety of ways to media output.

To date, no definite conclusions can be drawn regarding the assessment of the influence of the media on audiences. Whilst it is true that the media cannot be studied in isolation, studying it within its social context is no easy task.

Popular culture: definitions and theories

The concept of **popular culture** is complex and problematic. So far in this unit the media have been considered in terms of produced forms, their ownership, control, readership and audiences. Now we turn to the cultural forms which seem to stem from the people themselves.

Popular culture and identity

How do you decide which clothes to buy and wear? How do you choose between television and radio, and which programmes? Would you rather go to a disco, cinema or theatre? How do you make such decisions? Are you influenced by members of your family, friends, advertising campaigns or wider society, such as people you may see around you in a shopping mall? In essence, how is your personal identity affected by such external factors? Such questions and their answers are examples of the complex picture that makes up what we call popular culture.

A consideration of popular culture

- It can be useful in attempting to measure the attitudes and values of the mass consumer, rather than those at the leading edge of culture.
- It reflects the existing ideas of the people, rather than generating new ones. Its influence is often far less than the interest and discussion which it gives rise to.
- It is in a period of transition, since most of our ideas about what is right or wrong have been undergoing re-evaluation; 'no new dogmas have yet emerged victorious' in terms of the mirror of the world depicted by films.

The development of ideas on popular culture

F.R. Leavis, in *Mass Civilisation and Minority Culture* (1930), maintained that popular culture:

- catered for low, common values and, as such, was coarse, commercial and tasteless;
- threatened 'civilisation' by lowering standards and by pandering to profit motives, i.e. making its producers rich;
- meant that preserving English literature would be the only way of safeguarding 'high' culture. (Interestingly, much of the teaching of English literature throughout the education system has been influenced by such thinking and is supported by statements from Prince Charles and other members of the Establishment.)

R. Williams, in *Keywords: A Vocabulary of Culture and Society* (1976), noted that popular culture:

- adopted the viewpoint of the people, rather than the viewpoint of those with power over them;
- has tended to be identified by others, rather than by the people themselves;
- still carries notions of inferiority, for example the popular press is seen as different from and inferior to the quality press.

The development of ideas on popular culture has been linked to debates over definitions and theories:

- What or who forms popular culture? Does it come from the people themselves in relation to their interests and values, or is it a more subtle form of social control by those in more powerful positions? Is there any negotiation between such social groups?
- Do production and commercial factors influence popular culture? Do market and profit factors receive more consideration than the quality of what is produced?
- Does popular culture have an ideological function to get people to accept the dominant ideology of those who hold power over them? Or may elements of opposition and rebellion be detected within popular culture?

'High' and 'low' culture The idea persists that if it is popular then it is common, bad and perhaps even trash. This is exemplified in the review below of the *EastEnders* episode which included the death of one of its main original characters, 'Arfer' Fowler. The reviewer writes in terms of both its language and its content, including its reference to T.S. Eliot's comment! Interestingly, several other reviewers in national newspapers on that same day, for example *The Times*, were far more positive.

Television

Nancy Banks-Smith

PRECEDED by many signs and portents — a clutching of the forehead, a dreaminess about the old days — Arfer Fowler has died on his allotment from a cerebral haemorrhage. Everyone in **EastEnders** (BBC1) was astonished. It was the first indication that Arfer had a brain.

Before collapsing among King Edwards, Arfer wandered around the deserted Albert Square; it was a last stroll round a limited life and not unmoving. Everyone had gone to Ben's christening, leaving the Square swept clean of people and sluiced with unaccustomed peace. No sizzle of rashers from Kaf's caf. No roaring chorus from the Vic. No-one but David and Cindy, at it like knives as usual.

Birth and copulation and death, as T S Eliot once remarked after a rather brief visit to Albert Square.

You will be amazed to hear that Arfer, whose life seemed so circumscribed, once trod the boards. In Bob Monkhouse's autobiography (chosen by Pauline Quirke as the book to take to a desert island with the Bible and Shakespeare) he says that 25 years ago he appeared with Arfer and Del Boy at Weston-super-Mare in She's Done It Again!, a rib-tickler about a vicar whose wife has sextuplets. I must say I'm sorry I missed that.

There are not a lot of laughs in EastEnders. How often must Arfer, escaping from the crushing woes of the Square to his allotment, have leaned on his spade and heard, like the crash of a distant wave, the laughter at Weston-super-Mare as his trousers fell down.

At Ben's christening, the news of his death raised a wasp-like buzz of wozzes. "Woz wrong?" (Ruth) "'Ere! Woz goin' on?" (Peggy) "Woz you say?" (Ian) and, all together now, "Woz 'appened?"

In the credits one was touched to see that Arfer's name, like Abou ben Adam's, led all the rest.

Accustomed as we are to hospital drama, Walford Hospital was weirdly peaceful. No patients having a punch-up. No junior doctors yelling jargon. Above all, no one begging for Arfer's virtually unused brain.

Source: The *Guardian*, 22 June 1996

It is difficult to identify any fixed divide between 'high' and 'low' culture, however. Popular culture develops and takes on new forms: critics may discover some merit in what they once dismissed. Popular music, for example by the Beatles, may achieve an air of respectability, even 'classic' status; as may Hollywood films: *Blade Runner*, in its portrayal of the present and its future direction in terms of urban decay, endless shopping malls and progress towards ruination sets out themes which are core to postmodernism (see pages 331–2).

Problems associated with 'high' and 'low/popular' culture

For media producers, there may be a mass culture in that it attracts a huge audience. However, such an audience will undoubtedly be segmented and stratified in key sociological areas of age, gender, ethnic grouping and social class, and this, in turn, will reflect underlying diverse tastes, attitudes and values. Does, then, a mass audience exist?

- A mass audience may not exist in relation to those who receive media output. In other words, consumption depends on interpretation and appreciation, which vary considerably among consumers.
- Cultural tastes are socially constructed and audiences may be far from passive consumers of culture: they may well form highly active discriminating groups.

Folk culture

Folk culture, perhaps the 'parent' of popular culture, has been seen as a form of heritage, stemming from a past in which people accepted an agreed set of shared values which integrated them tightly into an organic community. Such an organic community displayed its own living culture in folk music, folk dances, festivals and so on. This way of living reproduced, through the generations, local skills and crafts; it was part of a patterned, ordered existence, growing out of the natural environment, seasonal changes and the historical traditions of the community.

It has been claimed that our thinking about folk culture has been cradled in romantic notions of the past, ignoring the reality of economic and cultural inequalities. The elite had their 'high' culture and the ordinary people had their 'folk' culture: each knew their place, particularly before the development of popular culture. However, the background to some idealised 'golden age' having its own authentic folk culture is difficult to locate even in historical and geographical terms.

Perhaps the nostalgic thinking behind a fanciful folk culture is a product of what appears to have been lost in contemporary society. It does, however, tend to undervalue the present and overvalue the past with its higher rate of illiteracy and general cultural poverty.

> *'Taste and style are socially and culturally determined. It is the power to decide upon the definitions of taste and style which circulate within societies which is important, rather than the remote possibility of finding universal and objective reasons for validating aesthetic judgements. The power to determine popular culture and the standards of cultural taste is not restricted to the economic and political power exercised by the mass culture industries, although these are obviously crucial for any adequate assessment of the overall process. It also includes, even if only as a secondary phenomenon, those*

> intellectuals, or producers of ideas and ideologies, with the
> power to attempt to set down guidelines for cultural
> discrimination, and the position from which to try to decide
> upon what people should like and dislike.'
>
> D. Strinati, *Popular Culture* (1995)

Think about it

- Is it possible to decide what people should consume or the popular culture which they should like or dislike? Since cultural tastes are socially constructed, to what extent do you think that they may exercise social control?
- There is a view that popular culture promotes 'low' common values and may be considered as common, commercialised and tasteless. How might sociologists respond to such a viewpoint, particularly in relation to the social structure of contemporary society?
- Can there be a fixed divide between 'high' and 'low' culture? How do you see each of these forms of culture? What examples of each form can you suggest and what are the reasons for your choices?
- What do you understand by the term 'folk culture'? Where would you place folk culture in relation to 'high' and 'low' culture within the structure of society?

Culture, subculture and identity

The terms 'culture' and 'subculture' have become widely used and, rather like 'high' and 'low' culture, can throw up more issues than explanations. Traditionally, within sociology, **subculture** has tended to be explained in terms of social, economic or ethnic groups that have produced their own particular style or values within the mainstream culture of society. Subcultural groups often seem to be represented by youth groups: the Teddy Boys in the 1950s gave way to the Mods and Rockers in the 1960s and then Skinheads and Punks in the 1970s. Remnants of these groups persist today, along with more recent groups.

Each group has had its own identity and style, often reflected in clothes, hairstyles, music, etc.

'A typical skinhead'

SHORT HAIR ~
LIKE DAD ONLY
DRAMATISED
INTO A STYLE

FLAT CAP
(OPTIONAL EXTRA)

EAR RING
(LATER SKINS
NOT LIKE DAD)

COLLARLESS
SHIRT

BRACES

DOC MARTENS

JEANS
ROLLED UP

Source: Adapted from
M. O'Donnell and J. Garrod,
Sociology in Practice (1990)

Think about it

- Select one subcultural group and discuss how it develops its own identity.
- What is achieved by its identify? What determines the extent to which such a group may affect wider society?

Despite their distinctiveness and the shock reactions they produce, particularly from the media and the 'adult' world, these youth groups have been located within mainstream cultural institutions such as the family, educational establishments and those in the world of work. Whilst they may seem to be deviant, it does not follow that they are delinquent; since, as S. Frith argues in the following extract:

'... it's not a **crime** to dye your hair green. Their styles depend on commercial teen culture (pop music most obviously) but weren't created by it – ted and mod and punk and skinhead styles certainly weren't dreamed up by businessmen. The young people involved aren't "classless" – they seem to be working class in social origin and setting – but neither are they obviously embedded in their parent cultures. British youth styles appear as bizarre in their local communities of family and neighbours as they do to middle class and media observers. Sub-culture does seem an appropriate term to get at these youth groups' sense of **difference** from society, as long as we continue to be clear that youth sub-cultures are, at the same time, embedded **in** society.'
S. Frith, 'The Sociology of Youth', *Sociology New Directions* (1985)

Subcultural theories British subcultural theory developed after World War II and tended to focus on working-class subcultures. Questions raised included issues of the relationship between the experiences of class-based groups and their subcultural styles. Do such deviant groups relate to working-class values? Why are such styles taken on by minority elements among the working-class youth groups? Attempts to answer such questions have included the following:

- S. Hall, in *Resistance Through Rituals* (1976), stated that working-class subcultural activities challenged middle-class values and formed working-class identity. In class terms, a skinhead gang represents 'us' against 'them'. This is carried out by developing a behaviour and a cultural style that sets the gang apart from the middle class and parades their rebellion.
  (a) The style is set by clothes, music, etc., and portrays the youth culture to which they belong.
  (b) The culture often encourages ritualistic behaviour, for example at football fixtures.
  (c) Their aggressive behaviour may be seen as a way of overcoming their lack of status and power.
  (d) Aspects of the culture have sometimes, via the media, been merged into the mainstream of society: nose studs and rings, Doc Marten boots, for example.

- J. Clarke, in *The Skinheads and the Magical Recovery of Community* (1976), stated that skinhead culture tried to recreate the working-class culture of the East End of London which had largely disappeared. The rise of the skinhead culture can be seen in terms of their exclusion from existing subcultures and their seeing themselves as under attack and under the authority of others. This is manifested by:
  - (a) their need for solidarity rooted in the solidarity of their working-class community; such solidarity having disappeared because of slum clearance, etc.;
  - (b) their support for local football teams, which helped emphasise the importance of 'territory' and provided a sense of identity;
  - (c) territoriality, solidarity and masculinity becoming ways of recreating a sense of community – significant aspects of such youth groups and their exaggerated styles.
- A. McRobbie and J. Garber, in *Working-class Girls and the Culture of Femininity* (1978), stated that working-class girls feel inferior within both their class and their gender so that:
  - (a) their fate as adults is in low-status work because they are put off from achieving high qualifications;
  - (b) they share an anti-school subculture and may seek status from deviant activities.
- E. Cashmore, in *Rastaman* (1979), discusses the importance of youth cultures for black youth, especially involvement in the Rastafarian movement which stems from the subculture of Jamaica as the result of deprivation and poverty. Originally the music developed from slavery and colonialisation; it makes constant reference to these roots. Rastafarianism was founded by Marcus Garvey, with the late Haile Selassie of Ethiopia regarded as a prophet. The promise is that the Rastas will one day return to their cultural home in Africa. Reggae music, though it has become a commercial sound, has a strong ideological content. It expresses Rastafarianism as:
  - (a) music and religion are important for black youth because these form the basis of popular nationalism (an identity with Jamaica);
  - (b) it is a source of black consciousness which takes them back to their African roots;
  - (c) it has a social significance since it is the religion and the music of deprived and discriminated-against blacks.

Resistance and ideology

A major difference between American and British subcultural theory relates to the use of the concept of ideology by British theorists. Working-class subcultures came to be seen as fringe activities symptomatic of contemporary capitalist societies. Lack of status and wealth was a driving force behind youth subcultures, which offered alternative values and alternative forms of success and reward. This formed the real insight by American sociologists which British sociologists had to apply to subcultural lifestyles.

To seek some explanation for skinheads in the late 1960s, for example, there was the need to examine not just their material circumstances (experiences at home and work) but their cultural conditions (which underwent little change at the time).

Youth subcultures solve ideological problems and to make sociological sense of them we need to understand the 'ideological conditions of existence'. S. Hall et al.'s *Resistance Through Rituals* (1976) includes a history of British youth groups not in terms of wages or job opportunities but in terms of changing ideas about leisure and style. P. Cohen summed this up in his study of skinheads:

> *'The hidden function of subculture is this – to express and resolve, albeit "magically", the contradictions which appear in the parent culture. The succession of subcultures which this parent culture generated can thus all be considered as so many variations on a central theme – the contradiction, at an ideological level, between traditional working class puritanism and the new ideology of consumption. . . .'*
> P. Cohen, 'Subcultural Conflict and Working Class Community', *Working Papers in Cultural Studies* (1972)

So, according to Cohen, a 'problem' for the young in Britain since World War II had been to unravel competing systems of meaning, i.e. traditional working class (emphasising workplace solidarity, community and family life) in contrast to middle class (emphasising educational opportunity and individual ambition). One response can be to create an 'image' and a form of group leisure that negotiates a path between such competing values, by presenting a new individual status (for example skinheads, punks, grungies etc.). The dominant culture (hegemony) of an adult world tends to look disparagingly at young people and youth culture and seeks to impose social order and control whilst expecting young people to 'accept' the existing values.

Cohen suggested that subcultures should be seen as ritual solutions to cultural contradictions and that such rituals often took the form of 'resistance'.

Recent accounts of subcultures

More recent analyses have tried to take on board criticisms of the 1970s work. They have tried to think about the connection between youth cultural styles and the transmission of class and gender relations from one generation to the next. P. Aggleton's study of middle-class youth and the transition from school to work, *Rebels Without a Cause* (1987), is one such work. This study was based on the sons and daughters of the new middle class, whose parents were teachers, designers, etc. The starting point was their apparent underachievement in a College of Further Education. The engaging descriptions of middle-class, chic lifestyles focused on relationships between the seemingly relaxed and informal social control often found amongst such middle-class families and their children's somewhat frustrating experience of education. The apparently permissive parental control is of particular interest. Such resistance as existed on the part of the young people was seen as contest rather than revolt – a bargaining for degrees of personal autonomy within the family's existing social relations. What is important is the power of parental culture in the socialisation process: traditional views of generation gaps and the like seemed non-existent.

'Youth culture is now replaced by style, and is firmly part of the consumption process. Youth culture is now expropriated from the young, especially working-class youth, and is consumed by the privileged elite amongst youth.'

M. Brake, *Changing Leisure and Cultural Patterns Among British Youth* (1990)

The privileged elite referred to by Brake may be seen as remnants of a youth market that has collapsed because of population changes, mass youth unemployment, the fall in earnings of those in employment and the growth of young people in full-time education. The latter rely on parental handouts and out-of-term hospitality to supplement a loan or grant which is annually eroded by inflation. Thus, the 'youth elite' increasingly shares products and services with other groups who have substantial purchasing power – working couples without children, for example. This means that:

'the spectacular subcultures of the 1950s and 1960s no longer exist. Because for many young people relative poverty means they must secure a culture identity via the productive use of industrial commodities ... the art of making do ... the creative discriminating use of the resources that capitalism provides ...'

J. Fiske, *Understanding Popular Culture* (1989)

But would a return to prosperity and a pick-up in the labour market for the young lead to a revitalisation of youth subcultures? Or have wider socio-economic changes, including the declining proportion of young people in society, combined to make this unlikely? Little evidence exists to allow us even to guess the answers!

Consumer culture and lifestyle

The consumer culture is seen as lacking in merit since it is a culture which encourages material aspirations focused on the purchase of goods and lifestyles. In the consumer culture aspirations are channelled by the 'desirability' of such goods and lifestyles.

SUPER-THIN MODELS WORRY US ALL, THIN GIRLS AND FAT WATCHES: these kinds of headlines appeared in most national newspapers in the summer of 1996. On the surface it was a row between the watch company Omega and *Vogue* magazine. Omega's brand director claimed that the images of two of the models in *Vogue* were promoting anorexia among young females. The editor of *Vogue* responded:

'models have always been thin and this debate has been going on for 20 years. The fact is that thin models are what people want to see. They don't want to see girls like themselves – good, solid size 14s.'

Alexandra Shulman

Dr Glen Waller, a specialist in eating disorders, had written to *Vogue* four years previously to protest against the imagery, following research into the negative impact thin models had on women: as a lone medical voice he feared that 'the culture of ultra-thinness will remain'. This view was shared by Susie Orbach, a psychotherapist, writing on the front page of the *Guardian* (see below). Her anticipation of Omega withdrawing its advertisements was in fact premature; and, ironically, the *Guardian*'s fashion pages the following day featured pale, wasted waifs!

'The thinness of the models is not new or dramatic, but its effect is shocking all the same'

Commentary

Susie Orbach

● ●

WOW. Such are dreams made of, Omega cancels its ads in Vogue as a protest against the use of skeletal models in the June edition.

Twenty-six years ago a group of women concerned about how the uniformly skinny physical representation of females in advertisements and fashion magazines found its way into the consciousness of young girls and women had the glimmer of an idea (now taken for granted) that there was a relationship between eating problems and the image of womanhood portrayed on billboards and in magazines.

Each year as the mannequins got thinner, young women struggled to find a way to mimic those images by transforming their own bodies.

The group of concerned women dreamed of boycotts. They would use their economic power to force manufacturers to present women in all their variety and to extend the range of what might be considered beautiful.

They knew that thinness was just the latest construction. After all, just a generation before, Sophia Loren's voluptuousness had reigned, bringing with it the same kind of distress to women who failed to meet that kind of curvaciousness. But this new aesthetic of thinness was particularly dangerous.

It just happened to coincide with that moment in history when women were beginning to demand that they take up more not less space in the world, when women attempted to be seen as more than (sexual) objects.

The campaigners were ineffectual. Bulimia, compulsive eating, anorexia entered the vocabulary. We learnt what torture such experiences were. Responsible citizens shook their heads and felt helpless about the pull of the thin imagery on their daughters.

The surprise on looking at the June Vogue is how familiar it all is. The thinness is not new or dramatic but shocking all the same.

It is the pictures of prepubescent bodies dressed up to look like sexually available women that magnetise us. The pictures combine vulnerability with an aggressive edge. They invite,

magnetise and bewilder all at the same time.

But Omega has withdrawn and hopefully this will set a trend. The work of countless women and men who have campaigned against the destructive power of such images of women could receive no greater reward than to have a younger generation see pictures of beautiful women in all shapes and sizes representing the full glory of femininity.

Source: The *Guardian*, 31 May 1996

Clearly, glossy magazines and their advertisements, including watches priced at thousands of pounds, form part of consumer culture. In essence, however, they form 'artefacts of meaning', peddling dreams of high priced consumer desirables via wafer-thin super models.

Think about it

- Consumer culture makes products such as designer clothing and expensive fashion accessories seem highly desirable. What examples can you provide of consumer culture from glossy magazines and advertisements? Do these examples reflect social stereotyping, and if so, how?
- What social problems can you think of that might be associated with 'selling dreams' or linking lifestyles and identities with products (look back at the section on artefacts of meaning on page 291)?
- Do you think that there actually exists a relationship between consumer culture and our personal identity (e.g. eating habits)?

Consumer culture and Marxism

It may well be claimed that the concept of consumer culture relates more to economic theory than to sociological theory. Sociologists, until quite recently, showed little interest in cultural and material consumption. Hence P. Bourdieu, in *Distinction* (1984) and *The Field of Cultural Production* (1993), is important; along with other Neo-Marxists, he relates cultural consumption to processes of cultural production along the following lines:

1. The driving force of popular culture is the need for cultural industries to achieve profits. Popular culture goes further than just how and why goods are produced: it is also about consumption and how and why goods are produced to make a profit by finding large markets.

    Hence, it may be claimed that Omega watches, by threatening not to advertise in *Vogue* magazine, gained far wider publicity from the resulting headlines and coverage by major newspapers than it did from the 185,000 monthly readership of *Vogue*.

2. An analysis of popular culture needs to consider both production and consumption. It seems unlikely that power and control in themselves can provide adequate explanation for consumer culture and its patterns of consumption.

    Hence, it may be claimed that popular culture may be seen in terms of cultural resistance to the capitalist ideology. Such a culture of conflict involves the making of social meanings by the masses in becoming critical of, for example, 'the culture of thinness'.

3. Certain goods become available for consumption, whilst others do not. The way in which consumer products become available may influence the way they are consumed and the meanings placed on them by consumers.

    Hence the 'normal' size-14 female, shopping for fashionable clothes, becomes aware of her weight through the images of models in glossy magazines and shop windows. She reviews her appearance and image in relation to products such as healthy-eating options and dietary aids, which, in turn, impacts on her self identity.

In summary:

> 'The main thrust of a great deal of cultural analysis in recent years has been towards the act of consumption and the part it plays in the creation of popular culture. Is the consumer to be regarded as a critical saboteur "expropriating" commodities and using them to create alternative cultural meanings, or as a postmodern style guru constructing "pick and mix" subcultural patterns "off the shelf" – an element of punk here, a bit of Teddy Boy there?'
>
> P. Manning, 'Consumption, Production and Popular Culture', *Sociology Review* (February 1993)

The emphasis has been on how we construct our popular styles through consumption. There is a danger of not paying sufficient attention to how these processes are related to production – something Marx always insisted on. Large multinational media conglomerates dominate areas of cultural production. The greater their dominance, the harder it is for consumers to 'demand' a variety of cultural options.

So where does this leave us? Clearly, the media conglomerates do not dominate all spheres of cultural production. There are specific subcultural sectors in which 'cultural activists' (some soccer supporters, 'indie' music fans, rave organisers, etc.) can apply their interests and enthusiasms to shape the cultural production process. However, such subcultural sectors are fragile and often vulnerable to incorporation into wider society. It remains the case that the process of cultural production shapes the nature of possibilities in popular culture. In focusing only on consumption, there is a danger of putting the cart before the horse.

Think about it

- Can individual identities and social values be shaped by the media conglomerates referred to above?
- How might consumption patterns play a part in the social control of our lives?

Modernism, postmodernism and popular culture

As we saw in Unit 1 (page 57), **modernism** is generally used to refer to the modern age in terms of the scientific and rational ideas which developed from the Middle Ages and Renaissance.

Postmodernists see the industrial world as having entered a new era in which our individual identities are determined by consumer symbols, ideals and choices, rather than group popular cultures.

D. Strinati, in *Popular Culture* (1995), identifies some important characteristics of postmodernism:

1. The breakdown of the distinction between culture and society: here Strinati refers not only to the way in which media images, in an increasingly media-saturated society, are dominating our sense of reality and how we define ourselves and the world around us; but also to the way in which the economy, in terms of consumption, is increasingly influenced by popular culture – it holds a vital role in deciding what we buy and why we buy it.

2. An emphasis on style at the expense of substance: in the field of consumption people are more interested in the packaging and design of goods than in the goods themselves, whilst the style and playfulness of much TV and many films is becoming more important than content, meaning and intellectual depth.

3. The breakdown of the distinction between high culture (art) and popular culture: everything can be turned into a joke or quotation. Andy Warhol's multi-imaged print of Leonardo Da Vinci's famous painting, the *Mona Lisa*, demonstrates how the uniqueness, the artistic aura, of the *Mona Lisa* can be violated: it becomes turned into a joke with its title *Thirty are better than one*. Warhol's work is famous for questioning – and creating – cultural icons; other well known examples are his prints of Marilyn Monroe and Elvis Presley and everyday consumer items like tins of Campbell's soup and Coca-Cola bottles. Strinati also refers to the way in which art is becoming more integrated into the economy both because it is used to encourage people to consume through its expanded role in advertising and because it becomes a commercial good in itself.

4. Confusions over time and space: for example, the growing immediacy of world space and time that has arisen from the media dominance. We know what is going on in Northern Ireland or the Middle East, virtually as it happens. This means that our previously unified and coherent ideas about space and time begin to become distorted and confused. Rapid international flows of capital, money, information, communication, and so on, disrupt the linear unities of time and the established distances of geographical space. Because of the speed and scope of modern mass communications, time and space become less stable and more confused. Films such as *Back to the Future* and *Blade Runner* (see page 323) also serve to exemplify the confusion in our sense of space and time.

5. The decline of the '**meta-narratives**' in a postmodern world: examples of meta-narratives include religion, science and Marxism, since all make universal claims to knowledge and truth. Consider also how we usually think of history, and then recount the plot of any film involving time travel in the same terms, using the concept of linear time. Compare such complex ideas with earlier science fiction accounts of time travel.

   With this comes the rejection of any absolute, universal claim to knowledge. Any theory making such claims has become increasingly open to criticism, and doubt. It is becoming more difficult for people to organise and interpret their lives in line with 'meta-narratives'.

An evaluation of postmodernism

The characteristics of postmodernism, outlined above, do beg some questions. It challenges sociological theories as 'meta-narratives' in decline and suggests that there has been a blurring of ideas in relation to time and place factors. Such claims seem to produce a virtual reconstruction of sociological theories, which almost amounts to a new 'meta-narrative' describing a 'pick-and-mix' lifestyle in the global framework of 'free-floating' media images. Postmodernism can thus itself be regarded as a 'meta-narrative'.

Other issues include the following:

- It is difficult to dismiss, or at least undermine, the scientific and rational developments of several centuries of modernism.
- The notion that the media has taken over 'reality' seems to be overstated.
- Bold assertions seem to have been made with little supporting evidence. This applies not only to ideas about 'reality' but also to important claims on how the media affects consumption patterns and lifestyles.
- Developments in communications and technology may affect time and place factors in the speed of information (and leisure) delivery, but the experience of such developments is not evenly distributed either globally or within particular societies between social classes and occupational groups.
- It is claimed that social group identities have become eroded and that popular culture, for example art and music, has become threatened or even reduced to a 'trash' culture. Such a claim is by no means new: in many areas of sociology, such as family and community, the world we used to know was far better.

In conclusion, the following extract may serve to draw together some crucial issues associated with modernism and postmodernism.

> 'Modernism may be neatly symbolised by cash and the supermarket. Postmodernity is perhaps best represented by the credit card and the shopping mall. Whereas in the 1930s the Model T Ford motor car came off the production line in any colour (provided it was black!), postmodern consumers in the 1990s are spoilt for choice. Consumption now often implies spoiling oneself. If modernism was about discipline and leisure, postmodernism is about excess and pleasure. Society and its elites can no longer dictate tastes and meanings ... with the collapse of shared cherished distinctions between high and popular culture, the blurring of perceptions of both image and reality, increasingly symbolised by such terms as "virtual reality" and "hyper-reality" ... all that is solid melts into air.
>
> 'The importance of choice and lifestyle has become fundamental to postmodernism. With changes in work patterns, family networks and electronic superhighways, individuals are bombarded by choices, information, images and styles. Questions of "Who am I?" "What sort of world do we live in?" were answered in modernism by shared occupations, community and national identity. However, the postmodern leaves individuals with growing feelings of insecurity, and of living in an uncertain world of risk and chance. It is no surprise that insurance is one of the growth markets in a world of unemployment, divorce, HIV/Aids, as well as global famine, the threat of nuclear war, terrorism, pollution and so on.'
>
> Adapted from S. Scraton and P. Branham, 'Leisure and Post Modernity' in M. Haralambos (ed.) *Developments in Sociology* vol. XI (Causeway Press, 1995)

Revision and practice tasks

Task 1: structured question

Before you attempt your answers, read the advice given below.

(a) Briefly explain the term 'youth culture'.   4 marks
(b) Outline how sociologists have attempted to portray and interpret any one youth subculture.   4 marks
(c) Why have sociological studies of youth subcultures tended to have been based on deviant groups?   7 marks
(d) Critically assess the view that deviant youth subcultures represent expressions of working-class resistance to social domination.   10 marks

Advice on response to structured question

(a) You need to show knowledge and understanding of the term in relation to age (transition) and culture (identity, values, etc.). You could give an example to aid your brief explanation, but this is not essential.
(b) As in (a), you need to show knowledge and understanding of the youth subculture you select. If you choose skinheads, for example, you should make reference to their appearance (hair, boots, etc.); you will also need to provide an interpretation of identity or symbols (behaviour, music, etc.), perhaps in terms of class, gender or ethnic background.
Note: parts (a) and (b) carry only 4 marks each. It is important that you read, and even mind-plan, each part carefully. Try to avoid duplicating your responses to each of these subquestions and realise their mark allocations; 4 marks should take up about seven or eight minutes' writing time in a clear logically ordered paragraph.
(c) You must show your ability to briefly discuss and analyse sociological studies (two or three should be adequate rather than a 'shopping list' of studies), in terms of such factors as public concerns about youth subcultures (moral panics, media coverage, deviancy amplification, etc.). Also worthwhile might be reference(s) to sociological attractiveness, empathy, supporting the 'underdog', labelling, etc.
(d) You should demonstrate in two or three well-structured and soundly developed paragraphs your ability to select and evaluate relevant evidence, in particular in relation to 'resistance'. S. Hall's *Resistance Through Rituals* (see page 325 of this unit) would be a good example to quote; the section on resistance and ideology on pages 326–7 is also relevant. Also worth considering is the contradictory nature of youth culture and subculture in comparison to mainstream youth groups who may conform rather than exhibit resistance. Is there a difference between transient fashions and style, and the reality of youth subculture?

Task 2: structured question

Use the general guidelines on pages 9–10 and the advice provided above to help you with the structured question below.

(a) Briefly explain the term 'moral panic'.   4 marks
(b) Provide an example of a recent moral panic and state why you consider it has arisen.   4 marks
(c) How have sociological studies of the news influenced our interpretation of it?
                                                                                  7 marks
(d) Discuss the problems faced by sociologists who attempt to assess the impact of television or film violence on their audiences.   10 marks

Source: Interboard 1997

Essay questions

1. Evaluate the viewpoint expressed by some sociologists that the mass media operate in ways which support the ideology of dominant groups.
2. Discuss the evidence for an increasing concentration of ownership of the mass media. Assess the extent to which owners of the mass media can exercise control over the content of the mass media.
3. 'People use the media to interpret and understand the world.' Critically examine the sociological evidence for this statement.
4. Discuss the claim that the mass media is primarily responsible for the production of stereotypical images of either gender or ethnic differences.
5. Evaluate the sociological argument of the claim that the mass media have created a mass culture.
6. To what extent can distinctions be drawn between 'high' and 'low' culture?
7. 'People use the mass media to interpret and make sense of the world.' Assess the sociological evidence for such a statement.
8. Explain and discuss the viewpoint that mass media effects may be best understood by studies of audience perception.
9. To what extent may it be claimed that the mass media is 'balanced' and 'impartial'?
10. Compare and contrast modernist and postmodernist interpretations of popular culture.

Ideas for coursework and personal studies

1. Select a major news item and study how it is covered in the different forms of the media – newspapers, magazines, TV or radio. How does the style and form of coverage vary between the media and within one particular medium? How might this variety shape the views of different individuals or social groups?
2. Conduct a study into the effects of violence on television on young children and adolescents. Think carefully about how you should approach this study and what difficulties you might encounter.
3. Carry out a study of:
   (a) the extent to which advertising may persuade people to buy things;
   (b) the extent to which consumption of three chosen products is influenced by lifestyle aspiration.
   If you choose to use a questionnaire/survey for your investigation, construct the questions carefully to be free of bias, and try them out on a few people before beginning to collect your data.
4. Study one television 'soap' in terms of the depiction of one of the following:

   • gender;
   • ethnicity;
   • social class.

5. Research the extent to which television and developments in communication technology reduce personal contacts between people within families and households and between individuals outside the household.
6. Construct and carry out research, using an interview schedule, as to whether television news coverage has less bias than other forms of news coverage.

Selected reading list

Folk Devils and Moral Panics, 2nd edn, Stan Cohen (Martin Robertson, 1980)

Forever Feminine: Women's Magazines and the Cult of Femininity, Marjorie Fergusson (Heinemann, 1983)

Hearth and Home: Images of Women in the Media, Gaye Tuchman et al. (Oxford University Press, 1978)

The Media, Brian Dutton (Longman, 1986)

The Media Guide, Steve Peak and Paul Fisher (eds) (Fourth Estate, published annually)

Policing the Crisis, Stuart Hall et al. (Macmillan, 1978)

Popular Culture, D. Strinati (Routledge, 1995)

Post Modernity, D. Lyon (Open University Press, 1994)

Resistance Through Rituals, S. Hall and T. Jefferson (eds) (Hutchinson, 1976)

Television News: Whose Bias?, Martin Harrison (Policy Journals, 1985)

Television Violence and the Adolescent Boy, W. Belson et al. (Gower Press, 1972)

7 The sociology of health and medicine

Introduction

This unit explores a range of sociological views on health and health provision in the UK. Sociologists investigating this area tend to focus either on the sociology of health, or on the sociology of medicine; this unit will look at both.

The sociology of health centres on people's experience of health and health care, including:

- definitions of health;
- the existence of inequalities in the experience of health;
- the existence of inequalities in access to health care;
- explanations for such inequalities;
- the consequences of such inequalities for a range of social groups.

The sociology of medicine centres on how health care is delivered, including:

- the relationship between doctor and patient;
- the medical profession and how doctors in particular possess considerable power via diagnosis, treatment, refusal to treat, etc.;
- state and private provision of health care;
- the development and social impact of the 'Care in the Community' policy;
- the growth of the voluntary sector and the role of carers.

■ **THE SOCIOLOGY OF HEALTH**

What is health?

The World Health Organisation (WHO) defines health as:

> '... *not merely the absence of disease and infirmity but complete physical, mental and social well-being.*'
>
> WHO (1946)

In broad terms we may identify two definitions of health: the **medical model** and the **social model**. The medical model is the definition of health put forward by doctors and health care professionals, and could be described as the official definition. The social model incorporates people's more general beliefs about health.

Which ever model of health is used, it is important to recognise that our concept of health is relative. In other words, a person's view of what is 'normal' health is influenced by factors such as their social class, where they live, their gender, ethnicity or age. Health may be seen, therefore, as a **social construct** – its meaning depends on the social environment at a particular place and time. It is even possible to argue that the definitions and classifications of disease are also social constructs; the symptoms and signs of disease tend to be based on concepts of **normality**, which itself may be interpreted in a variety of different ways (see page 344).

Comparing the two models

The medical model has been criticised for:

- its narrow focus on medical control of disease; and
- its limited usefulness for providing a community-based service.

The social model, by contrast, emphasises:

- the impact of the environment on health, for example pollution, bad housing, poor working conditions, etc.;
- the need for collective methods in the community to address health issues, specifically health inequalities;
- health promotion.

Alternative concepts of health

Various ideas have been put forward in an attempt to describe attitudes to the concept of health.

1. The **body as machine**: illness is accepted as a matter of biological fact and modern biomedicine is seen as the only valid type of treatment (medical model).
2. The **body under siege**: the individual is under constant threat from germs, diseases, stresses and conflicts of modern life.
3. **Inequality of access**: accepts the medical model but is concerned about unequal access to treatment.
4. The **cultural critique**: emphasises the 'social construction' of health and highlights how Western biomedicine has oppressed women, minority groups and 'colonial' peoples (social model).

5. **Health promotion**: emphasises the importance of a healthy lifestyle and personal responsibility, although it also sees health as a collective responsibility (social and medical model).
6. **Robust individualism**: emphasises the individual's right to live a satisfying life, with freedom of choice, e.g. to pay for private health care (political view, i.e. New Right).
7. **Willpower account**: emphasises the moral responsibility of individuals to use their will to maintain good health and avoid self-abuse such as drug taking (moral and political – New Right).
8. **God's power**: views health as righteous living and spiritual wholeness and God as the provider of health (spiritual and virtuous).

Source: Adapted from W. Stainton Rogers, *Explaining Health and Illness* (Harvester Wheatsheaf, 1991)

The medical model of health

This model sees the person as 'sick', 'ill', 'disabled', 'incapable' and in need of one or more of the following: **treatment** if medically ill; **institutionalisation** if incapable of fending for themselves, for example in cases of severe mental illness; **caring** if severely physically disabled. The medical practitioners, external agencies or carers focus on the person as *different*, i.e. not in 'normal health'.

- Health is viewed as the 'absence of disease' and as 'functional fitness'.
- Health services are geared towards treating sick and disabled people.
- A high value is put on the provision of specialist medical services in institutional settings.
- Doctors and other qualified experts diagnose illness and disease, and sanction and supervise the withdrawal of patients from productive labour.
- The main function of health services is remedial or curative – to get people back to productive labour.
- Disease and sickness are explained within a biological framework that emphasises the physical nature of disease: in other words, the medical model of health is biologically reductionist.
- It focuses on establishing abnormality (and normality).
- A high value is put on using scientific methods of research (**hypothetico-deductive method**) and on scientific knowledge.
- Qualitative evidence (given by lay people or produced through academic research) has a lower status than quantitative evidence.

The social model of health

This model suggests that individual and community health results from complex cultural and structural influences affecting particular groups of people – ethnic minorities, the elderly, women, for example. This interpretation of 'health' takes into consideration the wider social pressures affecting individuals' well-being. The social model focuses on the barriers and difficulties which prevent the 'ill' or 'disabled' person from having access to health and 'normality':

- lack of information or education on health care;
- lack of transport facilities to enable contact with doctors, hospitals, etc.;
- difficult access to buildings;
- lack of support from and contact with others;
- limited protection by legislation;
- lack of funds or limited access to financial support;
- few opportunities of work;
- preference for qualitative research focus.

What do sociologists mean by 'health'?

In the sociology of health and illness two of the most influential theoretical perspectives have been the **functionalist** or **consensus viewpoint** and the **social action theories. Conflict theories** and **feminist theories** have also raised critical questions about medicine and health care and in whose interests they are operating.

Functionalist (consensus) theories

Talcott Parsons studied the role of the medical profession in society, and in particular the relationship between doctor and patient, and described his theories and findings in his book, *The Social System* (1951). He saw the role of medicine as crucial to the effective running of society, with its key role being to keep people healthy or, if they became sick, to help them to get better and to allow them to be healthy contributors to society as workers, voters, parents, etc. Medicine, in this view, is a form of **social control**, seeking to ensure that the individual is well fitted to the needs and requirements of the social system. Parsons points out that doctors have a key position in determining a person's health status through:

- deciding how 'well' or 'ill' the person is;
- declaring them fit or unfit for work;
- prescribing drugs or vaccines to control behaviour, ward off infection or protect from disease;
- determining when or whether a patient's illness is either 'deviant' or 'imaginary'.

This perspective on the role of medicine reflects the medical model of health (see page 338).

Social action theories

Erving Goffman made a study of the behaviour of patients and their relationships with those who were treating or caring for them. In *Stigma* (1964), he described how individual patients adjusted to their disabilities. They 'managed' and 'presented' themselves in their relationship with doctors and medical staff in order to minimise the negative consequences for themselves. In *Asylums* (1961), Goffman showed how, in psychiatric hospitals ('total institutions'), mental patients adapted to their role of acceptance and powerlessness in relation to the staff.

Interactionists might say that illness is not just the existence of biological disease, but a function of how a particular disease (for example Aids) or the ill person (for example HIV positive) is perceived by others and how that perception is acted upon. Such perceptions of mental illness indicate how important the image or definition of the illness or the ill person can be. Illness is what a particular society, at a specific point in time, for certain groups or individuals, views it to be – with the medical profession playing a crucial role in the labelling (see page 345) of illness and ill people. The relationship here is essentially one of power and control as the 'staff' impose their rules on the inmates who, in turn, are expected to comply. Non-compliance can result in severe consequences for inmates. In the film *One Flew Over the Cuckoo's Nest* the use of lobotomy on the main character (played by Jack Nicholson), who was deemed to have behaved in a 'deviant' manner, represented a very severe punishment.

Conflict theories

Conflict theories put forward two key objections to the functionalist or consensus view of medicine:

- Medicine is not merely a supportive social institution, it also serves itself as a **profession**. E. Freidson, in *Profession of Medicine* (1970), notes the role of the profession is to justify its 'expert' status and to claim that its practitioners possess the power to diagnose who is ill, why, and how the patient should be treated.
- Medicine operates within a societal and economic framework of capitalism and this enables doctors to assist in the social production of health and illness. Whilst standards of living and health care have improved under capitalism, for Marxists such as L. Doyal, significant inequalities of health and illness still exist.

Feminist theories

Feminist theories on health, whilst far from unified, tend to focus on two key points:

- The health industry is seen to be dominated by men, particularly in the most powerful and specialist professional areas, for example transplant surgery; health policy is also male dominated (MPs and Civil Servants are predominantly men).
- The view of women adopted by the medical profession is seen to undervalue female patients and their health problems.

Research by R. Miles in *Women, Health and Medicine* (1988) suggested that doctors are likely to:

- see women as neurotic and emotionally unbalanced;
- attribute women's problems, whether social and psychological, to their biology being different from that of men;
- assume that the maternal instinct and motherhood are the key elements in a woman's life and that, therefore, any denial of this instinct will cause depression or other forms of ill health.

Postmodernism

Postmodernism tries to look critically at all the assumptions about health and ill health. Disease can be seen as a social construct – a concept based on assumptions within a society about what is normal or abnormal. Some postmodernists also question the practice of medicine by so-called medical experts. A wide range of 'expert' practices have been accepted at different times and in different cultures, not just the 'scientific' medicine of the twentieth-century Western societies. Acupuncture, faith healing and homeopathy are common examples. Postmodernists would argue that theories which seek to justify current practice serve to support medical intervention and the use of medicine as a form of social control.

Postmodernists also note how the idea of the 'healthy body' is constructed and how, through advertising and health promotion campaigns, it has a preferred shape and form.

Think about it

- Which of the theories noted above appears to match the doctor–patient relationship best? Explain clearly why you think that theory offers a clearer explanation than the others.
- Whose interests are best served by the 'construction of the healthy body'?

Illich's criticisms of modern medicine

Ivan Illich, in *Medical Nemesis* (1975), criticises modern medicine which he sees as having dangerous consequences. He suggests that medicine itself causes people damage in the following ways:

- Ill health (**clinical iatrogenesis**) is produced by medicine's engineering approach, the arrogance and incompetence of doctors and the unintended consequence of treatment (for example inadvertent infection, psychological distress, death). An example from November 1997 would be the 'incompetent breast-screening techniques' in Essex hospitals.
- The medical–industrial companies play a role in maintaining a sick society (**social iatrogenesis**), i.e. drug companies and manufacturers of life-support machines generate their profits from people being sick. Transplant surgery is an expensive growth area which is highly technological.
- Loss of capability of self care (**structural iatrogenesis**) results from people becoming sickly because of their dependence on others to do things for them.

For Illich, the 'culture of industrialisation' ensures that technology defines social organisation and, in this instance, health and sickness. He suggests that in order to resolve these difficulties society must be de-professionalised and de-industrialised. Illich sees health and freedom as being closely related. A person is only healthy when he or she has sufficient control over their own social and economic destinies.

Influences on health

Historically, disease was seen by medical practitioners and others as closely tied to poverty, which in turn was seen to be evidence of an individual's moral weakness. This reflects the influence of religion, which sees illness as punishment, and the concept of the **undeserving poor**:

This perspective was deeply embedded in the workings of the nineteenth-century Poor Laws, for example.

There has been an increasing emphasis within medical research on the role of individual behaviour as a cause of disease. Smoking, drinking, many aspects of diet and exercise are widely seen to be matters for individual choice and responsibility. Some surgeons refuse to treat smokers.

However, while personal behaviour may have an effect on health, so too do social position and the related advantages or disadvantages of particular social groups. These factors are referred to by sociologists as environmental influences.

Environmental influences on health

The environmental or socio-economic perspective on health differs from the medical model in that the emphasis is taken away from the individual. This perspective looks at the socio-economic factors affecting people's health, such as geographical location, class, sex, occupation and education, and at the study of epidemics or **epidemiology**.

The **Chadwick Report**, published in the mid-nineteenth century, recognised this way of defining health within a social context. It identified inadequacies in water supplies and poor drainage facilities for the disposal of refuse as the largest sources of disease in large cities. More recently, the **Black Report,** published in the 1980s, highlighted socio-economic factors determining health and the links between health and unequal distribution of wealth (see page 362). The government largely ignored the findings, however, and in 1992 published the *Health of the Nation* and the Scottish version *Scotland's Health – A Challenge to Us All*, which, in today's climate of consumerism and marketisation of services, put the main focus on health as the need for behavioural or lifestyle change. Under a heading 'Other influences', only a couple of lines acknowledged socio-economic factors:

> *'Health varies according to socio-economic standing and wealth . . . and certainly there is no general agreement on what are the most important factors.'*

Is health a social 'problem'?

For a personal trouble to become a social issue, it must be within the 'public domain' or, in other words, it must become an issue which affects many people. Society's collective concern then makes it a public issue and hence something which could be described as a **social problem.**

The definition of what constitutes a social problem is linked to the political structure within a society and the values of the dominant group. It is possible for those in power to suggest that the behaviour of one group challenges the values and threatens the interests of the rest of society in a way that might upset the status quo. Not being in a state of 'normal' health can be seen as being 'deviant' or abnormal (see Unit 10), unless an epidemic affects significantly large numbers of the population – such as the outbreaks of E-coli in Scotland in 1996 and meningitis at Southampton University in 1997.

The individualisation of social problems

An issue that is seemingly a social problem can be individualised or explained in terms of the behaviour of individuals. In the context of health, this perspective sees the individual as responsible for their own health; emphasis is placed on the individual's lifestyle. For example, Edwina Currie, then Junior Minister of Health, referred in 1989 to the poor diet of the people in the North of England and Scotland and linked this and their lifestyle to the high incidence of heart disease in the North as compared to the South.

This idea of individualising health is reflected in the **social pathology model,** which focuses on certain individuals' behaviour as a social problem and a threat to common social values. N. Manning, in *What is a Social Problem?* (1987), described social pathology as:

> *'. . . behaviour by individuals which transgressed social norms and threatened the supposed unity of a social system in which given social roles were essential functional prerequisites for the complex interdependence of modern society.'*

This model, focusing on individual lifestyles, and on personal choice and responsibility (see point 6 on page 339), reflects the dominant Conservative philosophy of individualising an issue, in this case health. This emphasis on individuals has been described as 'victim blaming' in that:

- it sees the social issue as comprising *individual* behaviour; and
- it suggests that what is needed is to 'change the victim'.

Health and normality – social reaction and labelling

Individuals who are seen as 'ill' are perceived to be different from others – illness is seen as a form of 'abnormality'. The form and extent of the 'abnormality' can result in very different social reactions. A person who has a headache or feels a bit stressed or depressed might not be treated in a negative way by friends, relatives and colleagues: their 'ill' behaviour may be tolerated and excused. However, where the stress or depression becomes long-term or deep-rooted or extreme, the social reaction might be less tolerant. In such a situation the reaction of others – avoiding contact or being unwilling to accept the 'ill' person's behaviour, for example – can itself serve as a reinforcer of a person's difficulties. Here once again the writing of Goffman in *Stigma* offers interesting examples of the process of social reaction and the likely response of the stigmatised individual (see page 345).

E. Freidson listed a number of medical conditions and indicated their relative seriousness in terms of deviance. This is shown in the following table. He was looking only at those types of 'deviance' for which the individual is not held responsible.

Level of seriousness	Illegitimate (stigmatised)	Conditionally legitimate	Unconditionally legitimate
Minor deviation	**Stammer** • partial suspension of some ordinary obligations • new obligations expected	**Cold** • temporary suspension of a few obligations • obligation to get well	**Facial pockmarks** • no change in obligations
Serious deviation	**Epilepsy** • suspension of some obligations • adopt new obligations	**Pneumonia** • temporary release from obligations • obliged to cooperate and seek treatment	**Cancer** • permanent suspension of many obligations • additions to privileges

Source: E. Freidson, *Profession of Medicine* (Dodd Mead, 1970)

The extent to which an illness is perceived as an abnormality or deviancy can be seen to be affected by how long-standing (chronic) the illness is. For people who have chronic illnesses, we can distinguish two sorts of results of their condition:

- the effects of their symptoms – their inability to walk, their dependence on other people for basic needs – which in turn may have an impact on the person's self esteem;
- the way in which others view the illness, or the person who is ill; the social reactions of others towards that person.

Chronic illness can affect the ill person's sense of self worth and their identity. This is a consequence of both the actual and the imagined reaction of others. It may also depend on the culture in which the ill person lives, which may adopt very different attitudes (positive or negative) towards different illnesses. The level of social interaction between the ill person and others can vary, depending on factors such as:

- where the person lives;
- what the illness is (Aids? cancer?);
- what their social status or position is;
- whether there are supportive friends or relatives.

Goffman's work on **stigma** and the **management of self** has been very influential in this area. **Stigmatisation** occurs where there is a difference between a person's individual identity (how they see themselves) and their social identity (how others see them). The social identity is often based on **stereotypes** and sometimes results in **labelling**, which can include expectations about how the ill person will behave. The likelihood of stigmatisation varies, depending (according to Goffman) on:

- the visibility of the condition or illness;
- the extent of other people's awareness of the illness;
- the extent to which the illness reduces the person's ability to communicate.

A process of labelling can occur. A person's illness can be seen as 'negative', causing the ill person to be avoided. This is illustrated in the diagram below.

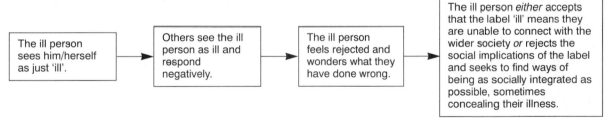

The ill person sees him/herself as just 'ill'. → Others see the ill person as ill and respond negatively. → The ill person feels rejected and wonders what they have done wrong. → The ill person *either* accepts that the label 'ill' means they are unable to connect with the wider society *or* rejects the social implications of the label and seeks to find ways of being as socially integrated as possible, sometimes concealing their illness.

The 'sick role'

Talcott Parsons, in *The Social System* (1951), argues that we can use illness to avoid doing unpleasant tasks such as 'going to work'. This he refers to as the 'sick role'. He suggests that there have to be ways of regulating illness, to prevent it from being used as an excuse. If we are sick, we have a duty to get better: we are obliged to follow doctor's orders. This perspective indicates that health and illness are not simply concerned with biological states but that they are linked to the roles we are expected to play in society.

'Sickness is a by-product of the nature and structure of our social existence, involving far more than the foibles of individual actions or excess.'

Labonte (1982)

Illness could be seen as an economic necessity: an army of professional groups, as well as drug and medical technology companies, derive their living from its treatment. If there was no such thing as 'mental illness', for example, there would be no need for psychiatric services or psychiatric drugs – the pharmaceutical business is a highly lucrative industry. It is therefore in the interests of certain powerful sections of society that we believe in the 'sick role' and in our duty to get well.

Health and deviance – the case of mental illness

The modern view of disease came about with the growth of scientific medicine in the nineteenth century, and is based on the idea of organs of the body not functioning properly. The diagnosis and treatment of such malfunctioning is the core of the medical function in Western industrial societies: medical science and practice centres on the identification (diagnosis), classification and treatment of diseases (see the medical model on page 338).

Mental illness in Britain, and elsewhere, constitutes an area of significant medical and social attention and has been identified by some researchers as a leading cause of disability, and ultimately death, in most Western societies. One woman in eight and one man in 12 will, at some time during their life, experience psychiatric care, while around 25 per cent of all hospital beds are occupied by mental patients. In the USA doctors write 200 million prescriptions for psychoactive drugs in the course of a single year – many to deal with stress or depressive illnesses, according to Kennedy (1983).

The medicalisation of social problems

In Western society mental health is dominated by psychiatry. The psychiatrist holds a powerful position in that he or she can convince others that certain kinds of behaviour challenge the values and threaten the interests of the rest of society. The psychiatrist can label someone whose behaviour is outside these values and beliefs as 'manic depressive' or 'schizophrenic'. This can have a dehumanising, stigmatising effect on the individual. The psychiatrist–patient relationship, then, is an example of how one group of people have the power to label another group as deviant. As Manning points out in *What is a Social Problem?*:

> *'The medicalisation of social problem victims is a neat strategy, for it accomplishes several objectives simultaneously. It removes the direct attribution of responsibility to the victim, yet retains an individualist focus. It draws on a powerful and legitimate source of both expertise and authority, yet diverts claims away from the political arena.'*

This idea concentrates on the individual's behaviour as the social problem and as a threat to common social values. Politically it is in line with the New Right's focus on individual responsibility. While it is only one way of seeing mental distress, it represents a political ideology on which wider social structures, such as social policy and funding, are based. It is an effective way of keeping what is essentially a social issue as a personal problem.

The perception of mental illness as deviance

E. Freidson (see page 344) showed how different conditions or deviances are viewed with different levels of seriousness. Freidson believed that, during the course of an illness, movement through the various categories of deviance is quite common – health and illness are changing processes, not static situations. In the case of a person becoming mentally ill, it is possible to see the development of an 'ill career':

'normality' → use of controlled drugs → stay in psychiatric hospitals

depending on the extent and form of 'deviant behaviour' of the mentally ill (or well) person.

Sociological research on mental illness

Diagnosis or labelling?

An important sociologist in this area is **Thomas Szasz**. He argues that mental illness was discovered in the mid-nineteenth century, when behaviour (or bodily function) was added to the study of anatomy (or body structure) as the subject matter of medicine. People who complained of pains, when physically they seemed quite fit, could now be described as suffering from a functional illness. Szasz made the following conclusions:

- Strictly speaking, disease can affect only the body, not the mind.
- Psychiatric diagnoses are stigmatising labels phrased to resemble medical diagnoses and applied to people whose behaviour annoys or offends others.
- Mental illness is not something a person has but something he or she does or is; therefore it cannot be subject to treatment or cure but it might be changed.
- The prestige and power of psychiatrists has been inflated by more and more phenomena being defined as within the scope of their discipline.

Problems with the medical model of mental illness

In *The Myth of Mental Illness* (1961), Szasz points out that the **medical model** of mental illness makes certain assumptions:

- that the symptoms of mental illness distinguish people who have them from those who do not and who are therefore not ill; that there is, therefore, a clear-cut distinction between the two populations;
- that, like a physiological illness, mental illness is an unfolding process which, if undetected, will grow to a point where it may endanger the effectiveness or even the life of the individual;
- that mental illness may be treated medically by physical treatments, such as electro-convulsive therapy and/or drugs, in which both the 'ill' individual and the doctor may believe.

One major point about Szasz's work is that it makes us question assumptions about **normal** behaviour, and makes us think about the psychiatrist as an official involved in a **labelling** process. It also makes us question what we take to be **abnormal** behaviour, and helps us to focus on the real personal and social problems faced by people living in a complex and demanding social world. Szasz is in danger of overstating the case, however, making us feel that nothing could be or should be done to mould the behaviour of people committing anti-social acts. There are certainly many psychiatrists who would argue that Szasz is misrepresenting their profession. In fact Szasz is only one of the **anti-psychiatry school** that emerged in the 1960s to attack the inadequacy of the medical model when applied to mental illness. Others of this school include Foucault, Cooper, Laing, Goffman and Scheff.

The film *One Flew Over the Cuckoo's Nest*, starring Jack Nicholson, provides some dramatic examples of the process of labelling and treatment (see also Unit 10, page 559).

The socio-economic model v. the medical model

Mental illness is not, however, simply a personal or individual matter. Evidence suggests that socio-economic factors such as housing, poverty and unemployment can affect a person's mental health and emotional well-being. A survey undertaken in an area of Edinburgh with poor housing conditions showed that out of 300 people interviewed, 61 per cent reported stress-type symptoms (Housing and Health Study, 1986).

While the medical/psychiatric model locates the cause of the problem with the individual, the socio-economic model focuses on wider social structures. If, for example, someone who is living in damp, overcrowded accommodation, visits their doctor complaining of stress-related symptoms, the doctor, being unable to rehouse this person, will probably prescribe tranquillisers. While tranquillisers may provide temporary relief, they may also create new problems, such as addiction. If the underlying cause of the problem remains unresolved, and the medication ceases to work, it is possible that the person will feel worse, but it might now be more difficult to decide why they feel this way – is it the medication or is it the unresolved problem? The issue can become clouded.

Think about it

S. Ramon, in his 1990 study, *Beyond Community Care*, quotes some mental patients:

'... to be a mental patient is to have everyone controlling your life but you – you are watched by your shrink, your social worker, your friends, your family, and then you are diagnosed as paranoid. ...'

'... to be a mental patient is to take drugs that dull your mind, deaden your senses, make you jitter and drool, and then you take more drugs to lessen the side effects. ...'

'... to be a mental patient is to participate in stupid groups that call themselves therapy, music isn't music, it's therapy, volleyball isn't sport, it's therapy. ...'

S. Ramon, *Beyond Community Care* (Pluto, 1990)

- Explain why some sociologists suggest that many people classified as mentally ill may not, in fact, be ill at all.

The sociology of disability

Disability may be more common than you think. A United Nations report in 1991 estimated that there are more than 500 million people – one in ten of the world's population – who suffer from some kind of impairment. The same report notes that at least 25 per cent of the 'entire population' are adversely affected by the presence of disabilities, and that of the 500 million disabled people in the world, 300 million live in developed countries, 140 million are children and 160 million are women.

Worldwide, 100 million people are disabled by malnutrition; and there tends to be a close link between poverty and disability. In Great Britain, statistics from the Office of Population Censuses and Surveys (cited by R. Davies in *Sociology Review*, April 1994) suggest that almost 6.25 million (14 per cent) of people aged over 16 years are disabled. The rate of disability increases from 12 per cent (for 65–69-year-olds) to 80 per cent (for over 75-year-olds).

Disablism – the status of disabled people

People affected by **disablism** fall into four broad groups:

- people with disabilities;
- their carers (usually a female member of the disabled person's family);
- the general public – society as a whole;
- professionals – in particular politicians, service providers and medical professionals.

Our concept of disability tends to be based on our ideas of what is 'normal'. It results not simply from a person's inability to see, walk, talk, etc., but also from society's exclusion of people with such inabilities. The Disabled People's International – an organisation committed to raising issues which affect people with disabilities – defined disability as:

> *'an impairment in the functional limitation within the individual caused by physical, mental or sensory factors; a disability is the loss or limitation of opportunities to take part in the normal life of the community on an equal basis with others imposed on people with impairments by physical and social barriers.'*
> C. Barnes, *Disabled People in Britain and Discrimination* (Hurst and Co., 1991)

Society's attitudes to disability

Society's attitudes to disability have in some measure been shaped by the way the economy has developed. Two hundred years ago, disabled people were largely cared for by their extended families, within a smaller, slower-paced, agricultural or small-scale industrial society. However, with the development of industrial society this changed. As families became more divided and society less willing to make room for disabled people, state provision (with its emphasis on 'need' and negation of 'rights') was seen as the way forward. Separate educational provision was provided for children with disabilities, for example. While the original, paternalistic thought behind such institutional provision was to shelter 'inadequates' from society, the notion grew that society needed to be protected from them. 'Socially abnormal' children and adults were thus invisible, silent – and **excluded**.

With the Education Act 1981, educational policy began to shift towards '**inclusion**' and today it is usual for children with various disabilities to be educated in 'ordinary' schools. Society as a whole, however, still tends to exclude disabled people.

Because of long-standing segregation of disabled people in institutions, day centres and separate educational establishments, and the absence of disabled people from public buildings and transport, there is in society a lack of understanding of impairment or disability. This allows fear, embarrassment and notions of the fundamental inferiority and 'otherness' of impaired people to perpetuate and become the catalyst for ongoing discrimination. For example, the official unemployment rate for disabled people in Britain in 1997 was 21.2 per cent, compared to 7.6 per cent for able-bodied people. The '**actual**' **unemployment rate** is probably even higher. The 'common sense' explanation for these statistics is that they reflect restrictions on work capacity caused by the physical or mental impairments of disabled people. However, this is contradicted by the evidence. Numerous studies which ask employers to evaluate the work performance of disabled employees reveal a high level of satisfaction. This suggests that contact with disabled people can change able-bodied people's perceptions of impairment. It also shows how people with impairments are disabled by prejudice as much as by material discrimination.

Those who hold the power to label make many assumptions on behalf of society about disabled people by judging their physical or mental appearance. In most cases they 'forget' about class, gender, race or sexuality, and group disabled people together merely because they are 'different'. But disabled people are not just disabled. They are male or female, black or white, homosexual or heterosexual, employed or unemployed, etc. Society generally refuses to see them in this differential way, however, and views them in a totalising way in regard to their disability.

> '*Bringing people into more personal contact . . . at least makes them more aware of the individual character of the disabled child or adult . . . they will eventually get . . . to see us as people first and as disabled second. [Then] they will have begun to see that we are also products of our social backgrounds and environments just like anybody else and not just a disability breed.*'
>
> Report of the Snowdon Working Party, 1976

Think about it

A study by G. Cumberbatch and R. Negrine (*Images of Disability on Television*, 1992) analysed six weeks of prime-time television broadcasts across all channels in 1988. The most striking feature they discovered was the virtual invisibility of disabled people outside news broadcasts and specialist programmes such as the BBC's *One in Four* and Channel 4's *Same Difference*. There were no disabled people in any of the current affairs programmes or game shows and they represented just 0.5 per cent of all the characters portrayed in fictional programmes.

* The survey mentioned above was conducted in 1988. From your own observation, do you think there have been any significant changes in the portrayal of disability?
* Comment on the sociological aspects of media images (or lack of them) of disability.

The medicalisation of disability

The medical model

The medicalisation of any social problem is a neat strategy, for it accomplishes several objectives simultaneously:

- It focuses on the individual (victim-blaming).
- It refers to experts for advice.
- It diverts responsibility away from the political arena towards the medical one.

World Health Organisation model of disablement

| Disease or disorder (intrinsic situation) | → | Impairment (exteriorised) | → | Disability (objectified) | → | Handicap (socialised) |

Source: M. Morgan et al., *Sociological Approaches to Health and Medicine* (Routledge, 1985)

The World Health Organisation's model of disablement resembles that of the labelling perspective in the field of mental health (see page 347); the expectation is that the disabled person's physical impairment fully explains their difficulty in obtaining employment, for example. Sociologists suggest, however, that **prejudices** contribute to the difficulties encountered by disabled people, and that these are social constructs.

The medical (or 'individual') model of disability sees the 'problem' of disability:

- as an issue concerning individuals;
- as deriving purely from lack of physical functioning;
- within the 'personal tragedy theory' of disability: disability is seen as a tragic event which occurs randomly and affects unfortunate individuals.

It places the disabled individual at the centre of a range of professions and special facilities which are there to 'help' them with treatment. Little attention or interest is paid to the wishes or desires of the disabled person.

The social model

The social model of disability rejects the basic ideas of the medical model. Here the disabled person has the capacity to challenge and to interact with a wide range of agencies and social situations. Whilst not ignoring the 'problem of disability', the social model locates this very firmly within the wider society. It suggests that it is not individual limitations which make disability so difficult for disabled people, but the lack of appropriate service provision and facilities and the existence of stigmatising attitudes on the part of professionals and policy makers. Restrictions placed on disabled people include:

- individual prejudice;
- institutional discrimination (inaccessible public buildings, unusable transport systems, etc.);
- segregated education;
- discriminatory employers;
- absence of inclusion;
- limitations in respect to policy and legislation by governments in meeting the expressed needs of the disabled;
- the potential impact (during 1998) of proposed government restrictions on disability benefits.

Disability – the medical and social models compared

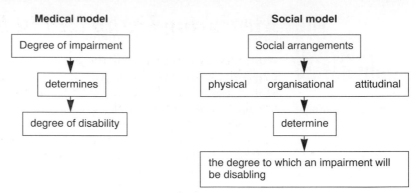

Medical model

Degree of impairment

↓

determines

↓

degree of disability

Social model

Social arrangements

↓

physical   organisational   attitudinal

↓

determine

↓

the degree to which an impairment will be disabling

Source: T. Davis 'Disabled by Society', in *Sociology Review*, April 1994

Think about it

- Construct a similar pair of models to show the pattern of mental illness as it is understood **medically** and **socially**.
- Add examples to your diagram.

The Disability Movement

May 1990: The Campaign to Stop Patronage demonstrates against the LWT Telethon

The development and promotion of a social model of disability is related to the growth of a civil rights movement amongst disabled people. In this context it is important to distinguish between organisations *of* and organisations *for* disabled people. Charitable organisations *for* disabled people such as Scope, Mencap, RNIB and RNID, are funded and run mainly by non-disabled people. They are sometimes felt by organisations *of* disabled people to be problematic because they can be seen as perpetuating disabled people's dependence on charity. Organisations such as the Disabled People's International and BCODP (British Confederation of Disabled People) are run by disabled people. They argue for 'Rights not Charity' and are highly critical of the fact that disabled people have not always had a voice in the voluntary organisations that supposedly are there to represent them.

Think about it

Anything is possible.

Scope – formerly The Spastics Society – is the UK's largest charity working with people with disabilities.

We changed because our name was offensive and hurtful to the people we work with.

We have become **Scope** because the name represents what we work to achieve – scope for people to live the life they choose.

In partnership with over 250 affiliated local groups, Scope works with people who have cp to make possible the things that others take for granted.

- In 1994, the Spastics Society changed its name to Scope. From a sociological viewpoint, what reasons can you suggest for (a) the change and (b) the choice of name? Comment on this in relation to 'labelling'.

Measuring health and ill health

Mortality

Mortality as a measure of the health of a society derives largely from available statistics. These offer insights into the main forms of illness which cause death by indicating how many people were certified as having died from, for example, a heart attack. Mortality or 'age-at-death' statistics can be compared over time by cause of death, by region, by social class, by occupation and so on. They also make it possible to predict how long a male or female may be expected to live and to compare life expectancies in, say, the 1990s with those for the 1970s or the 1890s and so on. The following table is a brief example.

| | Life expectation (years) | |
	Male	Female
1891–1900	44.1	47.8
1974–76	69.6	75.8
1989–91	73.2	78.8

Source: *The Health of the Nation* (HMSO, 1992)

As is the case with any statistical source, however, it is as well to remember that mortality figures only partially represent reality.

Key statistical data is collected on age-specific death rates, with the main reference points being the still-birth rate and the **infant mortality rate** (IMR), which is the number of deaths of infants under one year old in every 1000 live births. The IMR is considered to be a sensitive indicator of the general health of a society, as causes of infant deaths are often linked to social and living conditions, as well as the availability of health services which, of course, affect all age groups.

Changing patterns of mortality

The most significant improvement in mortality rates since the start of the 1900s has been amongst the very young. At the beginning of the twentieth century, one in ten children born died in the first year; the rate for 1991 was just less than one in a hundred, with more than 98 per cent of babies surviving their first year of life. However, there has been a general slowing down in the improvements in life expectancy in recent years. Life expectancy in Northern Ireland and Scotland tends to be shorter than in the rest of the UK.

The shift from deaths caused by infectious diseases such as smallpox or TB to a greater number of deaths from degenerative diseases such as bronchitis, cancer and heart disease has been a key feature of the patterns of ill health and causes of death in industrial societies.

Think about it
• Why might life expectancy in Northern Ireland and Scotland be shorter than in the rest of the UK?

The following table, showing a record of christenings, deaths and causes of death in the seventeenth century, offers an interesting historical perspective.

The diseases and casualties in the week beginning 20 December 1664 for London			
Abortive	2	Infants	3
Aged	24	Killed by a fall from a Scaffold at St Martin in the Fields	1
Bedridden	1		
Bruised	1	Lethargy	1
Cancer	1	Livergrown	1
Canker	1	Overlaid	1
Childbed	12	Palsie	1
Chrisomes	6	Plague	1421
Collick	2	Quinsie	1
Consumption	59	Rickets	8
Convulsion	25	Rising of the Lights	3
Dropsie	17	Rupture	1
Drowned in a Tub of Mash in a Brewhouse at St Giles in the Fields	1	Scowring	1
		Spotted Fever	28
		Stillborn	3
Fever	82	Stopping of the Stomach	3
French-pox	1	Suddenly	1
Frighted	1	Surfeit	17
Grief	2	Teeth	41
Griping in the Guts	13	Tiffick	3
Jaundies	1	Winde	1
Imposthume	6	Wormes	8
Christened	[Males 60] [Females 44] [In All 104]	Buried	[Males 951] [Females 855] [In All 1806] Plague 1421

Decreased in the Burials this Week 1413

Parishes clear of the Plague 26   Parishes Infected 104

The A size of Bread set forth by Order of the Lord Mayor and Court of Aldermen

A penny Wheaten Loaf to contain Nine Ounces and a half, and three half-penny White Loaves the like weight.

Source: Open University (1975) in K. Jones and G. Moon, *Death, Disease and Society* (Routledge, 1992)

Major causes of death in
the UK in 1931 and in
1991

The pie charts below show that within the sixty years from 1931 to 1991, there was a major shift in the causes of death in the UK, with cancers and circulatory diseases now claiming a much higher percentage.

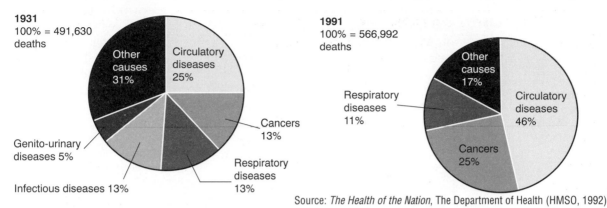

1931
100% = 491,630
deaths

Other causes 31%
Circulatory diseases 25%
Cancers 13%
Respiratory diseases 13%
Infectious diseases 13%
Genito-urinary diseases 5%

1991
100% = 566,992
deaths

Other causes 17%
Circulatory diseases 46%
Cancers 25%
Respiratory diseases 11%

Source: *The Health of the Nation*, The Department of Health (HMSO, 1992)

Morbidity

Morbidity is the term used by sociologists to mean rates of sickness as an indicator of the absence of health. It is measured either through available statistics – for example, time taken off work – or through self-reported illness in surveys of health. Statistical data may be obtained from hospital records, consultations between doctors and patients, government statistics on work absences, or specially commissioned social surveys. Morbidity measurement represents health negatively as a level of illness at a given point in time, suggesting that illness is a passing phase. Clearly this is not the case for everyone and, in the instance of someone who has a long-term illness, such a representation of morbidity is inaccurate. By emphasising time off work, the morbidity figures largely ignore those who are not in employment: the unemployed, the old, the very young and women who are not in paid employment. Even statistics which are collected from doctors' surgeries or from hospitals indicate only the extent of illness of those who refer themselves for treatment. People who do not consult medical practitioners are very unlikely to be taken account of in the morbidity statistics.

Data relating to morbidity is a useful guide to the state of the nation's health yet, as noted on page 353, the statistics are rather limited. The General Household Survey (of around 16,000 households) is carried out annually; it has provided personal recollections of episodes of ill health with attempts to distinguish between **acute illness** (which may be temporary) and **chronic illness** (long-standing illness which affects a person's daily life). There is also data available on the use of NHS services which may be taken as a measure of the amount of sickness for which there has been a consultation with a doctor or which has led to the use of hospital out-patient or in-patient facilities.

In 1993, B. Cox and others interviewed 9000 people for *The Health and Lifestyle Survey* (a follow-up to an earlier survey published by the Health Promotion Research Trust in 1982). The survey concluded that people's self assessments were fairly accurate, and suggested a relationship between subjective views of health and objective measures of it. Many such studies have found a 'submerged iceberg of sickness' in the community which is never brought to the attention of the medical profession.

■ HEALTH – A HISTORY OF INEQUALITY

Nineteenth-century industrial Britain was rife with inequalities, as Charles Booth's and Seebohm Rowntree's studies of poverty in London and York (see Unit 8, pages 394–5) and Charles Dickens's observations on Victorian society illustrate only too clearly. Major engineering projects were introduced to address issues of sanitation and fresh water supply as one way of improving social conditions, at least in the towns and cities. The tables below show some key data on the population and its health in the mid-nineteenth century.

Pauperism (per 1000 population, 1850 estimates)	
England and Wales	57.4
Scotland	41.8
Ireland	72.5

Life expectancy at birth (1850)	
Males	40 years
Females	42 years

Death rates (per 1000 population)		
Year	Adults	Infants
1840	22.9	154
1850	20.8	153
1860	21.2	162

Unemployment in some towns in the mid-nineteenth century				
Town	Numbers fit for work	Fully employed (%)	Partly employed (%)	Unemployed (%)
Liverpool (Vauxhall)	4 814	38	12	49
Stockport	8 215	15	35	50
Colne	4 923	19.5	32.5	48
Oldham	19 500	49	22.5	25.5
Wigan	4 109	24	62	38

Source: Rose (1972), Mitchell and Deane (1962), Hobsbawm (1964)

By 1858, the Medical Registration Act had created a unified medical profession. Soon after, medical care moved from the home to the newly formed hospitals. Developments in both institutionally-based medical care and the medical profession itself brought about some improvement in the health of urban dwellers, but inequalities of poverty remained throughout the nineteenth and into the twentieth centuries. Such inequalities had implications for the health, well-being and life expectancy of the most vulnerable sections of the population: the poor, the unemployed, the elderly, single parents, the disabled.

One of the aims of the **National Health Service** (NHS), established in Britain after 1945, was the eradication of inequalities of medical provision relating to social class and life chances. While a private sector was allowed to continue to exist, a national service based on compulsory insurance contributions by employers and employees was established to provide medical treatment and care for those in need. The service inherited from the previous voluntary and municipal agencies a number of problems of unequal provision on both a class and geographical basis, and a reluctance of some doctors to establish practices in the areas of greatest need. The aim of the NHS to alleviate and then eliminate such inequality went hand-in-hand with a wider range of policies designed to improve the environment of working-class people in order to curb the spread of disease. Re-housing schemes took people from inner-city slums to new estates and towns in or closer to the countryside, and steps were taken to improve safety regulations in factories, to reduce pollution and so on.

Research into social class and inequalities in NHS provision

Research by Noyce and others, published in the *Lancet* in 1974, found that the fewest resources still coincided with the geographical areas with low average family income. Cartwright and O'Brien, in an article in *Basic Readings in Medical Sociology* (1978), take this to be one of many contributory factors to the differential use of health services by social class. Other factors are:

- knowledge and education: studies quoted showed the higher up the Registrar General's scale (see Unit 2) the greater the knowledge of the means of transmission of disease and of effective family planning methods;
- attitudes and self confidence: the higher up the scale the greater the expressed criticisms of the service provided. Professional-class patients are more willing to ask questions, while the unskilled manual group often waited to be told;
- vulnerability: social conditions render working-class people more vulnerable to events that cause depression, for example loss of mother in childhood, large families, lack of confiding relationships and unemployment. Barbara Preston has noted that several diseases are class-related, with professional classes having only half the expected death rate from them, while unskilled manual workers have death rates at least 50 per cent higher than expected. These include deaths resulting from epilepsy, bronchitis, hernia, influenza, TB and pneumonia;
- relations with the GP: working-class patients found it more difficult to communicate their problems to what they saw as middle-class doctors – they required more consultations, but each lasted for a shorter period than those of their middle-class counterparts.

Despite the dramatic improvement in the overall health of Britain's population over the past 100 years, inequalities persist. In the 1970s, men and women in occupational class 5 of the Registrar General's classification had a two-and-a-half times greater chance of dying before retirement age than those in class 1; trends in death rates indicate that the gap between the health of the lowest and the highest social class groupings widened during the 1980s; and research data shows regional disparities with, for example, those living in the northern and north-west regions of England and Wales experiencing the highest death rates since 1945. At a more localised level, P. Townsend's study of Bristol in 1982 (in *Inequalities in Health*: the Black Report 1982) allowed different wards of the city to be compared, whilst the JCC (Joint Consultative Committee) (1985) showed that there were significant differences in the health experiences of those living in Manchester as compared with the rest of the country. People in less affluent areas of the city had far worse life expectancy than those in wealthier areas. In 1844, Friedrich Engels observed of Manchester:

> *'The manner in which the great multitude of the poor is treated by society today is revolting . . . they are deprived of all means of cleanliness, of water itself. . . . They are given damp dwellings. . . . I broadly accuse [the bourgeoisie] . . . of social murder.'*
>
> Friedrich Engels, 1845

Over 100 years later, as noted in the following article, it would seem that Manchester retains a poor health record.

OPCS study confirms link between social deprivation and ill health
Manchester 'least healthy place for men in England'

David Brindle, Social Services Correspondent

MANCHESTER is the most unhealthy place to live in England if you are a man, a government study yesterday suggested. Corby in Northamptonshire is worst for women.

Over the period from 1989 to 1993, Manchester had the highest death rate for men and the fifth highest for women, according to analysis by the Office of Population Censuses and Surveys.

Corby, the former steel town, had by far the highest death rate for women and the ninth worst rate for men in the 366 districts surveyed.

The study provides further confirmation of the link between social deprivation and ill health — a

Healthiest

MEN
East Dorset, Wokingham (Berks), Chiltern (Bucks), Elmbridge, Mole Valley (Surrey)

WOMEN
Broadland (Norfolk), East Dorset, Wansdyke (Avon), East Devon, Rutland

Unhealthiest

MEN
Manchester, Hammersmith & Fulham, Lambeth, Tower Hamlets, Southwark (London)

WOMEN
Corby, Easington (Durham), Middlesbrough, Salford, Manchester

link which has finally been acknowledged by the Department of Health.

Districts identified as having the lowest death rates for men and women are all in the more affluent South-west, East Anglia or the South-east outside London.

The OPCS says there has been no significant change over the past 30 years in differences between North and South in death rates, which are seen as an indicator of general health levels.

However, there have been changes in the rankings of regions.

Whereas the North-west was clearly the least healthy region in the early 1960s, it has since improved at the expense of the North, which now has the highest death rates for men and women.

Similarly, the South-west has displaced East Anglia as the region with the lowest death rate for women. The two regions also share the lowest rate for men.

In a separate study, the OPCS warns that generally improving death rates and life expectancy — now 74 years for men and 79 for women — do not mean that health standards are rising.

More people are developing cancers of the lung, bladder, pancreas, prostate and breast, the study says. The proportion of men classified overweight or obese rose from 39 per cent in 1980 to 56 per cent in 1993, and of women from 32 per cent to 46 per cent.

• An estimated 34 per cent of babies born in England and Wales in the third quarter of this year were outside marriage, the OPCS says, compared with 32 per cent last year.

Population Trends 82 (HMSO, £9.60).

Source: The *Guardian*, 8 December 1995

Sociological analyses of inequities in health

Inequities in health can be defined as differences which are unnecessary and avoidable and judged to be unjust and unfair. They include:

- restrictions of choice of lifestyle;
- inadequate access to health and other public services;
- poor and unhealthy working and living conditions.

Some of the influences on a person's health chances are shown in the diagram below. Bear in mind that a number of these, not just one, might contribute to good or poor health chances.

Health chances

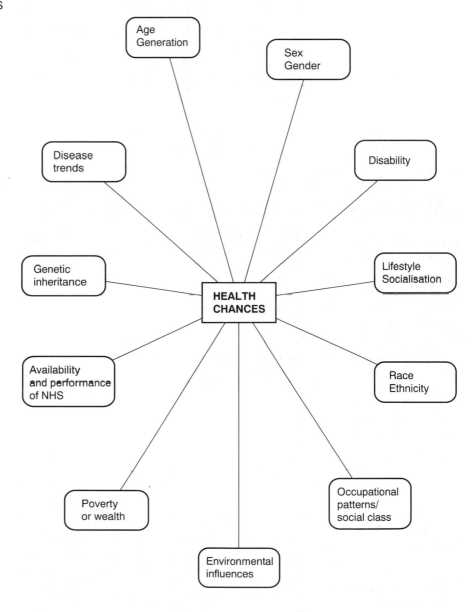

Source: L. Jones, *The Social Context of Health and Health Care* (Macmillan, 1994)

Sociologists are interested in whether inequities in health are increasing or decreasing; whether the gap between the healthiest and the least healthy is getting larger or smaller. Difficulties in developing reliable answers include:

- reliability of data: for example, in looking at definitions of suicide, the definition of cause of death on the death certificate may occasionally be influenced by social factors;
- changing classification of occupations and therefore of social class over time;
- change in the relative size of different sections of the population: the top two social classes have expanded, whilst all others have contracted.

Sociologists using statistics need to be aware of who compiles them and for what purpose. However, all the statistics in this area consistently show inequalities in health existing over time and between a range of groups.

Health and social class

The terms 'health' and 'social class' both involve certain problems of definition that are not apparent in everyday usage. Health is to some extent subjective, and a number of questionnaire studies have shown that many people feel below par on any particular day. Health is also something that has to be assessed relative to age: and we would not normally expect a healthy 80-year-old to behave in a similar way or to feel as physically fit as a much younger person. Nevertheless, it makes sense to think of health as an objective phenomenon, meaning absence of particular diseases or afflictions rather than as a positive state of affairs. The term 'social class' has been used in different ways by sociological theorists (see Unit 2), but the basic division between a manual working class and a non-manual middle class has been accepted as a basis for analysis in terms of health.

In *The Strategy of Equality* (1982), J. Le Grand found that public expenditure per person reporting illness is greater the higher the social group. Using market research socio-economic categories (see Unit 2, page 82), classes AB (the 'professional' classes) received 40 per cent more than classes DE (semi- and unskilled classes). Le Grand also points to the lack of take-up of preventive and other services which he attributes both to inadequate supply and an unwillingness or inability to demand services due to lack of transport and telephone, unhelpful staff, problems of communication, possible loss of earnings and so on.

This analysis outlines a situation rather than explains it, however. Marxist writers would point to the role of wealth and the nature of social structures under capitalism in terms of who is put at risk and who receives what forms of treatment. Some analysts might point to heredity and congenital factors, while others would point to cultural deprivation or the malfunctioning of the Welfare State. As Ian Kennedy noted in the 1980 Reith Lectures (see page 375), we should aim to improve health education and pay particular attention to those at the bottom of the socio-economic structure.

The histogram below illustrates the effect of social class on infant mortality. The figures include infant deaths where parents are unemployed: it would be interesting to see whether long-term unemployment produced a similar or different infant mortality rate to that of unskilled manual workers, for example.

Infant mortality, by social class of father (England and Wales, 1989)

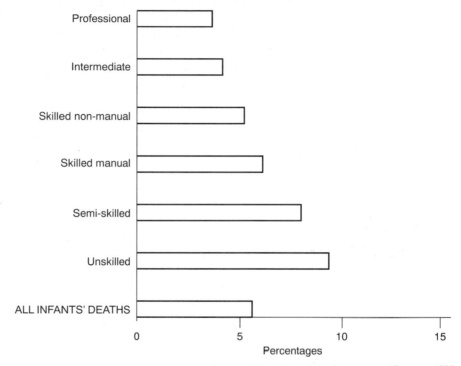

Source: Office of Population Censuses and Surveys, 1992

Several pieces of research have further stressed the link between both health and health treatment and social class. The Black Report on inequalities in health (see page 362) provided a great deal of evidence to this effect, with some important points being as follows:

- A child born at the bottom of the social scale is twice as likely to die at birth or in the first few months of life as a professional-class child.
- For every boy from class 1 who dies before his first birthday, there will be two from class 3N (skilled working-class) and four from class 5 (unskilled working-class).
- Of 38 causes of death for children aged between one and 14, 22 showed manual working-class children more at risk than the professional classes, with only asthma showing the reverse.
- For children under seven, the percentages not visiting the dentist and not being immunised against smallpox, polio, etc. rises the further down the scale. For example, the figures for smallpox immunisation revealed that only 6 per cent in social class 2 had not been immunised, as against 14 per cent for class 2, 16 per cent for class 3N, 25 per cent for class 3M, 29 per cent for class 4, and 33 per cent for class 5.

The Black Report (1980)

In his foreword to the Black Report (1980), the then Secretary of State for Social Services, Patrick Jenkins, noted:

> *'I must make it clear that additional expenditure on the scale which could result from the report's recommendations – the amount involved could be upwards of £2 billion a year – is quite unrealistic in present or any foreseeable economic circumstances. . . . I cannot, therefore, endorse the group's recommendations.'*
>
> Patrick Jenkins, 1980

Black Report recommendations: summary

1. The abolition of child poverty to be adopted as a national goal for the 1980s, by:

   - increasing the maternity grant and child benefit;
   - introducing an infant care allowance for under fives;
   - providing nutritionally adequate school meals for all;
   - mounting a child accident prevention programme.

2. A comprehensive disability allowance to be introduced for people of all ages.
3. Minimally acceptable and desirable standards of work, security, conditions and amenities, pay and welfare or fringe benefits to be drawn up.
4. Resources to be shifted more quickly towards community care and primary health care, to improve child health services, expand home help and nursing services for disabled people and extend joint care funding and programmes.
5. National health goals to be set after consultation and debate.
6. Local authority spending and responsibilities under the 1974 Housing Act to be substantially increased.
7. A Health Development Council to be established.
8. Research and statistical data relating to health, such as statistics on child health, income and health inequalities, to be improved.

In fact the government rejected the main recommendations of the Report.

The Black Report (1980) and *The Health Divide* (M. Whitehead, 1992) offer similar conclusions in respect to the relationship between social class and health.

Unemployment and health status

Unemployment and Mortality, a study by K. Moser in 1987, showed that mortality rates were higher for the unemployed than for the employed, and noted an 11 to 1 difference in attempted suicide rates with the incidence of suicide increasing the longer the duration of unemployment. There is much evidence that the prospect of unemployment can induce stress and that the experience of unemployment itself can have a detrimental effect on an unemployed person's health. Studies on unemployment and health tend to emphasise three key explanations:

- the physiological impact of the stress of unemployment;
- the importance of material resources, and, with long-term unemployment, a lack of access to these;
- a process of health selection, in which people already suffering ill-health are more likely to lose their jobs.

M.H. Brenner established a link between levels of production and unemployment and ill-health. In *Mental Illness and the Economy* (1977), he suggested that recession and wide-scale economic distress have an impact on health status indicators – infant mortality rate (IMR), maternal mortality and national mortality rates, especially on deaths ascribed to cardiovascular disease, cirrhosis of the liver, suicide and homicide, and rates of first admission to mental hospital. It has been suggested that the loss of a job is like a bereavement but is not accepted and respected as such. Unemployment can certainly bring the risk of prolonged stress with implications for physical and mental health.

Casualty crisis: how the NHS fails the homeless

Homeless people are being forced to rely on hospital accident and emergency wards rather than GPs – with deadly consequences. Simon Rogers and Camilla Berens report

According to a new report by Shelter, Britain's primary healthcare system is not only failing the homeless, it's also resulting in the waste of untold sums of desperately needed NHS cash. *Go Home & Rest?* exposes a system in which everyone loses out. Homeless people rely on accident and emergency (A&E) departments for basic healthcare, doctors and nurses have to deal with conditions that could have been dealt with by a GP and the NHS is stretched further by the massive waste of money and time.

Compiled from 51,000 London A&E clinical records, *Go Home & Rest?* is the largest ever single study of its kind. It shows that although 97 per cent of the population is registered with a GP, up to 70 per cent of homeless people are not.

The findings are mirrored in Scotland. Shelter Scotland, which will issue its own report on health and homelessness this month, says nearly all homeless Scots use A&Es rather than GPs.

Spokeswoman Tricia Marwick wants guidelines put in place to ensure all homeless people have access to GPs. "This will save lives and NHS resources," she said.

Robert Aldridge of the Scottish Council for Single Homeless said some GPs "covertly discriminated" against the homeless and prevented them registering. "Receptionists often say the practice is full, or the homeless are dropped from practice lists

'The homeless need long-term GP care. If they don't get it they die'

without explanation," he claimed. "But mostly the problem lies with GPs failing to ensure the homeless are aware of services."

Homeless life expectancy has plummeted in recent years, accompanying the rise in TB and other deadly illnesses among rough sleepers. Aldridge blames this on the difficulty in accessing GP healthcare. "A&Es just patch people up and send them on their way, but the homeless need long-term healthcare through a GP – if they don't get it they die," he said.

These problems led Lothian Health Board to establish an innovative 'homeless team' to address the health needs. Set up in 1995, the scheme, the only one in Scotland, offers drop-in homeless GP clinics four times a week. Peter McLoughlin, homeless services development manager, says the service aims to get homeless people registered with a doctor. "But," he explains, "it may be difficult for homeless people to have a GP. They may be moving around a lot or have a very chaotic lifestyle." He believes the challenge facing the health service is to make GPs more flexible to accommodate the homeless.

Philip Reid, a doctor who works with homeless people, admits that many of his colleagues won't register

homeless patients. "Most GPs don't like registering people who appear difficult, whether it's because they turn up drunk or because they just look shabby," he says.

Healthcare professionals are shocked by the massive waste of resources haemorrhaging as a result of this situation. The report reckons that while a typical visit to a GP would cost the NHS £15.49, inappropriate attendance at an A&E costs £44. That's a total extra cost of £60,000 a year to each hospital – nearly £3 million in Scotland and an additional £16 million in England.

But there are solutions. Several organisations run their own medical services and local authorities all over the country are funding projects to get homeless people registered. Some provide primary healthcare through doctors and nurses at hostels and day centres.

The report found that while 59 per cent of visits by homeless people to A&E were inappropriate, only 35 per cent of those receiving some form of attention attended casualty without reason.

But these projects are no substitute for the 24-hour-a-day, seven-days-a-week service that a good GP provides.

And healthcare professionals acknowledge it is ghetto-isation – one service for homeless people, isolated from mainstream healthcare, and another for the rest of us. ■

Additional reporting by Neil Mackay and David Milne

Source: Adapted from *Focus*

Think about it

- Explain why inequalities still exist in the following areas:
  - access to specialist health care facilities;
  - causes of death;
  - infant mortality;
  - life expectancy.

- Why are homeless people vulnerable to illness?
- What social factors contribute to their vulnerability?
- How might social policy be directed to assist vulnerable groups, e.g. the homeless and those in poverty?

Why does inequality in health persist?

The authors of the Black Report concluded that inequalities still existed and were affected by level of income, occupation, education, housing and lifestyle – none of which could be addressed by the NHS. They offered four major explanations as to why such inequality can still be found and suggested that the structural explanation was the strongest of these:

- The **artefact explanation** takes the view that social mobility is removing class differences and that the decline of the manual working class will ensure improvements. The inequalities debate sees ill health as a biological entity which differs between social classes.
- The **behavioural or cultural explanation** places emphasis on pathological (personal/individual) consequences of behaviour such as poor diet, drinking alcohol, smoking or lack of exercise. Inequality will reduce when people make healthier or more appropriate choices.
- The **health selection explanation**, a similar view to that of the nineteenth-century evolutionary theory (social Darwinism), suggests that people in ill health will inevitably fall to the bottom of society and that inequality will always be there.
- The **structural or materialist explanation** sees factors outside the individual's control affecting their life and health chances. Issues relating to the form and nature of employment or unemployment are critical, as is the person's position in society relating to, for example, home ownership, income, quality of life, living conditions and poverty (where few people have any real choice).

A range of factors which might influence health

External/environmental factors	Internal/individual factors

Physical environment

- Climate
- Heat/ventilation
- Water
- Infection
- Soil
- Pollution
- Air
- Toxicity
- Food
- Trace elements
- Waste
- Radiation
- Disasters

Socio-economic environment

General
- Local services
- Transport/traffic
- Recreation/open space/leisure
- Noise/crime/security
- Urbanisation

Specific
- Housing
- Employment/unemployment
- Occupation/working situation
- Disposable income/resources
- Life events
- Social networks

Genetic/biological/ethnicity

- Genetically determined disease or biological status
- Susceptibility or resistance to trauma and disease

Early experience

- Nutrition/housing
- Pollution/illness

Lifestyles/health-related behaviour

- Smoking
- Alcohol
- Diet
- Addiction
- Physical exercise
- Sexual practices

The expansion of private health services in recent years may be contributing to a further widening of the gap in health care between the classes. Ann Shearer, in 1981, estimated the number of people covered by private schemes to be in the region of 3.5 million; 1994 estimates put the figure as high as 5 million. While in the past this group would have been composed wholly of professional and managerial people, there has been an expansion of clerical and skilled manual subscribers. This may be a reflection of the social mobility of certain groups of skilled workers as suggested by the embourgeoisement thesis (see Unit 2, page 74), but the net result may be to further increase the deprivation of the semi- and unskilled groups.

Unequal access to health care

Access to, and distribution of, the health care system raises questions about the extent to which all citizens are able to gain equal access to assistance when and where they require it. N. Abercrombie and A. Warde, in *Contemporary British Society* (1994), identified three major problems associated with National Health Service provision:

- social class inequalities in distribution – evidence suggests that health care provision still favours the better-off, a situation which existed before the NHS came into being in 1948;
- geographical distribution – some areas are well provided for, some are not, so where you live becomes critically important;
- priorities of the medical profession – care of the elderly and the mentally ill tends to be under-resourced, whilst the high technology specialisms and more prestigious areas of provision tend to do much better.

We have already looked in some detail at class factors. The following sections look at problems of unequal access in the contexts of region, gender, age and ethnicity/culture.

Regional and local variations

As noted earlier, there are significant geographical variations in health and illness. Scotland, for example, has a 25 per cent higher rate of heart and circulatory disease than other parts of the UK. A North–South gradient has been identified, with general health being worse in the North and Midlands regions of England than in the South. M. Blaxter (1990) concluded that much of the North–South divide results from the greater concentration of poor physical and material environments, such as poor quality housing stock, in the North.

In Scotland, the Lothian Health Board noted in 1992 that over the previous year negative environmental influences on health showed a clear increase. Factors identified include:

- an increase in unemployment;
- a widening of the poverty gap;
- an increase in homelessness;
- more pollution;
- further environmental damage.

The Board cited research on children and young people, referring to major changes in the social structure of families, and external influences such as increased use of TV, videos and computer games, suggesting that children's health and general behaviour may be suffering as a consequence of such social and environmental changes.

Gender and health inequities

Women are the biggest users of health care facilities, largely because of their roles as child-bearers and child-rearers. There are, however, other interesting gender differences. Cause of death differs for men and women (see the table on page 367), and whilst women live longer than men they have higher rates of morbidity. However, if conditions associated with reproduction (childbirth) are excluded, the gender difference on morbidity (for 15–44-year-olds) virtually disappears.

Life years lost for those dying before age 65 (1989), ranked by specific type of disease				
Disease category	Male	Rank	Female	Rank
Heart disease	450 979	1	165 248	1
Lung cancer	115 751	3	68 686	3
Motor vehicle traffic accidents	123 799	2	40 195	6
Breast cancer	429	19	150 282	2
Cerebrovascular disease	64 484	5	63 350	4
Suicide and self-inflicted injury	82 161	4	24 050	9
Chronic obstructive pulmonary disease and allied conditions	47 398	6	42 058	5
Colorectal cancer	44 516	7	38 981	7
Cervical cancer	–	–	29 651	8
Pancreatic cancer	16 619	9	15 284	11
Due to alcohol	23 025	8	15 461	10
Diabetes mellitus	13 896	10	12 640	12
Bladder cancer	10 156	13	4 816	16
Diseases of the oesophagus, stomach and duodenum	9 242	15	6 254	13
Accidents caused by fire	8 845	16	5 700	14
Homicide and assault	6 390	17	4 636	17
Accidental drowning	10 624	12	2 239	18
Prostatic cancer	10 942	11	–	–
Accidental poisoning	9 783	14	5 168	15
Laryngeal cancer	4 476	18	1 028	19

Source: Adapted from Godfrey (1993: 186)

Think about it

Look at the table above.

- Identify the highest and lowest ranked causes of death (before 65) in terms of disease, for both males and females.
- Why might deaths in motor vehicle traffic accidents be higher for males than for females? Remember to use your sociological skills to draw up your conclusions.

Gender inequities in health are evident also among lone parents. J. Popay and G. Jones (1990) found that lone parents have poorer health than parents in couples, but that lone fathers were more likely to suffer long-standing illness. On other health indicators, some lone mothers tended to have a worse health record:

- they had poorer socio-economic circumstances;
- they tended to be younger, with less experience and thus fewer life skills;
- they were less likely to own their own homes;
- they were less likely to be in employment;
- they were more likely to be in receipt of means-tested state benefits.

Domestic division of labour

Whilst the impact of work on health and other issues has been examined in the public sphere, it is only relatively recently that researchers have begun to analyse this in the domestic sphere. The fact that most women take ultimate responsibility for household budgets in times of scarcity puts them at a disadvantage in terms of health. For example, it has been found that women are more likely to turn off the heating when at home on their own, and are more likely to ensure that men and children get enough to eat before they do themselves. This is not helped by the fact that within our society women's domestic labour is not granted any economic status; women are therefore likely to feel that they do not contribute to the economy of the household.

Women who are materially disadvantaged are exposed to greater health hazards in the home; however, there are also certain psycho-social aspects of motherhood that seem to be common to both rich and poor. The social and moral pressure to be a 'good mother' transcends social classes: even women in affluent households are likely to be economically dependent and in most households it is women who are responsible for caring activities such as the provision of food and children's clothes. This lack of control, Popay suggests, leads women to neglect their own needs in favour of those around them. It may be factors such as these which are likely to impact on women's higher levels of minor illness.

The diagram below summarises key factors affecting women's health status.

Key factors associated with women's poor health status

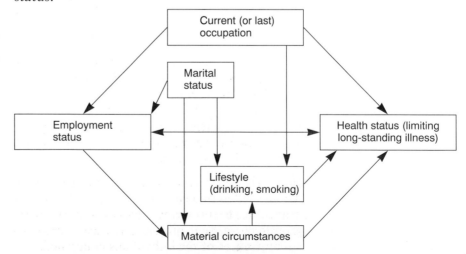

Factors associated with women's health status (restricted activity due to illness)

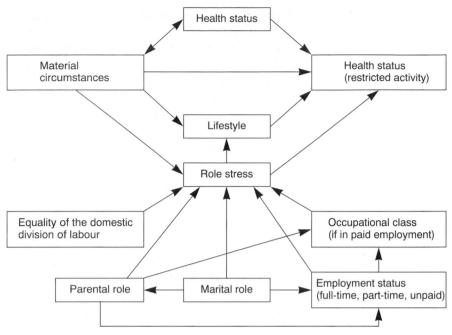

Source: Adapted from H. Roberts (ed.), *Women's Health Counts* (Routledge, 1990)

See also pages 388–90 on women's role as carers.

Age and health inequalities

Much attention has been given to the inequality in the distribution of health associated with age and, in particular, old age. In 1996, there were over 9 million pensioners (around one sixth of the population) in the UK; by the year 2040, about 20 per cent of the population will be over 60 years old. The numbers of the 'very old' (those over 85 years) are increasing rapidly. Sociologists and policy makers in the area of health often see the increasingly ageing population as a major problem. The elderly are:

- less likely to be economically active;
- more likely to be dependent on others;
- more likely to represent a cost to taxpayers (benefits, pensions, etc.);
- more likely to suffer from ill health (and therefore to need health care and state support).

In more specific health terms, old age is seen as leading to:

- increased dependency on state support for geriatric care;
- an increase in degenerative diseases;
- an increase in long-term sickness;
- more restricted activity/mobility;
- increased loneliness for single older people;
- increased need for personal care by family, hospital, residential care or social services support.

It is well documented that many older people have to live on a lower income, often in a situation of poverty, and that this can contribute to ill health. In general terms, illness and diseases tend to affect particular age groups more than others, often associated with the social situation or circumstances of the individuals concerned.

The table below shows significant differences between social classes in respect to the likelihood of their being vulnerable to chronic illness; it also shows, very markedly, the impact of age on the likelihood of becoming chronically ill.

Chronic sickness rates by social class and age, UK (1994)				
Socio-economic group	**Male**		**Female**	
	0–15 years (%)	**65+ years (%)**	**0–15 years (%)**	**65+ years (%)**
Professional	16	57	11	53
Unskilled	28	68	8	65

Source: Adapted from *Social Trends*, 1996

Ethnicity and health inequalities

Issues of 'race' and 'ethnicity' have received relatively little attention within the sociology of health and illness. Evidence suggests that the Asian community has a higher incidence of mortality from coronary heart disease than the general population and, with Afro-Caribbeans, are more at risk from circulatory diseases such as strokes. There are higher reported rates of mental illness amongst the Afro-Caribbean community, with the incidence of schizophrenia being higher than that of the general population. It is possible to suggest that diagnosis by psychiatrists tends to pathologise such groups or cultures and leads to racialisation – to view ethnicity, not class or material conditions, as the key factors in ill health.

A. McNaught (1984) suggests that health authorities have failed both to provide relevant health services, at the point of need, for ethnic minorities, and to develop appropriate strategies to address their needs. However, he sees the social consequences of social inequalities as having more influence on the health status of ethnic minority groups than ethnicity alone.

J. Nettleton's 1993 study noted that amongst Asian women there are lower rates of alcohol and tobacco consumption. In respect to health problems, the women interviewed tended to emphasise social isolation, fear and frequency of racist attacks and damp housing as the main negative influences on their physical and mental health. Here then the racial patterning of health and illness cannot be easily understood until and unless there is an appreciation of the wider experiences of people from ethnic minorities in the UK.

Think about it

- Explain why rates of illness may differ according to ethnicity. Use the information in the table opposite to support your views.
- Explain why smoking patterns differ depending on country of birth.

Summary of main findings of immigrant Mortality Study (England and Wales, 1970–78)	
Mortality by cause	**Comparison with death rates for England and Wales**
Tuberculosis	*High* in immigrants from the Indian sub-continent, Ireland, the Caribbean, Africa and Scotland
Liver cancer	*High* in immigrants from the Indian sub-continent, the Caribbean and Africa
Cancer of stomach, large intestine, breast	*Low* mortality among Indians
Ischaemic heart disease	*High* mortality found in immigrants from the Indian sub-continent
Hypertension and stroke	*Strikingly high* mortality among immigrants from the Caribbean and Africa – four to six times higher for hypertension and twice as high for strokes as the level in England and Wales
Diabetes	*High* among immigrants born in the Caribbean and the Indian sub-continent
Obstructive lung disease (including chronic bronchitis)	*Low* in all immigrants in comparison with ratio for England and Wales
Maternal mortality	*High* in immigrants from Africa, the Caribbean, and to a lesser extent the Indian sub-continent
Violence and accidents	*High* in all immigrant groups

Source: L. Jones

Men's smoking habits (left) and death rates among ethnic males and females (right)

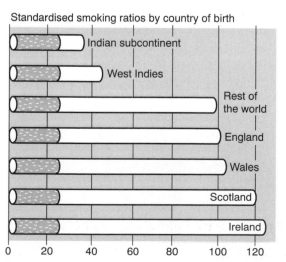

Standardised smoking ratios by country of birth

Indian subcontinent
West Indies
Rest of the world
England
Wales
Scotland
Ireland

0   20   40   60   80   100   120

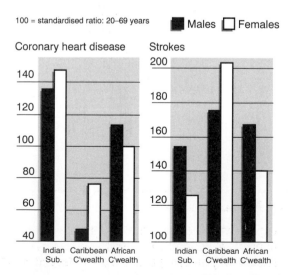

100 = standardised ratio: 20–69 years   ■ Males □ Females

Coronary heart disease   Strokes

Indian Sub. Caribbean C'wealth African C'wealth

Source: R. Balarajan, *Ethnic Differences*

Health inequalities and cultural factors

A number of sociologists have argued that certain social groups are more likely to experience various forms of cultural deprivation than others. We have seen that ethnic minority groups appear more vulnerable to certain health difficulties; the same pattern can be seen to affect other groups. It is suggested, for example, that the working class are much less likely to take their illnesses to their GP than the middle class and, as a consequence, may become more ill. There is considerable evidence that excessive alcohol and cigarette consumption, along with poor diet and bad housing, are likely to affect the health of members of the working class in a negative way. Such cultural-based arguments are often offered as explanations for the differing patterns of morbidity and mortality between different groups in the population, being linked to lifestyle, cultural preferences or limitations of opportunity. Poor health is seen to be caused by patterns of behaviour based on cultural preferences – how, for example, the different social classes apply their cultural knowledge to particular aspects of their lives, such as diet. The increased incidence of smoking (and use of high-tar cigarettes) amongst the working class compared to all other groupings exemplifies this phenomenon. It has been suggested by Edwina Currie, for example (see page 343), that certain groups need to be educated to improve their lifestyles and consequently their health.

Think about it

• What would sociologists say about the view that education would lead to improvements in lifestyle and, subsequently, in the health of sectors of the population?

■ THE SOCIOLOGY OF MEDICINE

The sociology of medicine differs from the sociology of health, as follows:

Sociology of health	Sociology of medicine
• looks at how people strive to maintain their health and the factors affecting their degree of success.	• tries to understand how individuals seek help from doctors and how this help is provided.

What does it mean to become a patient?

D. Tuckett, in his study, *Meetings between Experts* (1985), observed that many self-reporting patients are judged by doctors and consultants to be suffering from trivial complaints, while many people with severe medical difficulties make no effort to consult a doctor. Is our understanding of what illness, symptoms and trivial complaints are, a matter of objective criteria or subjective judgement on the part of both doctor and patient? As Tuckett reminds us, individuals can experience enormous suffering from a condition which medically does not exist, while many medically ill people accommodate themselves to a pattern of deterioration or even remain unaware of their condition for some time.

M. Wadsworth's study of the population of a London borough (*Health and Sickness*, 1971) found that between 75 per cent and 90 per cent of the population over the age of 16 suffered, in any period of two weeks, at least one painful and distressing symptom. However, only about 20 per cent of the total would have visited a doctor, less than 3 per cent attended the out-patients department of a hospital, and only 0.5 per cent were admitted as in-patients. The general findings of such studies are that there is no clear relationship between the seriousness of a symptom and the likelihood of requesting medical help.

One factor that goes some way to explaining this is the level of tolerance that people have to pain. Beecher's study (1977) of patients wounded in battle showed that quite different quantities of morphine were required to relieve the pain from what were apparently similar wounds.

Another factor is the availability of alternative courses of action to consulting a doctor – patent medicines, traditional remedies or other respected opinions. The decision as to whether or not to consult a doctor may be based on factors such as fear, feelings of inevitability or different definitions of symptoms and illness, which may be influenced by cultural factors. I. Zola, for example, found that Americans of Italian, Irish and Anglo-Saxon stock differed in their reasons for consulting a doctor, with Italians seeking help when their social and personal relationships were threatened, the Irish seeking approval for their actions, and the Anglo-Saxons seeking help when their work or physical activity was threatened. D. Tuckett quotes the findings of many other studies and concludes that different social groups have different norms and values concerning the recognition of symptoms and what it is appropriate to do about them. Added to this, however, is prior experience of medical services: individuals weigh up the possible costs and benefits involved before using the medical services. Various studies have shown that many decisions of dying people not to contact the doctor were based on realistic assessments of what could or could not be done for them.

The decision not to consult a doctor may also be influenced by past experience of feeling dependent and helpless; there is also low status in acquiring the position of patient. Financial loss, the effect on family relationships, and past experience of relations with a particular doctor may also be influential.

The doctor–patient relationship

The relationship between a doctor and a patient can be analysed in terms of power and subordination. Ian Kennedy, in his Reith Lectures on the theme 'Unmasking Medicine', in 1980, quoted the example of an assembly line worker who is bored with the tedium of his job and wants a few days at home. He then has to stake a claim to illness, but it is the doctor who has the power to grant or refuse the sick-note. Kennedy points out that health is equated with ability to work, with the doctor in the role of reinforcing the prevailing social and political attitudes and values.

Another aspect of the power of doctors is presented by D. Sudnow's 1967 study of patients declared 'dead on arrival' in American hospitals. Doctors had the power to determine what resuscitation efforts should be made, and Sudnow noted that factors such as age, social background and judgements on character were involved. Even some admissions to UK casualty departments have been shown to depend on whether the patient is deemed to be 'worthy', with 'vagrants' often refused access.

Tuckett puts forward a 'negotiation' model. The doctor may try to establish his or her image of authority by the use of a waiting room, uniform, equipment and administrative procedures; the patient, too, is negotiating during the consultation. Tuckett suggests a number of variables that may influence the relative power positions:

- the extent of the patient's need for help;
- the dependence of the doctor on income from the patient;
- the doctor's self esteem.

The patient tends to be in the much weaker situation: the doctor has many patients, but the patient – usually – has only one doctor.

Think about it

- Look at the table on page 375 and note down:
  – the pattern of access to the medical profession by social class and age;
  – all the factors you can think of which might explain this pattern.

- Summarise the key ideas from the information about Illich (opposite). Present a critical evaluation of Illich's views from a sociological functionalist position.

Percentage of the population reporting acute and chronic illness who consulted their doctor in the previous two weeks				
Socio-economic group	All ages		Over 65	
	1974	1985	1974	1985
Group 1 (professional)	25	27	32	32
Group 2 (intermediate)	27	28	31	26
Group 3 (skilled, non-manual)	31	32	25	30
Group 4 (skilled, manual)	33	29	26	28
Group 5 (semi-skilled)	33	30	26	28
Group 6 (unskilled)	31	34	28	39
Total	32	31	27	29

Source: Adapted from J. Le Grand et al., *Privatisation and the Welfare State*, 1989

The more traditional view of the doctor–patient relationship sees the doctor as an aid or resource to the patient. Beecher, for example, has noted the placebo effect of the patient's belief in professional help and treatment contributing heavily to its success. Other sociologists have put forward more controversial interpretations of the doctor's role, the most prominent among these being that offered by Ivan Illich.

Illich and Kennedy – critical views of the medical profession

Illich sees modern society as creating dependence of individuals on experts and technology. He argues that treatment-caused diseases now account for more suffering than traffic and industrial accidents. Illich claims that he is not against the use of medicines or the development of new ones, but rather is opposed to the domination of professionals who mystify their skills, claiming that only they know what is best for their patient.

A milder but somewhat similar approach was taken by Ian Kennedy in the series of Reith Lectures of 1980 under the title *Unmasking Medicine* (see page 374). Kennedy argued that the nature of modern medicine makes it positively damaging to the health and well-being of the population. He described doctors as new magicians and priests wrapped in the cloak of science and reason, while he would prefer to view a doctor as someone who can care. Like Illich, Kennedy attacks medical science for concentrating on reaction and responses to illnesses rather than on the prevention of them, and he points to the costs involved in terms of both finance and misplaced expectations. For Kennedy, the need is to:

• use medical resources more effectively;
• curb our continual use of medicine in the form of complex technology;
• improve the health education service;
• pay particular attention to the disadvantaged groups at the bottom of the socio-economic ladder.

It is, of course, debatable as to how valid are the criticisms of Illich and the more moderate Kennedy. Nevertheless, it is interesting that medical science has come under increasing attack at a time when the scientific approach to sociology is out of favour and environmentalists are pointing to the pollution and devastation caused by so-called scientific and technological advances.

The sociology of the medical profession

The doctor–patient relationship is of particular interest to sociologists, since most of us, when ill, would look to our local GP (general practitioner) for initial assistance. However, there is a wide range of health care professionals who deal with our needs. These include GPs, hospital doctors, anaesthetists, nurses, midwives, psychiatrists, psychiatric nurses, health visitors, dentists, opticians, etc.

Sociologists have long been interested in looking at these professional groups and seeking to understand and explain why they are so influential in our society. Many have begun by defining the characteristics of an ideal-typical profession. This model includes the possession of systematic intellectual knowledge, which requires extended education and specialised training. Qualifications provide the basis for the organisation of professionals into associations which regulate the conduct of their members by ethical codes of practice. These associations – in medicine, the two major bodies are the British Medical Association and the Royal College of Nursing – would claim to be more orientated to providing a public service than to enhancing their own self interests. H.L. Wilensky identified five necessary stages in the movement from occupation to profession:

1. the emergence of a full-time occupation;
2. the institutionalisation of specialist training;
3. the establishment of a professional association;
4. the recourse to legislation to secure the recognition and protection of the association;
5. the formulation of a code of professional conduct.

The model consists of a list of elements taken from certain old established professions, mainly law and medicine.

There are a number of key characteristics that distinguish a profession from an occupation:

- skills based on theoretical knowledge;
- the provision of training;
- offering a service for others;
- represented by a recognisable organisation;
- assessment of competence on entry and during practice, usually by examinations;
- a professional code of conduct or ethics;
- a claim to specific 'expertise'.

Doctors are socialised by their training into seeing themselves as 'experts', and society allocates them to that role and status. This expert status provides doctors with considerable power which, in turn, gives them much control over many aspects of the lives of disabled or ill persons. With respect to disabled people, this includes a key role in decisions over:

- whether unborn disabled babies should live or not;
- where disabled people live;
- whether they can or should work;
- what school they should go to;

- what benefits they should be entitled to;
- what services they should receive;
- whether they should have children;
- whether 'brain dead' patients must or should be kept alive by technology (though in some cases this decision has been taken by the courts).

Many of these decisions are based on considerations of what constitutes 'normality' for the non-ill and the non-disabled and are, therefore, a **social construct**.

The development of the medical profession

During the nineteenth century, medical practitioners sought to enhance their profession and ensure that they were the only group entitled to offer a medical service. This they did by joining together in a single profession, leading eventually to the formation of the British Medical Association (BMA). At the end of the nineteenth century, a range of trade unions and Friendly Societies began to offer insurance protection for sections of the working class. These organisations employed doctors on a full- or part-time basis, and gave the doctors access to a section of the population which had not previously had access to medical provision. The National Health Service Act 1946 strengthened the position of doctors within a state-run health service offering universal health care.

In the 1950s, doctors possessed the ability to determine which issues were or were not placed on the health policy agenda. Indeed, some policies were not pursued by government because of anticipated opposition by the medical profession. This clearly demonstrates the considerable influence of this professional group at the time. Their power and influence was further enhanced by the exclusion of non-professionals from the area of debate on health issues and policies. Any government intent on introducing change in the NHS or medical care generally had to take into account the views of the medical profession in order to alter policy. After the 1979 general election, however, Margaret Thatcher's government set out to challenge the power of professional groups such as doctors (as well as lawyers and teachers) and subsequently to alter many aspects of health care provision. This had direct consequences on medical professionals.

It has been argued that, well into the 1980s, doctors had a fair degree of professional autonomy:

- economic autonomy – the right to determine their own pay;
- political autonomy – the right of doctors to make policy decisions as the legitimate experts on health matters;
- technical autonomy – the right of the profession to set its own standards and to control clinical performance.

Since the mid 1980s, however, the monopoly position of the medical profession has been subject to critical scrutiny and a range of changes have affected their autonomy. Such changes include:

- changes in morbidity (degenerative diseases such as cancer and heart disease have replaced infectious diseases as the major influence on morbidity);
- more emphasis on preventative medicine;
- policy moves towards community care;

- primary health community-based initiatives;
- the growth of other specialised occupational groups, for example paramedics, physiotherapists;
- divisions between junior hospital doctors and consultants over hours, pay, conditions;
- NHS reforms since 1991, with more emphasis on managers rather than medical consultants running the Hospital Trusts;
- GP budget-holding, which has split those GPs with budgets from those without, the latter often being in poorer urban areas.

Marxist writers such as D. McKinlay and K. Stoeckle (1988) argue that the logic of capitalism is bringing about radical change in medicine and the medical profession. A loss of professional control has been identified in areas such as:

- the content of training;
- criteria for entrance to the profession;
- form and content of work;
- patient groups;
- tools of labour (equipment, drugs);
- means of labour (premises);
- amount of remuneration.

Reforms to the NHS have ensured that doctors working in the state system are now managed directly and have less say over the form and extent of their work, whilst those who work in the private sector are likely to be less controlled or regulated than their NHS counterparts.

The impact of changes on the professional role

Pressure for change from government and from patients (consumers) is likely to continue well into the twenty-first century. If the medical profession is to retain its position of importance in health care matters, some would argue, it will need to consider its relationship with its patients and the extent to which doctors retain power and control or not. R. Gomm (1993) refers to the health and welfare services as contributing to the oppression of the poorer and more vulnerable sections of society and suggests that it is possible to offer examples of ways in which such relationships (between doctors and patients, for example), might be altered for their mutual benefit. He notes three forms of relationship:

- a **disabling relationship**, where doctors would exploit patients for their own benefit. This is similar to the views of Ivan Illich;
- a **brokerage relationship**, where doctors serve as brokers or referents between a range of, for example, community services such as chiropody and the users/patients themselves;
- a **helping relationship**, where doctors work with users/patients to identify the most appropriate forms of health care provision to suit their particular needs.

All the relationships noted above, to differing degrees, still prioritise the power of the doctor, as noted by the functionalist sociologist T. Parsons (1955). Gomm suggests that all parties to a consultation, doctor and patient, should share their knowledge about the health issue.

The provision of health care

The providers of health care services can be categorised into four groupings, as illustrated in the following table:

Voluntary services	The private sector	The NHS, social services, housing, education and other departments	Informal carers
• Meals on Wheels	• Chiropodist	• Community nurses	• Family
• Charities	• Taxi services	• Occupational therapists	• Friends
• Housing associations	• Private residential and nursing homes	• Benefits advisers	• Neighbours
	• Private medical care		

- **Voluntary services** include a range of organisations which provide health care and basic social services. These organisations, often with charitable status, offer care to people at home, in supported or sheltered housing, in special projects such as hospices, and for specific groups such as single homeless people or people with various types of disability. Examples include Shelter and Marie Curie hospices.
- The **private sector** are providers who are running a health care provision business, and would include private nursing homes, BUPA and other large medical insurance companies, private hospitals and non-NHS doctors and dentists.
- The **public sector** – in this case the National Health Service – includes hospitals offering various services: accident and emergency facilities; psychiatric care; general care; teaching; maternity care; specialist care (for example Stoke Mandeville hospital for spinal injuries). It also includes GPs' practices, some dentists, some physiotherapists, community psychiatric nurses and health visitors. It is closely linked to educational and social service provision at local level, particularly through community-based meetings between different professionals, for example GPs, social workers, health visitors, etc.
- **Informal carers** is the term used to describe the caring for ill or dependent people by their families or the local community. The burden of informal care usually falls to women, who comprise the vast majority of informal carers.

All of these groups can be seen to contribute to an overall pattern of health and community care for the population. One of the key points for consideration for sociologists, however, is the extent to which each of these groups should provide such provision.

State or non-state health care?

State provision, under the principles on which the National Health Service was formed in 1947, included the following basic commitments:

- to be available to the whole population;
- to provide equal access to people in need of health care;
- to be free to all users at the point of use;

- to be comprehensive in what was provided;
- to provide health services of a good standard to everyone, irrespective of where they lived, who they were or how much they earned.

The NHS offered state provision which was based on the idea of being a public service and aiming to be egalitarian in ethos (treating all patients with equal respect). However, the form and level of provision in the late twentieth and early twenty-first centuries looks very different from that proposed in 1946. J. Allsop, in *Health Policy and the NHS* (1995), notes a number of reasons why state provision by the NHS has changed, particularly how it has changed since the 1970s. She identifies a number of problems which have led to a need to alter the form and extent of NHS provision:

- problems of management – seen as inefficient and wasteful;
- problems of resources – the demand for equipment etc. has increased as the range of available technology has mushroomed;
- problems of cost;
- problems relating to value for money – with increased political pressure for all public services to provide this;
- alternative ways of providing health care.

There is increasing evidence of the growth of the private sector as a provider of health care (see the tables below), although the public sector still pays for – and provides – the vast majority.

Private medical insurance	
1979	5 per cent of the population had private medical insurance
1981	7.3 per cent of the population had private medical insurance (1.87 million people)
1989	13 per cent of the population had private medical insurance
1991	12 per cent of the population had private medical insurance (3.43 million people)
1996	16 per cent of the population had private medical insurance

Provision and funding of care by the public and private sectors	Care provided by public sector		Care provided by private sector	
	Funded by public sector (%)	Funded by private sector (%)	Funded by public sector (%)	Funded by private sector (%)
Elective surgery (1986)	83	0	2	15
Long-term elderly care (1989)	44	20	7	29
Acute psychiatric care (1989)	93	0	0	7
Long-term mentally ill (1988)	82	18	0	0
Long-term mentally handicapped (1988)	82	18	0	0

Source: Adapted from B. Baggott, *Health and Health Care in Britain* (Macmillan, 1994)

In 1990, W. Laing's *Review of Private Health Care* estimated that the private sector share of UK hospital-based health care had increased from 7.5 per cent to 15 per cent since 1984. In 1989, P. Nicholl had already noted an increase of 48 per cent in the number of in-patients treated by private hospitals between 1981 and 1986.

Hospital funding

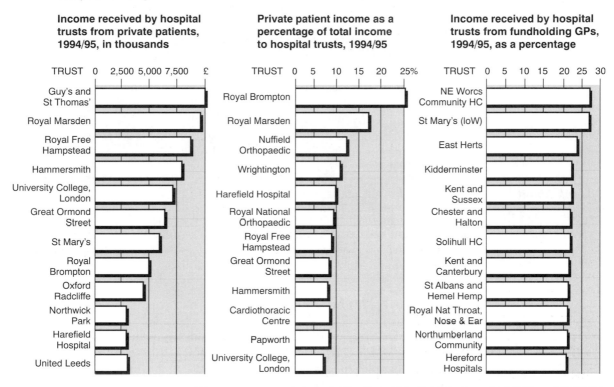

Income received by hospital trusts from private patients, 1994/95, in thousands

Private patient income as a percentage of total income to hospital trusts, 1994/95

Income received by hospital trusts from fundholding GPs, 1994/95, as a percentage

Fundholding GPs and non-fundholding GPs

Before 1991 there were no fixed medical budgets and patients were treated according to clinical need. From 1991 GPs had the choice of becoming fundholding or non-fundholding. Non-fundholders send their patients to hospitals where the health authority has already agreed a budget by purchasing a set number of procedures for a fixed price. Fundholders negotiate with their local health authorities to pay for all their patients' medical treatment outside the practice if they want to. They can then decide how and where that money should be spent. Approximately half the country's GPs became fundholders, though figures vary from region to region.

In 1997 the Labour government proposed the ending of the fund-holding system, as fund-holding practices were perceived as getting priority in hospital services.

Operation costs

There are no standard rates for operations within the National Health Service. One hospital may charge £8,000 for an operation that costs £1,500 elsewhere. A hospital will impose a high charge for a surgical procedure if it is not interested in performing it. A low price may well reflect the fact that a hospital has fulfilled its annual contract to the local health authority, and is offering an operation at a discounted price to attract extra custom to use up its surplus capacity.

Source: The *Guardian*, 28 May 1996

The free-market approach

This view sees the state health service in crisis, not as a consequence of inequalities of outcome nor of lack of resources, but rather as the consequence of the drain on the state of subsidised medical and welfare services. Proposals for change include:

- reorganisation and the setting up of private medical care;
- a shift of burden (for example of cost) to individuals and organisations via private health care (BUPA schemes, etc.)

In the USA, in 1984, V. Navarro looked at how the Reagan administration saw health and care provision as having a negative impact on the economy because of:

- too great an expenditure on health care and not enough on industry;
- the restrictive nature of health and safety legislation and its effects on the competitiveness of American industry;
- the bureaucratic inefficiency of the state's health schemes (proposing instead more privatisation of medical services).

Think about it

- Why, since the late 1970s, has there been an increase in private health care provision?
- What major difficulties have you identified in the provision of health care offered by the NHS?

Community care

Health care systems throughout the world are creating and developing frameworks for care based in the community. It is seen to be more relevant to people's needs (the needs of both carers and cared for) and a more cost-effective way of providing a service. The idea of community care is based on a number of key principles:

- more emphasis on care and support at home;
- the movement of caring professions to work in communities rather than in large-scale institutions such as psychiatric hospitals;
- the active engagement of members of the community (individually and collectively) in the provision of care for those in need;
- a move away from hospital-based services;
- emphasis on care for the elderly and the mentally ill in the community.

In the UK, the basic intention of community-care legislation was to meet the needs of individuals and groups who require long-term care. The problems of cost and value for money have been addressed during the last two decades of the twentieth century through the government's attempts to ensure that doctors (GPs specifically) offer a more efficient and cost-effective service to their patients, in their local communities. The closure of psychiatric hospitals and an increased move towards community care were seen as possible ways to reduce reliance on state provision. Indeed, 'Care in the Community' was intended to offer quality care, to reduce costs, to allow local communities (GPs, health visitors, community psychiatric nurses, midwives, etc.) to take more responsibility for health care, and to shift the emphasis of provision from 'treatment and care' to 'prevention' of illness and ill health.

The table below, indicating a continuous rise in the numbers of registered disabled people living in private households may be seen as 'proof positive' of the working of Care in the Community.

Estimated and projected numbers of people with disabilities living in private households, by age: Great Britain 1968–2001				
Age group	Degree of disability	1968–69 (000s)	1981 (000s)	2001 (000s)
16–64	Very severe	42	42	44
	Severe	120	123	131
	Appreciable	215	220	233
	Total	377	385	408
65–74	Very severe	35	42	37
	Severe	99	123	108
	Appreciable	206	257	224
	Total	340	422	369
75 and over	Very severe	80	109	126
	Severe	123	170	197
	Appreciable	172	240	278
	Total	375	519	601
16 and over	Very severe	157	193	207
	Severe	342	416	436
	Appreciable	593	717	735
	Total	1092	1326	1378

Source: Adapted from A. Harris, (HMSO, 1971) and 'Populations Projections 1978–2018 (HMSO, 1980) cited in J. Allsop, *Health Policy and the NHS* (Longman, 1995)

Meeting needs

According to R. Baggott's 1994 study, *Health and Health Care in Britain*, 60 per cent of the expenditure on hospital and community health services is spent on the elderly and children, 10 per cent on the mentally ill and 5 per cent on services for people with learning difficulties.

Many aspects of community care provision fall on the voluntary sector, with care being provided by close relatives (usually women) for dependent family members (the old, the very young, the ill or disabled). Richard Titmuss, a major writer on post-war social policy, warned in 1968 that the phrase 'community care' conjured up wishful images of 'warmth and human kindness, essentially personal and comforting' whereas in fact one consequence of the introduction of community care has been to focus provision on the family and, specifically, on 'privatised female care'. It is women who become the carers in the domestic environment of the home.

Carers

Many dependent people are cared for by relatives or friends who provide their services free of charge. There are 6 million of these informal carers in the UK, 6 out of 10 of whom are women.

How many?

14% of British adults are looking after someone who is mentally or physically disabled, ill or frail. One in 5 households contain someone who is caring for someone else.

How old?

The peak age for caring is 45 to 64. The lives of 1 in 5 people in this age group are restricted by their caring responsibilities. Carers look after people of all ages: see below.

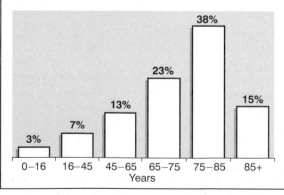

Who needs them?

Carers are looking after people with all kinds of disabilities:

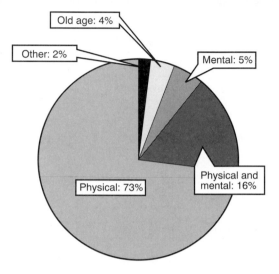

Old age: 4%
Other: 2%
Mental: 5%
Physical: 73%
Physical and mental: 16%

The consequences

■ 57% of all carers who spend more than 20 hours a week caring for someone in the same house cannot take a break of 2 days; 8% of them find it very difficult to get away for even 2 hours.

■ Half of all carers have long-standing health problems.

■ One fifth of all carers look after more than 1 person.

■ A quarter of them have been caring for someone for over 10 years.

Source: Adapted from the *Guardian*, 12 May 1992

Of the six million informal carers looking after sick, disabled or elderly people in the UK, a quarter of them spend 20-plus hours a week on care. Around 60 per cent of carers are women, with over a quarter of these in the 45–64 age group.

Community care recipients and agencies/providers

People who receive community care	Community care agencies/providers
• Elderly people • The chronically (i.e. long-term) sick and disabled • People with mental health problems • People with mental disabilities • Children	• Health authority community nurses, psychiatric nurses, mental handicap nurses, district nurses, health visitors • Other health staff, for example, bath nurses • Social services departments – social workers • Home helps • Meals on Wheels • Local authority residential homes • Sheltered housing (local authority) • Day centres • Voluntary provision such as St John's Ambulance and Red Cross • Self-help groups and community centres

Source: L. Jones, *The Social Context of Health and Health Care* (1994)

The Griffiths Report 1988

The Griffiths Report made recommendations for the provision of care in the community (see page 386). It set out a framework for those in need of certain types of health and social service provision to receive this within their local community rather than, as previously, in a long-term-stay institution.

In 1991, a White Paper 'Caring for People' offered four key components of community care as follows:

• services that respond flexibly and sensitively to the needs of individuals and their carers;
• services that intervene no more than is necessary to foster independence;
• services that allow a range of options for consumers;
• services that concentrate on those with the greatest needs.

A critical view of community care provision

The promotion of private residential care for the elderly has been a major government initiative; by 1989 only 43 per cent of long-term institutional care was provided in the public sector. Despite the government's commitment, a number of difficulties with the policy can be noted:

• problems of over funding;
• problems with planning;
• poor standards of community care provision – some private nursing homes offer poor service and little relevant or good-quality provision for the mentally ill. Informal carers are often in need of support which is rarely available.

Furthermore, critics suggest that increased use of the voluntary sector is an attempt to privatise health provision, creating difficulties with the NHS Hospital Trusts and services.

The Griffiths Report:
main findings

1.1 I recommend that the following steps be taken to create better opportunities for the successful and efficient delivery of community care policies for adults who are mentally ill, mentally handicapped, elderly or physically disabled and similar groups.

1.2 Central government should ensure that there is a Minister of State in DHSS [Department of Health and Social Security], seen by the public as being clearly responsible for community care. His role should be strengthened and clarified in the light of the other recommendations.

1.3 Local social services authorities should, with the resources available:

1.3.1 Assess the community care needs of their locality, set local priorities and service objectives, and develop local plans in consultation with health authorities in particular (but also others including housing authorities, voluntary bodies, and private providers of care) for delivering those objectives.

1.3.2 Identify and assess individuals' needs, taking full account of personal preferences (and those of informal carers), and design packages of care best suited to enabling the consumer to live as normal a life as possible.

1.3.3 Arrange the delivery of packages of care to individuals, building first on the available contribution of informal carers and neighbourhood support, then the provision of domiciliary and day services or, if appropriate, residential care.

1.3.4 Act for these purposes as the designers, organisers and purchasers of non-health care services, and not primarily as direct providers, making the maximum possible use of voluntary and private sector bodies to widen consumer choice, stimulate innovation and encourage efficiency.

1.4 To enable this to happen, local social services authorities must be put into a position to take a more comprehensive view of care needs and services.

1.5 Equally to enable action to be taken, local social services authorities will need confidence that their resources can match their responsibilities. Therefore:

1.5.1 Central government should arrange for the necessary transfer of resources between central and local government to match the defined responsibilities.

1.6 It is further recommended that:

1.6.1 Health authorities should continue to be responsible for medically required community health services, including making any necessary input into assessing needs and delivering packages of care.

1.6.2 General medical practitioners should be responsible for ensuring that local social services authorities are aware of their patients' needs for non-health care.

1.6.3 Public housing authorities should be responsible for providing and financing only the 'bricks and mortar' of housing for community care.

1.6.4 Authorities should have the power to act jointly, or as agents for each other.

1.6.5 Distribution of specific grants should take account of the extent to which consumers in a local authority area are able to meet the full economic cost of services.

1.6.6 The functions of a 'community carer' should be developed into a new occupation, with appropriate training so that one person can, as far as possible, provide whatever personal and practical assistance an individual requires.

Source: Department of Health, 1988

Walker (1993) sees the primary intention of community care policy during the 1980s and 1990s in the negative sense of reducing the role of health services in care provision. A major consequence has been the official encouragement of the private sector to take a more active part. With respect to residential homes for the elderly, the idea of consumer choice is often limited by conditions for admission: confused or demented people or those who are difficult to control are often excluded.

The policy of mental hospital closures was at first resisted by hospital staff, keen to protect their own interests. Their resistance was overcome, however, and the policy has succeeded in ensuring that the number of patients in hospital has been significantly reduced. Even so, critics have pointed to a number of difficulties associated with the rapid rate at which the change was implemented. These include:

- poor planning and preparation;
- limited consultation;
- under-resourcing in terms of finance, suitable alternative accommodation, appropriately trained and qualified community-based staff;
- lack of support for ex-patients.

Between 1975 and 1985 there was a 70 per cent increase in the number of people with mental disabilities in local authority homes and a 154 per cent increase of those in private homes.

Walker noted three key elements to the government's community care provision:

- fragmentation of providers;
- marketisation, involving the private sector (the potential 'opportunities' and 'risks' of this policy can be seen in the table below);
- decentralisation of administration and operations.

The opportunities and risks in an emerging community care market	
Opportunities	**Risks**
more choice for purchasers and service users	service fragmentation and loss of strategy
efficient division of responsibilities between agencies	wasteful duplication and rivalry
innovation and creativity	diminishing public accountability
devolved authority and budgets	inequalities and inequities in redistributing resources
developing quality and cost-effective services	putting cost and savings before quality
efficient management and information systems	raiding resources from direct provision
constructive consultation and cooperation	confrontation between commissioners and providers
partnership between providers	monopoly and duopoly provision
contracts define responsibilities and expectations	short-termism creates instability and uncertainties
consensus between purchasers and providers	special interest alliances exclude users

Gender and health – women, caring and carers

The emergence of a feminist sociology in the 1960s and 1970s brought an interest in the health implications of women's position in society. Initially, this interest focused on women as recipients of health care, particularly on the way in which women's health problems were defined within medicine, and on the medical control of all aspects of women's lives, especially their reproductive lives. Sociologists' interest moved from women's reproductive role, to their social role in the domestic sphere and then to the interaction between the many social roles that women fulfil. Graham's 1987 study, *Women, Health and the Family*, found significant and systematic differences in the health experiences of women and men in Britain.

Many factors have combined to broaden sociology's perspective:

- the realisation that, despite the National Health Service, social class inequalities in health remain and appear to be deepening;
- the increasing proportion of elderly people in the population;
- the concern of governments to reduce the costs of the NHS, thus directing sociology's attention to the world beyond the hospital;
- the development of health policies that stress health promotion in the community;
- the role that individuals can play in keeping themselves healthy.

Women's experiences, both of health and of health care, are seen by sociologists as related to their position in society, which is often based on their role as the caretakers of other people's health: in childhood, adulthood and old age. The sociology of women's health places a major emphasis on the connections between women's health and women's reproductive and caring role.

Within the sociology of health, feminist theory has placed some new areas on the agenda:

- the influence of material conditions on women's health, with studies exploring the effects of urban deprivation, housing, social isolation and poverty;
- the relationship between women's paid employment and their health, looking at women's reproductive and caring work, both paid and unpaid;
- their experiences of pregnancy and childbirth, of childcare and domestic labour, and of caring for the elderly and the disabled in the community;
- women's paid role as carers in the NHS and private medicine.

Across the range of health services, women are the major recipients. For example, while only 5 per cent of the elderly population in the UK are in hospital or residential care, the majority (over 75 per cent) of these long-term residents are women. The fact that it is not so much 'old age' as 'women's old age' that is being defined and managed in these institutional settings has only recently been highlighted as an issue for sociologists of health. As a result, sociology has barely begun to explore and to understand the consequences of this 'feminisation' of institutional care for those who live and those who work there.

Medical sociology's view of the patient's role was narrowly defined in relation to the roles of doctors and nurses. As a result, patients whose needs were met on a voluntary and non-professional basis received little attention. Yet we now know that most health care is provided by and in the community – by relatives, neighbours and friends. Recent surveys suggest that in the UK there are between one and two million people over 16 years of age with an appreciable or severe handicap who are being cared for in the community. Women outnumber men among this population, particularly among the older age group.

There are 1.2 million carers living in the community with children and adults whose disabilities are such that they need help with the tasks of daily living. In addition, it is estimated that there are around 130,000 carers supporting those with special needs who live alone. Added to this figure, there are 6.5 million parents acting as the primary carer to their children who, while not disabled, are under 16 years of age.

We know that 'care by/in the community' almost always means care by/in the family, with little support from outside. We also know that family care is a myth: one person tends to be identified as the main carer and, once identified, other relatives withdraw. In the vast majority of cases, the principal carer is a woman and a relative of the dependent person.

Studies of community care point not only to a link between women and caring, but also to a link between caring and loss of income. Lost work opportunities – through giving up a job, going part-time or not pursuing promotion – have a marked economic impact on carers. It is only in recent years that attempts have been made to quantify this economic impact. Studies suggest that women carers, like those they care for, tend to be economically dependent on the earnings of partners or on social security. Where carers have paid jobs, it is typically in the low-paid sector of the economy – working at times and in places that fit in with their caring commitments.

The NHS pyramid

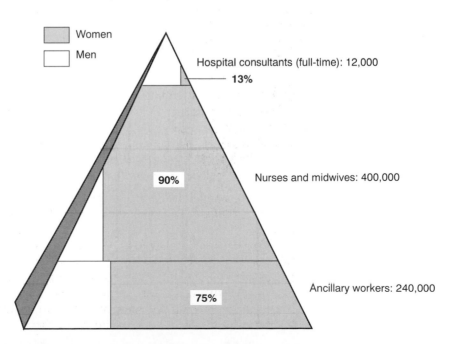

About 75 per cent of those employed by the NHS are women. However, while paid health work is largely women's work, it tends to be controlled by doctors and administrators who are men.

If we look at the composition of staff in old people's homes, we find that 80 per cent are women. Similarly, 75 per cent of the staff in children's homes are women. And nearly all home helps, nursery nurses and nursery school teachers are women. Caring in the community and caring within the labour market are not always mutually exclusive. A large number of women do both, caring at home for their family and taking on paid jobs where they provide care for others.

P. Simpkin (1979) refers to the notion of 'caring' as ideology, going on to state that it represents a form of moral and political control. Whilst his analysis was directed at the role of social workers (a caring profession), it is possible to argue that some of his ideas might equally apply to the position which women carers find themselves in. He offers the view that any helping relationship is, by definition, unequal, as one party is partly or wholly in the hands of the other. At the same time the carer will find themselves unable to obtain relief from the caring role.

Think about it

- Provide a list of reasons why women become the main carers.
- Having done this, consider how 'Care in the Community' might have affected women's role as carers.
- To what extent might government changes in health care be primarily economic? Offer a case *for* and *against* this view.
- In what ways has the focus of Sociology in respect to health care changed in the past twenty years?

Revision and practice tasks

Task 1: structured question

(a) Briefly explain how **two** aspects of people's occupations may influence their health. [4]

(b) Briefly explain **two** ways in which unemployment influences people's health. [4]

(c) Outline the evidence for the existence of **either** ethnic **or** gender inequalities in health in the UK. [7]

(d) Critically assess the view that class differences in health can be explained by different lifestyle choices. [10]

Total: 25 marks

Task 2: structured question

(a) Briefly outline how ideas of health and illness vary between societies. [4]

(b) Identify and briefly explain **two** factors, other than advances in medical care, which have improved the health of the population. [4]

(c) Outline the evidence for the view that individual differences in health and illness are not caused solely by biological or psychological factors. [7]

(d) Critically assess sociological explanations of class inequalities in health. [10]

Total: 25 marks

Essay questions

1. What sociological explanations have been offered for the continued existence of inequities in health in the UK?

2. Discuss the view that the medical profession possesses too much power.

3. To what extent can it be argued that doctor–patient relationships have become more equal during the last decade?

4. Is social class the most significant factor affecting a person's health? Support your view by referring to appropriate sociological research.

5. What impact has the introduction of community care had on any one designated group?

6. Discuss the view that community care initiatives have merely served to make disadvantaged groups (for example the mentally ill, the elderly) even more disadvantaged.

Ideas for course work and personal studies

1. Interview two health care professionals working in two different localities about the factors which contribute to ill-health within their locality. Compare the factors which are common to both areas, and those which differ.

2. Compare mortality rates from specific causes within a locality – 100 and 50 years ago – with those today, seeking to explain any differences you discover.

3. Research the extent to which cigarettes, despite controls, are still advertised, and how this affects the attitudes of young people – and perhaps their parents – towards issues of health and smoking.

4. Contact two or three major companies, and use other secondary sources available to you locally, to examine the extent of private health care in your locality. Carry out a small survey of the attitudes of both participants and non-participants, towards private health care.

5. Carry out a questionnaire-based survey in your locality to find out which age groups and social class groups seem to adopt healthy lifestyles in terms of their physical activity, work and leisure patterns, diet, etc.

Selected reading list

Asylums: Essays on the Social Situation of Mental Patients and Other Inmates, Erving Goffman (Aldine, Chigago, 1961)

Beyond Community Care, S. Ramon (Pluto, 1990)

'The Black Report', P. Townsend and N. Davidson in *Inequalities in Health*, P. Townsend, N. Davidson and M. Whitehead (eds) (Penguin, 1982)

Contemporary British Society, N. Abercrombie and A. Warde (Polity Press, 1994)

The Myth of Mental Illness, Thomas Szasz (Hoeber-Harper, New York, 1961)

The Outsiders, H. Becker (The Free Press, New York, 1963)

The Social System, Talcott Parsons (Routledge & Kegan Paul, 1951)

Stigma, Erving Goffman (Prentice Hall Inc., Englewood Cliffs, NJ, 1964)

'Unmasking medicine', Ian Kennedy (The Reith Lectures, 1980)

The Welfare State and Equality, H.L. Wilensky (University of California Press, 1975)

8 Poverty and welfare

Introduction

Britain's social services – education, health care, housing, social security benefits, etc. – constitute what is commonly referred to as the **Welfare State**. The term is used to describe the role of the state which seeks to make sure that there is a minimum standard of health, hygiene and living standards for all the population. The implication is that the Welfare State is a comprehensive and coherent institution that has successfully tackled a wide range of social problems. Such problems are significantly different from **sociological** problems, which relate to the theories and ideologies which form an ongoing debate.

This unit will include:

- the nature and extent of poverty, including its definitions, theories and explanations;
- the distribution of poverty, with reference to gender, ethnicity and social class, including the underclass debate;
- theories and ideologies of welfare, including welfare as social control, policies on the funding of welfare and the redistribution of wealth;
- the origins of the welfare system and social policy in terms of the role of the state and the private and voluntary sectors.

The nature and extent of poverty

Definitions of poverty

Particularly over the past century, there have been sociological and political debates about what is understood by poverty. A lot of the discussion has been about whether poverty should be defined in **absolute** terms or in **relative** terms. A tradition has been to define poverty in terms of the relationship between a person's income or resources and that which is required for a healthy life.

Absolute poverty

Important pioneering empirical research work was undertaken by **Charles Booth** (1840–1916) and **Seebohm Rowntree** (1871–1954). Booth's *The Life and Labour of the People of London* was published in 17 volumes between 1891 and 1903. Booth calculated that an income of 18–21 shillings was needed to maintain a moderate family with food, rent and clothing in London. Those with an income below this were in absolute poverty. A certain level of income was perceived as being the **poverty line**.

In 1899, Rowntree examined the extent of poverty in York. He consulted the work of Dr Dunlop, a nutritionist who had experimented with the diet of Scottish prisoners. Rowntree established an absolute poverty line based on the cost of providing 3500 calories per day for men involved in moderate muscular work and then adding to it the cost of clothes and shelter and adjusting it according to family size. He established, for example, that the minimum clothing needs of a young woman were:

> 'one pair of boots, 2 aprons, 1 second-hand dress, 1 skirt made from an old dress, shawl, jacket, 2 pairs of stockings, 1 pair of old boots worn as slippers, and one-third the cost of a new hat.'
> B.S. Rowntree, 1899

As a result of his research, Rowntree's *Poverty: A Study of Town Life* was published in 1902. It concluded, for example, that a worker with three dependent children and an income of less than 21s 8d per week was in '**primary poverty**'. To qualify for primary poverty:

> 'The children must have no pocket money for dolls, marbles or sweets. The father must smoke no tobacco and drink no beer. The mother must never buy any pretty clothes for herself or her children, the character of the family wardrobe as for the family diet being governed by the regulation "nothing must be bought but that which is absolutely necessary for the maintenance of physical health and what is bought must be of the plainest and most economic description".'
> B.S. Rowntree, *Poverty: A Study of Town Life* (Macmillan, 1902)

Those whose income was marginally above this, but who still did not have what Rowntree perceived as the 'basic necessities', were in '**secondary poverty**'. Rowntree calculated that 28 per cent of the population were in poverty, with 10 per cent of these in primary poverty and 18 per cent in secondary poverty.

Pictures of poverty in 1899

- No occupation. Married. Age sixty-four. Two rooms. The man 'has not had his boots on' for twelve months. He is suffering from dropsy. His wife cleans schools. This house shares one closet with eight other houses and one water tap with four others.

- Widow. Four rooms. Grandson (eleven) sleeps here. Parish relief. Woman takes lodgers when she can get them, but that is seldom. Do not know how she manages to live.

- Charwoman. Two rooms. Son twenty. Casual labourer. Husband in workhouse. Dirt and drink in plenty. This house shares one water tap with six other houses and one closet with two others.

- Retired soldier. Married. Three rooms. One child. Parish relief. Husband, after serving twelve years in India, receiving no pension. Dying of consumption; poverty stricken. This house shares one closet with another house.

- Tailor. Married. Four rooms. Six children, school age or under. Apparently very steady and industrious. Home fairly clean and comfortable. Landlord has warned them to 'look for another house' as he objects to so many children.

- Age 38. Labourer. Married. Three rooms. Six children, school age or under. Wife used to go out to work but cannot do so now. House clean, but damp and almost uninhabitable. There are eleven houses in this yard and three houses join at one closet.

- Bricklayer's labourer. Married. Two rooms. Three children, school age or under. Young wife. Both man and wife drink. Children dirty. Sanitation as at no. 31 . . . there is one ashpit for this yard; it is full to the top, and slime running down the walls.

Source: J. Roll, *Understanding Poverty* (Family Studies Centre, 1992)

In summary, Rowntree's attempts to show that there was a huge amount of poverty in England in the 1890s hinged on his maintaining that there were three essential costs to everyone:

- food, in terms of a basic diet to maintain good health;
- clothing, in terms of the minimum needed for protection against wet and cold conditions;
- housing, in terms of the average rent paid by working-class people at the time.

Interestingly, Conservative governments, particularly under Margaret Thatcher in the 1980s and 1990s, supported the notion of an absolute definition of poverty. They tended to argue that the aim of welfare benefits and social policy should not be to improve the living conditions of the poorer members of society but merely to ensure that such groups had a basic standard of living.

Think about it

- Rowntree considered three basic costs (food, clothing and housing) to calculate the extent of poverty in Victorian England. How might such basic costs be calculated a century later?
- What other essential costs do you think may need to be considered in relation to the poor of Britain today?
- What do you think might be the criticisms made of concentrating on an absolute definition of poverty?

The use of absolute criteria for defining poverty has been criticised for a number of reasons. Although termed 'absolute', calculations are based on subjective definitions of what is perceived as being necessary. Perceptions of what is necessary change over time and vary between individuals and families. Rowntree himself was aware that what is perceived as being poverty today will change as living standards rise tomorrow. For example, for his second survey of York in 1936, 'human needs' were increased to include possession of a radio, books, a holiday, beer and tobacco. Rowntree's 1899 research was repeated, using similar methodology, in York in 1936 and 1950. In 1936, 18 per cent of the population in York were considered to be in poverty, while by 1950 this figure had fallen to 1.5 per cent. It was perceived that poverty had been almost totally eradicated as a result of economic expansion (and full employment) and improvements introduced by the Welfare State. However, although there had been an undeniable rise in living standards for the vast majority of the population, this way of defining poverty began to be seen as inadequate. In particular, it ignored individual dietary requirements, the needs of particular localities and any comparison with the income of society as a whole. Researchers in the 1960s began to challenge the complacent belief that poverty had been overcome.

The advantages and disadvantages of an absolute definition of poverty

Advantages
- An absolute definition of poverty may be seen as clear and easy to understand and recognise.
- A relative definition of poverty (see below) may be seen as less useful as it is related to the general standard of living at a particular time in each society's history.

Disadvantages
- It relates to complex issues: it is difficult to specify essential costs which may well change even in the short term.
- There is the tendency to relate poverty and essential costs in society, and subgroups of society, in terms of life at the time.

Relative poverty Relative poverty is based on considering poverty in relation to general expectations in terms of everyday living standards of society as a whole during a particular period of time. Hence relative poverty considers not only necessities but also exclusion from what may be considered normal expectations by most members of a society. J. Galbraith stated that:

> *'People are in poverty when their income, even if it is adequate for survival, falls markedly below that of the community. Then they cannot have what the larger community regards as the minimum necessary for decency . . . They are degraded if they live outside the grades which the community regards as acceptable.'*
> J. Galbraith, *The Affluent Society* (Penguin, 1962)

In other words, relative poverty is being poor in comparison to the society in which the person lives, whether it is the UK or West Africa. For example, a person in West Africa may be considered to be rich if he or she possesses a bicycle, while in parts of the USA a person would be considered to be in poverty if he or she did not change cars every few years. Peter Townsend, in his study *Poverty in the United Kingdom* (1979) (see below), suggests that the sole indicator of poverty is not lack of money for food, shelter and clothing. It is also related to expected behaviour in that society. He gives the example of an old lady he interviewed who saw the purchase of a birthday card for a young relation as being more important than buying food for herself. In UK society it is considered to be normal or accepted behaviour to send such a card, and consequently it was crucially important for this old lady.

> '*Individuals, families and groups in the population can be said to be in poverty when they lack the resources to obtain the types of diet, participate in the activities and have the living conditions and amenities which are customary, or are at least widely encouraged or approved, in the societies to which they belong.*'
> Peter Townsend, *Poverty in the United Kingdom* (Penguin, 1979)

However, expectations change over time both within a society and between one society and another. As societies become more affluent, what was initially considered to be a luxury now becomes a necessity. In 1899, for example, a domestic fridge was virtually unknown. Today, in most countries of Western Europe, it is considered to be a necessity for the preservation of perishable foodstuffs, so a person without a fridge today would be considered poor in relation to the rest of that society.

> '*Poverty is relative because need is relative to social institutions and practices.*'
> Peter Townsend, *New Society* (August 1980)

Think about it

- Draw up and discuss a total list of 16 goods and services which you would consider to be basic necessities of life.
- How would you attempt to carry out a serious assessment of the extent of poverty in the area in which you live?

In 1965, Peter Townsend and Brian Abel-Smith published *The Poor and the Poorest*. They argued that people on National Assistance Benefit (NAB) (see page 430) had an income which was insufficient for them to have a standard of living comparable to the majority of the population: they considered that a sufficient income needed for this was NAB + 40 per cent.

Then, in 1968/9, Townsend undertook his massive survey of the extent of poverty in the UK, based on 10,000 individuals in 3250 households. His findings (quoted above) were published in 1979 under the title *Poverty in the United Kingdom*.

> *'The chief conclusion of this report is that poverty is more extensive than is generally or officially believed and has to be understood not only as an inevitable future of severe social inequality but also as a particular consequence of actions by the rich to preserve their wealth and so deny it to others.'*
> Peter Townsend, *Poverty in the United Kingdom* (Penguin, 1979)

Townsend's main findings were as follows:

- By the state's standard, nearly 5 million people were in poverty and a further 12.5 million were on the margins of poverty.
- By the relative income standard, 9.2 per cent of the sample households were in poverty and a further 29.6 per cent on the margins.
- By the deprivation standard (see below), over 25 per cent of people were living in poverty.
- The poor were widely dispersed throughout the country, although some areas showed a greater concentration than others.
- The groups most likely to be in poverty were: elderly people who had been unskilled manual workers, children in the families of unskilled manual workers, one-parent families.

Criticisms of Townsend's research focus on two areas. First, a number of critics from the Tory Right argue that he was measuring inequality rather than relative poverty. In particular, they argue that the fact that somebody is deprived relative to others in an affluent society does not indicate that he or she is in poverty. Rather, it indicates that in an unequal society some people are bound to be less well off than others.

The other area of criticism has been about the methodology used. Townsend used a **deprivation index**. He considered that a household was in poverty if its members, because of inadequate resources, were excluded from a normal, accepted lifestyle. Poverty can be gauged by measuring the extent to which people are deprived of amenities regarded as being normal by the rest of the community. To this end, Townsend asked questions from a list of 60 indicators of deprivation and from these he extracted 12 which he considered to be particularly accurate indicators of lifestyle. These were then used to compile a deprivation index. If people lived in a household where a significant number of these indicators of deprivation applied, then they were considered to be in poverty. The criticism of this has been that the criteria chosen tended to reflect a personal choice of poverty indicators rather than one which had been undertaken through prior research on customary behaviour – for example, people saying that they had not eaten a cooked breakfast may indicate personal choice rather than poverty.

Think about it

- How many items in Townsend's deprivation index (see page 399) apply to you, and for what reasons?
- Which items do you consider to be (a) really useful and (b) not particularly useful to indicate deprivation?
- Draw up and discuss your own index of deprivation, to apply to the UK now.

Peter Townsend's deprivation index

1. Has not had a week's holiday away from home in the last twelve months.
2. (Adults) Has not had a relative or a friend to the home for a meal or snack for the last four weeks.
3. (Adults) Has not been out in the last four weeks to a relative or friend for a meal or snack.
4. (Children under fifteen) Has not had a friend to play or to tea in the last four weeks.
5. (Children) Did not have a party on last birthday.
6. Has not had an afternoon or evening out for entertainment in the last two weeks.
7. Does not have fresh meat (including meals out) as many as four days a week.
8. Has gone through one or more days in the last fortnight without a cooked meal.
9. Has not had a cooked breakfast most days of the week.
10. Household does not have a refrigerator.
11. Household does not usually have a Sunday joint.
12. Household does not have sole use of four amenities indoors (flush WC; sink or washbasin and cold water tap; fixed bath or shower; and gas or electric cooker).

Source: Adapted from P. Townsend, *Poverty in the United Kingdom* (Penguin, 1979)

More recently, in their research into poverty in London, *Poverty and Labour in London* (1987), Peter Townsend et al. have continued to use a deprivation index, although they have updated the criteria and taken earlier criticisms into account. In particular, greater allowances have been made for variations in taste such as whether individuals were meat-eaters or vegetarians.

The advantages and disadvantages of a relative definition of poverty

Advantages
- Poverty becomes related to the normal expectations of the society.
- It may provide a realistic view of poverty and deprivation within society.
- It extends the concept of poverty to take account of not only basic material necessities, but also a range of other needs.

Disadvantages
- Taken to its extreme, it links inequality to poverty so that many people whose basic needs are met may feel deprived.
- It may blur the differences between 'needs' and 'wants', based on what people have come to expect.
- People may overlook differences within and across societies where expectation may vary considerably.

A social consensus definition of poverty This third definition of poverty reflects an attempt to offset the problems associated with absolute and relative definitions. With absolute poverty, for example, there are problems concerning what a 'necessity' in any particular society actually is. With relative poverty, there is the problem of it normally being based on levels of income – but the amount of money entering a person's home does not always reflect that person's standard of living, nor indeed their level of deprivation. It is often other factors, such as the existence of supportive relatives, efficient social services, the quality of the home and its immediate surroundings, that reflect varying levels of deprivation for people on similar incomes.

The **social consensus** definition of poverty, though originally devised by Peter Townsend, was refined by Joanna Mack and Stewart Lansley. For the television programme *Breadline Britain* (1983), they took into account the methodological criticisms of Townsend. They undertook prior research on customary behaviour by asking people to rank in order of importance the items they considered to be essential. These were then put together to arrive at a group of items agreed by a large majority of people (hence 'consensual'), rather than simply perceived by the researcher, to be necessities. Using these, Mack and Lansley were then able to work out a level of deprivation which the majority of the population felt to be unacceptable.

From their research it was calculated that 7.5 million people were in poverty, of which 2.5 million were children: i.e. 13.8 per cent of the population.

They repeated the research in 1990. The number of items perceived as being necessary had increased from 22 to 32, reflecting a rise in social expectations. (The 32 items are listed in the table 'Breadline Britain' on page 401.) The 1990 study also showed that the number of people in poverty had increased from 7.5 million to 11 million. During the 1980s there was considerable discussion as to whether poverty had increased or whether it was just that the differentials between high and low earners had widened. There would seem to be some evidence that poverty has actually increased. One explanation for this could be the relative erosion of the value of government benefits. In 1979, for example, pensions became indexed to prices rather than wages; while income support and invalidity benefits have not kept pace with average earnings.

The major criticism of Mack and Lansley, though, is that despite taking into account the methodological criticisms of Townsend, their definition of poverty (people without three or more essential items) could still be perceived as being arbitrary.

It seems that there can be no impartial definition of poverty. Poverty has become a political debate. Politicians and others influenced by **market liberal theories** (see pages 424–5) prefer to consider absolute definitions of poverty, which allow them virtually to disregard poverty in contemporary Britain. However, others influenced by what may be termed a **social democratic** viewpoint (see page 426) prefer relative definitions. They hold the view that social justice should do more for the poor than merely enable them to exist at a subsistence level, rather it should allow them the opportunities available to most members of society. Some **Marxist sociologists** maintain that notions of both absolute and relative poverty divert attention away from the social inequalities inherent within a capitalist class system which in itself generates poverty.

Think about it

- Study the items not included in the 1983 *Breadline Britain* survey (see opposite) and state why you consider these were included in the 1990 survey.
- What are your views on the statement in the Notes that 'in 1990 there were 11 million poor people'?
- Think about Mack and Lansley's social consensus definition of poverty compared with Carey Oppenheim's consensual poverty line, shown on page 402. List their similarities and differences.

Breadline Britain: A measure of deprivation in 1990

	A %	B %
A damp-free home	98	2
An inside toilet (not shared with another household)	98	–
Heating to warm living areas of the home if it's cold	97	3
Beds for everyone in the household	95	1
Bath, not shared with another household	95	–
A decent state of decoration in the home[2]	92	15
Fridge	92	1
Warm waterproof coat	91	4
Three meals a day for children[1]	90	–
Two meals a day (for adults)[4]	90	1
Insurance[2]	88	10
Fresh fruit[2]	88	6
Toys for children e.g. dolls or models[1]	84	2
Separate bedrooms for every child over 10 of different sexes[1]	82	7
Carpets in living rooms and bedrooms in the home	78	2
Meat or fish or vegetarian equivalent every other day[3]	77	4
Celebrations on special occasions such as Christmas	74	4
Two pairs of all-weather shoes	74	5
Washing machine	73	4
Presents for friends or family once a year	69	5
Out of school activities, e.g. sports, orchestra, Scouts[1,2]	69	10
Regular savings of £10 a month for 'rainy days' or retirement[2]	68	30
Hobby or leisure activity	67	7
New, not secondhand, clothes	65	4
A roast joint or its vegetarian equivalent once a week[3]	64	6
Leisure equipment for children e.g. sports equipment or bicycle[1]	61	6
A television	58	1
Telephone	56	7
An annual week's holiday away, not with relatives	54	20
A 'best outfit' for special occasions	54	8
An outing for children once a week[1]	53	14
Children's friends round for tea/snack fortnightly[1]	52	8

A = Proportion deeming items to be necessary
B = Proportion of households lacking each of the items

The description of items have been abbreviated
1 For families with children
2 Not included in the 1983 survey
3 Vegetarian option added in 1990
4 Two hot meals in the 1983 survey

Notes This table shows households which lacked items because they could not afford them.

Poverty was defined as a lack of three of these necessities. In 1990 there were 11 million poor people according to this definition, a rise from $7\frac{1}{2}$ million in 1983.

Source: Harold Frayman, *Breadline Britain 1990s; the findings of the television series* (Domino Films for London Weekend Television, 1991)

Carey Oppenheim's consensual poverty line	
Examples of items included	**Examples of items excluded**
Basic designs, mass manufactured furniture, textiles and hardware	Antiques, handmade or precious household durables
Prescription charges, dental care, eyesight test	Spectacles, private health care
Fridge-freezer, washing machine, microwave, food-mixer, sewing machine	Tumble-dryer, shower, electric blankets
Basic clothing, sensible designs	Second-hand, designer and high fashion clothing
TV, video hire, basic music system and camera	Children's TVs, compact discs, camcorders
Second-hand 5-year-old car, second-hand adult bicycle, new children's bikes	A second car, caravan, camping equipment, mountain bikes
Basic jewellery, watch	Precious jewellery
Basic cosmetics, haircuts	Perfume, hair perm
Alcohol – men 14 units, women 10 units ($\frac{2}{3}$ Health Education Authority safety limit)	Smoking
One week annual holiday	Holiday abroad
Walking, swimming, cycling, football, cinema, panto every two years, youth club, scouts/guides	Fishing, water sports, horse-riding, creative or educational adult classes, children's ballet/music lessons

Source: C. Oppenheim, *Poverty: The Facts* (Child Poverty Action Group, 1993)

Theories and explanations of poverty

There are a number of theories and explanations of poverty, ranging from the explanations of Victorian times which saw the laziness of individuals as being the main cause of poverty, through to the twentieth century where a variety of theories have been suggested for the incidence and prevalence of poverty. Rowntree's research in the 1890s made a significant contribution to our perceptions of the reasons for poverty. The table on the next page lists the main causes. It is interesting to note that whereas 'low wages' were the main cause of family poverty in 1899, by 1950 'old age' was the principal reason for families being in poverty.

The reasons put forward for poverty can be broadly classified into two groupings:

- Individual responsibility – the individuals are largely responsible for their own poverty, either through some fault of their own, or because it is passed on through a social group such as their family.
- Institutional failure – the poor are excluded from enjoying a decent standard of living through the actions of others.

Rowntree: 'Causes' of poverty			
due to:	Families in poverty		
	1899 (%)	1936 (%)	1950 (%)
Death	16	8	6
Illness	}6	4	21
Old age		15	68
Unemployment	2	29	0
Miscellaneous (including large family)	25	3	3
Low wages	52	42	1

Source: Adapted from K. Coates and R. Silburn, *The Forgotten Englishmen* (Penguin, 1970)

Individual dependency explanations

Individual responsibility

During the nineteenth century it was popularly believed that individuals were solely responsible for their own poverty. Idleness and drunkenness were seen as being major reasons for people being in poverty. The response to this was to make life as difficult as possible for the poor in order to cure them of their laziness and immorality. Although tabloid headlines would suggest that this is still a popular belief today, most sociologists look for more complex reasons to explain poverty.

The over-indulgent state

In this view the provision of welfare services by the state is seen to reduce people's incentive to work, making them dependent on the state. Poverty can be ended or greatly reduced by removing such provisions and giving 'social security scroungers' the incentive to work. Tabloid headlines condemning 'social security scroungers' would seem to suggest that this theory has a hold on popular ideology. Such a view was supported by a MORI poll in 1985, which suggested that 20 per cent of the people interviewed disagreed with the statement 'people living on supplementary benefit are in real need'.

In 1989, David Marsland, in an article titled 'Universal welfare provision creates a dependent population', suggested that the Welfare State created dependency through its provision of universal benefits. Unemployment benefits, for example, create incentives for people to stay unemployed and not to get a job. Individuals have expectations that the state will look after them 'from the cradle to the grave' and this in turn leads to a dependency and lack of personal initiative. Marsland believed that benefits should be targeted on those with the greatest need, such as the sick and disabled. His views had a considerable influence on Conservative Party policy from 1979 until 1997.

The culture of poverty Many New Right theorists have suggested that the poor have a lifestyle which leads them into dependency, which then becomes a habit from which they cannot escape. This results in a **'culture of poverty'**, to borrow a phrase devised by Oscar Lewis in his fieldwork in Puerto Rico and Mexico in the 1950s and 1960s. Lewis's studies, notably *The Children of Sanchez* (1961), identified whole communities whose values prevented them from taking advantage of opportunities to lift themselves out of squalor. Lewis argues that:

> *'The poor constitute a distinctive culture ... experiences, attitudes and values generated in poor communities are passed from one generation to the next in a never-ending cycle. [Feelings of helplessness, inferiority, resignation and fatalism lead them to be] not psychologically geared to take full advantage of changing conditions or increased opportunity.'*
> Oscar Lewis, *The Children of Sanchez* (Random House, 1961)

The application of the concept of the 'culture of poverty' to the industrialised West has been criticised by a number of researchers. In particular, they suggest that the characteristics displayed seem more of a response to prevailing conditions rather than an explanation for them. Ken Coates and Richard Silburn, in their research into St Anne's in Nottingham, supported this:

> *'. . . the poorer households could not be said to be culturally distinct from the richer. They appeared to respond to the same values, to share the same basic assumptions, to accept similar restraints. Their hopes for the future may not have been as high as those in mainstream society but there was no indication that this was due to a culture of poverty.'*
> K. Coates and R. Silburn, *Poverty: The Forgotten Englishmen* (Penguin, 1970)

The cycle of poverty or deprivation This is a development of the culture of poverty perspective, except that it sees individuals or groups as being inadequately socialised into the prevailing culture, rather than forming a distinct or opposition culture. Sir Keith Joseph, in the late 1970s when he was Secretary of State for Health and Social Services, maintained that there was a **cycle of deprivation** or disadvantage. He argued that:

> *'. . . the roots of much deprivation go back to infancy and early childhood when the child is developing emotional and social relationships and looking for models of behaviour . . . inadequate people tend to have inadequate parents and . . . inadequate parents tend to rear inadequate children.'*
> Sir Keith Joseph, *Stranded on Middle Ground* (Centre for Policy Studies, 1976)

He went on to stress how, in this cycle of deprivation, inadequate parents had large families that they could not hope to train to be anything other than inadequate parents, and so on. This is illustrated in the following diagram.

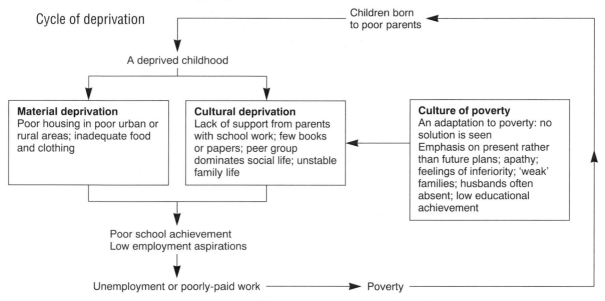

Cycle of deprivation

Mark R. Rank, an associate professor of social work and expert on poverty, welfare and social policy, analysed a national survey of 13,000 American households to define the extent of intergenerational welfare use. His findings, published in the *Journal of Marriage and Family*, June 1997, disprove the notion that welfare traps many of its recipients into a chronic cycle of dependency.

The study found:

- only 25 per cent of those receiving welfare said their parents had used welfare;
- only 10 per cent of those receiving current welfare grew up in households that frequently used welfare;
- only 5 per cent of all receivers of welfare were chronic welfare users, i.e. in four of the last six years, who grew up in households where parents were frequent users of welfare programmes.

Thus, while many politicians claim that welfare reform is essential to break the 'vicious cycle of dependency', Rank's study demonstrates that the vast majority of welfare recipients are first-generation users.

'So much of the welfare debate is based on this notion of chronic welfare dependency: freeloaders whose families abuse welfare from one generation to the next. Yet our analysis shows that this stereotype fits only a very small portion of the population,' Rank said.

Source: Adapted from *News Analysis*, Web site wupa.wustl.edu/re.24 August 1997

Think about it

- What do you consider might be the long-term effects of a cycle of deprivation for individuals and for society?
- Do you think that the cycle of deprivation is a cause or a result of poverty?
- Do you consider that the poor are victims of society rather than the cause of social problems for society?

Institutional failure

This theory suggests that people lose out in complex industrial societies, not through their own fault but through failures inherent in capitalistic societies. Economic growth, for example, may create inequalities in the labour market because some skills are needed more than others. Poverty is the consequence of this, particularly for groups such as the sick, the disabled and the unemployed, who are in a weak bargaining position.

> '*A major reason for the existence of poverty lies in the inequalities in occupational rewards, created by a highly stratified labour market. Large sections of the population are denied access to work which has good pay, security, and otherwise good conditions. The existence of poverty is thus related to the fact that Britain is a hierarchically organised society.*'
>
> Adapted from P. Townsend, *Poverty in the United Kingdom* (Penguin, 1979)

Marxist explanations

Marx saw the impoverishment of the proletariat as the inevitable consequence of capitalism. Although this may have not happened, there is an impoverished, low-wage sector and this can be perceived as being functional to capitalism in a number of ways. Bill Jordan, in his article 'Universal welfare provision creates a dependent population – the case against' (1989), sees poverty dividing the working class by creating a claimant class, which can be blamed for hardships inflicted on the rest. This claimant class can also be perceived as inhibiting wage demands by acting as a visible lesson of the problem of unemployment, while also providing a pool of cheap labour which can be hired or fired when necessary.

The distribution of poverty

Sociological and other studies have constantly pointed towards groups in society who are, or are likely to be, living in poverty. Whilst poverty is not evenly distributed in society, it does nevertheless tend to affect those groups who are disadvantaged in a variety of ways.

Groups in poverty

The number of people in poverty depends on the definition used, and varies according to whether poverty is defined as absolute or relative. However, the groups most likely to be in poverty are similar, irrespective of the definition used. Statistically, the groups most likely to be in poverty are:

- those who are unemployed;
- those who are low paid;
- single parents;
- long-term sick or disabled people;
- pensioners.

The following table shows how benefit spending is distributed by group.

Benefit spending by recipient group in Great Britain				
	1981/2 (£ million)	1986/7 (£ million)	1991/2 (£ million)	1995/6 (£ million)
Elderly	28 408	33 570	35 616	38 785
Long-term sick and disabled	5 941	9 264	13 698	21 208
Short-term sick	1 439	1 644	1 484	843
Family,	9 677	11 991	13 012	17 029
of which: lone parents	2 135	4 113	6 423	9 510
Unemployed	7 458	11 094	8 496	9 029
Widows and others	1 883	1 915	2 119	1 893
All benefit expenditure	54 806	69 478	74 425	88 787

Source: *Guardian Education*, 10 June 1997

These socially disadvantaged groups are similar to those identified by Rowntree in 1899. However, over recent years, ethnicity and gender have increasingly featured as an aspect of poverty. Afro-Caribbeans and some Asian groups are more likely to be in one or more of the above categories, while women form the majority of old people, single parents and the low paid. This is partly because they live longer, but also because disproportionately they have the financial responsibility of caring for young single families.

The unemployed Although unemployment is cyclical, its incidence has increased since the late 1970s. Structural changes in the economy have led to a reduction in manual and semi-skilled employment, particularly for males. In part, the increasing use of automation has meant a reduction in the number of employees involved in production. This has been reinforced by the globalisation of industry which has enabled multinational companies to site a proportion of their productive capacity in the Third World where wage rates are lower than the UK. This has led to semi- and unskilled workers in the UK being made redundant as they are in direct competition with workers in the Third World prepared to work for much lower wages. In particular, this has affected males and specifically those with low skill levels. By 1995, over 30 per cent of males in the UK with low educational attainment were unemployed, compared to approximately 10 per cent in the mid-1970s.

Other groups disproportionately affected by unemployment include Afro-Caribbeans and some Asian communities. Here the main factor tends to be racial discrimination by employers rather than low educational attainment.

It is not just the lack of income which leads the unemployed into poverty. A lack of basic skills makes it difficult for individuals to regain employment; while a lack of self esteem is reinforced by not having a job. Hence the unemployed frequently become trapped in a cycle of unemployment and poverty.

The low paid Low pay is officially defined as two-thirds of the average male wage; it is estimated by the Low Pay Unit that 45 per cent of workers in the UK are on low pay. The groups of people most likely to experience low pay are semi- and unskilled workers and part-time employees. Since 1979, these groups have increased as a proportion of the workforce, as their disposable income has fallen.

> 'The real incomes of the poorest tenth ranked by income after housing costs fell sharply from a peak in 1979 of £73 per week to just over £61 per week in 1991 (both at 1994 prices). This represents a return to the living standards of a quarter of a century ago.'
>
> For Richer for Poorer: the Changing Distribution of Income in the UK, 1961–1991 (Institute for Fiscal Studies)

There are a number of reasons for this fall in real incomes:

- A fall in demand for unskilled and semi-skilled workers: this has meant that their wage rates are rising more slowly than average wage rates in the economy as a whole.
- The increase in part-time working: the shift in the economy to short-time and part-time working has meant that the income for many groups of workers has been falling. In particular, this has affected females, especially those with young families.
- The redistributive effect of taxation changes since 1979 from direct to indirect tax: this has had a disproportionate effect on the low paid, reducing their disposable income.

Single parents Approximately 60 per cent of single parents are in poverty. Their income is, on average, less than that of groups of people without children. The 1990 Family Expenditure Survey stated that the average income of the poorest quarter of single people without children was £155 per week, while that of the poorest quarter with one child was £74 per week. Most of this group tended to be women and the increase in their number has contributed to the feminisation of poverty: full-time work is extremely difficult to obtain because of the responsibilities of childcare, while part-time work is often poorly paid. Thus many single parents are caught in a **poverty trap** and thrown onto benefits. Child Benefit, although it is now being upgraded annually, was frozen from 1987 to 1990, while the take-up for Family Credit is only at the level of 40 per cent of those eligible to receive it. In November 1997 the government reduced benefit to single-parent families by £10.50 per week.

There has been a significant rise in the number of one-parent families since the 1970s, mostly because of the rise in the divorce rate but also because of the increased acceptability of single parenthood. As a result, many women have become responsible for bringing up families on their own. From 1988 attempts were made to move single parents off state benefits and into the workforce. Other changes have included advice on jobs, training and childcare for lone parents with school-age children. In July 1997, the new Labour government started a programme which targeted 40,000 lone parents in eight regions of the UK, with an increase to 500,000 in October of that year. A second programme, aiming to train 50,000 childcare assistants was brought in to run from 1997 to 2002.

1m single mothers face call to seek jobs

By George Jones, Political Editor

ONE million single mothers will be put at the forefront of the Government's drive to reduce dependency on welfare benefits by Tony Blair today.

In his first major speech outside Westminster since becoming Prime Minister, he will announce plans to "help" lone parents to look for jobs and take advantage of new childcare facilities.

Although there is no plan to force single mothers to attend interviews at Jobcentres at this stage, compulsion and the docking of benefits is not being ruled out.

Mr Blair will underline his determination to help what he describes as the forgotten "workless class" by delivering the speech at a run-down housing estate in south London.

It will be the first of a series of speeches that Mr Blair will make around the country in an attempt to demonstrate that he is keeping in touch with the concerns of the voters.

The speech will set out Mr Blair's long-term approach to reform of the welfare state and the guiding "philosophy" of his Government.

He will describe the 1960s as being concerned with the State, the 1980s about the individual and the late 1990s and early part of the next century about "community".

The drive to get single mothers back to work will be a key element of the "welfare to work" package, which will form the centrepiece of Gordon Brown's first Budget early next month.

After reports that single mothers would be "forced" to look for work, Downing Street officials went out of their way yesterday to emphasise that the proposals in Mr Blair's speech were aimed at "helping" them back into the jobs market.

Officials said that many single parents felt "trapped" on benefits; they did not know how to go about finding work or childcare facilities.

"We want single parents who want to work to be seen at employment offices and made aware of what's on offer."

The Government is proposing that money could be diverted from the profits of the mid-week lottery to help set up after-school clubs, where children could stay until mothers finished work.

Source: Adapted from the *Daily Telegraph*, 2 June 1997

Think about it

- What do you think are the major issues associated with the drive to reduce dependency on welfare benefits?
- What measures would you think worthy of political debate in providing more opportunities for lone parents to remain in or enter paid employment?

The long-term sick and disabled

The sick, particularly the long-term sick, and also the disabled, are often included under the same broad heading in sociological texts, while coverage of their situation in relation to poverty tends to be scant and ambiguous. Disease, illness, handicap and disability are terms which are frequently used interchangeably. The concept of 'sickness behaviour', including reference to the 'sick person role', is used by sociologists such as T. Robinson in *Worlds Apart: Professionals and their clients in the Welfare State* (1978) to show how the meanings and experiences of sickness represent a wide range of states shaped, often, by life experiences and group values. Hence the long-term sick may be medically defined and socially labelled which may account for their low levels of income, financial assistance and welfare benefit. The ambiguity extends to statistics on the sick, and these need to be treated with some caution, as shown by the data below which lump together, without explanation, NHS activity, the sick, disabled people, the mentally ill and people with learning disabilities!

National Health Service activity for sick and disabled people: In-patients		1986	1991–92	1994–95
Acute	Finished consultant episodes (thousands)	6 763	7 285	7 566
	In-patient episodes per available bed (numbers)	40.1	49.6	55.1
Mentally ill	Finished consultant episodes (thousands)	278	293	316
	In-patient episodes per available bed (numbers)	2.9	4.2	5.4
People with learning disabilities	Finished consultant episodes (thousands)	58	62	59
	In-patient episodes per available bed (numbers)	1.2	2.2	3.2

National Health Service activity for sick and disabled people: accident and emergency, out-patients and day cases		1988 (000s)	1991–92 (000s)	1994–95 (000s)
Accident and emergency services	New attendances	12 663	13 397	14 482
	Total attendances	16 606	16 289	16 880
Out-patient services	*Mentally ill*			
	New attendances	247	280	342
	Total attendances	2 146	2 120	2 520
	People with learning disabilities			
	New attendances	4	4	6
	Total attendances	35	46	71
Day case admissions	Acute	1 207	1 894	3 049
	Mentally ill	13	1	2
	People with learning disabilities	4	1	2

Government estimates put the figures for people with some disability at approximately 6 million, of whom 360,000 are children. The group tends to be disproportionately represented in poverty statistics, possibly because a high proportion are pensioners. This is largely a reflection of the increasing lifespan of the population, who are in turn more likely to experience disabilities in old age. Of the group under pensionable age, approximately one-third are living in poverty. Despite government legislation requiring companies to take on a proportion of disabled employees, they are often limited to specific types of employment. These jobs are frequently low skilled and consequently poorly paid. If not in employment, disabled people are often totally dependent on benefits.

Pensioners

In 1971, 52 per cent of families in poverty were old age pensioners. By 1992, this figure had fallen to 28 per cent, but it has remained at this level for a number of years. This is largely because pensions are now increased annually according to the retail price index (RPI) rather than the average rise in wages. The disparities in poverty apparent in old age reflect the disparities pre-retirement. Those most at risk from poverty are those who have been low paid during their working life, who have no work-related pension and are totally dependent on state benefits. Pensioners with company pensions are relatively affluent.

The impact of social class, gender and ethnicity

Social class and poverty

Peter Townsend (see page 397) noted that the majority of the unemployed, the low paid, the sick and the disabled have or have had unskilled or semi-skilled jobs. Such jobs normally pay the lowest rates, carry the least security and are unlikely to include pension schemes or other forms of rewards or benefits.

It is interesting to note how the risk of poverty is distributed (see the diagram below). The risk of poverty may also be related to time periods within life cycles – unemployment and retirement clearly increase the poverty risk.

Proportion of UK population living in poverty (below 50% average income after housing costs)

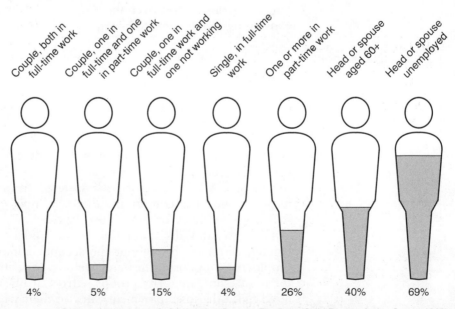

Couple, both in full-time work — 4%

Couple, one in full-time and one in part-time work — 5%

Couple, one in full-time work and one not working — 15%

Single, in full-time work — 4%

One or more in part-time work — 26%

Head or spouse aged 60+ — 40%

Head or spouse unemployed — 69%

Source: Adapted from C. Oppenheim, *Poverty: The Facts* (Child Poverty Action Group, 1993)

Some Marxist writers take the above points much further. For example, John Westergaard and Henrietta Resler, in *Class in a Capitalist Society* (1975), maintain that by subdividing the groups in poverty we are ignoring or even attempting to hide their common social class position. Other Marxist writers consider that the inequalities within a capitalist class society are shown to be the main causes of poverty. For such writers, the Welfare State provides a 'smoke screen', since it has been introduced by the ruling class in order to prevent any move towards revolutionary change. The Welfare State identifies the poor predominantly with the lowest element within the proletariat, and is the price paid by the ruling class in its attempt to maintain social harmony.

Gender and poverty   Peter Townsend et al., in *Poverty and Labour in London* (1987), referred to a 'feminisation of poverty' and identified four groups which make up most of the women in poverty:

• women looking after children, relatives or other dependants, on an unpaid basis, unable to enter waged employment;
• lone women with young children, whether or not they are in waged employment;
• elderly women reliant upon state pensions, particularly those living alone;
• women on low earnings which, even when combined with other household earnings, do not enable them to rise above the poverty line.

The majority of the poor in Britain are women. There were estimated to be about 5 million women in poverty throughout the 1990s; 60 per cent of adults receiving Income Support were women. Over 70 per cent of the low paid were women: the Low Pay Unit calculates this percentage to total 6.34 million. Low pay has become associated particularly with part-time and often short-contract women workers in service industries. It is noteworthy, too, that 96 per cent of lone parents on Income Support are women, and over three times more women than men on state pension require Income Support.

Ethnicity and poverty   It is difficult to obtain accurate statistics on ethnicity and poverty, especially at a national level.

Koushika Amin and Carey Oppenheim, in *Poverty in Black and White* (1992), refer to a local study by Islington Council in London. This study stated that 40 per cent of ethnic minorities, compared with 30 per cent of whites, were living in poverty as defined by Townsend as an income less than 140 per cent of supplementary benefit level. The study also found that 37 per cent of Afro-Caribbeans, 35 per cent of Asians and 47 per cent of Irish suffered from material deprivation in terms of working conditions, diet, clothing, housing, etc. (compared with 33 per cent of (other) whites).

Ethnicity and discrimination seem to have gone hand-in-hand in Britain, certainly throughout the second half of the twentieth century. Employment opportunities and welfare benefits have been problematic for most ethnic minority groups. Afro-Caribbeans and Asians have suffered twice the unemployment rates of their white counterparts, regardless of their educational qualifications. It was estimated that, in 1997, unemployment among ethnic minorities was well above 20 per cent compared with 10 per cent for whites. These groups are also more likely to earn lower wages than whites and to become trapped in the semi- and unskilled sectors of the labour market. Colin Brown, in *Black and White Britain* (1984), found that, in 1982, the average weekly earnings for full-time white male workers were £129, for Asians the figure was £110.70 and for Afro-Caribbeans it was £109.20.

Links between ethnicity and poverty operate in other spheres too. In the British social security system, to claim higher levels of disability allowances or certain types of old age pensions, proof of residence in the UK for ten out of the previous 20 years may be required. Carey Oppenheim, in *Poverty: The Facts* (1990), found evidence that some from ethnic minorities were put off claiming means-tested benefits in case this affected the chances of relatives gaining UK residence rights.

'Deserving' and 'undeserving' – the underclass debate

Historically, there has always been a distinction between the **deserving** and the **undeserving** poor. The underlying belief that some people are poor because they do not conform to current social values and therefore need to be disciplined can be traced back to Elizabethan times, when an Act of Parliament in 1531 made a distinction between 'licensed' begging by 'genuine' cases (deserving poor) and non-deserving beggars. The latter were to be whipped and sent back to where they had come from.

In recent years the idea that there is an underclass has emerged. It is described using similar imagery to that displayed by the Victorians in their notion of the deserving and undeserving poor. The deserving poor are perceived to be those who have an appropriate attitude to work or whose poverty is unavoidable because of their circumstances, for example because they are sick or disabled. A number of commentators on the New Right, for example Peter Marsland (see page 403), believe that benefits should be targeted at this group and not be given to those who are capable of fending for themselves, i.e. the 'undeserving' poor. This distinction between deserving and undeserving poor is particularly favoured by the political Right, as it reflects their belief in individual responsibility and minimum intervention by the state in welfare. They have attempted to address the links between class and poverty by distinguishing between deserving and undeserving poor and between 'rough' and 'respectable' working class. The underclass is seen to be the undeserving poor: a group without employment, culture or class, who do not conform to social values and therefore must be disciplined and changed.

According to the American New Right writer Charles Murray (see Unit 3, pages 126–8), the UK has an underclass and it is growing rapidly. The poor are to blame for their poverty because they choose or are conditioned to act in a certain way. This view is reinforced by surveys which show that an increasing number of the UK population regard the poor as responsible for their own poverty. Many people believe that they could find work if they chose to do so. The reality of poverty is, however, at variance with this; a large proportion of people in poverty are already in work. The problem is that they do not earn enough to keep themselves out of poverty. Of the remainder, a large number are unable to find work because of long-term sickness or disability.

The persistence of poverty

The persistence of poverty, especially in relation to the distribution and possible redistribution of wealth and income, remains the subject of an ongoing debate. Surveys, such as that carried out by the Health Visitors' Association in 1996, relate living conditions for many in the twentieth century to those of the previous century, as described in the following article.

Rickets, TB and poor nutrition: Dickensian diseases return to haunt today's Britain

Health visitors report reveals a nation failing children born into poverty

Susan Emmett

Lighting the cooker and leaving the oven door open is the only way that Tracy McCormack can afford to heat the front room of her house in north-west London. The bedrooms are cold and damp, the doors have been taken away because of damage by woodlice, and her two-year-old is recovering from pneumonia.

Ms McCormack, 25, a mother of two, is one of the many whose living conditions match those of the 19th century, according to a national survey by the Health Visitors Association.

The new study – which follows the revelation in the *Independent on Sunday* yesterday of government figures showing that one in three British babies is born into poverty – was compiled by 500 health visitors and found widespread child malnutrition, poor living conditions and a high number of people struggling with fuel debt and service disconnections.

It paints a bleak picture of families living in overcrowded housing. Nearly three-quarters of health visitors care for families in these conditions and 48 per cent have caseloads including families who have to share kitchens and bathrooms.

The health implications of this hardship read like a passage from Dickens. Nearly one-third of health visitors found tuberculosis among their clients last year. According to the chairman of the British Lung Foundation, Dr John Moore-Gillon, the disease is concentrated in poor areas and has been on the increase since 1988. "Tuberculosis has never gone away. But we are witnessing an increase whereas we expected to see a continuing decrease," he said.

Two-thirds of health visitors encountered iron deficiency among the families they cared for, 93 per cent had to deal with cases of gastroenteritis and 4 per cent reported cases of rickets.

The findings also show a high number of households having their gas, electricity, telephone and water cut off. The majority of these households include children.

Living on less than £80 a week from benefits, Ms McCormack can hardly afford her bills. She spends only £16 a week on food; essential items such as nappies are carefully rationed. Unless she can find £70 overnight, her phone, which takes only incoming calls, will be cut off and she will not be able to communicate with her absent, unemployed husband. He left on their fifth wedding anniversary after several rows over money.

But keeping her children warm and the electricity bill low is her greatest worry. Coal at £4 a bag is too expensive for her to consider lighting the fire and she cannot afford to run an electric heater all the time. Her children wear several layers of clothes, but that did not shield Cally, two, from pneumonia. Since the disease sent the child to hospital in an ambulance a year ago, she has regularly revisited the doctors and only recently finished another course of antibiotics.

"Pneumonia is a serious thing," Ms McCormack said. "Having pneumonia as a kid can affect her later on in life. She was so dehydrated they couldn't even get a needle into her veins. I don't think my cold

This 1875 engraving (left) shows the grim Victorian poverty described by Dickens. Today, Cally, two (right), is recovering from pneumonia in the flat her mother, Tracy, cannot afford to heat
Photograph: Glynn Griffiths

house helped her condition because it starts off as a cold and just gets worse and worse." Despite her child's continuing illness, Brent council says it cannot afford to install central heating in Ms McCormick's home this financial year, although the situation will be reviewed next April.

Jackie Carnell, director of the Health Visitors' Association, is concerned that social conditions in Britain are returning to those of the last century. "It is a tragedy that as we now approach the end of the 20th century, the many improvements in health and welfare are being undermined by the effects of desperate poverty on a national scale."

Bleak House 1996: The ghosts of poverty past

'It is a black, dilapidated street, avoided by all decent people; where the crazy houses were seized upon, when their decay was far advanced, by some bold vagrants, who after establishing their own possession, took to letting them out in lodgings. Now, these tumbling tenements contain, by night, a swarm of misery. As, on the ruined human wretch, vermin parasites appear, so, these ruined shelters have bred a crowd of foul existence that crawls in and out of gaps in walls and boards; and coils itself to sleep, in maggot numbers, where the rain drips in; and comes and goes, fetching and carrying fever ...'
Charles Dickens in *Bleak House*, published in 1853

'It is a chilly, dank room even with the tiniest flicker of heat that can be afforded – a flame from the oven. But that is still better than the rest of the flat, which gets no heat at all. It lacks suitably thick walls and even doors to insulate from the winter wind. The children catch colds. The colds turn into pneumonia. £4 for a bag of coal is too expensive and an electric heater is beyond her means. The local council can't afford to install central heating this year, so she will wait until it can reconsider her case in April. Maybe by then her two-year-old will be over the pneumonia that has kept her under medical care for the past year.'
Life for Tracy McCormack in Harlesden, London, 1996

Source: The *Independent*, 25 November 1996

Think about it

- What surprises you most about the living conditions experienced, by many, in 1996, according to the Health Visitors' report?
- What do you consider might be done to improve the standards of living of children in poverty?
- How do you think sociologists might interpret reports received about poverty?

After World War II, with the creation of the British Welfare State, **benefits** were intended to meet the duty of the state to help the poor and to provide a **safety net** for all members of society. In the 1960s and 1970s, welfare seemed to focus on preventing the worst off from slipping well behind the better off. By the 1980s, the focus had shifted to the effects of so-called 'welfarism' in terms of its costs and impact on those receiving welfare benefits: there loomed the threat of an emerging dependent underclass. This, in turn, led to a 1990s' view that welfare dependency does little for the state and little too for individuals who come to depend on state benefits.

However, despite the above generalised views on the development of the state welfare system, there remains no real consensus, or agreement, on how welfare benefits should operate. Frank Field, the Minister for Welfare Reform in the Labour government elected in May 1997, admitted that basic questions still need to be asked about the aims and nature of welfare. The removal of Family Income Support from lone parents in late 1997 and the intention to review disability payments reflects the government's commitment to get people 'into work and off benefit'. He referred additionally to the state welfare system as an 'engine for social advance and betterment'.

Patterns of distribution of income and wealth

Sources and distribution of income

A common measure of living standards is disposable income, which is the amount of money people have to spend or invest. It consists of income from all sources, minus income tax, national insurance contributions and local taxes. Households receive income from many sources, as shown in the following tables. Wages and salaries make up more than half of all household income, although they fell by 12 per cent between 1971 and 1995. During this period, income from private pensions and annuities doubled its share of total income. This change is partly a result of the growing number of elderly people in the UK and the increased likelihood of them having occupational pensions.

Household income						
Source of income	**1971 (%)**	**1976 (%)**	**1981 (%)**	**1986 (%)**	**1991 (%)**	**1995 (%)**
Wages and salaries	68	67	63	58	58	56
Self-employment income	9	9	8	10	10	10
Rent, dividends, interest	6	6	7	8	9	7
Private pensions, annuities, etc	5	5	6	8	10	11
Social security benefits	10	11	13	13	11	13
Other current transfers	2	2	2	3	2	3
Total household income (= 100%) (£ billion at 1995 prices)	314	365	398	472	573	599

Source: *Social Trends*, 1997

Sources of household income: by household type, 1994–95					
		Earned income (%)	Investment income (%)	Contributory cash benefits (%)	Non-contributory cash benefits (%)	Gross household income (= 100%) (£ per week)
Retired households	Single person	–	39	45	16	137
	Couple	2	52	39	7	246
	Other	16	37	32	15	301
Non-retired households	Single person	80	8	4	9	266
	Lone parent Dependent children	37	12	1	49	203
	Non-dependent children only	71	9	10	10	340
	Couple No children	87	9	3	2	498
	Dependent children	88	4	1	7	537
	Non-dependent children only	88	6	3	3	660
	Other	76	9	5	11	503
All households		73	12	8	8	381

Source: *Social Trends*, 1997

The tables above show that:

- lone parents with dependent children received nearly half their income from non-contributory cash benefits, such as Income Support and other benefits to supplement low incomes;
- retired households received most of their income either from investment income, such as occupational and personal pensions, or from contributory cash benefits such as the state retirement pension;
- couples with non-dependent children had the highest gross income, consisting mainly of earnings. Such households had more people of working age than other household types;
- earnings represent at least three-quarters of gross income for most households, except for retired and lone-parent households who rely more on social security benefits.

Sources and distribution of wealth

The unequal distribution of wealth in the UK has remained unchanged over a considerable period of time. In 1993, half the population owned 93 per cent of marketable wealth, as illustrated in the first table on page 418. Marketable wealth consists of those things that can be sold or cashed in, such as property or shares. The table shows that wealth distribution fluctuated only very slightly between 1976 and 1993, although there has been a tremendous increase in total marketable wealth.

Distribution of wealth		1976 (%)	1981 (%)	1986 (%)	1991 (%)	1993 (%)
Marketable wealth	Percentage of wealth owned by:					
	Most wealthy 1%	21	18	18	17	17
	Most wealthy 5%	38	36	36	35	36
	Most wealthy 10%	50	50	50	47	48
	Most wealthy 25%	71	73	73	71	72
	Most wealthy 50%	92	92	90	92	93
	Total marketable wealth (£ billion)	280	565	955	1 711	1 746
Marketable wealth less value of dwellings	Percentage of wealth owned by					
	Most wealthy 1%	29	26	25	29	26
	Most wealthy 5%	47	45	45	51	51
	Most wealthy 10%	57	56	58	64	63
	Most wealthy 25%	73	74	75	80	80
	Most wealthy 50%	88	87	89	93	93

Source: *Social Trends*, 1997

Net wealth distribution of the personal sector [See page 420.]	1971 (%)	1981 (%)	1991 (%)	1995 (%)
Life assurance and pension funds	15	17	26	34
Dwellings (net of mortgage debt)	26	36	36	26
Stocks, shares and unit trusts	23	8	11	15
National Savings, notes and coins and bank deposits	13	10	9	10
Shares and deposits with building societies	7	8	8	7
Other fixed assets	10	11	5	5
Total net wealth (£ billion at 1995 prices)	1 207	1 459	2 658	2 830

Source: Adapted from *Social Trends*, 1997

Redistribution of income through taxes and benefits, 1994–95 [See page 420.]						
Average per household	**Bottom fifth (£ per year)**	**Next fifth (£ per year)**	**Middle fifth (£ per year)**	**Next fifth (£ per year)**	**Top fifth (£ per year)**	**All house-holds (£ per year)**
Wages and salaries	1 180	3 830	10 230	17 820	28 250	12 260
Imputed income from benefits in kind	10	20	100	310	950	280
Self-employment income	260	510	1 050	1 550	6 160	1 910
Occupational pensions, annuities	280	780	1 300	1 520	2 220	1 220
Investment income	170	260	500	800	2 420	830
Other income	140	200	190	250	340	230
Total original income	2 040	5 600	13 380	22 250	40 330	16 720
plus Benefits in cash Contributory	1 930	2 290	1 620	1 050	680	1 510
Non-contributory	2 730	2 180	1 540	900	490	1 570
Gross income	6 700	10 080	16 540	24 200	41 510	19 800
less Income tax and NIC	270	760	2 300	4 360	9 350	3 410
less Local taxes (gross)	570	550	630	680	790	640
Disposable income	5 860	8 760	13 610	19 150	31 370	15 750
less Indirect taxes	1 740	2 070	3 090	3 960	4 810	3 130
Post-tax income	4 120	6 700	10 520	15 190	26 570	12 620
plus Benefits in kind Education	1 600	1 250	1 390	1 200	670	1 220
National Health Service	1 790	1 720	1 660	1 460	1 270	1 580
Housing subsidy	80	80	40	20	10	50
Travel subsidies	50	60	60	90	130	80
School meals and welfare milk	80	20	10	10	–	30
Final income	7 720	9 840	13 690	17 970	28 640	15 570

Source: Adapted from *Social Trends*, 1997

Property forms a major part of personal wealth, as shown in the table at the bottom of page 418. Those who have wealth worth over £500,000, however, hold more of such wealth in stocks and shares than in any other form. The distribution of marketable wealth is therefore even more unequal if property value is not included, with over half the wealth of the UK owned by just 5 per cent of its population (see the table at the top of page 418).

The personal sector (see the table at the bottom of page 418) consists mainly of individuals living in households and institutions, but also includes private businesses and life assurance and pension funds. The percentage of net wealth held in dwellings after taking away mortgage debt has declined since 1988 when house prices started to fall in some parts of the UK, especially in the South-East of England. One reason for the fall in the percentage held in stocks, shares and unit trusts was a change in the pattern of investment towards life assurance and pension funds. The amount of wealth held in life assurance and pension funds has continued to grow, and since 1993 has replaced dwellings as the largest component of wealth.

Income distribution and redistribution

The average incomes of various groups of households are shown in the table on page 419. Households receive income from non-governmental sources such as employment, pensions, investments, etc.: this is referred to as 'original income'. Cash benefits from the state, for example retirement pensions and Income Support, are added to original income to give gross income. This income is then reduced by income tax, national insurance contributions (NICs) and local taxes to leave disposable income. The deduction of indirect taxes, for example VAT, results in post-tax income. Households also benefit from government expenditure on services such as education and health; adding in estimates of the value of these services gives a household's final income. In 1994–5 the average 'original' income for households in the bottom fifth of the distribution was about £38,000 less than the average for those in the top fifth. After the addition of cash benefits and benefits in kind, and the deduction of direct and indirect taxes, the difference was reduced to £21,000.

Think about it

- Do you think that a **minimum wage** policy might serve to protect the incomes of the poorest paid or threaten their employment?
- What measures, if any, do you think are worthy of consideration in relation to income and/or wealth redistribution?
- How reliable are the various types of data which have been referred to in this section of the unit?
- If income and/or wealth were to be redistributed from the rich to the poor, what might be the consequences
  – socially
  – economically
  – politically?

Wages and income

Much of the political debate in Britain about the economy has centred on the issue of a national minimum wage. This is favoured by those opposed to 'poverty wages' but opposed by others who claim a national minimum – £4 per hour was one figure mentioned – would make British business uncompetitive and would increase unemployment.

A minimum wage is also championed by those who point to the widening gap in income between rich and poor over the past 15 years. Between 1980 and 1993 the top 1% of income earners in Britain, some 262,000 people, enjoyed an average increase in income of almost £94,000, while the 13 million who make up the bottom 50% had seen a rise of just £4,000 (see Figure 1). All of this means, of course, that disposable income at the top is increasing while such income is falling for the bottom 50% (See Figure 2).

Internationally, too, low wages for much of the British and Northern Ireland populations means that in the 1980s the UK became one of the poorer nations in the European Union (see Figure 3). Figures published by the European Commission in 1994 show that in 1991 wealth per head in the UK was 98% of the European average and 30% of Britons lived in regions with only 90% of the European average. On Merseyside the figure was just 77%, making the region eligible for substantial Commission aid.

Is the UK now destined to be a low wage economy for the majority? How can the economy stand huge pay rises for the well off but little for the poor? Would a minimum wage also improve production and stimulate the economy; or would it further drive up costs and feed the dole queues?

John Williams

Figure 1
Winners and losers in incomes, 1980–93

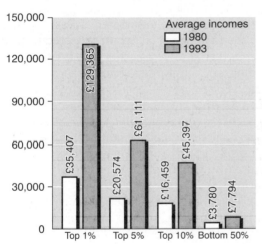

Figure 2
Distribution of disposable household income after housing costs in UK

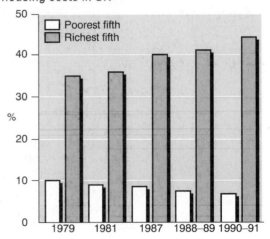

Figure 3
National averages gross domestic product per capita

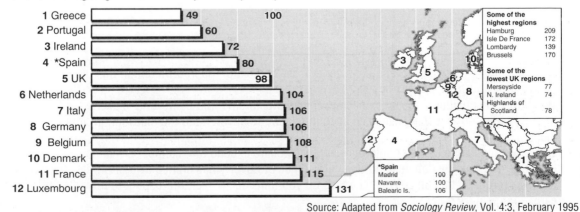

Source: Adapted from *Sociology Review*, Vol. 4:3, February 1995

The persistence of poverty – the ongoing debate

In 1995, a report from the Joseph Rowntree Foundation, a charity supporting independent research into social policy, found that the poorest 20–30 per cent had not benefited from 18 years of Tory rule. The foundation avoided stating that absolute poverty, as opposed to relative poverty, had increased. However, a figure in a government household survey, which the report quoted, implied that this was the case for the bottom 10 per cent. The report influenced political debate due to its challenge of the 'trickle down' theory, which holds that economic betterment at the top will filter through to the bottom.

However, another report, published in May 1997 and funded by the Joseph Rowntree Foundation, showed that government spending in kind (the 'social wage') – on services such as education, health and housing – has helped to cushion pay inequality. Previous estimates of the widening of the income gap between rich and poor had not taken account of such welfare benefits.

The foundation disputed suggestions that it had eaten its words and stated that the new research showed that inequality would have been even greater but for the effect of the social wage. The foundation's 1997 report stated that the cash incomes of the poorest fifth grew by 6 per cent between 1979 and 1993 and by 13 per cent when the 'social wage' was included.

Such research cast doubt on the 'poor-get-poorer' thesis. A study commissioned by Peter Lilley, the former Social Security Secretary in the mid 1990s, showed that incomes of the lowest earners were rising faster than any others. The spending of the lowest tenth of earners had increased by 30 per cent since 1979, with 84 per cent owning a fridge-freezer, 75 per cent a video and 57 per cent a car.

As the economy improves, the average income rises. So does the poverty line. Poverty may now be defined as inequality in incomes. One analyst, for example, has considered that a couple with three children, living in a £70,000 house and earning £20,000 a year, could be considered as poor under this definition.

It would seem that the whole debate on the persistence of poverty, and the distribution of wealth and income, shifted away from its roots in the mid-twentieth century so that by the late 1990s terms such as 'welfarism' have been replaced by those such as 'mutuality' and 'stakeholder', as illustrated in the following article.

Think about it

- Read the article on page 423 and consider it in the context of the information in this unit on the *distribution* and *persistence* of poverty.
- What do you consider is meant by such terms as 'welfarism', 'mutuality' and 'stakeholder'? Can you think of other terms which have been used in relation to poverty and the distribution of wealth and income?
- Why does the Prime Minister hold the view that welfare expenditure cannot be maintained?
- How do you think the debate about the persistence of poverty has shifted away from its roots based on its coverage in this unit? What changes do you think seem likely, in respect to poverty, during the early 21st century?

Labour draws up ten-year plan for welfare reform

BY JILL SHERMAN
CHIEF POLITICAL CORRESPONDENT

HARRIET HARMAN and Frank Field have drawn up a ten-year programme to reform the welfare state, including proposals to replace cash benefits with other forms of help.

The Social Security Secretary and her deputy have put together an ambitious plan to curb the £90 billion social security bill stretching well into the next century. They are said already to have submitted a rough outline of the scheme, which focuses on different ways of supplementing state support, to the Prime Minister.

Tony Blair has already made clear that welfare reform is one of his top priorities and he called Mr Field to Downing Street only days after he became Prime Minister to urge him to "think the unthinkable".

One of the most far-reaching ideas is a scheme to review the balance between cash benefits and community care for the sick and the disabled.

Ms Harman is looking at the whole range of disability allowances and assessing whether some payments could be replaced by providing help for disabled people in the home. In the long term this

Field: he was urged to think the unthinkable

approach could be extended to other benefits. Sources said Ms Harman was keen to "redress the balance between cash benefits and care".

Another area which Mr Field is particularly keen on is setting up new institutions to offer benefits to individuals — or "mutuality", as the buzzword in Whitehall would have it. Friendly societies or trade unions could offer individuals insurance against sickness, unemployment or long-term care.

Mr Field is also keen to give people a greater stake in their own benefits by making them more aware of how their money is being spent. One idea is to transform the National

Insurance contributions scheme to make it more autonomous and managed for its contributors. Each person would be given an individual account, with annual statements of where their cash was going.

The ten-year programme which has been drawn up for Mr Blair is said to have included three options for the current benefit system:

☐ Supplementing state provision with private-sector funding. One example is the proposed stakeholder pension to supplement the basic state pension.

☐ Replacing existing schemes altogether, especially means-tested benefits. One suggestion is a new care pension, which would be given to those looking after dependents, to replace existing carer allowances.

☐ New programmes, such as the universal mortgage insurance scheme.

The ideas are said to be at an early stage, with the details still to be fleshed out. But Mr Blair has made clear to his European colleagues over the past week that welfare reform should now be at the top of every country's agenda, arguing that European economies including Britain's could no longer sustain the current high levels of welfare payments.

Source: *The Times*, 10 June 1997

Theories and ideologies of welfare

This section considers some of the main theories and ideologies on welfare, and also **social policy** and **social control**. Clearly ideologies have become linked to social policy in relation to basic issues such as how society should be organised by the state, in terms of evaluating the wants and needs of its members. Five main theories are outlined in the following pages:

- functionalist theory;
- market liberal theory;
- social democrat theory;
- Marxist theory;
- feminist theory.

Functionalist theory

Functionalist or, in its contemporary form, structural functionalist theory stresses two important functions of state welfare:

- social policies contribute to the overall well-being of members of society so as to enable the maintenance of the social system;
- welfare assists in social integration, which is essential in order to ensure value consensus, particularly within advanced, complex societies.

These functions are discussed in depth by Talcott Parsons in *The Social System* (1951) and by Neil Smelser in *Social Change in the Industrial Revolution* (1959).

Structural functionalists have applied their views on welfare to poverty and social policy in the following ways:

- Poverty may be seen as functional to society since it makes the better off feel good about themselves and society.
- Poverty provides stimulation and incentives for the poor to work hard, achieve success and strive for upward social mobility, even if this means accepting basic, poorly paid jobs.
- Social policy, in providing a welfare system, limits the poverty of groups who may find themselves marginalised: this helps to integrate such groups and promotes social control.

Therefore, for structural functionalists, an appropriate welfare system – and even poverty itself – may be seen as useful in maintaining harmony within society.

Criticism of functionalist theory

- Whilst functionalist theory is systematic and extensive, its emphasis on social stability does not allow it to account for often quite dramatic changes within society, for example the increase in the UK in the number of homeless people and people with HIV/Aids.
- There tends to be an overemphasis on value consensus, which changes over time, as, for example, in the wide ranging views as to what constitutes relative poverty in a particular society.
- It concentrates on social order and control. Thus, it overlooks the conflict and coercion which a social policy and society itself may exert on, for example, lone parents or the unemployed.

Market liberal theory

Market liberal theory maintains that a free market is the best form of organisation for a capitalist economy in order for it to maximise its cost-effectiveness and efficiency. Accordingly, state intervention needs to be kept to a minimum. Such thinking led to the development of the New Right, particularly under Margaret Thatcher's leadership as Prime Minister from 1979 until 1990. It was influenced by the writings of the American economist Milton Friedman and the Swiss philosopher Friedrich Hayek, both of whom suggested that:

- excessive interference by the state, combined with the power of the trade unions, had limited capitalism, cutting off its economic potential;
- high taxes, state control of industry and high levels of public expenditure were unnecessarily hindering economic freedom;
- the state had acted too weakly in exerting its social control in terms of law and order (see Unit 10, pages 506–7).

Vic George and Paul Wilding have stated that:

> 'Every economic system needs a legitimising ideology and capitalism is no exception. Such values as individualism, inequality, competition, and private property are essential to a capitalist economic system ...'
>
> Vic George and Paul Wilding, *Ideology and Social Welfare*
> (Routledge & Kegan Paul, 1985)

Market liberal theory, according to George and Wilding, is critical of welfare systems (and prior social policy) in the following areas:

- A welfare system interferes with individual freedom. Individuals become forced to contribute to benefits which they do not seek or may not even want. This can cause an unwelcome redistribution of resources from the rich to the poor.
- A welfare system overloads government; as a complex system, it can have unpredicted outcomes. Concessions to pressure groups can be prompted as a 'vote motive', i.e. to gain their votes at elections.
- A welfare system is inefficient – state welfare services become too expensive and too large to run. They may also become unresponsive to the needs of those they are intended to serve.
- A welfare system leads to inefficient planning: officials can decide, sometimes incorrectly, on their clients' wants and needs. An open market provides competition and more choice for clients.
- A welfare system creates dependency; it does not allow people to become more responsible for themselves and their families.

Criticisms of market liberal theory

- The ideology of the New Right, in governments led by Margaret Thatcher and John Major, led to policies which reduced state expenditure on welfare. This further disadvantaged a wide range of groups, who became disaffected – contributing to the overwhelming defeat of the Conservatives in the general election of 1997.
- The welfare system, particularly in relation to the NHS, demonstrates the problems of introducing health and medicine into a 'free' market. Indeed, there arose a debate as to whether there was a hidden agenda – one of undermining the NHS.

- Available evidence demonstrates that a competitive market in health and welfare often results in unequal access to the provision and might create in some areas a poorer level of service, i.e. NHS Trust hospitals running out of money.

Social democrat theory

Social democrat theory maintains that the welfare system should not hinder individual initiative, but enable people to widen their opportunities. For example, lone parents, rather than being subsidised to stay at home and receive benefits, should be encouraged and provided with childcare support to return to education and training or to enter the employment market. According to social democrats, a similar principle can be applied to other groups, such as school leavers, the unemployed and the homeless.

> 'With a few inevitable exceptions, welfare should be an investment in productive people, not a last resort for the incompetent.'
> Ralph Miliband, *Reinventing the Left* (Polity Press, 1994)

Anthony Crosland (1918–77), Labour politician and writer, had suggested, by the 1960s, that it was no longer desirable for the state to control major industries, financial institutions, etc. He maintained that there should develop a pluralist approach to ownership of the means of production, leading to a mixed economy with the type of ownership – whether central, local, public/private, etc. – being determined by circumstances. To a large extent Crosland's ideas may be seen to represent the social democrat viewpoint, and to fit in well with the post-1997 Labour government's policies. This viewpoint also includes the following:

- There needs to be some collective welfare provision by the state to address the problems of living in a capitalist free-market economy, for example unemployment, poverty, etc.
- A free-market economy can be inefficient and wasteful in terms of labour and resources; education and training may not meet the immediate skills required by the employment market.
- Certain needs, which tend to slip outside market forces, such as the welfare of the disabled and the elderly who are not profitable in an enterprise culture, have to be addressed.
- Social stability cannot necessarily be entrusted to a capitalist free market; loyalty to the state and good citizenship, linked to welfare rights and benefits, help to reduce conflicts which arise from the inequalities in the economic system.

Criticisms of social democrat theory

- There are areas in the social democrat approach to a free-market economy in which a state still needs to control and iron out problems. Hence high taxes may be required, which, whilst in the welfare interests of citizens, tend to be unpopular right across society.
- Welfare benefits and services provided mainly by the state, but alongside voluntary and other organisations, can become costly and piecemeal. This may not meet the wants or needs of either welfare providers or client groups.

Marxist theory

Marxist theory emphasises welfare and social policy as serving the control needs for the capitalist system. Marxists maintain that the capitalist state serves the interests of the capitalist class in the long term. In the short term, decisions made by the state may seem to favour the subject class (the proletariat), rather than the ruling class, but this provides a 'smoke screen' of false consciousness.

The subject class may enjoy a 'feel-good factor' through home or share ownership, but this inevitably serves the capitalist interests behind such schemes. Essentially, since the subject class of workers try to sell their labour for the highest price, they compete – and even at times conflict – with capitalists, who attempt to maximise profits by cutting costs, particularly labour costs.

The main points associated with Marxist theory on welfare and social policy are noted below.

- Capitalists gain from the Welfare State, as it provides them with a healthy and educated workforce, including a reserve army of labour maintained by the benefits system.
- The welfare system was not intended to end poverty or to reduce inequality, but as a concession by the ruling class to enable people to survive in the capitalist system. Their gratitude for the means of survival helps to prevent social unrest: the working class becomes 'educated'.
- In general the working class are looked after by the state: they are told that they are 'stakeholders' in society. In return, loyalty and obedience are expected, and social control is maintained.

Some contemporary Marxists adopt a more positive view towards welfare and social policy. For example, Ian Gough, in *The Political Economy of the Welfare State* (1979), considered that the increases in welfare benefits during the 1960s and 1970s were due to working-class pressure on the state. Similarly, Klaus Offe has written:

> *'The contradiction is that capitalism cannot exist with the welfare state, neither can it exist without the welfare state.'*
> Klaus Offe, 'Some contradictions of the modern welfare state', *Critical Social Policy*, vol. 2, no. 2 (1982)

Criticisms of Marxist theory

- Marxist theory, steeped in ideology, maintains a highly uncomfortable view of welfare provided by the state in a capitalist economy. Accordingly, Marxists often adopt a negative attitude to any attempts by the state to address social problems such as poverty and unemployment for which, they consider, the capitalist system is responsible.
- There arises an unclear view of the relationship between the Welfare State and the subject class. Welfare and social policy help to maintain the capitalist system and therefore form an important part of a continued class struggle. However, evidence tends to show that collective provision does not threaten capitalism and indeed, in reality, Marxists seem to join in the clamour to fight against cuts in welfare benefits and services.

- Other major issues, particularly in relation to gender and ethnicity, tend to be excluded from Marxist theory. When such issues do appear, they are considered in the context of capitalism and class struggle. It would appear that Marxist theory has tended to marginalise such dimensions in terms of welfare and social policy.

Feminist theory

Feminist theory views the state, and its welfare provisions, as supporting the interests of the ruling class and, in particular, male domination or patriarchy. Feminists influenced by Marxist thought, such as Michele Barrett in *Women's Oppression* (1980), argue that the state supports the ideal of a nuclear family with the father as the breadwinner and his wife and children economically dependent on him. This not only perpetuates patriarchy, but serves capitalism and acts as a control system over women. Women's relatively low pay increases capitalist profits based on the ideology of the family wage. Furthermore, unwaged domestic labour has been seen as a natural function of women, which in turn lightens the state burden of responsibility for childcare, the disabled and the growing number of elderly people. Therefore, for feminists, the state plays an important role in constructing and maintaining the domestic spheres, and so continues to subordinate, exploit and control women.

Other points associated with feminist theory on welfare and social policy include the following:

- The family/household system represents a small-scale version of the Welfare State which relies on unpaid domestic labour, the value of which, in personal, emotional and financial terms, remains largely unrecognised.
- Women seem to be expected to take on the burden of the state in relation to looking after children and sick and elderly relatives; 'community care' developments have relied upon this expectation.
- Women, even in the labour market, are concentrated in low-paid, part-time jobs, which often lack security and wider benefits.
- Unequal treatment is widespread: for example, cohabiting males can claim benefit for female partners but females have no such right. Since women normally have time away from the labour market, for example for childbirth and family support commitments, they become disadvantaged through gaps in national insurance payments and contributions to pension schemes. This leads to lower levels of benefits, particularly during retirement.

Criticisms of feminist theory

- Whilst Marxist feminists seek to abolish the family/household system described above, there are many other branches of feminism expressing different viewpoints. Radical feminists see men as responsible for the oppression of women; whereas the more liberal strands of feminism consider reform possible through women achieving positions of power from which they can make improvements.
- Gill Pascall, in *Social Policy – A Feminist Analysis* (1986), maintains that since there are a range of feminist approaches to welfare there is 'no single feminist social policy'. Feminist approaches to welfare and social policy sometimes appear to be contradictory because the Welfare State seems to control the lives of women and to reproduce an

ideology that places them into caring, maintenance domestic roles. However, it has also been supportive of women in terms of improved legislation, for example the Equal Pay Act 1970 and the Sex Discrimination Act 1975. In addition, social policies in relation to equal opportunities may have helped to narrow the gap between males and females in public examination results and in terms of access to higher education.

Think about it

• Identify examples of how welfare policy, whether increasing or decreasing the level of welfare provided by the state, can be seen as a means of **social control**.

The development of social policy on welfare

The role of the state

During the twentieth century, the state has become increasingly involved in dealing with what it sees as social problems, replacing the parishes and local authorities and organising their work into a national framework.

State involvement in welfare pre-1945

The first direct state involvement came with the Poor Law Act 1601, which made parishes responsible for **poor relief**. Before this, poor relief had been an individual's responsibility. By the nineteenth century, the demands of industrialisation, urbanisation and the economic dislocation caused by the Napoleonic Wars were putting strain on this system of poor relief, which came to be seen as inadequate. This coincided with a change in thinking regarding the recipients of welfare. People were now considered to be responsible for their own success or failure: if you were unemployed or in poverty, it was your own fault. This led to the Poor Law Amendment Act of 1834. Apart from the old and sick, who continued to receive 'outdoor relief', all poor relief was to be given in workhouses where conditions were deliberately made as bad as possible. The notion that individuals were responsible for their own poverty did not, however, put an end to the problem of poverty.

Successive governments continued to increase their involvement in social welfare, notably through the Public Health Acts of 1848 and 1875, which set up **local health authorities**, and the Education Act 1870, which meant that for the first time the government accepted responsibility for the provision of elementary education (see Unit 4, page 167). During the late nineteenth century, the idea that all individuals were totally responsible for their own salvation was gradually replaced by an attitude that the state should intervene to correct the worst imbalances created by the economy. The provision of free breakfasts for the poor in London in the late nineteenth century (depicted in the illustration on the next page) is an example of such state intervention.

Free breakfast for the poor in Whitecross Street

Source: Peter Joslin, The *Illustrated London News*, 5 January 1878

Among the factors prompting this change of attitude was the research on poverty carried out by Rowntree and Booth (see pages 394–5), which demonstrated that up to one-third of the populations of London and York were living in poverty. Another factor was the medical checks on volunteers for the Boer War (1899–1902), which revealed that a large proportion of them were unfit for military service due to ill health.

Between 1906 and 1914, the Liberal government introduced a number of significant reforms. These included:

- provision for old age pensions, a national insurance scheme, free school meals and medical inspections;
- Labour Exchanges for the unemployed;
- Wages Councils which laid down minimum wages for low-paid workers in certain industries.

The Welfare State, 1945 onwards

The term 'Welfare State' as we know and understand it was largely the creation of the 1945–51 Labour government, following the publication of the **Beveridge Report**, *Social Insurance and Allied Services*, in 1942. Beveridge attempted to conquer what he perceived to be the 'five great social evils' – want, ignorance, disease, squalor and idleness. To solve the problems associated with these, the Labour government undertook the following:

- **want** (or **poverty**): this was tackled by the provision of National Assistance, a means-tested benefit payable to people with no other income, or to top up other benefits, such as family allowances.
- **ignorance:** new secondary schools were built to provide free secondary education for all.
- **disease:** the National Health Service was set up to provide free medical treatment for all.
- **squalor:** the public sector was encouraged to help provide rented housing, while New Towns were set up to rehouse slum families.
- **idleness:** the government adopted Keynesian economic policies in order to ensure full employment (i.e. below 3 per cent). J.M. Keynes has argued that unemployment in the 1930s had been caused by a lack of demands for goods and services. If such demand could be increased by government spending, unemployment would fall.

Family Guide to the
National Insurance
Scheme, HMSO 1948

FOREWORD
by The Rt. Hon. James Griffiths, M.P.
MINISTER OF NATIONAL INSURANCE

THE 5th July 1948 will be a great day in the development of our British Social Services. On that day we shall see National Insurance, including Industrial Injury Insurance, in full operation, supporting—and supported by—Family Allowances, the National Health Service and National Assistance. We have indeed come a long way from the Old Age Pensions Act of 1908 (which gave the 5s. a week pension at 70), to this new system of Social Security which provides help for childbirth, in sickness, in unemployment, in bereavement, and in old age.

The system will provide for everybody without exception: men, women and children, young and old, rich and poor, married and single, employer and employed, those working on their own account, and those not working at all.

This booklet tells you how much you must pay each week and what benefits you will receive in return. It is not possible, of course, to set out all the details in such a short guide, and I am afraid you will find some parts complicated, and perhaps difficult to apply to yourself. If you are in doubt on any point please ask your nearest National Insurance Office for help. You will find the staff there very ready to give you all the help and explanation they can.

The success of this great Insurance Scheme depends upon the willing co-operation of every one of us. Our benefits must be paid for out of our contributions and our taxes. This scheme is, therefore, more than an Act of Parliament; it is an act of faith in the British people. That faith, I know, is not misplaced.

James Griffiths

Source: Peter Joslin

Think about it

Read the above extract describing the aims of the National Insurance Scheme.
• How much do you think 5 shillings a week in 1908 would amount to in relation to current prices?
• Would the comments expressed about the food for the family still be relevant today?

From the 1950s until 1979, the **collectivist approach** to welfare provision remained the dominant ethos. Although, by the late 1970s, economic problems and the desire by governments to balance the Budget had forced successive Labour and Conservative governments more and more towards the targeting of benefits to what they perceived to be the most needy cases, commitment to the Welfare State remained strong.

The political consensus between the two major political parties was broken by Margaret Thatcher's election in 1979. This produced a move away from collectivism and towards an emphasis on the responsibility of the individual, reflecting the ideas of earlier periods. The Thatcher government came into power with the avowed intent of 'rolling back the frontiers' of the state, specifically with ideas of reducing public expenditure and taxation. Alongside this was the notion that more services were to be provided by the private sector. Their ideas represented a break with the ideas of successive post-war governments. The culmination was the Social Security Act 1986, which became operational in 1988. The major provisions of the Act were as follows:

• the replacement of Supplementary Benefits by Income Support. The main effect was to reduce benefit level for a number of people;
• the introduction of Family Credit in place of Family Income Supplement. This provided a higher benefit sum but fewer were eligible to claim it;

- the introduction of the Social Fund as a discretionary payment to cover items in excess of normal weekly expenditure. It replaced a system of one-off, single-grant payments and was introduced partly to help hardship cases no longer covered by Income Support. However, payment is generally a loan rather than a grant and has to be paid out of the claimant's subsequent benefits. Furthermore, there is only a limited amount in the Social Fund each year.

The above developments represented a shift from a **universalistic approach** to a **selectivistic approach** to welfare. The universalistic idea is based on the notion that the Welfare State helps promote common and equal citizenship; while the selectivistic approach represents the idea that the Welfare State provides a safety net for the poor and infirm, who are to be identified by **means testing** with benefits targeted at them.

Universal v. selective approaches to state welfare benefits		
	Universalistic	**Selectivistic**
Aims	• To benefit all who are in need in order to promote the common good, and to achieve greater equality.	• To target benefits to those identified in greatest need, via means testing, and to act as a safety net.
Advantages	• Makes sure that all who are in need obtain benefits, and overcome any ignorance or stigma associated with such benefits.	• Targets benefit to help the most needy rather than those with resources who could become subsidised by the state.
	• Helps overcome the poverty trap by providing benefits even for those on low incomes.	• Benefits savings could be used to provide more or better services or to lower taxation.
	• Provides a relatively cheap system to administer benefits.	• Provides a less costly system since fewer qualify or receive entitlement to benefits.
Disadvantages	• Many people can claim benefits and it is costly for the state to provide and maintain.	• Requires more administration in a more complex system, which could become more time-consuming and costly.
	• People may become reliant on benefits rather than on their own resources, resulting in welfare dependency.	• Means testing and targeting can create a bureaucracy leading to communication problems and errors in recording and judgements.

Think about it

- Do you think that the selectivistic approach to state benefits might be seen as more appropriate in contemporary society? If so, why is this the case? If not, why not?
- What case can you put forward to retain the universalistic approach despite the mounting costs for society?
- How do you think sociologists might apply universal v. selective approaches to areas other than state welfare benefits, such as education and training or crime and deviance?

Some benefits which were formerly universal were now means tested, while others were not increased in line with inflation. The ideas behind the Social Security Act of 1986 were supported by further legislation and measures in a number of areas:

- Since 1988, there has been a failure to raise Child Benefit, a universal benefit paid to mothers, in line with inflation.
- Prescription charges have increased dramatically from 20p in 1979 to £5.65 in 1997; charges have been introduced for dental and eye checks.
- The Council Housing programme has been reduced, with tenants being given the opportunity to buy council houses. Housing Benefit has not been increased annually and has not kept pace with inflation.
- Care in the Community (see Unit 7) has replaced institutional care for mentally ill, elderly and disabled people. Numerous psychiatric and geriatric hospitals have closed down, with care being provided by voluntary organisations, local authorities and the family. This has been criticised as being ill thought out and badly funded, as well as for shifting the burden of care on to women in the family.
- In education, schools were encouraged to opt out from local authority control, and an increasing use of selection by ability has tended to favour the articulate middle class.
- Market principles have been introduced into the provision of health care.
- Privatisation was a policy commitment of the Thatcher government and has led to the contracting out of a number of services, such as the cleaning of schools and hospitals and refuse collection, to the private sector. This was seen as increasing accountability and reducing state outgoings on unnecessary welfare expenditure.

The effects of the 1986 Social Security Act – notably a reduction in the value of benefits and a reduction in the number of those able to claim benefits – together with the deregulation of the labour market, led to a sharp decline in the welfare rights of a substantial section of the population. In May 1988, a study of the 30,000 people who had consulted the Citizen's Advice Bureaux during that month was published:

Main findings of the study

- Stricter means testing meant higher rates of non-claiming.
- Some claimants who took a job found themselves worse off as the amount of work people could do and still claim Income Support was cut from 30 to 24 hours.
- People in work and claiming Family Credit were frequently worse off because their mortgage interest payments were no longer made for them.
- Single parents in work and claiming benefit found their childcare and work expense payments cut.
- Grants for tools and clothing to help people start work were no longer available.
- Benefits were no longer payable during the first two weeks of work.
- Cuts in Housing Benefit left the majority worse off.
- Compensation for the loss of free school meals was inadequate.

Source: Adapted from P. Trowler, *Investigating Health, Welfare and Poverty* (Collins, 1996)

The provision of welfare services

The state sector

Central v. local state welfare provision

Although much of the state's involvement in welfare provision today is in association with the private and voluntary sectors (see pages 435–7), sociologists generally consider the state to be the main provider of welfare in the UK. Welfare provision is a huge task which needs to be carried out in a complex society. There has remained the need for the state to hold a coordinating role over the wide range of central government and local authority services.

Central government welfare services

Department of Social Security
Social Security benefits, e.g. old age pensions, child benefits.

Department of Health
National Health Service, including: hospitals, general practitioners, dental services.

Department for Education and Employment (DfEE)
Coordination of local education authority (LEA) provision, funding, further and higher education and grant maintained schools, employment and training. Job centres, training schemes for the unemployed, Training Enterprise Councils.

Department of Transport
Motorways and trunk roads, subsidies to rail services, transport safety standards.

Home Office
Prisons, special hospitals, probation service, Metropolitan Police Service, coordination of police forces nationally.

Local authority welfare services

Social Services Departments
Homes for the elderly and children, fostering and adoption, home helps, social work services.

Housing Departments
Local authority (council) housing provision.

Local Education Authorities (LEAs)
LEA controlled schools, adult education, youth and community services.

Environmental Health Departments
Maintain standards in housing, food hygiene in restaurants, shops, etc.

Department of the Environment
Central government funding for local authorities, coordinating town and country planning, environmental protection.

Other local services
Including fire services, waste disposal and recycling, libraries, parks and swimming pools, sports and leisure centres.

Source: Adapted from P. Taylor et al., *Sociology in Focus* (Causeway Press, 1995)

Think about it

- Consider any *one* service above, for example education and training. Think about its activities, which have been listed briefly above. How could you find out more about these activities and how effective they are?
- In some areas of welfare service, for example health, there now seems to be a considerable overlap between central and local provisions. How do you think this might be explained?
- Think about changes that you might wish to make in terms of responsibility for central and local welfare services. How would you justify your changes?

Welfare pluralism

Before the Welfare State developed fully, after World War II, other sectors of society were involved in, and in some cases responsible for, welfare provision. These other sectors have continued to operate, often alongside the state. **Welfare pluralism** has developed, whereby the state may be recognised as a major provider, but is not the sole provider of welfare. Indeed the boundaries are often not clear cut. This section will consider the State's involvement in welfare provision in relation to the private and voluntary sectors.

Writers such as Norman Johnson in *The Welfare State in Transition: The Theory and Practice of Welfare Pluralism* (1987) maintain that there are two major aims of welfare pluralism:

- **decentralisation:** the process of reducing state power into other, particularly more local, sectors and organisations;
- **participation:** the encouragement of wider involvement in both the policy making and the delivery of welfare.

Johnson considers that welfare pluralism was supported by the Conservative government up to 1997. He has criticised such pluralism as relying too much on the voluntary sector and on the exploitation of women.

The private sector

The private sector refers mainly to the welfare services provided by private means, for example by private companies. Such organisations charge for services provided and normally seek to make a profit.

From public to private 1948–98

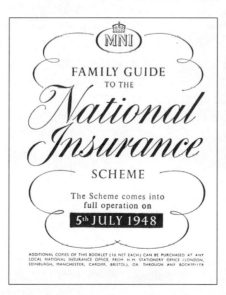

The private sector includes:

- private health insurance and pension schemes;
- private hospitals (and also private-sector work in NHS hospitals);
- private care for the elderly (in residential homes and within the community);
- private universities, colleges and schools (including nurseries).

Those who are responsible for and manage residential units, nurseries, etc., are usually self-employed. Childminders, for example, normally work in their own homes after becoming registered with their local social services department. The income for many providers in the private sector comes from their clients. Private residential homes, however, tend also to rely on fees paid by the Department of Social Security (DSS). Since the NHS and Community Care Act 1990, there have been changes in funding which have led to the local authorities needing a 'top up' from clients or their families.

Private v. public provision of welfare services		
	Private welfare	**Public welfare**
Model	• 'Residual model' (also market liberal view)	• 'Institutional model' (also social democrat view)
Main ideas	• Those members of society in most need should be identified and aided by welfare agencies via means testing, etc.	• All members of society should think positively about welfare needs with the 'strong' supporting the 'weak'.
Writers include	• F.A. Hayek, *The Road to Serfdom* (1976)	• R.M. Titmuss, *Commitments to Welfare* (1968)
	• M. & R. Friedman, *Free to Choose* (1980)	• R. Pinker, *Social Theory and Social Policy* (1971)
Main debate	• Freedom and choice benefits all and allows individuals to become more responsible citizens.	• Only those who can afford it actually have freedom and choice, while those in need become marginalised.
	• Provides greater equality of opportunity members of society to compete as both providers and consumers of welfare.	• Members of society often have unequal resources and this can lead to widening divisions within and between providers and consumers of welfare.
	• Allows for more efficient and cost-effective private delivery of welfare provisions.	• Private delivery of welfare provisions, profit based and sectionalised rather than meeting fully extensive welfare needs.
	• Society can benefit from the considerable savings of free enterprise in an open market, with potential for lower taxes and improved welfare services for society as a whole.	• Society may not gain benefits if savings made are spent on advertising and marketing of welfare services, whilst lower taxes may even increase social inequalities.

Think about it

- Consider how welfare services might become affected by the government returning to a more 'institutional model'.
- What do you think have been the benefits of the developments since the 1980s of the 'residual model'?
- Do you consider that welfare pluralism might be adapted to meet both the private and public provisions of welfare services? How?

The voluntary sector

The voluntary sector refers mainly to organisations formed to serve a common purpose. Many such organisations were set up in the nineteenth century. For example, in 1870, Dr Thomas Barnardo (1845–1905) founded the first Boys' Home in London for orphaned and homeless children. Examples of other voluntary organisations include the National Society for the Prevention of Cruelty to Children (NSPCC) and the Women's Royal Voluntary Service (WRVS).

The main characteristics of organisations in the voluntary sector are as follows:

- Whereas most of the state-sector welfare services are set up by Acts of Parliament, the voluntary sector has remained largely outside such Acts.
- These are non-profit-making organisations whose management committees are unpaid and which are registered as charities. However, some of the larger voluntary organisations pay their staff, who may well be as qualified as their counterparts employed in the private or state sectors.
- Some voluntary-sector organisations offer services on a self-help basis not provided by the state, for example Alcoholics Anonymous. Others complement the state sector, for example MIND, the mental health charity. Elsewhere, links have been established between the two sectors, as in the case of Care in the Community programmes.

Robert Page, in *Social Policy* (1993), considered that voluntary organisations held advantages in terms of their welfare provision:

- They often use a high number of unpaid volunteers and have a less costly administration.
- The voluntary sector has greater opportunities for innovation and can respond quickly to new issues such as HIV/Aids.
- They can supplement state provision where state services are less able to cope because of increased demand, for example Help the Aged's provision for elderly people.
- They provide opportunities for 25 per cent of women and 20 per cent of men to care for each other and add to the welfare of their communities via the voluntary sector.

Formal and informal welfare

Whilst **formal welfare** refers mainly to the welfare provisions set out legally in terms of central government and local authority welfare services, **informal welfare** becomes more apparent in the voluntary sector. Also, for many members of society, informal welfare is provided by family, relatives, friends or local support groups.

Family and community in the provision of welfare

Women and the family

The history of social welfare, from Elizabethan times to the present day, repeatedly emphasises the importance of the family. In fact, prior to the formation of the Welfare State, the informal sector of welfare, i.e. family, friends and neighbours, provided a number of functions currently provided by the Welfare State. Government policies regarding the family did not become established until after World War I, mainly because there arose the desire to:

- maintain strong family structures so that the family can carry out the activities of education, training, etc.;
- provide a healthy environment for growing and living in families;
- avoid social welfare costs and activities by increasing the amount of mutual aid families could provide.

The nature and extent of care provided by the family has changed during the twentieth century, caused by changes in political philosophy, a reduction in state provision for welfare and the effects of an ageing population.

Despite increasing geographical mobility and an increase in the divorce rate, there is evidence that families continue to provide social care for their relatives. In particular, Peter Willmott, in *Urban Kinship Past and Present* (1988), found that in London during the 1980s people had regular contacts with their relatives and frequently relied on them for friendship and support. It appears that increasing geographical mobility has not reduced the support networks of the extended family as people maintain regular contact through cars and telephones. A study by Janet Finch in 1989 suggested that:

> *'People in late twentieth century Britain do not necessarily do less for their relatives than they have for the past two centuries ... but they do have to work out the nature of their relationships and the patterns of support associated with them, in circumstances which are very different from the past.'*
>
> J. Finch, *Family Obligations and Social Change*
> (Polity Press, 1989)

This has been reinforced by legislation providing tax allowances for dependent relatives.

Family care, especially for elderly people, is frequently provided by women. L. Balbo's article *Crazy Quilts* (1987) suggested that their role in welfare was similar to that of a patchwork quilt:

> *'They (women) patch together resources to meet human needs ... This packaging of resources requires intelligence, planning, creativity, time and hard work. And just as in a patchwork quilt, the end result is design, logic and order.'*
>
> L. Balbo, 'Crazy quilts' in S. Showstack (ed.) *From a Woman's Point of View* (Hutchinson, 1987)

The role of women as carers and supporters of their family in need has been encouraged by the government's community care policies, one consequence of which has been to increase family involvement in the care of people in the community. In practice this has meant that more women have become carers:

> 'At the most conservative estimate, there are 1.3 million people in Britain acting as principal carers for elderly relatives, children with disabilities or chronically sick and disabled adults.'
>
> Gillian Parker, *With Due Care and Attention* (Family Policy Studies Centre, 1985)

In 1990, a survey conducted by the Equal Opportunities Commission found that three times as many women as men were looking after elderly and disabled relatives. In all research to date, caring for sick and elderly relatives is perceived as a female role except where husbands are looking after sick or disabled wives.

Changes brought about by Care in the Community (see Unit 7) have further increased the stereotype that the role of carer is a female role, while the community of friends and relatives only provide a small proportion of assistance.

Conclusion

As stated in the Introduction of this unit, it is often assumed that the Welfare State forms an all-embracing, close-knit institution which addressed, certainly during the second half of the twentieth century, a range of social problems particularly for disadvantaged groups. However, its development was piecemeal; a large number of policies and reforms were responses to specific social pressures rather than the result of long-term planning. Sociological debates have raged over social problems, such as: Are those in poverty to blame for their circumstances? Should welfare benefits be universally available or selectively targeted? Should the family and community become more involved in welfare? Whatever values are agreed by sociologists and others, one thing seems clear: these debates undoubtedly will continue, in relation to issues of poverty and welfare well into the twenty-first century.

Revision and practice tasks

Structured questions

1. (a) Briefly explain what is meant by 'absolute poverty'. (4)
   (b) Outline two differences between 'absolute poverty' and 'relative poverty'. (4)
   (c) Explain how difficult it might be to break out of the 'cycle of deprivation'. (7)
   (d) Critically assess the arguments in favour of more selective targeting of State welfare benefits. (10)

   Total: 25 marks

2. (a) Briefly explain what is meant by a 'culture of poverty'. (4)
   (b) Outline **two** problems faced by sociologists in attempting to measure the extent of poverty in contemporary society. (4)

(c) 'Most people living in poverty are women.' Explain this statement. (7)

(d) Critically assess the view that policies designed to eliminate poverty only cause increased dependency. (10)

Total: 25 marks

Source: Interboard Paper 1, Summer 1996

3. (a) Identify and explain **two** of Beveridge's 'five giant evils'. (4)

(b) Using examples, briefly explain what is meant by 'universal benefits and services'. (4)

(c) Outline the arguments in favour of the development of 'community care' policies in the last two decades. (7)

(d) Critically assess New Right views of the relationship between inequality and welfare. (10)

Total: 25 marks

Source: Interboard Paper 1, Summer 1997

Essay questions

1. Discuss how the different definitions and explanations of poverty merely represent the views of different ideologies.

2. 'Some maintain that the persistence of poverty may be associated mainly with the attitudes and actions of the poor themselves.' Evaluate this viewpoint.

3. Assess critically the responses of social policy makers, since the 1980s, to either lone parenting or the ageing population.

4. Examine the view that contemporary social policies help to maintain rather than overcome either gender inequalities or racial discrimination.

5. Evaluate the contribution of New Right thinkers to an understanding of the nature and extent of poverty.

6. 'The Welfare State may have addressed major issues surrounding poverty, but it has done little to achieve its original goal of eliminating it.' Explain and assess this view.

7. Examine the view that surveys and statistics on poverty are very limited in terms of interpreting both the nature and extent of poverty in the United Kingdom.

8. Assess different sociological viewpoints on the roles of the family and other agencies in the provision of welfare.

9. Examine the view that the Welfare State has produced a dependency culture and that there has arisen the need for a more selective targeting of welfare benefits.

10. What is the 'mixed economy of welfare'? Does such a mixed economy deliver welfare more effectively than other possible arrangements? (See advice on response to this, below.)

Advice on response to essay question 10

First, identify clearly the 'mixed economy of welfare' in relation to developments in social policy since 1979, and pick out key trends such as privatisation, community care and residualisation, i.e. help given only to those in greatest need, rather than as a universal right.

You then need to identify relevant examples of the various aspects of the mixed economy of welfare, for example council housing v. owner occupation; private and occupational pensions v. state pensions; private health insurance v. the NHS. Present clear evidence, especially in relation to delivery, impact and other alternative welfare arrangements.

It is important that you evaluate the arguments surrounding effectiveness; show your awareness of competing definitions of effectiveness, for example economic efficiency v. economic equality, etc.

Remember to make sure that your material is presented logically and coherently, and that it focuses directly on the exact essay question.

It might be helpful to prepare a detailed essay plan (see Unit 3, pages 158–9).

Ideas for coursework and personal studies

1. Carry out a study to identify, describe and evaluate any one group who may appear to be living in poverty near to where you live or study.
2. Update a major study into any aspect of welfare, poverty or social policy. Start with your notes and textbooks, then gain more specific literature or, if available, seek information from the Internet.
3. Research into the effects on a small sample of women, and on other relationships within a family or household, of caring for a disabled or elderly relative at home.
4. Conduct a participant observation study at your local branch of the Benefits Agency. Make research notes on your observations, for example on the attitudes and behaviour of those waiting around, lining up in queues, or on the interaction between enquirers, claimants and officials.
5. Carry out a survey of attitudes towards poverty, focusing on attitudes towards poor people known personally to your sample group and towards those living in poverty whom they have read about. What does your sample consider to be the possible causes and cures for those living in poverty?
6. Interview a sample of people aged 60 and above about poverty during their lifetime. How do they consider ideas (or definitions) about poverty may have changed?

Selected reading list

The Children of Sanchez, Oscar Lewis (Random House, 1961)

The Life and Labour of the People of London, 17 vols., Charles Booth (Macmillan, 1891–1903)

The Poor and the Poorest, Peter Townsend and Brian Abel-Smith (G. Bell & Sons, 1965)

Poverty: A Study of Town Life, B.S. Rowntree (Macmillan, 1902)

Poverty in Black and White, Kaushika Amin and Carey Oppenheim (Child Poverty Action Group, 1992)

Poverty in the United Kingdom, Peter Townsend (Penguin, 1979)

Poverty: The Forgotten Englishmen, K. Coates and R. Silburn (Penguin, 1970)

'Universal welfare provision creates a dependent population', David Marsland in *Social Studies Review* (P. Allan, November 1989)

'Universal welfare provision creates a dependent population – the case against', Bill Jordan in *Social Studies Review* (P. Allan, November 1989)

The Welfare State in Transition: The Theory and Practice of Welfare Pluralism, Norman Johnson (Wheatsheaf, 1987)

9 Community, nation and development

Introduction

This unit looks first at the issue of community. It presents:

- debates among sociologists on the subject of community;
- their attempts to define community;
- communitarianism and the concept of citizenship;
- urban and rural society, and the nature and impact of urbanisation;
- community studies and the range of approaches taken by sociologists in carrying these out.

The unit then goes on to consider a much wider 'community' – the concept of nationhood. It looks in particular at:

- what is meant by a nation and what is meant by a nation state;
- the nature and role of nationalism and its potentially racist aspects;
- the relationships between nations in a post-colonial world, but one where supra-national powers of a new and different nature influence society.

Finally, this discussion will lead on to a consideration of issues relating to globalisation and development:

- how we define developed, underdeveloped, developing countries;
- the inequalities between countries and their sociological implications;
- questions relating to aid to the developing world and North–South relations;
- the impact of rapid growth and urbanisation in developing countries.

■ SOCIETY AND COMMUNITY

The study of the community is an area of particular interest to students of sociology, both for its methods and for its findings. Research into 'community', for example, provides many examples of the use of participant observation, since almost all the studies rely on the researcher living within the community. This method is combined with interviews, questionnaires, surveys and scrutiny of official documents.

It is worth reading at least two or three community studies, as they provide information on a wide variety of sociological topics such as family life, gender and age stereotypes, schooling, subcultures, deviance, work and leisure, political behaviour and the impact of social class. Some of the key community studies are outlined on pages 500–502 of this unit.

Influential sociologists' studies of the community

Nineteenth-century sociologists saw society as being held together by close family and community ties; they believed that the breakdown of these ties might lead to social disorder and chaos. Expecting that the changes brought about by the Industrial Revolution – the decline of feudal obligations, the move to large cities to work as factory 'hands' – would lead to a weakening of the old social bonds, they set out to find evidence that other controlling influences on human behaviour continued to exist, to see how people related to each other without chaos and to discover whether people still had a sense of their 'place' in society.

Emile Durkheim examined this 'new' society for evidence of disintegration (for example suicide). In his famous study on suicide, Durkheim remarked how people who lost the ability to identify with society's 'norms' were more likely to take their own lives (see Unit 10, page 515).

Ferdinand Tonnies observed a change which took place during the process of industrialisation to do with a loss of a 'sense of place'. He identified a move from what he termed **Gemeinschaft** (a strongly bonded sense of community) to **Gesellschaft** (a weaker association between people):

- In a small-scale Gemeinschaft society, people are valued for their **ascriptive status**, i.e. for what they *are* rather than for what they *do*. Ascribed roles reduce conflict and increase a sense of 'knowing one's place'. This is reinforced by a lack of social and geographical mobility. The local culture is fairly homogeneous (i.e. there is little variation in status or values), since there is limited division of labour. The family and the church provide the bases of the society's values; their codes of behaviour are clear and accepted. Gemeinschaft community, then, promotes traditional values, and its inhabitants feel attached to the locality. There are solid relationships linking the inhabitants and a clear sense of 'stability' and 'order'.

- In a Gesellschaft society, these community ties are weakened by social change which comes about as people's means of earning a living change. Greater social and geographical mobility disrupts the settled patterns and values that existed before. Kinship ties are no longer of prime importance in influencing where people live or work. Association between people is more likely to be by economic exchange, by impersonal contractual bonds.

Nineteenth-century writers saw a move from 'community' to 'conflict', in parallel with that from the 'sacred' to the 'secular' society, and from 'tradition' to 'modernism'. The old order had been changed by the industrial and democratic revolutions, and the new order, its outlines still unclear, was often the cause of anxiety. Similar debates and concerns continue in the writings of sociologists today as they study urban and rural life, the city as a place and the existence – or not – of the elusive 'community'.

Definitions of 'community'

In 1955, G.A. Hillery catalogued 94 definitions of community, and the only factor that was common to them all was that community concerned people! Of his 94 definitions:

- 69 agreed that community includes social interaction, area, some ties or bonds in common;
- 14 included some common characteristics other than area;
- 15 defined community in terms of a rural area.

Is 'community' a description or a value judgement?

The concept of community is not only used as a descriptive term there is also an evaluative component. As a descriptive term, it has been used to describe social relationships in particular geographical areas, such as villages, towns, districts of a city, suburbs or slums. It has been used evaluatively in statements such as 'This area is a real community; that one isn't.' Sometimes the word is also used to refer to non-geographical units where people share interests rather than a locality, as in 'a community of scholars'.

Communitarianism

This term is generally taken to mean being in favour of community. It has been adopted by both the political Left and Right, yet with very different usage. Prime Minister Tony Blair, for example, has referred to it frequently as representing his view of 'communal relationships'. According to Amitai Etzioni, communitarianism represents:

> *'a new moral, social and public order based on restored communities, without allowing Puritanism or oppression.'*
> A. Etzioni, *New Statesman and Society*, 3 March 1995

Communitarians tend to express concern about the tendency for communities to be replaced by a set of Gesellschaft relationships and to argue that we need to return to the 'real' community of Gemeinschaft, where human relations are intimate and where:

> *'because a community shares its values there can be no fundamental moral conflicts; roles and relationships cohere and cannot conflict.'*
> Plant, *Community and Ideology* (Routledge & Kegan Paul, 1974)

The family and the community

Traditional family patterns tend to be identified with the stability of the community. This is the main focus, for example, of Etzioni's argument when he stresses the importance of addressing what he views as 'the parenting deficit' – also the name of his 1993 study.

> *'The family was always entrusted with laying the foundations of moral education. In the renewed community we envision, raising children is a job for both parents.'*

Some communitarians, including Etzioni, believe the 'new' community can be achieved by forms of neighbourhood self regulation, such as imposing curfews and compulsory community service on teenagers. Examples of such measures already exist in the USA and are proposed for the UK by the Labour government; one such scheme was introduced in Paisley and Hamilton in Scotland in October 1997. In Philadelphia, communitarian policies mean that homeless people who refuse to comply with job-search regulations will be denied entry to local authority emergency shelter; whilst in New Orleans a curfew has been instituted to ensure that young people are not outside late at night.

Communitarianism and postmodernism

At the heart of the debate surrounding communitarianism is the debate between modernism and postmodernism (see Unit 1, pages 57–9). Communitarianism represents postmodernism with its ideas of replacing the Welfare State, class and power relations with 'community' as a way of engaging with people and tackling the problems of society. Community, in this view, is classless, it is unproblematic and consensual and ignores conflicts. Etzioni asks:

> *'Should anyone in our community be allowed to starve? No. But communities will differ about how they do this. Many will not want to give money, but may establish a soup-kitchen, or a work-for-food plan.'*
> A. Etzioni, the *Guardian*, 13 March 1995

Thus, communities will deal with 'their problems' individually but without questioning the structures of society which allow people to starve.

The British Labour Party in the 1992 general election had already begun its journey along the postmodernist road. This involved:

- recognising the popular belief in the importance of consensus in determining community values;
- seeing that Marxist doctrines were outmoded and that talk of class or class interests were a liability in a changed world.

Under Tony Blair's leadership, the party's 'communitarianism' took on board this appeal to 'decency' and indeed adopted parts of the Conservative Party's image, with the commitment to be 'the party of aspiration and ambition'. According to Blair (as quoted in the *Guardian*, 23 March 1995), communitarian (and now New Labour) ideals and rules are ones which:

> *'we all stand by, fixed points of agreement which impose order over chaos'*

– an appeal to the idea that there is an unproblematic consensus of shared values.

Citizenship and the dissenting citizen

The intention of this developed communitarianism is to enable people to become 'good citizens' and, for this purpose, to be responsible for themselves and for others. This move towards a more advanced 'citizenship' aims to support stability and order.

The idea of citizenship as outlined by Blair and Etzioni is one where rights are less important than responsibilities and duties. This is not new – in 1992 the former Conservative Education Secretary, John MacGregor, and his Labour shadow, Jack Straw, both agreed that:

> 'pupils should be trained in citizenship. This training should include the teaching of individual duties and responsibilities ... respect for the law and training to understand how society works.'

This view was echoed in 1996 by the Department for Education and Employment.

Citizenship is also connected to the level of equality or inequality in society – a problem not addressed by communitarianism. J. Kingdom aptly summed up the problem:

> 'Education, income, health and housing are the means through which we become free to participate in the life of the community – the essence of citizenship. There can be no communal state under capitalism without a citizenship-based welfare state.'
>
> J. Kingdom, *Government and Politics in Britain* (1992)

Think about it

In the 1980s, the poll tax was an issue over which many people became 'active citizens'; these 'communities of resistance', however, were fiercely opposed by the Establishment. Etzioni would not perhaps have approved of them either, since a central part of their campaign was non-payment of the poll tax (in other words breaking the law) which would not be part of the democratic process. This is a problem with communitarianism and its assumption of **consensus** and shared values: how to include, within communities, groups with different morals and values.

- In the case of the poll tax, how do the values represented by those who 'rebelled' against it fit in with the idea of community consensus as the basis of the society's value system?

- Which groups in society might be excluded if the ideas of communitarianism were to be applied, and why?

In a climate of increasing public concern about the perceived breakdown of society, communitarianism has gained currency and has influenced the policies of both the Democratic Party in the USA and the Labour Party in Britain. However, communitarianism tends to view community as essentially 'good', homogeneous and unproblematic; its assumption of shared values could lead to exclusion and discrimination. Its apparent moral and authoritarian stance has also led to its ideas being closely connected with those of the New Right.

Locality, culture and the sense of belonging

Urbanisation

The following statistics, drawn from census data, show the percentage of the UK population living in towns from 1801 to 1991. What is evident is a significant growth in this percentage up until the early 1950s, followed by a slight decline into the 1990s.

Percentage of the population living in towns, UK

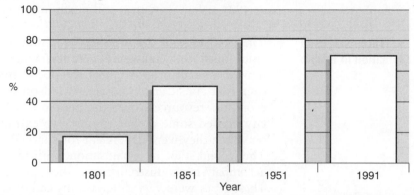

It is argued that the development of **urbanisation** (i.e. the growth of population living in towns and cities) in the UK was closely linked to the development of industrial capital, factories and an industrially located working population (as opposed to employment in agriculture). Conversely, the changes that took place in the composition of industry, particularly the decline of manufacturing industry, since 1951, appear to have resulted in a decline in the urban population. This process of **de-urbanisation** has tended to increase since the 1970s for a number of reasons:

- Changing employment patterns: as industry has moved out of the central areas and been replaced by smaller working units or has disappeared altogether with the growth of the service sector, people have less need to congregate within the towns and cities.
- Commuting: more working people are able to travel into the urban areas by public or private transport.
- Changing access to technology: the increasing availability of computers, telephones, faxes, etc. allows communication without the need for all workers to be in the same place ('tele-cottage' provision, e.g. BT networks in the Highlands of Scotland).

The sociological debate about the effects of urbanisation on community is problematic and ongoing. At one level there is evidence that community, in the pre-industrial sense of the word, all but disappeared in the nineteenth century as a result of industrialisation and urbanisation. In pre-industrial society, community had great significance, with towns and even villages often having a high degree of self sufficiency and political autonomy. Industrial society was marked by an increasing division of labour and growing central state authority. There was a steady shift from social relationships based on close personal ties of loyalty and deference to relations based on formal and legal contracts.

In general, the most highly industrialised countries are also the most highly urbanised. It is difficult to know which factor causes the other, but it is clear that each contributes to the other, and that as industrialisation has spread, so the proportion of the population living in towns has grown, although many cities in the UK, for example Manchester and Liverpool, have had falling populations since the 1960s.

Whilst this process of de-urbanisation can be seen in many of the industrial cities of the developed world, it is occurring at a much slower rate compared to the process of urbanisation across the world as a whole. In some developing countries, as we shall see later in the unit (page 493), urban growth is still much in evidence.

Three stages of urbanisation in Britain

1. **The first stage of urbanisation** was that from the first emergence of cities until the eighteenth century, when a few small-sized cities housed a small proportion of the population. Leaders of those cities exercised considerable power, based on either religious, military or economic resources, over the people in the surrounding area: every city needed some power resource to extract the agricultural surplus on which they were dependent for survival.

2. **The second stage of urbanisation**, with the very rapid growth of cities accompanying industrialisation, took place between 1811 and 1851. These cities were very different: instead of small craftsmen working in individual workshops, there were great factories and mills powered by steam engines and organised for large-scale production. Factory work required many hands, and rows of back-to-back houses, cramped and overcrowded, without sewage or public health facilities, dominated the area surrounding the factory. The factory managers and owners moved to the outskirts. In spite of widespread infectious disease, towns increased in size as more workers moved from the land to the factory.

3. **The third stage of urbanisation** has been labelled **metropolitanisation**. This is where the rate of increase in urban populations as a proportion of the whole population slows down or stops. Instead of there being many towns of roughly equal size, populations concentrate in 'conurbations'. Further technological improvements allow industrial production to decentralise, but the headquarters of firms tend to be in the big centres, together with the service sector, insurance, accounting, advertising, and so on. In Britain, 40 per cent of the population now live in the seven conurbations of Greater London, West Midlands, West Yorkshire, Manchester, Merseyside, Clydeside and Tyneside, with large numbers of people commuting to work each day rather than living close to their employment.

Another way of analysing these stages is by classifying them in terms of the dominant type of employment:

- Pre-industrial economies are mainly **agricultural**; the **primary sector** of the economy is dominant.
- As workers move to employment in industry and the proportion on the land declines, the economy becomes one in which the **secondary sector (manufacturing industry)** predominates.
- In the post-industrial phase associated with metropolitanisation, there is no longer a majority employed in industry. The **service sector** – white-collar, office jobs with middle-class status in welfare, education and public relations, etc. – employs much of the workforce.

Shifts in the structure of occupations influence the social relationships in the locality in many ways.

Urbanisation in developing countries

In most developing countries (see the section beginning on page 478), urbanisation is happening *before* industrialisation; thus giving rise to some new ideas on the relationship between urbanisation and industrialisation. In India, for example, people are forced off the land by population pressure and drift to the towns without there being industrial work for them. A 'revolution of rising expectations' makes people desire a better standard of living: contact with more developed societies shows this as a norm. One of the features of this 'revolution' is dissatisfaction with rural life and with traditional authority or caste restrictions.

There is also a tendency in developing countries for one or two cities to grow disproportionately: half of the biggest 'urban agglomerates' in the world are found in Africa, Asia and Latin America. Many of the inhabitants of these cities have no work, eking out a living by begging, whilst many others do messenger or service jobs which would be mechanised in an industrial society. Shanty towns, health hazards and slums are chronic (i.e. troublesome and ongoing) symptoms of stage 2 urbanisation as described above, whilst transport problems are acute (i.e. troublesome but short-term). Towns are often seen to represent modernity, however; voluntary associations give members practice in the new forms of social relationships – which are very different from those in rural communities.

Where urbanisation grows at a rate that is not matched by industrialisation, a serious lack of resources will sustain poverty, overpopulation and instability. Where town life is not embedded in a local culture, 'anomie' (see Unit 5, page 228) and social disorganisation is often found to be chronic.

Is community disappearing, or just changing?

There is a body of opinion which suggests that community is ceasing to exist. The theoretical starting point for this in sociology is associated with the views of F. Tonnies (see page 443), who believed that the process of urbanisation and industrialisation was causing the old patterns of community life in rural villages to break down, to be replaced by contractual relationships in new associations. In his view, the old unity of the village community was being displaced by competitiveness and self interest within the city. This Gemeinschaft/Gesellschaft distinction is summarised in the following table:

Gemeinschaft	Gesellschaft
• Community	• Association (society)
• Kinship (blood ties)	• Rootless nuclear family
• Neighbourhood (sense of place)	• Atomistic society (impersonal, mobile)
• Relationships (intimacy, friendship)	• Instrumental relationships (for particular ends)

Similar views were stated by Louis Wirth in his study *Urbanism as a Way of Life*, based on Chicago in 1938. Wirth saw the size, population density and cultural mixture of the city as preventing the development of any feelings of community, but rather creating tensions and social problems.

Further support for the view that community is disappearing is offered by studies of rural areas in Britain, where conflict seems to be replacing solidarity. Pahl (1965) studied the area within a 40–50-mile radius of central London, in which he identified what he calls 'metropolitan villages', inhabited by a wide variety of potentially conflicting social groups. From his sample of 400 people (from a population of 23,000), he found, for example, potential divisions between the newcomers and the traditional rural inhabitants, and between members of the middle class who were seeking rural tranquillity and urban labourers in search of affordable accommodation. Similarly, Howard Newby, in his East Anglia studies (1980), has indicated the growing division between the rich and the poor in East Anglia. Relatively rich farmers have now been joined by rich commuters, while the poor agricultural labourers have been further impoverished by cutbacks in local services such as public transport. This situation can also be noted in the Scottish Highlands, where local crofters are being displaced by English immigrants who, with new technology, are able to conduct their work using telecommunications. One effect has been a considerable increase in the price of property, with a negative impact on local people's ability to buy property in the area.

Some writers in the Marxist tradition would argue that Tonnies's theory was ideologically based. The main problem with it, however, revolves around definitions (see page 444). G.A. Hillery (1955) located over 90 different usages of the term 'community' by social scientists, and D. Lee and H. Newby (1983) isolated three basic strands in the different usages of the term 'community' by sociologists, each of which would give different answers as to what community is:

- Firstly they point to the geographical usage of the term as involving a group of people living in a particular area. If this were to be accepted as the definition, then clearly communities still exist.
- The second definition involves regular patterns of interaction without predicting what relationships will be like. If this is accepted then the research by Young and Willmott in Bethnal Green, London, in 1957, *Family and Kinship in East London* (see Unit 3), by Gans (1962) in Boston, and so on, would indicate the continuation of the community even if it is to some extent being threatened by rehousing schemes.
- Finally, Lee and Newby suggest that a feeling of identity or communion is the all-important element. If this is the case, then it would become meaningful to talk about a whole range of communities in Britain: professional, religious and ethnic communities, for example.

Think about it

- Do you feel part of a 'community' – or of more than one community? If so, how would you define it/them? Ask your family and friends what they consider the 'community' to be.
- Based on your answers to the question above, can you come up with a general definition for 'community' which you feel is a satisfactory sociological definition?
- If you were asked to undertake an investigation into the existence of a 'local community', whom would you consult, and why?

Community and locality

Does the nature of a community depend on where it is? G. Simmel, in *The Metropolis and Mental Life*, was the first person to relate the concepts of Gemeinschaft and Gesellschaft to specific localities. He investigated the relationship which the city promotes between the individual and the urban world in which he or she lives. For Simmel, urban life is rational, resulting from the increased pace deriving from social and economic differentiation, as opposed to rural life, which is based on feelings and emotional relationships. He regarded the city as the seat of the money economy, which encourages matter-of-fact treatment of people and things; and he identified what later became familiar urban social evils: impersonality, isolation, dehumanisation and alienation. These, he saw, produce eccentric behaviour, an exaggerated search for individuality and self identity within the unstable framework of metropolitan life; the individual becomes:

> *'a mere cog in an enormous organisation of things and powers which tear from his hands all progress, spirituality and value.'*
>
> G. Simmel (1964)

Simmel, like Tonnies, feared the loss of community in modern society. However, in contrast to Tonnies, Simmel related this solely to the growth of the city as a unique form of social organisation.

The idea that a rural locality determines a harmonious community lifestyle has been subjected to wide-ranging criticism. Oscar Lewis, who studied Tepoztlan in Mexico during 1949, was its first critic. He emphasised:

> *'the underlying individualism of Tepoztlan institutions and character, the lack of co-operation, the tensions between villages within the municipo, the schisms within the village, the pervading quality of fear, envy and distrust, in interpersonal relations.'*
>
> Oscar Lewis, *The Children of Sanchez* (1949)

Doubts concerning urbanism as a way of life were also cited by a number of community studies which established the existence of 'some disturbingly Gemeinschaft' communities in the centre of large cities: for example, Young and Willmott's studies of Bethnal Green in East London, which was later termed an urban village; the studies of Hoggart (on Hunslet, in 1957) and H.J. Gans (*The Urban Villages*, in 1962). Louis Wirth, in his Chicago studies, appeared to overlook Gemeinschaft-style neighbourhoods within the urban system.

It has also been found that commuter villages in the countryside, like urban villages, are difficult to position within the rural–urban continuum. Pahl, for example, (1965) revealed villages consisting wholly or partly of rural commuters and others who lived in the countryside but worked in towns and cities. Other 1960s' studies of rural communities (for example, the work of Williams and Littlejohn) illustrate that many rural areas cannot be classified as examples of Gemeinschaft: rural Britain contains the business rationality, geographical mobility, loneliness, anonymity, class conflict, etc., which are held to be typical of the Gesellschaft society.

The study of suburbia

With neither the rural nor the urban end of the spectrum typifying the way of life expected of them, sociologists turned their attention to 'suburbia'. The stereotypical suburban homogeneous housing estates, with endless streets of identical houses containing lifestyles of similar relentless conformity, have been portrayed as representing vast transit camps for the upwardly mobile commuting middle-class executives devoted to the consumption of consumer durables and 'keeping up with the Joneses'.

An upper-middle-class suburb was studied by Seeley et al. in 1963 to test whether or not it was a 'real' community. It was difficult to draw the line round the suburb: residents were seldom born there, nor did they expect to live there for the rest of their lives; and the men generally worked in the nearby city, so the community was not bonded by shared work. Nevertheless, Seeley et al. argued that the suburb was a 'real community' because of the relationships between the residents, their institutions and their shared values, particularly their shared purpose, and their focus on their children.

> '*Its major institutional focus is on child-rearing and all the suburb's institutions, the school, the church, the community centres, the clubs, directly or indirectly, are geared to turning out young people to the specifications accepted in the community. In so far as these communities tend to be of people of similar age and stage in the life-cycle, and of roughly similar income and status, attitudes to the children are more homogeneous than in a neighbourhood of an equivalent size in a city area.*'

Seeley et al., *Suburbia* (1963)

Features of suburban life

- Life is centred not on the neighbourhood or the street, but on the home.

- The 'home-centredness' is reflected in a strong emphasis placed on obtaining consumer durables.

- There is relatively less emphasis on contact with relatives and relatively more on choosing, making and keeping friends, often from a fairly wide geographical area and not just from the neighbourhood or street.

- Where households are made up of husbands and wives, there is more emphasis on sharing tasks and sharing friends.

- There is fairly high participation in a variety of informal and formal organisations, with friendships developing out of this voluntary participation.

Source: Adapted from N. Abercrombie and A. Warde, *Contemporary British Society* (Polity Press, 1994)

The stereotypical 'myth of suburbia' is also subject to criticism. After moving into the suburb of Levittown, H.J. Gans (see below) discovered that it was not a totally homogeneous community and that most inhabitants had settled there for 'house-related' as opposed to 'job-related' reasons.

The Levittowners (1962)

Gans studied the beginning of a Chicago suburb in Levittown, with a largely middle-class population. Nearly half of those interviewed said they had come to settle permanently. They, too, focused on the family; but friendships here emerged on the basis of shared interests rather than aspiration, material accumulation, or social class. Informal and later formal clubs and associations sorted people by their interests and social class, so that in a short time each organisation tended to be homogeneous, though a great diversity of organisations existed. Gans noted too the difference between 'locals' and 'cosmopolitans', a difference which cut across the divisions of class and religion, and found it a useful concept for analysing community networks. He emphasised that so much suburban life was home-centred that many residents are 'sub-locals', with little energy even for local community affairs. He suggested that the community was divided by social class (56 per cent lower-middle-class white-collar workers, 18 per cent professional and 26 per cent manual workers); religious affiliation; and differences between locals and cosmopolitans.

In Britain, there is evidence to support the view that there is no necessary causal connection between the shift in the location of residence to suburbia and the adoption of a particular lifestyle. Willmott and Young, in *Family and Class in a London Suburb* (1960), and Colin Bell, in *Middle Class Families* (1968), for example, demonstrate that extensive geographical and social mobility did not necessarily mean that Gemeinschaft-type social relationships would be dissolved, only that they were less dependent on locality.

Think about it

- Do you consider that the 'community' in which you live meets Tonnies's conditions of Gemeinschaft or Gesellschaft or neither? Give reasons for your view.

Rural–urban theories

Patterns of rural life: ideal-typical features

- It is organised as a community with people frequently meeting and being connected to each other in lots of different ways.
- People have close-knit social networks; in other words, one's friends know each other as well as oneself.
- Most inhabitants work on the land or in related industries. There is a high proportion of jobs that overlap and there is a relatively simple division of labour. Most workers are relatively unspecialised farm labourers.
- Most people possess an ascribed status fixed by their family origin. It is difficult to change the status through achievement. People are strongly constrained to behave in ways appropriate to their status. This status spreads from one situation to another, irrespective of the different activities in which people engage.
- Economic class divisions are only one basis of social conflict. Various strategies are developed to handle potential conflicts that cannot be overcome because people keep meeting each other. Generally, social inequalities are presumed to be justified, often in terms of tradition.

Source: Adapted from N. Abercrombie and A. Warde, *Contemporary British Society* (Polity Press, 1994)

Ferdinand Tonnies and **Louis Wirth** are the two most important socio-logical sources on the urban/rural divide; their comments need to be considered in any study of the characteristics of urban life or the decline of community. In the 1940s, R. Redfield referred to rural life as the 'folk society', being small, isolated and homogeneous, with a strong sense of group solidarity. He saw behaviour as tending to follow traditional pat-terns and lacking experiment and intellectual reflection. Redfield's main emphasis, however, was that urban–rural differences should be seen as a continuum rather than a dichotomy. This approach was taken up by writers such as T. Lynn Smith who, in *The Urban and Rural Worlds* (1991), saw the principal characteristics of rural and urban areas becoming blurred. Smith attempted to distinguish rural lifestyles in the following ways:

- Occupation: the agricultural basis of rural life in an essentially natural environment contrasted starkly with urban life. Within each rural group, however, Smith admits to significant distinctions, such as that between crop farmers and livestock farmers.
- Size of community: based on the agricultural need for a considerable area of land per person, large farming communities are almost an impossibility.
- Population density: the need to reside close to the land makes popula-tion density low, and this has secondary effects on the intimacy of social relationships and educational standards.
- Environment: agriculture is the principal determinant of the environ-ment; the physical environment subjects people to its direct influence.
- Social differentiation: in rural areas thousands of small, relatively independent and unrelated units develop. Associates tend to have sim-ilar backgrounds, beliefs and behaviour patterns.

- Social stratification: the number of strata in a rural area is much reduced, with all tending to take an intermediate position.
- Social mobility: people tend to be more attached to their social status, with less desire or opportunity for mobility.
- Social interaction: a general lack of it, with visitors rare. Those relationships that do develop tend to be permanent and personal.
- Social solidarity: unity based on similarities rather than interdependence, informal and non-contractual with a consciousness of being similar to each other.

P.H. Mann, in his study *An Approach to Urban Sociology* (1970), notes the following differences between rural and urban areas in relation to Britain:

- Urban areas have a preponderance of women over men.
- Rural areas have more young people aged 5–24, fewer of the 25–54 group and about the same number of over 55s.
- Only agriculture distinguishes rural and urban areas in occupational terms. Building, transport, clerical and commercial occupations are found equally in both, although unskilled manual workers are more commonly found in conurbations.
- Foreign-born people are more commonly found in urban areas, with the south being more attractive to them than the north.
- The birth rate is slightly higher in rural areas, while infant mortality and the death rate are higher in urban areas.
- Diseases of the epidemic type are much more common in urban areas and, perhaps surprisingly, there are more doctors in rural areas.

Criticisms of the rural–urban thesis

The rural–urban dichotomy has been a very influential thesis in sociological theory; nevertheless it has come under attack from many quarters. Mann's study, mentioned above, cast doubt on the theories of rural–urban divisions, revealing instead important differences in Britain between the north and south:

> *'The differentiation between north and south was often more real than the differentiation between rural and urban.'*
> P.H. Mann, *An Approach to Urban Sociology* (Routledge & Kegan Paul, 1970)

Among the most important criticisms raised are the following:

It is ideological
It can be argued that the image of a rural utopia preceding urbanisation is a myth designed by a reactionary ideology. Marxists would point to the conflicts between master and slave, feudal lord and serf as characterising earlier epochs. A study of Westriggin in Scotland by K. Littlejohn, for example, revealed traditional patterns of stratification in a rural area – a perspective still noted in crofting communities in the Scottish Highlands in the 1990s. Tonnies's concept of a stable community can also be attacked by historical evidence; M. Anderson has produced data to show that considerable movements of population took place within the rural sector in early nineteenth-century England.

It selected the wrong unit for analysis

Wirth's study of Chicago (see page 450) viewed the city as a social whole and suggested the impossibility of observing good community relationships developing on this large-scale area. This view has been criticised by R. Pahl, who quotes a wide range of different studies to show the existence of numerous small communities encapsulated within the city boundaries. Within these smaller communities, regular patterns of interaction take place and people identify with their own particular community.

Urbanism is not the cause of social problems

L. Castells, a Marxist, has argued that the social problems of the city are the product of capitalism rather than of urbanisation. In his view, monopoly capitalism leads to the centralisation of business organisations in the main cities, thereby encouraging immigration from surrounding areas. Capital is unwilling to provide the means of reproduction of labour power (housing, health facilities, education, transport, etc.) and so it is left to the state to do so. The state, in turn, has inadequate resources, and so urban social movements arise to challenge the social order and its inadequate provision of facilities.

Modern communications

The mass media ensure that the same messages are carried to every area within a state or even continent. As M. Stewart has argued, an isolated farm homestead in the American Midwest is far more part of urban society, in terms of outlook, contact and background behaviour, than town dwellers in a less developed country. Similarly, modern means of transport have tied the rural area into the urban economy, with urban and rural areas both meeting the commercial needs of the other. In the UK, British Telecom and the Highlands and Islands Development Board (in Scotland) have developed sophisticated telecommunications provision in numerous rural villages.

The changing rural scene

Pahl showed that the 'metropolitan villages' in apparently rural areas outside London (see page 450) contained a greater social mixture than could be found within a similar area of a city: traditional farmers and agricultural labourers; large property owners who were tied by both property and tradition to the village; the salaried who had chosen to live in a rural landscape and commute to work; retired urban workers who had accumulated sufficient capital to settle in such areas; urban workers with limited capital who found it easier to buy reasonable accommodation away from the city; and a rural working class that originated in the village and retained its home there but commuted to the city for low-paid work.

Re-housing initiatives

A policy of rehousing was adopted by the Labour government in Britain after 1945 and continued by its Conservative successors. The policy was in part a response to the devastation caused by the war, but more so a recognition of the poor living conditions of large sections of British society.

New Towns One element of this policy involved the creation of **New Towns** which could offer new employment and living opportunities to the overspill population from the large inner-city areas of London and Liverpool, for example.

The first group of New Towns to be established after 1945 were:

- Basildon, Bracknell, Crawley, Harlow, Hatfield, Hemel Hempstead, Stevenage and Welwyn, all in the area surrounding London;
- East Kilbride and Glenrothes, in Scotland;
- Newton Aycliffe and Peterlee, in County Durham;
- Corby, in Northamptonshire;
- Cwmbran, in South Wales.

These were followed by a second generation of New Towns including:

- Cumbernauld, in Dunbartonshire;
- Skelmersdale, in Lancashire;
- Milton Keynes, in the East Midlands.

Some, such as Welwyn and Stevenage, were based on existing towns, while others, such as Peterlee, were almost entirely new projects.

New council estates A second element of the rehousing policy was the building of **council estates** on the edges of towns and cities, such as Kirby on the fringes of Liverpool. These would have their own shopping centres and perhaps recreational facilities, but they would not be sufficiently large to constitute towns in their own right.

Policy intentions The initial aim of these developments was to eradicate or at least alleviate social problems. Many of the inner-city areas had suffered war-damage, and some people had temporarily been rehoused in prefabricated buildings. In some areas there was overcrowding, while in many others there was poor sanitation. Moreover, the decline of some traditional industries such as shipbuilding was beginning to make its mark in terms of unemployment, and the New Towns were designed to attract new industries that would have an industrial site and an available labour force on hand. Finally, the dirt and pollution of some areas, with the smoke-created smogs of the early 1950s, were creating a health problem which, it was believed, could be solved by a policy of rehousing in more rural areas.

However, many of the New Towns and estates were quickly associated with new social problems (see below).

Sociological studies A number of studies by sociologists and other researchers have involved explicit comparisons between traditional working-class communities and the new areas in which they were rehoused following urban clearance. Early studies noted several unforeseen developments. Mann, for example, notes that:

> '[after] the early years of settling into their new homes and getting the young families under way, parents and children seemed to find the New Towns dull places.'
> P.H. Mann, *An Urban Approach to Sociology* (Routledge & Kegan Paul, 1970)

He notes that neighbourhood activities never developed to the extent intended, and many of the New Towns were not large enough to sustain leisure organisations such as cinemas, dance-halls and theatres.

Other developments that have been identified as a result of rehousing include the following:

Changing family patterns   In *Family and Kinship in East London* (1957), Young and Willmott found that the movement of people from Bethnal Green to Greenleigh led to declining contact with the extended family (see Unit 3). Before moving, the average husband saw one or more of his relatives on 15 occasions in a week, but this declined to between three and four after moving. The figures for the average wife were even more dramatic, falling from over 17 to between two and three. This led to a certain amount of isolation, with family sickness becoming a minor disaster as no relatives were on hand to help. Hannah Gavron, in *The Captive Wife* (1966), illustrated empirically how marital tensions can develop as a result of this pattern of isolation.

The development of a privatised existence   Young and Willmott quote several examples of failure to develop patterns of friendship with neighbours. Complaints about the unfriendliness of neighbours were regularly made, and even

> *'where relations have not been severed, there is little of the mateyness so characteristic to Bethnal Green'.*
> Young and Wilmott, *Family and Kinship in East London*
> (1957)

Young and Willmott explain this in terms of different places of origin within the East End of London, the low population density that does not encourage sociability, and the few points of contact with both pubs and shops being at some distance from the houses.

Changing identities   Those people still living in Bethnal Green felt that those who had moved had become 'stand-offish', and some of the residents of Greenleigh noted the same characteristics of their neighbours. Young and Willmott explain this in terms of the improved status the woman, in particular, feels of her home. The improved houses necessitated better furniture and the need for more sophisticated means of communications, for example via the telephone rather than 'popping round for a chat'.

Vandalism and crime   Many rehousing schemes have been associated with an increase in vandalism and crime, with some areas, such as Kirkby near Liverpool and Westerhailes in Edinburgh, being regarded (perhaps unfairly) as hot-beds of vandalism. Some researchers have noted the role that the design of certain estates and tower-blocks may have in creating this. It can be argued that the anonymity of the new place of residence without feelings of community make vandalism and crime easier to commit with little risk of being caught.

Lack of employment   Economic developments have meant that many of the New Towns have failed to become the havens of employment for which they were designed; Skelmersdale and many of the others have very high rates of unemployment.

All these findings reflect the lack of a community in the area of resettlement; increasing unemployment levels in many of them is likely to increase these problems. However, there is a danger of using rehousing as a scapegoat for social problems that are more widespread, and many of the criticisms made of the New Towns and council estates have been overstated. On the question of crime, it is still the inner-city areas such as Toxteth in Liverpool and Balsall Heath in Birmingham that record the highest number of offences, and the racial and social problems exhibited in recent years in St Paul's in Bristol, Brixton and Notting Hill in London, for example, would seem far more serious than those of the New Towns. David White points out that in Milton Keynes:

> 'Vandalism is rare enough for a headmaster to make a point of showing me an isolated example – eight windows of his school broken.'
>
> David White, *Families* (1992)

Undoubtedly, loneliness and feelings of isolation are to be found in rehoused communities. David White concedes that in Milton Keynes there is a high rate of marital breakdown and that the number of people satisfied with life there has declined. But for those in employment such feelings can be off-set by use of the telephone and car, allowing contact with the extended family at least in times of crisis.

As Goldthorpe and Lockwood found from their Luton study, many people have voluntarily left traditional working-class communities to rehouse themselves on private housing estates, which exhibit many of the characteristics of council estates, as soon as they are financially able. It may be that the new housing situation fails to live up to expectations and that this induces feelings of nostalgia for a more communal life, while the disadvantages and inconveniences of the latter are forgotten.

Power, social policy and social conflict in urban and inner-city society

As towns grow, some factories move out; business and shopping districts spread, invading the residential zone; the city edges are extended by developing suburbs; and the **inner-city area** is left with obsolete housing, slums, single-room dwellings for migrants, problem families and the homeless. These 'twilight zones' contain a high concentration of the unsettled, transient young, and have the highest rates of delinquency, mental illness, divorce, illegitimacy, illiteracy and suicide. Ghettos may develop where homogeneous groups – distinguished by skin colour, country of origin or religion – reside, whether by choice or as a result of discrimination in housing allocation and provision. Some disadvantaged groups may get stuck here, as a permanent lower class ('underclass'), cut off from opportunities for upward mobility.

In 1981, Britain saw considerable disturbances in urban areas such as Brixton, Toxteth and Moss-side, where young people – both black and white and very often unemployed – rioted, looted, burned and attacked the police. Durkheim's fears about the loosening of bonds of social solidarity in modern conditions appeared to be well founded. The responses of the Establishment (noted in the Scarman Report, 1982) also showed clearly the gap in the social experiences between the two groups of black and white youth. More recent events in Oxford, Cardiff and Newcastle in 1991, and Manningham in Bradford and Chapletown in Leeds during 1995 and 1996, appear to contribute to the view that such disturbances are an irregular but grave indication of difficulties in inner-city areas.

The Report by Lord Justice Scarman and J. Beynon's book *The Scarman Report*, published in 1983, provide useful reference points raising issues related not only to the riots themselves but also to the living situation and economic circumstances of people living in these communities. Within urban and inner-city areas a number of identified social problems have been noted by sociologists which appear to recur over time:

<u>Poverty and deprivation</u>   Charles Booth in the late nineteenth century noted the levels of poverty in the inner city, findings which would be substantiated by a series of reports and research studies today, for example: a study by local government leaders in the North of England (1982); the Barclay Report on Tower Hamlets (1985); the Scarman Report (1982) on inner-city riots.

<u>Unemployment</u>   Particularly high levels of unemployment exist for young people from ethnic minorities in some inner cities. There is a view that the lack of employment opportunities in such deprived areas may contribute to the development of an 'underclass' as defined by Charles Murray in 1990 (see Unit 3, pages 126–7).

<u>Riots</u>   From the early 1980s to 1996 there have been a number of riots in English inner-city areas (see above).

<u>Housing for ethnic minorities</u>   Housing policies and the poor quality of 'ghettoised' housing, together with overcrowding and racial discrimination, create difficulties for ethnic minorities trying to obtain good quality housing.

Education Poor quality educational provision exists in these areas and there is a tendency for it to be under-resourced with high levels of truanting and poor exam results.

It is suggested that many inner-city residents are too isolated or poor to engage in collective action about their deteriorating situation. At the same time the growth of a drug-culture and drug-related crime, as well as urban riots, create a climate of fear in some inner cities. Charles Murray's suggestion that an underclass is developing in these impoverished areas poses a suggested threat to social order and may lead to harsh social policies on benefits, law and order, and crime.

The megalopolis

In stark contrast to the deprivation of some inner-city areas is the culture of affluence of the 'megalopolis'. Between the late 1960s and the mid-1990s, R. Jewson suggests it is possible to identify the development of the megalopolis, accompanying the post-Fordist era of production. Some towns and cities now have a global dimension as headquarters of transnational corporations or computer-software industries. Examples would be towns and cities along the M4 corridor (London–Bristol), the M11 corridor (London–Cambridge) and the M8 corridor of 'Silicon Glen' (Edinburgh–Glasgow). The features of the megalopolis include:

- de-urbanisation;
- a wide variety of small settlements;
- decentralisation of jobs and capital;
- decentralisation of retail businesses (i.e. to green-field hypermarkets);
- limited state intervention;
- development of consumer culture.

As noted by Robson (1988), decaying inner-city areas can be found within the growing megalopolis. To the above list of features, therefore, we can add:

- decline of the thriving inner cities;
- decline of inner-city public services and revenue;
- urban riots.

Think about it

Indicators of inner-city deprivation can be listed as follows:

- population loss;
- high levels of unemployment;
- high proportion of long-term unemployed;
- large number of lone-parent households;
- high proportion of people over pensionable age;
- significant number of houses without an inside toilet;
- large proportion of people without higher degrees or diplomas;
- high ratio of people with unskilled or semi-skilled jobs.

Which, if any, of these aspects do you feel are more likely to feature in an urban context than a rural one? Give reasons for your answers.

Major sociological studies of community

Whilst the theme of community is being revisited in sociology in the 1990s, it was first studied in depth in the period 1950–74. The selected reading list for this unit (pages 500–502) provides evidence of how important the topic has been for sociological study; many of the issues raised in the early stages of the sociology of community are still highly relevant today.

Think about it

This section of the unit has looked at the concept of community and at the ways in which sociologists have debated the form and extent of community relationships in an industrial society such as the UK.

- What lists of advantages and disadvantages can you now draw up for urban and for rural communities, from a sociological point of view?
- How do you understand the relationship between community and citizenship?
- Is the existence of community under threat?

■ SOCIETY AND NATION

Nationhood: what does it mean?

- What is a **nation** and by what characteristics can it be identified?
- What is the relationship between **nationalism** as a political doctrine, a consciousness of **nationhood**, and what is often called **patriotism**?
- Why should a nation be a recognised unit of government and what are the political implications of such a situation?

The nation, the state and the nation state

Words like 'the nation', 'the state' and 'the country' are often used interchangeably. Until 1991, for example, the USSR was referred to as a single state containing 15 republics (a number of which sought independence) and 128 officially recognised ethnic and linguistic groups. Should we say that Britain is a single nation or a 'united kingdom' containing four nations: England, Scotland, Wales and Northern Ireland? What will it be called when Scotland and Wales set up their own parliaments?

The nation

A **nation** can be defined as a cultural entity, a collection of people bound together by shared values and traditions, for example a common language, a common religion and a common history, and usually occupying the same geographical area.

This, on the face of it, seems simple enough, but does not always work. The Palestinians, for example, while seeking to establish themselves as a nation in the Middle East, cannot meet the criterion of 'geographical area'.

The following characteristics are typical of a nation:

- a political entity, defined by state boundaries;
- a geographical unit, defined by 'natural frontiers' or by some historical territorial identity, for example 'the English nation';
- a people conscious of their common identity and unity, revealed through a distinctive national culture or collective political action;
- a people, defined by some common 'objective' feature of their social life, for example common language, ethnic or social origins, religion or shared economic life.

Putting these elements together creates an 'ideal' of nationhood, a people with their own state and homeland, a developed national culture and consciousness, and social homogeneity. This represents what most **nationalists** would wish their nation to be. (See pages 466–9 for a discussion on nationalism in the UK.)

The state

A **state** is considered to be a political association which:

- enjoys sovereignty (see page 471);
- possesses supreme or unrestricted power;
- is located within defined territorial borders.

Max Weber's definition sees the state as the agency within society which possesses the monopoly of legitimate violence. The idea behind this view is that in well ordered societies, sectional violence (such as that used by the IRA) is considered illegitimate. Violence may only be used, legitimately, by the central political authority and those to whom it delegates such entitlement.

The nation state   There is also the modern concept of the **nation state** – a state possessing clearly defined borders in which the boundaries of state and nation are linked together.

All these definitions are problematic once we start to look closely at specific, 'real' examples. Whilst cultural features such as shared language, religion, history, traditions etc. might commonly be associated with nationhood, there is no blueprint nor any objective criteria for this to allow judgements which can conclusively establish where and when a nation exists. Do the people of Northern Ireland, for example, belong to the 'British nation', the 'Irish nation' or to a separate 'Northern Ireland' or 'Ulster nation'? Whilst nations are certainly bound together by a shared culture or cultures, the make-up of nations can be very diverse (i.e. heterogeneous).

It is often considered that the sharing of a common language might ease the process of development of a nation; language is viewed as one of the clearest symbols of nationhood. A common religion can also be a potent symbol. In Northern Ireland, for example, religion expresses common moral values and spiritual beliefs. People speaking the same language (English) are often divided by religion, with Protestants largely favouring unionism and continued links with Britain and many Catholics seeking to establish links within a unified Ireland.

Nations may also be based on a sense of racial unity. This was evident in Germany at the time of Nazi power, with the German word for people, *Volk* – which refers both to cultural unity and to blood ties – being emphasised. The significance of race has also been highlighted by far-Right groups such as the National Front in Britain and France, and by supporters of apartheid in South Africa. Such groups use the law, violence or propaganda to campaign against non-white access to employment or immigration. In Britain, the National Front sought the repatriation of non-white immigrants on the grounds that multi-racialism undermines national unity. In 1997 in places such as Dover the National Front and others demonstrated against Czechs and Slovaks who claimed that they were being persecuted because they were Romanies, and sought to live in Britain.

Nationalism

Nationhood is related to both state and nation. It has been subject to shifting definitions, though B. Anderson, in *Imagined Communities* (1983), offers four key characteristics:

- The nation is *imagined* in as far as it carries the image of 'communion' or 'social interaction', even with and between people who never meet.
- Nation is *limited* because it has finite yet potentially elastic boundaries.

- It implies *sovereignty* in the sense that the people who comprise it have the right to determine their own future, as shown for example by the 1979 and 1997 referendums on devolution for Wales and Scotland.
- Nation implies *community*, a sense of deep comradeship amongst the people.

The greater attention given by sociologists, in recent years, to nationalism and the nation state has been accompanied by a more critical attitude towards these areas of study:

> *'The prevailing image of nationalism in the West today is mainly negative ... [this negative evaluation] contrasts with the favourable attitude of nineteenth-century liberals and radicals, and later conservatives, towards the doctrine of national self-determination.'*
>
> Anthony Smith (1987)

Theories of nationalism

Marxist theories

Marxist theories of nationalism have tended to emphasise the connection between the rise of the bourgeoisie and the emergence of the nation state. The relationship between nationalism and industrialisation/modernisation was formulated most fully by Ernest Gellner, in the 1960s, in a model which brings together economic and cultural factors. His main argument is that:

> *'... as the wave of industrialisation and modernisation moves outward, it disrupts the previous political units [which are] generally either small and intimate ... or large but loose and ill-centralised.'*
>
> Ernest Gellner

The 'two prongs of nationalism', he suggests, 'tend to be a proletariat and an intelligentsia': the former is first uprooted and then gradually incorporated in a new national community; the latter provides new cultural definitions of group membership which are widely diffused with the development of mass literacy and a national education system which industrialisation itself makes necessary, in order to weld together the different groups.

Max Weber was an ardent nationalist whose political sociology was guided by the principle of the 'primacy of the interests of the nation state'. Emile Durkheim's sociology was guided by a concern with the 'regeneration of France', the overcoming of profound internal divisions, especially between classes, and the recreation of 'solidarity'.

The much greater interest which sociologists have shown, since World War II, in nationalist movements and the formation of nation states is easily understandable, since it coincides with an upsurge of nationalism directed specifically against the economic and political dominance of the Western nations – where the great majority of sociologists live and work – which has created entirely new situations, and new problems for those nations.

Nationalism has been described as asserting the primacy of a group relationship based on a common language, culture and dialect – sometimes a common religion – over all the other claims on a person's loyalty. The history of nationalism derives from:

> 'a doctrine invented in Europe at the beginning of the 19th century [which] holds that humanity is naturally divided into nations and that nations are known by certain characteristics which can be ascertained and that the only legitimate type of government is national self-government'
>
> J. Eccleshall (1986)

This view suggests that nationalism comprises:

- a political doctrine (not merely a 'state of mind');
- a specific theory of political legitimacy;
- a claim that national identity is essential to social life;
- a principle and a form of political organisation (in most, but not all, cases).

Nationalism is an immensely powerful force; first, because it is sustained by a deep-rooted sense of belonging to a territorial and cultural community and, second, because this sense of belonging has become firmly attached to the nation state in a process of political development which is now several centuries old, and has taken on the character of a sacred and unalterable principle of political organisation. Evidence of the power of nationalism can be seen in the break-up of the Soviet Union after 1989, and the violent upheavals in the former Yugoslavia between Serbs, Muslims and Croats. Significant nationalist movements can also be noted with the vigorous separatist movements in Ireland, Scotland and Quebec in Canada.

Local nationalism

Local nationalism grew in many countries during the 1970s: Corsican and Breton in France, Quebecker in Canada, Basque and Catalan in Spain. It is hard to pinpoint the cause for this upsurge in local separatism. Economics plays a role: local nationalists usually claim their regions are shortchanged by their central governments. Nationalists often emphasise their regions' distinct languages and cultures and demand that they be taught in schools. Some of the impulse behind local nationalism is the bigness and remoteness of the modern state, the feeling that important decisions are out of local control, made by faraway bureaucrats. And often smouldering under the surface are historical resentments of a region that once was conquered, occupied and deprived of its own identity. Whatever the mixture, local nationalism sometimes turns its adherents into radical activists willing to take large-scale violent action to get their way.

Nationalism in the UK

The simplistic view of the British system as a unitary, homogeneous and stable polity faltered in the late 1960s. First the Irish and then the Welsh and Scottish nationalists showed how 'multinational' the UK was and how divergent were many of its regional political cultures.

In addition to the low-level civil war in Northern Ireland, Scotland and Wales present problems of regionalism. Wales has been a part of England since the Middle Ages; the thrones of England and Scotland were united in 1603, and in 1707 both countries agreed to a single

Parliament in London. But old resentments never quite died. Wales and Scotland were always poorer than England, provoking the feeling among Welsh and Scots that they were economically exploited. In the twentieth century the political beneficiary of these feelings has been the Labour Party, which holds sway in Wales and Scotland, with no Conservative MPs being elected in either country in the 1997 general election (in which the Conservative Party represented itself as the 'party of the Union'). The growth of Plaid Cymru (meaning 'Party of Wales') and the Scottish National Party was evidenced in the 1974 election when the Welsh Nationalists won three Commons seats and the Scottish Nationalists eleven. After the 1997 election they held four and six seats respectively (an increase of two seats for the SNP over the 1992 result).

Welsh nationalism

In Wales, culture has been at the heart of nationalism. Although Plaid Cymru, founded in 1925, claims the right to a seat for Wales in the United Nations, it has traditionally based its programme on the views of its founder, J. Saunders Lewis, who once declared the movement 'not a fight for Wales's independence, but for Wales's civilisation'. This civilisation is identified with the Welsh language and the promotion of literary and musical forms which flourished in feudal times.

Economics also provides a spur for nationalism in Wales. Although Wales does not have oil, the Welsh, like the Scots, feel economically exploited by England.

The Welsh language, the ancient Celtic tongue of Cymric (pronounced *kim-rick*) is perhaps the most important symbol for Welsh nationalists. About one Welsh person in five still speaks Cymric, but most are elderly, and popular use of the language has declined dramatically. In recent years, however, there has been an upsurge of people learning it and Welsh is now officially equal to English within Wales. The provision of a Welsh TV channel has ensured linguistic distinctiveness and may contribute to both linguistic and cultural diversity.

Scottish nationalism

The claim for independence from England and the rest of the UK rests on the presumption of a distinct Scottish nation. Scotland, it is claimed, was a nation state long before the Act of Union (1707) with England; but rather than securing an equal partnership, the Union has reduced Scotland to a subordinate and peripheral status. It did, however, leave intact the essentials of a distinct national life – an education and legal system, a national church and, until recently, a national economy. Scots, too, have retained a distinct sense of identity, of political behaviour and a tradition of literary work. The purpose of the Union was to put Scotland on the map as part of Britain's growing commercial and political empire: its decline, claim the nationalists, means that Scotland must express its individuality in another forum, the United Nations.

In the case of Scotland, ethnic and cultural issues have largely been overshadowed by regional economic and social justifications for self government. The Scottish National Party (SNP), founded in 1934, was formed chiefly in response to the collapse of Scotland's prosperous Victorian economy, a shift of ownership and control of local resources south of the border, and indifference to this at Westminster. This theme pervades party ideology today.

The discovery of oil in the North Sea off Scotland in the 1960s underlined the economic basis of Scottish nationalism. Oil offered Scotland the possibility of economic independence and self government, of becoming something more than a poor, northerly part of Britain. 'It's Scotland's oil!' cried the Scottish Nationalists, whose electoral fortunes rose with the offshore discoveries.

Over the last 30 years, major divergences have occurred between Scotland and England with respect to the electoral success of the main political parties. While the SNP has increased its share of the vote in Scotland, the Conservative vote has collapsed. In 1997 no Scottish Tories were elected.

Modernity and postmodernity – the Scottish dimension

Given that Scotland is dependent on external political and economic forces, its capacity to control its destiny and to become more of a self-governing society may seem limited. Nevertheless, Scotland provides an important sociological test case for the proposition that the quest for greater self determination occurs in the context of the globalisation of economic, political and cultural power – not as a contradiction to this globalisation but as part of the process. In a world where the nation state of the nineteenth century seems to be losing its reason for existence, Scotland's future seems bound up with major shifts in political and social arrangements at a global level.

Scotland as a nation, and the assertion of nationalism more generally in the late twentieth century, set it at the centre of current sociological concerns. The fact that it can claim to be a nation without being a state in the conventional sense does not mean that it remains an anomaly in the modern world, as judged by the more traditional perspective of 'modernity'. Rather, Scotland becomes an example of those tendencies threatening to break up and remake the world political order, an order in which the correspondence between states, societies and nations is no longer clear-cut. (See David McCrone (1993), *Scotland – the Sociology of a Stateless Nation*.)

English nationalism   England has long been a nation state. It has created an intense patriotism (see page 464), but no classic nation-building nationalist ideology. Instead, the political and social system is legitimated by a pre-nationalist doctrine of parliamentary sovereignty, which extends also over Scotland, Wales and Northern Ireland. England's predominance in the Union, her relative isolation from foreign invasion, her position until recently as a world economic and political power, and the long absence of any menacing revolutionary politics, have ensured that nationalistic rhetoric is mainly deployed by established leaders in defence of practices hallowed by tradition, or by their claims for the spirit of 'English' parliamentary freedom.

English nationalism in the 1990s has been most evident in the strong element of opposition to further integration into the political and monetary systems of the European Union. Anti-European feelings were crystallised in the campaign of Sir James Goldsmith's Referendum Party in the 1997 general election. This single-issue party campaigned for a referendum in which the British people would be given the opportunity to vote on the country's future relationship with the European Union. They won no seats in the election but did secure between 3 and 4 per cent of the vote. The Conservative opposition in 1997 still adopted a sceptical European position whilst the Labour government was still not committed to European monetary Union (EMU). On a less political level, the way in which the 'little Englander' mentality, anti-European feelings and nationalist sentiments may be expressed as a negative view of 'other nationalities', has often been seen at its strongest in the context of sport, particularly when the England football team confronts other nations. A study of this phenomenon in terms of clashes between national groups of fans outside the UK has been made by John Williams et al. from Leicester University, in their book *Hooligans Abroad* (1984).

Nationalism's links with racism

There is a dimension of English nationalism which seeks to emphasise race both within the Conservative Party in the person of, for example, Norman Tebbitt, and in overtly racist organisations such as the National Front or the clandestine Combat 18 (a hardline splinter group from the British National Party). Since the 1958 Notting Hill race riot in London, we have had to face the fact that there is a race problem in Britain and that there are no easy solutions to the attitudes of white nationalists towards black immigrants or their descendants.

Nationalism, empire and the rise of racism

Race relations in Britain have their roots in the legacy of empire. In 1948, Britain legally made the peoples of its many colonies British 'subjects', entitled to live and work in the United Kingdom. Although the colonies were granted independence in the 1950s and 1960s as members of the British Commonwealth – a loose organisation of countries that call the Queen their nominal sovereign – their people were still entitled to emigrate to Britain. The 1950s saw the arrival in the UK of West Indians from the Caribbean, followed by Indians and Pakistanis. Many immigrants took the lowliest jobs which the British had not wanted. (The immigrant population in 1997 is about 5 per cent of Britain's total.)

   White resentment soon grew, with some believing that the immigrants wanted their housing and jobs. Britons began to discover they were racists, sometimes violent racists. In 1967, the openly racist National Front Party was formed, advocating the expulsion of all 'coloureds' back to their native lands. Young men, some supporting the Front or the rival National Party, went in for murderous 'Paki bashing', with slogans such as 'Rights for Whites'. During the 1970s votes for the two small parties grew, although neither won a seat in Parliament. Such low-level support continued through to the 1990s.

Patterns of migration and settlement

Over the course of the centuries, many groups have migrated to Britain and settled in various parts of the country. For example, Jewish and Irish immigration occurred in the seventeenth century, although most Jewish migrants came to Britain between 1870 and 1914, fleeing persecution in parts of Europe, whilst between 1820 and 1910 there was a large influx of Irish immigrants who settled in London and the major west-lying cities of Manchester, Glasgow and Liverpool. During and after World War II, large numbers of refugees arrived, including, by the end of 1945, around half a million Polish refugees.

   In the period 1945–61, as we saw above, recruitment for employment in Britain, to meet the needs of a growing economy, saw the arrival of immigrants from the New Commonwealth. The table on the next page gives details of the numbers involved.

   Since 1961, and as a consequence of the 1962 Commonwealth Immigrants Act, there has been a marked reduction in immigration from the New Commonwealth. According to Haralambos and Holborn (1995) the numbers declined from 136,000 in 1961, to 68,000 in 1972 and 22,800 in 1988, with a slight rise in 1992 to 27,000.

Estimated net immigration from the New Commonwealth, 1953–1962					
Country of origin	West Indies	India	Pakistan	Others	Total
1953	2 000	–	–	–	2 000
1954	11 000	–	–	–	11 000
1955	27 500	5 800	1 850	7 500	42 650
1956	29 800	5 600	2 050	9 350	46 800
1957	23 000	6 600	5 200	7 600	42 400
1958	15 000	6 200	4 700	3 950	29 850
1959	16 400	2 950	850	1 400	21 600
1960	49 650	5 900	2 500	−350	57 700
1961	66 300	23 750	25 100	21 250	136 400
1962	31 800	19 050	25 080	18 970	94 900

Source: Layton-Henry, *The Politics of Immigration* (Blackwell, 1992)

Immigration and race relations policies in the UK

Throughout the 1960s and 1970s there developed a broad political consensus in the UK on the 'control and integration' strategy for immigration and race relations. Such strategies have been criticised both for being too harsh and inhumane and for being too liberal.

Race relations legislation in the UK

The government has sought to combat racial discrimination through a series of Race Relations Acts, the first of which, introduced in 1965, sought to prevent racial discrimination in certain public places. It set up a Race Relations Board to receive complaints of discrimination and, if necessary, to take action. A further Act was passed in 1968 which sought to prevent discrimination in housing, employment and commercial services. This allowed the Race Relations Board to use the courts if a dispute could not be amicably resolved. In addition, the Act also set up a new body, the Community Relations Commission, to seek to promote 'harmonious community relations'.

The continuation of discrimination led, in 1976, to a third Act and the establishment of the Commission for Racial Equality (CRE), which replaced both the Race Relations Board and the Community Relations Commission. This new body has the power to conduct its own investigations of organisations (for example pubs, clubs, employers, local authorities) to find out whether they are discriminating against someone on the grounds of race.

If discrimination is discovered, the CRE can require the organisation to change its practice and then check that this has been done. Finally, individuals who believe they have been discriminated against on racial grounds can take their case individually to the courts or to an industrial tribunal, sometimes with legal support from the CRE.

That the policies and legislation have failed to combat racism is considered to be the result of the following factors:

- The 1976 immigration legislation may have inadvertently resulted in appeasing, legitimising and encouraging the racism of the electorate by identifying black people, not white racism, as the problem and by practising racial discrimination at the point of entry.

- This state institutionalisation of discrimination led to a system of internal surveillance of black residents. Every black was a potential criminal, as exemplified by the police raids on workplaces in the early 1980s in search of illegal immigrants and the legal attempts to stop asylum seekers obtaining welfare benefits in 1996.
- Successive governments have failed to educate the electorate. A high-profile anti-racist campaign, plus a determined attempt to provide more resources to support the new settlers in the 1950s and 1960s could perhaps have limited the problems we face today.
- The anti-discrimination legislation of 1972 was not only a case of too little, too late, it was also contaminated by the laws on exclusion. If the government refused to admit people on the grounds that their skin colour would cause problems, why shouldn't a factory owner do the same?
- A harsher analysis depicts the race relations legislation, central and local government funding, and the commitment to equal opportunities and anti-racist policies as intended to inhibit black self-organisation and as tokenism intended to create a 'black middle class' and suppress conflict without redressing injustice.

Most critics, however, accept that the 1976 legislation and the increased role of the CRE represented an attempt to offer more vigorous enforcement and that the legislation has some role to play in an anti-racist strategy.

Issues of sovereignty: the UK and the European Union

All modern nation states involve an apparatus of government laying claim to specific territories and possessing formalised codes of law, backed by the control of military force.

Defining sovereignty

The territories ruled by traditional states were always poorly defined. All nation states, by contrast, are **sovereign states**, with clear-cut borders defined by international law (though some are disputed). Anthony Giddens offers a definition of the concept of nation state: a political apparatus, recognised to have sovereign rights within the borders of a demarcated territorial area, able to back its claims to sovereignty by control of military power, many of whose citizens have positive feelings of commitment to its national identity.

Sovereignty is a legal and a political concept, with a long history that can be traced back to the writers and philosophers of the Roman Empire. For most of the past two centuries, it has been understood to mean that a state, which is independent, possesses the exclusive and sole authority over a specific people and territory. The government of this state exercises the final and ultimate, or sovereign, authority within its borders. Sovereignty, then, is characterised by the claim to exclusive jurisdiction over people and territory; a claim which is legally recognised by other states. It is also characterised by the notion of the 'sovereign equality of states'.

The sovereignty of the UK

A difficulty in relation to sovereignty, as defined opposite by Maidment, and the UK is that the UK no longer retains *exclusive* jurisdiction over people and territory; it has ceded formal control over certain issues to the institutions of the European Union (see the diagram below and also Unit 11, page 587). The degree and extent of this diminution of sovereignty was not extensive when Britain joined the European Community in 1973; over 30 years later, however, the erosion of sovereignty is still the subject of much debate.

EU institutions and their relationships with each other and with national bodies

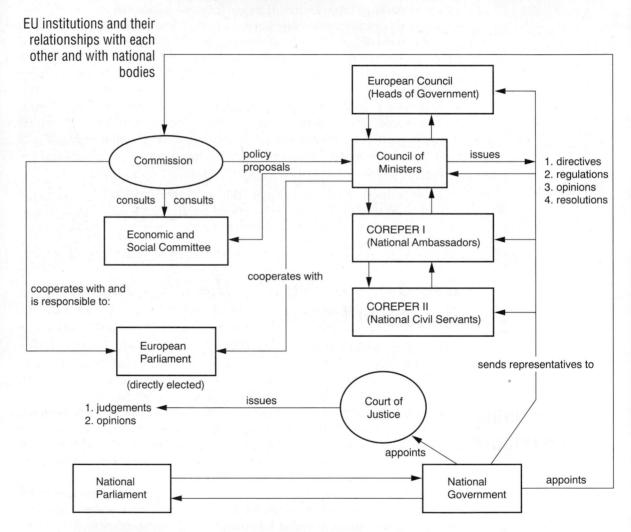

Britain's membership of the European Union

Britain's profile as an EC member changed almost beyond recognition in the second half of the 1980s. Three sets of factors combined to make Britain a more 'normal' EC member:

* With time and experience, Britain has become familiar with the new European arena and this in turn has brought respect and a willingness to exploit the new opportunities.
* The agreements so vigorously pursued on 'agro-budgetary' issues came to constitute a structural righting of old grievances.

The UK, sovereignty and Europe

The following is a summary of the key points relating to sovereignty as outlined by Maidment, their effects on the British view towards the EC (later the EU) and the debate about Britain's being 'in or out of Europe':

- Sovereignty is a legal and a political concept.
- It is characterised firstly by the claim to exclusive jurisdiction over both people and territory and, secondly, by what is known as the sovereign equality of states.
- There is a tension between the notion of sovereignty and the realities of global power. Sovereignty, nevertheless, is an important component element of a nation's political consciousness.
- Paradoxically, the enhancement of a country's autonomy or control of its own affairs may be improved by the diminution of its sovereignty.
- Initially, the UK chose not to be a founder member of the European Community because it believed that it continued to be a global power.
- The growing realisation that this was no longer the case convinced a broad coalition of cross-party opinion that the UK should join the EC; an application to be a member was submitted by a Conservative government in the early 1960s.
- The issue of sovereignty continues to be a concern, particularly with opponents of British membership.
- Membership of the EC has resulted in a loss of sovereignty, which has been further reduced by the development of the single European market.
- The single European market would not have been possible without a loss of sovereignty.
- The British government believed the trade of sovereignty for power to be worthwhile.
- More recently, a number of adverse judgements by the Court of Human Rights against the British government, the apparent erosion of the power to legislate in Britain (for example over fishing quotas) and the BSE 'crisis' of 1996 have hardened the British government's attitude towards Europe.

- The changing ideological constellation in British politics began to find expression in European terms: neo-liberalism in the Thatcherite version began to be articulated as a recipe for the wider European economy, both by the government and by exponents of an even purer variant of economic liberalism.

The role of the UK government in relation to its component territories, both regional and national, has been a source of debate, with the powers of the establishment in London striving to ensure that the complications of Brussels do not lead to undue interference. This was explicitly an issue during the devolution debate of the 1970s, and has surfaced again with the re-emergence of the Scottish National Party as a serious political force, and the imminent creation of Scottish and Welsh parliaments.

Concerns about sovereignty have frequently provided the rhetorical cover for those in the UK who fear the erosion of British, or more correctly English, identity under the weight of continental and, for some, Catholic influences. A quarter of a century of British membership has not overcome these doubts. A powerful emotional appeal for the retention of an independent British identity remains one of the features which distinguishes British political debate on Europe from that in most other member states.

Political implications British membership of the European Union has had political implications in terms of UK domestic politics; it remains a contentious issue. There are also wider political implications: the possibility of member states acting together as a political power bloc was one of the motivations for Britain joining the Community in 1973. For Britain, the prospect of EC member states acting together looked increasingly attractive as other avenues for the UK maintaining a world status (for example the Commonwealth and the 'special relationship' with the USA) were receding in significance.

Economic implications

The economic attractions of joining the EC were a major influence in Britain's applying for membership. The EC offered a 'common market' which has assumed increasing significance for the British economy.

In the first nine years of membership, British exports to EC countries increased by 27 per cent a year, compared with 19 per cent average annual growth in UK exports to the rest of the world. After 20 years of membership, British dependence on the EC was well established: in 1973, 36 per cent of British exports went to EC countries; by 1996, this figure had risen to 60 per cent, with exports to Germany alone exceeding those to Japan and the USA combined. The UK also has attracted significant inward investment: by the end of 1996, 43 per cent of total Japanese investment in Europe and 35 per cent of US investment had gone to the UK (much of it to Scotland).

Sociological implications

The impact of Europe – and in particular the 'Social Chapter' of the 1994 Maastricht Treaty – affects a wide range of social issues, including:

- protection for employees;
- a minimum wage;
- funding for projects in deprived areas under urban aid arrangements.

Judgements by the European Court of Human Rights have related to sociological aspects of work: for example judgements in favour of women having the same retirement age and the same level of pay as men; and judgements in favour of part-time workers having conditions of employment equivalent to those of their full-time colleagues.

The continuing debate on the social dimension of Britain's membership of the EU illustrates a strand in the changing form of domestic politics in the UK. The Conservative government was united in resisting the calls for a European social charter or any further social legislation – a stand apparently supported by British business opinion (see also Unit 5). However, subsequent to the Labour Party being elected to government in 1997, the Foreign Secretary, Robin Cook, committed the new government to the introduction of the Social Chapter as soon as was possible.

Think about it

- What sociological questions are raised by Britain's membership of the European Union?
- What are the advantages/disadvantages of a supra-national body such as the European Parliament or the European Court having authority superior to that of individual member nations?
- Find out what has happened as regards the introduction of the Social Chapter in the UK since the 1997 election. Has there been any sociological comment on this?
- In this section of the unit we have looked at the ideas of 'nation' and 'state'. How do you see these two concepts relating to each other?
- What tensions can you identify between national and supra-national authority and what sociological impact might these have?

■ GLOBALISATION

Globalisation is the process whereby political, economic, social and cultural relations in any one society become increasingly influenced by external or global factors which, in turn, have profound consequences for an individual's life experiences. For example, the development of global communications has enabled people in the UK to obtain almost instant access to news from all over the world. Such a communications industry has no 'national' boundaries and tends to be owned by corporate business which is not located within any one nation state.

K. Robertson (1992) has marked out the historical phases of the move towards globalisation as follows:

- Phase 1 – the germinal phase (1400–1750): the development of national groupings and religious movements, for example Catholicism.
- Phase 2 – the incipient phase (1750–1870s): the emergence of nation states and trade on an international scale.
- Phase 3 – the take-off phase (1870s–1920s): the advent of liberal democracy and communism; the first stages of global communication and transportation; global warfare (for example World War I) and global sporting activity (for example international football, the Olympics).
- Phase 4 – the struggle-for-hegemony phase (1920s–60s): the inter-state conflict and competition between the 'super powers' (USA, USSR and China); the development of the United Nations, the European Community, GATT (General Agreement on Tariffs and Trade), nuclear deterrence, global inequality, colonial independence movements.
- Phase 5 – the uncertainty phase (1960s–2000): the end of the cold war; the collapse of the Soviet Union; concerns over the environment and the growth of nationalism; public disillusionment with political solutions to social and economic problems in the West; and the growth of religious fundamentalism in the East (for example Islam) and the West (for example sects and deinstitutional religion).

S. Sklair (1991) notes the existence of a new 'transnationalist capitalist class' which is not constrained by national territorial borders and which now controls the world capitalist economy. **Transnational companies** (TNCs) influence not only the developed world but also developing capitalist economies such as Poland and Hungary and Third World economies which might be ripe for exploitation. Sklair argues that TNCs seek to:

- control production of rapidly changing markets, for example computer software development;
- remain innovative through the use of technology – what Schumpeter calls 'creative innovation';
- maintain low production costs – by implication keeping wage costs low and productivity per worker high;
- diversify their operations and maximise profitability wherever in the world there is the most potential.

Think about it

In *Global Shift* (1992), P. Dickens identifies the following three characteristics of transnational companies (TNCs):

1. control of economic activities in a number of countries;
2. an ability to take advantage of geographical and social differences between countries, primarily the natural physical properties and social resources created by government policies;
3. the flexibility to shift resources and operations between locations.

- Study the financial pages of a national newspaper for a week, and identify news items relating to the largest companies. Can you identify which are multinational or transnational? In your town, are there branches of multinational or transnational companies?
- What might be the sociological implications of each of the three characteristics identified by Dickens?

For Marxists, the existence of this new class of 'global capitalists' poses a potential threat to workers in those countries that are used for production. Whilst short-term benefits might allow workers to be employed and investment to take place, in the long term – since the aim is to maximise profits – the investment and employment advantages may quickly disappear if higher profits can be earned elsewhere. In the context of the UK, it is possible to identify TNCs in the high-technology bases along the M4 corridor in England ('Silicon Valley') and along the M8 corridor in Scotland ('Silicon Glen'), which are dominated by American and Japanese computer software and hardware companies who wish to gain access to the European market.

With TNCs comes a new **international division of labour**, whereby the companies look for low-wage economies with little or no trade union activity and often employ workers on short-time contracts for low hourly rates and with limited job security. Car manufacturers such as Nissan, for example, have been encouraged to set up their production plant in Sunderland and to apply their working practices to the UK workforce. Often women are employed on a part-time basis and this, in its turn, can have a marked impact on the employment opportunities for male workers. We saw in Unit 5 how the movement to post-Fordist production processes has radically altered employment practices and created a small core of technically skilled and relatively permanent employees; has allowed more development of computer controlled production; and has deskilled the majority of employees whose employment terms and conditions are often poor.

In respect to the wider social impact of globalisation, D. Becker (1987) has suggested that a growth of **consumerism** has been positively fostered by TNCs to ensure profitability. Sports companies, for example, in the wake of Euro '96, Wimbledon and the Olympic Games, seek to sponsor sporting events and athletes, to buy up TV advertising of their products and to maximise their market share. The global media have an important role to play in the selling of these 'products' to the public through the use and direction of transmitted ideologies which seek to project the message that prospective consumers should aspire to owning Reebok or Nike trainers, that they should drink Coca-Cola or drive a Renault.

Globalised information and communication systems, owned and controlled by TNCs, will also seek to project ideas which are favourably disposed towards **global capitalism**. This, in its turn, could lead to the development of a shared, linguistically and societally uniform, **'global culture'**.

Anthony Giddens (1994) uses the term 'disembedding' to refer to the ways in which social relations have been removed from local contexts and given a global framework. This 'globalising process' is, for Giddens, potentially damaging to the development of close and meaningful personal contact between individuals and groups. Within the UK, the impersonal nature of modern communication – TV as opposed to conversation – and the impact of industrial restructuring (particularly large-scale unemployment) have arguably contributed to significant changes in the UK in the latter part of the twentieth century.

■ THE DEVELOPMENT OF SOCIETIES AND STATES

Definitions and explanations of development

Development studies arose in the aftermath of World War II in relation to the growth of anti-colonial independence movements. The current focus of much of development sociology is organised around issues of deprivation and want. T. Lawson, in *Sociology Reviewed* (1993), notes that sociologists seek to identify differences between societies on the basis of their different stages of development. He offers a range of classifications as follows:

- **developed world** v. **underdeveloped world;**

OR

- developing societies: for example **First World** (developed), **Second World** (developing) and **Third World** (undeveloped);

OR

- Western capitalist societies (First World) and the socialist economies of Eastern Europe (Second World) (until 1990) = **the North** v. undeveloped countries (Third World) = **the South;**

OR

- Third World societies (the **underdeveloped** countries) made poorer by First World;

OR

- advanced capitalist (postmodernist) societies of the West v. the collapsing communist societies of Eastern Europe.

Whichever 'definition' is adopted, there is one fact which informs the debate: the disparity between 'rich' (developed) and poor (developing/underdeveloped) countries. About 75 per cent of the world's population live in 'poor' countries, which collectively hold about 17 per cent of the world's wealth, 10 per cent of the world's manufacturing industry and 20 per cent of world trade and investment.

What then constitutes the Third World when compared to the First World (the North/South division of countries)? A number of indicators of Third World 'status' might include:

- a tendency to have a larger agricultural than industrial workforce;
- a tendency to rely on a limited number of raw material products for export;
- relatively poor diets;
- high levels of illiteracy;
- a colonial past.

T. Barnett, in *Sociology and Development* (1988), pinpointed three meanings of development which may be considered of relevance:

- **Development from within:** change can occur as a result of the society itself.
- **Development as interaction:** change occurs because of interactions with others, for example other countries or capitalist enterprises.
- **Development as interpenetration:** change occurs as a result of any number of reasons, the interrelationships between societies being so complex.

Aidan Foster-Carter's study, *Development in Sociology* (1993), identifies four senses of the word development:

1. **economic development**, which is usually linked directly to economic growth, for example expansion of manufacturing industry;
2. **social development**, where the redirection of poverty and inequality are important and an increase in employment necessary (these have been considered key welfare requirements of development);
3. **political development**, which tends to look (from a Western perspective) at the extent to which a country is deemed to be democratic;
4. **cultural development**, which relates to the extent to which the existing culture(s) in any one country can be sustained, or whether it (they) may change and be influenced by others.

Indicators of development

- degree of urbanisation;
- literacy rates and vocational training;
- newspaper circulation;
- political democracy (as measured by the existence of a multi-party system and the regular executive transfer through secret ballot elections);
- free enterprise;
- secularisation (i.e. the institutionalisation of 'rationality' as the dominant behavioural norm);
- degree of social mobility;
- occupational differentiation;
- large number of voluntary associations including, for example, trade unions;
- national unity (as opposed to ethnic and denominational factionalism);
- nuclear-family patterns;
- independent judiciaries.

Source: Adapted from Hoogvelt, *The Sociology of Developing Societies* (Macmillan, 1985)

Sociological theories of development

As the study of development overlaps the boundaries of economics, sociology and political science, academics from each of these disciplines have tried to determine the concept. **Economists** have distinguished relative levels of development in terms of gross national product (GNP) and income per head of population. (GNP is the value of all goods and services produced in a country during one year.) In 1995, the extreme contrast between the USA and Burundi in Central Africa was measured by per capita income figures of $13,220 and $87 respectively. Others have tried to use a more refined approach of socio-economic development indicators, such as life expectancy at birth, per capita daily consumption of animal protein, average number of persons per room and newspaper circulation per thousand population. **Sociologists** have focused on status on the basis of achievement, the specialisation of roles and individualism as some characteristics of the more developed society.

The complexity of the issue has led some writers to substitute for development concepts such as nation-building, modernisation and social change. Like 'development' itself, however, these contain ambiguities, inconsistencies and value judgements. As a result of this confusion, it is essential to identify the definition or interpretation used by each writer on the subject of development. Some writers see development in terms of values and awareness, some in terms of institutional growth and specialisation and others in raw economic terms.

'Development' – whose interpretation?

The term 'development' tends to have certain evaluative overtones.

- A common interpretation is that it can imply progress. However, in recent years some aspects of economic development have been criticised as being harmful both to individuals and to society as a whole. Pressure groups such as the Friends of the Earth, and writers such as Ivan Illich have taken this view. Illich has seen a pattern of environmental pollution emanating from so-called technological progress; and individual self sufficiency has been eroded rather than enhanced by many technological innovations. The relevance of this criticism depends on personal beliefs, but it is useful to be aware that development in all its respects may not be universally welcomed.
- Secondly, the term development can give the impression of a clear path from a particular form of society or economy to another. The acceptability of this may also depend on personal belief, but again it is important to be aware of the overtone and to be able to identify it in the writings of the many commentators on development.

The early development of the social sciences took place in the context of and with reference to the period of the Industrial Revolution. The prime focus for early sociologists was the transition from pre-industrial society with its agricultural base and rural communities to the industrial society of Western Europe, with its industries, cities and apparently contractual associations. With the belief that the laws of human behaviour were ready and waiting to be discussed by sociologists, many of the early writers in this field attempted to transform their observations and commonsense assumptions into theories of development. Among the early writers were Comte, Spencer, Tonnies, Durkheim and Pareto.

Auguste Comte Comte developed an evolutionary approach to man's (sic) development, based on the rationalisation of human thought. He identified three stages of development, in which completely different explanations dominated man's view of his world:

- The 'theological' stage: in this stage, the world was explained in terms of supernatural powers and beings, with little attempt to extend knowledge.
- The 'metaphysical' stage: in this stage the world was explained in terms of abstract ideas, but little was done to apply these to the solution of human problems.
- The 'positive' stage: this involves the use of scientific principles developed from empirical studies that enable man to understand and dominate his world. Comte viewed the sociologist as the one with the task of developing such principles and theories so that peace and harmony could be achieved.

As with many of the theories of development outlined below, Comte's approach is open to attack as being ethno-centric. We can accept that his description of the development of human thought is correct in relation to his own society, but he then makes the assumption that all other societies will develop along the same path and that the present stage is the ultimate one.

Herbert Spencer Spencer saw evolution in terms of growth rather than particular stages. According to his model, a pattern of development could be traced in terms of small hunting societies becoming – by virtue of growth, differentiation and specialisation – modern industrial societies.

The analogy of society with a living body became a fundamental aspect of functionalism, and Spencer's ideas were clearly of importance in influencing later writers such as Talcott Parsons.

Ferdinand Tonnies Tonnies, with his concepts of Gemeinschaft and Gesellschaft, viewed development in terms of a dichotomy between two forms of society. Unlike Comte and Spencer, he did not see it as an evolutionary process with a gradual pattern of change or several distinct stages.

Emile Durkheim Durkheim also saw a dichotomy between a simple society with little division of labour and collective values, and modern society with a complex division of labour and individualism. More than many of the others, Durkheim identified modern society as having problems, with individual aspirations not always coinciding with the interests of the whole society. The weakening of social ties, according to Durkheim, contributed to a state of normlessness or anomie.

Vilfredo Pareto The approach of the Italian sociologists Vilfredo Pareto and Gaetona Mosca was that society remained essentially the same and did not in fact develop. To them change was an illusion, with apparent transformations of social revolutions constituting no more than stages of a cycle. They focused on political power, and saw the inevitability of one elite group being replaced by another, whatever the ideological commitment involved. As soon as power is obtained, steps are taken to consolidate and maintain it, which in turn leads to the overthrow of the incumbent elite and its replacement by another.

Marx's theory of development

While the early development theorists have all had an impact on subsequent writers, the writings of Karl Marx have had a much more significant effect.

Marx regarded the economic infrastructure of society as the fundamental cause of both the conditions of it and its pattern and rate of change. He stated, for example, that one century of the capitalist mode of production contributed more to economic development than the whole age of feudalism.

Marx traced the evolution of society in terms of several stages or modes of production. In the first stage, property was communally owned by the tribe. In Western society, this was replaced by the period of antiquity, with the emergence of private property and the division of society into classes of citizens and slaves. This was in turn replaced by feudalism, in which a pattern of land tenure and mutual obligation distinguished the nobility from the serfs. Marx envisaged the feudal system of production being replaced by the capitalist system, with the bourgeoisie owning the means of production and the proletariat selling its labour power on the market. Unlike the serf, the proletarian had no rights to the means of production; through the exploitation of his labour power, vast amounts of capital were accumulated. This process involved the alienation of the worker from both his labour and capital: his work was imposed on him by the capitalist and he did not receive the financial rewards of his labour.

Weber's theory of development

Weber's approach to development was similar to that of Durkheim and Tonnies, in that he focused on the transition from pre-industrial to industrial society. Weber stressed the rationality of industrial society: means were adapted to meet ends, there was a systematic organisation of the decision-making process, and unquestioning belief was replaced by reason.

Weber also stressed the rationality of capitalism in calculating profit and loss possibilities in a scientific manner that could never have characterised a cottage industry. He saw a spirit of capitalism stimulating change and improvement, opposing traditional values which involved unwillingness to change. He also saw the religious values of hard work and asceticism as enhancing the economic development of society.

Many writers have stressed the opposition of Weber to Marx; in terms of his emphasis on ideas contributing to rather than being the product of economic change, this is justifiable. However, much of what Weber had to say echoed rather than refuted Marx's ideas. He too analysed the role of expanded markets and the agricultural revolution in the development of capitalism.

Weber stressed the positive aspect of reason and rationality in contributing to efficiency, and the technical efficiency of bureaucracy as a means of decision-making. However, he was no Utopian, and he had less to offer for the future than Marx's communist mode of production. He saw dangers of regimentation and the loss of individuality as possible products of the development of bureaucracy (reflected perhaps by Tonnies and Durkheim who saw industrialisation and urbanisation as negative aspects of development).

Some key questions in development theory

Many of the questions that have worried contemporary theorists of development can be identified in the writings of some of the classical theorists referred to above.

Is development a gradual process or a series of stages? Tonnies and Durkheim saw development in terms of a polar dichotomy between pre-industrial and industrial society, while others such as Comte and Marx identified a series of evolutionary stages. These patterns will later be identified in writers such as Rostow and Parsons.

Does social change imply disruption and strain? For Marx, strains and contradictions are inbuilt into each of the modes of production until the final communist stage, while Durkheim identified the problem of anomie or normlessness in modern society and Tonnies wrote of the conflict and self interest of Gesellschaft. The question remains as to how far change itself creates new social or personal tensions.

Is development a unilinear and inevitable process? For Marx, the pattern of transition from primitive communalism through the feudal and capitalist modes to the final communist stage is mapped out, although intervening factors such as the state and ideas may delay or hasten the demise of each stage. Comte and Spencer also identified evolutionary processes that would culminate in the creation of a particular type of society. However, of concern to later social scientists are questions as to whether there is only a single path, whether there can be regression or decay as well as development, and whether it is possible to predict such a thing as a final stage of development.

Are economic, physical, cultural or political factors the prime movers?

Marx saw the economic infrastructure of society as ultimately responsible for whatever changes take place, although other factors can have some role to play. Max Weber added the importance of values in determining economic change, with the Protestant ethic combining with a favourable economic situation to produce the rise of capitalism. Later writers have also become involved in this debate, with some pointing to the role of drive and determination, the need for achievement and the existence of an entrepreneurial class willing to take risks; while others have pointed to climate, the availability of natural resources, and international power as the most important factors.

Can development be planned?

The early theorists saw development as an unconscious process. In the modern world, however, with much more effective international communications systems, people in less developed countries see the higher living standards elsewhere and wish to accelerate or initiate the process of development in their own societies.

Contemporary models of development and underdevelopment

The early sociologists were essentially concerned with the development of Western European society. Since the early 1950s, however, the focus has largely altered to look at developments in those countries that have yet to industrialise.

This changed focus reflects the break-up of the British, French and Belgian colonial empires, and the arrival on the world stage of a whole array of new nations. The expressed desire of the leaders of many of these states to develop their economies and establish themselves politically, socially, economically and culturally as the equals of the developed states has given social scientists the opportunity to be viewed as experts, whose interpretation and professional advice could facilitate the process of development. Economists such as R.N. Dumont have been foremost in acting as professional advisers to governments of African states, but sociologists have also been important in producing models of development and offering explanations as to why development projects have been successful or not.

The **sociology of development** links together a wide variety of theorists, but they share a similarity of approach. Each of them traces an evolutionary pattern of development from a form of pre-industrial society to the present-day modern industrial or post-industrial society. Each also sees cultural factors as playing an important role in the development process – although, in one view, cultural change is seen as the precursor of development (for example, McClelland), while in another cultural change has to come hand-in-hand with economic change if strain is to be avoided (for example, Parsons). Finally, each theory stresses the importance of internal factors in the development process, with external constraints on development being largely ignored.

Modernisation theory

Modernisation theory can be viewed as an updating of nineteenth-century social evolutionary theory (see Comte, Spencer, Tonnies), offering the view that societies evolve in the same direction over time and presenting a 'march of progress' view.

Parsons's functionalist approach

The emphasis on the problems of urban and industrial development by writers such as Durkheim and Tonnies was taken up by Talcott Parsons and his followers. Durkheim and Tonnies had identified the dangers of normlessness and moral breakdown produced by the replacement of traditional communities. Parsons developed this in terms of social strain which reflected a lack of harmony in the process of development and could lead to a breakdown of stability and order. He suggested that in a closely integrated social system, a change in one aspect of society or its environment would require adaptation on the part of others; until that adaptation takes place there is incompatibility and therefore strain. According to this view, the process of modernisation can mean that:

- new occupational structures may be at odds with the stability of family, culture and so on;
- new elites may clash with the claims to obedience of traditional rulers;
- difficulties can develop as one set of values is displaced before a new one is fully established.

The result may be social disintegration, unless there emerges a successful process of adaptation or the creation of new institutions and values that make possible a reintegration of society.

Rostow's economic model

W. Rostow produced an evolutionary model which traces the pattern of development from a traditional society to the age of high mass-consumption, and suggested that any society can be placed at one of five stages of development:

1. **The traditional society:** at this stage there is adherence to long-standing practices which do not eliminate completely the possibility of some technical innovations. However, a ceiling on growth exists because of the lack of scientific understanding. Attitudes are described as being a long-run fatalism, and power lies in the hands of landowners rather than some form of centralised organisation.
2. **The pre-conditions for take-off:** during this stage there is greater awareness of the role of education, investigation and experimentation. Economic progress is seen as both attainable and desirable, and enterprise is encouraged. Banking and investment develop, and new manufacturing techniques come to light. However, progress is slow, and the development of a centralised national state to oppose the traditional landowning interests takes time.
3. **The take-off:** this Rostow sees as the great watershed in the life of modern societies, when traditional objections to change are overcome and growth becomes a normal condition. New industries develop and profits are reinvested, thus stimulating new patterns of demand for both goods and services. New agricultural techniques develop side by side with industry, and growth becomes self sustaining.
4. **The drive to maturity:** in this stage annual reinvestment of profits and taxation revenue rises to between 10 per cent and 20 per cent, new industries are launched and greater self sufficiency of the economy is attained. Some 60 years after take-off begins (40 years after the end of take-off), what may be called 'maturity' is generally attained.

5. **The age of high mass-consumption:** in this final stage, people gain sufficient income to purchase more than their basic necessities. Resources are directed more towards social welfare and security than to further technological expansion, although steady growth continues.

Rostow's model is interesting and serves as a significant alternative to a Marxist analysis. However, it suffers from generalisations, and the assumption that the modern Western society stands at the end of the development process is clearly open to challenge. From the rapid changes that have taken place in the world economy, space exploration, social attitudes and so on, it can be seen that what we have at present or what we can reasonably foresee for the future is not the end of a developmental process. It is also far from clear that there is a single path to development; events in Saudi Arabia, Singapore and Taiwan in recent years have shown how the process can be speeded up and whole stages omitted. The theory can be criticised as being a form of **economic determinism**.

Think about it

- Which of the models of development that you have looked at in this section of the unit do you find most convincing? Explain why this is the case, comparing it with at least one other model.

The sociology of underdevelopment

The sociology of underdevelopment has grown in significance in recent years as a reaction to the sociology of development. It too links a wide variety of writers sharing some similarities in approach. Each of them focuses on the role of outside powers in influencing and distorting the development process. Each also examines the way such outsiders have exploited the less developed countries and grown rich at their expense. Finally, each rejects development theory as a non-historic and ideological description of events.

Convergence theories

Convergence theories see all modern industrial societies becoming similar in their format and intention, with similar developments in culture, social structure, politics and economics. Among the leading contributors to this debate are Daniel Bell, Clark Kerr and Ralf Dahrendorf.

Daniel Bell: *The Coming of Post-Industrial Society (1973)*

Bell argues that a new type of society has evolved in Western Europe and the USA in recent years and will continue to grow. This society is based on knowledge as the central resource, with professionals, academics and scientists providing the information necessary for society to maintain itself. The knowledge-centred and service-orientated economy renders irrelevant the Marxist analysis of capitalist society in terms of production, ownership and exploitation.

According to Bell, economic prosperity brings social improvement by achieving:

- decreasing patterns of inequality;
- the blurring of significant class distinctions;
- the creation of a more open system of mobility; and
- a consequent decline in class ideology.

Skills and education replace birth and property as the basis of political power.

Clark Kerr (et al.): *Industrialism and Industrial Man (1978)*

Kerr argues that all industrial societies are converging towards a pluralistic industrialism, in which the essential role of the state is to regulate competition between groups. The logic of industrialism necessitates a particular pattern of development, whatever the ideological pretensions of the society. Kerr argues that all industrial societies pass through four stages:

- increasing social mobility, with the selection of employees on merit;
- decreasing differences between strata;
- the expansion of a middle strata;
- social status, rather than ascribed characteristics, increasingly reflecting income and occupation – more 'meritocratic'.

Whilst Bell has been criticised for seeing knowledge as an independent variable in its own right, so Kerr is criticised for seeing technology as independent in any social system (**technological determinism**). His theory has been challenged by studies showing a growth rather than a reduction in inequality in states such as Sweden and the United Kingdom, and status inconsistency of the affluent manual worker and the continuation of a conflict between classes in Britain. Many of the growing service industries involve low-paid female workers rather than an expanded middle stratum; and, since 1981, according to the Child Poverty Action Group, poverty in Britain has risen dramatically, whilst the richest sections of the population have become more affluent.

Ralf Dahrendorf: *The New Liberty (1959)*

Dahrendorf, like Bell, stresses the importance of social improvement rather than economic growth as the prime aim of post-industrial society. He suggests that the main pattern of conflict is no longer between the proletariat and the bourgeoisie, but between the large firms with their privileged employees, and the rest of society.

Think about it

- Which of the theories on development above appears the most convincing and why?
- How would development theorists explain the decline of Britain as a world power in the second half of the twentieth century?
- Explain what is meant by
  - technological determinism
  - economic determinism
  - mass consumption
  - cultural development.

Development theory: a critical overview

Development theorists			
	Underdevelopment theorists (primarily Marxist) (e.g. Harris)	**Modernisation theorists (primarily functionalists)** (e.g. Sutton)	**Modernisation theorists (primarily Weberian)** (e.g. Myrdal)
Explanations for why the Third World remains poor	Exploitation by rich colonial powers	• lack of capital investment • failure to develop products for export • lack of stable political structures • failure to reform traditional social structures	• lack of an ideology of social and economic progress • lack of trained, literate administrators • lack of an ethic of rationality
Factors affecting the process of development	Failure to escape the influences of Western exploiters will inhibit change.	• the ability of developed societies to exert influence • the acceptance of highly developed Western societies as appropriate models for change	• the introduction of well-organised educational structures • the presence of an educated modernising elite to impose new values on the society • charismatic leadership
Attitudes towards the development of Third World countries	While the capitalist societies continue to exert influence on them, there is little chance of social change. .	• The influence of Western developed societies can only be beneficial. • The technology and ideology of free enterprise will speed development.	The chances of introducing progressive ideologies are good: the benefits can be seen through the media (for example, the 1995 Live Aid concert to raise funds for famine relief was viewed by 1500 million people in 140 countries).

Source: Adapted from P. Selfe, *A Level Sociology* (Macmillan, 1993)

Think about it

• In 300 words outline the key points of similarity and difference between underdevelopment and modernisation theories.

The relationship between the developed and the developing worlds

The poorest 40 countries in the world produce about 5 per cent of the GNP of the richest 40 countries: they are 20 times poorer. This gap between the rich (developed) countries and the poor (developing) countries is likely to grow even wider into the early part of the twenty-first century. The reliance of the Third World countries on the export of their cash crops to the industrial economies makes them very vulnerable both to changes in global consumption and to climate change (drought, for example, can lead to the failure of a main cash crop). None the less many poorer economies aspire towards development and some seek to copy the processes of industrialisation of the 'developed' countries.

Alternative development strategies

From 1945 to 1973 **aid** dominated considerations of development and the relations between the First and Third Worlds. This aid included:

- **Direct foreign investment (DFI):** although not strictly aid, modernisation theorists would see such investment by foreign companies as being 'a good thing' and akin to aid.
- **Military aid:** whilst not development aid, military aid could be said to bolster regimes which might be seeking to develop. In fact it tends to impoverish many Third World countries who incur crippling debts in purchasing military equipment.
- **Overseas development assistance (ODA):** distributed for specific development projects, this category accounted for the largest amount of development aid.
- **Private loans:** whereas ODA money is restrictive, loans from Western banks offer more freedom to the receiving countries.
- **Voluntary aid:** given by charities such as Oxfam, this accounts for a very small proportion of total aid money.

The use of aid is also a means of bolstering *First* World economies:

> 'Our foreign aid programs constitute a distinct benefit to American business. The three main benefits are:
>
> 1. Foreign aid provides a substantial and immediate market for United States goods and services.
> 2. Aid stimulates the development of new overseas markets for US companies.
> 3. Aid orientates national economies toward a free enterprise system in which US firms can prosper.'
>
> Eugene Black of the International Monetary Fund (IMF), quoted in T. Hayter, *Aid as Imperialism* (1991)

Aid since 1973

By the late 1970s, largely as a result of economic crises in many First World countries, private loans had become the single largest source of development money. Massive rises in interest rates in the 1980s meant that many Third World countries, unable to repay the loans or even the interest, were left with huge debt repayment burdens. For example, in

1984, the net flow of capital into Latin America was minus $30 billion: the cost of repaying debt interest was more than the amount of aid coming in. Brazil refused to pay back its aid interest.

Aid – who gives what and how does it work?

Givers

Since 1969 DAC* members have repeatedly promised to give the UN target of 0.7% of their GNP in aid to poor countries. The promise was reaffirmed most recently at the Social Summit in Copenhagen in 1995. But the 0.7% target has never been hit, or even grazed. In 1994 the average aid given by DAC members stood at 0.3% of GNP – less than half the target and the lowest level in 20 years. If rich governments stick to their current plans, it is certain to fall further. Only Norway, Denmark, Sweden and the Netherlands have ever reached the 0.7% of GNP target; the US gives the smallest percentage of its GNP of all donors. Japan is now by far the world's largest donor. At about $5 billion a year, aid given by charities is less than 10% of the 'official' aid. It, too, has been declining in recent years: their grants to the South fell by 6.2% between 1992 and 1993.

Bad shot

Most estimates suggest that less than 20% of aid ever reaches poor people directly. Two-thirds of the world's poor live in 10 countries that together receive less than a third of official development assistance. The Arab States have more than six times the per-capita income of South Asia, yet in

* **DAC = Development Assistance Committee** of the OECD, to which all major aid donors belong.

1992 (shortly after the Gulf War) they received more aid. Populations whose governments spent more than 4% of Gross Domestic Product (GDP) on armaments in 1992 received more per-capita aid ($83) than those with military spending of less than 2% GDP ($32). The message is clear: aid is intended to serve the strategic and other interests of the donors and not to eradicate the poverty of recipients.

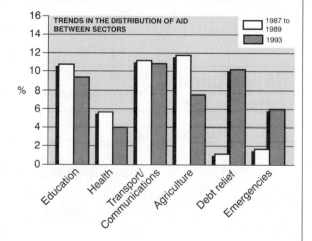

The chart shows how aid has shifted away from spending on health and education – the core tasks of poverty reduction – towards debt 'relief' and emergencies. In fact, overall, considerably more than half the total is not 'aid' at all, but returns to the donors in interest payments and purchases of goods and services.

Source: Adapted from *New Internationalist*, November 1996

Think about it

• What advantages are there for Britain in providing aid to Third World countries?
• What difficulties can be created for countries that are in receipt of aid?

The Brandt Report (1980)

According to Willy Brandt, the North (First World) could develop its manufacturing industry by producing to meet the needs of the South (Third World), as well as giving the South access to the North's markets. The positive sentiments which the Brandt Report generated, however, have had little apparent impact on the issue of development.

Development directions

Rather than the mutual relations which the Brandt Report sought to foster, changes in the 1980s and 1990s appear to be towards the encouragement of foreign companies to invest in Third World (and some First World) countries. Japanese companies investing in Singapore, Taiwan, South Korea and Malaysia, for example, indicate a long-term view that such developing economies hold the key to the future. In the UK, development agencies such as the Scottish Development Agency have succeeded in attracting foreign companies (often TNCs) to set up plants there, though the economic crisis in late 1997 in Asia has curtailed the development of the new Hyundai plant in Dunfermline.

Think about it

- Why do you consider that the ideas contained in the Brandt Report (see page 489) have not yet been fully implemented?

Development strategies – case studies

The following summaries look at two differing economies and their development strategies.

India: developmentalist/modernisation theory

India is seeking to make rapid progress in both industrial and technological fields in order to compensate for more than 300 years which were lost under colonial rule. Many Western industrial enterprises, with the direct help of local capitalists and bureaucrats, and using India's cheap and plentiful supply of labour, are continuing to install increasingly high-tech processes into the Indian economy.

There is a growing awareness of the pitfalls of modernisation as a way of 'progress', however. A group called Lokayan has rejected the notion of 'Third Worldism', with its implications of 'catching up' with the industrialised Western and Eastern bloc countries. Also, there is an:

> *'unfortunate assumption . . . that when technology arrives here, it is transferred. We are finding that the technology often just gets transferred to the premises of the subsidiary, not into the society as a whole. It stays within the walls of the factory.'*
>
> S.K. Goyal of New Delhi University

Thus it may be seen that modernisationist development is doing little to effect significant changes in the basic structure of the Indian economy. Affluence is being generated, but it is distributed only amongst the few urban and rural middle classes. For the vast majority of the already impoverished population the future remains bleak. International 'modernisation' intervention, whether by direct capital investment or through so-called 'aid' programmes, seems to have the effect of establishing the dominance of the controlling group even more firmly.

Taiwan: statist theory – an emerging paradigm

The Japanese saw in Taiwan the ideal opportunity to acquire an offshore garden capable of providing abundant and cheap produce. They introduced into the island economy a small number of industries which were closely connected with agricultural production, such as factories for the production of inorganic fertilisers and others to process and pack agricultural produce for export.

The role of the State has been to ensure the availability of a docile workforce so that policies of economic expansion could be carried through effectively, regardless of the human cost.

A number of theorists have pointed out that Taiwan is a model of **free market capitalism** – testimony to the claims of the modernisationist theories. Others have pointed to the dependency induced in Taiwan by successive foreign powers, and emphasise the role of Taiwan's powerful regime in maintaining a sense of autonomy when confronted with overseas 'aid' packages.

The 'Taiwan phenomenon' shows up the inadequacies of both developmentalist and dependency theories. Apart from the introduction of new technology, the internal structure and characteristics of the traditional institutions have remained intact. Further, the traditional institutions and values seem to be highly compatible with the concept of a powerful, authoritarian regime. A major element in dependency theory – the notion that a local elite in the pay of an external economic power will enforce external controls – fails to match with the reality of Taiwanise economic affairs. Statist theory, then, combines aspects of both developmentalist and dependency theories to produce a new explanation for a country's development.

Colonialism: the exploitation of the Third World

Nineteenth-century colonialism was seen to be a valuable political instrument to allow the West to further develop its interests. Colonies were established in Asia, Africa and South America by foreign countries such as Britain, France, Germany, Belgium, Portugal, Spain and Italy. Such colonies were:

- a source of cheap raw materials;
- additional markets for goods manufactured in Europe;
- providers of wage-labour to work the plantations and mines;
- territorial areas ruled by a system of law and order which suited the colonial administration.

Most of the colonies became independent nations only after World War II (post-1945).

Lenin, the architect of the 1917 Russian Revolution, saw the relationship between **imperialism** (colonialism) and capitalism as follows:

- Capitalist firms, supported by the political and military strength of European governments, set up in the colonies to maintain profitability.
- Access to raw materials was made possible at low cost.
- It was important to develop a transport infrastructure in the colonies.
- Such developments led to the concentration and centralisation of capital in transnational firms.
- Conflict between the colonial power and local workers and peasants was inevitable.
- Colonial powers would seek to exploit the Third World countries (then colonies) and make them dependent on the colonisers for economic survival.

Effects of colonialism

European countries dominated their colonies for a variety of purposes, which were largely economic but which also included the establishment of military influence and the 'civilising' of populations through Christianity.

Early penetration by European countries was based on the destruction of domestic industries, the exploitation of the colonies for food, cheap labour and raw materials, whilst at the same time opening up new markets for Western manufactured goods. In addition, Britain, for example, through the Navigation Acts, prevented exports from its colonies and used military force (as in the case of the Chinese opium war) in order to gain access to trade.

After the initial period of expansion, in order to extend their economic domination, colonial powers forced the development of monocultures – i.e. single crops grown in large quantities to be sold in bulk to Europeans. Unilever, for example, profited from the exploitation of Africa's resources of palm trees, from which oil was extracted and processed and then sold as soap in Britain.

The colonial powers also sought to influence ideas about the populations of the colonies and the colonising nations. Within Britain this 'hegemony' (Gramsci's term) took the form of indicating that the colonial power was superior, that its people possessed greater intellect and were more 'civilised', and that control over the internal affairs of the colony – reinforced by the military where necessary – was therefore justified. Within the colony itself, the dominant hegemony (British) reinforced the idea of British superiority and applied this to employment procedures and criminal and civil justice. The resulting racial inequality and racism can be seen still to influence some British attitudes to others both in Britain and overseas (see pages 469–71).

Demographic change

The 1981 World Development Report noted that by the year 2000 the total world population will be 6 billion, of which 5 billion will live in the Third World. Whereas the population of the developed world is predicted to rise by 300 million by the year 2010, the developing countries' population will expand by 2500 million over the same time-scale – leading to estimated world population figures of 10 billion by 2050 and 11 or 12 billion by 2100.

A growing population may seem desirable, even necessary, in a country seeking to encourage economic growth, as a means of addressing labour shortages and ensuring that labour costs are kept low. The very high rates of population growth in Third World countries, however, are of major concern. Pressure on food resources, large-scale migration, land availability, and the potential for high levels of ill-health, poverty and disease are considered likely to be problematic when an economy is unable to sustain a growing population.

Reasons for high birth rates in Third World countries

- economic insecurity: children are potential earners;
- status of women: they have little choice about childbearing;
- religious influences;
- poor education;
- poor access to and lack of use of contraception.

Urbanisation and industrialisation

Patterns of change in agricultural production, along with population expansion, have resulted in mass migration to the towns and cities of the Third World, creating major population concentrations with slums or shanty towns on the periphery.

It is estimated (see the table below) that by the year 2000 approximately 3 billion people will live in cities; Mexico City will have a population of over 25 million. Eight of the ten largest cities in the world will be in South America or Asia.

Current estimates suggest that city-based patterns of living will continue into the twenty-first century, with the attendant problems of overcrowding, pressure on housing, sanitation, education, transport, etc., and the continuing existence of squalor, disease, poverty and starvation.

The top ten cities (population in millions)					
1950		1980		2000 (est.)	
City	Pop.	City	Pop.	City	Pop.
New York	12.3	Tokyo	16.9	Mexico City	25.6
London	8.7	New York	15.6	Sao Paulo	22.1
Tokyo	6.7	Mexico City	14.5	Tokyo	19.1
Paris	5.4	Sao Paulo	12.1	Shanghai	17.0
Shanghai	5.3	Shanghai	9.9	New York	16.8
Buenos Aires	5.0	Buenos Aires	9.9	Calcutta	15.7
Chicago	4.9	Los Angeles	9.5	Bombay	15.4
Moscow	4.8	Calcutta	9.0	Beijing	14.0
Calcutta	4.4	Beijing	9.0	Los Angeles	13.9
Los Angeles	4.0	Rio de Janeiro	8.8	Jakarta	13.7

The growth of the Third World city was also influenced greatly by colonialism to serve, initially, the interests of colonial investors.

T. Zerner (1964), however, saw the growth of new urban centres in the Third World as progressive, as encouraging individualism and assisting in the removal of 'tradition', thus promoting progress and change. Others, such as M. Castells, see problems not of 'adjustment', 'assimilation' or 'integration', but of class relations and class politics in the urban environment. Social problems – such as poverty, inadequate health care, poor nutrition and bad housing – become aspects of class relations, issues over which social classes fight political battles.

Urban migration What pushes people towards cities? The 'push' factors include land degradation, lack of land, unequal land distribution, droughts, storms, water shortage, religious conflicts and local economic decline. 'Pull' factors, pulling people towards cities, include work opportunities, higher incomes, 'bright lights', joining other rural refugees, freedom from oppressive ways of living and access to health care and better education.

The city now: a checklist of advantages and disadvantages

Urban advantages

- lower costs per person or per household for the provision of water, sewers, drains, rubbish collection, telecommunications and most forms of health, educational and emergency services*
- higher population concentration, reducing demand for land for building and transport
- greater potential for reducing use of fossil fuels
- greater potential for reducing use of motor vehicles
- less need to travel at all

Urban disadvantages

- diseases spread more easily
- airborne and industrial pollution
- noise and traffic accidents
- overcrowding
- inadequate housing
- poor quality water supplies
- very high land and property prices in some districts

* However, the limited resources available in many of the cities of the developing countries do not easily allow even the basics of sanitation and housing issues to be addressed.

Issues of development

Development and gender issues

Women form roughly half the population of the world, yet in the developing countries the position of women appears to be even less equal in many respects than it is in the West. Policy making in social, economic and political areas tends to overlook the needs of women, as if they were invisible. This is often the result of assumptions made by the planners, who are usually men. Such assumptions include:

- Men are the principal workers in society.
- Men are the heads of households.
- Men are the primary breadwinners.
- Men's wages comprise the family income.
- Women and men have equal access to education.
- Women and men have equal access to credit.
- Women and men eat similar proportions of food in the families.

All these assumptions have been shown to be incorrect in the context of developing countries. According to *New Internationalist*, for example, women in Africa do 60–80 per cent of all agricultural work and grow more than three-quarters of all of the food consumed.

D. Amaduire (1987) and other black writers are critical also of the assumptions and portrayal of Third World women by First World feminists. K. Zabaleta, for example, noted in 1986 how many Latin American women read about themselves in the writings of North American academics, who write in English, which is not the women's language.

According to L. Brydon and D. Chant (1989), the obstacles to women's move towards equality with men in the developing countries relate to the reproductive sphere. The double burden of women's reproductive and productive work needs to be considered if women are to derive any benefit from development. These writers suggest that women in the Third World should be given the opportunity to participate fully in the formation of policy and to have their contributions to development recognised. In other words, the question of political power is critical.

Policies for women

'This is the point that needs impressing upon all those policy advisors, policy makers, policy implementers, at national and international levels, who wish to "include women in development", "enhance the status of women" etc. The single most important requirement, the single most important way of helping, is to make resources and information available to organisations and activities which are based on an explicit recognition of gender subordination, and are trying to develop new forms of association through which women can begin to establish elements of a social identity in their own right, and not through the mediation of men. Such organisations do not require policy advisers to tell them what to do, supervise them and monitor them; they require access to resources, and protection from the almost inevitable onslaughts of those who have a vested interest in maintaining both the exploitation of women as workers, and the subordination of women as a gender. The most important task of sympathetic personnel in national and international state agencies is to work out how they can facilitate access to such resources and afford such protection – not how they can deliver a package of ready-made "improvements" wrapped up as "women's programmes".'

D. Elson and R. Pearson, *Women and Development*
(Routledge, 1981)

What has happened to women in the Third World?

It is undoubtedly the case that colonialism and development have changed the lives of women in the Third World. Colonial governments introduced education for women, they attempted to protect women from some very unpleasant experiences such as female circumcision. But, at the same time, they had their own ideas as to how women should behave and what work it was appropriate for them to do. The social transformations brought about by capitalist development are, therefore, ambiguous.

Changes in technology

Changes in technology, and the dominance of men in areas of decision-making are likely to ensure the continuance of an unequal position for women in terms of access to paid employment, education and an equitable share of distributed food.

The negative impact of technology

The introduction of a range of new technology has had a dehumanising effect on workers in developed economies and on the peasants in developing economies. In the former, computer technology has deskilled workers (see Unit 5), causing unemployment through job losses and hardship for many; whilst in the Third World economies, farming technology has altered land use: fertilisers have polluted the soil and tens of thousands of peasants have lost their livelihoods and homes.

Such development leads to what may be called cultural alienation, where people lose contact with social norms and values (anomie – see Unit 10, page 515) and lose the power to influence their own lives (alienation).

Development and employment

The process of economic development, linked as it is with economic growth, carries positive advantages for a country's population. These anticipated improvements may include a higher standard of living, better health care, lower mortality, better housing and improved educational opportunities. The experiences of the so-called 'Tiger economies' (the rapidly growing Asian economies) seem, in part, to follow this pattern, but – as in the developed countries – not all of a developing country's population benefits from national advances. Whilst the opportunities for business and technology sector employment appear buoyant, there are many who are unable to access the new labour market at all, and may conversely see their former livelihoods disappearing. Often, workers who move from rural to urban areas in search of employment find difficulty in obtaining anything other than a meagre subsistence as industrialisation places strong downward pressure on wages. Indeed, the Asian stock-market 'crash' of 1997 caused the collapse of employment in Thailand, a trend which also affected Hong Kong and Indonesia.

Development and education

There is a generally held view that education is crucially important in order to set up the right conditions for development. Such development would generate economic growth and ensure further investment in education, and the effective socialisation of literate and numerate citizens.

In some Third World countries, fewer than 50 per cent of children attend primary school, whilst the percentage for secondary schooling often falls below 40 per cent. (In 1991, it was 5 per cent in Tanzania, 80 per cent in Kuwait.) In India it was estimated in 1995 that there were over 250 million illiterate people.

In poor rural areas there is limited educational provision, and what there is tends to offer a curriculum with a European flavour, reflecting colonial influence. Educational provision, where it is offered, generally favours boys and men, with limited access to girls and women.

Colonial powers were often concerned that the provision of education might foster feelings of confidence, aspiration and knowledge, and that this might lead to the colonial peoples beginning to question the colonial's power. They also recognised, however, that education could be used effectively to **socialise** the population into accepting the legitimacy of colonial power to rule over the country and to benefit from trade.

Development and health

It has always been assumed that a healthy population and workforce will aid economic development, whilst an unhealthy population would be associated with poverty and underdevelopment. However, it is now recognised that the relationship between health and development is not a simple one-way affair. 'Development' may affect health both positively and negatively, although, for the poor, particularly in the Third World, post-war development has often brought little advantage. Whilst development brings the potential for improved diet, housing, social change and reductions in infectious diseases, it is often associated with degenerative diseases (for example strokes, cancer, etc.). Increased stress and exposure to environmental pollution, for example, can be seen as negative side-effects of modernisation and detrimental to health. On the whole, modernisation theorists have not as yet fully considered the possible negative effects of development on Third World populations or the impact of Western diseases.

Seers (1979) sees 'development' as a form of improvement, with certain conditions being necessary to assist in the drive for better health in the Third World:

- the capacity to buy food and physical necessities;
- a job (paid or otherwise);
- equalisation of income distribution;
- adequate education levels.

A concern in the Third World is that Western medical interests may tend to dominate instead of ensuring that primary health care (PHC) approaches, which seek to involve and address the needs of local people, are adopted. Resources for health in the South tend to be minimal and, as in other areas of inequality between the First and Third Worlds, a very long way behind the industrialised nations.

The World Bank (1980) noted a number of features which appeared to characterise Third World health and health care:

Availability and accessibility
- Health facilities are largely inaccessible, especially to women and children.
- Urban and rural differences and inequalities persist in health care.
- Availability of services and treatment, for example access to X-rays or drugs, is often unpredictable and differentially allocated (i.e. between, for example, urban and rural areas).
- Official health provision is often ineffective, with a 'black economy' of medicine and limited public provision.
- Economic and physical barriers, for example time and transport, exclude many people.

Systematic factors and training
- There is little emphasis on preventative medical care.
- Hospitals are often prioritised over primary health care (PHC).
- Increased costs of health care have a disproportionate effect in Third World countries.
- Poor training is often a problem.
- There is a lack of community participation.

Political and social importance
- The emphasis is often on 'slogan-led' health care.
- The state assumes responsibility for health care but rarely provides it effectively or efficiently.
- Social security systems are either limited or non-existent.

Environmental conditions
- Housing, working and travel conditions often pose a threat to health, with few environmental controls.
- Disasters such as floods, droughts and fires drain resources and put pressure on existing health care provision.

Think about it
- The latter part of this section looked at issues of globalisation and development. Identify some possible social effects of globalisation on (a) developing and (b) developed countries.

Development and the environment

Economic growth and resource depletion

It is becoming clear that the world cannot sustain its recent levels of economic growth, industrial development and use of natural resources. This applies especially to Third World countries, where economic pressures are putting significant strain on resources such as minerals, trees and oil.

- The Caribbean *produces* around 40 per cent of the world's bauxite, but *consumes* little of the end-product, aluminium.
- The United States *consumes* about one-third of the world's aluminium, but *produces* only 2.8 per cent of the raw material.

The constant drive for economic growth amongst the developed nations serves to increase the inequalities in developing economies, as resources move from the latter to the former. In the so-called 'Tiger economies' of Asia, the drive for rapid economic growth at almost any cost is predicted to continue well into the twenty-first century, while even in the UK there is no coherent policy on energy conservation.

Pollution

Evidence from the former Soviet countries shows how much pollution can be created (with no controls) in an attempt to industrialise. The nuclear accident at Chernobyl in 1986 is still leaking radiation into the ground and the surrounding area may be contaminated for hundreds of years. In Nigeria, local people have been campaigning against the pollution caused by multinational oil companies. During 1997 Asian countries up to 1,000 miles away were affected by the burning, for land development, of forest in Indonesia. The sun had not shone in Kuala Lumpur for two months and cases of breathing difficulties increased 100 fold, stretching medical provision to the limit. The 'smog' only lifted temporarily when heavy rain fell in October 1997, to return again within weeks.

The 'Green' and the 'Brown' agendas

- The North pollutes both globally and locally, but has the means to reduce some of the impact of pollution. Its environmental concerns often therefore focus on global issues, such as resource depletion, that have been pushed out of sight. This is sometimes called the **'Green agenda'**.
- The people of the South mostly pollute locally, but they often don't have the means to reduce the impact of their pollution. Their concerns tend to focus on things like untreated sewage and poor water quality. This has become known as the **'Brown agenda'**.

The Brown agenda tends to be ignored by the international community, with governments, international agencies, research institutions and environmental professionals concentrating their efforts on the 'Green agenda' of deforestation, global warming, resource depletion and biodiversity. The central concerns of the Brown agenda are cities' poor air quality and dirty water, which can make the inhabitants sick within a few hours. The immediacy of this agenda adds to the urgency of reducing poverty.

Agenda 21

This was the 800-page blueprint for **sustainable development** agreed by the world's leaders at the 1992 Rio Earth Summit. It involves strengthening environmental commitments and integrating economic, social, quality-of-life and local democracy issues. In the UK, Agenda 21 has been accepted by 60 per cent of local authorities:

- 198 authorities have started state-of-the-environment reports.
- 134 are developing their own local sustainability indicators.
- 182 have adapted or created new public consultation procedures.
- 187 are seeking to adopt an environmental management system.

Revision and practice tasks

Task 1: structured question

(a) Briefly explain what sociologists mean by a 'community study'. [4]

(b) Identify, with examples, **two** methodological problems that sociologists face in studying 'communities'. [4]

(c) Assess the contribution of any **one** community study you are familiar with to our understanding of **either** rural **or** urban life. [7]

(d) Evaluate the view that studies of communities tend to 'romanticise' their ways of life. [10]

Total: 25 marks

Task 2: structured question

(a) Briefly explain what is meant by 'community as a local social system'. [4]

(b) Identify two contrasting communities in your locality. Briefly justify your choices. [4]

(c) Indicate the main problems a sociologist might encounter in the study of communities. [7]

(d) Examine the view that the people of Britain can usefully be regarded as a national community. [10]

Total: 25 marks

Source: Interboard Specimen Paper, 1994

Essay questions

1. Explain briefly what is meant by the terms 'urbanisation' and 'de-urbanisation'.

2. Identify and explain two reasons for the fall in the size of the rural population in Britain during the twentieth century.

3. Critically evaluate what sociologists mean when they discuss 'community'.

4. Identify and explain at least five features which you might expect to find in a rural community which would make it different from living in a large city.

5. Identify and explain the major disadvantages of living in a rural area compared to living in a large city.

6. Identify and explain reasons why the official crime rate in urban areas is about twice the rate of rural areas.

7. Discuss why the distinction which is sometimes drawn between rural and urban lifestyles might be misleading.

8. Explain why there has in recent years been a fall in the size of the population of cities in Britain.

9. What criticisms have sociologists offered in respect of the concept of communitarianism?

10. What is a 'nation'? Choosing examples from at least two nations, show how the idea of nation might be socially constructed.

11. Outline the social consequences, for the United Kingdom, of closer ties with other EU countries.

12. Discuss the view that national boundaries mean very little under the impact of globalisation.

13. Critically evaluate the ideas contained in 'Modernisation Theory'.

14. Discuss the view that 'the relationship between the First and Third Worlds still disadvantages the latter'.

15. Evaluate the impact of transnational corporations on developing countries.

16. Discuss the influence of (a) colonialism and (b) globalisation on a developing country's economy.

Ideas for coursework and personal studies

1. Set up interviews with a range of people in an identified community in order to obtain views about the provision of overseas aid.
2. Devise a questionnaire and interview people in your locality to ascertain what, for them, constitutes 'Nation'.
3. Investigate the existence of nationalism within any identified nation state, e.g. Scotland, Wales, England, Northern Ireland. If you wish, identify links between sporting events, nationalistic behaviour and press coverage.
4. Interview a sample of people living in either an urban or a rural community and evaluate what advantages and disadvantages they see in either urban or rural life.
5. Interview a sample of elderly people who have lived in a rural community for most of their lives and evaluate a recording system to analyse how they feel that living patterns have changed during their lifetime.

Selected reading list

Class and Conflict in an Industrial Society, Ralf Dahrendorf (Routledge & Kegan Paul, 1959)

Community and Association, Ferdinand Tonnies (Routledge & Kegan Paul, 1955)

Community Life, Graham Crow and Graham Allan (Harvester Wheatsheaf, 1994)

Contemporary British Society, N. Abercombie and A. Warde (Polity Press, 1994)

Development in Sociology, Vol. IX, Aiden Foster-Carter (Causeway, 1993)

Family and Class in a London Suburb, P. Willmott and M. Young (Routledge & Kegan Paul, 1960)

Globalization, K. Robertson (Sage, 1992)

Government and Politics in Britain, J. Kingdom (Polity Press, Cambridge, 1992)

Industrialism and Industrial Man, Clark Kerr et al (Heinemann 1962)

Investigating Society, Robert G. Burgess (ed.): Chapter 2 'Community Studies' by J. Herman Gilligan and C.C. Harris (Longman, 1989)

The Parenting Deficit, A. Etzioni (Demos, New York, 1993)

Sociology, 2nd edn, A. Giddens (Polity Press, Oxford, 1993)

The Sociology of Community, C. Bell and H. Newby (eds) (Frank Cass, 1974)

The Urban Villages, H.J. Gans (Allan Lane, 1962)

Major classic studies on community

The studies outlined below are the most important studies on community which were published during the 1960s and 1970s and are useful reference points for today's study of community.

- **C. Bell and H. Newby, 'Community studies', in W.M. Williams (ed.)** *Studies in Sociology* **series (Allen and Unwin, 1971):** a very good introductory textbook with an excellent bibliography. It provides comprehensive and critical coverage of the main research on community at the time.

- **J.M. Beshers,** *Urban Social Structure* **(Free Press, New York, 1969):** an examination from a functionalist perspective of the social characteristics of residential areas and the influence of location on the general social structure of the city.

- **J. and R. Darke,** *Health and Environment: High Flats* **(Centre for Environmental Studies, University papers. CES UWP 10, 1970):** looks at interrelations between health and environment. It provides a summary of evidence on living in high-rise flats with the stage in family life cycle being a major factor, e.g. very young children increase demands on parents.

- **N. Dennis, 'The popularity of the neighbourhood community idea' in R.E. Pahl (ed.)** *Readings in Urban Sociology* **(Pergamon Press, 1968):** a critical examination of various concepts of community. It suggests that 'community' is best seen as 'locality social intercourse', as the centre of a set of common experiences and as setting local norms and informal control mechanisms.

- **H.J. Gans,** *The Levittowners* **(Allan Lane, 1962):** a participant observation study, in which it is reported that people moved to the suburb of Levittown (Chicago) because they wanted a house, not for reasons of a 'suburban ideology' or to experience more intense interpersonal relationships! Gans argues that the most important result of suburban experience is the sorting out of people according to their social characteristics, thus providing a different social area in which they might interact. 'Levit' refers to the builders who built the houses in the suburb which Gans investigated.

- **B.J. Heraud,** *Sociology and Social Work: Perspectives and Problems* **(foreword by N. Timms) (Pergamon Press, 1970):** argues for a sociological as opposed to a psychological perspective in the analysing of social problems in a community context.

- **G.A. Hillery, 'Definitions of community' in** *Rural Sociology* **20 (1955):** The task of the paper is to ascertain the extent of agreement among definitions of community (see in particular 'Areas of agreement', pages 111–123). Ninety-four definitions are classified by content and subjected to quantitative and qualitative analyses. There are wide variations but most are in basic agreement that community consists of persons in social interaction within a geographic area and having one or more additional common ties.

- **J. Klein,** *Samples from English Cultures* **(Routledge and Kegan Paul, 1965):** The first part of this book describes life in three different communities – a London district (Branch Street), a Liverpool district (Ship Street) and a Yorkshire mining town (Ashton). Three subcultures are analysed on a locality basis. The second part examines child-rearing practices. Klein's approach is social psychological, hence her emphasis on the importance of early socialisation and personality development as an explanation for the vicious circle of social deprivation. Structural constraints of macro socio-economic forces are largely ignored.
- **P.H. Mann,** *An Approach to Urban Sociology* **(Routledge and Kegan Paul, 1970):** Chapter 7 is particularly good on theoretical considerations.
- **N.W. Polsby,** *Community Power and Political Theory* **(Yale University Press, 1970):** Polsby criticises the assumptions of the 'stratificationist' approach to power and suggests a 'pluralist' model which recognises the existence of competing groups within any community. He argues that power is not concentrated within a single group in society, but relates to a large number of different issues.
- **M. Stacey, 'The myth of community studies',** *British Journal of Sociology* **vol. 20, no. 2 (1969):** Stacey argues from a functionalist perspective, in favour of 'a local social system'. The author believes that such systems help to preserve stability and order, offering support to those encountering difficulties.

10 Crime, deviance and control

The uniform of the Hooligan: 'All of them have a peculiar muffler twisted round the neck, a cap set rakishly forward, well over the eyes, and trousers very tight at the knee and very loose at the foot.'

Introduction

'Hooligans', as the cartoon above refers to them, are only one of many examples of people considered to be showing deviant – or criminal? – behaviour. The cartoon shows such people existed well before the twentieth century.

This unit looks at the meanings of 'deviance' and 'crime' and how our understanding of these terms forms part of our understanding of society as a whole.

- **Deviance** refers to any form of social behaviour which strays from what may be seen as 'normal' or socially acceptable. Whilst deviance may include criminal activities, it goes far wider than this. Deviance needs to be seen as relative to the ideas of social normality, which vary greatly between different societies at different times.
- **Crime** or **criminal activities** are most commonly defined in terms of breaking the laws of a particular society. However, not all criminal activities will necessarily be seen as deviance: minor traffic offences, for example. Most car drivers, at some time, will exceed the speed limit or drive through a red traffic light.

Think about it

'Hooligans, deviants or criminals?'

Look at the cartoon above.

- What difference does it make whether the couple on the motorbike own it or not? What if they intend to ride it?
- What could or should be done about groups hanging about on street corners in noisy, urban areas? Is it a social problem? Why, or why not, would you consider it to be a social problem?
- Have you ever behaved in a deviant manner, for example by dressing in such a way as to draw attention to yourself? Have you ever knowingly carried out a criminal act, for example in relation to alcoholic drink laws?

The relationship between deviance and **control** is complex; as too is the issue of what constitutes deviant or criminal activities. This unit attempts to cover these complexities and will include:

- a consideration of the nature of deviance and how it has been defined;
- how controls on crime and deviance are operated by society;
- traditional theories and explanations of deviance from biological and psychological as well as sociological viewpoints;
- subcultural theories, including deviancy amplification and the role of the mass media, folk devils and moral panics;
- critical contemporary approaches including neo-Marxism, New Left realism, feminism and New Right realism;
- measurement of crime, the uses and limitations of crime statistics, British Crime Surveys, victim and self-report studies;
- the distribution of crime and deviance by age, gender, ethnicity, locality and class;
- role of the police, the courts and prisons;
- asylums and the issues of non-culpable deviance and suicide.

Crime and deviance defined by society

What may be considered normal varies across different societies and cultures and across time. What constitutes a crime in a particular culture is often related to the dominant value of that culture or what most members of that society consider to be worthy at the time. Furthermore, within any one society, at any time, there are a wide variety of different sets of values. For example, male homosexual behaviour was illegal in the UK until 1969; then, following the recommendations of the Wolfenden Report (1967), private homosexual acts between consenting adults were **decriminalised** (no longer categorised as criminal acts). This represented a major change in relation to the role of criminal laws in respect of control of private conduct; it signalled the idea that crime does not reflect absolute standards but changes over time and between cultures.

K.J. Erikson, in *Wayward Puritans, A Study in the Sociology of Deviance* (1966), shows how in New England, USA, in the seventeenth century, religious crimes (i.e. crimes against religious dogma and associated moral codes) were the most noticeable of all crimes; whilst other (for example economic) crimes seemed to be treated less harshly: thieves were treated leniently if they became repentant. The Puritans who had fled across the Atlantic to Massachusetts believed that the Church should consist of 'visible saints' or people who could be seen to be amongst the Elect of God. Their laws were based on the Bible, and in cases of doubt church ministers would set a rule that was justified with reference to the Bible. By contrast, in the UK and the USA in the twentieth century, it is economic crimes that are generally treated harshly, attracting far heavier penalties than do religious blasphemy or disrespect. Definitions of crime can thus be seen to change in relation to wide social changes and social values.

What a society sees as deviant in terms of its culture also varies considerably, as the article on page 506 shows.

The article demonstrates, for example, different ideas towards homosexuality; in New York it was viewed mainly as a deviant act, whereas in Iran 90 per cent viewed it as a criminal act even when carried out in private by consenting adults.

For sociologists, deviance usually refers to behaviour or activities which do not seem to fit in with the expectations of the majority of members of a particular society and which receive their disapproval. Since deviance is such a relative concept, it is far more complex than it may at first appear.

Related to the concepts of crime and deviance are the issues of **marginalisation** and **discrimination**. Even after the 1969 changes in the law regarding homosexual acts, gay men and women in the UK remain marginalised (i.e. seen to be on the edge of society) and discriminated against. It may be argued that mentally ill and disabled people are discriminated against and, by extension, disabled by society – the concept of mental illness as non-culpable deviance is taken up on pages 557–9.

Perceptions of Deviance in Six Cultures

To find out prevailing attitudes in different cultures about the deviant nature of nine specific acts, Graeme Newman (1976) administered questionnaires to representative samples from six cultures: India, Indonesia, Iran, Italy (specifically Sardinia, a subculture), the United States (specifically New York City), and Yugoslavia.

One central question Newman asked was, "Do you think this act should be prohibited by law?" His premise was that if people felt strongly that an act was deviant, they would want it to be illegal and would want the police (rather than the family, government officials, or doctors) to act as the agent of social control.

Here are some highlights of the responses:

Robbery (with physical injury to the victim). Regarded overall as the most serious crime. The predominant view in all cultures was that it should be illegal. (But in Sardinia, which has a tradition of violence, only 50 percent of the subjects said they would report a robbery to the police.)

Misappropriation of public funds (by a government official, as by embezzlement). Rated the second most serious offense overall. The Yugoslavians, citizens of a socialist country, criminalized the theft of "social funds" more than all other samples.

Factory pollution of the environment. The vast majority of all six samples (ranging from 93 percent of Yugoslavians to 99 percent of Indians) regarded this act as deviant. However, all countries preferred to report this act to a government official rather than to the police.

Incest. The feeling in all cultures was that incest should be illegal. Five of the six cultures disapproved by 94 to 98 percent; in New York the proportion disapproving was much lower, 71 percent.

Homosexuality. A majority in all cultures (from 71 percent in Yugoslavia to 90 percent in Iran) thought that homosexuality should be against the law even when performed in private by consenting adults—except in New York, where only 18 percent thought so.

Taking drugs. Regarded as criminal by a majority in all cultures.

Abortion. General disapproval, but the New York and Yugoslav samples showed a preference for decriminalization.

Public protests (such as political demonstrations). The predominant response for Sardinia and New York was to regard protest as not just noncriminal, but nondeviant. The other four cultures were deeply divided.

Not helping (for example, failing to go to the aid of a holdup victim). Drew the widest variation in responses in all cultures, probably because it is difficult to establish the circumstances under which this act would be criminal. New Yorkers were the least inclined to want to make this act a crime.

Almost everything anyone does violates somebody's standards, somewhere.

Source: G. Newman, *Comparative Deviance. Perception and Law in Six Cultures* (Elsevier, New York, 1976)

Think about it

- Why is it that different cultures appear to adopt differing views towards the actions noted in the article above?

Social control

This refers to control, exercised in a variety of ways, to curb and prevent deviant behaviour. Sociologists divide social controls into two main groups – informal and formal.

Informal control

These controls are based on unwritten rules and acceptance of social norms. They form a close part of everyday life, through agencies of socialisation such as the family, the school, peer groups and the mass media.

- In conforming to established norms, individuals usually receive acceptance and rewards as positive sanctions; they are shown respect, for example, or are trusted with personal matters.
- Individuals who break these norms receive negative sanctions for their deviant behaviour; for example ridicule, disgust or being 'sent to Coventry'.

Norms exist alongside sanctions to reinforce **conformity**.

Formal control: the law and the courts

Formal control is based on written rules and on laws of the state which are passed by government and then interpreted in courts of law. Negative sanctions with specific penalties, for example fines or imprisonment, are imposed (see also pages 554–5).

As well as serving as a deterrent, the law also controls actions in a more subtle way. As it comes to be accepted that the law is morally right, people believe that it should be obeyed. Respect for justice underlies the social functions of the law.

Social functions of the law

1. Maintaining public order
2. Protecting property
3. Encouraging cooperation by all citizens
4. Communicating moral standards
5. Regulating social life
6. Moderating the struggle for power by giving legal status to the recognised authority.

Think about it

- Identify examples of
  a) formal control
  b) informal control
  in the following contexts:
  – schools or colleges
  – the workplace
  – on the streets.

Biological, psychological and sociological explanations of crime and deviance

Biological (or physiological) theories

Biological (or physiological) theories tend to explain crime and other forms of deviant behaviour as being biologically based. In other words it is considered that some people are more inclined to become criminals because of their genetic background, often expressed in terms such as 'faulty genes' or 'hereditary factors'.

Theorists associated with this approach include the following:

- **Paul Broca,** an early French anthropologist; he claimed that the brains and skulls of convicted criminals differed from those of the more law-abiding members of society.
- **Cesare Lombroso,** an Italian criminologist in the late nineteenth century; he claimed that criminals had an innate tendency to anti-social behaviour – hence he proposed the idea of *il neo noto* (the born criminal). The *neo noto* was characterised by certain physical characteristics:

  'enormous jaws, high cheek bones ... handle-shaped ears found in criminals, savages and apes.'
  Cesare Lombroso, *Crime: Its Causes and Remedies* (1911)

- **William A. Sheldon,** an American; in the 1940s he linked biological structure with criminal behaviour. He distinguished three types of biological physique or build, and claimed that people of one particular type – which he termed 'mesomorph' – were well-developed, muscular and active. They were more likely to be aggressive and delinquent than 'ectomorphs', who were of a thin, fragile physique, or 'endomorphs', who were of a fat, weak physique.

Is there a biological basis for criminal and deviant behaviour?

- **Sarnoff Mednick**, working with fellow-sociologists in Sweden in the 1980s, used EEGs (electro-encephalograms) to measure the level and pattern of electrical activities in the brain. Six hundred Swedish boys and girls, aged up to 17, were given EEGs several times while awake and while asleep. Twelve years later, Swedish police records were examined and it was found that offenders had had a distinctive EEG pattern even though over six years had elapsed between the test and the date of the crimes. Mednick maintained, in *The Causes of Crime* (1987), that some inherited biological characteristics can play a part in causing criminal activity.
- **Hans Eysenck**, a British psychologist; he virtually made it his life work to emphasise the importance of inherited characteristics. His sophisticated biological approach argued that there is a link between genetically based personality characteristics and criminal behaviour, particularly extroversion or outward-going personality. Extroversion (and introversion) is inherited and based on genetic make-up. Eysenck tested prisoners and found them more extroverted than the wider population.

In the UK, various claims have been made about genetic causes of criminal behaviour in terms of inherited, abnormal chromosomes. Normally, females have two X chromosomes whilst males have one X chromosome and one Y chromosome, although some men have an additional Y chromosome. Research by S. Mednick et al. in *Biology and Violence* (1982) suggests that XYY men are more likely to be involved in violent crimes. Ann Moir and David Jessel, in *A Mind to Crime* (1995), maintain that biology is a control factor in crime; their data suggests that 89–95 per cent of all crime is committed by men because:

- the male brain has a lower level of the neurotransmitter (brain chemical) serotonin, which is responsible for the control of impulsive behaviour;
- higher levels of testosterone make men readier to engage in aggression.

Criticisms of biological (or physiological) theories

The very idea of a born criminal type not surprisingly causes considerable debate. It tends to assume that the key factor in criminality is the innate or genetic background of the individual, and underplays other important sociological concerns such as social class, gender, etc. I. Taylor, F. Walton and J. Young, in *The New Criminology* (1973), for example, suggest that lower-working-class males may appear more frequently in criminal statistics because their more manual forms of employment may produce the physical fitness and robustness associated with 'mesomorphs' (see William Sheldon above). Similarly, chromosome abnormality may lead to deviant physical appearance and hence the feeling of being apart from 'normal' life; such individuals may be drawn to deviant and even criminal activities.

The focus has tended to be on male criminality. Considerations of genetic or physical make-up have been applied predominantly to men; females do not seem to fit into this framework. Female writers on crime such as Otto Pollack in *The Criminality of Women* (1950) and more recently Anne Campbell in *The Girls in the Gang* (1986) have challenged such thinking.

Several of the major contributions to biological theories have been based on institutionalised criminals, i.e. those in prison. This assumes that all convicted criminals are guilty; also – if those studied are to be considered typical – it assumes that most criminals are caught.

Psychological theories

Psychological theories are similar to biological (or physiological) theories – indeed in some textbooks, studies such as those of H.J. Eysenck and S. Mednick are given as psychological theories – as they also associate crime and deviance with particular personality types. However, whilst biological theories are often seen in terms of genetic or hereditary background with lifelong consequences, psychological theories more often consider the individual's background. They consider especially the person's early childhood and parent–child relationships. Two major theorists associated with this approach are Sigmund Freud and John Bowlby.

Sigmund Freud (1856–1939)

Freud, an Austrian Jew, was a founding figure of psychology and also of the theory and practice of psychoanalysis and therapy methods (i.e. talking things out to a trained therapist). He put forward a developmental theory of personality which stressed the importance of early experience. The formation of 'normal' personality involves the negotiation of each developmental stage. Socialisation occurs in psycho-sexual stages which need to be worked through satisfactorily to avoid personality problems or abnormalities. For example, Freud saw the first 12 months of life as an oral stage of development in which gratification was obtained mainly by the mouth: too little or too much gratification could lead to anxiety manifested in a fixation on sucking or biting which may later result in greed.

With his daughter Anna (1895–1982), Freud fled to England from Nazi-occupied Austria. Anna Freud pioneered work on child psychoanalysis.

John Bowlby

A British psychologist, Bowlby is linked to psychoanalytical theories in his suggestion that damage can be caused by the separation of mother from infant. In *Child Care and the Growth of Love* (1963), Bowlby found that some forms of juvenile delinquency were linked to maternal deprivation in the early years of childhood.

Bowlby stressed the need for intimate mother–child relationships in order to prevent the development of a psychopathic personality characterised by an impulsive, emotionless, guiltless disregard for others which could lead to violent criminal behaviour. In other words, according to Bowlby, a child's emotional experiences could be capable of causing deviant and criminal behaviour.

Criticisms of psychological theories

Central to the psychological theories are issues of child development which, it may be claimed, contain value judgements in terms of what is 'normal' or 'successful' development and its consequences. Freud's theories have been developed and modified by his followers (neo-Freudians), based on their experiences as psychoanalysts. They have emphasised social and cultural influences on personality and view Freud's emphasis on sex and psycho-sexual stages as outdated. The concept of psycho-sexual stages has also been criticised as arbitrary and misleading: any important developmental stage, for example walking, can be either gradual or sudden – the ages at which individuals enter stages are likely to vary.

A relatively closed system of psychoanalysis, set within its own narrow framework of principles and practice, is bound to be based on its theoretical background and training. Hence its evidence may well be seen to be connected to that small and self-supportive group of practitioners.

Freudian theories can explain only some aspects of crime and deviance. Whilst a relatively small number of criminals may have personality disorders, it seems unlikely that this would be true of the majority. It is doubtful that even those involved in similar criminal activities would share similar psychological disorders.

Maternal deprivation theory

Linked to the psychoanalytical theories of John Bowlby and others have been studies on the long-term effects of maternal deprivation. As early as 1959, B. Wootton, in *Social Science and Social Pathology*, pointed out that the loose definition surrounding this concept made evidence unreliable. By 1976, A.M. Clarke and A.A.D.B. Clarke, in *Early Experience, Myth and Evidence*, had gathered evidence to demonstrate that the importance of early childhood in forming adult personalities had been overstated and the resilience of young children underestimated. So, within 20 years of Bowlby's evidence being published, the pendulum had swung back to suggest that it does not matter to the infant whether its rearers are its biological parents or others. Research has shown that the child can form attachment bonds, even multi-role bonds, to people other than its biological parents.

Beliefs based on the mother–child bonding relationship and the dependence of the fragile infant, it is claimed, are peculiarly Western and peculiarly modern. For example, N. Fox, in *Attachment of Kibbutz Infants* (1977), noted that child-rearing in Israel within the kibbutz (or agricultural community-based farming project) was shared between parents and professional child-rearers: mothers and child-rearers became interchangeable attachment figures. Throughout history, parents have been assisted by others: family members, governesses, nannies, childminders and, in more recent times, nurseries, crèches and playgroups – with no significant changes in patterns of crime and deviance.

1972 saw the publication of the first edition of a key text: *Maternal Deprivation Reassessed* by M. Rutter et al., a major reviewer of Bowlby's work. By this time Rutter had also started work on his famous study *Fifteen Thousand Hours* (1979) (see Unit 4, page 190). Rutter claimed that schools do significantly affect child development and educational achievement, though they may not be able to remedy the effects on personality development of maternal deprivation.

It can be seen from the above that, in relation to psychological theories of crime and deviance, quite complex factors are involved. Whilst some violent crimes are carried out by individuals, others are committed by groups; it seems improbable that psychological characteristics are shared by separate individuals or even among members of the same group.

Psychological profiling

A more recent development in psychological theories of crime and deviance has been the use of psychological profiles or offender profiling. In 1994, **Paul Britton**, a forensic psychologist, completed a profile for the police of the killer of Rachel Nickell, whose body was discovered on Wimbledon Common. This led to the entrapment of Colin Stagg who was later released.

Britton is not alone as an 'offender profiler'. Professor **David Canter**, Head of the Investigative Psychology Unit at Liverpool University, has provided help to police in more than 100 criminal cases. Canter criticised Britton's techniques as having 'no systematic or scientific basis', and did not mention Britton in his book on investigative psychology, *Criminal Shadows* (1994). Indeed, Canter had agreed to act as a defence witness if Colin Stagg's trial had proceeded.

Britton and Canter represent two different schools of **forensic psychology**. Canter is an environmental psychologist, interested in social interaction and the way environment shapes behaviour; he will look, for example, at whether a criminal binds his victim or tries to disguise his appearance. Britton, with some expertise on the personalities and characteristics of people convicted of sexual assaults, takes an individual-based approach.

There have been numerous examples of psychological profiles being wrong. One notable case was that of Albert de Salvo, the 'Boston Strangler', who murdered 13 women between 1962 and 1964. Before de Salvo's arrest, an American psychologist suggested that the police should be looking for a flamboyant homosexual with an accomplice. De Salvo was aggressively heterosexual and worked alone! Nevertheless, despite such criticisms, we may be witnessing the dawn of a new approach in relation to psychological theories of crime and deviance.

Sociological theories
Theories of crime and deviance

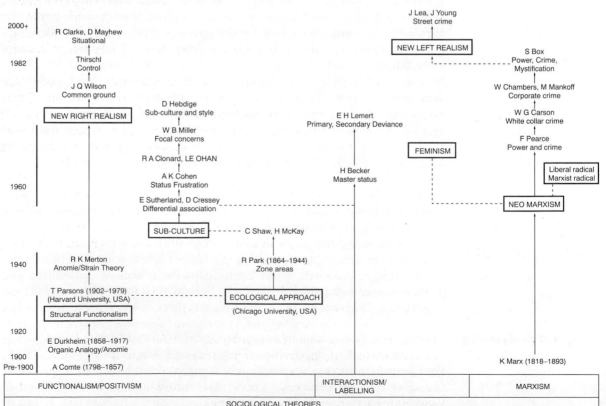

Sociologists tend to be rather dismissive about the non-sociological theories of crime and deviance. Crime and deviance, for sociologists, occur within a social setting and framework, and are studied in terms of the **social interaction** which takes place between members of society and those who make and carry out the rules. The rule makers, supported by rule enforcers, interact with the rule breakers.

The social interaction between those who make and apply rules, and those who break them.

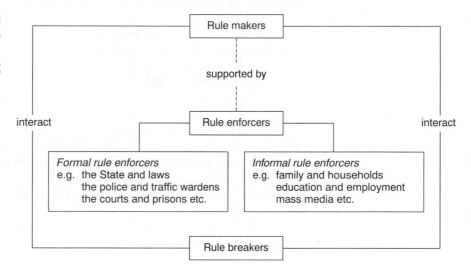

The most common traditions in sociological theories of crime and deviance, discussed below, may be seen as broad and, to some extent, overlapping. However, these traditional perspectives are important as they form the building blocks for the development of different sociological viewpoints on crime and deviance from the early nineteenth century onwards.

The classical theories of functionalism and Marxism developed in the nineteenth century. Functionalism, in the form of structural functionalism, continued to develop throughout the twentieth century. It was challenged in the mid-twentieth century by interactionism, which itself was challenged by neo-Marxists and other contemporary theories including feminism and both the New Left and New Right.

Classical functionalism and positivism

Classical functionalism may be seen as having developed from positivism and the work of the French social thinker **Auguste Comte** (1798–1857). In the early nineteenth century, Comte maintained that positivism, or empirical knowledge which could be observed, measured, tested and proved as accurate, was the only real form of knowledge – as in the physical sciences. Such knowledge could be used to describe and explain social behaviour. It is worth considering Comte's views in relation to the ideas and methods of Caesar Lombroso (see page 508). Many of the early studies of crime and deviance, including Emile Durkheim's classic study of suicide, *Le suicide* (1897), tended to reflect positivism. Indeed, positivist approaches to crime and deviance have persisted throughout the twentieth century, particularly in attempts to measure, or even overcome, crime. The following charts illustrate positivist approaches to crime and deviance.

Truancy rates[1], whilst at school, of prisoners[2] compared with the general population[3] (left); time to reconviction[4], by gender and age[5] (right)

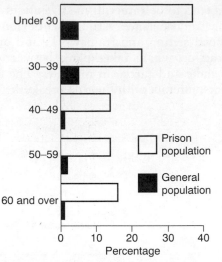

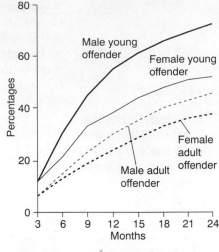

[1] Percentage who mostly played truant from school after the age of 11
[2] Prisoners in prison in England and Wales, excluding juveniles
[3] Great Britain figures

[4] Time between discharge from prison in 1991 and first reconviction for a standard list offence

[5] Adults are aged 21 and over on the sentencing date; young offenders are aged under 21 on the sentencing date

Source: *Social Trends*, 1994

Advantages of positivism

Positivism has the following attractions:

- Criminologists who wish to apply their knowledge and techniques may see advantages in their findings adopting a more 'scientific' status.
- Criminal and deviant acts can be made more explicit, often in the form of bold numerical data, which may carry more weight with the general population (consider, for example, the usefulness of measures of truancy).
- It produces 'evidence' for sociologists and others seeking to develop penal and sentencing policy. Both Michael Howard and Jack Straw (Conservative and Labour Home Secretaries in 1997) cited much evidence in support of their political position.

Criticisms of positivism

- The methods used to calculate criminal and deviant acts may be suspect: just how accurate can calculations of, for example, sexual and drug offences be? (See also pages 534–40.)
- Criminal and deviant acts may be seen, at least by the actors themselves, as meaningful actions rather than cold statistics. The release of IRA or other 'political' prisoners, for example, raises the question – overlooked by positivists – as to whether their actions may or may not be viewed as criminal.

Classical functionalism and Emile Durkheim

Emile Durkheim (1858–1917) was probably the first sociologist to produce a broad sociological theory of deviance. He considered that deviance was *universal* (and normal), *relative* and *functional*.

- **Universal** (and normal) refers to the deviants present in all societies who act against its norms and shared values: hence deviance may be considered universal, i.e. found in every country across the world.

- **Relative** refers to different social groups possessing different ideas about norms and shared values: hence deviance is relative to particular countries or localities.
- **Functional** refers to deviant acts which receive widespread disapproval, thereby serving to support socially acceptable behaviours: hence, providing deviant acts do not become excessive, these can serve a functional purpose and reinforce norms and shared values. New Age Travellers, for example, may serve to reinforce the more socially acceptable household and general living patterns in the UK.

Durkheim referred to a 'boundary-maintaining' function, which drew the line between acceptable and non-acceptable behaviour. For Durkheim, a limited amount of deviance could benefit society, but the balance was very important since too much deviance could threaten society and even cause its ruin.

Durkheim and anomie   **Anomie** means normlessness or a lack of norms. For Durkheim, anomie occurs under severe social strain. The Wall Street stock exchange crash in 1929 is often used as an example of anomie: wealthy stockbrokers committed suicide by leaping from their skyscraper offices rather than attempting to cope with their financial ruin and its social implications. More recently, in the UK, there have been over 30 cases of suicide associated with financial losses at Lloyd's shipping insurance company, among them former Sea Lord Sir Richard Fitch, who lost £300,000 after joining Lloyds in the late 1980s: he committed suicide as a result in February 1994.

Writing in the early 1900s, Durkheim saw society in terms of traditional, small-scale settings with strong community bonds. As society developed, it became more complex and the moral consensus or shared values about the rules of living were weakened: its members and their families became more isolated and uncertain about norms and values. A state of anomie set in.

An anomic state of affairs is harmful for individuals and for society as a whole:

- When members of society have to 'go it alone' without support from others, tragedy – which might otherwise have been averted – can occur. The case of the Lloyd's Names, referred to above, is a case in point.
- When the 'boundary-maintaining' function becomes blurred, there is the increased risk of members of society crossing a boundary. An example of this might be when the legal limits for the consumption of alcohol are exceeded.
- When community bonds become weakened, individuals are less likely to seek or receive approval from other members of society or to express disapproval. This was demonstrated in Rwanda in 1994, when genocide went seemingly unchecked and those fleeing into exile were seen living in disease-ridden camps squatting over United Nations food supplies.

Thus Durkheim's contribution to theories of crime and deviance suggested that, unlike other nineteenth-century commentators, he viewed deviance not as being based on the acts of individuals but as a major aspect of society itself.

Criticisms of Durkheim

Durkheim seems to offer little, if any, explanation for the following:

- why some members of society are more likely than others to commit deviant acts;
- how the power dimensions operate (in all societies some members possess social control in framing and carrying out its legal system);
- whether the majority interests of society are, in reality, overlooked by those in power.
- who, in fact, defines what is deviant.

Structural functionalism and R.K. Merton

Robert K. Merton, the American structural functionalist, developed Durkheim's concept of anomie into what has become known as **strain theory**. He identified the strain or stress which exists when 'success' – often represented by financial rewards or high incomes – becomes the main target (the goal) of individuals within society but when this is difficult for most people to achieve in a socially acceptable way (the means).

- For Merton, the dysfunction between goals and means as an explanatory theory of crime and deviance may be seen as 'structural' because it relates directly to the social structure of, for example, the USA.

- Merton did not consider that all individuals who became blocked from their pathway to financial rewards and success would become anomic; but there were some fairly clear-cut expectations: those on the bottom rung of the social ladder wished to improve their living standards but had low expectations of doing so; those on the top rung have much higher expectations of success.

Merton and anomie

R.K. Merton further contributed to the development of the concept of anomie in relation to strain theory with a model illustrating how individuals might choose different degrees of conformity or non-conformity. This is shown in the following table:

Response	Cultural goals	Cultural means
1. Conformity	+	+
2. Innovation	+	−
3. Ritualism	−	+
4. Retreatism	−	−
5. Rebellion	+ −	+ −

+ Individuals believe in society's cultural goals; they use socially acceptable means of achieving their goals

− Individuals do not believe in society's cultural goals; they reject the goals or the means of achieving them.

+ − Individuals reject the goals or the means and use their own or new ones.

Conformity (numbered **1** in Merton's model) occurs when individuals accept society's goals and the means of achieving them. The cultural goal may be success achieved by means of hard work by law-abiding citizens. The alternatives to conformity, numbered 2 to 5, are explained below.

Responses towards deviance, based on R.K. Merton's model of anomie

2. **Innovation**   Innovators try to achieve success but they reject the normal methods or means and turn to theft, vandalism, etc. These individuals may feel no guilt as they may have been socialised to the values of the deviant subculture which accepts such means.

3. **Ritualism**   Ritualists continue to work within the system but give up trying for success. They may be office workers, for example, stuck in a rut and simply 'going through the motions'. Ritualism occurs when the means to the goals are accepted but the individual loses sight of the actual goals.

4. **Retreatism**   Retreatists abandon both the goals and the means of achieving them, and become alcoholics, tramps, etc. Retreatism occurs when an individual withdraws from society. Unlike the innovator's deviant subculture response to society, retreatism may be seen as an individual adapting to society.

5. **Rebellion**   Rebels reject goals and the accepted means of success and replace them with their own goals and means, for example political or religious extremists or revolutionaries. Such individuals often come from a background of radical political views, for example Sinn Fein, the political wing of the IRA. This response differs from the previous three since it is seeking to adopt a new agenda and to create a new society rather than to adapt within the existing society.

Source: Adapted from K. Browne, *An Introduction to Sociology* (Polity Press, 1992)

Criticisms of R.K. Merton's theory of anomie

- It requires us to accept that the central value system of the USA (in the 1930s) was known and acknowledged: everybody wanted to achieve the 'American dream' and financial success, even those who 'retreated' or 'rebelled'.
- Can we accept the strange effect of conformity causing deviance in the form of anomie because deep down all Americans wish to conform to American values?
- It does not explain why individuals choose one form of deviance rather than another. Merton does argue, however, that different types of innovation and ritualism reflect different emphases in socialisation between the middle and working classes, with the latter being less socialised and feeling less guilty.
- It provides no definition of crime and deviance.
- It offers no explanation of the separation between means and goals.
- It concentrates too much on the individual and not enough on other important factors, for example deviant subcultures and the power of the state to define crime and deviance.
- I. Taylor, P. Walton and J. Young, in *The New Criminology* (1973), argue that Merton's theory of anomie implies that the poor are likely to become criminals because they do not have the means to achieve their goals and are therefore more likely to become innovators. However, if the poor are under pressure to innovate why do such a relatively small percentage commit crime? On the other hand, any overrepresentation of the lower classes amongst offenders could also be explained by certain police strategies, bias of the courts, etc.
- The theory seems to have a middle-class bias in that it assumes that all criminals and rule-breakers accept and cherish middle-class goals.

Many delinquent activities, however, do not appear to be aiming for material gains. What material goals are football hooligans pursuing, for example? The assumptions in the theory do not necessarily apply to real life. People do not share the same social beliefs!

However, the concept of anomie does have its strengths. It attempts to explain criminal behaviour, perhaps more so than deviant acts, in terms of the structure and culture of society, rather than in terms of individual characteristics.

Social disorganisation and ecological theories

Shared values and social stability are emphasised by both Durkheim and Merton. Various factors may contribute to disturb such social stability, of which **social disorganisation** has been identified by several sociologists. They consider that the **ecology** or the **urban environment**, with its population size and movements, could produce social disorganisation. Its indicators might include delinquency, illegal drug use, prostitution, alcoholism, etc. These might exist in areas (or zones) of shifting populations, where control mechanisms are more likely to break down and criminal and deviant activities are more likely to flourish.

Major factors associated with social disorganisation and ecological theories and studies include:

- Since crime is an urban phenomenon, it seems reasonable that some of its causes lie in the social effects of urbanisation.
- Following Robert Park, working in Chicago in the 1920s, the 'Chicago School', as it became known, laid the basis for an ecological model of crime. In *Juvenile Delinquency and Urban Areas* (1942) Clifford Shaw and Henry McKay showed that male rates of delinquency were highest in the first of the five concentric zone areas – i.e. in the **inner-city zone** or **business centre** as shown in the diagram below. This first zone, originally occupied by the wealthy, had by the late 1920s begun to fall into decay and to be occupied by immigrant workers, with poverty, poor housing, unstable family conditions and social disorganisation being much in evidence.

Map of Chicago showing zone rates of male juvenile delinquents, 1927–33

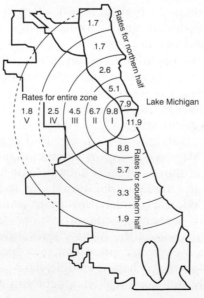

The delinquency rates are shown in terms of the proportion of delinquents as a percentage of the total male population of each zone.

Source: C. Shaw and R. McKay, *Juvenile Delinquency and Urban Areas* (University of Chicago Press, 1942)

Criticisms of ecological theories

- They fail to explain how social disorganisation originates, and do not account for organised criminal activities.
- They are **deterministic**, tending to assume that people respond to their environment in a passive way and play no active role in deciding their behaviour.
- They assume that everyone in a 'zone of transition' would become delinquent. Why, then, do certain individuals not become delinquent, even when they mix with criminal groups?
- They are **circular** in their argument: crime and deviance are used to illustrate social disorganisation which in turn is used to account for juvenile delinquency.

Interactionist and labelling approaches

These theories form a fundamental criticism of traditional positivist criminology. They maintain that the positivist perspective involves often incorrect assumptions about the nature and explanation of crime and deviance, tending to present their subject matter as easily identifiable and more or less black and white. Rather than pursuing the causes of crime, labelling theorists analyse the social processes by which the behaviour of some individuals comes to be labelled as officially criminal; they look at the consequences and implications for these individuals.

In the 1960s and 1970s, Howard Becker claimed that in objective terms there is no such thing as deviance – an act only becomes deviant when it is so labelled. We may take as an example two men seen kissing in a street. Many people, who cannot identify with what they see, react by labelling the men as 'queers'; they categorise the men and the act as deviant, in order to 'make sense' of the situation which appears to be a distortion of their picture of reality.

Labelling is a reaction by the audience – i.e. society – to produce a sense of order in social relations. Becker gives an example of a brawl involving young people in a low-income area: the police may see this as evidence of delinquency, whereas if it had happened in a high-income area they would be more likely to see it as just 'youthful high spirits'.

Thus important points for interactionist and labelling approaches are as follows:

- Those who observe an act of deviance may view it one way, whereas those who commit the act may view it differently. If individuals are labelled as deviant by those in a position to make the label stick (the police, for example), then those individuals become deviants.
- Deviance is not the direct behaviour of a person; rather it depends on the interaction between the person and the observer.
- The attachment of a deviant label has important effects on how individuals are seen by society and on how they see themselves, and on the resulting patterns of interaction between them and others.
- If someone is caught and branded as a deviant, a process of **stigmatisation** occurs: this involves the re-evaluation of one's public identity by others. The new status makes it increasingly difficult for an individual to retain his or her normal identity. The label, through its stereotyping effect, oversimplifies what the deviant 'is' and so the labelled individual is seen as nothing but what his or her label suggests.
- It is not simply a label but a 'master-status', which may override a person's status as a parent, neighbour or colleague: he or she will be

associated with the negative qualities and characteristics normally linked with the label, and will start to see him- or herself in terms of that label.

Two major interactionist and labelling studies are summarised below.

Edwin H. Lemert, *Humans, Their Deviance, Social Problems and Social Control* (2nd ed. 1972)

Lemert stressed that, for an understanding of juvenile delinquency, the motivation and activities of those reacting to delinquency was more important than the motives and actions of the delinquents themselves. Unlike positivist approaches which assume that social control arises out of the existence of deviance, Lemert argues that social control actually leads to deviance: the deviance lies not in the act itself but in the responses of others to the act. The deviant then responds to other people's reaction. Hence, for Lemert, there are two stages:

- primary deviance: the original act that becomes defined as deviant;
- secondary deviance: the deviant's response to society's definition of the original act.

An example might be an alcoholic or a drug addict who cannot gain a respectable career because of the discovery of his or her primary deviance. He or she may then drift into unconventional (or unusual) occupations where his or her deviance does not make much difference. These marginal occupations, in the field of contemporary music, for example, can be termed secondary deviance.

Howard S. Becker, *Outsiders: Studies in the Sociology of Deviance* (1963)

Becker maintains that 'social groups create deviance by making rules . . . and by applying those rules to particular people and labelling them as "outsiders".' The word 'career' is often used to describe the path of an individual entering an occupation or profession, going through training, starting work, becoming successful, and so on. Becker uses the analogy of the career to show what happens when an individual becomes a deviant. He views such an individual as starting on a deviant career and eventually reaching the 'status' of 'outsider'. However, Becker's labelling theory seems better at explaining secondary deviance than primary deviance.

Interactionist and labelling approaches

Advantages	Criticisms
<ul><li>Based on their belief that no act is in itself criminal, they represent alternatives to positivist approaches, which assume that the 'facts' of crime can be found in an analysis of statistics.</li><li>They consider that deviant behaviour is the product of meanings from social interactions.</li><li>They maintain that criminals do not differ significantly from non-criminals: it is unlikely that any adult has not committed a crime during his or her life.</li><li>Rather than searching for causes, they analyse the process during which behaviour comes to be defined as 'deviant'.</li><li>They do not adopt an absolute view of crime, but hold that attitudes as to what is considered deviant change over time and place.</li><li>They consider that the witnesses or observers of actions are as much a focus of research interest as the actors themselves.</li></ul>	<ul><li>It may seem that there is an overconcern for offenders and for those in marginal areas of deviance, e.g. homosexuals.</li><li>They fail to explain the origin of deviance, implying that it is the result of a label being attached.</li><li>Deviants appear as rather passive victims of the observers of their actions; deviance is underplayed.</li><li>They imply that deviants act without gaining pleasure from their behaviour or that they seek the label 'outsider' to gain status over others.</li></ul>

Subcultural theories

A society may be seen as a homogeneous group with its own dominant culture in terms of its norms and shared values. However, there may exist within a society many smaller groups which, whilst subscribing to the dominant culture, may have their own subcultures and their own norms and values. Such small groups may include immigrant groups, youth groups and religious groups. Edwin Sutherland and Donald Cressey's **differential association theory**, set out in the box below, implied that individuals learned to be criminal by mixing with 'others of similar interests and backgrounds'. Working from within the tradition of the Chicago School (see page 518), their main interests were in street gangs and delinquent subcultures.

E.H. Sutherland's differential association theory

- Deviant behaviour is learned.
- It is learned in interaction with others.
- Criminal behaviour is learned mainly in intimate personal groups.
- The learning includes (a) techniques of committing the act, and (b) the specific direction of motives, drives, etc.
- Motives and drives are learned from definitions of the legal codes, in other words a person learns reasons for either obeying or violating rules.
- A person becomes deviant because of an excess of definitions favourable to violation of law.
- Differential associations may vary in frequency, duration, priority and intensity.
- The process of learning criminal behaviour by association with criminal and anti-criminal patterns is the same as in any other learning.
- While criminal behaviour is an expression of certain needs and values, this is unexplained because non-criminal behaviour may be an expression of the same needs and values.

Source: Adapted from Edwin H. Sutherland and Donald R. Cressey, *Criminology* (10th edn, 1978)

Subcultures arise, according to Albert K. Cohen, when the mainstream culture sets goals but does not provide the means for them to be achieved. Cohen terms this 'status frustration'. In *Delinquent Boys: the culture of the gang* (1955), Cohen argues that delinquent subcultures, in which there is a conscious rejection of the norms and values of schools and society, arise as a reaction to status frustration. Within delinquent subcultures, individuals receive status from their peers for deviant acts such as shoplifting and vandalism. (Note the similarity of Cohen's argument with Robert Merton's 'innovation', described on pages 516–17.)

W.B. Miller, in *Lower Class Culture ...* (1968), is critical of both Merton's anomie theory and Cohen's status frustration. The differences of opinion within the school of subcultural theorists revolve around the relationship between the 'subculture' and the wider society in which it is located. Both Merton and Cohen view the delinquent subculture as a reaction against a lack of opportunity and a failure to attain mainstream goals. Miller's theory suggests that working-class delinquent subcultures develop independently from the mainstream culture. For Miller, delinquency does not involve a striving for middle-class values, but rather a process of acting out what he terms the **focal concerns** of a working-class subculture. These 'focal concerns' are distinct cultural activities, such as a concern for toughness, masculinity and the pursuit of excitement, that develop within the subculture and are conformed to over a number of generations.

Criticisms of subcultural theory

Subcultural theory has never been totally rejected: social theories have used at least some of the concepts employed by subculturalists. One critic, David Matza, in *Delinquency and Drift* (1964), argues that most deviance is quite normal. All individuals, whatever their social class, have deviant values lying just under the surface and occasionally 'drift' in and then out of deviancy. Matza emphasises few differences between deviants and conformists: there is little evidence of the existence of a permanent deviant subculture. For Matza, techniques of ritualisation are adopted by a delinquent in order to justify his or her actions. Joy-riding for instance, is explained as a search for fun rather than stealing. Hence Matza and other contemporary critics accuse subcultural theory of over-estimating and overemphasising the amount of delinquent activity.

Deviancy amplification and moral panics

What happens to an individual who is labelled a criminal? The label may brand him or her; it may even form a **stigma**, damaging the individual's image and self image, affecting his or her future behaviour and the way others may view or treat that individual. One development of this social reaction towards individuals who become labelled as criminal or deviant has been termed **deviancy amplification**. The process of deviancy amplification may be explained as follows:

- The seriousness of what may initially be no more than an uncommon event becomes exaggerated and distorted – it is amplified.
- Amplification leads to the media taking an interest which in turn may lead to a real or assumed group of deviants becoming identified and negatively labelled.
- This leads to a 'moral panic' (see Unit 6, page 301) associated with the activities of the deviant group who become blamed for the ills of society, and portrayed as folk devils.
- This 'new' and socially unacceptable 'problem', in needing to be addressed, attracts even further media attention.
- The general public and police become sensitised, and on the lookout for the growing 'moral panic', which, fuelled by media coverage, may lead to increased arrests and further treatment by the courts.

Processes involved in the development of deviancy amplification and 'moral panic'

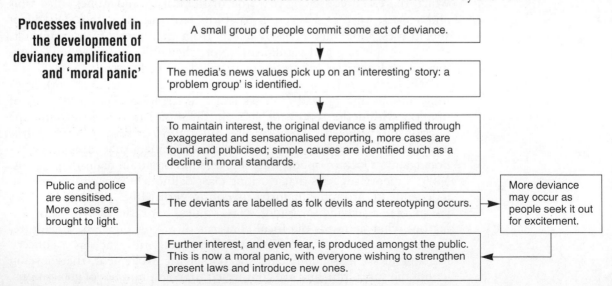

A small group of people commit some act of deviance.

The media's news values pick up on an 'interesting' story: a 'problem group' is identified.

To maintain interest, the original deviance is amplified through exaggerated and sensationalised reporting, more cases are found and publicised; simple causes are identified such as a decline in moral standards.

Public and police are sensitised. More cases are brought to light.

The deviants are labelled as folk devils and stereotyping occurs.

More deviance may occur as people seek it out for excitement.

Further interest, and even fear, is produced amongst the public. This is now a moral panic, with everyone wishing to strengthen present laws and introduce new ones.

The idea of deviance and amplification by the media was first forward by L. Wilkins who, in *Social Deviance* (1964), pointed to minority groups becoming the target of exaggeration and distortion. Being labelled as 'folk devils' provides a deviant subgroup with an identity. Stan Cohen, in *Folk Devils and Moral Panics* (1972), explored how such processes operated in relation to the ill-formed alarm and 'moral panic' associated with Mods and Rockers in the mid-1960s.

According to Cohen, the Mods and Rockers consisted mainly of groups of youths with different clothing, music styles, etc., but they were treated by the mass media as though they represented something much more serious than a youth-based subcultural reaction to social and economic circumstances. The press, television and other social groups defined their activities as a 'problem' and began the process of their formation into subcultures, particularly after minor scuffles in Clacton, Essex, on Easter Sunday 1964. This 'problem' was conveyed to the public as a conflict between 'heroes' and 'villains': the hue and cry against these moral outcasts resembled the historical practice of witch-hunting with its scapegoating effects or blaming for social ills. Hence social 'problems' became represented as modern-day 'folk devils', with exaggerated claims being made about both Mods and Rockers. Events were exaggerated in the vocabulary used by the media: YOUNGSTERS BEAT UP TOWN – 97 LEATHER JACKET ARRESTS, for example, appeared in the *Daily Express*, though in fact only 24 of the 97 people arrested were charged, and only a few were charged with offences involving violence. Cohen referred to 'the control culture' represented by the police, the courts and members of the local community who started to respond to the 'moral panic': seaside towns, especially during bank holidays, became very heavily policed.

Examples of moral panics and folk devils

1960s
Mods and Rockers
Sexual Permissiveness
Drug abuse
Student militancy
Trade union power

1970s
Mugging
Political violence (IRA, PLO)
Trade union militancy
Social security 'scroungers'
Youth culture (punks, skinheads)

1980s
Drug abuse (glue-sniffing, heroin, crack, ecstasy, etc.)
Black youth (inner-city riots)
Football hooliganism, lager louts
Greenham Common women
AIDS
Homosexuality
Acid House parties
Striking coal miners

1990s
New Age Travellers
Rottweilers and pit bull terriers
Religious cults
'Satanic' ritual abuse of children
Joy-riding
Saddam Hussein

Source: Adapted from K. Browne, *An Introduction to Sociology* (Polity Press, 1992)

In *Policing the Crisis* (1979), Stuart Hall et al. made an in-depth study of street crime (see also the section on New Left realism, page 527). They looked at the moral panic around mugging in the 1970s in terms of social class changes and race relations in the UK, and linked moral panics to broader ideological issues. Their social reaction theory is bound up with theories of the state and ideology and the relationship between law and order; they identified struggles within the state in response to economic changes. They maintained that once the UK no longer had an empire to exploit, wealth depended on the exploitation of the working class. However, according to Hall's findings, street crime itself tends not to be between classes or racial groups, so it does not give rise to any real redistribution of wealth; the poor (whites and blacks) steal from others in similar poor socio-economic circumstances.

Criticisms associated with deviancy amplification and moral panics

- Initially the concept of deviancy amplification was only tentatively put forward and it lacked any academic testing or support.
- The conditions and circumstances under which it does not take place have not been formulated, nor has the occurrence of deamplification.

Contemporary critical approaches to crime and deviance

Critical theories of crime and deviance may be seen in terms of the challenges to functionalism and interactionism made by neo-Marxists and other contemporary theorists, including feminist and New Right thinkers.

Marxist approaches

Marxist analysis of crime and deviance is not easily explained because it has to be understood in terms of wider debates about the nature of society. It is based on an examination of crime in relation to the power structure of society and sees crime as a product of the nature of capitalism.

- Marxists maintain that labelling theorists raise issues of power but fail to deliver a sufficiently coherent and structurally based view of the operations of power in defining acts as criminal.
- Marxist writers have traditionally been concerned about whether the law can be unbiased. They draw a basic distinction between the infrastructure (or economic base) of society and its superstructure (i.e. the legal, religious and political aspects of society). The infrastructure determines the superstructure, so the law reflects the interests of the wealth-owning ruling class and the state passes laws which support these interests.
- Marxists attempt to move criminology away from a focus on the 'criminality' of the poor and into categories taken from biology, psychology or positivistic sociology.

Neo-Marxist approaches

Some Marxists would argue that because the state has 'relative autonomy', not all laws serve the interests of the ruling class but rather benefit the 'subject class'. They point to the Factory Acts, for example, which provided protection for industrial workers by setting minimum safety requirements. Other neo-Marxists have replied that such laws provided little benefit for the subject class because of the way in which they were administered. F. Pearce holds probably the most realistic Marxist position and maintains that:

> 'The majority of laws in Britain and America work in favour of the capitalists, yet many laws also benefit the other social classes, not only because the system needs a healthy, safe population of producers and consumers but also because it needs their loyalty.'
>
> Frank Pearce, *Crimes of the Powerful* (Pluto Press, 1976)

If crime is seen as essentially a working-class activity, how do we account for white-collar crime, crime committed by persons of respectability and high social status in the course of their occupation? This type of crime, for example tax evasion and breach of factory and company acts, can include clear breaches of the law.

Because white-collar crime is often seen as 'normal business practice' and is hard to detect, it is often successful. W.G. Carson's study, *White Collar Crime* (1971), sampled 200 firms in south-east England and found that every firm had committed some violation in the four-and-a-half years studied – and this was before the advent of computer fraud. The offences were rarely prosecuted and usually only received official warnings.

Neo-Marxists maintain that crime is more widespread than official statistics indicate. Also, at least in terms of money, crime is a ruling-class not a working-class phenomenon. This is because of the selective administration of the law. An interesting examination of corporate and white-collar crime is provided in a study by William Chambliss and Milton Mankoff: *Whose Law? What Order?* (1976).

In relation to the administration of law, Mike Fitzgerald, in *Prisoners in Revolt* (1977), argues that class differences are clearly visible in the prosecution and punishment of offenders. Prisons in the UK (along with all capitalist societies) are full of working-class people; this distracts attention away from the activities of the powerful, which are potentially more harmful and dangerous for the majority of the population. I. Taylor and colleagues note that there has been an increasing amount of work which has attempted to 'demask the crime-free facade of the ruling-class'.

Neo-Marxists and structural theorists have constantly pointed to the double standards which seem to be at work in the administration of law. One has only to look at the differences in the definition and punishment of those guilty of social security fraud and those involved in tax evasion or fraudulent trading. Roger Levitt pleaded guilty to fraudulent trading in 1990 and was sentenced to 180 hours' community service. Then Levitt moved to the USA to become chief executive of a New York-based boxing company. An extradition order by the Department of Trade and Industry failed, in late 1997, with Levitt seeking compensation!

Corporate crime from a Marxist viewpoint

Steven Box, in *Power, Crime and Mystification* (1983), argues that corporate crime is more extensive and more damaging than individual crime. Most of this 'crime' – using harmful chemicals in food, producing dangerous goods for profit, overcharging, for example – is not even regarded as illegal.

Corporations are rarely prosecuted for their crimes. Matters of health and safety, dishonest advertising or insider trading are, Box argues, treated sympathetically and leniently through agencies such as the Health and Safety Executive and the Advertising Standards Authority and rarely result in criminal legal proceedings. The fraud squad is discouraged from involvement in financial crime in the City of London, which is expected to police itself. Even when legal proceedings follow, the judge is likely to take a lenient view, as for example in the case of Geoffrey Collier, who was convicted in 1987 of illicit trading in shares. He was given a fine and a one-year suspended sentence. The judge, Mr Justice Farquharson, was lenient because Collier, who had lost his membership of the Stock Exchange and his £250,000-a-year job, faced an 'uncertain financial future'. It is unlikely that a burglar with a far more uncertain financial future would be treated so leniently. Indeed, in the USA, a stockbroker involved in illegal trading worth $20 million was fined and given a suspended sentence by a judge who, the day the case was tried, sent an unemployed black shipping clerk to prison for a year for stealing a television set.

Some American Marxists analyse business corruption as organised crime with links to political processes. William Chambliss, in *On the Take: From Petty Crooks to Presidents* (1978), used observation to show that leading members of Seattle's ruling class were behind organised crime in the city. He got his evidence by hanging around in bars and gambling joints for several years. He argued, on the basis of his substantial evidence, that:

> '[crime is not a] by-product of an otherwise effectively working political economy, it is a main product of that economy.'
>
> William Chambliss (1978)

Furthermore, crime networks are inevitable in capitalist society.

Source: Adapted from L. Harvey and M. MacDonald, *Doing Sociology* (Macmillan, 1993)

A recent American publication and TV documentary have suggested that assassinated president John F. Kennedy had close links with the mafia, a charge which has also been made against the American singer Frank Sinatra. Such links, it is contended, ensured Kennedy's initial election to the American Senate, the platform for his eventual election as president. In addition, it is claimed, he had a number of sexual liaisons (including with the film star Marilyn Monroe) whilst projecting the image of a faithful husband. Such 'deviant' activity was reportedly covered up by presidential aides. More recently President Nixon resigned from the presidency rather than risk 'impeachment' and possible criminal prosecution over the 'Watergate affair'.

Think about it

- In what ways do you think corporate crime is similar to white-collar crime? In what ways do you think it is different?
- Why does corporate crime tend to remain relatively invisible?
- What do you consider to be the problems associated with reporting or dealing with corporate crime?
- What difficulties might you encounter in attempting to research the incidence of crime in your area?

New Left realism (NLR)

A development of Marxist approaches to crime and deviance can be found in what has been called New Left realism or NLR. It is regarded as controversial by many Marxists. Unlike the traditional Marxist view of crime, which focuses on white-collar crime, NLR focuses on street crime. It considers that, whilst white-collar crime and corporate crime are more widespread than is shown by official statistics, what matters to many people, especially in inner-city areas, is the crime carried out by young, working-class, white and black youths (essentially street crime), largely carried out by and against working-class people. New Left realists pay particular attention to three causes: relative deprivation, subculture and marginalisation.

Relative deprivation refers to a group's experiences when it feels deprived in relation to other similar groups:

• In the UK, the media stress the importance of success and the purchase of material goods: individuals are socialised into a value-system which promotes a middle-class lifestyle.
• It is the relative deprivation experienced by certain groups in society that explains their high levels of criminality.

Subculture: This is a restatement of the subcultural theories explained on pages 521–2. It forms the collective solution to groups' problems:

• If a subculture shares its relative deprivation it will develop lifestyles that enable it to cope with its problems.
• Crime is only one aspect, usually quite small, in the process of cultural adaptation to oppression. There may well be a link with drug abuse.

Marginalisation refers to the marginal groups who use violence and riots as political action:

• They do not have organisations to represent them in political life; they lack clear political goals.
• Rather than having clear-cut grievances, they feel general discontent, often in relation to their future.

The key ideas of New Left realism are set out by John Lea and Jock Young in *What Is To Be Done About Law and Order* (1984). The aim of these two British criminologists was to dispel the mythology associated with crime created by those on the political Right and by 'Left idealists': those Marxists who have an almost romantic picture of the criminal as a political activist or what we may call 'the-mugger-as-Robin-Hood syndrome'. They cite, for example, the case of Anthony Williams, a Scotland Yard Financial Officer, who commenced his vast fraud activities in 1986 when he was asked to arrange the financing of a long-term operation against organised crime! On 20 May 1995, Williams received a seven-and-a-half year jail sentence for the fraud of £5 million. He admitted numerous counts of theft, and 535 others were taken into consideration. Nevertheless, the vast amounts of money that he spent revitalising and creating employment opportunities for the pretty but rundown and impoverished Scottish Highland village of Tomintoul could make him eligible for the classic Marxist role of Robin Hood criminal hero. The question is: was Williams's criminal activity an attempt at wealth redistribution or was it based on self interest and a desire for personal wealth and status?

A comparison of Marxist and NLR approaches to crime and deviance		
	Marxist	**NLR**
Crime statistics	• incorrect, biased and ignore middle-class, white-collar crime, etc.; • bias in law operation and policing.	• correct, reflecting concerns of most people including working-class crime; • accepts middle-class, white-collar crime greater than statistics reveal.
Causes of crime	• repressive biased laws; • class struggle, poverty; • unemployment, etc.	• the outcome of relative deprivation, subculture and marginalisation.
Who commits crime?	• all groups; • ruling class as real criminals.	• all groups; • young, male, working-class as main offenders.
Values	• manipulated by ruling class via media, education, etc.	• same as for Marxists, but with people creating own subcultures in response to their problems.
Policing	• repressive and reflecting capitalist interests.	• repressive, but reflecting will of the majority.
Attitude to policing	• mostly negative and repressed, so search for means to fight them.	• mostly positive; trouble occurs when there is a breakdown in communication.
Female crime and deviance	• no specific comments; • accept females have lower crime rates because of their exclusion from means of production.	• no specific position; • accept that females have lower crime rate.
Race crimes	• black crime rates higher because of biased policing and historical oppression.	• extreme marginalisation with West Indians having higher crime rates than Asians because of relative deprivation, subculture and marginalisation factors.
General attitudes to be adopted	• crime is seen as a form of rebellion against capitalism and, as such, as a good thing; • criminals are to be admired as expressing a challenge to mainstream capitalist culture.	• crime mostly affects working class, who need sympathy and assistance from police; • need to work towards the re-creation of working-class communities, etc.

Source: Adapted from S. Moore, *Investigating Deviance* (Collins Educational, 1991)

Criticisms of NLR

- It draws on the work of subcultural theorists (see page 521) which accepts high crime rates among lower classes who form subcultures in response to their circumstances.
- It suggests that lower-class criminal values are similar to those of the dominant values of capitalism, i.e. selfishness, aggression, etc.
- It provides a structural sociological explanation, but offers no account of the way individuals interpret their actions; in other words, it offers little explanation of different motives for criminal acts.
- It lacks an exploration of the experiences of both the victim and the offender, tending to rely simply on the victim's perceptions of crime.
- It emphasises class at the expense of other major considerations such as gender and ethnicity.
- It focuses on street crime, at the expense of other types of crime; although sound use is made of crime statistics, no conclusions are drawn about the involvement of other classes and ethnic groups in crime.
- It makes considerable use of statistics collected in the USA which may not represent the statistics of other capitalist societies.

Priest advocates shoplifting from 'evil' superstores

BY MICHAEL HORSNELL

A CLERGYMAN yesterday advocated shoplifting from supermarkets in retaliation for the damage he claimed they did to local communities. The Rev John Papworth said that theft was justified and added: "I don't regard it as stealing, I regard it as a badly needed reallocation of economic resources."

The 75-year-old Church of England priest, Mr Papworth, stood by his defence of shoplifting from superstores, which he condemned as "places of evil and temptation" that had forced small shops out of business.

Mr Papworth, who assists with services at St Mark's Church, St John's Wood, told *The Times*: "You can steal from a person – though you must not – but you cannot steal from a thing. These huge shops are the enemies of civilisation, creaming off profits, promoting unemployment, causing widespread bankruptcies of small businesses."

Source: Adapted from *The Times*, 15 March 1997

Think about it

- What can you suggest as (a) sociological justifications for the views expressed by Mr Papworth and (b) possible sociological effects of his expressing these views?

Feminist approaches

For feminists, there are two key questions:

1. Why do so few women commit criminal acts? (Prisons are still largely a male preserve, with males accounting for 96 per cent of all prisoners.)
2. For what reasons do such women commit these acts?

Feminists maintain that 'malestream' theories have failed both to address these questions and to provide any answers.

Although there is no single feminist theory – feminist approaches to crime and deviance take several forms, including liberal, socialist, Marxist and radical feminism – one major feature of feminism in relation to crime and deviance is that in virtually all of its forms there tends to be an emphasis on **patriarchy** and **oppression**. In general, feminists consider that:

- women are controlled by men, both inside the home and in the employment market;
- women have been pushed to the sidelines and become virtually invisible because of the prevalence of sexist theories which underplay female involvement in criminal and deviant activities.

Feminists, then, have challenged myths about the nature and extent of female participation in crime and deviance. The issues they have examined include the following:

- Socialisation processes, from an early age, lead to different values being developed between the sexes. It is put forward that females are more passive and less aggressive than males and therefore commit fewer violent crimes. Hence females are more likely to be convicted of crimes associated with their traditional gender roles, such as shoplifting and prostitution.
- Tighter controls exist for females, both in the family and in their public lives; what is seen as deviant behaviour may be linked to this sexual inequality. S. Lees, in researching *Losing Out: Sexuality and Adolescent Girls* (1986), showed that no respectable lad would go out regularly with a 'slag'; that girls hated to be labelled as a 'tight bitch'; but that no equivalent terms existed for males.
- The male domination of sociology: whilst the majority of sociology students have been female, its teaching – particularly in higher education and at lower academic levels – and even its textbooks have been mainly male-dominated. Male-based assumptions have led to studies of males, by males, in male-dominated subcultures such as street crime, drug taking, etc. This tendency has been termed **vicarious identification**, i.e. male sociologists become attracted to and choose to study subcultural activities of delinquents which appeal to them.
- Although there are female delinquents who seek excitement in much the same way as their male counterparts and become involved in violent acts and also burglary (as discussed by E. Player in *Women in Crime in the City* (1989), such females seem to receive far less attention than their male counterparts.

Social reaction has disputed the belief that women are treated more lightly than men by the police and courts because of what may be termed 'a chivalry factor'. P. Carlen, in *Women's Imprisonment* (1983), states that courts may actually be harsher for those who disturb or challenge the social norms and expectations of the male sex. S.A. Russon, in *Women and the Law: The Uses of Images of Femininity in the Courts* (1984), maintains that females who commit social security frauds and murder tend to receive harsher sentences than males.

P. Abbott and C. Wallace conclude that most feminists would agree that women commit fewer and less serious crimes than men:

> 'Also, while it is true that more women have become involved in crime in recent years, this seems to have been mainly petty crime and male crime has also increased during the same period.'
> P. Abbott and C. Wallace, *An Introduction to Sociology: Feminist Perspectives* (Routledge, 1990)

As two girls face charges of manslaughter following the death of a fellow teenager, **Yvonne Roberts** looks at the facts behind female violence

Women on the verge

ON MONDAY NIGHT, in Corby, 13-year-old Louise Allen died. She had been surrounded by a crowd of girls after intervening to stop a fight. Two fellow 13-year-old girls have been accused of her killing. Allen's headmaster, James Platt, in expressing his grief, endeavoured to retain a sense of proportion.

"Incidents like this happen in every town in every corner of every land," he said. "I don't think there is a culture of violence. Nobody set out on Monday night to kill anybody."

The difference, of course, is that "incidents like this" have traditionally always been the business of a certain type of lad. Undeterred by James Platt and in ignorance of precisely what occurred, yesterday's headline in The Sun read: "Kicked to death by 30 schoolgirl yobs."

Much of the press will now be pre-occupied, yet again, with apocalyptic visions of a "new" breed of female: violent, lawless, minus testosterone, but fuelled by something infinitely worse — feminism.

But *is* female violence on the increase? And if it is, who is to blame? Is it feminism? Or today's fight for survival on the streets, in which drugs, poverty and joblessness make no exceptions for gender? Or is something far more complex also afoot — a combination of influences as complex as that which triggers violence in men?

Officially, female violence appears to be rising. Over the past five years, *reported* female violent crime has risen by 12 per cent — four times the rate of male violent crime. Since 1973, offences involving women carrying out robbery, murder, assault and drug-related crimes have increased by a staggering 250 per cent. In practice, however, the number of offences remains small. In 1984, 5,300 women were found guilty of violence against persons; in 1994, the figure was 9,700.

What is obviously not known is the amount of unreported crime, the scale of random acts of physical abuse carried out by women. It isn't difficult to come across stories. A fracas in a mini-cab office: a woman waits, three teenage girls jump the queue. She objects. They punch, kick, black her eye, slap her. She is too frightened to make a report.

Female violence may be statistically small, but daily experience tells many of us that female *aggression* appears to abound. The restraints are off and feminism has helped to lift those restraints. The woman who screams abuse in her car, the belligerent teenager, the mother who beats hell out of her tiny child.

In the 19th century, criminologists were convinced that, biologically, women were too "nice", too programmed for nurturing, to give life — or living — a kick in the teeth. Hence a violent woman was out of the norm,

> 'Women may commit violence for many reasons — poverty, boredom, isolation, fear, greed, kicks. Just like men'

mad or bad. Many women were and are extremely violent, but only to themselves: self-mutilation, anorexia, drug abuse.

Cases of extreme female savagery have never been difficult to find — Rosemary West and Rwanda being the most recent examples — but judges, like others, have held dear to the mad or bad categories. In 1992, Maria Rossi and Christina Molloy, both 18, who had terrorised their neighbourhood for years, murdered Edna Phillips, a pensioner, using a dog chain, a knife, broken glass and scissors. The judge called them "evil products of the modern age".

Since the eighties, popular culture has shown women doing it for themselves — murder and mayhem, that is — as psychofemmes. Interestingly, in film, while we've had the mad and the bad (Basic Instinct, Single White Female), we've also had what approximates to real life: "nice" women drawn into violence by circumstance (Thelma and Louise); not so nice women who enjoy what they're doing, not least because it is lucrative (The Last Seduction); and the just plain nasty. In Blue Steel, the heroine explains she is a cop because "I like slamming people's heads against the walls."

Equality means that today, in fantasy *and* in real life, women too can become rapists, serial killers, psychopaths, sadists and all-round bad guys. In her book Deadlier Than The Male, Alix Kirsta writes that women may commit violence for many reasons — poverty, boredom, isolation, fear, greed, kicks, desire for attention, power and dominance, and in self-defence. Just like men.

Critics will argue that feminism has destroyed the female ideal and with it the civilising hold it had on women's behaviour. Others will counter that too many women paid too high a price for that idea — trapped in economic dependency and powerlessness to the point at which their own lives were (and are) at risk.

Ann Lloyd, in Doubly Deviant Doubly Damned, Society's Treatment of Violent Women, reminds us that females are still more likely to be the recipients of violence than the instigators. She also points out that, if prison populations are any guide, then the same type of woman gets convicted now as years ago: the violated, the ill-educated, the survivors of that most brutalising of experiences, being "in care".

Arguably, if feminism has encouraged women to look to self-esteem, the importance of education and the need to take control of one's life, then it just might have prevented some women from joining the group who are abandoned in Holloway or who live by violence.

And it may yet persuade others that raising a fist in defiance is best left as a symbolic gesture.

Source: The *Guardian*, 2 May 1996

Think about it

- Do you consider that there is a new breed of violent and lawless females in contemporary society?
- To what extent may it be claimed that feminists have helped to release female criminality?
- Do you think that self abuse or anorexia can be viewed as extreme violence? What societal influences can be identified as contributing to these 'problems'?

New Right realism

New Right realism includes a number of contemporary approaches which attempt to provide direct answers to practical questions of crime and deviance. They have been welcomed by policy makers, including politicians and those involved in the criminal justice system, in that they put forward the need for a firm line and stiff punishments to stem increasing crime rates. Three major approaches to the diverse range of **social control theories** are:

- common ground theories, for example J.Q. Wilson's *Thinking About Crime* (1977);
- control theories, for example Travis Hirschi's *Causes of Delinquency* (1969);
- situational theories, for example Ron Clarke and Pat Mayhew, editors of *Designing Out Crime* (1980).

Common ground theories

These assume that people act rationally and that those who break the law act both illegally and immorally. Such a model of human behaviour has been termed the 'economic man' model, on the basis that decisions are made as to whether certain actions are worth taking in relation to their benefits: people commit crime if its benefits are greater than its costs (i.e. risk of being caught and imprisoned). Is it worth, for example, committing company or computer fraud for, say, £1 million if, based on recent trials, the risk might be one year's imprisonment?

J.Q. Wilson, a main figure in recent American criminology, has had much influence in both the USA and the UK. Wilson points to the rising crime rates during the 1960s (see the graph below) when radical measures were taken to reduce poverty in both countries. Increased affluence can be linked to increased, rather than decreased, crime levels.

The rise in crime, 1960–70

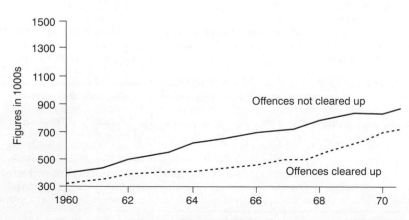

Source: *Criminal Statistics for England and Wales* (Home Office)

Control theories
These arose out of the research and thinking of Travis Hirschi: rather than asking why people commit crime, control theories ask why they do not do so. The thrust of such theories is presented not so much as a matter of what we need to know about crime and deviance but more what we need to know in order to do something about it. Hirschi revolutionised criminology by posing such questions. His idea that anyone could become criminal in appropriate circumstances forms the basis for this type of social control.

Hirschi believes that individuals are linked to society by four bonds:

- attachment: how people care about others' opinions;
- commitment: the amount of personal investment that people put into their lives, for example through education, business or organising a reputation for virtue;
- involvement: a person with a wide range of interests and activities may be too busy to become involved in crime;
- belief: the intensity or degree of belief that it is necessary to obey laws.

How far a person conforms to these bonds represents the extent to which they either feel linked to society or feel free to deviate.

Steven Box, in *Deviance, Reality and Society* (1971), though seen as a neo-Marxist, asks what factors strengthen or weaken an individual's bonds to society and suggests the following key issues:

- secrecy: the chances of people concealing deviance;
- skills: the knowledge required to commit deviant acts;
- supply: the equipment needed to be deviant, for example drugs or weapons;
- social support: peer approval;
- symbolic support: the extent to which the wider society gives support and approval.

Situational theories
These emphasise the immediate feature of the environment in which an offence may take place. They reflect the belief that theories produced so far have not stemmed crime rates, especially among the young. Introduced by members of the Home Office Research and Planning Unit, in particular R. Clarke and P. Mayhew, they oppose what they term 'dispositional theories', based on the histories and motives of delinquents, and consider it better to present crime and delinquency as the behaviour of reasonable people forming judgements in response to particular situations. They stress the importance of the following:

- target hardening, which makes crime more difficult, for example property marking, reinforced phone kiosks, improved locks and bolts, etc.
- surveillance, or informal control such as the design of buildings, street lighting, etc. which makes crime more visible and easier to control by the police and public.

Conclusions on New Right realism
- It deals quite efficiently, if rather provocatively, with the carrying out of crime in certain situations.
- It tends to be limited in terms of what it actually covers, and this is not what many other sociologists might prefer to research.
- It assumes that potential criminals follow a relatively simple and rational pattern of behaviour, but such assumptions may be considered limited if predictions fail to match behaviour.

The measurement of crime and deviance

How much crime and deviance takes place? This very important question is actually very difficult to answer. The measurement of deviance, in its sociological sense, is far from straightforward. Both saints and sinners may be seen as 'deviants' – neither Mother Teresa nor Rosemary West were 'normal' in their activities. As the extract on page 506 shows, almost anything anyone does violates someone's standards of 'normality'; any attempt to measure deviance has to take on board not just individual or group activities but also factors of time and place.

The measurement of crime statistics may seem more straightforward: official crime figures for England and Wales are published each year by the Home Office, as illustrated in the following table. According to the 1995 statistics, total recorded crime had fallen for the third consecutive year.

Notifiable offences recorded by the police (England and Wales, 1995)

NOTIFIABLE OFFENCES RECORDED BY POLICE		
Summary of Offences	**Offences in 1995 (000s)**	**%***
Violence against the person	217.5	−1
Sexual offences	30.4	−5
Robbery	68.4	14
Total violent crime	**316.3**	**2**
Burglary	1,244.2	−1
Total theft and handling stolen goods	2,459.6	−4
(of which vehicle crime)	1,323.5	−4
Fraud and forgery	134.3	−8
Criminal damage	917.0	−1
Other notifiable offences	52.2	8
TOTAL OF ALL OFFENCES	**5,123.6**	**−2**
*Percentage change over 1994		

Source: The Home Office, 26 March 1996

The usefulness of official crime statistics

Sociologists and students of sociology tend to be highly critical of official crime statistics. Crime statistics are difficult to interpret; they are based on notifiable or indictable (serious) offences, the commonest of which is theft (about 50 per cent of all recorded crime), followed by burglary (about 25 per cent), but there may be omissions, for example criminal damage of less than £20 in value. The 2 per cent fall between 1994 and 1995 in total offences shown in the table masks, for example, a 14 per cent rise in robberies. Furthermore, recorded levels of crime include only those offences which people feel they should or wish to report to the police and which are accepted by the police. Not only are many crimes not reported; of those that are, the police may regard the matter as too trivial and time-consuming or may refuse to accept an account or may decide that there is not enough evidence. The police may even consider the person reporting the crime as unreliable – a drunk, drug addict or tramp, for example. Official crime statistics may therefore provide some 'facts' about crimes, but they have been socially constructed and form what may be termed the 'end-product' of a complex series of human decisions.

In spite of their shortcomings, official crime statistics do, however, serve some useful functions:

- They provide some idea of crime levels for different offences and for different categories of crime, in relation to age, gender, ethnicity and social class.
- They allow for comparisons to be made for both **indictable** (serious) offences and **non-indictable** (less serious or summary offences such as minor motoring offences); and also comparisons from one year to the next, over periods of time, and across and between different countries.
- Through the mass media, in particular television and newspapers, they give the general public some information on the circumstances relating to criminal activities.
- They form the basis for theories and explanations, relating to crime, deviance and control, for sociologists and others.
- They assist in determining policy in terms of allocating funds and other human and technological resources to attempt to control criminal activities. The map below gives some indication of different levels of funding in different areas of the UK, in terms of the cost, per head of the population, of operating police services (the upper end of the range was £220 for the Metropolitan Police, while the lowest cost was £83 in Cambridgeshire). Nevertheless, such figures cannot be taken as a simple reflection of crime levels, as can be seen by comparing the two sets of data below. Nor can it be taken as a measure of efficiency since, for example:
  - there are exceptionally high costs for some forces who regularly have to monitor large public events such as marches;
  - some forces provide specialist training used by other forces.

Notifiable offences by police force areas, 1994 (left). Police area forces, net cost per person, 1994–5 (right)

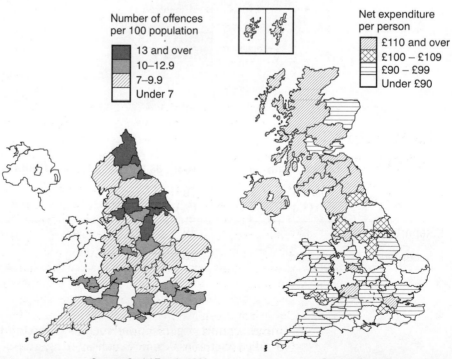

Number of offences per 100 population

- 13 and over
- 10–12.9
- 7–9.9
- Under 7

Net expenditure per person

- £110 and over
- £100 – £109
- £90 – £99
- Under £90

Source: *Social Trends*, 1996

Source: *Social Trends*, 1996

Limitations of official crime statistics

Even when made public by the Home Office, crime data is subject to 'internal' challenges and is treated with caution by observers and those in authority in relevant areas, such as government ministers and the police. A major limitation of official crime statistics has already been mentioned: they include only those crimes recorded by the police. Many different types of crime remain undiscovered or unreported. The significance of this hidden or 'dark figure' of undiscovered or unreported crime is illustrated by the following graph and table, which show an estimate of the proportion of offences actually recorded by the police.

Percentage of offences recorded by police, 1995

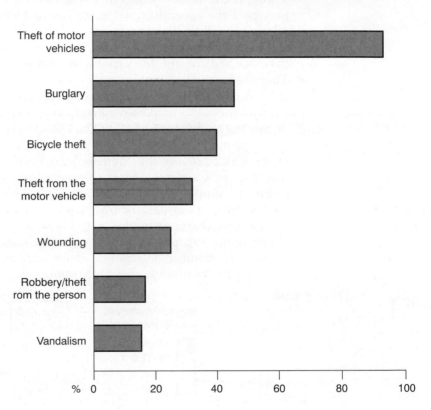

Source: HMSO, 1995

Crimes reported and recorded, as a percentage of crimes committed				
	1981 (%)	1991 (%)	1993 (%)	1995 (%)
Reported	36	49	47	46
Recorded	22	30	26	23

Source: British Crime Survey, Home Office

Crimes against organisations such as company fraud and shoplifting and so-called victimless crimes such as drug abuse are not covered by these percentages.

The British Crime Survey (BCS)

As we have seen, statistics of recorded crime cannot alone be used 'safely' as an indication of the true extent of crime. The British Crime Survey aims to provide a more complete picture of the extent of crime than can be given by police figures. In 1992, for example, official crime figures showed a record 5.7 million offences, whereas the British Crime Survey that year estimated a total of 15 million criminal offences – almost three times the official number.

The British Crime Survey (BCS) is carried out by the Home Office in England and Wales; to date it has been carried out five times – in 1982, 1984, 1988, 1992 and 1994, each report measuring crime in the previous year. Before the first BCS in 1982 there were no estimates of unrecorded crime. The 1992 BCS asked 10,000 people aged 16 and over whether they had been victims of crime in the previous year; in 1994, the sample was 14,500 people aged 16 and over. Each BCS supports the unreliability of official crime statistics:

TRENDS IN CRIME: FINDINGS FROM THE 1994 BRITISH CRIME SURVEY

Pat Mayhew, Catriona Mirrlees-Black and Natalie Aye Maung

KEY POINTS

▶ The BCS estimated a total of 18 million crimes in 1993 against individuals and their property. For BCS crimes which can be compared with police statistics, incomplete reporting and recording mean that only just over a quarter are estimated to end up in police records.

▶ Between **1981 and 1993**, for those crime types that can be compared, the number of crimes recorded by the police increased by 111%; the BCS showed a lower rise of 77%. The divergence in the figures is due to a smaller increase in vandalism and violence according to the BCS.

▶ Recorded crime shows a larger rise than the BCS mainly because a greater proportion of crimes are now reported to the police than in 1981. In the case of vandalism and violence, more reported crime may also have been recorded by the police.

▶ From the most recent figures — **1991 to 1993** — for those crime types which can be compared, recorded crime figures have risen by 7%, whereas BCS figures rose by 18%, reversing the previous pattern. The greater rise in BCS offences was apparent across most offence categories.

▶ Police figures of crime since 1991 may have risen less steeply than the BCS because the proportion of crimes reported to the police has fallen.

▶ The risk of being a victim of crime is generally higher for those in inner cities, council and rented accommodation, and flats. The risks are also higher in the north of England. Risks of contact crime are highest for men and younger people.

Source: Research Findings No. 14, Home Office Research and Statistics Department, September 1994

Levels of reported crime, England and Wales, 1993				
	Wounding (%)	Domestic burglary (%)	Vandalism (%)	All offences (%)
Reported	54	69	27	47
Recorded	24	41	14	27
Cleared up	19	8	2	5
Resulting in caution or conviction	14	2	2	3

Source: *Social Trends*, 1996

The BCS does not, however, provide a complete account of crime. Many crimes, such as fraud, drug offences and crimes against businesses, cannot be covered in a household survey. Also, like any crime survey, it is prone to error, resulting mainly from the difficulty of ensuring that samples are representative, but also due to the frailty of respondents' memories, their reluctance to talk about their experiences as victims and their failure to recognise certain incidents as relevant to the survey.

It should also be noted that the simple addition of unreported crimes to the official crime statistics does not necessarily give an accurate picture of crime rates. The official statistics themselves are skewed as a result of the different practices adopted by police forces across the country. One police force, for example, may have a policy of not recording thefts of goods valued at less than £20, whilst this threshold may be £10 for another police force.

Think about it

- Using the tables on page 536, the 'key points' on page 537, and the information on reported and unreported crime above and on page 539, construct an argument *for* and *against* the view that crime statistics assist sociologists to understand what is happening to crime in Britain.

Influences on the reporting of crime

As indicated in the following graph, there are many reasons why crimes are not always reported. Some of the most common reasons are listed below the graph.

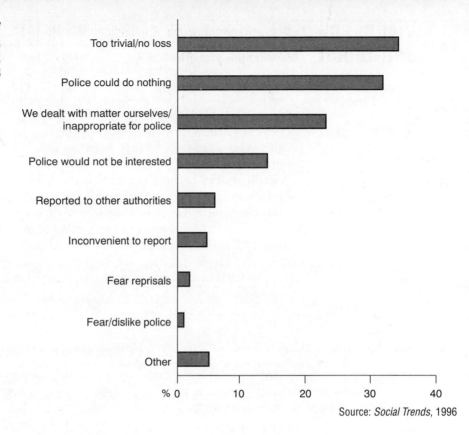

Unreported crime, by reason for not reporting, England and Wales, 1993

Source: *Social Trends*, 1996

- The incident might be too petty to report; particularly if it involved no loss or damage, or the loss was small.
- A victim may see little point in reporting an incident if he or she feels that the police could not do anything about it – by either recovering item(s) or catching the offender(s).
- The victim may fear embarrassment by the police or in court. The Rape Crisis Line estimate that two out of three rape victims do not report the crime because of embarrassment; they fear the police may fail to take them seriously, or they may be made to feel it is their own fault they were raped.
- In the case of 'victimless crime' – some crimes benefit both parties and there is no obvious 'victim', e.g. the sale of cigarettes and alcohol to those under age – reporting it will harm all concerned.
- The victim may fear reprisals if the crime is reported, for example the blackmail victim may be afraid of the consequences of reporting the blackmailer, as also may be the case with incidents involving the illegal supply of drugs or underage sex.
- A crime may be considered a private matter that those involved would rather deal with themselves, for example theft within a family.
- There may be no awareness that an offence has been committed. 'Lost' property may have been stolen, for example, and while the media may report cases of hoax gas meter readers, etc., there may be people who never realise they have been the victim of a hoax or similar crime.

Victim and self-report studies

The British Crime Survey exemplifies how victim and self-report studies can be used to try to overcome some of the problems associated with official crime statistics.

Victim studies

Victim or victimisation studies are designed to research the number of people who admit to having been victims of crime, whether or not reported to the police.

Victim studies became popular in the USA in the 1960s. R. Block, in his paper to the American Society of Criminology, *A Comparison of Victimisation, Crime Assessment and Fear of Crime in England and Wales, the Netherlands, Scotland and the United States* (1987), pointed out that victim studies indicate that overall only about one-quarter of the serious crimes actually committed are reported to the police. While there are merits to the victim study system there are also drawbacks, as indicated in the table below.

Advantages of victim studies	Disadvantages of victim studies
• They may provide a more reliable measure of crime rates and official crime statistics, and prove more useful for annual, national and international comparisons. • They enable the 'dark figure', not revealed in some crime statistics that uncover only the 'tip of the iceberg', to be more effectively calculated. • They receive from respondents information as to whether or not they have been victims of crime, and if so which types of crime and whether or not they were reported to the police. • They can be grossed up from samples, rather than distorted by police practices and the criminal justice system.	• People may have some difficulty in remembering accurately whether, and how often, they may have been victims of crime. • There may be a tendency to exaggerate victimisation, either through bravado from a physical attack or through misinterpretation – e.g. a knock on the door may be taken to be an attempted burglary. • The underestimation of crime, as with official crime statistics, still occurs, since some people never realise they have been victimised – e.g. petty theft. • There persist weak areas in such data collection – e.g. domestic violence and sexual offences.

Self-report studies

These studies involve asking people about their own illegal activities and whether or not they have been discovered. They are usually based on anonymous questionnaires or interviews, which include information on social characteristics such as age, gender, race and social class. Self-report studies have shown that:

- illegal activities or criminal behaviour, whether petty or serious, are distributed right across the population;
- the differences between males and females or between working- and middle-class people are much less than official crime rates indicate;
- therefore, since many contemporary sociologists have based their theories on official crime statistics, such theories may be challenged.

Advantages of self-report studies	Disadvantages of self-report studies
• As with victim studies, they may provide a more reliable measure of crime rates. • They locate a far greater number of offenders than provided by official crime statistics. • They can be compared with official conviction rates to find out a range of interesting information – e.g. which offenders are most likely to be convicted.	• There tends to be a natural inclination, despite the guarantee of anonymity, either to hide one's own criminal activities or, in the case of juveniles, to exaggerate such behaviour. • Under-reporting may still occur, due to dishonesty or forgetfulness. • The selective nature of a questionnaire or interview, in terms of what it covers, can produce important omissions in terms of criminal acts not included. • The representativeness of the sample may seem doubtful; many self-report studies have taken place in schools and excluded truants and dropouts, and such studies may tell us little about adult crime.

Fear of crime Fear of crime has received considerable attention from sociologists and has been a continuing theme for those involved in British Crime Surveys.

POLICE SAY FEAR OF CRIME IS EXAGGERATED

Young men, not old ladies, are most at risk from violent crime, say the police in a new publication launched today. While most victims of assaults know their attackers, and statistics show that the elderly are the least likely to be attacked, it is they who most fear being mugged in the street or attacked in their homes.

A fact sheet, 'Your Police are Making a Difference', launched today by the Association of Chief Police Officers, with the support of the Police Federation and the Police Superintendents' Association, urges elderly people not to become housebound through exaggerated fears of being attacked. It acknowledges that there have been horrific crimes against old people which rightly attract wide media coverage, but points out that for every incident of mugging reported to the police, there are 45 serious accidents at home. Yet surveys show that twice as many people say they are worried about being mugged than fear being hurt in an accident. For every homicide victim, five people are killed in road accidents.

Britain is one of the safest countries in Europe. While people living in England and Wales run a 1 in 90 risk of being a victim of violence in one year, compared with the 1 in 75 European average, a third of Britons say they feel unsafe, compared with only a quarter of all Europeans.

The fact sheet says: "Fear of crime is not caused by crime alone. It is also caused by unruly behaviour, shouting and bad language, and by the signs of an uncaring community which does nothing about rubbish and damage. Working in partnerships we can tackle crime; the causes; the symptoms and the fear."

Source: Adapted from the Association of Chief Police Officers, *News Release*, 6 September 1996

The following table has been extracted from the 1996 British Crime Survey data on fear of crime in England and Wales.

Fear of crime[1]: by gender and age, 1996								
	Males				Females			
	16–29 (%)	30–59 (%)	60 and over (%)	All aged 16 and over (%)	16–29 (%)	30–59 (%)	60 and over (%)	All aged 16 and over (%)
Theft of car[2]	28	23	19	23	30	26	22	26
Theft from car[2]	26	20	16	20	22	21	16	20
Burglary	18	18	18	18	27	26	25	26
Mugging	12	11	13	12	28	25	26	26
Rape	–	–	–	–	44	31	22	32

[1] Percentage of people aged 16 and over who were 'very worried' about each type of crime.
[2] Percentage of car owners.

Source: British Crime Survey, Home Office: *Social Trends*, 1997

From this it can be seen that those who experience most fear of crime are women and the elderly. However, with the notable exception of assaults to predominantly female victims, these two groups were not the most common victims of crime. According to victim surveys, most assaults take place outside the home, although this is affected by the fact that domestic disputes are less commonly reported even to sensitive survey interviewers. Also, very little is known about the frequency of party-related assaults – assaults by family or relatives – which seem to pose a greater threat to women than assaults by strangers in public places.

The Islington Crime Survey

This famous survey, led by Trevor Jones and Jock Young, was one of the first local studies of crime. It was conducted in the inner London borough of Islington, and its findings underline the reality of the fear of crime, as exemplified by the following extract:

Studies like the Home Office's well-known British Crime Survey have revolutionised thinking about crime. By asking people direct about the crimes they have experienced, such studies give us a much more reliable measure of the extent of crime. In particular, they allow us to chart the 'dark figure' of crime previously unknown — about half of which turns out to be serious crime . . . the London borough of Islington last year commissioned the Centre for Criminology at Middlesex Polytechnic to conduct a survey of the extent of crime in the area, and to assess the public's evaluation of police performance. A random sample of 2,000 households were surveyed.

It is sometimes suggested that crime, although frequent, is a minor irritant, given the range of problems the city dweller has to contend with. The public, on this view, suffer from hysteria about crime. Panics abound—particularly about mugging, sexual assault and violence—which are out of touch with reality.

But the inner city dweller is not the average citizen. Our study, with its ability to focus in on the highly victimised, indicates the realism of their fears.

It is scarcely odd that 46 per cent of people in Islington should admit to worrying 'a lot' about mugging, given that over 40 per cent of the borough's population actually know someone (including themselves and their family) who has been mugged in the last twelve months. Nor is it unrealistic to worry about burglary when its incidence runs at five times the national average.

Why are women more fearful about crime than men, when most studies show they have a far less chance of becoming victims? Our survey suggests that, in the inner city at least, their fears are perfectly rational. Women here are more likely to be victims of crime than men.

Source: T. Jones and J. Young, 'Crime, police and people', *New Society* (24 January 1986)

The Islington study showed that:

- crime had a tremendous impact on the people living in that urban borough, with one-third of households having been victims of serious crimes such as burglary and vandalism;
- such residents rated crime as a major problem second only to unemployment;
- fear of crime shaped people's lives, with one out of four people not venturing outside their homes after dark and 28 per cent feeling unsafe in their homes;
- over 50 per cent of women in the borough never or rarely ventured out after dark because of fear of crime – amounting in effect to a curfew on women;
- assault rates varied by age and by ethnic group, as shown in the table:

Assault rates: by age, race and sex (Rates per 1000 householders)				
		Age		
Race	Sex	16–24	25–44	45+
White	Males	401	174	50
	Females	588	311	20
Afro-Caribbean	Males	438	228	124
	Females	414	492	44
Asian	Males	143	206	112
	Females	87	150	250

Such fear of crime may be interpreted as hysteria, if seen in the context of BCS findings that a statistically 'average' person aged 16 or over can expect a robbery once every five centuries, an assault resulting in injury once every century and a burglary every 40 years. However, the Islington inner-city resident is not an 'average' citizen and the area's levels of victimisation reinforce the realism of the residents' fear of crime.

Think about it

- Do you consider that official crime statistics are useful? What purpose do they serve? Whose purpose do they serve?
- If you have a fear of crime, what facilities might be available to you in order to combat such a fear?
- Are female crime figures likely to increase as women seek and gain greater opportunities outside the home?
- Find out about the early 1990s 'zero tolerance' campaign and its view on violence against women. Contrast this feminist campaign with the use of 'zero tolerance' policing strategies against criminals and the homeless which have been applied in some British cities in the late 1990s.

Is the crime rate increasing?

Increases in recorded crimes need not necessarily mean that more crimes are being committed or that people are at greater risk of being victims of crime. Such increases could be explained by a variety of factors, which suggest that more offences are being discovered but not necessarily that more offences are being committed:

- Police training and equipment are becoming more sophisticated – for example the use of computers, forensic science, genetic fingerprinting and DNA profiling.
- Higher policing levels, increased recruitment and detection specialists (see above) all tend to lead to increasing detection rates.
- Changing police attitudes and policies towards some offences, such as prostitution, kerb-crawling or drink-driving, have led to greater determination on the part of the police to prosecute certain offenders. This may create an impression of a rise in these crimes, when it is simply the police making extra efforts to prosecute such crimes and hence catching more offenders.
- Changes in the law have made more things illegal: marital rape, for example, became illegal in 1991.
- Improved communications, such as mobile phones and radar devices, make the reporting of crime easier.
- Changing attitudes to serious offences such as rape may have resulted in a greater proportion of rapes being reported. This may also apply to other traditionally 'taboo' crimes such as domestic violence and child abuse.

Notifiable offences recorded by the police: by type of offence						
	England & Wales		Scotland		Northern Ireland	
	1981 (000s)	1995 (000s)	1981 (000s)	1995 (000s)	1981 (000s)	1995 (000s)
Theft and handling stolen goods,	1 603	2 452	201	222	25	33
of which: theft of vehicles	333	508	33	38	5	8
theft from vehicles	380	813	–	71	7	7
Burglary	718	1 239	96	74	20	16
Criminal damage	387	914	62	87	5	4
Violence against the person	100	213	8	16	3	5
Fraud and forgery	107	133	21	22	3	5
Robbery	20	68	4	5	3	2
Sexual offences,	19	30	2	3	–	2
of which: rape	1	5	–	1	–	–
Drug trafficking	–	21	2	8	–	–
Other notifiable offences	9	29	12	65	3	2
All notifiable offences	2 964	5 100	408	503	62	69

Source: Home Office; The Scottish Office Home Department; Royal Ulster Constabulary: *Social Trends*, 1997

- People may have more possessions to lose, and more people have insurance policies. Insurance claims often require a police report, so more crime is reported: nearly all car thefts, for example, are reported so that people can claim the insurance money. Rising numbers of recorded burglaries may simply reflect more people with household contents insurance policies.
- There are more opportunities for crime in modern society: increases in the number of motor vehicles has led to a large rise in auto-related crimes; the increase of huge self-service supermarkets has made shoplifting easier; new technologies have made electronic money laundering easier (as illustrated in the article below); and so on.
- Some crimes may have increased not because people have become more dishonest but because it has become easier to commit those crimes; greater availability of illegal drugs, for example, has led to a large growth in drug and drug-related offences.

Organised crime finds hiding place for loot on Internet

Dan Atkinson in Lisbon

FRAUDSTERS and money launderers are colonising the Internet in an attempt to escape the surveillance of police and regulators around the world, a conference was told yesterday.

"Electronic money laundering will boom, traditional paths are already highly supervised," said Dr James Backhouse of the London School of Economics.

Criminal, terrorist and drug related funds will be switched into virtual money or "e-cash", moved around the world and later translated back into conventional money. One reliable money laundering route, he said, would be to set up a front company on the Internet supposedly supplying information services; in fact, it will act as a clearing house for tainted funds. Dr Backhouse was speaking to delegates from police, judiciaries and law firms around the world at the international conference on money laundering and economic crime held in Lisbon.

A critical difference, according to Dr Backhouse, separates the Internet's financial systems from conventional credit and debit cards. These leave an audit trail of transactions for the police but "e-cash removes most of these records".

At present the point at which the electronic money is turned back into hard cash could make the fraudsters vulnerable. But, said Dr Backhouse, ever more goods and services are being offered for sale on the Internet and priced in e-cash. Because of this the money need never return to the conventional banking system. In addition, new currencies created on the Internet will exist independent of central banks.

Earlier in the conference John Moscow, a senior investigator for the state of New York, warned that any "mischievous financial transaction that passed through US territory" may be pursued and prosecuted by the American authorities. With two thirds of world trade denominated in dollars, and with most of those transactions clearing through New York, the scope for American action is clearly wide. A former fraud squad officer said security and intelligence officers in the US had found themselves with time on their hands after the end of the Cold War and were now focusing on the underworld.

Serious Fraud Office assistant director Chris Dickson launched a stinging attack on Austria, claiming its secret bank accounts hold an estimated $140 billion (£93 billion), much of it the proceeds of crime and terror.

The Channel Islands were also criticised for their softly softly approach to investigating foreign tax fraud and fraud on the EU itself. Mr Dickson said the Seychelles was "a particularly brazen example" of an offshore tax haven turning a blind eye to criminal and terrorist funds.

Source: The *Guardian*, 24 April 1996

The more closely we look at crime statistics, the more problematic they become; and the more cautious we must be about generalisations based on these figures. It may be that we are becoming a more 'criminal' nation as the increase in crime rates would suggest, but this cannot be assumed. It is important to be aware of other possible reasons for such an increase, as outlined above. We must also bear in mind that full enforcement of the law is impractical. The police have to use some discretion. If the police recorded and acted on every crime they knew about, they would be overwhelmed with paperwork and the courts would be flooded with cases.

The social distribution of crime and deviance

Crime and deviance by age

Through the 1990s the media drew attention to the problem of juvenile crime, with reports of armed robberies, assaults and 'car-jackings'. A widely reported case was the murder in February 1993 of two-year-old James Bulger: while on a shopping trip in Bootle with his mother, he was taken off and killed by two ten-year-old boys playing truant from school. Newspapers were full of articles asking what had become of British morality. The trial of the two boys attracted worldwide attention, with 120 journalists in attendance. The judge suggested that the two young murderers may have been influenced by watching violent videos.

Evidence shows that among young offenders, a relatively small number of individuals are responsible for a large proportion of crimes. The cost of this to society was illustrated very specifically in 1996 when the Chief Constable of Nottinghamshire gave details of the cases of four teenage boys who had committed 765 offences between them, totalling £458,000 in insurance, legal and policing claims.

In August 1994, an analysis of youth crimes was published by the Central Statistical Office under the title *Social Focus on Children*. This report collates much of the available data on young people and crime, and provides an official snapshot of various social groups; the intention is to repeat the exercise every five years to build up long-term data. *Social Focus on Children* found that there has been a drop in the number of young people involved with crime. In England and Wales, the number of 10–16-year-olds found guilty of offences, or formally cautioned, fell by almost 35 per cent between 1981 and 1992 from 214,300 to 139,900. Part of the explanation might lie in demographic changes – there are now fewer 10–16-year-olds in the population. Also, it might be explained by the police becoming willing to use informal (unrecorded) warnings. The authors of the report feel, however, that neither of these factors provides the full explanation, although they conclude that the reasons remain not fully understood.

The murder of the toddler Jamie Bulger, referred to above, raised public awareness of juvenile crime and prompted calls for more effective measures by the police and courts in relation to young offenders. The data given on page 548 shows how the legal system deals with children at different ages.

Think about it

The following table shows some interesting differences between offence rates in different age groups. Bearing in mind that the 21–34 age band is by far the widest range (14 years, compared with the four-year ranges 10–13, 14–17 and the three-year range 18–20), the age group 14–17 is clearly a peak age for most criminal offences.

Offenders found guilty of, or cautioned for, indictable offences: by gender, type of offence and age, 1995						
		10–13 (%)	14–17 (%)	18–20 (%)	21–34 (%)	35 and over (%)	All aged 10 and over (= 100%) (thousands)
Males	Theft and handling stolen goods	8	24	16	37	15	160.9
	Drug offences	–	13	24	53	10	71.9
	Burglary	8	30	20	37	5	43.9
	Violence against the person	4	21	14	43	17	41.8
	Criminal damage	10	24	15	39	12	12.2
	Sexual offences	4	14	8	30	45	6.8
	Robbery	7	36	19	32	6	5.3
	Other indictable offences	1	8	17	58	17	52.4
	All indictable offences	5	20	18	43	14	395.2
Females	Theft and handling stolen goods	12	28	12	32	16	60.1
	Drug offences	–	10	19	56	16	7.9
	Burglary	12	43	15	24	4	1.9
	Violence against the person	8	36	11	34	12	7.7
	Criminal damage	8	27	13	35	17	1.2
	Sexual offences	6	13	6	50	24	0.1
	Robbery	7	55	16	20	2	0.5
	Other indictable offences	–	9	15	59	16	5.0
	All indictable offences	10	26	13	36	15	84.4

Source: Home Office; *Social Trends*, 1997

- Why do you think this peak occurs in the 14–17 age group, and why do you think the rate drops again for many offences in the age group 18–20? Think about possible factors such as: family, or the judicial system as applied to different age groups.
- Which is the one category of criminal offence whose rate does not drop from age group 14–17 to 18–20? Can you suggest reasons for this?

Under 10

You cannot be guilty of a criminal offence.

You can be taken into local authority care if you are beyond the control of a parent or guardian. In extreme cases, with the permission of the Health Secretary, you can be put in a secure community home.

POLICE POWERS

If you are detained by the police they can:
- search you
- carry out an "intimate search"
- take your fingerprints and photograph
- take a non-intimate body sample (nail scrapings)
- take an intimate body sample (blood, semen)

THE CHILD'S RIGHTS

Parents must be informed of a juvenile's arrest and detention. Arrested juveniles:
- have a right to inform someone else of their arrest and to communicate privately with a solicitor
- have a right to silence
- should be interviewed in the presence of a parent or another adult who is not a police officer

10 – 13

A child over 10 is capable of a criminal offence, but can only be convicted in court if he/she knows the difference between right and wrong.

Greater use is being made of informal methods instead of courts: eg caution by police, making amends such as repairing damaged property.

Persistent offenders can be dealt with by Youth Courts except in cases of murder or manslaughter which are heard in adult Crown Courts.

For grave crimes this age group can be put in secure community homes.

Very disturbed and highly delinquent children can be placed in a secure Youth Treatment Centre until the age of 18, but only with the Health Secretary's permission. Such cases are very rare.

Young offenders who appear in court can be:
- fined or made to pay compensation (parents or guardians are ordered to pay);
- put under the supervision of a social worker or probation officer;
- given an "absolute discharge" for trivial crimes. This means they are not punished.

14 +

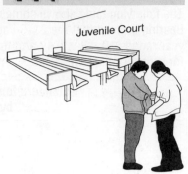

Juvenile Court

Between 14 and 16, a child is legally defined as a "young person" and presumed to know the difference between right and wrong.

The same penalties apply as for the 10 to 13 age group but the risk of a custodial sentence increases.

From 14–17: youngsters accused of serious offences, which for an adult would carry a maximum sentence of 14 years in prison, can be tried by the adult Crown Court.

15: offenders can be locked up in a Young Offender Institution for 2 to 12 months. They can also be held in police custody to await trial if no secure local-authority accommodation is available or if the court decides that this is necessary to protect the public.

16: offenders can be ordered to do community service, can be put on probation and are liable to pay fines or compensation themselves.

17: offenders are still dealt with by Youth Courts but can be held in custody in the same way as an adult if they are thought likely to go missing or commit another crime.

Source: The *Guardian*, 2 March 1993

Think about it

- What factors do you think need to be taken into account when the police or courts are dealing with young offenders?
- At what age should a young offender be held fully responsible for a serious crime he or she has committed, such as murder or burglary?
- Do you think that harsh treatments for young offenders might be of benefit to them and/or to society as a whole? Justify your view.

Crime and deviance by gender

The section on feminist approaches to issues and theories of crime and deviance (see pages 529–32) addresses the major gender issues in relation to crime and deviance.

Criminal studies tend to support the idea of crime as a male phenomenon. Figures from the late 1980s suggested that males were five times more likely to commit crime than females, while the data in the table on page 547 and in the graph below seem to reinforce the perception of the offender as more likely to be male. However, the extent of female criminal activity, as represented in statistics, is often questioned and it has been argued that far more female crime exists than is recorded. One suggested reason for this is that police attitudes to female offenders committing minor, non-indictable crimes may be more lenient than they are to males, with the result that many female crimes remain reported but unrecorded.

Generally, it is believed that when women are involved in crime, it is usually for minor offences such as petty theft, which may receive cautions rather than custodial convictions. Also, it is held that if women do appear in court, they can use 'biological' reasons to explain their action – 'crime of passion', for example – which can result in the judge passing a more lenient sentence. Indeed, when women do break the 'norm' and act contrary to society's expectations of them, it can cause massive public concern and fascination – much greater than might be the case if a similar offence were committed by a man. This can result in the female offender becoming a 'folk-devil': examples of this have been the cases of Myra Hindley, still a focus of press attention decades after her conviction, and Beverly Allitt, convicted in 1993 of murdering four babies in her care, who became the focus of deviancy amplification (see page 522) as the 'killer nurse'.

Known offenders as a percentage of the population, by gender and age, 1995

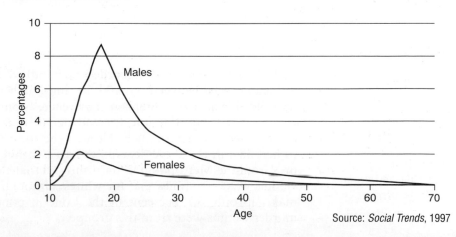

Source: *Social Trends*, 1997

Crime and deviance by ethnicity

Only relatively recently have sociologists turned their attention to ethnicity in relation to crime and deviance. After World War II black immigrants were stated to be 'more law-abiding than the general population' according to the research of Z. Layton-Henry in *The Politics of Immigration* (1992). However, this did not remain the case, and by the 1970s friction had arisen between the police and the black community.

In 1981, Lord Scarman's report, *The Brixton Disorders*, considered that policing tactics in Brixton, London, which were intended to cut 'street crimes' by stopping and searching suspects on the streets, led to discrimination against Afro-Caribbeans. Since Afro-Caribbeans tended to have a 'street culture', their presence on the streets was high, and they were more likely to be stopped, searched and arrested. The Scarman Report included the following recommendations:

- an improvement of police community relations;
- an increase in recruitment to the police from ethnic minority groups.

Critics, however, maintained that the recommendations, many of which were never carried out, conveniently distracted attention away from the real discontents and problem areas of society; indeed, in 1985 race riots occurred in Toxteth, Tottenham and Birmingham. Various sociological studies have been carried out in relation to these disturbances:

- Toxteth: G. Gaskill and P. Smith, in *How Young Blacks See the Police* (1982), studied the hostility felt by young blacks who collectively seemed to have experienced the police in negative terms of prejudice accompanied by feelings of despair and distrust.
- Tottenham: M. Harris, writing in *New Society* (1985), said that what happened in Tottenham should not be described as a race riot, since half of those charged were white: however, the shooting by the police of an Afro-Caribbean mother of six seemed to have been what sparked off the riot.
- Birmingham: E. Ellis Cashmore, in *Re-writing the Script* (1985), argued that government and local authorities had become 'out of touch' with the position of black youth in modern society, and that black youths had suffered from economic insecurity, deprivation and enforced idleness. In 1987, in his book *The Logic of Racism*, Cashmore describes the findings of in-depth interviews carried out with 800 people in and around Birmingham. He found racism to be present in all classes and age groups, and wrote that 'most people are conservative for no reason more mysterious than that they want stability'.

In 1992 there were 7793 recorded racial attacks. The true figures were estimated to be between ten and 20 times higher. In April 1993, an 18-year-old black man, Stephen Lawrence, standing at a bus-stop in Eltham, south-east London, was murdered by a gang of white youths in an unprovoked racial attack. He was the fourth black or Asian person to be killed in racial incidents in the area within a two-year period. Figures from the Metropolitan Police showed that the murder rate for black victims was three times that for whites: although Afro-Caribbean people make up only 6.8 per cent of the London population, 20 per cent of murder victims were from this group.

Issues of sociological debate on crime and ethnicity

<u>Criminalisation and ethnicity</u>   Afro-Caribbean males represent more than 10 per cent of the prison population and they are seven times more likely than white males to be sent to prison. Explanations that have been put forward include the following:

- The British criminal justice system is considered racist and discriminating against those from minority ethnic groups, particularly Afro-Caribbeans.
- A higher proportion of the Afro-Caribbean ethnic group also belong to the class and economic groups which make up the majority of the prison population.

There is limited research evidence to judge these explanations, although some sociologists consider that racism and discrimination in key spheres such as employment lead Afro-Caribbeans towards criminal activities. The police and the courts may see this group in negative, stereotypical ways.

<u>Realist approaches</u>   Developments in criminology and sociology have turned to crime as a real and serious threat to law and order – a threat which requires some swift solutions. The two main approaches are New Right realism and New Left realism (see pages 527 and 532). From New Left realism, key elements in understanding attitudes to crime and ethnicity are as follows:

- Relative deprivation: black youths feel deprived of – and blocked off from – the financial and material benefits they see around them.
- Subculture: this becomes a collective solution to group problems; crime forms a group cultural response to feelings of oppression.
- Marginalisation: black youths are pushed to the edge of society and towards criminal activity because of low academic success and high levels of unemployment.

<u>Cultural explanations</u>   The existence of a correlation between high unemployment levels and crime rates has been long debated. Other cultural explanations for crime have included the decline in the traditional two-parent family, the effect of tower-block living on communities and the influence of television.

Think about it

- How do you think sociologists have influenced the perception of the link between unemployment and crime?
- To what extent do you think that tower blocks and housing estates may have contributed to high crime rates?
- How might the apparent collapse of the family, lack of parental authority and the age of television be linked to a high crime rate? Can unemployment also be added to these factors?
- What problems might arise for sociologists in attempting to carry out research into these questions?

Crime and deviance by social class

Earlier sections of the unit have made general reference to crime and deviance in relation to social class. The traditional sociological perspectives each have their own interpretation of this link.

Structural functionalist theory

- assumes that criminals and deviants might serve a functional and useful purpose in reinforcing, by their negative activities, mainstream middle-class 'norms' and values. However, such norms and values may not be reflected precisely across all social groups.
- suggests that anomie, as defined by R.K. Merton, is an important factor. The theory attempts to explain criminal behaviour in terms of the structure of society, by which the 'strain' of striving for the dream of financial security and success is placed particularly on the working class.

Marxist theory

- examines crime and deviance in terms of the power structures of society. Laws reflect the ruling class interests at the expense of the subject class: the state passes laws to support the interests of capitalism.
- asks how middle-class and corporate crime can be accounted for if crime is seen as essentially a working-class activity carried out by deprived and marginalised groups. One suggestion has been that individuals who have committed criminal acts might be judged by a hierarchy within their own class.

Social class differences are evidenced by the punishments received by offenders. Prisons in capitalist societies are largely populated by those from working-class and ethnic minority groups. This may be seen to distract from the often far more lucrative criminal activities of those higher up the social stratification scale.

Crime and deviance by locality

Several approaches have been made by sociologists to establish possible links between crime rates and locality, ranging from the ecological studies of the Chicago School based on the American urban environment in the 1920s, to the New Left realism based on the concept of street crime in Britain in the 1980s. The urban environment has been the focus of attention, with relatively high crime rates in inner-city areas. Some of these areas seem to carry not only an increased risk of serious crimes but also an increased fear of crime (including relatively minor disturbances such as rowdiness or petty vandalism). Two London studies presented in *Confronting Crime*, edited by R. Matthews and J. Young (1986), the Islington Crime Survey and Broadwater Farm, showed that about one-third of households in these areas had suffered burglary, robbery or sexual assault within the previous 12 months. This rate is in fact not vastly different from that revealed by the 1994 British Crime Survey findings which estimated 18 million crimes were committed against people or property in England and Wales as a whole.

Criticisms of locality studies of crime and deviance have pointed to their positivist approaches based on the collection of criminal statistics, which tend to be unreliable and do not provide a complete picture. Also there seems to be a tendency for such studies to be overdeterministic and to depict the locality as passively accepting what is happening. This fails to explain why, in most cases, the people within a locality fear rather than accept or associate with criminal acts and deviant behaviour.

The role of the police

Of key concern is the relationship between law and order on the one hand and individual freedom on the other. There seems to have arisen a feeling of unease about the role of the police and their relations in general with society. Some of the reasons for this include the following:

- Society has moved away from respect for the law as an accepted social norm; moral codes have changed. The police constable is especially vulnerable to this new attitude that holds little respect for authority:

    'His natural, accepted authority has gone; his right to intervention is queried and his slightest failing is magnified.'
    Richard Thackrah, *Policing the Nineties. In Whose Interest?*
    (PAVIC, 1994)

- Society is less homogeneous. Some notable confrontations with police have included black and other non-white citizens who often claim to be victimised by the police.
- New methods that have been introduced to make the police more efficient have at the same time made them more distant – the increased use of computer technology, for example.
- The increased size of the criminal justice system and, in particular, the police force (see the table below) has reduced the element of personal contact which once, it is often claimed, allowed the police to become part of the local community.
- There have been a number of cases of proven (and suspected) misconduct by the police, including assault of prisoners. There is more widespread use of informers, and as crimes of violence and terrorism have increased, police methods – rightly or wrongly – have become less 'kid glove'.
- Until recently, complaints against the police have been investigated by the police themselves (normally by a Chief Constable of another force). Calls for more independent inquiries are widespread and are now being acted upon.

Employment in the criminal justice system		1971 (000s)	1981 (000s)	1991 (000s)	1995 (000s)	(Rates per 10 000 population)	
						1971	1995
Police service	Police	109	133	142	141	20.0	24.8
	Civilian staff	31	41	51	57	5.6	10.0
	All police service	139	174	192	198	25.6	34.8
Prison service		17	24	33	40	3.5	7.8
Probation service		–	13	18	18	–	3.5

Source: *Social Trends*, 1996

The Sheehy proposals

The main recommendations of the **Sheehy Report** into police responsibilities and rewards, published in 1993, are outlined in the box below.

Recommendations of the Sheehy Report

1. New pay scales to allow for overlapping between the ranks; points awarded for the experience and skills that a job demands.
2. The ranks of Chief Inspector, Chief Superintendent and Deputy Chief Constable should be abolished, and rank structure simplified.
3. Fixed-term appointments should replace 'jobs for life'; pensions to be more flexible.
4. Existing police regulations should be replaced by a national non-statutory Code of Standards.
5. Normal retirement age should be raised to 60 for all ranks and in all forces.

The Sheehy Report recommendations were intended to further and support the positive attributes of the police service; Sheehy argued that they should improve the ability of the police service to manage itself and its role more effectively.

The key issues for sociologists, within the debate on Sheehy's proposed reforms of the police, are how the proposals might affect police morale in the short term and policing strategies in the long term. Decreased levels of pay and fewer opportunities for promotion may cause changes which are then reflected in attitudes and policing tactics. There seems to be an increasing split between the need for military policing in crisis situations such as riots and armed robberies, and the need for 'friendly' community policing, for example foot patrols, which relies on the cooperation and support of the general public.

The role of the courts

Laws in England and Wales consist of three main types (Scotland has its own, different, legal system):

*   **common law:** passed down through the centuries to form rules commonly accepted as law;
*   **statute law:** laws passed by Parliament and written in statute-books (or law books). Each Act of Parliament adds to statute law;
*   **case law:** when a court case takes place and a judge decides a ruling on a point of law such a decision forms the basis of future law. Case law is based on the law of the land and the interpretation given by other judges.

English law is also divided into criminal law and civil law. **Criminal law** covers offences committed by individuals against society, ranging from serious crimes such as murder to petty theft. There are two types of offences, or activities breaking the law: indictable and non-indictable.

*   **Indictable offences** are serious offences tried before a jury; they may now be tried by magistrates (see below) if the accused agrees.
*   **Non-indictable offences** are less serious and are heard in a magistrates' court with no jury.

About two million defendants are found guilty each year – the majority for non-indictable offences.

The **civil law** deals with the rights, duties and responsibilities of individuals in society in relation to one another. A civil wrong or injury by one person to another is known as a **tort**.

The courts are an important element of the judicial system in the UK, operating independently of government and Parliament and in support of democratic processes. The role of the courts may be summarised as follows:

- They provide fair trials and ensure sound verdicts to those being prosecuted for alleged offences.
- They demonstrate equality of treatment, regardless of class, gender or racial background.
- They allow the accused the right to defend himself or herself or have legal representation in magistrates' courts, or in Crown Courts presided over by judge and jury.

The role of the courts and the extent to which they fulfil the above has been the subject of wide sociological debate. J. Lea and J. Young's *What is to be done about Law and Order?* (1984) and D. Scraton et al.'s *Law, Order and the Authoritarian State* (1987) are just two of the many texts involved in this debate. Approaches to the debate follow similar lines to the various approaches to theories of crime and deviance (see pages 512–34). For example, functionalists would consider courts as having the vital function of marking the boundary of acceptable behaviour to serve the interests of society, while Marxists would argue that the courts are a product of capitalism and serve the interests of the rich and powerful.

The role of prisons

Prisons may be defined as institutions run by governments for detaining convicted criminals. They are intended to accomplish at least four goals:

1. The separation of criminals from society: prisons achieve this when convicts reach the prison gates. It is considered important to protect society from individuals who commit extreme acts which are not acceptable to society. Prisons are one of several options: capital punishment, for example, might be an alternative in cases of murder.
2. The punishment of criminal behaviour: prisons are, for most, unpleasant places in which to spend time. They are often crowded, degrading, boring and dangerous. Not infrequently, prisoners are victims of each others' violence. Inmates also are constantly supervised, sometimes harassed by prison officers and deprived of normal means of social, emotional, intellectual and sexual expression. Prison may be considered a severe form of punishment.

3. The discouraging of criminal behaviour: rising crime figures suggest that prisons have failed to achieve this goal. There are some good reasons for this. First, by their very nature, prisons are closed to the public. Few people know much about prison life, nor do they think about it often. Inmates who return to society may brag to their peers about their prison experiences in order to recover their self esteem. For the prison experience to act as a deterrent, the very unpleasant aspects of prison life would have to be constantly brought to the attention of the population at large. Television series based on prison life may perhaps serve such a purpose. Another reason why prisons may fail to deter criminal behaviour is that punishment can hardly discourage undesired behaviour if the likelihood of being punished is minimal. The argument about the relative merit of different types of punishment is limited when there is a high probability that whichever forms are used will be applied to all (or most) criminals.

4. The reform and rehabilitation of deviants: during the eighteenth century, prisons, asylums and hospitals became separate institutions. Murder became recognised as the most serious offence. As human rights developed, so the killing of another person represented the ultimate attack on the rights of an individual. Hence prisons took on the role of attempting to reform wayward deviants into accepting conformity. However, even within prison, conformity may be viewed differently by its inmates:

Social roles in a women's prison

The prison is one of the most visible agents of social control. Its purpose is well known: to punish and perhaps to rehabilitate society's criminal deviants. What is less well known is that this purpose is undercut by the existence of an informal social system among prisoners. This inmate society has its own clearly defined structure of social roles, most of which are considered deviant by the "outside world." Ironically, inmates who take on roles that involve cooperation with prison officials are considered deviant by other inmates.

Sociologist Rose Giallombardo (1967) conducted a field study of the hierarchy of social roles in a progressive prison for women. She found that the lowest social role is that of *snitcher*. For revealing forbidden inmate activities to the prison staff, the snitcher is despised. Other prisoners punish her by singling her out for public scorn and ridicule, a strong sanction known as "signifying."

Sharing the bottom of the social ladder with the snitcher is the *inmate cop*, or *lieutenant*, a prisoner who has been given some authority over other inmates. She is despised for her disloyalty and resented for her power.

Inmates who cooperate with prison officials are considered deviant by other inmates.

Another outcast from prison society is the *square*, an inmate who is thought of as an "accidental prisoner" whose real loyalty lies with the prison administration. A square may also be a prisoner who does not take part in homosexual activities. The square is not only ostracized and distrusted but also pitied by other prisoners.

A final "deviant" inmate role is that of the *jive bitch*. A deliberate troublemaker, she breaks promises and distorts information, sometimes to break up lesbian relationships.

At the opposite end of the social spectrum are the "good-guy" roles. *Rap buddies* are especially close friends. *Homeys* are inmates from the same home town. A *connect* is an inmate with a "good" prison job who helps other inmates obtain scarce goods (such as cigarettes and extra food) and information. A *booster* makes a business of stealing prison food and supplies and selling or trading them to other inmates. A *pinner* acts as a lookout, warning other inmates of unreliable prisoners or approaching guards. In the upside-down social hierarchy of a prison, pinners are the most respected and trusted members.

Source: M.S. Bassis et al., *Sociology: An Introduction* (Random House, 1980)

The prison population in the UK is rising, as shown in the table below. Over the last 40 years, remand prisoners (i.e. those charged and awaiting trial) have made up an increasing proportion of the prison population; the table illustrates that although the number of untried prisoners has fallen by 1000 since 1986, they still represent a fifth of the total prison population.

Population in custody in prison establishments					
		1981 (000s)	1986 (000s)	1991 (000s)	1992 (000s)
Average population	Males	48.9	52.5	49.7	50.0
	Females	1.6	1.8	1.7	1.8
	Total	50.5	54.3	51.4	51.8
Remand prisoners	Untried prisoners	5.9	9.6	8.6	8.6
	Convicted prisoners awaiting sentence	2.3	1.7	2.0	2.1
	All remand prisoners	8.2	11.3	10.6	10.7
Sentenced prisoners	Adults	29.3	32.0	33.7	34.3
	Young offenders	12.6	10.7	6.8	6.5
	Other sentences	–	–	0.1	0.1
	All sentenced prisoners	41.9	42.7	40.6	40.9
Non-criminal prisoners		0.4	0.2	0.3	0.3

Source: *Social Trends*, 1995

Asylums and the issue of non-culpable deviance

Mental illness and disability

Up until the twentieth century, certain 'deviant' forms of behaviour may have been termed 'mad'. Attitudes, as well as treatments, have since changed.

Anthony Giddens, in *Sociology* (2nd edn 1993), points out that workhouses (effectively prisons), from the seventeenth century onwards, provided shelter and food for the sick, the aged and the mentally ill. These inmates were incarcerated in the workhouses for several hours a day and forced to work. It was not until the eighteenth century that hospitals, asylums and prisons began to be separated out, each taking on more specialised roles. By the nineteenth century, asylums and, more specifically, mental illness had become recognised by the medical establishment. Mental illness became 'medicalised', taken over by medical practitioners and seen as a disease requiring treatment rather than punishment: people could be placed in an asylum, even against their will, although a medical doctor's certificate was required.

Today, mental illness is seen as:

- a social phenomenon and as such forming part of a social construction since it has been socially defined as inappropriate;
- not usually as easy to define as physical illness and more often seen as 'a state of mind';
- dependent on the context in which it is displayed.

'Deviance' and informal controls

In the context of mental illness, medical psychiatric care can be seen as one form of informal control of deviance (see page 506), as indicated in the following article.

Vitamin 'cure' for violent offenders

VIOLENT criminals could be treated with vitamins in an effort to lower their aggression levels.

An experiment in the technique is planned in an attempt to reduce the number of assaults on staff at Aylesbury Young Offenders Institution in Buckinghamshire.

Bernard Gesh, who will head the trials, said he believed an enhanced diet could affect the production of serotonin, a chemical whose level in the brain is thought to affect aggressive behaviour.

'If you have a well-balanced diet the chances are your brain chemistry is going to be in better shape in the same way your body is going to be in better shape,' Mr Gesh told BBC2's Newsnight.

Professor Malcolm Lader of the Institute of Psychiatry in London, who has been examining the impact of drugs on serotonin levels, suggested drug treatments might help curb aggression in prisoners. He said giving patients drugs such as Prozac raised serotonin levels, making them less aggressive. Low levels of serotonin have been found in violent men.

He even suggested some inmates might be forced to take such drugs.

'I think a form of compulsion — with a lot of safeguards and appeals and so on — might be appropriate,' he said. 'There are times when patients are fairly irrational in why they don't take medication.'

A spokesman for the Prison Service said it was aware of the proposal to carry out a nutrition-based study but insisted discussions were still at a preliminary stage.

Source: The *Daily Mail*, 12 September 1996

Think about it

- What other factors do you think sociologists might consider in relation to the extensive use of drugs which attempt to treat personal and social problems?
- How might violent criminals react to the use of vitamins as treatment for their aggression? What problems might sociologists find in trying to research the success or otherwise of such treatment?

The functionalist Talcott Parsons considered medicine as a form of social control. By defining a person's condition as deviant (Parsons refers to the 'medicalisation of deviance'), medicine controls that person's behaviour in such a way that any threat he or she poses to society can be minimalised. Deviant behaviours such as alcoholism, drug addiction and suicide are defined by medical experts as evidence of deviance or sickness. Once a certain class of behaviour – or even a particular political or religious allegiance – is defined as 'deviant', the question arises as to whether this poses a social problem.

Other informal controls include education (the hidden curriculum), and the mass media (promotion of the ideology of the powerful and supporting established power structures), as discussed in their respective units of this book.

Erving Goffman's classic study *Asylums* (1961) was based on his research into mental institutions in Washington, USA, in the mid-1950s. Goffman maintained that asylums, along with other 'total institutions' such as hospitals and prisons, can cause rather than cure mental illness. He cited the following reasons:

- All aspects of life are spent in the company of many others, in the same place and under one authority.
- Each day's activities are firmly regimented and a tight schedule is established by a formal code of rules administered by officials of the institution.
- *'They are forcing-houses for changing persons; each is a natural experiment in what can be done to the self.'*

Mortification, according to Goffman, is the process which individuals go through in total institutions and which involves losing their former personality. This mortification strips inmates of their self concept by:

- removing personal items such as clothing, jewellery, etc., which tends to take away individuality, and imposing standard hair cuts, mass uniform, etc.;
- limiting communication and self expression by imposing appropriate ways of addressing each other, the staff, etc.;
- forcing individuals to live under lock and key with little if any freedom of speech, movement, etc.

The film *One Flew Over the Cuckoo's Nest*, based on Ken Kesey's book of the same title, portrays a rebellious mental patient finally overcome by a lobotomy, a controversial treatment which involves destroying parts of the brain, which reduced the patient (Randall McMurphy, played by Jack Nicholson) to a 'vegetable'. The book was based on research into the effects on patients of being in a mental institution, and shows patients' general reactions – including initial mortification. Another film looked at the treatment of a Hollywood actress, 'Frances Farmer', in an American psychiatric hospital. This true story also depicted how she underwent electro-convulsive therapy and then a lobotomy.

Reintegration Patients, on being discharged from an asylum, may find reintegration into society problematic. 'Disculturation' effects, even if temporary, involve the patient's inability to fit back into the norms and values of the outside world after what may have been a lengthy period of incarceration. The stigma of being an inmate, of an asylum or a prison, may take longer to overcome than disculturation – even trying to regain entry into the family or the workplace may be an uphill struggle.

Revision and practice tasks

Task 1: data response question

Offenders aged 14 to 17 sentenced for indictable offences: by type of sentence

Item A

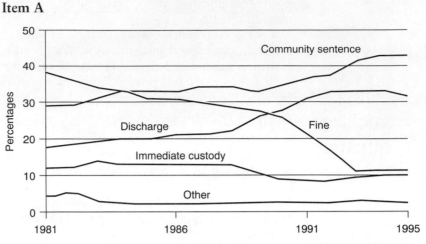

Source: *Social Trends*, 1997

Item B

Risk of being a victim of crime: by type of area, 1995 (England & Wales)			
	Indices[1]		
		Inner city	Non-inner city
Household offences	Home vandalism	110	100
	Burglary	180	90
	Vehicle vandalism	145	95
	Vehicle thefts	150	95
	Bicycle thefts	165	95
	Other household theft	140	95
	All household offences	125	95
Personal offences	Assaults	140	95
	Robbery/theft from person	185	90
	Other personal theft	105	100
	All personal offences	135	95

[1] All areas = 100.

Source: *Social Trends*, 1997

(a) Study Item A and briefly explain:
  (i) indictable offences
  (ii) major trend lines   [4 marks]

(b) Study Item B and state:
  (i) why households risk being victims of crime, particularly in inner city areas;
  (ii) why the risk of personal offences may be relatively less in non-inner city areas.   [4 marks]

(c) Outline how any one sociological approach to crime and deviance might assist our understanding of young offenders. [7 marks]

(d) Evaluate the usefulness of statistical data on crime and deviance such as provided by Items A and B. [10 marks]

[Total: 25 marks]

Task 2: structured question

(a) Briefly explain what sociologists mean by 'folk devils' and 'moral panics'. (4)

(b) Outline the possible causes and effects of any two 'moral panics'. (4)

(c) Outline how any one subcultural theory might assist our understanding of juvenile delinquency. (7)

(d) Examine the view that crime is, and will remain, an essentially male activity. (10)

(Total 25 marks)

Essay questions

1. All acts which are criminal may be seen as deviant but not all deviant acts are seen as criminal. Explain, discuss and illustrate this statement (see sample essay in Task 3).

2. How successfully can official crime statistics be employed to help in our understanding of the concepts of deviance, crime and control?

3. Assess the view that labelling deviance is a reaction by the audience to produce a sense of order in social relations.

4. How far do subcultural theories contribute to sociological explanations of deviance?

5. Discuss how deviance may be created by the ways in which agents of social control define and categorise certain individuals and groups.

6. Do social control and the legal system serve to enforce the will and interests of the ruling class?

7. Examine and illustrate the processes involved in the development of the concept 'moral panic'.

8. To what extent might it be argued that the emancipation of women has lessened control factors and is leading to higher female crime rates?

9. Discuss the view that critical contemporary approaches challenge functionalist and interactionist theories of deviance and control.

10. Critically examine the view that the apparent high rates of criminal activities among working-class males and certain ethnic minority groups has been produced by policing techniques, inadequate official statistics and a biased legal system.

Task 3: sample and essay task

Read the following example of a response to essay question 1 above. Note not just its content, but its introduction, development, structure and conclusion.

Having read through the essay carefully, your task is to reduce it to an essay plan. Read back over relevant sections of this unit and other sources.

Then draw up your own essay plan for the following essay title:

• Explain the difference between crime and deviance and discuss why only some deviant acts are classified as criminal.

All acts which are criminal may be seen as deviant but not all deviant acts are seen as criminal. Explain, discuss and illustrate this statement.
This much quoted statement or conundrum attempts to draw some distinction between criminal and deviant acts. Generally, it is accepted that most, if not all, crime is deviant, but not all deviancy is criminal. There is a fundamental difference between the two, which this essay will seek to address.

Deviancy is the breaking away from what is socially accepted as normal behaviour. Normal behaviour is established through a consensus or agreement of society's norms and values. Thus, if a person behaves abnormally, they can be termed deviant. Where deviancy becomes criminal, however, is when behaviour becomes destructive to the smooth running of society. So, for example, in societies where marriage is the normal starting point for a family, a lone parent or a couple deciding to have children without getting married would be seen as deviant. On the other hand, murder and burglary are criminal acts because they are harmful to other members of society *and* they conflict with the existing legal practices laid down as lawful within that society.

What is seen as deviant and what is seen as criminal is open to interpretation. For example, 'jay-walking' (crossing or walking in the street with no regard for traffic) is considered dangerous and illegal, and therefore a criminal offence, in many states in America. However, it is not classed as a criminal act in Britain. Although only a minor example, this difference in interpretation may in part be caused by the difference in values – and the norms that derive from them – that relate to the two countries. Thus, in America, the 'jay-walking' law may be seen as a suitable way of protecting its citizens from unnecessary dangers, whereas in Britain it may be seen as rather petty and possibly even an infringement on an individual's freedom to cross a road.

Thus it can be seen that it is difficult and misleading to refer to a specific society since, within any one society, at any time, there is a wide variety of different sets of values. Until it was legalised in 1969, male homosexual behaviour was considered a criminal activity in the United Kingdom. Legal changes can be highly controversial, however: in spite of the change just referred to many gay men and women remain marginalised (or seen on the edge of society) and discriminated against for what is still seen as deviant behaviour. Disability may also be seen in this way; indeed it may be argued that disabled people are disabled by the society in which they live, by the way society and its social institutions operate and also by the attitudes and beliefs that non-disabled people hold about disabled people.

Emile Durkheim argued that deviancy was functional to society as it provided an outlet for innovation and change. Columbus was regarded as a deviant when he suggested sailing over the edge of the horizon in an attempt to find another route to the East. If he had not done so, the false idea that the world was flat would not have been corrected so soon. His 'deviancy' from accepted norms brought about a significant change in awareness of the world and, ultimately, in the social, economic and political composition of the world. Durkheim also argued that a certain amount of crime was necessary to reinforce the norms and values accepted by the majority of the society. Whereas deviancy can be moulded into a new way of thinking, high levels of crime are dangerous for society because they reflect a weakening of the norms and values and indicate that reinforcement as well as possible changes are needed.

Deviancy can serve to reinforce socially acceptable behaviour; Durkheim referred to a 'boundary-maintaining' function which drew the line between the acceptable and non-acceptable. Whilst deviancy could benefit society, the balance was critical: too much deviance could threaten society and even cause its ruin. Durkheim's 'boundary-maintaining' function may be explained as marking the boundary of acceptable behaviour which can be spelt out to all members of society, for example by means of the criminal justice system including the use of symbols such as wigs and gowns. Such symbols represent legal authority developed over centuries by those with experience in matters of law and order. Also reflected are the wishes of the people in legitimating social change – making marital rape illegal in the United Kingdom, for example, in 1991. A boundary testing function whereby extreme acts of crime and deviance draw members of society together and strengthen their mutual bonds, was exemplified on the Isle of Wight, in early 1995, when three highly dangerous life-serving prisoners escaped from Parkhurst Prison.

By contrast, Marxist views on deviant and criminal acts are based on a concept of the structure of capitalist society as protecting and promoting ruling-class interest: laws in effect ensure the maintenance of an economic system based on private ownership and profit accumulation. The competition to gain wealth encourages selfishness and aggression at the expense of the overall well-being of society. Too often, the end is claimed to justify the means, and the drive to be financially successful, to gain economic or other forms of power, may lead to criminal activities. Deviations such as squatting can be viewed in terms of the frustrations produced by a capitalist system. The law reflects the interests of the ruling class and ensures it remains unthreatened, through the state passing laws which support its interests. Marxist writers have traditionally been interested in, and very dubious about, the unbiased nature of the law.

In conclusion then, deviancy and crime may be simplistically separated but the two concepts vary in definition from society to society according to their respective norms and values. A certain amount of deviancy must be permissible (in contrast to crime which is non-permissible) in order to bring about change and to allow for individuality; although, as Durkheim noted, without criminality it would be more difficult for law-abiding citizens to know what constituted 'normal'/non-deviant/non-criminal behaviour. Thus, despite Marxist views on the nature and structure of capitalism, some deviant behaviour must remain legal to allow for the basic human rights of opinion and freedom.

Ideas for coursework and personal studies

1. Carry out research, with a manageable sample, perhaps using an interview schedule, to find out people's views as to whether or not they consider society has shared values, as suggested by structural functionalists. You may find it most straightforward to focus on a particular area of interest such as forms of deviant behaviour – motoring offences, for instance.

2. Using a map of the area in which you live, devise a method to find out if criminal activities take place in distinctive zones. Do such zones follow the concentric pattern identified by the ecological approach of the Chicago School, or do they follow a different pattern. If they follow a different pattern, does that pattern in some way mirror features of the environment?

3. Devise a small research programme to investigate whether traditional male stereotypes of deviant behaviour or criminal activity can be applied to females. Perhaps such a programme might be used to carry out a study of a specific female subcultural group.

4. Conduct an observation study in a Magistrates' Court or Crown Court. Take note of the various offences with which defendants are charged, the judgements which are reached, and what factors seem to have influenced such judgements. Take particular note of the gender/appearance/ethnic background of the defendants.

5. Select a group such as teachers, nurses, or local community care or social workers, and investigate whether, and if so, how, the members of this group label its 'clients'. You should also attempt to include observations of the origins and effects of any labelling processes which you detect.

Selected reading list

Crimes of the Powerful, Frank Pearce (Pluto Press, 1976)

Delinquency and Drift, David Matza (John Wiley & Sons, 1964)

Folk Devils and Moral Panics, Stan Cohen (2nd edn Blackwell, 1987)

Girl Delinquents, A. Campbell (Blackwell, 1981)

Humans, Their Deviance, Social Problems and Social Control, 2nd edn, Edwin H. Lemert (Prentice-Hall, 1972)

Juvenile Delinquency and Urban Areas, Clifford Shaw and Henry McKay (University of Chicago Press, 1942)

The New Criminology, I. Taylor, F. Walton and J. Young (Routledge & Kegan Paul, 1973)

Outsiders: Studies in the Sociology of Deviance, Howard S. Becker (Macmillan, 1963)

Policing the Crisis, Stuart Hall et al. (Macmillan, 1979)

Power, Crime and Mystification, Steven Box (Tavistock, 1983)

The Sociology of Youth Culture and Youth Subculture, M. Brake (Routledge & Kegan Paul, 1980)

Suicide: A Study in Sociology, Emile Durkheim (1897) (Routledge & Kegan Paul, 1970)

What Is To Be Done About Law and Order?, John Lea and Jock Young (Penguin, 1984)

Whose Law? What Order?, William Chambliss and Milton Mankoff (John Wiley & Sons, 1976)

11 Power and politics

There's more than one way to make friends and influence people . . .

Introduction

Power and politics, as an area of study for sociologists, raises broad questions about society's decision-making processes: who holds or gains power to influence the lives of others and how do they do so? This decision-making takes place through a range of processes from debates in Parliament to discussions in a household; while most of the processes involve persuasion, some involve the taking of power by force. The focal points of this unit, the sociological aspects of power and politics, include:

- sources and definitions of power and authority;
- political institutions and decision-making processes, including pressure and interest groups, and the mass media;
- political participation, party membership and support, and voting behaviour;
- protest and social movements, including feminism and environmentalism;
- the distribution of power;
- powerlessness and marginality in terms of age, class, gender and ethnicity.

Power and authority

Sources and definitions of power and authority

'A Prince should have no other aim or thought, not take up any other thing for his study, but war, and its order and discipline, for this is the only art that is necessary to one who commands.'

Niccolò Machiavelli (1469–1527), *The Prince*

'Knowledge itself is power.'

Francis Bacon (1561–1626)

'Unlimited power is apt to corrupt the minds of those who possess it.'

William Pitt the Elder (1708–70)

'I repeat . . . that all power is a trust – that we are accountable for its exercise – that, from the people and for the people, all spring and must exist.'

Benjamin Disraeli, 1st Earl of Beaconsfield (1804–81)

'Power tends to corrupt and absolute power corrupts absolutely. Great men are almost always bad men.'

1st Baron Acton (1834–1902)

Think about it

- Consider and discuss the above quotations about power.
- Is there any quotation with which you particularly agree or disagree? If so, explain why.
- Try to provide your own quotation to describe an important aspect or view of power in contemporary society.

Power, obedience and ideas of liberty

The concepts of 'power' and 'obedience to authority' have been debated among both political philosophers and sociologists. Plato and Socrates, writing in Ancient Greece over 2000 years ago, considered these concepts to be central to the understanding of society. **Plato** (427–348 BC) wrote in *The Republic* about the ideal state: a community in which property was to be owned in common and which was governed by aristocrats or philosopher-kings, who would train the young. **Socrates** (469–399 BC), Plato's teacher and friend, rather than go against a wrong decision by a court of law that he was corrupting the morals of the youth of Athens, in Ancient Greece, committed suicide.

It is generally considered, however, that **Aristotle** (384–322 BC) was the founder of the scientific approach to political theory. His *Politics*, which classified governments as monarchies, aristocracies and democracies, according to whether they were controlled by one person, a select few or many people, combined an investigation of the facts with a critical inquiry into possible ideals; this provided a challenging model of political theory.

By the Middle Ages, issues relating to power and obedience had widened. **Niccolò Machiavelli** (1469–1527), the Italian philosopher and statesman, turned to power politics in his classic text *The Prince*, a realistic evaluation of the possibilities and problems associated with governments seeking to maintain power and obedience.

The English philosopher **Thomas Hobbes** (1588–1679) also emphasised power and obedience. In *Leviathan*, he argued that the monarch's power should be unlimited, because the state was based on a social contract in which people accepted a common superior power to protect them from their own brutish instincts. Another seventeenth-century English philosopher, **John Locke** (1632–1704), agreed with much of Hobbes's social-contract theory but stated that all people have certain 'natural rights' (to life, liberty and property) which cannot be taken from them unless the people agree: he argued that governments could be legitimately overthrown if they failed to protect these rights.

Locke's views can be detected in the USA's Declaration of Independence on 4 July 1776, which announced America's separation from Britain. Its main author was **Thomas Jefferson** (1743–1826). The famous preamble declared that all men are created equal and have inalienable rights to life, liberty and the pursuit of happiness. There followed a detailed list of acts of tyranny committed by King George III of England and his ministers and Parliament against the American people. The document has 56 signatures. The US Constitution was the second declaration of liberty to come out of the American Revolution. Its first ten amendments, known as the Bill of Rights, established guarantees of civil rights.

Shortly after the American Declaration of Independence, the French Revolution of 1789 ended the feudal system in France and introduced representative government. In the political thinking of the leaders of the French Revolution, liberty was seen as a natural right of man, a right to act without interference but requiring voluntary submission to necessary limitations in order that the benefits of organised social existence might be enjoyed. Challenging the theory of the divine right of kings to rule as representatives of God, this new theory held that the source of all governmental power was the people, and that tyranny began when the natural rights of men were violated. From the French Revolution came the Declaration of the Rights of Man and of the Citizen, which served as a model for most of the declarations of liberty adopted by European states in the nineteenth century.

More recently, the issue of national liberty has been expressed in the struggles of small states and colonies to be free from foreign political or economic control and to achieve their own independence. Closely related to this have been the efforts of national or racial minorities, such as the French residents of Quebec, Canada, to win political autonomy or independence within a country.

Issues related to individual liberty in the twentieth century include how to preserve and extend civil rights, such as freedom of speech and freedom of the press. As nations have grown in size and social complexity, governments have claimed greater powers to restrain individuals and groups. Critics of this development believe that it threatens individual liberty. Others believe that only if government is granted such powers can the complex problems of a heavily populated and increasingly mobile world be addressed.

A challenge to traditional ideas of liberty was the Russian Revolution of 1917. The Soviet state that resulted – in line with the Marxist theory on which it was based – held that all previous forms of liberty were ideologies of the ruling classes and did not benefit the masses. Real liberty was possible only by overturning class exploitation and installing collective ownership of the means of production. The initial success of the revolution raised hopes of a new period of human freedom. However, the economic disasters which followed and the terrorist dictatorship of the 'police state', especially under Joseph Stalin, led people to assume that communism leads inevitably to dictatorship.

Other threats to liberty during the twentieth century were posed by the totalitarian governments of Italy, Germany, Spain and the Soviet 'satellite' communist states of Eastern Europe. In these countries civil liberties were destroyed, the rights of the individual were subordinated to the requirements of the government, and those who defied official policies were terrorised into submission. Freedom was restored in Italy and in West Germany (now part of the United Federal Republic of Germany) after World War II, and in Spain after the death of its dictator, Francisco Franco, in 1975.

Totalitarianism

Totalitarianism refers to a political ideology in which all social, political, economic, intellectual, cultural and even spiritual activities serve the interests of the rulers and ruling ideology of the state. One form of totalitarian state is **autocracy**. The older autocracies were ruled by a monarch or other titled aristocrat who governed by a principle such as the divine right of kings. People could live and work in relative independence, provided they did not involve themselves in politics. The modern totalitarian state, however, is ruled by a political party, usually with an ideology claiming universal authority and not tolerating any rival claim. People are made dependent on the wishes and whims of the political party and its leaders.

Countries whose governments are usually seen as totalitarian include Germany under the National Socialism of Adolf Hitler; the Soviet Union under Joseph Stalin; and the People's Republic of China under the Communist rule of Mao Zedong (Mao Tse-Tung). Other governments that have been referred to as totalitarian include Italy under Benito Mussolini; North Korea under Kim Il-Sung; and Iraq under Saddam Hussein.

Think about it

- What distinguishes totalitarian governments from more democratic forms of government?
- In what ways may democratic governments seem to act in totalitarian ways?
- Do you think that the wider use of identity cards and fingerprinting could move a democratic state towards totalitarianism, or may it justify such practices as in the interests of its citizens?

Authority, legitimacy and ideology

Most of the terms associated with power and politics, although widely used, often prove difficult to define accurately. We have looked at the concepts of power and obedience. Now, in turning to 'authority', we find that a common understanding of this concept is based on the power to secure obedience from individuals and groups in society. Authority may taken many forms, ranging from how it may be exercised within the family, in the education system, to its use in legal and military contexts.

Authority   Authority is often accompanied by sets of rules, sanctions and symbols. Symbols of authority range from the academic gown to the legal wig, from the police car to the military tank, even the size or type of chair. In each case, the symbol carries the message that authority is legitimate power.

Max Weber on power and authority

The concepts of 'power' and 'authority' may seem much the same thing, with both requiring obedience. Weber, however, drew a distinction:

- Although power cannot be equated with physical force, the threat or the use of force may be important in terms of a position of power. The individual with power in a social relationship is generally free from restraint in their own actions and can shape those of others accordingly.
- Authority may be distinguished from power, since authority is *legitimate*. In other words its use is accepted as right and proper by those willing to obey. Their obedience is based on loyalty to the office held by a particular leader, the personal attraction of a leader or the benefits to be gained by general obedience to a political system.

It should be noted that Weber wrote in German, and that problems have arisen in translating his work into English. A paper by I. Walliman et al., *Misreading Weber...* (1980), identified eight different translations of Weber's writing, each carrying a different interpretation. Walliman et al. provide the following version of Weber's definition of power:

> 'Within a social relationship, power means any chance (no matter whereon this chance is based) to carry through one's* own will (even against resistance).
> (* individual or collective).'
>
> I. Walliman et al., 'Misreading Weber', *Sociology* vol. 14 no. 2 (1980)

P. McNeill and C. Townley, in *Fundamentals of Sociology* (1986), suggest that there are two broad concepts of power, both of which regard power as a property of a social system rather than of an individual acting in a social situation. It is on this point that many critics have taken issue with Weber (or with the most common translations of Weber's definition of power). Weber seems to be stating that 'power is the probability that one actor in a social relationship will be in a position to carry out his or her own will despite any resistance'. This suggests that power is what Y does to Z. Walliman et al. attempt in their translation to consider Weber's intention. They take out the reference to 'an actor' and use an asterisk to indicate that the 'one' in 'one's own will' could be an individual or a group. According to such an interpretation of Weber's writings, power can be exercised as a group phenomenon, in which actors are little more than agents.

Weber identified three sources of authority:

- **Traditional authority** is based on traditions and customs. It involves a belief in the right of the holder of a high social position to give commands, since that has become the established pattern of life. An example is **patrimonialism** in which the state becomes the extension of the personal household of the ruler; Weber refers to the Pharaohs of Ancient Egypt. Patrimonial authority is characterised by a centrally controlled state; modern attempts at patrimonial authority can be evidenced in the actions of Jean-Bedel Bokassa of Central Africa and of the former Shah of Iran.

Another form of traditional authority is **feudalism**, which involves a contractual relationship between rulers and their subjects. Feudalism in Britain in the Middle Ages saw all-powerful monarchs retaining their position through war, coercion (force) and the granting of lands to supporters. The film *Braveheart* is a dramatic depiction of feudalism in a thirteenth-century Scottish context.

- **Charismatic authority** is based on personal charisma or magnetism and the exceptional personal qualities of the holder. What matters is not whether the leader really possesses such qualities, but rather that the followers believe that this is the case. A charismatic leader is capable of diverting people from traditional patterns of allegiance into a new course. Two obvious examples of charismatic authority are Jesus Christ and Mohammed, each of whom played a major role in challenging the social order of the time and establishing new patterns of belief.

  In the 1950s and 1960s, American political scientists in particular tended to label prominent political figures as charismatic leaders; the persons so chosen included Nasser in Egypt, Nkrumah in Ghana, Sukarno in Indonesia, Tito in Yugoslavia and John Kennedy in the USA. John F. Kennedy (1917–63) was elected the youngest ever President of the USA in 1961, and held charismatic authority, making direct appeals for public commitment with particular attention to civil rights, until his assassination in November 1963 in Dallas, Texas.

  The attempt to create the image of a charismatic figure is certainly discernible in the personality cults of Stalin (the USSR), Mao Tse-Tung (China), Kim Il-Sung (North Korea) and Fidel Castro (Cuba), and many leaders in developing countries use their press to cultivate an image of dynamism and importance. However, while Kennedy's premature death helped to enshrine his 'charismatic' image, the subsequent fall from power of several of the other leaders who had been seen as charismatic casts some doubt on the use of the term. It is now more often used as a description for a leader whose attractive personality or photogenic appearance contribute to a 'media-friendly' style.

- **Rational-legal authority** is based on the law or written rules, and is likely to be found in modern states such as Britain. Those making the rules are seen as having the right to do so, and wider society would expect to benefit from their obedience to the rules. As with traditional authority, it is the office rather than the individual that commands respect and obedience, and decisions are made and applied by a rational and impersonal bureaucracy. It is from rational-legal authority that British political leaders have stressed the role of the **electoral mandate**: if a policy is contained in the winning party's election manifesto, then, it is argued, it should be put into practice as a legitimate sequel. (This ignores the fact that more people in total probably voted against the party and its manifesto than supported it.)

It is possible to identify institutions, such as the Church, the monarchy or the Cabinet, which consist of a mixture of all three of Weber's forms of authority. By definition, forms of familial authority, such as patriarchy and matriarchy, rely on tradition, although these also attempt to gain the support of rational-legal sources. The Director of Public Prosecutions or the Inland Revenue tend to have rational-legal authority, whereas the rugby captain or the televangelist (see Unit 12) claim charismatic authority.

Notwithstanding Weber's comments, the distinction between power (which depends on physical force) and authority (which may take one or a mixture of the forms described above) is not always clear cut. Power backed by force can become 'routinised' into accepted authority; the authority of today's political leader may be the power of yesterday's terrorist. Power can become authority by means of ritual and ceremony which routinise the exercise of power by one group over another, making it part of everyday expectations.

The routinisation of legitimated power

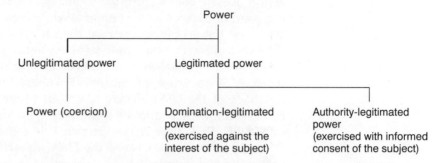

> '*What makes the difference between "naked power" and authority or domination is legitimation – a justification of power which is regarded as acceptable (by both superiors and subordinates).*
> *Weber provides three kinds of legitimacy – hence three kinds of authority: traditional, charismatic and rational-legal. Authority is legitimated power. "Legitimation" does not necessarily imply that someone is cynically manipulating someone else. The term refers to what people consider to be justifiable reasons for some action or institution.*'
>
> Adapted from Sociology "A" level 1990, National Extension College Trust Ltd.

Weber's three forms of authority were **ideal-type**; they would rarely, if ever, exist in their pure form. However, they do offer a useful insight into the sources and nature of authority, and perhaps help to explain the behaviour of political leaders who have sought to conform to aspects of them.

Legitimacy   Legitimacy, as the word suggests, is based on what is legitimate or legal; it is a distinctive feature of being lawful, for example a lawful political action. Legitimacy is often created by common consent; the acceptance of the legal rules adopted reinforces their legitimacy. However, although it may seem fairly straightforward, legitimacy needs also to be seen in relation to particular legal rules in particular societies at specific points of time. For example, poll taxes levied on individuals, regardless of their income, wealth or other payment of taxes, have led to challenges to their legitimacy. Resentment over a poll tax introduced in England in June 1381 by King Richard II caused what has become known as the Peasants' Revolt. The leader of the peasants, Wat Tyler, marched on London to force the King to abolish this poll tax, which had been imposed to fund a war against France. Similarly, the controversial community charge (dubbed the 'poll tax'), introduced over 600 years later by Margaret Thatcher and intended to spread local tax burdens across all residents, was reformed after considerable social unrest and widespread political marches: it contributed to Thatcher's resignation as Prime Minister in November 1990.

Legitimacy may be associated with particular countries, governments and political acts. If a government is overthrown by another political group, the response – particularly in the case of a bloodthirsty, military coup – may be that this is an illegitimate act: such extreme political action usually goes against the legal constitution of a country. However, if a coup does receive the support of the people whom it claims to represent, and the people accept this, then it achieves legitimacy. States may achieve legitimacy once diplomatic recognition by other countries and international organisations has become acknowledged, as evidenced recently in the case of Eastern European countries and the former republics of the USSR. There is a wide range of national constitutions establishing their countries' legitimacy. The United Kingdom's constitution dates back over many centuries, but there exist no written legal documents, as in the case of the USA; nevertheless, both countries are nationally and internationally accepted as legitimate.

Ideology The term 'ideology' refers to any system of ideas and beliefs, often political in nature, held by an individual or like-minded group. More specifically, it has become associated with any system of ideas which legitimates the subordination of one group by another. The concept was first coined by Antoine Destutt de Tracy (1755–1836), who used the word simply to refer to the 'science of ideas' in the period of social optimism in France leading up to the French Revolution (1789–92). He conceived it in terms of a comprehensive encyclopaedic knowledge, able to break down prejudice, and of use in social reform. Ironically, in a complete reversal of its initial usage by Destutt de Tracy, ideology has since come to mean a particular set of beliefs, often dogmatically held.

This modern interpretation of the concept of ideology developed during the nineteenth century, when it gained theoretical importance. In *The German Ideology* and other writings, Karl Marx and Friedrich Engels use the term to describe an essentially flawed or prejudiced interpretation of reality which fails to take account of fundamental material conditions and constraints. Marx and Engels stressed two key factors in relation to ideology:

- It provides a world view based on the interests of one group – the ruling class.
- The world view provided by a ruling ideology is a distorted one, since the interests of the ruling class represent the interests of a minority group rather than humanity in general.

During the twentieth century the concept of ideology has had enormous effects on world civilisations. Examples of ideological conflict include the 'crusade against fascism' in World War II and the Cuban Crisis of 1962 in which President Kennedy of the USA alleged that Russian defensive missile sites were being constructed in Cuba. This led to a blockade and international crisis until President Kruschev of Russia agreed to dismantle the missile bases. In ideological terms, Cuban communism has remained an embarrassment to American capitalism because of the geographical closeness of the two countries and the continued Cuban involvement in left-wing regimes and revolutionary movements. In the post-World War II period, the ideological conflict between the USA and the USSR, known as the Cold War, could be viewed as one of the most extensive worldwide political, economic and psychological struggles.

Think about it

- What norms and values have you accepted from an early age, and how have these influenced your personal development?
- How might your norms and values have influenced your own political action (or lack of it)?
- Do you think that feminism and environmentalism are beliefs or ideologies? What distinctions would you make between beliefs and ideologies?

The exercise of constraint

We have already noted how writers such as Hobbes and Locke considered that a social contract formed the basis of political decision-making: there is the need for people to accept a common superior power who acts in their interests and in the greater interest of the country as a whole. Therefore, the exercise of constraint in order to allow political processes to operate may be seen as justifiable, even, in some cases, to the extent of using coercion or force. Quite often the threat of fines or imprisonment places a firm constraint on people. Most countries, regardless of how democratic the government may be, use some form of constraint: inevitably individuals or groups will not agree with some laws, by-laws, rules, conventions, etc., and such individuals must be constrained or forced to conform in the interests and security of others.

If an individual makes a personal decision to join a club or a college by volunteering to do so, a social contract is formed and rules are freely taken on board. If subsequently those rules become unacceptable to the individual, who no longer wishes to comply with, for example, rules relating to regular attendance or no smoking areas, that individual may then need to leave or run the risk of being expelled. It is because countries, for the most part, do not hold these kinds of options, that they build a system to exercise constraint and, if necessary, force people into compliance.

Where there are varying definitions of power and constraint, the ones which will be dominant will be the definitions supported by those members who are already in institutional or socially defined positions of power in the society. It is important to note that the dominant groups tend to define power in functionalist terms. Interactionists remind us that the social order is dependent on the way we define the social situation. We will look at these different approaches in more detail below.

Think about it

- Think of an incident or occasion, in your own experience, in which one person's power prevailed over the group. Did you exercise constraint or challenge such power?
- What were the characteristics of such power and constraint?

Different approaches to power and authority

This section provides a basic outline of the different approaches to power and authority. Theories relating to the nature of power are looked at in more detail on pages 602–609.

The functionalist approach to power and authority

According to the American functionalist, Talcott Parsons, society is based on value consensus, or a system of shared values providing legitimacy to those selected to make the decisions. In this, functional, approach, obedience to the decision-makers follows, because they embody the wishes of the whole society and make decisions according to agreed rules in the interests of the majority.

This is a similar approach to Weber's concept of rational-legal authority, whereby people obey the rules of others because they consider that the decision-makers hold the right to make those rules. Nevertheless, the functionalist idea of consensus is problematic in contemporary societies, which are complex: it seems unlikely that shared values can in reality be shared by all. For example, a decision to build a new road system may please motorists but not environmentalists who may actively campaign to resist the development. The functionalist approach may explain why individuals obey rules virtually without challenge most of the time, but it does not provide an explanation for the exceptions. Furthermore, critics of Parsons and the functionalist approach consider that such an approach to power is both simplistic and naive. They argue that it merely provides a sociological backdrop to rationalise the views of the political power-holders. They hold that Parsons has failed to understand how power is often used to promote sectional interests rather than serving society as a whole.

The interactionist approach to power and authority

The American sociologist, George C. Homans, considers that power is based on the rewards which an individual obtains from a leader, such as material goods or symbolic status. This approach was developed by Peter Blau in *On the Nature of Organizations* (1974), which notes how socialisation trains an individual to feel a moral obligation to repay benefits received. In a stable relationship, what is given and what is received should balance out, so that neither party feels overly obliged to the other. If this is not the case and the relationship is to continue, then the main beneficiary will feel an obligation towards the other and will become willing to equalise the relationship by obeying an instruction of the other. Hence a relationship can develop similar to Weber's idea of feudalism, whereby each party honours an obligation. Blau terms this **socialised morality**.

Although the interactionist approach can be used to interpret many examples of obedience to authority, it provides only a partial explanation. It overlooks all those authority relationships which are brought about not by choice but by the deliberate coercion of one person or group by those who hold the authority to constrain, or if necessary coerce, by the use of sanction or force.

The conflict approach to power and authority

In the conflict approach adopted by Marxists, wealth ownership leads to control over the coercive apparatus of the state. Anarchists go even further and stress the fundamental illegitimacy of power. A number of Marxist writers have considered elements of coercion by the state to enforce obedience.

Marxists, in particular the French neo-Marxist Louis Althusser (1918–90), have also drawn out the significance of factors that make the threat or use of force unnecessary to obtain obedience. Naked force itself is fragile, and as soon as people recognise this, domination cannot be maintained. It is necessary therefore to persuade people to obey the system. Althusser argued that capitalist power was maintained through the state in two ways:

- by **repressive state apparatuses** (**RSA**s) such as the police, army and courts;
- by **ideological state apparatuses** (**ISA**s); he points to the role of the family, the school, the mass media, the church, etc. in spreading ideas that legitimate the social order with positive reasons provided for obedience.

S. Bowles and H. Gintis show how the school system rewards conformity and punishes innovation and rebellion so that obedience to the authority of a future employer becomes 'natural' (see Unit 4, page 187).

Conflict approaches adopted by both Marxist and non-Marxist writers emphasise the role of coercion or the background threat of it. The Marxist approach views the oppression of a whole class by both physical force and the **hegemony** or domination of ideas. A major contributor to the debate on hegemony was the Italian Marxist Antonio Gramsci (see page 607).

Hegemony is an important concept within the Marxist approach. It originally referred to the dominance of one state over a group of others. The conquest of European territory by Napoleon was seen to have created a French hegemony over continental Europe. The term has since become more commonly used to refer to a group holding power, either by force or by shared agreement, and to the ideology which is associated with that group and which is therefore dominant over others.

A radical alternative view of power and authority

Steven Lukes, in *Power, A Radical View* (1974), suggests that power has three dimensions, which he refers to as the 'three faces of power':

- **Success in decision-making**, in which individuals or groups hold different policy preferences; they influence decision-making on a range of issues. Those who become most successful in getting their own way will have most power. In reality, the usual situation in Western democracies is that no one individual or group dominates decision-making but that several important groups wield political power.
- **Managing the agenda (or non-decision-making)**, in which political power may be used to obstruct the discussion of some issues and prevent decisions being made. Individuals or groups with power may manage the political agenda of debate to prevent alternative actions or to limit the range of discussion. In effect, any decisions become non-decisions. There are parallels here with agenda setting in the mass media, discussed in Unit 6 (see page 298).

- **Managing desires (or manipulating the wishes of others)**, in which desires can be shaped and the wishes of others manipulated. Individuals or groups may be persuaded to accept, or even made to desire, something which may not be in their interests, for example directorships in tobacco or military arms companies. Thus the income and status of the powerful may be further increased. The 'cash for questions' scandal in July 1994, for example, revealed that two Conservative MPs had each accepted £1000 in return for putting a written question to a minister. As a result, the Nolan Committee, led by Lord Justice Nolan, was formed:

> 'to examine current concerns about the standards of conduct
> of all holders of public office, including arrangements relating
> to financial and commercial activities ...'

The Nolan Report, published in May 1995, recommended that MPs should disclose their employment contracts and earnings from outside interests.

Further views of power and authority

The constant or fixed sum approach   This maintains that there is a fixed (or even, some consider, zero) amount of power and that the more of it that one group holds, the less there is available to the rest of society. An unequal distribution of power furthers the sectional interests held by some at the expense of others.

The variable sum approach   This was put forward by Talcott Parsons in *Sociological Theory and Modern Society* (1967). It rejects the above and maintains that power can increase or decrease in relation to how effectively a government can achieve its goals. For example, in Serbia, in 1996–97, anti-government demonstrations brought its capital, Belgrade, to a standstill: those who were not officially in power prevented the achievement of social goals by those who were. According to the variable sum approach, the power held by any one person or interest group can sometimes seem to be outside the control of those who officially wield power.

Other sociologists, including Michael Mann in *The Sources of Social Power* (1993), claim that modern institutions, for example political establishments, military forces and business corporations, have increased their power in the contemporary world and have achieved greater 'organisational effectiveness'.

Think about it

- What examples can you think of, other than those provided, to illustrate Steven Lukes's 'three faces of power'?
- Do you consider, in relation to the sociological views expressed so far in this unit, that there may be further faces or dimensions of power and authority?
- Think about the points in the following table and try to provide examples to illustrate both functionalist and Marxist approaches to power, in relation to social relations and who benefits. Can you think of any 'typifying phrases' which match your further examples?

Functionalist and conflict approaches to power and authority		
	Functionalist	**Marxist**
Social relations:	Based on consensus, shared values	Based on conflict, exploitation
Who benefits:	Everyone	The group with power
Typifying phrases:	'Let's all pull together and we'll all benefit.'	'If you win, I lose.' '… you have nothing to lose but your chains.'
Emphasis on:	Liberty	Equality

Politics in relation to the institutions of state and government

The state and its government may be seen as forming the basis for political power and authority in most advanced societies. 'Stateless societies', which do not possess a central political system nor even a defined location, such as the Palestinians in the Middle East or the Kurds in northern Iraq, do exist; however, here we consider what may be termed the modern state and its government.

Weber provided a definition for the state:

> 'a human community that successfully claims the monopoly of the legitimate use of physical force within a given territory.'
> Max Weber, *Economy and Society: An Outline of Interpretive Sociology* (University of California Press, 1978)

In modern Britain, the 'given territory' or specific geographical area consists of England, Scotland, Wales and Northern Ireland. The government, in Westminster, has within its power the legitimate right to use force to suppress terrorism in Northern Ireland, for example. The force used by other groups to achieve their ends – the Irish Republican Army (IRA) or the notorious Kray twins, for example – is not considered legitimate. Only the state and its government can use the legal system, via the police and the criminal courts, to imprison people; only the state and its government can declare war on another state.

The idea that modern nation states developed in Europe with the rise of capitalism formed the basis of Weber's classic text, *The Protestant Ethic and the Spirit of Capitalism* (see Unit 12, page 622). For Weber, bureaucratically organised states, based on rationalisation, arose as the result of the development of capitalism. Written rules and efficient management through bureaucratic procedures developed along with capitalist states. Such states developed centralised systems with elected or specifically appointed specialists; there was less reliance on the traditional forms of arrangement based on birthright or custom.

Marxists, particularly, have criticised Weber's definition of the state. They consider that a state may refer also to insitutions which maintain ruling-class dominance, in other words the capitalist state. For Marxists, the modern state provides political decision-making processes which permit capitalists to accumulate wealth.

Institutions of state and government in modern Britain

The state

'The state' refers to the permanent institutions with political power within a defined geographical area. Such institutions do not change when a new government is elected (or new political leaders). State institutions in Britain include:

- bodies which oversee laws, for example the courts;
- public bodies (or 'quangos': quasi-autonomous non-governmental organisations), which carry out many of the functions of government, for example allocating public funds;
- local and regional government, which make decisions for themselves or carry out services decided upon by central government;
- Parliament (even though its personnel may change – particularly at general elections);
- the civil service, which maintains stability (unstable governments do not have a civil service);
- the armed forces, including the security or intelligence services, which hold a key role in the protection of the state and its citizens.

In Britain, the Head of State is the monarch, the one person who has the authority to speak on behalf of the state. However, although the Queen may have the authority to speak for all her subjects, it is not expected in a modern democracy that she should do so without guidance; she is held accountable to the people for what she does. In the majority of modern states, the Head of State is elected and is normally known as 'President'.

The government

'The government' refers to elected ministers who claim the authority to run the state (see above). Whereas the institutions of the state are permanent, the government can change. It represents a temporary majority in Parliament, based on the results of the previous general election. By their votes, the people give it a temporary authority to control the institutions of the state and pass laws according to a manifesto put before them at the election.

The idea that the government controls and runs the institutions of the state does not provide a full understanding of the relationship between the two. The following points need also to be taken into account:

- During its term of office, the British government effectively *is* the state. All major national decisions – the timing of elections, the appointment of ministers, the taking of military action – are made by the government.
- The Head of State (the monarch) has reserve powers which may be used in exceptional circumstances. Thus the Queen *could* dismiss a minister or the whole government, and could refuse to give royal assent to laws; in practice, however, this rarely if ever occurs.
- Parliament has the power to veto government legislation. Though rarely used, this is a real power.
- Membership of the European Union has made the situation more complicated. In some areas of jurisdiction, such as trade and environmental protection, the Council of European Ministers is the govern-

ment of the UK. Apart from leaving the EU, there is nothing the British government or Parliament can do about the Council's decisions where there is no national veto available. Similarly, the permanent institutions of the EU – the European Commission, the European Parliament and the European Court of Justice – have now become part of the state.

Summary of ideas of power and authority

- Different approaches to power and authority define and use concepts such as authority, legitimacy and ideology in different ways. Hence they hold different views and arrive at different conclusions about how power is gained and maintained, particularly in advanced Western societies.
- Many sociologists view the state as the main legitimate source of power. Analysis of politics in relation to the institutions of state and government is an important but complex task.
- Various political systems put forward different definitions and sources of power and authority in modern societies. Even democracy takes a variety of forms; and some see it as a vague concept embraced in different ways in different nation states.

Political parties in the UK since the 1970s

The Conservative Party

During the 1970s a group of leading Conservatives met at Selsdon Park, Surrey, and set out a new conservative strategy against the background of the early signs of economic recession. Their 'Selsdon Man' views favoured:

- a reduction in state intervention in the economy;
- a move towards a freer market economy;
- tax cuts;
- controls over trade union power.

Conservative Prime Minister Edward Heath (1970–74) was persuaded to adopt these strategies but economic crises brought them to a halt despite their popularity within the party. The next Conservative Prime Minister, Margaret Thatcher (1979–90) continued the policies and the label 'New Right' took hold. During the 1980s and 1990s, internal divisions between the right and moderate wings of the Conservative Party increased, with the picture further complicated by divisions over policy on Britain's place in the European Union. John Major's leadership (1990–97) ended with the massive Conservative defeat in the general election of 1997 and he was succeeded by William Hague, who promised a 'fresh start and a fresh future' for the Conservative Party.

The Labour Party

The decline of the Labour Party in the late 1970s was reinforced by their election defeats in 1979 and 1983. The initial reaction to the Conservatives' 'New Right' movement was a swing to the left in the Labour Party under the leadership of Michael Foot (1980–84). In 1981 a splinter group formed the Social Democratic Party (SDP), which attempted to re-establish the traditional Labour ideology – for a time, in partnership with the Liberal Party – to replace Labour as the major opposition party. The attempt failed, however. In 1984 Neil Kinnock replaced Foot as the Labour leader, bringing more moderate views back to the fore and 'purging' extremists on the left of the party (the 'Militant' wing). His successors after Labour's third successive election defeat in 1992 (John Smith, 1990–94, and Tony Blair from 1994) continued along the moderate route, Smith broadening the democratic base of union politics and Blair pushing the party into a centre-left position with a move away from the traditional commitment to public ownership of industry and the utilities. Such moves, and public appeal, helped Tony Blair to secure 419 seats in parliament, and a huge majority of MPs in the House of Commons in 1997.

The Liberal/Liberal Democrat Party

After the brief appearance of the SDP (see above), the collaboration between the new party and the Liberals led to a merger and the renaming of the party as the Liberal Democrats in 1988.

Under the leadership of Paddy Ashdown (from 1988), support for the Party among the national electorate remained at a fairly steady 15–20 per cent, despite some dramatic victories in by-elections and a good power base in local government. However, despite obtaining only 17 per cent of the votes in the general election of 1997, they did achieve a record number of 46 MPs in the House of Commons. The Party's policies, though emphasising the civil rights and social responsibilities of the individual, are not ideologically attached to either the 'left' or 'right'. During the Labour Party's shift towards the right in the mid-1990s, the Liberal Democrats became perceived as the representatives of some of the more traditional 'left' values, for example in their seeking to maintain the Welfare State so as to provide a reasonable living standard for all citizens and to protect more vulnerable groups. Another traditional 'plank' of the Liberal platform has been their campaign for electoral reform, aiming to replace the current 'first-past-the-post' system with a system of proportional representation. They also propose (in a policy also traditionally associated with the Labour Party) that the House of Lords should be replaced by an elected second chamber.

'Minority' political parties

Formed in 1985 (from the former Ecology Party), the Green Party's highest level of support came in the European elections in 1989 when it gained 15 per cent of the (European-wide) voters' support. This led to its environmental policies being taken more seriously by the larger parties, particularly by the Liberal Democrats.

In the UK, nationalist parties developed in the 1970s, reflecting the frustration felt by the Welsh and Scottish people at being subject to London-based policies imposed by a party which only a very small minority of Welsh and Scottish voters had supported. The parties all have a greater degree of political and economic independence from the UK as their main goal. By 1974 the Scottish National Party had gained over 30 per cent of Scottish votes and Plaid Cymru, the Welsh nationalist party, 11 per cent of the votes in Welsh constituencies. During the 1980s, such support fluctuated but it grew again in the 1990s as disillusion with the Conservative Party – perceived as mainly Anglo-centric – increased, as did doubts about the Labour Party's real commitment to granting any meaningful level of independence to the separate nations. (For more on the nature and role of nationalist parties, see Unit 9 pages 467–90.)

Other minor parties in the UK include extreme groups such as the British National Party (BNP) on the right and the Socialist Workers' Party on the left. Although both parties (particularly the BNP) have had some (controversial) success at local government level, neither has ever had a candidate elected as an MP.

There are also some single-issue parties, the largest of which (unless the Green Party may be seen as single-issue) in recent years has been the Referendum Party, established by business tycoon Sir James Goldsmith (1933–97), who campaigned for a referendum on Britain's future place within the European Union. Despite a high profile campaign in the 1997 election, the Referendum Party gained no seats, but did receive about 2 per cent of the votes.

UK general election results 1974–1997: the number of seats and percentage of votes won by each of the main parties											
	1974		1979		1983		1987		1992		1997	
	seats	votes (%)	seats	votes (%)	seats	votes (%)	seats	votes (%)	seats	votes (%)	seats	votes (%)
Conservative	277	36	339	44	397	42	376	43	336	42	165	31
Labour	319	39	269	37	209	28	229	32	271	35	419	47
Lib/LibDem	11	18	11	14	23	25	22	23	20	18	46	19
Scots Nats*	11	30	2	17	2	12	3	14	3	22	6	22
Plaid Cymru*	3	11	2	8	2	8	3	7	4	9	4	9

* Percentage of vote only in Scotland and Wales respectively

The functions of political parties

Decision-making processes

Decision-making processes amongst the electorate and political parties may be seen to work in the following ways:

- Electoral processes influence party policies. In order to gain electoral success and govern, political parties need to establish party manifestos and programmes reflecting what they consider to be the desires and interests of the electorate.
- Failure by the ruling party, in its policy-making, to reflect the interests of the people may allow new parties to emerge, as in the case of the Social Democrats referred to above. The policies of new parties, even if representing the people only on a single issue, such as the Referendum Party, can have an effect on electoral processes.
- Disregarding the opinion of the electorate can be to the peril of a political party, particularly if it forms the government. The Conservative Party won the 1987 election with a majority of 102 seats, but following its implementation of the unpopular 'poll tax' (see pages 571–2), it was defeated in a series of by-elections and by 1992 its majority had fallen to 21 seats. Sleaze issues also damaged the Conservative Party, as demonstrated by the defeat of Neil Hamilton, at Tatton, by the television reporter Martin Bell, in the 1997 general election.

- It is dangerous for political parties, or their members, to represent sectional interests, as evidenced by the Nolan Report, 1995 (see page 576). To retain credibility, it is necessary for a broad spectrum of interests to be represented.

Political parties transform wide-ranging opinions on a variety of topics into a narrower range of choices, generally presented in opposition to those of the other major party or parties. It is claimed that parties make possible the representation of the mass of the people in the following ways:

- By selecting candidates for national or local office, they enable the electorate to make a clear choice between 'opposed' parties.
- They put forward policies which the electors can evaluate and vote for if they approve.
- They unite the mass of the people on national matters, rather than simply expressing local opinions.
- They offer an avenue for the politically ambitious person who wishes to seek office and/or election.

Political parties, then, are supposed to create opinion, to aggregate it, to coordinate a series of policies and to provide a forum for the selection and promotion of potential leaders. In order to win elections, no party can afford to be seen only to consider the views of one class or sector of the electorate: the need to win elections acts as a pressure towards consensus. Since World War II, this has often led the two major parties in the UK to pursue goals within 'the middle ground' – a policy which party activists tend to find insufficiently radical.

From a sociological viewpoint competition between two or more political parties forms a healthy element in a representative parliamentary democracy – as stated below by the American functionalist Seymour M. Lipset:

> *'Democracy in a complex society may be defined as a political system which supplies regular constitutional opportunities for managing the governing officials, and a social mechanism which permits the largest possible part of the population to influence major decisions by choosing among contenders for political office and decision making processes.'*
> Seymour M. Lipset, *Political Man* (Mercury Books, 1963)

Think about it

- Who do you know who 'transforms wide-ranging opinions on a variety of topics into a narrower range of choices'? Consider some issues, such as the benefits of staying on at school or college or a new job for a family member. Which individuals regularly form alliances and with what impact on family decisions? Who has the role of 'ideas person' whose ideas others debate and note? Who points out the long-term implications of a suggestion? (Is it the 'instrumental' father-figure (see Unit 3, page 136)? Who decides when the growing children can take responsibilities in different arenas?
- How well do you consider that the representation of the mass of the people is made possible by the four different processes given above?
- To what extent do you think a representative parliamentary democracy exists in Britain?

Pressure groups and interest groups

Pressure groups attempt to influence political policy-making without seeking to form a government. Pressure groups normally concentrate on specific issues, while political parties need to cover a broad range of issues. Because pressure groups often draw attention to issues which might otherwise be overlooked or even ignored by the major political parties, they may be seen as an essential element of democracy.

Categorising pressure groups

Although pressure groups vary in their aims, organisations and methods, traditionally they have been broadly categorised as either promotional or protective groups:

- **Promotional (or 'cause') groups** support a specific cause or moral concern, rather than safeguard the interests of, say, a sectional group of society. Some promotional groups seek to recruit large numbers to the cause to impress MPs; others put more emphasis on the quality of support for their cause. In recent decades there has been a rapid increase in support for environmental causes. Friends of the Earth is a well-known example of a promotional pressure group concerned with protecting the environment.

- **Protective (or 'sectional interest') groups** represent the interests of a section of society. Such a group's main purpose is to protect its members; its membership is normally restricted. Examples include the National Farmers Union and professional interest groups or associations such as the BMA (British Medical Association).

Selected pressure groups: aims and membership		
Pressure group	**Main aims**	**Members (approx.)**
Friends of the Earth (FoE)	To preserve and protect the environment	200,000
League Against Cruel Sports	To end blood sports	30,000
Liberty	To defend and extend human rights and civil liberties in the UK	5,000
Motor Cycle Action Group	To campaign on behalf of motorcycles	22,000
National Farmers Union (NFU)	To look after the interests of farmers	150,000
Royal Society for the Protection of Birds (RSPB)	To conserve and protect birds and their environment	850,000
Worldwide Fund for Nature (WWF)	To preserve and protect wildlife species and their habitat	200,000

Think about it

- Based on the information given in the box above state whether each pressure group might be considered a promotional (or 'cause') group or a protective (or 'sectional interest') group.

Whilst it might seem convenient to divide pressure groups into promotional and protective interest groups, many groups have shared characteristics:

- Some promotional (or 'cause') groups may share protective (or 'sectional') issues, for example the Council for the Protection of Rural England (CPRE) which sees itself as campaigning on behalf of future generations for the preservation of National Parks, Green Belt areas and features of the countryside such as hedgerows and woodlands which are essential for the ecological system.
- Some protective (or 'sectional') groups may share promotional (or 'cause') issues, for example Amnesty International, which campaigns for greater awareness and observance of human rights, particularly on issues of political imprisonment, the death penalty, torture and political asylum.
- It is dangerous to assume that 'promotional' groups are morally superior to 'sectional' groups. When politicians and others refer to 'vested interests' and those with 'axes to grind', they are usually pointing at sectional interests. However, democratic society needs to take account of the views of those who may lose out through government decisions.

Pressure groups of either type often build up a wealth of specialist knowledge; this can be useful to government policy-makers. Friends of the Earth, for example, have specialist knowledge and data on the situation and protection of endangered animal and plant species and the natural environment, which could be used as a factual basis for the construction of policy on pollution, if the political motivation is there.

Insider and outsider groups

Wyn Grant, in *Pressure Groups, Politics and Democracy in Britain* (1989) prefers the use of the terms '**insider**' and '**outsider**' groups:

- Some protective groups may be considered insider groups, since they may be consulted by the government and their views invited during policy-making – for example, the Royal National Institute for the Blind (RNIB).
- Some promotional groups, for example the Royal Society for the Protection of Birds (RSPB), may similarly be considered insider groups. However, promotional groups seem most likely to be outsider groups with less access to those in power.
- Outsider groups may try to become insiders by collecting information and data and by carrying out well documented campaigns, which may raise their profile and esteem among MPs – for example the Ramblers Association.
- There is a price to pay for being an insider group, since such groups may seek to constrain or even 'screen out' excessive demands from their members which a government may view as unreasonable or unacceptable.
- 'Prisoner' groups are groups which find it difficult to break away from an insider relationship with the government, either because they depend on government sponsorship – for example English Heritage – or because they are in the public sector.

Grant's categorisation of
pressure groups

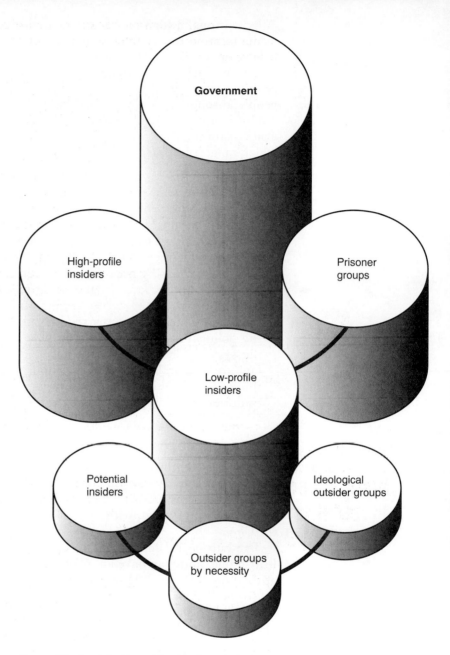

Source: Wyn Grant, 'Insider and Outsider Pressure Groups', *Social Studies Review*, January 1990

Wyn Grant distinguishes between low-profile and high-profile insider groups, according to the extent to which a pressure group puts itself in the public eye via the media. A low-profile strategy might concentrate on background links and contracts with government rather than statements via the mass media. Few groups would seek such a low-profile, almost secretive arrangement, since the media helps to set the political agenda. However, some groups prefer not to use the media so as not to spoil their close relations with policy-makers.

By contrast, a high-profile strategy involves the conscious use of the media to project or enhance the group's position. For example, the Confederation of British Industry (CBI) changed its low-profile strategy, based on reaching 'informed opinion' via the quality press, to a high-profile strategy with attempts to reach the rank-and-file, i.e. ordinary people, through mass circulation newspapers and television.

Outsider groups tend to be broader-based than insider groups. Unlike insider groups, they are not bound by any constraints and so have a wider range of strategies open to them. Grant places outsider groups into three categories:

- 'Potential insider groups', a transitional category, would like to become insider groups but face the problem of gaining the government's attention for consultation on certain policy areas. They may seek to mount a successful campaign via the media and parliamentary contacts.
- 'Outsider groups by necessity' may seek to become insider groups but may lack political knowledge and understanding of how the political system operates.
- 'Ideological outsider groups' tend not to become closely involved with the political system because they seek to challenge, or even change, the system. They may consider that certain practices, permitted by law, are so morally wrong that virtually *any* preventative action is justified. Various animal liberation groups have carried out raids on laboratories and even placed bombs in retail stores.

A peculiarly British phenomenon

Whilst no categorisation of pressure groups can be watertight, the distinction between insiders and outsiders seems to represent a system traditionally peculiar to British culture and the British style of government. Certainly the distinction would seem less appropriate to a relatively 'open' political system, with more access for pressure groups, such as in the USA.

The European Union seems to operate a more open system than the British one, and may have an increasing influence as decisions are taken at the European level. However, the transfer of decision-making authority to the European institutions is a slow and complex process, and the national arena will continue to be important throughout the 1990s and beyond.

Summary of pressure groups

- Pressure groups are organisations with a formal structure.
- Pressure groups have precise goals and seek to influence others.
- Pressure groups do not concern themselves with a full range of policy issues; their goals are narrower.
- Pressure groups are not political parties or parts of such parties.
- Pressure groups operate on any public decision-making body to which it is appropriate.

Supra-national organisations and globalisation

Supra-national institutions and organisations are those which have powers over and above the powers of any member-nation's government. Examples include the North Atlantic Treaty Organisation (NATO), the United Nations Organisation (usually referred to as the UN) and the European Union (EU). Britain belongs to all three organisations and all, to some degree, influence its foreign policy – and some aspects of its domestic policy.

The European Union

Probably the most debated example of supra-nationalism, in Britain, is the EU with its mixture of supra-national and intergovernmental institutions (see Unit 9). Such a mixture means that, on some issues, member states can oppose proposals which they feel are disadvantageous, although on others, decisions are made at the European level and must be adopted by member states. As we saw in Unit 9, policy-making in the EU is carried out by five main institutions – the Council of Ministers, the European Commission, the European Parliament, the European Court of Justice and the European Council of Heads of Government.

Population of member states of the EU and the number of votes each has in the Council of Ministers

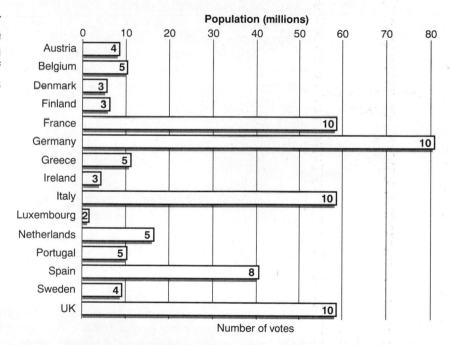

Source: Adapted from the *Guardian*, 16 March 1994

Background to the EU

Winston Churchill, as British Prime Minister, first put forward the idea of a united Europe in a speech on 19 September 1946, strange as that may now seem in relation to the hesitations expressed by his successors, particularly Margaret Thatcher, John Major and many senior Conservative politicians. Churchill suggested a 'United States of Europe'. Despite Churchill's initial suggestion, however, Britain actually declined subsequently to become a founding member of the first European body, the European Economic Community (EEC) in 1957.

Britain joins the EEC Britain's first application to join the EEC was in 1961. Negotiations continued until 1963 when the French President, Charles de Gaulle, rejected Britain's application. Britain applied again in 1967, but this was again vetoed by de Gaulle. Only after de Gaulle's retirement in 1969 was the British government able to negotiate its entry into the EEC. In 1971 Edward Heath, the Conservative Prime Minister, held talks with de Gaulle's successor, Georges Pompidou. In 1972, Heath signed the Treaty of Accession and on 1 January 1973, Britain became an EEC member.

The EEC referendum, 1975 British unease about EEC membership remained, however, in particular for three reasons:

- Many British politicians did not share the vision of Europe enthusiasts such as Jacques Delors (later President of the European Commission 1985–94) who looked forward to the creation of a European supra-national structure.
- Since Britain had not been a founding member, it had to accept existing policies which it had not created.
- There was a price to pay for membership in terms of Britain's trading links with non-EEC countries, in particular its wide Commonwealth; trade with non-EEC countries was penalised.

After the British general election in 1974, the newly elected Labour government agreed to renegotiate Britain's terms of membership and held a referendum. The referendum, held in 1975, resulted in a 67 per cent vote in favour of remaining in the EEC. However, misgivings persisted, as Britain's contribution to EEC funds was high, trade with non-EEC countries was still penalised, and – because Britain's agricultural sector was relatively efficient – there has been little gain from the EEC's Common Agricultural Policy (CAP).

> 'British membership of the EC was advocated on pragmatic economic grounds. Britain thought it was joining a common market – an economic organisation – and played down the political consequences of membership.'
> A. Geddes, *Britain in the European Community* (Baseline Books, 1993)

The EEC since 1979 After 1979 and the election of Margaret Thatcher as Prime Minister, there was further criticism of Britain's contribution to the EEC budget; Britain was the second largest contributor. After a long battle over Britain's contribution, a rebate was eventually agreed in 1984.

The Single European Act of 1986 was supported by Thatcher and her allies, since a free, single market would mean greater deregulation and less governmental intervention. It was also supported by Jacques Delors, but on the grounds that it would restart the move towards greater European integration. The European **exchange rate mechanism** (ERM) had developed by 1987, ensuring that each member's currency would 'be virtually fixed in relation to the others'. This entailed spending restraints for many members, with considerable impact on welfare benefits, particularly state pensions, with people being encouraged to take out personal, private pensions rather than depending on state provision. The

British government, having joined the ERM, left it soon afterwards and the question of rejoining it became one of the major debating points at the 1997 general election. Gordon Brown (Chancellor of the Exchequer) stated in October 1997 that entry would not take place before 2002.

The ongoing debate about the future of Europe seems likely to continue well into the twenty-first century.

Globalisation

Globalisation goes beyond supra-nationalism: it refers to the growing interrelationship of world events (see Unit 5, pages 231–3 and Unit 9, pages 475–7). What happens in any one nation state or supra-national organisation has become increasingly linked to events right around the globe.

Some sociologists are now challenging whether the nation state should continue to form the basis of the sociology of politics. They put forward the case that international organisations cut right across individual nations. Transnational corporations (TNCs) have developed from multi-national companies and hold worldwide interests. Western culture, in the form of Coca-Cola, Levi jeans, etc., can now be found virtually everywhere: some sociologists refer to the world as a 'global village'. A. McGrew, in *A Global Society* (1992), views globalisation as the process by which events, decisions and activities in one part of the world have important consequences for those in quite distant parts of the globe. In April 1986, for example, the explosion at the Chernobyl nuclear power station in the USSR led not only to high radiation levels over 50,000 square kilometres of land in the immediate area, but also to contamination in 20 nation states, including Britain. The environment recognises no political boundaries, as global warming continues to testify.

Issues relating to supra-nationalism and globalisation

- Daniel Bell, in *The World and the United States in 2013* (1987), considers the nation state is:

  'too small for the big problems of life and too big for the small problems of life.'

  For example, the unity of a nation state may be threatened by nationalist and regional movements within it, such as Britain's relationship with Northern Ireland, Scotland and Wales; but the sovereignty of a nation state may become challenged by bigger organisations beyond it, as demonstrated by Britain's relationship with the EU.
- K. Bonnett, in *Power and Politics* (1994), suggests that there is a move towards increasing unity at a global level but with increasing fragmentation at a national level. As more links are forged between nation states, the power of each individual state decreases. The EU and its laws affect its member states in such a way that citizens can take their governments to the European Court.
- D. Heald, in *Democracy and the New International Order* (1993), considers that political power is shifting from national to international settings, along with attempts to cope with major global problems such as climate change. Eventually, he foresees some form of world parliament as an international centre for pressing global issues, including food and water supply and distribution, Third World debt, ozone depletion and reduction of the risk of nuclear war.

Summary of supra-nationalism and globalisation (see also Unit 9)

- Supra-national political organisations such as the UN (United Nations), the European Union (EU) and NATO (North Atlantic Treaty Organisation) have developed since 1945.
- With the end of the Cold War and the collapse of European state socialism, the world is no longer divided into huge opposed political power blocs.
- Political, economic and commercial activities are developing on a worldwide basis.
- The contact and interrelationship between nation states has grown greatly.
- Military power can operate globally, with the use of intercontinental missiles, spy satellites, etc.
- Ideas and culture move swiftly and more rapidly across the world than ever before.
- Economic activity involves not only world trade, but also globally integrated production.

Think about it

- What examples can you provide of the multinational status of items clearly associated with Western culture? Have there been attempts to prevent this from happening?
- How might you carry out a sociological investigation, on a local scale, of the claim that the world has become a 'global village'?

Political participation

Ideas of citizenship

Citizenship refers to the holding of specific rights by individuals in a nation state which cannot be removed except by legitimate means. It denotes the membership of a native or 'naturalised' person of that nation state. The rights of citizenship carry with them duties: whilst freedom of expression may be a right, there are duties in respect of what can be said or written so as to prevent the infringement of the rights of others.

In Ancient Greece and Rome, citizenship was granted to prominent members of society. They benefited from legal privileges, sometimes including participation in political decision-making. This pattern of citizenship lapsed in the Middle Ages when it was replaced by the absolute right of the monarchy to hold all rights over their subjects by virtue of divine appointment (see Unit 2, pages 65–6). The concepts of rights and citizenship then developed further after the American War of Independence and the French Revolution at the turn of the eighteenth century.

In contemporary Western democratic nation states, there may be some division drawn between the terms 'citizen' and 'subject': citizens have rights under the laws but are subject to obligations such as obeying the laws. In Britain – a monarchy – citizens are technically 'British subjects'.

Whilst the concept of citizenship includes important ideas in relation to political participation, towards the end of the twentieth century it is widely debated, not only in countries with monarchs such as Britain, but also in states lacking a parliamentary democracy. The European Union provides an interesting case: the relationship between member states goes beyond free economic trading to form international political alliances, and produces a scenario in which individuals are both European citizens (as indicated by the European passport) and national citizens or subjects.

Citizenship in contemporary Britain

The rights and obligations of British citizens form part of the unwritten British constitution – a mixture of tradition, written documents and statute laws dating back to the Magna Carta, signed by King John in 1215, limiting his absolute power. As centuries passed, various Acts of legislation have defined the rights and liberties of British citizens. For example, the right to worship freely was established by a number of Acts, including the Catholic Emancipation Act of 1829, which also allowed Catholics to stand for Parliament. Slavery was ended when an Act abolishing the slave trade came into effect in 1833. Sex Discrimination Acts were passed in 1975 and 1987.

The rights of British citizens were further extended by two international agreements on human rights:

- The United Nations Declaration of Human Rights, in 1948, established rights which governments were meant to grant to their citizens.
- The European Convention on Human Rights, signed in 1950, set out the rights which all citizens in Europe could expect; it also established a Commission of Human Rights and a European Court of Human Rights to secure the Convention.

Basic rights of citizens in Britain today include:

- freedom from arbitrary arrest or unjustified police searches;
- freedom of conscience in matters of religion and politics;
- freedom of expression;
- the right to protest peacefully;
- social freedoms, for example the right to marry, divorce, etc.;
- the right to vote and to stand for election;
- the right to a fair trial.

Debates about citizenship in the 1990s

In the 1990s, the issue of what citizenship should be has received wide discussion in the UK:

- The Conservative government under John Major tried to promote the idea of 'active citizenship'.
- Pressure groups and opposition parties have expressed concern that laws passed in the 1980s and early 1990s have led to limitations of British citizens' basic rights.

In the 1980s, rising crime and rising public spending levels led the government to look for solutions to these problems which did not involve governmental intervention. One solution was to suggest that responsibility for society's problems did not lie with the government, but with the whole community. Every British citizen, in other words, had a duty to take an active part in solving society's problems. This fitted the ideology in the Conservative Party, and provided the government with ways of deflecting criticism. To promote the idea of active citizenship, John Major launched the Citizen's Charter in 1991. Since the development of this charter, public services have had to set themselves performance targets laid out in separate charters available to the public. By 1995, over 40 charters had been published, including, for example, the Patient's Charter and the Charter for Further Education.

The other reason for the emphasis on citizenship from the mid-1990s was the concern by some pressure groups and opposition parties that, since 1979, Conservative governments had disturbed the basic rights of citizens. Examples include measures preventing miners from travelling around the country during the miners' strike of 1984/5, and incidents during anti-poll tax demonstrations in which protesters complained that their rights to peaceful public protest had been violated (see also Unit 9, page 446).

Criticisms surrounding citizenship in Britain

Criticisms in relation to the political participation of citizens in contemporary Britain include the following:

- There are major political institutions that are not democratically elected but which hold powerful political positions, including the monarchy and the House of Lords.
- Democracy should consist of more than basic rights, such as freedom of speech, and should have participatory elements so that citizens become more involved in government. Innovations such as push-button voting, however, appear to be more of a threat than an opportunity for creative citizenship. Rather, democracy should allow greater participation in, and control by, citizens in the provision of, for example, education and health services at both national and regional levels.
- More radical approaches – including Marxist – maintain that citizens cannot participate in political power sharing when widespread economic inequalities continue to exist. Most citizens belong to the proletariat, but wealth inequalities favour the ruling class who seek to keep the role of the citizen to a minimum level; even with an apparently representative democracy it is the representation of the ruling class which is, in reality, being maintained. Citizen's Charters create a 'false consciousness' as an illusionary device of citizen power, according to this view.

Think about it

- Think of five points you would want to address if you were drawing up a Citizen's Charter. Give a sociological basis for each of your choices.

Party or pressure group membership

In the final quarter of the twentieth century, political commentators have noted the decline in **party alignment,** i.e. the extent to which people identify with a particular political party. This decline in political party membership has been paralleled by an increase in pressure group membership. In 1996, Peter Riddell, a political commentator, claimed that party politics had become a fringe activity: only about two per cent of adults are active members of the main political parties.

However, parties remain essential in any representative system, providing coherence for decision-making and recruiting political leaders. With declining membership comes the risk that parties may become less representative. Membership of some of the larger pressure groups compares well with that of the two major political parties. RSPB membership at 850,000, compares quite closely with Conservative Party membership, just under 1 million, and Labour constituency membership of about 700,000.

Party support and voting

Whereas pressure group membership tends to reflect the particular interest of that group, party political support and voting seem to be of a more individual or even personal nature. In modern democracies, individuals may well express their views both in the home and outside it, but they vote in private. Sociologists and others carrying out research into party support and voting often tend to point towards the degree to which voting may be linked to social characteristics of individuals and groups within society. However, such research has opened up considerable debate and even uncertainty about party support and voting.

Political socialisation and voting

Shared social characteristics, particularly in relation to social class and family backgrounds, tend to lead to the support of a particular political party. *Political Change in Britain* (1974) has become a standard text on this subject. Research by the authors, D. Butler and D. Stokes, pointed towards two important factors:

- **Political socialisation** Children often followed their parents' voting behaviour. Families, geographical locations and employment could also influence how the young voted.
- **Partisan alignment** People tended to align or identify with the political party which traditionally represented their social class backgrounds. Working-class manual and unskilled workers voted Labour, whereas middle-class, white-collar and skilled workers voted Conservative.

In the 1960s, the partisan alignment viewpoint was widely accepted:

> *'Class is the basis of British party politics, all else is embellishment in detail.'*
> P. Pulzer, *Political Representation and Elections in Britain*
> (Allen and Unwin, 1967)

Nevertheless, partisan alignment could not explain the following 'problems':

- **deviant voting**, which describes the behaviour of those who do not vote for the political party considered to represent them in social class terms: for example manual workers who do not vote Labour or non-manual workers who do not vote Conservative;
- **deferential voting**, or the tendency of people to defer to those considered more able or better suited to govern. Working-class voters might defer to the traditional authority of the Conservatives rather than vote Labour. According to R.T. McKenzie and A. Silver in *The Working Class Tory in England* (1968), such deferential voting accounted for about a half of the working-class Conservative voters;

- **secular voting**, where secular matters or practical considerations such as financial benefits or improvements to living standards, influence the way people vote. McKenzie and Silver suggested that it was secular voting and not deferential voting that accounted for working-class Conservative voters.

The notion of secular voting has remained an influential factor some three decades after its initial conception. It has continued to help to explain the often volatile and unpredictable voting patterns in Britain. In the 1992 general election, for example, some voters – referred to as 'switchers' – changed their minds about how they would vote at the very last moment, thus causing a late and unpredicted swing away from Labour.

De-alignment issues

The traditional view of political alignment put forward by Butler and Stokes and others has been criticised in that it does not take account of the changes in voting behaviour which have taken place during the last quarter of the twentieth century. For example, increasing numbers seem to have turned their backs on identifying with particular political parties as once they, and their parents, had done. Ivor Crewe, a major political commentator, along with Bo Sarlvik, in *Decade of De-alignment* (1983), identified the following major trends:

- a decline in the share of the vote for the two main parties from over 90 per cent in 1970 to about 75 per cent in the 1980s. This was to the benefit of other political parties, including the Liberal and Social Democratic parties (which merged to form the Liberal Democrats in 1988);
- a fall in partisan alignment: fewer voters seemed to identify strongly with any particular party; voting behaviour seemed to have become more volatile and less predictable;
- class de-alignment, or a fall in the influence of social class background on voting. This was marked most by a decline in the number of manual workers voting Labour, from nearly 65 per cent in 1966 to less than 50 per cent in 1992.

Tactical voting

This occurs when people vote for another party rather than their party of preference, in order that that party may then have a better chance of gaining the seat. For example, some Conservative voters may switch their vote to Liberal Democrat to provide a greater challenge to a possible Labour victory in a particular seat. To be effective, tactical voting may require some sound information about voting intentions and likely outcomes. Another type of tactical voting may be 'negative voting', whereby voters may choose a candidate to demonstrate their opposition to a party or candidate, as when Martin Bell (Independent) gained his seat at Tatton in the 1997 general election. One possible consequence of such tactical voting on a large scale could be to let a third party win an evenly contested marginal seat.

Issue voting   Some commentators consider that issues (or policy preference) have increased in importance in recent years. The electorate, they claim, is becoming more rational in their voting behaviour. M. Franklin, in *Decline in Class Voting in Britain* (1988), for example, concluded from his research that issues played a major part in determining why people preferred to vote for a particular party. Hence the Conservative Party won general elections in 1987 and 1992 because its policies attracted self interest – increased home and shares ownership, for example.

The importance of issue voting has, however, been challenged:

> '*Does the voter pick the party because of its policies or choose the policy positions because they are favoured by the party he or she supports?*'
> J. Benyon and D. Denver, 'Mrs Thatcher's electoral success',
> *Social Studies Review*, vol. 5, no. 3 (January 1990)

Party politics cannot be seen solely in relation to specific issues. Other factors need to be considered, including the relative importance placed on certain issues by voters, and the influence of the mass media.

Does social class still influence voting?   Some sociologists criticise notions of class de-alignment and hold that social class continues to influence voting behaviour. Anthony Heath and his colleagues, writing in the mid-1980s, considered, in *How Britain Votes* (1985), that changes in the social class structure itself had been more important than class de-alignment, particularly in relation to the declining support for the Labour Party prior to 1997. According to Heath et al.:

- the class structure has changed. This has been more important than class de-alignment. Because of employment changes, by the 1980s the working class had fallen to about 30 per cent of the population; this has accounted for virtually half the decline in Labour votes;
- there needs to be an alternative view of the class structure. They considered that a structure based on economic interests would be more appropriate than the traditional, broad manual and non-manual occupation divisions. They provided five 'new' social class groups:

  (i) *salariat:* managers, supervisors, professionals, semi-professionals;
  (ii) *routine non-manual workers:* clerks, salesworkers, secretaries;
  (iii) *petty bourgeoisie:* farmers, small business owners, self-employed manual workers;
  (iv) *foremen and technicians:* manual workers with autonomy or in supervisory positions;
  (v) *working class:* all other manual workers.

Ivor Crewe has argued that the decline in class voting – people voting according to the traditional class alignment of parties – has been important because if fewer people are voting for their 'natural' class, this demonstrates a weakening of class alignment in general. Furthermore, Crewe has maintained that changes in voting patterns within social classes have been more important than the relative sizes of social class. After the 1997 election victory New Labour sought to claim that it 'represents' all socio-economic groups in the UK.

Other factors influencing voting

Sociologists and others interested in the factors influencing voting patterns and behaviour seem to have focused their attention on class alignment and de-alignment. However, a wide range of other factors require some consideration. These include the following:

Gender   Until 1974, women seemed more likely than men to vote Conservative. One explanation was that women tended to be home-based and not part of the male world of paid employment, trade unions and industrial conflict: male manual workers had been socialised into attitudes sympathetic to Labour. Since 1979, however, studies such as P. Walsh et al.'s *Gender and Voting* (1991) have claimed that this difference has almost disappeared.

Ethnicity   In 1983, Afro-Caribbean and Asian voters were the most solidly Labour of any identified group of electors. Such support for Labour has been explained in class terms – a disproportionate number of black voters are working class. Most Afro-Caribbeans and Asians say they vote Labour because of the party's support for the working class. However, non-manual black voters are also much more likely to vote Labour. This suggests that ethnicity is a factor in voting behaviour – according to T.A. Sewell, in *Black Tribunes: Black Political Participation in Britain* (1993), Labour is seen as more sympathetic towards ethnic minorities.

Region   Traditionally the Labour Party has been stronger in the North of England, Wales and Scotland than in the South. Ivor Crewe, in *Why Mrs Thatcher was Returned with a Landslide* (1988), maintained that with Labour's loss of working-class support in southern England, it had become 'a regional class party'. In 1987, 28 per cent of manual workers in the South voted Labour, compared with 57 per cent in Scotland and the North of England.

The mass media   Some sociologists have argued that the mass media has become an important influence on voting. Parties most successful in using the media may accrue votes, and media bias may also seem to be effective. For example, after the Conservative victory in 1992 the traditionally strongly pro-Tory *Sun* claimed 'It was *The Sun* wot won it'. Five years later, in the campaign for the 1997 election, the *Sun* switched allegiance and supported Labour leader Tony Blair. Rupert Murdoch too offered at least tentative support for New Labour prior to the election and the press in general tended to be less anti-Labour than they had been in any general election since 1945.

See Unit 9 for more detail on the influence of the media.

Think about it

- What do you consider to be the most important factors influencing the way people decide to vote at a general election?
- To what extent is it possible to judge how people may vote in relation to their family background, employment, etc.?
- What problems exist for social scientists in attempting to carry out surveys of people's voting intentions prior to a general election?

Protest and social movements

Feminism

'A starting point for feminism is the belief that men and women are not equal in society and that women are systematically subordinated or oppressed. Unlike traditional political thinking, which has either defended or ignored gender inequality, feminism sees this as a central issue and as a political movement tries to change it.'

Adapted from V. Bryson, 'Feminism', *Politics Review*, vol. 4, no. 1 (September 1994)

Feminism can be traced back to the late eighteenth century, when, during the French Revolution, women's republican movements sought the goals of liberty, equality and fraternity for all, regardless of sex. But the *Code Napoléon*, based on Roman law, wiped out any such hopes in Europe. In England, Mary Wollstonecraft wrote *A Vindication of the Rights of Women* (1792), the first major feminist work, which sought equality in revolutionary terms.

By the twentieth century, the issue of suffrage (the right to vote in political elections) had become the main target for British and American feminists. Despite large and sometimes violent campaigns, they met with considerable resistance. In 1893, New Zealand became the first country to give women the vote. Elsewhere, women had to wait until after World War I to win the right to vote. In the United States of America, the Nineteenth Amendment to the Constitution became law in 1920, partly in recognition of women's war contributions as paid and volunteer workers. In Britain, women over the age of 30 gained the vote in 1918; the age was reduced to 21 in 1928. Female suffrage was gained in the former Soviet Union in 1917, and in Germany, Poland, Austria and Sweden in 1919. Later, women won the vote in France (1944), Italy (1945), China (1947) and India (1949). In Kuwait, Jordan and Saudi Arabia, women are still denied the right to vote.

In the 1960s, changing economic and social circumstances encouraged a resurgence of feminism. Lower infant mortality rates, increasing adult life expectancy and improved contraception gave women greater freedom from childcare. Such developments led to many families seeking two incomes; the rising divorce rate also pushed more women into the job market. In the late 1980s, women accounted for more than 40 per cent of the workforce in Britain, France, Germany and the USA.

In the late 1960s and early 1970s, feminists organised women's rights groups. Attention was given to consciousness-raising to make women more aware of their shared disadvantages. They were inspired by texts such as *The Second Sex* (1949) by Simone de Beauvoir, *The Feminine Mystique* (1963) by Betty Friedan, *Sexual Politics* (1969) by Kate Millett, *The Female Eunuch* (1970) by Germaine Greer and *Gyn/Ecology* (1979) by Mary Daly.

By the 1980s, feminists began to consider the possibility that Western society was demonstrating a post-feminist backlash against the legal and social gains made by women. Texts such as *The Beauty Myth* (1990) by Naomi Wolf and *Backlash* (1992) by Susan Faludi concentrated on how the gains of the feminist movement were losing ground, citing, for example, opposition in the USA to abortion.

Environ- mentalism

Environmentalism has become a major issue in recent decades. With concerns about world population growth, industrial developments and technological advances, there has arisen an increased concern about the relationship between humans and the use and abuse of the world we inhabit. Environmentalism may be seen to be based on the principles outlined below:

'There needs to be a balanced relationship between humans and their environment. Other ideologies, including feminism, are rooted in interpersonal relationships. By contrast environmentalism stresses that humans are just one of many species. Since people can change the environment they need to accept responsibility for its survival.'
Source: Adapted from *British Politics*, R. Bentley et al.
(Causeway Press, 1995)

Concerns about the environment are not new. The first recorded environmental group was The Commons, Open Spaces and Footpaths Preservation Society, founded in 1865.

Environmentalists may be divided into four broad categories:

* single-issue campaigning organisations, for example Friends of the Earth, Greenpeace;
* advocates of environmental protection within other organisations and institutions, such as the Church, education and professional bodies;
* developers of relevant theories and practices for environmental protection, for example organic farming, renewable energy technology;
* 'Green' political parties.

In the 1980s, a wide range of environmental policies were developed. In some countries Green parties were formed. A growing number of local projects demonstrated how these policies might work. People began to accept environmental protection as a matter of everyday concern, alongside unemployment, access to health care, pensions and other forms of insecurity. Membership of environmental organisations grew at a faster rate than that of political parties.

By the mid-1990s, the need to integrate environmental protection with social and economic policies has led environmental activists to form strategic partnerships. For instance, Greenpeace worked together with a group of insurance companies and the G-7 group of developed countries to influence the first review of the Convention on Climate Change agreed at the United Nations Conference on Environment and Development (commonly known as the Earth Summit), held in Rio de Janeiro in June 1992. In April 1996, in the UK, Real World was founded – a coalition of over 30 pressure groups concerned with issues of the environment, development, social justice and democratic renewal, and united by what members see as the root cause of their individual areas of concern.

Think about it

* In the run-up to the 1997 general election, the *Independent* newspaper published the following articles about attitudes towards politicians among those in the 18–24 age group, particularly in the context of environmental issues. Read the articles and then answer the questions that follow.

The Gospel according to Swampy

Issues take precedence over politics for young people, survey shows

Clare Garner

Disillusioned with politics and alienated from the system, young people of today are turning their back on the traditional democratic process, according to a report published today.

Although young people (18- to 24-year-olds) represent a section of the electorate significant enough to swing marginal votes, only 40 per cent are likely to vote at the general election – a figure that slumps as low as 14 per cent among the black population.

While young people are more likely than their elders to participate in voluntary work, they are turning their backs on mainstream politics and the

My generation: the anti-roads protester Swampy, whose views on politics and direct action are mirrored by many of today's young people

Youth priorities

■ While 55% of 18- to 24-year-olds had done some form of voluntary activity in the previous year, only 51% of the population as a whole had. *Source: Voluntary Centre UK*
■ Membership of Amnesty International's Youth Section rose from 1,300 in 1988 to 15,000 in 1995. *Source: BYC/M-Power, 1995*
■ Three out of five young people voluntarily participate in youth work. *Source: Agenda for a Generation, UK Youth Work Alliance, September 1996*
■ Only two in five 18- to 24-year-olds are likely to vote at the next general election. *Source: Mori/TUC, August 1996*
■ 86% of young blacks aged 18–25 say they are not certain to vote at the next general election; 4.7% of the adult population in England and Wales are not registered to vote. The highest proportions of missing voters are amongst 21- to 24-year-olds. *Source: Treasury Figures*

established forms of participation. As shown by the emergence of individuals like tunneller Swampy and 16-year-old activist "Animal" in the recent anti-roads protests in Devon and elsewhere, the youth of today is more likely to get involved in direct action. They believe that getting

involved in politics does not make a difference – and that those that do get involved do so for the wrong motives.

The report – entitled *The Kids are Alright?* and compiled by London Youth Matters – will be launched today by Cardinal Basil Hume. It reveals that Thatcher's children have more faith in Chris Evans and Gary Lineker as role models for their finances. The Chancellor of the Exchequer came equal bottom with Mystic Meg, with the support of only one in a hundred young people.

Bernard Donoghue, chair of London Youth Matters, the umbrella organisation for youth organisations in the capital, asked: "As politicians launch for the nearest camera crew, and young people become the soft target for those wanting to jump on the moral bandwagon, who is to provide a positive spin for a scapegoat generation? Someone has to ensure that their voice is heard, and ensure that the system makes an attempt to reconnect with them," he said.

In 1993, a survey by Social and Community Planning Research showed that 8 per cent of the total UK population had no interest in politics. The equivalent figure for young people in the Youth in Politics survey from 1995, quoted by *The Kids Are Alright?*,

shows that the equivalent figure for young people is 24 per cent.

Young people's definitions of politics vary, however: 58 per cent of 22- to 25-year-olds believe politics are about things that affect their lives; 20 per cent say that politics are what goes on in Parliament; and 21 per cent say politics means nothing to them.

Individual issues tended to stir young people more than getting involved in politics generally: 73 per cent said they supported help for the homeless, 71 per cent rights for the disabled, 66 per cent the NHS, and 64 per cent animal rights.

Thirty two per cent said they had protested and 13 per cent were in favour of damage in support of animal rights. Other issues they cared about included support for single parents (56 per cent), employment issues (55 per cent), combating pollution (54 per cent), cracking down on nuclear power/weapons (52 per cent) and women's right to abortion (50 per cent).

Quoting a survey by Volunteer Centre UK (1991), the report argues that it is unfair to suggest that just because young people do not participate in mainstream politics they are apathetic. In the survey, 55 per cent of 18–24-year-olds had done some form of voluntary activity in the previous year, compared with 51 per cent of the population as a whole.

'Register to vote and naff up your ballots'

Daniel Hooper – better known as the roads protester Swampy – has a vote, but he has no intention of using it, **writes Clare Garner**.

He doesn't believe in voting: all politicians are as bad as each other and by voting for any of them he would be endorsing what is, in his view, a bankrupt system.

Election day on a road protest site will be the same as any other day for 23-year-old Swampy, who came to fame during the A30 evictions at Fairmile in Devon last month. "I'll probably be having some breakfast, doing the washing up, digging a bit of tunnel and putting up a tree-house," he said yesterday. "I don't feel that any of the parties represent my opinion at all and I don't agree with the political system. If you put people in power they generally get corrupted by power, as is quite clear from seeing the corruption that's around at the moment."

Whilst he admits it would be "quite nice" to see the back of the Conservatives, he doesn't believe Labour would be any better. "I don't believe it would make any difference," he said. "For instance, most of the road building consortiums are now donating money to the other side [Labour], so they are going to be just as corrupt. Take the Criminal Justice Act. Labour has never said they're going to stop that one. They just sit on the fence because they don't want to upset people and lose votes."

It is, he feels, time for the country to turn its back on the political system and prompt change through direct action. "The best way to deal with politicians is to fight them, but at the same time ignore them," he said. "They can't rule our lives if we turn away from them. The more people do that, the more the system is going to break down. Now more than ever, people are ignoring them and they don't feel as powerful as they did before.

"People aren't interested any more in what politicians have got to say. We're only actively encouraging them by voting. Yeah, register to vote and naff up your voting papers *en masse*."

In Swampy's book, politicians have only themselves to blame for the state of the country. "The amount of damage they are doing is phenomenal," he said. "How the hell can they blame that on young people – or anyone else for that matter. I mean, they're destroying the planet left, right and centre, they're pumping pollution into the air, they're sending people to war, and it's all about money."

But, he added, being young in the Nineties is not all bad. "It's exciting times in a way because there are a lot of things going on and we can make a change if people get active now. Rather than voting it would be better if everyone took their own action. I think we can change things in a different way."

Source: The *Independent*, 17 February 1997

Think about it

- To what extent do you think it is a valid protest to refuse to vote?
- Do 'alternative' parties such as the Green Party provide a genuine alternative for those who share the views expressed by Swampy? Give reasons for your answer.
- What reasons can you suggest for the following facts cited:
  (a) 86 per cent of blacks aged 18–25 said they were not certain to vote in the election.
  (b) Young people are more likely than their elders to take part in voluntary work.
  (c) A footballer and a DJ/TV presenter came top of the list of 'role models for their finances', while the Chancellor of the Exchequer ranked equally with Lottery result predictor Mystic Meg.

Think about it

Sociologists and political scientists have traditionally set out the wide range of political ideologies by using a line or horseshoe model, as illustrated below. Generally, the ideologies of the left have tended to favour greater equality and the state-controlled redistribution of wealth, whilst those of the right consider equality to be undesirable or unachievable and tend to emphasise wealth creation. These models, though in some ways now dated in relation to today's party politics in the UK, serve as a useful representation of the left–right pattern.

Line model

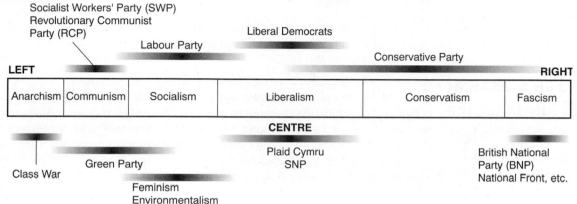

Horseshoe model

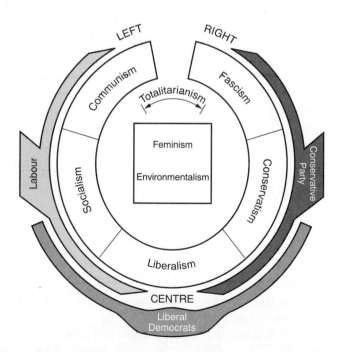

- What do you think are the advantages and disadvantages of using terms such as the 'left' and the 'right' to label political attitudes and positions? Do they influence social classifications?
- What problems might arise when line or horseshoe models are used to view political ideologies?
- Can you suggest a model which might give a better representation of today's political ideologies in the UK?

The distribution of political power

The distribution of political power may be seen in terms of five conflicting views about the nature of powerful groups in society.

- the classical democracy view;
- the Marxist view;
- the classical elitist view;
- the power elite view;
- the pluralist view.

This section of the unit examines each of these views of the powerful, and looks at the related concepts of hegemony and oligarchy.

The classical democracy view

As we have seen, the classical view of democracy argues that power is given by the people to a government. They do this by voting others into office or taking office themselves and, by so doing, they give their consent to government. In this case the powerful are only representatives of the people. They do not hold power on their own account, and they can be recalled from office if they fail to please the electorate. This is the view to which the other four theories relate.

The Marxist view

This is a class-based theory. This view states that the powerful form a ruling class; that is, members of the dominant group share the same economic position in the relations of production. The role of the state is limited. Critical decisions may never reach the political arena, so those who are making them – the controllers of the industrial and finance capital organisations – are not accountable to others in the society. This is why Marxists seek the public ownership of the means of production, so that the proletariat (the non-owners of the means of production) will be able to influence their economic and hence political destinies.

The dominance of the ruling class is not maintained simply by coercion, though the maintainance of the status quo by state officials by enforcing law and order is seen as exploitative and coercive. Marx's important insight was that the dominant ideology, the accepted frames of mind of a society, reflects and legitimates the social system. The ideology makes it seem that what are in fact the interests of the dominant class are for the good of the whole society. The phrase 'What's good for General Motors is good for America' is a classic demonstration of this. This legitimisation is reinforced by the mass media, taught in the schools, and forms the accepted values into which the young are socialised. So widespread is the acceptance of this view that coercion of the proletariat is rarely required.

J. Westergaard and H. Resler, in *Class in Capitalist Society* (1976), examined the results of decisions rather than studying the process of decision-making to support their view that because of the general acceptance of the ruling-class ideology in Britain, the capitalist class rarely has to exercise its power actively, i.e. the police and army are not used against the people directly.

Not all Marxists agree that capitalism dominates the state and makes it an instrument of the bourgeoisie. Jurgen Habermas calls himself a

Marxist, but his work is less dogmatic than most, although 'His writing is about as accessible to the average man (even an average honours graduate) as an engineering textbook in Swahili,' as P. Wilby puts it in his article *Habermas and the language of the modern states* (1979). However, Habermas's work remains important because of his central idea that modern capitalism faces a crisis not just of economics, but of legitimacy – hence the title of his famous text, *Legitimation Crisis* (1973).

Habermas's argument can be summarised as follows:

- Capitalist legitimation used to be achieved through the values of the market: rewards were won by the hardworking and enterprising. More recently, with technology making evaluation of individual effort difficult, individual initiative and talent do not seem so clearly related to reward. Fewer small businesses flourish, so there are fewer chances for the resourceful individual to set up on his or her own. The gap in income between the low-paid workers and the unemployed is small.
- There is the need for a new legitimation. The one that is dominant is the legitimation of the expert. The scientist and the technologist determine many decisions with far-reaching effects on our lives in terms of rationality and efficiency. This threatens debate about values, and depoliticises the masses who have not the expertise to participate and who can only choose between opposing teams of administrators who are themselves in the hands of the experts.
- This depoliticisation coincides with increasing state intervention in private areas of our lives. When eventually the state fails to solve the problems of inflation, employment and economic growth, then what is its function? Its other activities in representing and protecting the ruling class would, Habermas argues, be exposed in this situation, and a crisis of legitimation would arise.

Habermas has argued that this crisis is now upon us and that as a result, third parties whose common factor is that they are anti the government machine – such as ecology parties and nationalists – are growing in importance.

The classical elitist view

Elite theory maintains that there will always be a small organised group who, based on their superior talents, exercise power over a large disorganised mass. (See also the discussion of oligarchy on page 608.) Because the mass is always powerless, democracy in any strict sense is impossible; though Gaetona Mosca, in *The Ruling Class* (1939), noted that openness among an elite makes possible the representation of a wider range of interest. Vilfredo Pareto, in *A Treatise on General Sociology* (1963), in which he focused on the psychological qualities of elites, referred to two types of elite:

- 'lions', who were able to act forcefully, gain and keep political power, for example military dictators;
- 'foxes', who relied on cunning, and manipulated people, for example Western political leaders.

According to Pareto, the two types of elite replace each other over time, leading to a circulation of elites.

D. Berry, in *Central Ideas in Sociology* (1974), referred to a variety of elite ideologies. At different times men (rarely women) have claimed the right to rule because of their specific qualities (for example strength), their revelations from a god, or because of their technical and expert knowledge. Pareto has been criticised for being too simplistic and for assuming a 'circulation of elites' regardless of the variety of ideologies. Both Pareto and Mosca tend to underestimate the ability of the masses to achieve any form of political power.

Think about it

- What are the psychological characteristics of foxes and lions in Vilfredo Pareto's classical elite theory, and how does the 'circulation of elites' operate?
- Can you think of examples of 'foxes', 'lions' and the 'circulation of elites' in British politics?
- In which political systems does Pareto's theory apply? Think of an example of a political system where Pareto's theory does not seem to apply.

The power elite view

The power elite view is similar to the classical elite view, except for the different process of recruitment to elite positions. The power elite view states that the structure of modern organisations is such that power is largely monopolised by those at the top.

Distinctions may be drawn between the psychological explanations of elite dominance put forward by Pareto and Mosca, and the institutional explanations of Robert Michels, C. Wright Mills and F. Hunter. C. Wright Mills, in an influential study *The Power Elite* (1956), argued that the elite in the USA derived their power from their positions in business, government and the military. Those who occupied the top positions in these three areas of influence tended to move between the three at the highest level, to hold directorships or positions in more than one simultaneously, and to be strongly united by the similarity of their social background.

This view implies that the elite rule in their own interests and that, like the Marxist view, such an elite rule is not accountable in the political process. The mass media plays an important part in focusing the attention of the woman or man in the street on private and unpolitical matters, while the power elite, unchecked, pursue their own interests.

G.W. Domhoff, in *Who Rules America?* (1967), aimed to test out Mills's assertions in detail. Domhoff analysed the background and education of those who held political office to see whether or not they formed a distinct social group – a national upper class that was a governing (or ruling) class. This he defined as:

> *'a social upper class which receives a disproportionate amount of the country's income, owns a disproportionate amount of the country's wealth and contributes a disproportionate number of its members to the controlling institutions and key decision-making groups in that country.'*
> G.W. Domhoff, *Who Rules America?* (Prentice Hall, 1967)

Domhoff studied the composition of leadership groups to determine whether or not the leaders came from any given socio-economic class or ethnic or religious group; he also studied the decision-making process in different 'issue-areas' to see who constituted the decision-making group for various issues. He concluded that a group of less than 1 per cent of the US population was upper class, which, though also a governing class, did not rule alone. Most of the non-upper-class leaders, however, were selected and trained by members of the upper class and, therefore, tended to share the same goals and values.

This pattern is not uniquely American. R. Miliband writes of Britain:

> *'What evidence conclusively suggests is that in terms of social origin, education and class situation, the men who have manned command posts in the state system have largely been drawn from the world of business and property, or from the professional middle classes. Here, as in every other field, men and women born into the subordinate classes which form, of course, the majority of the population, have fared very poorly ... In an epoch where so much is made of democracy, equality, social mobility, classlessness and the rest, it has remained a basic fact of life in advanced capitalist countries that the vast majority of men and women in these countries have been governed, represented, administered, judged and commanded in war by people drawn from other economically and socially superior and relatively distant classes.'*
> R. Miliband, *The State in Capitalist Society* (Quartet, 1973)

Elite recruitment in Britain

A range of studies show that British elites are largely recruited from the existing elite, though they are open to new members who have academic success (and sponsored mobility through the old grammar schools and the universities – see Unit 4). The existence of such elites does not prove that they rule in their own interests and at the cost of others, however. This is hard to establish, and the evidence used to make this assertion is hard to determine. Nevertheless, inherited wealth seems an important factor in elite recruitment in the UK. P. Stanworth and A. Giddens, in *Elites and Power in British Society* (1974), found that only 1 per cent of companies were chaired by those from working-class backgrounds, as opposed to over 65 per cent of companies chaired by those from upper-class backgrounds. This, and similar studies, points to continuing economic inequality in Britain, with elites seemingly protecting their own interests. However, W. Grant and D. Marsh, in examining the CBI's influence on four government decisions affecting business interests, found that:

> *'The CBI had little consistent direct influence on the political policies pursued by the government.'*
> W. Grant and D. Marsh, *The Confederation of British Industry* (Hodder and Stoughton, 1977)

The distinction between the **ruling class** and the **ruling elite** is not an easy one. The important point is that theories of the ruling class are theories about economic dominance, whereas theories about elites are about those who hold the top positions in political institutions.

Summary of elite theory

- Rather than power to the people, democracy brought new bases of elite membership.
- Modern elites are an inevitable consequence of psychological differences between elites and masses and the organisational requirements of modern societies.

In its more recent form, elite theory has modified its pessimism about modern democracy, arguing that:

- different bases of elite power have important social consequences; and
- a democratic competition between rival representative elites constitutes the best practicable form of modern government.

The study of elites and the testing of elite theories has been controversial. While some researchers have pursued a 'reputational' approach, asking respondents 'Who holds power?', others, including Robert Dahl, have argued that only the careful study of actual decisions can establish who in fact is powerful. Even this, however, is not decisive, since the study of overt 'decisions' fails to explore the existence of 'non-decisions'. In many circumstances the balance of power may be such as to preclude political debate or political contest so that no overt point of decision is observable.

Source: Adapted from the *Collins Dictionary of Sociology*, edited by David Jary and Julia Jary (Harper Collins)

Hegemony

This term comes from the Greek word *hegemon*, meaning leader or ruler; it was defined as 'intellectual and moral leadership' by Antonio Gramsci (1891–1937), an Italian Marxist, in his *Selections from the Prison Notebooks*. Gramsci maintained that:

- the bourgeoisie exercise hegemony in capitalist society because of their dominant ideas and values, and convince groups to consent to such domination;
- revolution is needed if the proletariat is to challenge ruling-class hegemony; this requires the intellectual and moral development of the proletariat, subject class;
- the subject class can only challenge ruling-class hegemony by forming its own alliances and power blocs similar to those of the ruling class.

Criticisms of Gramsci's view of hegemony include the following:

- It places too much emphasis on 'intellectual and moral leadership' as maintaining the dominant ideas and values of the ruling class.
- It underestimates the strength of the economic structure of capitalism as **its source** of political power.

Contemporary hegemony

Despite the above criticisms, Gramsci's views of hegemony have been used by several contemporary theorists. Particularly influential has been Stuart Hall's *Hard Road to Renewal* (1988), an account of Thatcherism in Gramscian terms. Hall considered the complex relationship between state policies and class interests (during Mrs Thatcher's term of office as Prime Minister from 1979 until 1990) along the following lines:

- There arose opportunities for those who were politically active to reset the political agenda with their own ideas and values.
- Powerful political groups formed a new alliance, built around a revised political programme, and claimed to serve national interests.
- Opposing groups became excluded, and their power undermined and diminished.
- Such new dominant political ideas became accepted and even broadly popular: hegemony became established.

More specifically, Hall argued that Thatcherite ideology had attempted to establish a hegemony around New Right ideas and values, attempting to redefine how people saw their own political identity and interests. This was accompanied by changes in the balance of political forces – between employers and trade unions to the detriment of trade unions, for example – and a reshaping of the power structure of society. Just how successful were such attempts can still form an interesting debate, as indicated by unresolved tensions such as the following:

- The political agenda cannot be a one-way process; any ideology within a parliamentary democracy will face limiting forces (see, for example, the popular opposition to the community charge/poll tax).

- New internal political forces can only become established if the institutions and practical means are available and resistance can be overcome (as was shown, for example, in the difficulties faced in establishing health trusts as a cost-effective measure to provide adequate medical and health care for all).

- International policies, developed to serve powerful political and economic interests, may be presented in terms of the national interest, but this can lead to conflict as happened, for example, with the stabilisation of European exchange rates in 1992.

Think about it

Hegemony   used in the nineteenth century to refer to one state or ruler having political dominance over another. In the twentieth century its use has been extended by the Italian Marxist Antonio Gramsci (*Selections from the Prison Notebooks*, 1971) to refer to relationships between social classes as in 'bourgeois hegemony'. It is now commonly used to indicate a state of consensual dominance of the powerful group or class in a society over the ruled. It covers the whole range of ideas and values – not just the political – involved in the ruling group's view of the world, e.g. the role of the media.

A ruling class to which legitimacy is given has achieved hegemony: its rule is accepted without question and alternatives are not considered. A **hegemonic class** imposes its own views on society as a whole. It may be contrasted with another of Gramsci's concepts, a **corporate class** which pursues its view of society within a structure determined outside its own control. Hegemony is rare, though groups in power often seek it. Although power may be achieved by force, hegemony rests upon agreement with a specific set of norms and values. Hence, the formal educational system is important in achieving hegemony. Some analysis of education has been carried out in terms of attempts to reach, impose and preserve a state of hegemony. Such analysis directs attention to the relations of the cultures of the classes or groups in any society, and to the success or otherwise of the hegemonic class in imposing its culture upon other classes or groups.

Source: Adapted from M. Mann, *Macmillan Student Encyclopaedia of Sociology* (Macmillan, 1983).

- Based on the definition given above, to what extent do you consider it reasonable to view Margaret Thatcher's period of leadership in Britain as hegemonic?

- In general terms, how may hegemony be linked to the Marxist perspective on the distribution of political power?

- In Britain how might it be said that the populace are subjected to hegemonic control? By what means is such control maintained?

- In which nation states, since World War II, has political power rested upon hegemony and with what effects?

Oligarchy

The term 'oligarchy' is of Greek origin and refers to a form of government in which political power was controlled by a few citizens. Such citizens acted in their own interests rather than for the benefit of the people they governed.

Oligarchy has developed to refer to a small elite group of decision-makers: these are usually elected representatives or full-time paid officials. This produces a bureaucracy. However, oligarchic structure soon disposes of any democratic principles: democratic ideals tend to be replaced by hierarchical control. Robert Michels (1876–1936) referred to this as 'the iron law of oligarchy'. In *Political Parties*, published originally in 1911, he explained how the zest for Western socialism had become dampened by oligarchy. Michels' views were based on his study of the German Socialist Party.

A number of contemporary studies have supported Michels' 'iron law of oligarchy'. S.M. Lipset et al., for example, in *Union Democracy* (1956), researched an American printers' union, the International Typographical Union (ITU). They found that the ITU retained its democratic organisation but considered that this was based on particular historical and cultural circumstances. The researchers concluded that this trade union was an exception rather than the rule, and still supported Michels' 'iron law of oligarchy'.

Think about it

- Consider a bureaucratic organisation such as a large company or educational institution and note whether its structure makes democratic principles difficult or easy to achieve? Why?
- Which group(s) may be described, in your opinion, as oligarchic?

The pluralist view

Having looked at five conflicting views about the nature of powerful groups in society, we now look at a sixth, the pluralistic view. This view sees power as shared equally between competing interest groups. Whilst power does not rest in the hands of the ordinary member of a group, but in those of the elites at the top, it is limited by the veto of other groups. Politics, in this view, is a process of bargaining, in which many groups can veto the initiatives of others and few can get their own way without compromise. The role of government is to act as broker between the groups – often groups within the party in office – who may withdraw their support if they cannot exercise some sway in matters that affect their interests. Classical pluralism sees society as made up of many different groups pursuing different interests. It developed from Weber's thinking, as outlined earlier in this unit (see pages 569–71). The pluralist view fits well with the dominant ideology in the USA, where most research studies have been undertaken. Indeed, the French political thinker Alexis de Toqueville (1805–59) commented over 150 years ago, in *Democracy in America*, that American society held democratic potential because of its tolerance of many interest groups.

A famous contemporary classical pluralist text is Robert Dahl's *Who Governs?* (1961). Dahl studied local politics in New Haven, USA in terms of three main issues:

- local political decision-making – in relation to an urban renewal programme for the city centre;
- political nominations – who was elected to political posts, particularly that of mayor;
- education policies – on the new locations for schools, teachers' salaries, etc.

He found the following:

- Political decision-making was not uniform: even elected members of the same group were often disunited and in competition with each other.
- The economic issues group was most active in relation to the urban renewal programme, but there was little group solidarity.
- Political influence was no greater in the economic issues group than in 'about half a dozen other groups in the New Haven Community'.

Dahl noted that, in order to discover where political power lies, it is necessary to examine 'concrete' decisions to see which groups achieve their aims/goals.

Pluralists see political power widely distributed across society. No single elite group exists, but a range of groups compete for power. No one group can secure a monopoly of power and manipulate the system to its advantage, since competition ensures limited risk of power abuse. There are also a number of fundamental safety mechanisms and devices to ensure that a minority cannot abuse power. Regular elections and the freedom to form pressure groups, for example, ensure that people have some form of guarantee that power will not be abused. Also, even if various groups do not agree fully on every issue, there is a basic consensus on norms and goals.

Critics of pluralism include Peter Bachrach and Morton Baratz. In *The Two Faces of Power* (1962) they consider that merely examining decision-making neglects a second and important process: that of 'agenda control' of debate. They argue that political power lies in the ability to block issues from receiving serious consideration (see also page 575). As noted earlier, S. Lukes extends this idea to include a 'Third Dimension of Power'.

Pluralism, in summary, is based on a theory of countervailing power, which argues that when one interest threatens to dominate others, counterbalancing forces will develop among existing groups or new groups will come into being.

Summary of theories on the distribution of political power

Each of these theories links with a differing explanation of why and how the distribution of political power exists and how changes come about:

- For Marxists, political change arises as a result of the inevitable conflict of interests between the ruling class and the working class.
- Other conflict theorists also argue that change is inevitable, but the reason they give links to their explanation that authority relationships will always be unstable.
- Classical elite theorists believe that the 'circulation of elites' is inevitable as decadence makes the ruling group vulnerable, or because there arise situations calling for skills which the group in power doesn't possess (diplomacy or forcefulness, for example).
- Pluralist theorists and consensus functionalists do not believe that conflict is inevitable. If conflict occurs, it indicates a malfunction of the system. For these sociologists, change may arise in response to new situations which alter the balance of political power between groups, or to remedy and reform existing arrangements which do not work smoothly.

Powerlessness and marginality

This unit, so far, has focused on power, with particular reference to its definitions, its sources and its distribution. However, there are a number of groups in Britain and in other advanced Western societies which may be described as 'powerless'. Not only do they lack power, but they have become **marginalised** and pushed to 'the outside edges' of society. Marginality refers to social groups which may be considered as part insiders, part outsiders. It may be related to age, class, gender, ethnicity or other factors. However, it is often the complex interrelationship of these factors which serves to compound the powerlessness and marginality that such social groups experience on a daily basis from their positions on the sidelines of society. Whilst it is difficult to separate out specific factors such as age, class, gender or ethnicity as the prime cause of marginality, some pointers are offered below.

Age

Increasing proportions of young people, in an extended period of dependency often into their mid-20s, spend part of their time in one-parent households. As a result they experience poverty and marginality from a young age. In 1996, 70 per cent of single mothers received income support.

At the other end of the age spectrum, the powerlessness of the elderly may seem even more disturbing:

> '*It is hard enough at the best of times for the elderly (and other groups such as patients in mental hospitals, abused children) to win a place on a crowded political agenda. Often it takes a major scandal (e.g. horrendous media coverage about cruelty in children's homes or geriatric institutions) to make politicians take notice.*'
>
> Adapted from M. Bury and J. Macnicol (eds), 'Aspects of ageing' (*Social Policy Papers*, no. 3, 1990)

In *Family Change and Future Policy* (1990), edited by K. Kiernan and M. Wicks, education and training programmes for the disadvantaged young and income support for families are foreseen as developing in the twenty-first century. The impetus, they suggest, may not be social so much as economic, because children from disadvantaged households will form the next labour force and 'quality children become quality workers'. At the other end of the age scale, for those aged 65 plus (15 per cent of the population in Britain), the loss of their 'social connected-ness' – i.e. loss of roles and responsibilities – can lead to stigmatisation and discredited status in political terms (though they retain the facility to vote and join pressure groups such as Help the Aged); only the elite, including those holding high status political positions, are exempt.

Class

As in most areas of sociology, in the study of the sociological aspects of politics, class forms a complex range of issues. This applies particularly to powerlessness and marginality in politics. In 1992, the *Economist* published a table of the 100 'top people' in Britain, of whom 66 were males from public schools: proof that the 'old boy network' (see also Unit 4) still holds wide influence in Britain.

Members of professional classes may brush with marginality during periods of economic uncertainty. Teachers and lecturers, for example, despite their academic qualifications, may find themselves employed on an hourly basis or on short-term contracts (often of just one year), with no power to improve their contracts or conditions of employment. They may experience unemployment when a short-term contract comes to an end. Nevertheless, it is certainly the lowest ranks of society who seem to suffer the most.

Beggars and the homeless are marginalised and stigmatised. They are also politically powerless: with no fixed address, they lose their right to vote. Along with other marginalised groups, such as the long-term unemployed, single parents and the elderly, they carry negative labels: the 'underclass', the 'New Rabble', etc., which compound their marginality. Membership of these groups may even be seen as ascribed – in other words you are more likely to be marginalised if you have black or brown skin, for example, if you are female or if you have a mental or physical disability.

Accurate statistical information on the homeless is hard to obtain. Figures are kept only for those who are legally eligible for housing – families with children and those considered vulnerable. The Department of the Environment keeps statistics on the number of households for whom local authorities have accepted responsibility to provide accommodation: the total number in the 12 months ending March 1996 was 119,870. Comprehensive research on single homelessness in London was carried out in the form of a survey by the University of Surrey for the Salvation Army in 1989. It found at least 75,000 people homeless in London. In 1994, Shelter estimated that there were around 140,000 single homeless people nationally. The most visible and publicised group, rough sleepers, account for only a small fraction of homeless people.

Rough sleepers

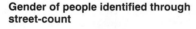

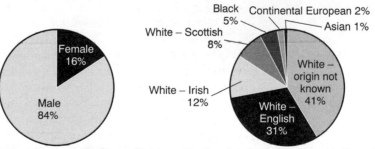

Source: Street-count by Homeless Network carried out in November 1995

Gender

Whilst women are underrepresented in politics, their lives are dominated by policy-makers who are mostly male. In Britain, women account for 52 per cent of the population yet hold under 20 per cent of the seats in the House of Commons: even after the 1997 election in which the figure almost doubled, there were only 120 female MPs, representing only 18 per cent of the total 659 MPs. Participation in politics is linked to a number of key resources, including financial means and personal contacts, and these seem more likely to be accumulated by males than females. Other factors accounting for female powerlessness and marginality include the following:

- **Socialisation processes:** what is learnt from an early age can shape adult political norms and values. Socialisation, by the family, education, the mass media, etc., often involves gender-role socialisation. Ambition and aggression, which may be seen as forming important ingredients for political success, may also be seen as 'unfeminine'. Hence socialisation processes may serve to marginalise females who, with a few exceptions, accept politics as a male-dominated, power-based activity. For functionalists this seems reasonable; but for Marxists and many feminists, powerlessness and marginality enable the state to reproduce capitalism in which females need to remain subordinated in its patriarchal system.

- **Biological differences:** policy decisions about female access to fertility treatments, abortions and maternity-leave conditions have, for the most part, been dominated by male politicians, whilst females tend to remain responsible for family life and for the care of children, the elderly and the disabled. It is even asserted that females are not suited to political life because of such family commitments! At its crudest level, biological differences support female powerlessness and marginality by reinforcing their childbearing and 'natural' home-maintenance roles.

- **Traditional attitudes** extend beyond those associated with the biological differences between men and women. Traditional attitudes and values include the idea that, since women are not legally prevented from entering politics, it is a fair system. Also the belief exists that women are not interested in politics; their marginality and lack of political power is due to their own decisions, even their own fault. This has led to the view that women may be seen as virtually irrelevant to power and politics. It ignores the fact that gender politics forms an integral part of politics. However, to assume that females and males form homogeneous groups is dangerous: there are women who are very active party political members and trade unionists, just as there are men who are passive and even disillusioned about politics – perhaps because of their feelings about the Child Support Agency and other economic or employment issues.

Ethnicity

Ethnicity usually relates to the non-white-skinned members of British society, although there have always been substantial numbers of the white-skinned population from ethnic groups, such as the Irish and those from European countries. The census of 1991 showed that of a population of nearly 55 million only about 5 or 6 per cent was black or brown skinned, though there was a wide variety of ethnic backgrounds.

The Runnymede Trust *Bulletin* (no. 247, July/August 1991) noted that white people tended to overestimate the number of black people living in Britain. Even Margaret Thatcher, in 1978, the year before she became Prime Minister, warned that Britain could become 'swamped' with immigrants. The 1991 census figures showed that this attitude was deliberately provocative. However, politicians still 'played the race card' in the 1990s. Their belief that there is political mileage in such views is confirmed by surveys of public attitudes and statistics, for example of reported racial attacks (which increased from 4383 in 1988 to nearly 8000 in 1992, according to the 1992 Crime Survey from the Home Office which recorded 140,000 episodes of racial harassment or attack).

Ethnic minority groups are also marginalised in terms of employment. Employment Department figures in 1994 showed that unemployment rates amongst Afro-Caribbeans, Bangladeshis and Pakistanis were higher than average. When ethnic minority groups do find employment, it is not usually in high status jobs:

> '*Ethnic and racial minority groups make up some 6% of the population of Great Britain and 4.7% of its working population. They make up less than 2% of the teaching profession, less than 2% of solicitors, 1% of police officers; they are virtually absent from the top levels of the civil service and the armed forces; there are no black judges and very few barristers; and there are none at the top levels of our major financial institutions.*'
>
> J. Edwards, 'The politics of racial equality', *Politics Reviews*, vol. 2, no. 2 (Philip Allan, September 1991)

Many sociologists consider that ethnicity and political powerlessness may be linked to lack of opportunities for ethnic minorities, particularly within education and employment (see Units 4 and 5).

The major political parties maintain that candidates from ethnic minorities are at no disadvantage in the selection process, but the small number of ethnic minority candidates selected, and some particular cases such as that of John Taylor in Cheltenham in 1991, seem to dispute this. For the 1992 general election, 23 ethnic minority candidates were selected to fight seats for the three main parties (nine Labour, eight Conservative and six Liberal Democrats). Although the main parties claimed that they wanted more candidates from the ethnic minorities, few of those selected stood for safe seats. In 1987, four black MPs were elected; they all kept their seats in 1992, when the total number of black MPs rose to six (about 1 per cent of MPs!). After the Labour victory of 1997 there were still only nine ethnic minority MPs in the House of Commons.

The election of candidates from ethnic minority groups may lead to more being selected. However, the fall in such candidates from 28 in 1987 to 23 in 1992, combined with the lack of public debate on this issue, may suggest that the struggle for greater ethnic minority representation in the House of Commons is far from over. If this remains so, the ethnic minorities may continue to be powerless and marginalised.

Think about it

- With the greater educational achievement of girls, the increasing number of women in the workforce and over 100 women MPs elected in the 1997 general election do you think that this will lead to more women taking up careers in politics? Justify your view.
- What are your views on beggars and homeless people? Who is to blame for their powerlessness and marginality? What could be done to attempt to relieve such apparently increasing social problems?
- Why do you think that most white members of British society overestimate the percentage of the population from ethnic minority groups? Carry out a survey among your family, friends and colleagues. How might the representation of ethnic minority groups be improved?
- What aspects of the British system do you think might allow those in ethnic minorities to become more widely involved in regional and national government?

Revision and practice tasks

Task: structured question

(a) Briefly outline what Marxists mean by the relative autonomy of the state. (4)

(b) Distinguish between the repressive state apparatus and ideological state apparatus. (4)

(c) Outline, with examples, what Marxists mean by hegemony. (7)

(d) Assess the claim that the UK state is controlled by a ruling class. (10)

(Total: 25 marks)

Source: Interboard Sociology, Paper 2, June 1996

Essay questions

1. Compare and contrast two sociological theories of the distribution of power (see **guided essay**, below).

2. Examine the claim made by some sociologists that there is a dominant ideology in advanced Western societies.

3. To what extent may it be claimed that contemporary Britain has a ruling elite?

4. Explain and discuss any **two** of the concepts below:
   - ideology;
   - hegemony;
   - oligarchy.

5. 'Pressure groups tend either to support or to hinder a political democracy.' Explain and discuss.

6. Discuss how appropriate it may be to draw distinctions between promotional and interest groups.

7. Evaluate what political commentators consider to be the key factors in determining voting behaviour in contemporary Britain.

8. To what extent does the role of the state in contemporary Britain conflict with Britain's membership of the European Union?

Guided essay

Compare and contrast two sociological theories of the distribution of power.

1. Precise and concise opening paragraph, addressing the question and setting the scene:

There are various sociological theories regarding the nature and distribution of power in advanced Western societies. This essay will examine the pluralist theory and the Marxist theory. By comparing and contrasting the two theories, it will endeavour to uncover the differences and similarities which exist between them.

2. Pluralist theory: background, concepts, etc.:

Whilst elite theory and Marxism argue that power is concentrated in the hands of a dominant minority, from a pluralist perspective, power is shared by a range of groups in society. The French founder of the pluralist perspective, Alexis de Tocqueville, considered that a democratic political system needed its members to have many interests. He maintained that democracy would not work if one element in society dominated all others since this could lead to a 'tyranny of the majority'. The dominant faction would become permanent and then neglect the wishes of others. Complex societies tend to separate into a variety of social groups, each able to focus upon its own particular concerns. This leads to organisations formed to represent these interests. As the range of occupations increases, so too does the number of specialised organisations representing particular interests in society, known as 'interest groups'. From a pluralist perspective, politics is a competition between 'interest groups', each seeking its own advantage. Since there is no dominant group politics is seen in terms of a compromise. Robert A. Dahl, in *Who Governs?* (1961), supports this view and suggests that because there is competition for power this makes sure that it is not abused.

Clearly, not all members of society can be directly involved in the political arena and so their interests are represented by their 'group'. J. Urry and J. Wakeford (eds), in *Power in Britain* (1968), considered that it was both inevitable and necessary that power elites should exist since people need as their representative the best able to lead. The leaders who stand for the various interest groups are often referred to as elites, so the pluralist perspective is often referred to as 'elite pluralism' as opposed to 'classical pluralism'.

3. Development of pluralist theory:

According to pluralists, power is not in any one centre, but is more widely spread across society. They maintain there is no single elite group existing but a variety of groups competing for power: no single group can achieve a monopoly of power and manipulate the system to its own advantage. Competition limits the risk of power abuse. Even though various groups do not agree fully on every issue, there is a basic consensus on norms and values. There are also a number of safety mechanisms to ensure that a minority cannot take advantage. Regular free elections, pressure groups and the freedom to form such groups, ensure citizens have some kind of guarantee that power will not be misused.

4. Criticisms of pluralist theory with broader reference:

Critics of pluralism, including Peter Bachrach and Morton Baratz in *The Two Faces of Power* (1962), state that simply studying decision-making overlooks a second process by which power is wielded – that of 'agenda control': political power also lies in the ability to block issues from receiving serious consideration. Other challengers of pluralism claim that all major interests in society are represented within the political arena of capitalism. Hence those opposed to the capitalist mode of production are unable to achieve their aim of a more collective mode of production through the existing political structure. The French Neo-Marxist, Louis Althusser, refers to 'ideological state apparatus' (ISAs), which operate to protect the interests of the ruling class and, as such, are likely to give 'bad press' to any group which opposes the status quo. In this way, it can be seen that whilst there may be apparent freedom for the formation of pressure groups, there exist ideological controls which subtly but effectively block oppositional views.

5. Marxist opposition to pluralist theory:

The Marxist perspective rejects the idea that power is based on trust and directed by those in authority for the benefit of all. On the contrary, power is seen to be held by a ruling group in society in order to exploit the masses. The dominant group uses power to further its own interests which are in direct conflict with the interests of those subject to its power. The forces of production are owned by a minority, the ruling class. There seems some illusion of democracy, but reality is different. This can be compared with the pluralist view, which, although viewing political resources as widely distributed throughout society, does not suggest the existence of an egalitarian society. On this point there is a similarity between the two theories, but in broader terms they can be considered as contrasting theories.

6. Linkage between Marxist and pluralist theories (comparing and contrasting):

Whereas Marxists believe that economic and political power are closely linked (to possess economic power is to possess political power), pluralists believe that economic influence or power is not a prerequisite for political power. For pluralists, anyone in a group can develop their own concerns, leading to the formation of an organisation to represent those interests, whether to protect their own occupational group or wider issues about which they may feel strongly such as the environment.

7. Criticism of Marxist theory:

A criticism of Marxism is that it fails to recognise the extent to which ordinary people can join pressure groups etc. and influence government decisions – notwithstanding the controlling effects of ISAs and other subtle forms of control such as socialism.

8. Concluding paragraph, reflection of key points in relation to essay title:

In conclusion, although power can be seen through many different theories, there are criticisms in each one. Considering both the Marxist and pluralist theories of power, we can see that although there is at least one point of similarity – i.e. both agree that we have not achieved, and will probably never achieve, a more equal sharing of power – there are many contrasting viewpoints. These derive from one major difference: pluralists consider that power is shared among interest groups which work to the advantage of the masses, whereas Marxists view power as being held by one particular group at the expense of the masses.

Ideas for coursework and personal studies

1. Carry out a survey in your own locality into people's views *either* on their general attitudes to politics or to specific politicians *or* on a specific issue such as the future of the monarchy or Britain's membership of the European Union. (Make sure your sample is manageable but broad, i.e. not just among your family or friends. Draw carefully on the sociological aspects of your assignment.)
2. Prepare and carry out an interview questionnaire in relation to age or gender and political attitudes and activities. (Similar advice as given above applies again here.)
3. Carry out a content analysis of the mass media in relation to one or more political issues for a specified period of time. Consider carefully the form or forms of both media and the issue(s) to be covered. To what extent does the content analysis reveal neutrality or bias? What other evidence may support your evaluation?
4. Compile a case study of a local political or environmental issue such as an urban development or a bypass scheme. How does media coverage of this issue reflect the attitudes and opinions of those whose lives are most affected? What are the views of these people on the impact they are able to have on political decision-making processes?
5. Carry out a survey of a pressure group by gathering its literature and interviewing a reasonable cross-section of members. Consider and evaluate its tactics and decision-making processes in its attempts to influence government and/or public opinion.

Selected reading list

Black Tribunes: Black Political Participation in Britain, T.A. Sewell (Lawrence & Wishart, 1993)

Decade of De-alignment, Ivor Crewe and Bo Sarlvik (Oxford University Press, 1983)

Decline in Class Voting in Britain, M. Franklin (Oxford University Press, 1988)

Elites and Society, Tom Bottomore (Routledge, 1993)

'Gender and voting', P. Walsh et al. in *Sociology Review* (Philip Allan, November 1991)

Hard Road to Renewal, Stuart Hall (Verso, 1988)

How Britain Votes, Anthony Heath et al. (Pergammon Press, 1985)

Legitimation Crisis, J. Habermas (Heinemann, 1973)

On the Nature of Organizations, Peter Blau (J. Wiley & Sons, New York, 1974)

Political Change in Britain, D. Butler and D. Stokes (Macmillan, 1974)

Power, A Radical View, Steven Lukes (Macmillan, 1974)

'Power and politics', K. Bonnett, in *Developments in Sociology*, vol. 10, M. Haralambos (ed.) (Causeway Press, 1994)

Pressure Groups, Politics and Democracy in Britain, Wyn Grant (Philip Allan, 1989)

The State in Capitalist Society, R. Miliband (Quartet, 1973)

The Power Elite, C. Wright Mills (Oxford University Press, 1956)

Who Governs?, Robert A. Dahl (Yale University Press, 1961)

12 Religion and ideology

'I've established a religion that really appeals to people.'

Introduction

Despite the material pressures of modern society, illustrated by the cartoon above, many people look to religion for answers about the meaning of life. By linking events to divine intervention and supernatural forces, religion tries to interpret, cope with and even complete everyday experiences. Religion is a considerable social force; not only can it unite – or divide – groups in society, it has considerable influence on moral codes and individuals' behaviour.

Religion involves beliefs and the rituals that express those beliefs in a wide range of private and public ceremonies of worship. Sociologists, however, tend to look behind such beliefs and rituals and focus on the concept of **ideology**. An ideology is a pattern of shared ideas (or even commonsense knowledge), believed by its adherents to be factual and analytical, which seeks to explain and legitimate the social structure or culture of a social group.

This unit will look at:

- beliefs in society: materialism and idealism;
- sociological theories of religion in terms of its influence on stability and integration, conflict and change;
- the relationship between religion and social structure;
- types of belief, with reference to the sacred and the profane, supernaturalism, magic and ideology;
- religious beliefs, practices and influences in relation to churches, denominations, sects and cults;
- the role of different religions in a multicultural society;
- indicators of religiosity and secularisation, including revivalism, new religious movements and televangelism.

Contrasting theories of religion

Materialism and idealism

Some theorists see social reality in terms of fixed structures and systems, while others see it as more fluid, to be understood as a continuous process of changing interpretation and intervention. These social theories have been referred to respectively as materialism and idealism.

- **Materialism** suggests that the world is made up of material or physical objects which shape our minds and ways of thinking. Nothing exists that is not physical matter or at least dependent on physical matter – and this includes our minds, housed in our physical brains.
- **Idealism** suggests that the world exists in our minds and can be changed by altering the ways in which we think.

Social theories may be deemed materialist or idealist, according to which of the above interpretations they tend towards when considering the material or economic forces that shape social life.

Karl Marx was a major critic of materialist theories. He considered that society could not be seen simply as part of the material world 'out there' in a timeless, unchanging form. For Marx, it would continue to shape and be reshaped by human intervention which is capable, by ideas and perceptions, of changing the material and social world:

> 'The ideas of the ruling class are, in every age, the ruling ideas, i.e. the class which is the dominant material force in society is at the same time its dominant intellectual force.'
> Karl Marx and Friedrich Engels, in R. Pascal (ed.), *The German Ideology* (Lawrence and Wishart, 1939)

Idealism, conversely, could take an active form with ideas serving to transform society. Marx suggests that the world exists in people's minds and it is capable of being changed by them:

> 'Man makes religion, religion does not make man. But man is no abstract being encamped outside the world. Man is the world of man, the state society.... Religion is the general theory of that world, its encyclopaedic compendium ... its universal source of consolation and justification.
> 'Religious distress is at the same time the expression of real distress and also the protest against real distress. Religion is the sigh of the oppressed creature, the heart of a heartless world, just as it is the spirit of spiritless conditions. It is the opium of the people.'
> Karl Marx, *The Critique of Hegel's Philosophy of Law*, trans. N.I. Stone (Charles H. Kerr, 1904)

Marx, then, identifies two forms of relationships in which people become involved. One is with objects, on a material or physical level; whilst the second is with other people, on an intellectual and emotional level. People therefore can be seen:

- objectively – as *passive* objects, affected by their environment; or
- subjectively – as *active* subjects, who can affect their physical and social environment.

Religion and ideology as sources of stability

Durkheim

For Marx, religion was an ideology which had for centuries deluded ordinary people into integrated, stable, social relationships conforming to capitalist ideology. Emile Durkheim, a founding figure of functionalism, also saw religion as a source of **integration**. However, whereas Marx saw the stabilised system as alienating and repressive, an effective means of pacifying people (through the promise of a better afterlife), Durkheim regarded the stable integration of society as necessary and beneficial in building the unity of its members into a moral community with shared values.

In his classic text, *The Elementary Forms of Religious Life*, the final book published during his lifetime, Durkheim maintained that society formed the basic means by which people organised and explained all their ideas. He analysed this relationship between society and its members by the use of two concepts:

- **collective representation** or the ideas that a group of people hold in common. These are social rather than individual and need to be seen as 'social facts' external to any individual in a society;
- **collective consciousness** or the sum total of all 'collective representations'. This forms the coherent views of the world and shared beliefs held by a particular society.

Sources of stability were of key interest to Durkheim. He stated that religion, which he described as:

> *'a unified system of beliefs and practices relating to sacred things . . .'*

served as a source of stability, and as a means of integration for society, in the following ways:

- It provides ultimate *meanings of human experiences and behaviour*, i.e. explanations by means of which individuals and societies can make sense of their lives.
- In requiring definitions of reality, society needs a common frame of reference for social action which is maintained by an *overarching view of reality* – this is provided by religion.

A Jewish wedding ceremony

- By drawing its members together in activities of celebration, religion sustains *value consensus*.
- Religion marks the rites of passage of a society: major status changes such as adulthood, marriage and death are accompanied by religious ceremonies in the *sharing of a common belief system*.

In *The Elementary Forms of Religious Life*, Durkheim set out the findings of his studies of religion in Australian aboriginal society. He concluded that religious worship is society worshipping itself, and thus providing itself with a major source of stability and integration.

Criticisms of Durkheim's views on religion

- To some extent Durkheim's views are based on studies of primitive societies. For example, in *Primitive Societies*, with his student Marcel Mauss, Durkheim attempted to show the basic differences between modern and primitive societies by studying the ways in which the latter categorise various phenomena of human experience. More complex modern and multicultural societies experience far greater difficulties in achieving and upholding shared values.
- Whilst religion may be important in promoting and maintaining stability, it is difficult – in view of the rifts and divisions which seem to exist in most religions – to go along with Durkheim's view that religion may be interpreted as society worshipping itself.
- There seems to be a conservative element to religion as seen by Durkheim and other functionalists, who tend to emphasise its role of stability and integration. But religion has also brought about *social change* – sometimes quite radical, as in the case of the Islamic revolution in Iran and liberation theology in Latin America. Religion does not necessarily produce stability and integration. Who would have considered, for example, that Yigal Amir, a 15-year-old Jewish extremist, would assassinate the Israeli Prime Minister Yitzhak Rabin in November 1995?

Religion as a source of change within society is discussed below in relation to the work of Max Weber.

Religion and ideology as sources of conflict and change

Karl Marx maintained that the main source of conflict leading to social change was based on the economic arrangements which surrounded capitalism and which formed the social relations of production; these included, according to Marx, the religious ideas and values held at any particular point in time. Religion was important: it imposed a passive acceptance on the workforce. It was no accident, therefore, that the USSR and the communist regimes of eastern Europe, influenced originally by Marxism, repressed religion and preached atheism, instead emphasising allegiance to the ideology of communism.

Weber

Max Weber challenged Marx's **economic determinism** – the belief that everything is determined by economics – by showing how economic processes themselves depend upon what goes on in the minds of people and, in particular, upon their ideas and beliefs. Weber did not seek to replace the economic determinism of Marx with a religious determinism. On the contrary, he emphasised the interrelation of the various factors. His key concept was that of **elective affinity** – the process by which certain ideas and certain social groups 'seek each other out' in history. To take the example of Confucianism: Weber did not consider that Confucianism either *produced* the Chinese bureaucratic system nor that it was merely a *reflection* of the system; he believed that, whatever might have been the original motives of Confucius and his followers, Confucianism became *a religious and ethical system which met the needs of a particular class of people* in China. In other words, the group of people, and the ideas, **elected** each other because of the natural **affinity** between them.

Weber – like Marx – set out to demonstrate the importance of ideas and beliefs by an analysis of the beginning of capitalism in Britain. Weber's book, *The Protestant Ethic and the Spirit of Capitalism*, defined capitalism as 'the pursuit of profit and forever renewed profit', and in terms of 'rational business transactions'. Weber investigated the extent to which religious beliefs and values influenced the development of the spirit of capitalism. He wrote of how, particularly under charismatic leadership (originally those who 'have received the gift of grace' in the New Testament Bible), radical change is introduced, with incredible after-effects. The radical social change that occurred in nineteenth-century Britain was, in Weber's opinion, associated with the activities of religious groups. In particular, among such religious groups, was **Calvinism** – a strict version of the Protestant faith named after its founder, a French priest, called **John Calvin** (1509–64).

Key aspects of Calvinist religion/ideology

- It is based on the idea of **predestination** – the belief that all events in our lives are predetermined and nothing can alter this. Since God knows everything, past and future, then our futures must be set from birth. Accordingly so is our destination at death – either for heaven or hell – and there is nothing we can do about it.
- Those destined for heaven, Calvin termed the **Elect**. However, even Calvinists do not know with any certainty if they are among the Elect, so it is necessary to search for signs. Weber argued that this 'salvation anxiety', rather than producing despondency, led to the hope that signs of reassurance of selection and salvation might be discovered.
- The **work ethic** is central to Calvinism. Signs of favour from God are gained by hard work. Work is a 'calling'; combined with self discipline and the avoidance of idleness and time-wasting, it is rewarded by earthly material success. Unnecessary leisure or laziness detracts from the glory of God, as does alcohol, gambling, sexual pleasure and material comfort. Calvinists in nineteenth-century Britain threw themselves into their work; rather than wasting their wealth, they saved and re-invested in their businesses.
- Calvinists became, in effect, 'God's tool on earth'. As part of their obedience to the work ethic, they looked, in a rational way, at maximising their efficiency rather than relying on traditional methods of production. In Weber's view, such a calculating, rational view of the world was needed for the development of capitalism.

The above seems contrary to most commonly held perceptions of Christianity and its non-materialist teachings. Nevertheless, for Weber, the Protestant ethic, with the constant seeking of a state of grace to achieve an emotional union with God and salvation, encouraged both the 'spirit of labour' and the 'spirit of capitalism'. It helps to explain why **industrialisation** took place in Britain ahead of other nations. Religions such as Catholicism in Europe and Buddhism in Asia did not create, according to Weber, appropriate conditions for the development of industrial capitalism.

Criticisms of Weber's views on religion

- Some societies held capitalist ethics and structures before Calvinism developed.
- The development of capitalism may be accounted for in other ways. Imperialism, piracy, international trade and so on brought huge amounts of wealth to countries. Successful forms of early capitalism may have been achieved by non-religious groups – as seems to be the case in many contemporary societies.
- M. Rodinson, in *Islam and Capitalism* (1977), criticised Weber's portrayal of oriental beliefs. Rodinson argued that Islam did in fact seem to promote the division of labour, trade and the development of a market economy. He suggested that it was not religion which initiated or even blocked capitalism but other factors such as colonialism and wars.
- Critics have argued that Weber misinterpreted the economic ethics of the world religions he researched, and failed to produce sufficient representative empirical data in support of his theory.

However, G. Marshall, in *The Protestant Ethic* (1991), offers a defence for Weber. He argues that Weber did not claim that Calvinism was the only factor in the development of capitalism since it was also necessary to have:

- separation of business and household capital;
- rational bookkeeping and allied technology;
- a sound structure of law and administration, and the rational spirit within a culture.

Marshall also states that:

> 'It seems to be the fate of Weber's Protestant ethic thesis to be interpreted anew by each generation of scholars in the light of their aims, particular concerns and obsessions . . . visions of modernity can convincingly be extracted from Weber's essays. This may mean simply that they are ambiguous. But it may also be that they pose in uniquely stark form the central interpretative problem of sociology; namely, how to understand the objective meaning of social action in terms of the interests and ideas of those involved.'
>
> G. Marshall, 'The protestant ethic' *Sociology Review*
> (September, 1991)

Subjectivity and meaning

Peter Berger and Thomas Luckmann, in various texts including their *Sociology of Religion and Sociology of Knowledge* (1969), provide an **interpretive approach**. They maintain that religion is produced by people subjectively interpreting, and finding meaning in, their lives: people's lives are based on a deep-rooted religious dimension. It is the *subjectivity of people's personal experiences* which, according to Berger and Luckmann, should be the focus for sociologists studying religion: this is the very essence of how people make sense of the world around them.

It was Weber's thinking that provided the starting point for Berger's writings. For Weber, the modern world and the development of capitalism had been accompanied by a process of 'rationalisation': bureaucracy needed to develop to provide more efficient institutions. Nevertheless, Weber understood that this carried a cost. Berger takes up Weber's line and talks about 'rationalisation' or reason replacing faith, causing 'dis-enchantment': the world becomes 'demystified' and its previous magic and mystery slowly disappear. Over the twentieth century, people's lives have been transformed from being unified and integrated within a set and stable framework to becoming fragmented and diverse in rapidly changing patterns of social life. This has led traditional religion into a credibility crisis: people now encounter many alternative belief systems and lifestyles. In contemporary multicultural society, each religion competes both with other religions and with secular belief systems; there is a wide range of non-religious doctrines or theories from which followers seek to gain the meaning of their existence.

Religion, knowledge and power

For Berger and Luckmann the sociology of religion forms part of a wider sociology of knowledge. They maintain that every society has its own body of knowledge which has been assembled by that society. For example, the knowledge required by Aborigines in their use of religious totem poles is markedly different from the knowledge required by the Pope deciding on the Catholic Church's policies regarding abortion.

The possession of this kind of religious 'knowledge' is one of the means by which the forces of social control – namely the state and its law-making processes – make elite claims to legitimate power. Religion also serves to legitimate social institutions by placing them in a sacred framework of reference: secular law is often rooted within religious law, for example the Ten Commandments.

The legitimisation provided by religion is also evident in its depiction of society and its establishment as created by God rather than by human beings. Historically important concepts along these lines have included the 'divine right of kings' (the claim that the monarch is appointed as an agent of divine will) and 'Papal infallibility' (the Pope appointed, and held to be beyond challenge, as God's representative).

Natural disasters, disease and death are events to which we try to attach meaning – the ways in which we do this become part of the reality of each society. If this is not achieved then the order gained through social institutions will not survive. It is often religion that offers meaning and explanations for major life events, particularly death.

Religion thus provides explanations in relation to ultimate questions that are accepted as knowledge by its believers. Religion or religious knowledge is therefore a very effective form of power in terms of the legitimisation it provides since, unlike other forms of legitimisation, only religion offers meaning for the ultimate realities of life and death.

Think about it

- What examples can you provide to explain how religion forms part of a wider body of knowledge? For example, which religious symbols or festivals do you consider contribute to the body of knowledge which characterises a particular society?
- Think about how religion forms an important part of the power structure, and control over people's lives, in both Western and Eastern societies.
- How do you consider religion might provide meaning and even comfort to people who experience personal tragedies and national disasters?

The relationship between ideas and social structure

Ideas, particularly religious ideas, do not exist in a vacuum – they fit in with the wider structure of society. Belief systems (see page 627) operate within society and, through the interaction of members of a society, can influence people's behaviour.

Islamic countries in the Middle and Far East exemplify how ideas can influence social structure. Civil law and Islamic religious law, in a country such as Iran, amount to the same thing: all areas of private and public life are governed by the Koran, the holy text of Islam. Whereas in the UK, ideas of religion are sometimes seen as distinct from the social structure in everyday terms, the Islamic code makes its ideas felt clearly in everyday life with, for example, the prohibition of alcohol and severe punishments for adultery, theft, etc.

The close interweaving of religious 'rules' and social structure, although particularly obvious in extreme cases such as the 'ethnic cleansing' in the former Yugoslavia in the 1990s, is prevalent in all societies to differing degrees. The social structure of most Western societies is undergoing considerable change and there is a constant reassessment of the relationship between traditional religious principles and current beliefs and practice. An example in the UK was the Archbishop of Canterbury's tacit acceptance, for the first time by the Church of England, of cohabiting couples as no longer being considered to be 'living in sin', as described in the article on page 626.

Think about it

- Do you think that changes in religious views precede or follow changes in the social structure of society?
- What examples can you provide of the interweaving of 'religious rules' in social rules or conventions even when religious practice seems to be at insignificant levels?
- Do you think that religious leaders should express their views about how the nation should behave on matters such as cohabitation or abortion? Give reasons for your response.

Dr Carey's best speech

THE Archbishop of Canterbury spoke in favour of marriage yesterday. That ought to be no more news than Gary Lineker speaking in favour of football. But it *is* news in the context of the General Synod of the Church of England, and good news too, because Dr Carey made the most powerful speech of his archiepiscopal career, and what he said needed saying.

Dr Carey was discussing the Synod's report *Something to Celebrate*, which attempts to give a guarded approval to cohabitation and wishes to dispense with the phrase "living in sin". He rejected the conclusion of the report with an argument which was both thoughtful and humane. Rather than impugning the motives of those who cohabit, the Archbishop acknowledged that many who do so manifest true love for one another. But what he demonstrated with great clarity was the falsity that the choice of who lives with whom, and in what manner, is a matter only for the couple themselves.

One of the most important features of marriage is that it takes place before witnesses, so acknowledging that "the wider society is involved". The "solemn, public promises" of the Christian wedding service, said Dr Carey, bring this out. Each marriage depends upon that wider society "in a thousand ways". Cohabitation, on the other hand, tending to be "provisional and private", pretends that it can exist *in vacuo*, which is anti-social. And just as society assists or ought to assist marriage, so marriage assists society. Its security and interdependency and provision of love for children provide a basis for individual development, physical well-being and moral growth for which nothing else can substitute. Every child of a successful marriage, is also, if one is going to be coldly arithmetical about it, a huge saving to the social services.

If Dr Carey had wished to be blunter still, he could have cited many examples all round us to confirm what he was saying. The breakdown of marriages and of other sexual relationships has an effect not unlike the effect of injury in the First World War. It inflicts psychological damage not only upon the direct victims but on others who love and depend upon them. It often invalids them out of happy and generous participation in society for months, years, sometimes for ever. And long after its visible wounds have healed, it still causes nightmares. As a result, literally everyone suffers. We have only to look at the recent marital difficulties in the Royal Family to see how true this is. When the Prince of Wales married Lady Diana Spencer in 1981, the public rejoicing was genuine and important, part of a great collective wish to live according to standards of love and trust. Now that their marriage has failed, it is misery instead of happiness that ripples out towards all of us, damaging national self-esteem, and making those who are married feel beleaguered.

Source: The *Daily Telegraph*, 1 December 1995

Belief systems and types of belief

Belief systems 'Belief systems' refer to ideas which individuals and groups hold to be right and true: these systems offer guides and codes for their behaviour and also tend to justify such behaviour.

- Belief systems do not necessarily take the form of a clear set of consistent and ordered ideas. Individuals and groups may hold beliefs and celebrate major festivals without knowing why: these beliefs may have been passed down to them by parents and others, as exemplified by the article below.

Christmas — Its Origin

BY *AWAKE!* CORRESPONDENT IN ITALY

JUST three days before Christmas 1993, Pope John Paul II acknowledged that the celebration of Christmas is not rooted in the Bible. Regarding the date December 25, the pope admitted: "On that day in pagan antiquity, the birthday of the 'Invincible Sun' was celebrated to coincide with the winter solstice." How, then, did Christmas begin? The pope continued: "It seemed logical and natural to Christians to replace that feast with the celebration of the only and true Sun, Jesus Christ."

"In other words," wrote journalist Nello Ajello in *La Repubblica*, "someone had Jesus born on an imaginary, fabricated, false date." When did this fabrication take place? A press release from the Vatican stated: "The festival of Christmas appeared for the first time in 354 [C.E.]."

What about January 6, Epiphany, which commemorates the coming of the Magi to visit the newborn Jesus? "Much evidence leads us to believe that the choice of January 6, like that of December 25 for the Roman holiday celebrating the birth of Jesus, was also influenced by a pagan anniversary," continued the press release. "In Alexandria, in fact, on the night between January 5 and 6, pagans used to celebrate the birthday of the *god Aeon* (god of time and eternity).... It would seem that the Church wanted to Christianize this festival."

Jesus never authorized his followers to merge true worship with pagan customs. Rather, he told them to teach "all the things *I* have commanded you." (Matthew 28:19, 20) Furthermore, when confronted by the religious leaders of his day, Jesus asked them: "Why do you break the command of God for the sake of your tradition?" (Matthew 15:3, *New International Version*) That same question may well be asked of so-called Christians who perpetuate pagan customs today.

Source: *Awake!* (published by Jehovah's Witnesses), 8 December 1995

Think about it

Christmas is a widely celebrated religious festival but few people realise or acknowledge its pagan origins; many are not familiar with the Christmas story itself.

- Think of examples of religious festivals and the symbols and ceremonies associated with them. How much background knowledge and understanding do you have of such festivals and what have been your sources of information?
- Of what sociological interest might be the pagan origins of religious festivals?

- Belief systems vary and produce very different ideas about what is right and true, as in the contrast which may be drawn between magic (see page 629) and religion. Sociologists need to examine such ideas in their own terms, as used by the people who subscribe to them.
- Belief systems make claims about truth and represent knowledge in both general and institutionalised forms. Such claims attempt to provide answers to the world and our lives. 'Experts', whether theologians, sorcerers or scientists, provide and defend their 'knowledge claims' and thus enter into power relationships or ideological realms. This is discussed below (pages 632–5) in the section on political and religious ideologies.

Different types of religious belief

Shared characteristics of religious beliefs

Despite the existence of many different types of religious belief, all religions seem to have certain things in common.

- Most divide the world into:
  - the **sacred** or that which is holy, which inspires awe, and must be treated with special respect; and
  - the **profane** or everyday non-sacred things that can be handled casually. The word 'profane' has also come to refer to attitudes which are disrespectful to the sacred.
- All religions include a set of beliefs or convictions about the truth or existence of things that cannot be proven by ordinary means.
- All religions prescribe **rituals** or procedures for maintaining the relationship between humans and their God or gods, spirits, etc. A ritual is a traditional, stylised form of communication with the deity that reaffirms religious beliefs.

The variety of religious belief

The following brief accounts describe just a few of the many different types of religious belief and practice.

Supernaturalism   Often found in small traditional societies, supernaturalism is the belief in wide impersonal forces that carry across into all aspects of life. The Melanesians of the South Pacific call such forces *mana*. They maintain that a skilled hunter or a woman who bears many healthy children has great *mana*. *Mana* can be good or bad, however. A warrior who is captured by his enemies has bad *mana*. *Mana* is not the same as luck: it exists in the universe and can be won through prayer and ritual or lost by going against taboos.

Animism   Animism is a belief in more clearly defined supernatural beings such as spirits and demons. In a sense, the Animist may be seen to live in an enchanted forest: rock and streams are alive with spirits and demons. At any moment a person or an object may be invaded by one of these supernatural beings and used by them for good or evil. They are not 'gods' in the Western sense; they are not worshipped, but they exist and must be dealt with. In Western societies, belief in the devil, superstitions and the fear of ghosts have animistic overtones.

Totemism   This is based on the 'totem', as used by North American tribes, but has become more widely applied. Totemism reveres particular objects, animals and plants as possessing supernatural powers. Kinship groups in primitive societies often had their own totems and allied rituals. In more advanced societies, totemic beliefs may be linked to military groups and football teams in the form of flags, badges and mascots, and can be recognised in our referring to certain artefacts as 'cult objects' (see also Unit 6, page 291).

<u>Theism</u>   Theism is the belief in a God or gods who oversee human affairs. Gods reveal themselves to humans in different ways. These divine encounters are preserved in myths and holy books that offer humans the promise of understanding the universe and obtaining salvation.

- **Monotheism** is the belief in a single all-knowing and all-powerful deity. Three of the world's major religions – Judaism, Christianity and Islam – are monotheistic.
- **Polytheism** is the belief in many gods and goddesses. Another of the world's major religions – Hinduism – is polytheistic.

The difference between monotheism and polytheism is not absolute. Some polytheists consider one deity more powerful than the others – the mother or father figure among gods. In some areas of the world, Catholicism (essentially monotheistic) borders on polytheism: saints are believed to have the power to intervene in human affairs and are 'worshipped'.

According to Max Weber, the failure of monotheism in some societies was caused by the powerful vested interests of religious 'experts' who relied upon a multitude of gods.

<u>Abstract idealism</u>   This is the belief in a holy way of thinking and behaving. Religions of abstract ideals do not have 'gods' in the Western sense, although they do revere holy men. Rather, they emphasise the quest for a higher state of being, a higher level of consciousness or awareness; their claim is to point to the 'Way'. Buddhism and Krishna Consciousness are examples. By following the 'Noble Eightfold Way' of right living, Buddhists can gradually eliminate suffering through successive reincarnations until they reach the ultimate goal of nirvana, the state of complete redemption.

Magic, science, religion and Ideology   Max Weber pointed to the differences between urban and rural forms of religion, and saw the latter as more inclined towards magic.

> '[Magic is] the influencing of events by the use of potions, chanting or ritual practices.'
> Anthony Giddens, *Sociology* (2nd edn 1993)

Under such a definition, if Communion wine may be considered as a potion, then the most important Catholic ritual may be seen in terms of magic. However, magic is generally considered to be practised by individuals rather than by communities of believers.

Individuals may turn to magic when faced by bad luck or danger. Bronislaw Malinowski (1884–1942), the British anthropologist, in *Magic, Science and Religion and Other Essays* (1944), described the magical rites of Trobriand Islanders in the Pacific, performed prior to dangerous canoe voyages but not before fishing in calm, local waters.

A wide range of cross-cultural studies have examined relationships between magic, science, religion and ideology. The following is an outline of just one major work in this area.

The Azande of Sudan

Edward Evans-Pritchard, in *Witchcraft, Oracles and Magic Among the Azande* (1937), his classic study of the Azande of Sudan in Central Africa in the 1930s, found that the religious beliefs of the Azande were based on:

- magic and witchcraft: an oracle was consulted when someone suffered from bad luck to establish the source of the witchcraft;
- ruling-class control: the Princes of the Azande were exempt from witchcraft accusations. Each Prince owned an oracle which was used to decide upon accusations of witchcraft between commoners;
- legitimation of privileges: the Princes of the Azande held their privileges by tradition and mythology. The special status of the 'knowledge claims' of the Princes and their oracles maintained order and control; as Evans-Pritchard puts it,

> *'Privileges invested in one class in society require the halo of the myth.'*
> Edward Evans-Pritchard, *Witchcraft, Oracles and Magic Among the Azande*
> (Clarendon Press, 1937)

The ideology of such a belief system seems to serve two purposes:

- It helps to offset worries caused by events which cannot be accounted for, by blaming an individual within a community.
- Conflict between competitors or rivals within the community becomes reduced via witchcraft. This cannot be dismissed as irrational: such ideas do seem to work when the basic assumptions are accepted by a community.

Nevertheless, Evans-Pritchard concluded that Azande beliefs about magic and witchcraft did not form a consistent body of ideas. His sympathetic approach to such a culture, however, has led to an interesting debate on the relationships between magic, religion and science and how all three may be seen as belief systems.

Personal knowledge

M. Polanyi, in *Personal Knowledge* (1958), argued that three factors interact to maintain belief systems:

- 'Circularity of ideas': each idea becomes explained in relation to another allied idea which upholds the stability of all related ideas and beliefs. If one belief is challenged, it is defended by referring to another belief which in turn is often rooted in the original belief.
- 'Subsidiary explanations for difficult situations': in magic, religion and science, conflicting evidence is seen as abnormal and need not be taken seriously. Explanations such as wrong interpretation or poor practice are put forward, thus allowing the evidence to be easily dismissed.
- Rejecting alternative world views: by using the legitimacy of existing world views held by 'experts' to undermine the challenges of rival views, we can refuse to accept alternative belief systems.

Polanyi's points make us reflect on the validity of scientific 'knowledge claims' and to question how unbiased and neutral these claims might be in their accumulation of the evidence on which the universal laws of the physical world are based.

Science as a belief system

T.S. Kuhn, in *Scientific Paradigms* (1972), reinforces the views of M. Polanyi. He refers to the 'dogmatism of mature science', which he sees in:

- a commitment to a particular way of seeing the world (a paradigm) and the adoption of a common ideological commitment to this accepted view when undertaking science; and
- the drive being not to reveal the unknown but to obtain and accept the known, in a relatively closed set of self-fulfilling ideas:

> '. . . a paradigm tells scientists about entities with which the universe is populated and the way members of that population behave. . . . It informs them of the questions that may be legitimately asked about nature, and the techniques that can be used in the search for answers to them.'
> Adapted from T.S. Kuhn, *Scientific Paradigms* (University of Chicago, 1972, p. 93)

So, in this view, science, as well as religion, may be seen as a belief system which insists on a certain way of viewing the world.

Stephen Hawking, in his famous lecture at the Royal Albert Hall, London, *Does God Play Dice in Black Holes?* (22 November 1995), commented that:

- Science assumes that the physical world follows natural laws which once understood could be used to predict the future, which is impossible.
- The deterministic view of science based on the eighteenth-century French philosopher P.S. Laplace's views of a God-mathematician who knows the positions and speeds of every particle in the Universe, and their future, is mistaken.
- All evidence points to God being a gambler who throws dice on every possible occasion.
- Twentieth-century science, particularly quantum theory and the uncertainty principle, had shown that the Universe is constructed in a way which cannot be determined. Thus the laws of science in their present form suggest that God still has a few tricks up His sleeve.

Think about it

- To what extent do you think that the laws of science can be used to predict the future? Do you consider that to be impossible? Does this make a nonsense of trying to establish, in a 'scientific' way, patterns of social events and behaviour?
- What do you consider to be the key points of difference between religious beliefs and scientific understanding?

Political, religious and racial ideologies: competitors or allies?

Political, religious and racial ideologies share some common features:

- They require faith in a set of beliefs.
- They serve to reflect and justify the interests of particular groups, including political and religious leaders and ethnic groups.

Throughout human history, religion has played a dual role in society. This has been of particular interest to sociologists over the last hundred years or so.

- One role of religion has been to *challenge* the values and practices of non-religious members of society and even inspire radical social change. It may be claimed that Christianity as a movement corrected the excesses and injustices of the Roman Empire. In more recent times, the Shah of Iran was overthrown in an Islamic Revolution; in 1979 Ayatollah Khomeini, after 15 years' exile, was installed as the religious leader of Iran until his death ten years later.
- Another role of religion, as we have seen, has been to *serve* and *legitimise* the existing social order. The emperors and kings of Europe ruled 'by divine right', appointed by God; so too did much earlier leaders such as the pharaohs of ancient Egypt. Part of this role, in ideological terms, has been not just to encourage the poor and disadvantaged to accept their lot with the promise of rewards in the next world, but also to maintain that what happens in life is simply the just outcome of rules that are the best that are available and that things are as they should be. It is in this role that religion was termed the 'opiate' of the people by Marx; because it serves as a consolation or 'escape', and encourages acceptance of hardship, it helps to preserve the status quo.

Gary Marx, in his study *Religion – Opiate or Inspiration of Civil Rights Among Negroes* (1967), showed how religion played both these roles in the context of black churches in America.

Challenge and inspiration: the black church provided the American political civil rights movement with its ideology, most of its leaders and, particularly in the south of the USA, its organisation. The black church was one of the few black-owned and black-operated institutions in the USA. It was the one place where blacks could gather, in private, without arousing the suspicions of whites. The Reverend Martin Luther King, Jr., spoke for the 'social gospel' tradition in black churches:

> *'Any religion that professes to be concerned with the souls of men and is not concerned with the slums that damn them, the economic conditions that strangle them, and the social conditions that cripple them is a dry-as-dust religion.'*
> Martin Luther King Jr.

Opiate: some black religious groups in the USA, such as the Holiness Church, fostered a passive attitude among American Negroes. Many such gospel churches expressed the belief that God had His reasons, the suffering of black people was God's will – but that change would come about in His own way at His own time.

Gary Marx maintained that the more traditionally religious groups were less likely to express impatience over the slow pace of assimilation or to resent discrimination. He found that the more worldly religious groups, such as the Black Muslim Movement, functioned as an inspiration for action and change. Other less worldly gospel churches functioned as an opiate and an obstacle to political change.

Civil religion – a marriage of politics and religion?

The term 'civil religion' has been used to describe ritual or patterned events which may not seem directly to involve religious practices or beliefs, but which generate loyalty and collectivity in similar ways to religious rituals. Examples of civil religion in the UK are civic occasions such as royal garden parties, the state opening of Parliament, and even the annual Oxford v. Cambridge boat race – or more personal events such as a registry office wedding.

The American sociologist Robert N. Bellah, in his article *Civil Religion* (1967), drew on Emile Durkheim's idea of the 'collective consciousness' of religion (see page 620). Bellah argued that whereas Christianity and Judaism, for example, could not draw total allegiance from all Americans, civil religion could do this since it draws on shared traditions linked to the history of the country. Thus American Thanksgiving Day with the traditional family gathering plays a unifying national role: the turkey meal symbolises the four wild turkeys served to the founding pilgrims of Plymouth Colony in 1621.

Civil religion can thus serve to unite and integrate nation states. In 1996 the Olympic Games in the USA and the Euro '96 football championship in England provided examples of nation states putting their faith in supporting, with fervour, their national teams. However, Bellah points to the negative as well as the positive aspects of civil religion, as described in the article on page 634.

Think about it

- Provide examples of civil religion and explain your choices.
- Explain why religion might play a key role for minority groups in society. Offer specific examples to support your views.
- Why are sociologists interested in the practice of religious rituals/ceremonies? Offer examples and justify your choice in sociological terms.

Civil Religion in the US

In July 1979, with the United States beset by energy shortages, inflation, and other problems, President Jimmy Carter delivered an impassioned television speech warning of "a crisis of confidence" threatening to destroy the American social and political fabric. Religious themes echoed through this speech so strongly that the next day's newspaper accounts compared it with a sermon. Indeed, in his half-hour speech the President used the words "God," "faith," and "spirit" eleven times, invoked the names of patriot-martyrs like John and Robert Kennedy and Martin Luther King, Jr., and closed with these words: "Let us commit ourselves to a rebirth of the American spirit. Working together with our common faith, we cannot fail."

Although the Constitution of the United States mandates a strict separation between church and state, sociologist Robert Bellah (1967) argues that there is nevertheless an important religious dimension in American political life. What President Carter referred to as the American "common faith," Bellah has called "the American civil religion." Bellah says that this collection of beliefs, symbols, and rituals does stand apart from established church religion in the United States; but all the same, it parallels religious belief in that it helps to sustain the legitimacy of the American system of government by perpetuating the concept that the very existence of the nation is a reflection of the will of God.

Civil religion has been present since the earliest days of the republic, Bellah observes. In his first inaugural address, George Washington spoke of "that Almighty Being who rules over the universe," and of the "propitious smiles of Heaven" that can be expected only by a nation that respects "the eternal rules of order and right which Heaven itself has ordained." Since Washington, no President has delivered an inaugural address without mentioning God. Over the years, civil religion has also come to be expressed in such holidays as Thanksgiving and Memorial Day, in mottoes like "In God We Trust," in shrines such as the Tomb of the Unknown Solider, and in rituals such as the recitation of the Pledge of Allegiance, with its "one nation under God...."

The civil religion, Bellah points out, has its negative aspects. An ideology based on God, country, and flag has been used to attack nonconformist groups and ideas. The United States has used its concept of itself as a "new Israel" with a "Manifest Destiny" of conquest and domination to justify such dark chapters as the mistreatment of the American Indian and the attempt, in Vietnam, to defend a freedom that was more imagined than real.

At its best, though, American civil religion has been able to avoid conflict with established churches while building up powerful symbols of national identity that can be used to inspire deep levels of personal motivation for the attainment of national goals. And with its prophets and martyrs, sacred places and scriptures, and solemn rituals and symbols, Bellah concludes, the civil religion has kept alive the motivating spirit of those who founded the United States: the obligation of both the nation and its individual citizens to carry out God's will on earth.

Source: *Sociology: An Introduction*, M.S. Bassis et al. (Random House, New York, 1980)

The relationship between religion, politics and national identity

The relationship between religious and national identity is particularly obvious when it becomes part of a clash of political interests, as in the familiar case of Northern Ireland. In historical terms, Catholicism – the majority religion – has been linked with Irish nationalism, whereas Protestantism has been linked with that section of the population in Northern Ireland who seek to retain loyalty with Great Britain. In Poland, to take another example, many see Catholicism as an inseparable part of their national identity and remained loyal to the Catholic church throughout the communist period when atheism was the official line. Feelings ran particularly high when a Polish cardinal was elected Pope (John Paul II) in 1978. In the post-Soviet era, the dual loyalty to religion and nationhood seems likely to continue despite the defeat of Lech Walesa's party in November 1995 and an apparent swing back to communism.

However, religion as an embodiment of national identity and political interest can be a powerful force even when it takes less dramatic forms than the more obvious examples of Ireland and Poland. The links between the Church of England and the Establishment – the focus of considerable media attention in the 1990s, not for the first time – provide a more subtle example.

The Church of England and the Establishment

K. Medhurst and G. Moyser, in *Church and Politics in a Secular Age* (1988), consider how the Church of England tries both to care for and to criticise the Establishment (i.e. that sector of society holding power and influence). They discuss the Establishment of the Anglican Church (i.e. its status as the official national church with the monarch as its head), which, whilst linked to the Church's political involvement in the state, raises some important issues:

- The Establishment of the Church of England is an arrangement between the Church and the State which sets the framework for political initiatives rather than being a political initiative in its own right.
- The Establishment allows certain channels of political activity, for example the right of some Bishops to hold seats in the House of Lords, and gives some official weight to the Church's pronouncements on political and social issues. An example of one such pronouncement concerned responsibility for problems in urban priority areas, and is outlined in *Faith in the City – A Call for Action by Church and Nation* (The Commission on Urban Priority Areas, 1985).
- One element of the Establishment provides the Church of England with unique authority: regardless of attendance statistics, the Church has a geographical presence in all areas of England, which gives it a national profile in most major issues of popular debate. This influence, however, does not extend to the other countries of the UK, where the Anglican Church is in a minority.
- There is a widely held notion that the Church of England serves the interests and is the protector of society as a whole.

The Establishment of the Church of England dates back to King Henry VIII who, by 1536, had passed Acts to set up a national Anglican Church. This denied the Roman Catholic Pope (from whom Henry VIII had received his title 'Defender of the Faith') any power over the Church of England. In effect the King had reintroduced the ancient right of a Christian monarch to exercise power over the church in his kingdom. Despite conflict between the State and the Church in the centuries which followed, the Church of England has remained in its position as the 'national' church and the one close to the sources of power.

Think about it

- Should there be a separation between the Church and the state/monarchy? What effects might this have on the Church of England's role in English society?

Religious beliefs, practice and influence

Church, sect, denomination and cult

A wide range of religious beliefs and practices make up the institutional settings and distinct forms of religious associations. However, as most people are born into a religion and it can be difficult to go against such ties, religious associations usually include many different types of people.

Churches

In many sociological texts which touch on the subject, sociologists seem to use a confusing variety of interpretations of the term **church**. Some use it to refer to different religious traditions (Christianity, Islam, etc.), while others, conversely, discuss 'religion' but only within the relatively narrow context of the Christian tradition, referring mainly to the Catholic and Protestant churches or faiths within Christianity. A church could perhaps best be defined as an established religious organisation in the Christian tradition, most of whose members are born into the religion. The obvious examples in England are the Church of England (or Anglican Church) and the Roman Catholic Church. The 'mainstream' churches aim to be inclusive, i.e. to welcome anyone as a member and provide a spiritual base for society as a whole. Some – usually smaller – churches are less tolerant of religious differences and display considerable diversity in their interpretation of religious scriptures and traditions. Most churches employ full-time, professional clergy in an often complex hierarchical structure. Services tend to be formal and member participation limited, with much use being made of rituals, though some groups (such as the Society of Friends, or Quakers) have no ordained priests or ministers, and no formal rituals in their gatherings.

Sects

A **sect** is a smaller, less firmly established religious group, often created by a splintering away from a more traditional institution. Initially at any rate, a sect gains most of its members through conversion from other religions or from people who had no affiliation previously. Sects tend to be exclusive, i.e. separating themselves from wider society and excluding those whom they consider unworthy. Sects tend to adhere to their own doctrine more literally than the mainstream groups; to see their own truth as the only truth; and to focus on the hereafter. Clergy – often part-time, and sometimes lay (unordained) leaders – preside over informal, often emotionally charged services. Members tend to withdraw from other social involvements and to focus their lives on the sect.

Ernst Troeltsch, in *The Social Teachings of the Christian Churches* (1931), developed the thinking of his friend Max Weber and drew differences between a church and a sect along the lines indicated in the following table. (Note that 'church' here focuses on the Christian tradition.)

Think about it

• Using the paragraphs on churches and sects above, summarise the key ideas in brief note form.

Church	Sect
Accepts values of existing social order, serves as a means of integration.	Indifferent towards or rejecting of existing social order.
Delegates control to a specialised ministry with its own hierarchical structure.	A more equal sharing of responsibility with participation in administration and services. If central authority exists, it tends to be in a single charismatic leader.
Appeals to the higher classes.	Connected with the lower classes, the propertyless and social outcasts.
Conservative – works with the State and supports the dominant groups in society.	Radical and in opposition to the world, rejecting its values and even withdrawing from life outside the sect.
Exercise of choice by members; an institutionalised framework but no strong control over social life.	Total commitment required of its members; a non-institutionalised setting but strong control over social life.
Emphasis on the relationship between individuals and the institution.	Emphasis on fellowship and integration with sacrifice of worldly pleasures and devotion to religious life.
Examples Church of England, Roman Catholic Church, Greek Orthodox Church	*Examples* Jehovah's Witnesses, Moonies, Plymouth Brethren

H. Richard Neibuhr, in *The Social Sources of Denominationalism* (1929), considered that sects did not last long and tended either to become denominations (see page 638) or to cease to exist. He maintained that:

- voluntary adult commitment does not carry through to subsequent generations;
- commitment to the sect weakens as other competing concerns, such as socialisation and education, lead to contact with the outside world;
- the death of a charismatic leader often threatens the survival of the group; rarely can a replacement be found and the group cohesion often falls apart;
- the ideology of a sect contains the seeds of its own destruction. In striving to work hard and save money, upward social mobility occurs: such success tends to make members less hostile to the outside world, and turn 'to denominations as the influence of social success'.

Denominations A **denomination**, as indicated above, may be seen as a form of religious organisation midway between a church and a sect; it has been seen by many sociologists as developing from a sect. As sects become established, it is argued, they tend to develop a more structured hierarchy and bureaucracy, and soften their once radical attitude to the outside world; the example of Methodism is often cited. However, as noted by Ian Thompson in *Religion* (1986), an opposite direction may be taken; a denomination may develop into a sect. The Salvation Army exemplifies a movement from a denomination to a sect, as does Jim Jones's People's Temple, which began as part of the American Christian Church.

Cults The concept of a **cult** is a broad one and not easy to categorise. A cult is the least structured and least formal type of religious organisation, though they can impose strict discipline on their followers and may be very tightly knit and secretive. They are often relatively short-lived, small groups, consisting of like-minded members who reject the values of the outside world even though they may not have a clearly set out theology or ideology. Instead the cult is likely to demand of its members that they soul-search and unlock their spiritual potential in order to gain self realisation. Sometimes members are allowed also to maintain other religious links – indeed, cults may combine elements of various religions or, like sects, derive from or operate alongside other religions. Like a sect, a cult may form around a charismatic spiritual leader. Examples of cults include forms of spiritualism, transcendental meditation and astrology.

The difference between a sect and a cult is not clear-cut, and can depend largely on the viewpoint of the person providing the definition.

Think about it

- What are religious sects and how, in your opinion, do they differ from (a) cults, (b) denominations?
- What attraction might sects have in terms of religious worship?
- Why do you think that sects and cults tend to attract negative media coverage?
- Using the paragraphs on denominations and cults above, summarise the key points in note form.
- Draw a diagram of key points from your notes on churches, sects, denominations and cults on a sheet of A4 paper, highlighting points of contrast between them.

The changing nature of beliefs and institutions

Indicators of religiosity and of secularisation

Religiosity and **secularisation** have come to be seen as opposite sides of the same coin. The term 'secularisation' has been used to refer to the process in which the extent of 'religiosity' (people being religious) has declined and the influence of religion over important aspects of social life and over individuals and groups in society has dwindled.

There has arisen among sociologists a religiosity v. secularisation debate, centred on the issue as to whether and to what extent religion has decreased in terms of its importance in the everyday lives of those living in modern society.

Larry Shiner, in *The Concept of Secularisation in Empirical Research* (1971), underlines some of the uncertainty associated with the concept of secularisation by considering a possible range of its meanings. This is summarised in the following list.

Meanings of secularisation	Difficulties and issues
• *The decline of religion:* previously accepted symbols, doctrines and institutions lose influence.	• How to identify the 'golden age' from which the decline started?
• *Increasing conformity with this world:* society becomes absorbed with the practical tasks of the present.	• How to measure 'conformity with this world'?
• *The disengagement of society from religion and religious values:* religion is more of an inward life with little or no influence on social institutions. There is a separation of religion from political life.	• It is not easy to know at what point secularisation has occurred when religion is still associated with political institutions: for example, the British monarch is Head of the Church of England.
• *The transposition of religious beliefs and institutions:* knowledge and behaviour once understood to be grounded in divine powers are transformed into purely human responsibility.	• It cannot always be proved that secular belief systems contain elements deriving from religious beliefs (e.g. that the capitalist ethic had religious origins).
• *The world is deprived of its sacred character:* people and nature become seduced by rational/causal explanation and manipulation. This starts from the assumption that humankind has become largely independent of religion.	• Some argue that human beings have always been religious and that the sacred may have been temporarily pushed into the unconscious and now is finding new forms of expression.
• *A general movement from a sacred to a secular society:* all theories of change become grounded in secular rather than sacred explanations.	• This is a general theory of change and does not relate specifically to religious change.

Source: Adapted from P. Selfe, *Work Out Sociology* (Macmillan, 1993)

Shiner concludes that a variety of meanings have become associated with religiosity and secularisation in order to suit the needs of those using these concepts (see pages 645–6 for criticisms of the concept of secularisation). Indeed Shiner has even recommended that the concept of secularisation be abandoned and other more neutral concepts be adopted – 'religious transposition', for example.

The 'traditional' secularisation debate

Bryan Wilson, in *Religion in a Secular Society* (1966), argued that the established churches had declined in terms of their power and membership. In *The Anglican Church and its Decline* (1974), he furthered his line of argument; this is summarised (with updated statistics) as follows:

- Religious practices and participation have declined throughout industrial societies. In the UK, this has affected the Church of England more than other denominations: Wilson referred to the decreased numbers baptised, confirmed and married in the Church of England. Baptism, for example, fell from about two-thirds in 1950 to about one-half in 1970.
- Enrolled adult membership of the Trinitarian churches (i.e. those professing belief in the Trinity of the Father, Son and Holy Spirit) stood at 6.4 million in 1995, representing less than 14 per cent of the UK population aged 16 and over. Overall membership fell by 25 per cent between 1970 and 1995, although the Orthodox Church and some of the free churches increased their membership. The following tables illustrate the trends in more detail.

UK membership of Trinitarian churches			
Trinitarian churches	1970 (millions)	1980 (millions)	1995 (millions)
Roman Catholic	2.7	2.4	2.0
Anglican	2.6	2.2	1.7
Presbyterian	1.8	1.4	1.1
Methodist	0.7	0.5	0.4
Baptist	0.3	0.2	0.2
Other free churches	0.5	0.5	0.7
Orthodox	0.2	0.2	0.3
All Trinitarian churches	8.8	7.4	6.4

Source: Adapted from *Social Trends*, 1997

Think about it

- Identify the key trends in Trinitarian church membership from the table above.
- Offer explanations for the trends.

Projection of religious components of the UK population 1975–2000						
	1975	**1980**	**1985**	**1990**	**1995**	**2000**
Anglican	2 297 871	2 179 458	1 895 943	1 727 977	1 785 273	1 584 090
Baptist[1]	235 884	239 815	243 099	230 921	223 407	220 317
Roman Catholic	2 605 255	2 457 053	2 281 340	2 200 844	1 915 417	1 783 831
Independent[1]	240 200	236 881	229 569	225 525	206 244	200 362
Methodist[1]	576 791	520 557	474 290	451 732	401 087	366 820
New Churches[1]	2 060	10 137	35 351	77 454	109 601	135 200
Orthodox	196 850	203 165	223 741	265 968	288 560	320 420
Other Churches[1]	147 083	141 439	137 415	135 488	135 611	133 764
Pentecostal[1]	101 648	127 068	136 669	162 499	196 531	211 476
Presbyterian	1 589 085	1 437 775	1 322 047	1 214 032	1 099 587	986 915
TOTAL	7 992 727	7 553 346	6 979 464	6 692 440	6 361 318	5 943 195
of which *Free Churches*	1 303 666	1 275 895	1 256 393	1 283 619	1 272 481	1 267 939
Percentage totals of adult population	18.5	16.8	15.1	14.3	13.4	12.5

[1]The six components of the Free Churches

Source: *UK Christian Handbook: Religious Trends No. 1 1998/99*, Christian Research/Paternoster Publishing, 1997

Statistics

The accuracy of statistics on religion, as in other areas of sociology, needs to be carefully examined. How useful are statistics on church attendance in the UK if gathered on Christmas Day, for example? And what about unexpected factors such as a rise in church membership caused by parents anxious to gain places for their children in Church of England primary schools?

Furthermore, it is not easy to compare church membership between countries (see page 643), partly because not all churches have membership lists. In Finland, for example, 'active' church members are those who vote in Church Council elections; while in the case of Roman Catholics, the criterion is the number attending mass.

Think about it

Declining appeal is felt by all faiths

BY RUTH GLEDHILL

THE Church of England and the Jewish community are the first religious bodies to produce evidence of what is a widespread trend.

Monsignor Kieran Conry, spokesman for the Roman Catholic Church, said the loss of young people was being felt in his as in all the Churches, although central figures had not been collated to establish the scale of the decline.

The Catholic Church's Birmingham diocese leads the field in working with young people, employing four priests and four lay members in this area. For 50 years, a centre in Stratford-upon-Avon has run week-long courses for teenagers and parish groups visit at weekends. The centre has proved so successful that in July the diocese is opening another near Alton Towers.

Father John Seeney, who runs the centre, said: "Young people find the Church very insignificant in their lives. Society does not see spiritual values as central to life, and maybe the church environment is not attractive to them. But I think there is a great hunger among young people for God, and for something deeper.

"Music is very important here, and the young people go home singing songs and hymns."

Britain's 300,000-strong Jewish community is also fighting the loss of its youngsters on a tide of secularisation and assimilation. Nearly half of Anglo-Jewish men aged under 30 have a non-Jewish partner, according to the Institute for Jewish Policy Research, and nearly half of under-35s do not belong to a synagogue.

The Chief Rabbi, Dr Jonathan Sacks, launched Jewish Continuity, a body which aims to keep young people wedded to the Jewish faith with a series of educational and other programmes.

Most synagogues have classes where youngsters are taught Hebrew and the reasons behind ancient Jewish traditions. Increasing numbers of synagogues of all traditions are holding more social events and special services for youngsters.

The Methodist Church, which has an active core membership of people under 26, last year accepted a radical charter for change. The young people themselves put forward *Charter 96*, which called for churches to develop the use of audio, video, drama, visual aids and a full range of music in worship. "Make the message relevant," it said.

Source: *The Times*, 11 April 1996

- What do you think may be the factors behind the decline in active church membership predicted through to 2000, shown in the table on page 641?
- Do you think that churches, and other religious groups facing declining membership, should change their views or their style in order to attract more members and therefore to continue to perform a particular social role?

- Religious practice has declined in affluent societies, where other intellectual, cultural and social interests are receiving greater attention. In particular, there has been a growing inclination in most west European countries to regard organised Christian religion as somewhat irrelevant, as indicated in the graph on page 643.

  However, while statistics may portray a decline in attendance or membership of mainstream churches in the UK, some religious movements – for example, Jehovah's Witnesses and Mormons – have experienced revival on an international scale.

Active church membership: European comparison, 1990

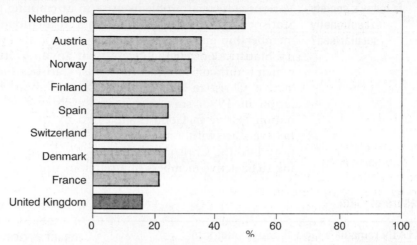

Source: *Social Trends*, 1994

- As a social institution, the Christian church in Western Europe has declined: many of the churches' social functions, for example in the fields of health and education, have been taken over by state agencies. Some religious bodies, particularly in inner-city areas, have adopted a much broader welfare role – exemplified by the work done in St Martin-in-the-Fields in central London – and indeed many people now see the church as a general welfare service agency to be turned to in times of emergency. Science and technology are seen as able to explain the previously unexplainable; and the mass media, particularly television, newspapers and magazines, have become the modern pulpits.

- Secularisation of a kind is taking place even within the churches. Mass in the Roman Catholic Church, for example, is no longer said in Latin, and practices such as abortion or homosexuality, which would have once been considered heresy, receive wide debate within and across churches. Some denominations have joined forces and, as Bryan Wilson stated: 'Organisations amalgamate when they are weak rather than when they are strong, since alliance means compromise and amendments of commitment.'

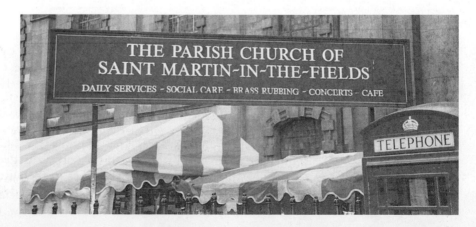

Is today's society exceptionally secularised?

Various statistical problems arise in attempting to answer this question. Statistics tend to be based on church attendance or claims of official membership and, as noted above, are not always representative of reality. Statistics on religion give little if any indication of strength of belief, which is difficult to measure. Whilst statistics showed the UK to have an 'active' Christian church membership of about 15 per cent of the population in 1990, surveys repeatedly show that over two-thirds of the nation believe in God, as indicated by the article below. Clearly many believers are within non-Christian faiths, but many others must be those born into the Christian tradition who retain some belief while not wishing to be active members of a religious organisation.

A Measure of Faith

BRITAIN remains a God-fearing country in spite of repeated claims from church and political leaders that religious belief has fallen in the latter half of the 20th century.

Large numbers in Britain believe in God and life after death, according to a survey published yesterday. In the survey of 19,000 people in 14 countries, all Christian except for Israel, the United States leads in belief in God, but in Ireland more people pray daily.

Britain was eighth in belief in God and life after death but eleventh in daily prayer. The survey, carried out in 1991, shows that most people believe in God and that there is a revival of belief in life after death.

Professor Andrew Greeley, author of the report, said: "It is the reverse of everything that the theories of secularisation and religious decline lead us to anticipate. God is not dead, she is alive and well even in Britain."

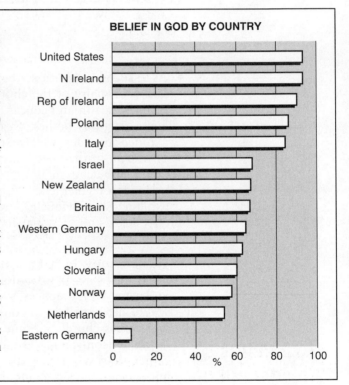

BELIEF IN GOD BY COUNTRY

Source: *The Times*, 19 May 1993

The supernatural still holds importance for many people, who express beliefs, not in churches, sects, denominations or cults but in 'subterranean theologies' such as horoscopes and the occult. The growth of 'fringe sects' may also indicate that people are fulfilling their religious needs in a wide variety of forms.

It can be argued, as a different perspective on the secularisation debate, that no golden age of religion ever really existed as a peak from which to decline. Even in Victorian England, only about 40 per cent of adults attended church regularly, according to the census taken in 1851; those attending church services were mostly from the upper and middle classes and may well have been influenced by social as much as religious factors. Historical research has tended to show that only a moderate commitment to religious belief was common amongst the English working class. Moreover, religion still seems to play an important role in everyday life: various forms of worship continue not only in religious institutions and schools but also via the mass media, particularly television and radio. Religion also plays a major role as a source of comfort during private and public crises, as well as being the basis for the celebration of ceremonies associated with rites of passage such as birth, marriage and death.

Revivalism

Some religious commentators consider that there has been a revival in interest and involvement in religion in the late twentieth century, both inside and outside religious organisations. This is perceived within the Christian tradition but perhaps more strikingly in the growth of fundamentalist Islam in the Middle and Far East.

Bryan Wilson's claims of secularisation, made in the 1960s, have since been challenged by writers such as J. Eldridge who stated tha:

> 'To dismiss all contemporary [religious] movements as irrelevant both in practical terms, and as providing clues for an understanding of social consciousness, is an astonishing thing to do.'
>
> J. Eldridge, *Religion: Where the Action Isn't* (Macmillan, 1988)

Another factor is that religious experience on a personal level is hardly reflected in official statistics. D. Hay and G. Heald, in their study *Religion is Good For You* (1987), found that about half of British adults had had what they termed a religious experience, whilst nearly one-fifth claimed an awareness of the dead (usually a deceased relative). There are other ways of identifying an interest in or attachment to religious traditions. I. Bradley, in *Religious Revival* (1987), claimed that nearly 60 per cent of the British population listened to or watched religious programmes; for example, each week 8 million viewers watch BBC's *Songs of Praise*.

Criticisms of the concept of secularisation

Criticisms of the concept of secularisation began in the 1960s when David Martin pointed to disagreement over its definition and its role in the propaganda of anti-religious groups. David Lyon, in *Rethinking Secularisation* (1985), outlined various reasons for reconsidering the concept of secularisation in relation to developments in science and the changing nature of belief and institutions:

- There is less need for total scientific explanations on such questions as the 'material' universe in the nineteenth-century (scientific) sense.
- A wide range of activities are now seen as religious.
- Many studies of religion in the UK have been based on a simplified form of history, which sharply contrasts the state of society before and after the Industrial Revolution. They have assumed that changes taking place in religion are all in the same direction – towards increasing secularisation, which cannot be reversed. However, recent evidence points to the growth of new religions and of evangelical Christian churches.

- There have been few attempts to compare secularisation in different societies and those carried out have usually proved to be inconclusive.
- Most studies of secularisation have tended to see it as an impersonal social process, but it is individuals and groups who are responsible for secularisation, not impersonal, abstract forces.

Lyon concludes that a major problem confronting individuals in a changing world relates to their own identity. In the past, the identity of the individual came from a small group within which he or she lived, such as family, village and religion. It has become accepted that the break-up of such groups in a rapidly changing society may cause the individual to lose his or her sense of identity. It has also been put forward that many modern social movements, both religious and secular, ranging from the National Front or the Socialist Workers' Party to the Moonies or Scientology, have come about as part of the search for 'identity'.

Links between religion and social position

There is a relative lack of sound research data on most aspects of religion, including in relation to stratification. Reasons for this may include:

- the wish of individuals to preserve their privacy on matters of religious belief and affiliation which they may well view in personal rather than public terms;
- the desire to avoid the use of labels by organisations; for example, perhaps the Church of England does not want to be associated only with the Establishment and the middle class but seeks an image of openness among its membership;
- religious organisations' apparent indifference towards research, with information seeming to be collected and used in a wide variety of ways;
- problems with differences in research methods. Social scientists use qualitative attitude surveys, with long in-depth interview techniques, whilst in religious spheres quantitative research methods are often used, whose results are quite difficult to interpret. Nor is it easy to cross-refer between the two kinds of research or to use them together.

Church statistics, particularly membership data, as we have seen, seem to provide rather dubious estimates of what is actually happening. Not until the 1851 census was religious attendance surveyed (see page 644), but even then it was only on a voluntary basis. A modern source of reference is the annual publication *UK Christian Handbook* (edited by P. Brierley and H. Wraight). This provides, mainly in directory form, large amounts of religious membership data, but there is very little, if any, information on social class backgrounds.

A number of social surveys have shown the willingness of people to associate with Christian denominations. For example, the table opposite provides results from a Gallup poll: over 90 per cent of those questioned expressed some affiliation, and of these 60 per cent saw themselves as belonging to the Church of England.

Religious denomination: composition by social class						
		Social class				
		AB (%)	C1 (%)	C2 (%)	DE (%)	All (%)
Denomination	Church of England	59	58	61	61	60
	Church of Scotland	7	8	7	8	7
	Free Church	11	12	7	10	10
	Roman Catholic	11	9	11	13	11
	Other	2	6	5	4	4
	None	10	8	9	5	8
Attendance	Once a week or more	20	14	9	11	12
	Up to once a month	11	12	5	5	7
	Just now and again	25	17	18	22	20
	Christmas/Easter only	2	4	8	1	4
	Special occasions only	19	27	34	32	30
	Never	22	26	28	29	27

Source: Devised from a self-report study by Gallup Poll in 1979. Adapted from I. Reid, *Social Class Differences in Britain* (3rd edn, 1989)

It is noteworthy that, according to the data in the above table, there was little variation in religious affiliation between the social classes. Where social class difference was marked this was in terms of church attendance. Regular attendance showed a general decline across the social classes, with attendance by those in AB classes amounting to about twice that of those in DE; C1 (non-manual) regular attendance rates were significantly higher than those of C2 (manual) rates. 'Very regular' attendance, by all classes, was only 12 per cent.

Local surveys tend to show that whilst churches may appear to be middle-class institutions, there are definite national and local variations. For example, L. Burton, in *Social Class in the Local Church* (1975), compared the social class backgrounds of two Midland Methodist churches (one suburban, the other on a housing estate) in relation to the local populations. In the suburban church, he found middle-class membership predominant among both ministers and church members: 93 per cent of ministers and members (compared with 46 per cent of the local population) were from middle-class backgrounds. The contrast was even greater on a nearby housing estate, where 56 per cent of the church membership, but only 16 per cent of the local population, were from middle-class backgrounds. Among those involved in church activities, though not church members, working-class people accounted for 12 per cent in the suburban church, but 69 per cent in the estate church. Similar research was carried out, with similar findings, by J. Harris and P. Jarvis in *Counting to Some Purpose* (1979).

Religion in a multicultural society

In a multicultural society containing a range of ethnic groups, such as the UK or the USA, religion can be seen to provide:

- a support mechanism for those of shared language and with similar attitudes and beliefs among a much larger host nation;
- a means of assimilation, or at least acceptance, into a geographically fluid and socially mobile society;
- cultural identity via meaningful institutions which preserve value commitments and a sense of worth in an otherwise alien world.

Sociologists use the term 'culture' to refer to a shared way of life. Cultural identity may include belonging to a particular religion, and in a multi-ethnic or multicultural society this interpretation and role of religion as representing cultural 'differentness' can be especially important. It can be a positive, unifying factor within a community, but can also create a 'them and us' attitude between different groups. This danger was highlighted by the effects of the *fatwa* or religious death sentence pronounced by the late Ayatollah Khomeini of Iran on author Salman Rushdie, after the publication of his book *The Satanic Verses* in Britain, in 1988. The book was felt by many Muslims to be heretically anti-Islam, so there was some support for the *fatwa* among British Muslims – this produced something of a culture clash between the Muslim community and those outside it.

SALMAN RUSHDIE AND MUSLIM BRITAIN: CULTURE CLASH

The publication of Salman Rushdie's *The Satanic Verses* and the late Ayatollah Khomeini's subsequent *fatwah* is of profound cultural significance as well as, of course, a personal tragedy for Rushdie. The importance of the continuing conflict around *The Satanic Verses* is that it has brought into sharp focus several key issues of ethnic relations in Britain. First, it has directed public and media attention towards a large section of Britain's Asian community – specifically, the one million plus who are Muslims. Previously, Asians have tended to attract less attention than Afro Caribbeans and this has allowed mistaken impressions to develop. Secondly, the strongest initial reaction to the order of death against Rushdie among white Britons came from a group previously publicly well-disposed to Britain's black population – liberal intellectuals. Thirdly, the crux of the matter is that the Rushdie conflict has raised the issue of ethnic cultural *incompatibility* in a way that cannot be avoided. The stark possibility is that certain cultural assumptions of Muslims may contradict those of the majority of Britons. In this case, the incompatibility is a conflict over two contradictory principles; the religious right and necessity to punish a blasphemer versus the right of an artiste (and other citizens) to freedom of expression. The latter is a core value of liberal, secular society. The following two quotations – the first from Ayatollah Khomeini's *fatwah* and the second from a response by the author Anthony Burgess – fully illustrate this collision of principle:

'I call upon all zealous Muslims to execute them [Rushdie and his publishers] quickly, wherever they find them, so that no one will dare to insult the Islamic sanctions. Whoever is killed upon this path will be regarded as a martyr, God willing.'
(*The Observer*, 19 February 1989)
'To order outraged sons of the prophet to kill him and the directors of Penguin Books on British soil is tantamount to a *jihad* [holy war]. It is a declaration of war on citizens of a free country and as such it is a political act. It has to be countered by an equally forthright, if less murderous, declaration of defiance.'
(*The Independent*, 15 February 1989)

Source: M. O'Donnell, 'Culture and Identity in Multi-Ethnic Britain', *Social Studies Review*, Vol. 5:3, January 1990

The singer Cat Stevens, who converted to Islam and took the name Yusuf Islam, ran into controversy when he expressed support for the *fatwa*. His opinion was particularly of interest to the media not only because of his former celebrity status but also because he had been a founder of what was to become Britain's first Muslim state secondary school. This also raised the sensitive issue of whether 'minority' religions in a multicultural society should be allowed to run state-supported schools within a nominally Christian state.

Britain to get its first Muslim state school

By Jonathan Petre
Education Correspondent

BRITAIN'S first Muslim state school is expected to open in London next year after Government advisers supported an independent Islamic school's bid for public funding.

The school in Brent, north London, was founded by Yusuf Islam, formerly the pop star Cat Stevens. Mr Islam made public his support for the Ayatollah Khomeini's fatwa against Salman Rushdie for his book The Satanic Verses. He said at the time: "The Koran makes it clear if someone defames the prophet then he must die."

Dr Patrick Sookhdeo, director of the independent Institute for the Study of Islam and Christianity, warned that Muslim state schools could become hotbeds of extremism. "How are we going to be sure that teachers are sticking to the curriculum and are not promoting an Islamic message?" he asked. "Islam is different to Christianity and liberal Judaism because it is a political as well as a social religion. If you link Islam with an ideological framework, urban deprivation and racial tensions, then you have the possibility of extremism taking hold."

But Dr Azam Baig, the principal of Islamia, said that such fears stemmed from ignorance. "There are other denominational schools, such as Church of England and Roman Catholic, so why not Muslim?" he said. "Prejudice against us goes back to the crusades. We are trying to produce good British Muslims. It is fear of the unknown. When people see Muslim schools in the state system, they will accept us."

Mr Islam's initial efforts to gain voluntary-aided status were rejected. Many Muslims blamed politics for the rejection. Dr Ghayasuddin Siddiqui, leader of the self-styled Muslim Parliament, said: "Muslims felt very aggrieved. We just want to contribute to society. At a time when the authority of the churches is breaking down, it is important that we have Muslim believers who wish to make sure that society has a moral bottom line."

If Islamia is allowed into the state sector, other independent Muslim schools shall follow – 44 have opened in the last 15 years. There could be as many as one million Muslims of school age by the year 2000.

Source: Adapted from the *Daily Telegraph*, 22 December 1996

Think about it

• In the article above it is argued that Islam can offer a moral set of values to a society which seems to have all but lost its traditional religious values. Does it matter if an 'incoming' religious tradition aims to supply a society's system of moral values?
• What might be the reasons put forward by those opposed to the granting of state support for a Muslim school? Explain possible reasons and think about the sociological implications of granting or refusing to grant such support.

The issue of education is only one aspect of the wider question of how to strike a balance between integration and identity. Most 'minority' religious groups within a wider society that is largely secular, but rooted in the Christian tradition, reach some sort of compromise between full integration into the 'host' society's system and total segregation. For example, many Jews attend non-Jewish schools, but there is still some pressure within the community (particularly among orthodox Jews) not to 'marry outside', and to preserve the Jewish heritage in the family.

It is difficult to generalise about the role of religion in a multicultural society, for various reasons:

- Culture and its religious elements are constantly changing, not static, as for example when first-generation immigrants are replaced by the following generation, or when a particular crisis such as the Salman Rushdie affair brings about a heightened cultural and religious awareness in a community.
- Cultural integration between religious groups is a complex procedure and may differ widely between different strands within broader groups (between Orthodox and Reform or Secular Jews, for instance).
- Cultural separatism can be caused by perceived threats to ethnic religious groups, which may, when feeling threatened, retreat into the traditional values of their culture, supported by religious leaders.
- Cultural interchange may occur, making the distinction between different cultural or religious groups harder to identify. For example P. Gilroy, in his study *There ain't no black in the Union Jack* (1987), describes minority cultures as 'syncretic' in that they select values from other cultures and incorporate them into their own. Conversely, members of the 'host' culture can be attracted to, and 'help themselves' to, elements of the 'minority' culture, such as music, food or lifestyle.

Ethnic minorities within the Christian tradition

In the UK, membership of the main Christian denominations has been, in general, declining. However, this is not always the case: as demonstrated by the Baptist and Pentecostal Churches whose membership consists largely of people of African or West Indian origin. West Indians, who were amongst the first of the coloured immigrants to arrive in the UK, and came from islands scattered across the Caribbean, shared a common history of slavery and a dominant white culture. Their background often included schooling taught in standard English, and many were Christians who attended church regularly. Statistics of Christian church attendance have rarely made any reference to the ethnic background of their membership.

Ethnic minorities and non-Christian religions in the UK

Although the presence of non-Christian religions in the UK is relatively small, interesting points to note include the following:

- It is estimated that by the year 2000, Muslims will have increased to the point where their numbers exceed both Methodist and Baptist church memberships. Islam is a world religion founded by the Prophet Mohammed in the sixth century. Muslims believe in one God, Allah, and that Mohammed was the last and greatest prophet who taught people how to live along the principles outlined in their holy book, the Koran.

- Hindus and Sikhs have also increased in numbers but, unlike Islam, neither Hinduism nor Sikhism is proselytising (i.e. seeking to convert new members from outside) and their numbers therefore have not increased as rapidly as those of Muslims.

- Hindus originate mainly from the Punjab and Gujarat and form the largest of the South Asian ethnic minority groups in the UK. However, relatively few remain within Hinduism, the major religion of India, perhaps because of a desire to leave behind the caste system which is fundamental to Hinduism. Sikhs, who come mainly from the Punjab, therefore form a larger religious minority in the UK than do Hindus, even though the numbers of immigrants from Sikh areas were originally smaller.

- The beliefs and values of the ethnic groups in the UK have been far from static. It seems that in the case of the Asian groups who originally came to Britain with different cultural and religious backgrounds, they initially tended to fall away from religious observance in the UK, until their own cultural and religious institutions became established.

- The Jewish community in the UK has remained statistically fairly static during the latter third of the twentieth century. Many Jews fled to the UK to escape pogroms or religious purges in Russia, from the 1880s to 1914, and then again after the Russian Revolution in 1917–18; later, more came to Britain fleeing from the Nazi extermination campaign in Hitler's Germany. They settled in areas such as East London, close to their place of arrival, and although suffering from a variety of forms of anti-Semitism, settled and prospered in the UK while retaining their religious identity and many aspects of their traditional culture.

There seems to be some limited evidence of a plurality of both Christian and non-Christian religious groups within the multicultural make-up of the UK. Its importance is difficult to judge, although – particularly in relation to the activities of some Muslims – it is difficult to ignore such a dimension, especially in such areas as politics and religious education.

Think about it

- To what extent do you think that the religion of an 'incoming' minority ethnic group can be affected or changed by Christian traditions and festivals?
- What do you consider to be the main issues associated with the assimilation or integration of ethnic groups into the 'mainstream' culture of the UK – if there is such a culture?

New Religious Movements (NRMs)

New Religious Movements, or NRMs, are not really new at all and have existed as long as there have been historical records. There have been periods in which many movements have come into existence and others in which few have been formed. Sociologists' main concerns are with those social factors which bring about and promote the development of such movements, and also factors that inhibit or prevent their growth at other times.

The formation of NRMs

William Sims Bainbridge and Rodney Stark, in *Cult Formation: Three Compatible Models* (1979), suggest that there are two stages in the formation of NRMs:

* the production of new ideas; and
* getting these ideas socially accepted.

This is particularly the case with the formation of cults.
    Bainbridge and Stark also identify three main models:

* The **psychopathology model**: cults are invented by individuals suffering from mental illness. There is little evidence for this, though cult founders often have ideas that differ from those that are accepted in normal society.
* The **entrepreneur model**: the founders of cults are rather like businessmen or women who set out to form an organisation in order to make money. Some founders of cults have made fortunes out of their members: for example Sun Myung Moon, the founder of the Unification Church (or Moonies).
* The **evolution model**: cults evolve and are formed into subcultures by like-minded individuals who get together to pursue their own interests.

During the 1960s, many young people in Britain and the USA began to reject the affluent society and attempted to 'drop out'. This period saw the development of a 'counter-culture' and also a drug-culture, involving 'flower people', hippies, Western Zen groups, Hindu sects and a wide range of NRMs. By the 1970s, the counter-cultures had dwindled. The foundations for many of the new movements were insecure: perhaps they had attempted to reverse the swing of the pendulum too early, since the affluence of the 1960s was short-lived. Some of the NRMs which began in the 1960s – for example the Moonies – did survive and continue to flourish, but many seem to have disappeared.
    A new wave of movements sometimes referred to as New Age Movements grew in the 1980s and 1990s. Such movements have become linked to environmental issues and personal development.

The 'functions' of NRMs

T. Robbins and D. Anthony, in *New Religious Movements* (1978), surveyed such movements and identified four social effects or functions:

* **Integrative:** Various studies have suggested that NRMs have the effect of bringing back alienated young people – perhaps from a drug-culture – to the major institutions of society; in this way they offer

useful functions for the society. Some movements may provide an outlet for dissatisfied young persons who might otherwise turn to crime.

- **Disintegrative**: Some studies have suggested that new religions help to break down the norms of existing societies and promote social change. Cults such as the Moonies have been seen as 'dangerous' by governments who have taken measures against them.
- **Socio-cultural transformation**: In the 1960s, hope was often expressed that the 'counter-culture' would lead to a constructive cultural revolution and that a peaceful revolution would be achieved by spreading the values of the counter-culture.
- **Irrelevance**: Some studies, however, have maintained that new religious movements, such as cults, are marginal and have no real part to play in modern society. Bryan Wilson (see page 640) claims that secularisation has transformed modern society and that religion has now become unimportant and even irrelevant. His view has, however, been challenged by the wide interest in new religions, and by the continuing large membership of institutional churches, particularly in the USA and other parts of the world.

Since there is such a vast variety of NRMs with widely differing functions, it is worth noting that some NRMs may have integrative, disintegrative or transformative consequences at different periods in their history. Some may be disintegrative in certain ways, transformative in others as well as having some integrative functions. Some NRMs may seem socially irrelevant, but may go through a series of stages ranging from being highly relevant to seemingly irrelevant. Irrelevant movements may become relevant because of changes in the movement or in society itself.

Pitirim Sorokin (1889–1968), a Russian-born American sociologist, provided an explanation of the variations in the development of NRMs in *Sociological Theories of Today* (1966). Although somewhat dated, it is nevertheless interesting to note that Sorokin's model views NRMs as the outcome of situations in which the individual is denied the legitimate expression of his or her psychic (religious) needs within the existing religious institutions. Sorokin saw NRMs as part of a pendulum swing between extremes of culture ranging from 'sensate' to 'ideational':

- 'sensate culture': based on the physical senses and viewing gods and the supernatural as an illusion;
- 'ideational culture': based on ideas, thoughts and feelings, with the only reality being above the senses, so that great importance is attached to the supernatural.

Sorokin used this model to study the history of Western civilisation. He argued that when a culture reached its extreme form, reaction to it would take place and the pendulum would begin to swing back. The extreme form of 'sensate culture' would be seen in the process of secularisation, in which even the churches become secularised in changing their attitudes towards divorce and abortion, and even accepting of the values of science and materialism – particularly in modern consumer society.

Types of NRMs

As NRMs have developed, sociologists have found terms such as 'sects' and 'cults' difficult to manage. Hence the concept of NRMs has tended to become adopted as an 'umbrella' term. A notable attempt to identify different types of NRMs has been made by Roy Wallis in *The Sociology of New Religions* (1985). Wallis put forward the view that NRMs differed in type according to how each viewed the world:

- **World-affirming**: NRMs which accept the world. Some of these may not even seem to be of a particularly religious nature. They help their members or 'clients' to cope with life, or give them more satisfactory or successful lives. Transcendental Meditation would be an example.
- **World-accommodating**: NRMs which remain within society, even if disillusioned with its secular nature. They offer help to their members often by making them more aware of their 'inner power' or inner divinity. An example might be Siddha Yoga.
- **World-rejecting**: NRMs which are critical if not hostile to the secular world. They encourage members to distance themselves from virtually all other religious groups and see themselves as the sole provider of salvation. Jehovah's Witnesses would be an example.

Wallis's analysis is illustrated in the diagram below which shows a range of NRMs:

Types of New Religious Movements (NRMs)

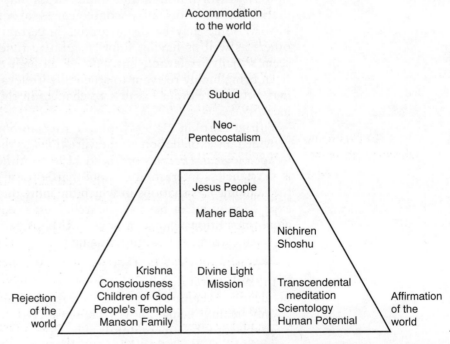

Source: R. Wallis, *The Elementary Forms of the New Religious Life* (1984)

Some problems do arise with this analysis, however:

- Not all NRMs are actually new; many have a well-established historical tradition – Krishna Consciousness, for example.
- Not all members of a particular NRM share exactly the same attitude. This may range from total commitment to limited participation, as is the case with Transcendental Meditation (TM), for example.

- James A. Beckford, in *Cult Controversies* (1985), found Wallis's analysis worthwhile but commented that it is difficult to categorise NRMs on the basis of how each type views the world.
- More critically, Rodney Stark and William Sims Bainbridge (see also page 652) see virtually any categorisation of NRMs as flawed. They found that lists of characteristics of NRMs vary considerably in every religious movement.

Televangelists and the rise of televangelism

Amidst the secularisation debate, attention has turned towards the power of the mass media and in particular the power of televangelists. From the 1960s, fundamentalist evangelists began to preach on television and to dominate religious broadcasting in the USA. Reasons for this domination of the media have included the following:

- Mainstream religion, particularly the Church and its major denominations, felt uneasy about preaching via television.
- Mainstream religion felt even more uneasy about the need to raise funds by this method; also airtime can prove a very expensive medium of preaching.
- Preaching by television became an effective way of converting the 'unchurched'. Televangelists pioneered techniques for 'pretending' that their relationship with each individual via the television screen was personal.
- Televangelists developed highly skilled techniques which appeared as natural religious fervour. Religious broadcasters such as Jim Bakker, Jimmy Swaggart and Pat Robertson, whilst remaining cool under the stress of media appearances, allowed themselves displays of emotion to move their audiences towards them and religion.

The decline of televangelists in the 1980s

After its initial emergence and development in the USA in the 1960s, televangelism started to decline by the 1980s. Reasons for this include:

- **Market saturation:** too many televangelists began to swamp the broadcasting channels in a market which did not respond to such a rapid growth.
- **Political involvement:** several televangelists supported Ronald Reagan's successful presidential campaign in 1980, but this proved less successful for them in terms of their subsequent viewing audiences.
- **Political activity:** when Reverend Pat Robertson revealed his ambitions to become President as part of a powerful 'new Christian right' movement in the USA, his viewing figures fell.
- **Scandals:** towards the end of the 1980s, several televangelists became disgraced and ruined by scandals involving sex and finance. For example, Jim Bakker received a prison sentence for helping himself to millions of dollars from his Praise The Lord ministry, despite his $1.1 million annual income.

The return of televangelists in the 1990s

Following the decline of televangelism in the 1980s, a revival seemed to be occurring in the 1990s – and even spreading across the Atlantic to several European countries, including Great Britain. The reasons for this include the following:

- **Political activity**: Reverend Pat Robertson, despite his demise in the 1980s, remained a powerful political figure. His Family Channel reaches over 90 per cent of all cable TV homes in the USA and over 50 per cent of all households. Providing televangelists can fund their activities, this will maintain their high profile in religion, mass media and politics.

$140m empire of a prince of televangelism

THE electronic church, or televangelism, may be down but it is by no means out.

The popularity and financial success of media ministries took a knock from the scandals of the mid-Eighties but many are still thriving. Dr Billy Graham is probably the best known televangelist, although he actually does very little broadcasting.

Another well-known figure, not only on America's airwaves but also in the world of politics, is Pat Robertson, founder of the **Christian Broadcasting Network**. Set up in 1960, CBN is now a $140 million (£93 million) a year media empire, airing Christian-inspired programmes across the US and 50 foreign countries.

It also includes a production company, an international relief agency and a radio station. Robertson usually presents its flagship The 700 Club, a news magazine programme and the longest running religious broadcast show ever.

The bulk of its revenues are raised through telethons, broadcast to obtain pledges and gifts of financial support. Quinton Shulze describes Robertson as the religious equivalent of Ted Turner, head of news network CNN.

Beyond CBN, Robertson has set up a university and a law firm and is chairman of the publicly quoted **International Family Entertainment**, parent of The Family Channel, which reaches 58 million cable subscribers. It bought **MTM Entertainment** from the former South East England broadcaster **TVS**. Robertson is also active in politics. He claims two former US presidents in his family tree and a shared ancestry with Winston Churchill. Ordained a Southern Baptist minister in 1961, he quit in 1987 just before announcing his candidacy for the US Presidency.

His campaign gained 9% of the Republican vote but he decided to suspend his candidacy and endorse George Bush instead. Two years later, he set up the Christian Coalition, a national organisation dedicated to restoring the greatness of America through a return to moral strength, and designed to educate people about the electoral process.

It has 850 chapters in 50 states, and observers believe that if and when Robertson returns to his presidential ambitions, the coalition will be activated as a political movement to support his efforts.

Nancy Amerrmana, a sociologist at Amory University in Atlanta, said: "I am not convinced that they have disappeared but they are certainly less visible at a national level. I think they have retreated to the local level where they are working on developing grass-root support and infrastructure.

"They will be back. In the next decade, we will see them return as senators and probably presidential candidates too."

Source: The *Evening Standard*, 18 May 1994

- **Para-personal communication:** televangelists establish a seemingly personal bond with their audience, despite the somewhat impersonal nature of television, by claiming personal knowledge and an interest in individual viewers.
- **Computer technology:** this has become used to simulate personal interaction. Televangelists can pray for individuals with personal problems via a computer printout of the names received. Technicians can scan letters and place names and addresses with a summary of the writer's problem into a computer. The computer programme can then generate a sensitive response and appropriate Bible reading. Modern multimedia technology can efficiently achieve sound and vision of a quality that might normally reach only the first few pews in a large church.
- **Secondary pay-offs:** quite apart from its religious content, televangelism acts as an important form of entertainment and 'spiritual nourishment' – whether through lively gospel music or famous celebrities who have become 'born again' Christians. Religious broadcasting has also become important in terms of Christian schools, fundamentalist colleges, publishers and television and film companies.

However, doubts have been expressed as to whether televangelism serves its basic purpose – to convert its audiences to Christianity. About 25 per cent of the population in the USA are already committed Christians and they provide the major audience for televangelism. Nevertheless, this is an impressive statistic in the modern world; American evangelists and televangelists now seem to be seeking further audiences beyond the USA, including in Great Britain. Anglicans in Britain (less than 15 per cent of the population) consider that televangelism will not be able to compete with the game shows and soap operas so popular with British viewers.

Think about it

If televangelism cannot compete with rival claims on our attention and loyalties, can religion as a whole 'compete' in a consumer society? Some church leaders have decided that the best policy seems to be 'If you can't beat them, join them', at least as far as advertising the 'product' is concerned.

Committee opens door to a brighter, better way to spread the Word

THE Church of England has finally resolved its moral dilemma over advertising, announcing yesterday that its brand of Christianity is ready for the hard sell. The advertising industry, on the other hand, was not quite so sure.

As the Church of England's communications committee announced there was no ethical bar to advertising, Robert Saville, a copywriter with the GGT agency, said: "If it was an ordinary product, like a chocolate bar, and so many people who have tried it have rejected it, you would be very worried."

But advertising is not the only answer. "Alternatively, change the product. The Church has got to make itself a more interesting, relevant and, even, a more entertaining product."

Canon Colin Semper, the communications committee chairman, accepted yesterday that some of the faithful believed advertising was "supping with the devil". It could, however, be a "creative, effective, appropriate, even amusing" means of getting the Christian message across.

The committee's 60-page report, entitled Paying the Piper, stops short of suggesting future campaigns.

Paul Slaymaker, managing director of DFSD Bozell, said: "no doubt what it should be: 'Back to Basics' — it's a useful phrase going begging at the moment, and we know that the Church of England can be more tolerant of naughty vicars than the Government can be about its naughty ministers."

Di Lowe and Stuart Gill at Ogilvy and Mather suggested a Hello!-style magazine, featuring celebrities at home, giving their positive thoughts on Christianity. "They would have to be the kind of people you would not normally associate with the Church, people like Chris Evans, Ian Wright of Arsenal and members of Take That," suggested Ms Lowe. "Anybody but Cliff Richard, in fact."

Slim Foster returned to the Christian fold three years ago after a break of 20 years, although not because of church advertising, he hastily added.

"I don't think you sell the Church, I think you put forward what the Church is offering, inviting people to make a leap of faith."

Those seeking assistance in this leap of faith could do worse than to contact the Rev Robert Ellis, a strong advocate of church advertising who orchestrated a television campaign for Lichfield dioceses in January 1993. "Our aim was to keep alive the rumour of God, it was not about bums on pews," he said, defending the decision to spend £7,000 on 10 TV slots.

Source: The *Guardian*, 22 February 1994

- Is the advertising of religion any different from the advertising of material goods? Why/why not?
- What does this kind of 'packaging' of religion tell us about social priorities?
- How and why do you think that the advertising of religion might be aimed at any particular social group, by class, gender, age or ethnicity?

Revision and practice tasks

Task 1: stimulus response question

1. Consider the stimulus material below and answer the questions which follow. Advice on how to answer this question is given on page 657.

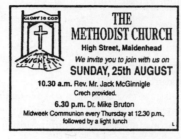  

Source: *Maidenhead Advertiser*, 23 August 1996

(a) Identify any **two** religious organisations which sociologists may term as denominations. Briefly explain your choices. (4)

(b) Explain what is meant by a sect and a cult and provide examples of each. (4)

(c) Briefly discuss the extent to which secularisation can be measured. (7)

(d) Evaluate the usefulness of secularisation in relation to the importance of religion in contemporary society. (10)

(Total: 25 marks)

Source: Interboard, Summer 1997

Advice on response to stimulus response question

(a) You need to identify two religious denominations, for example Methodists, Baptists, etc., and provide some elaboration of each – for example: Baptists seek full immersion under water as an important initiation ceremony into Christianity – or a more general accurate elaboration of denominations (see page 638 of this unit). This carries only 4 marks, so whilst you need to demonstrate your knowledge and understanding of this term you also need to be brief. (4)

(b) This is similar to (a) above, but is more clearly targeted: 2 marks are given for the meaning of each term.

- a sect is indifferent towards, or rejects, the existing social order; for example Jehovah's Witnesses, Hare Krishnas;
- a cult is a loosely structured group of like-minded members; for example Order of the Solar Temple, Japanese Aum Doomsday cult. (4)

(c) For this subquestion you need to show your ability to select and interpret how the extent of secularisation can or cannot be measured. The chart on page 639 and its accompanying text will be useful here. (7)

(d) This subquestion carries 10 marks and demands a clear and accurate demonstration of your ability to evaluate the sociological arguments relating to the usefulness of the concept of secularisation for considering the role of religion in contemporary society. Recent criticisms surrounding the secularisation debate are provided on pages 639–47 of this unit and follow on from the more standard literature on this important area of the sociology of religion. (10)

(Total: 25 marks)

Task 2: structured question

2. Answer the questions which follow.
   (a) Identify **two** features of secularisation. (4)
   (b) Identify and illustrate **two** criticisms of the secularisation thesis. (4)
   (c) Outline the evidence for the secularisation of the UK. (7)
   (d) Examine the reasons for the changes in institutional religion in the UK. (10)

(Total: 25 marks)

Source: Interboard, Summer 1996

Task 3: structured question

3. (a) Briefly outline **two** sociological differences between churches and sects. (4)
   (b) Sects are likely to contain individuals with certain social characteristics. Identify and briefly explain **two** such characteristics. (4)
   (c) Outline and illustrate **three** types of New Religious Movements. (7)
   (d) Evaluate sociological explanations of why people join New Religious Movements. (10)

(Total: 25 marks)

Source: Interboard, Summer 1997

Essay questions

1. 'Religion is the sigh of the oppressed creature . . . It is the opium of the people.' Outline Marx's contribution to the sociology of religion and evaluate the viewpoint that dominant religious beliefs are inevitably linked to economic and political interests.

2. Functionalists tend to emphasise stability and integration but religion has also affected social change, sometimes quite radically. Evaluate the contribution made by functionalists to the sociology of religion.

3. Assess the evidence which might support or challenge the claim that religion fulfils important functions in contemporary society.

4. 'In contemporary society religion is in competition with sports events, the mass media and Sunday trading. It might be claimed that religion is not winning this competition.' Explain and evaluate this statement.

5. Critically examine sociological explanations for the emergence of new religious movements.

6. To what extent do you consider that new technologies offer new opportunities for religious beliefs and practices?

7. 'Sociologists disagree about the meaning and extent of secularisation, but they seem to be in general agreement that it is happening.' Explain and discuss this statement.

8. To what extent is it useful in sociology to compare the fanatical support for a famous sports team with fanatical support for a religion?

Ideas for coursework and personal studies

1. A study in relation to what might be meant by the term 'secularisation'. Perhaps a sample could be selected and asked its views on beliefs about God, attending religious services, etc. Contrasting viewpoints might be obtained from religious ministers. Try to ensure that you organise such a wide range of questions systematically so that you have a manageable focus for your study.

2. A survey of observance of one chosen religion or denomination in some depth using both secondary and primary sources. This would provide some opportunity for ethnographic research, including an observation study, in relation to the commitment or lifestyles of the members of religious groups. You should explore sociological issues such as the impact upon and interpretation of such religious groups by members of wider society (public opinion as conveyed by media coverage, etc.).

3. A study of religious conformity in terms of the attitudes of religious groups to their own religion and how this affects their family life, children's education, etc. You might choose a sample from a particular religious group and compare their attitudes towards a number of topical issues with another group with little, if any, apparent commitment to religion.

Selected reading list

'The Anglican Church and its decline', Bryan Wilson, *New Society* (5 December 1974)

The Concept of Secularisation in Empirical Research, Larry Shiner (Penguin, 1971)

The Elementary Forms of Religious Life, Emile Durkheim (Collier Books, 1961)

The Protestant Ethic and the Spirit of Capitalism, Max Weber (Charles Scribner's Sons, New York, 1958)

Religion, Ian Thompson (Longman, 1986)

Religion in a Secular Society, Bryan Wilson (C.A. Watts, 1966)

The Religious and the Secular, David Martin (Routledge & Kegan Paul, 1969)

'Rethinking secularisation', David Lyon, *Review of Religious Research* (1985)

The Social Sources of Denominationalism, H. Richard Neibuhr (The World Publishing Company, New York, 1929)

The Social Teachings of the Christian Churches, vols. I and II, Ernst Troeltsch (1931) (University of Chicago Press, 1981)

A Sociology of English Religion, David Martin (Heinemann, 1967)

'The sociology of new religions', Roy Wallis, *Social Studies Review* (Philip Allan, September, 1985)

'Sociology of religion and sociology of knowledge', Peter Berger and Thomas Luckmann, in *The Sociology of Religion*, R. Robertson (Penguin, 1969)

Bibliography

Abbott, P. and Wallace, C., *An Introduction to Sociology: Feminist Perspectives* (Routledge, 1990)

Abercrombie, N. and Warde, A., *Contemporary British Society* (Polity Press, 1994)

Aggleton, P., *Rebels Without a Cause* (Falmer, 1987)

Allan, G., *Family Life: Domestic Roles and Social Organisation* (Blackwell, 1985)

Allen, T., 'Upheaval, affliction and health', in Bernstein, H. et al. (eds), *Rural Livelihoods* (Open University, 1992)

Allsop, J., *Health Policy and the NHS* (Longman, 1995)

Althusser, L., *Lenin and Philosophy and Other Essays* (New Left Books, 1971)

Amin, K. and Oppenheim, C., *Poverty in Black and White* (Child Poverty Action Group, 1992)

Anderson, B., *Imagined Communities* (Verso, 1983)

Anderson, M., *Family Structure in 19th Century Lancashire* (Cambridge University Press, 1971)

Andreski, S., *Elements of Comparative Sociology* (Weidenfeld & Nicolson, 1964)

Argyle, M., *The Social Psychology of Work* (Penguin, 1974)

Aries, P., *Centuries of Childhood* (Penguin, 1962)

Aristotle, *The Politics*, trans. Barker, E. (Oxford University Press, 1946)

Bachrach, P. and Baratz, M., 'The two faces of power', *American Political Science Review*, 56 (1962)

Baggott, R., *Health and Health Care in Britain* (Macmillan, 1994)

Bainbridge, W.S. and Stark, R., 'Cult formation: three compatible models', *Sociological Analysis* no. 40 (1979)

Balbo, L., 'Crazy quilts', in Showstack, S. (ed.), *From a Woman's Point of View* (Hutchinson, 1987)

Ball, S.J., *Beachside Comprehensive: A Case Study of Secondary Schooling* (Cambridge University Press, 1981)

Baltzell, D., '"Who's Who in America" and "The Social Register": Elite and Upper-Class Indexes in Metropolitan America', in Bendit, R. and Lipset, S.M. (eds), *Class, Status and Power* (The Free Press, New York, 1953)

Bandura, A. et al., 'Imitation of film mediated aggressive models', in *Journal of Abnormal and Social Psychology*, 66 (1) (1963)

Barker, E., *The Making of a Moonie* (Blackwell, 1984)

Barnes, C., *Disabled People in Britain and Discrimination* (Hurst and Co., 1991)

Barnes, J., *Who Should Know What?* (Penguin, 1978)

Barnett, T., *Sociology and Development* (Hutchinson, 1988)

Barrett, M., *Women's Oppression* (Verso, 1980)

Barry, A., 'Black mythologies: the representation of black people on British television', in Twitchen, J. (ed.), *Black and White Media Show* (Trentham Books, 1989)

Barthes, R., *Mythologies* (Cape, 1972)

Batley, R., *Local Government in Europe* (Macmillan, 1991)

de Beauvoir, S., *The Second Sex* (Penguin, 1949, trans. 1953)

Becker, D. et al., *Post Imperialism* (Boulder, Lynne Rienner, 1987)

Becker, H.S., *Outsiders: Studies in the Sociology of Deviance* (Macmillan, 1963)

Beckford, J.A., *Cult Controversies* (Tavistock, 1985)

Beechey, V., 'Women and production', in Kuhn, A. and Wolfe, A. (eds), *Feminism and Materialism* (Routledge & Kegan Paul, 1978)

Bell, C. and Newby, H. (eds), *The Sociology of Community* (Frank Cass, 1974)

Bell, C., *Middle Class Families* (Routledge & Kegan Paul, 1968)

Bell, D., *The Coming of Post-Industrial Society* (Heinemann, 1973)

Bell, D., 'The world and the United States in 2013', *Daedalus*, vol. 116, no. 3 (1987)

Bell, N. and Vogel, E. (eds), *A Modern Introduction to the Family* (The Free Press, New York, 1968)

Bellah, R.N., 'Civil religion in America', *Daedalus* no. 96 (winter 1967)

Belson, W. et al., *Television Violence and the Adolescent Boy* (Gower Press, 1972)

Benyon, J., 'The Scarman Report', in Benyon, J. and Solomon, J. (eds), *Roots of Urban Unrest* (Pergamon, 1987)

Benyon, J. and Denver, D., 'Mrs Thatcher's electoral success', *Social Studies Review*, vol. 5:3 (P. Allan, January 1990)

Berger, A.A., *Media Content Analysis* (Sage, Beverley Hills, 1982)

Berger, B. and P., *The War Over the Family* (Hutchinson, 1983)

Berger, P. and Luckmann, T., *The Social Construction of Reality* (Penguin, 1967)

Berger, P. and Luckmann, T., 'Sociology of religion and sociology of knowledge', in Robertson, R., *The Sociology of Religion* (Penguin, 1969)

Bernstein, B., 'A socio-linguistic approach to social learning', in Worsley, D., *Modern Sociology: Introductory Readings* (Penguin, 1970)

Bernstein, B., *Class, Codes and Control*, vol. 1 (Routledge & Kegan Paul, 1973)

Berry, D., *Central Ideas in Sociology* (Constable, 1974)

Beschers, J.M., *Urban Social Structure* (The Free Press, New York, 1969)

Beynon, H., *Working for Ford* (Allen Lane, 1973)

Blau, P., *On the Nature of Organizations* (J. Wiley & Sons, New York, 1974)

Blau, P. and Schoenherr, R.A., *The Structure of Organizations* (Basic Books, New York, 1971)

Blau, P. and Scott, W.R., *Formal Organizations* (Routledge, 1963)

Blaxter, M., 'The social patterning of health' in *Developments in Society*, 12 (Causeway Press, 1996)

Block, R., 'A comparison of victimisation, crime assessment and fear of crime in England and Wales, the Netherlands, Scotland and the United States' (Paper to the American Society of Criminology Annual Conference, Montreal, 1987)

Bonnett, K., 'Power and politics', in Haralambos, M. (ed.), *Developments in Sociology*, vol. 10 (Causeway Press, 1994)

Booth, C., *The Aged Poor* (Macmillan, 1894)

Booth, C., *The Life and Labour of the People of London*, 17 vols (Macmillan, 1891–1903)

Booth, W., *In Darkest England* (Salvation Army, 1890)

Bott, E., *Family and Social Networks* (Tavistock, 2nd edn, 1971)

Bottomore, T., *Elites and Society* (Routledge, 1993)

Boulton, Mary, *On Being a Mother* (Tavistock, 1983)

Bourdieu, P., 'Cultural reproduction and social reproduction', in Bourdieu, P., *Distinction: A Social Critique of the Judgement of Taste* (Routledge, 1984)

Brown, R. (ed.), *Knowledge and Cultural Change* (Tavistock, 1973)

Bowlby, John, *Child Care and the Growth of Love* (Penguin, 1963) (First published in 1951 by the World Health Organisation as 'Maternal care and mental health')

Bowles, S. and Gintis, H., *Schooling in Capitalist America* (Routledge & Kegan Paul, 1976)

Box, S., *Deviance, Reality and Society* (Holt, Rinehart & Winston, 2nd edn, 1981)

Box, S., *Power, Crime and Mystification* (Tavistock, 1983)

Box, S. and Cotgrove, S., *Industry and Society* (Allen & Unwin, 1970)

Brake, M., *The Sociology of Youth Culture and Youth Subculture* (Routledge & Kegan Paul, 1980)

Brake, M., *Comparative Youth Culture* (Routledge & Kegan Paul, 1985)

Braverman, H., *Labour and Monopoly Capital* (Monthly Review Press, New York, 1974)

Brenner, M.H., *Mental Illness and the Economy* (Harvard University Press, 1977)

Brierley, P. and Wraight H. (eds), *UK Christian Handbook 1998–99* (Christian Research, 1997)

Brown, C., *Black and White Britain: The Third PSI Survey* (Policy Studies Institute, 1984)

Browne, K., *An Introduction to Sociology* (Polity Press, 1992)

Brydon, L. and Chant, S.,*Women in the Third World* (Edward Elgar, 1989)

Burnham, J., *The Managerial Revolution* (Putman & Co, 1943)

Burns, T., *The BBC: Public Institution and Private World* (Macmillan, 1977)

Burns, T. and Stalker, G.M., *The Management of Innovation* (Tavistock, 1961)

Burton, L., 'Social class in the local church', in M. Hill, *A Sociological Yearbook of Religion in Britain* (Student Christian Movement, 1975)

Butler, D. and Stokes, D., *Political Change in Britain* (Macmillan, 1974)

Campbell, A., *Girl Delinquents* (Blackwell, 1981)

Campbell, A., *The Girls in the Gang* (Blackwell, 1986)

Canter, D., *Criminal Shadows* (HarperCollins, 1994)

Carlen, P., *Women's Imprisonment* (Routledge & Kegan Paul, 1983)

Carson, W.G., 'White collar crime', in Carson, W.G. and Wiles, P. (eds), *Crime and Delinquency in Britain* (Martin Robertson, 1971)

Carstairs, V. and Morris, R., *Deprivation and Health in Scotland* (Aberdeen University Press, 1991)

Cashmore, E., *Rastaman: The Rastafarian Movement in England* (Allen & Unwin, 1979)

Cashmore, E., 'Re-writing the script', *New Society* (1985)

Castells, M., *The Urban Question: A Marxist Approach* (Edward Arnold, 1977)

Castells, M., *City, Class and Power* (Macmillan, 1978)

Central Statistical Office, *Social Focus on Children* (HMSO, 1994)

Chambliss, W., *On the Take: From Petty Crooks to Presidents* (Indiana University Press, 1978)

Chambliss, W. and Mankoff, M., *Whose Law? What Order?* (J. Wiley & Sons, New York, 1976)

Chandler, J., *Women Without Husbands* (Macmillan, 1991)

Charmaz, K., 'Loss of self', in *Sociology of Health and Illness* 5 (1983)

Chester, R., 'The rise of the neo-conventional family', in *New Society* (9 May 1983)

Chibnall, S., *Law-and-Order News* (Tavistock, 1977)

Cicourel, A.V., *The Social Organisation of Juvenile Justice* (Heinemann, 1976)

Clarke, A.M. and Clarke, A.A.D.B., *Early Experience, Myth and Evidence* (Open Books, 1976)

Clarke, J., 'The skinheads and the magical recovery of community', in Hall, S. and Jefferson, T. (eds), *Resistance Through Rituals* (Hutchinson, 1976)

Clarke, J. and Critcher, C., *The Devil Makes Work: Leisure in Capitalist Britain* (Macmillan, 1985)

Clarke, R. and Mayhew, P. (eds), *Designing Out Crime* (HMSO, 1980)

Cloward, R.A. and Ohlin, L.E., *Delinquency and Opportunity* (The Free Press, New York, 1961)

Coates, K. and Silburn, R., *Poverty: The Forgotten Englishmen* (Penguin, 1970)

Cockett, M. and Tripp, J., *Children Living in Re-ordered Families* (J. Rowntree Trust, 1994)

Cohen, A., *The Symbolic Construction of Community* (Routledge, 1989)

Cohen, A.K., *Delinquent Boys: The Culture of the Gang* (The Free Press, New York, 1955)

Cohen, P., 'Subcultural conflict and working class community', in *Working Papers in Cultural Studies 3* (University of Birmingham, 1972)

Cohen, S., *Folk Devils and Moral Panics* (Martin Robertson, 2nd edn, 1980)

Comte, A., *The Positive Philosophy/Cours de Philosophie Positif* (Bell & Sons, 1986)

Cooper, D., *The Death of the Family* (Penguin, 1971)

Coser, L.A., *Masters of Sociological Thought* (Harcourt Brace Jovanovich, New York, 2nd edn, 1977)

Coulson and Riddell, *Approaching Sociology* (Routledge & Kegan Paul, 1991)

Cox, D. et al., *The Health and Lifestyle Survey* (The Health Promotion Research Trust, 1993)

Crewe, I., 'Why Mrs Thatcher was returned with a landslide', *Social Studies Review* (P. Allan, September 1988)

Crewe, I., 'Why did Labour lose (yet again)?', *Politics Review*, vol. 2, no. 1 (Philip Allan, September 1992)

Crewe, I. and Sarlvik, B., *Decade of De-alignment* (Oxford University Press, 1983)

Critcher, C., Bramham, P. and Tomlinson, A., *Sociology of Leisure* (Chapman and Hall, 1994)

Crow, G. and Allan, G., *Community Life* (Harvester Wheatsheaf, 1994)

Cumberbatch, G. and Negrine, R., *Images of Disability on Television* (Routledge, 1992)

Cummings, E. and Henry, W., *Growing Old* (Basic Books, New York, 1961)

Curran, J. and Seaton, J., *Power Without Responsibility* (Methuen, 1985)

Dahl, R., 'The concept of power', in *Behavioural Science* 2 (1957)

Dahl, R., *Who Governs?* (Yale University Press, 1961)

Dahrendorf, R., *Class and Class Conflict in an Industrial Society* (Routledge & Kegan Paul, 1959)

Dalton, M., *Men Who Manage* (J. Wiley & Sons, New York, 1959)

Daly, M., *Gyn/Ecology* (Beacon Press, Boston, 1979)

Darke, J. and R., 'Health and environment: high flats' (Centre for Environmental Studies, vol. 10, 1970)

Davie, R. et al., *From Birth to Seven* (Longman, 1972)

Davies, T., 'Disabled by society', in *Sociology Review* (April 1994)

Davis, F., 'Deviance: disavowal', in Lindismith, A.R., Strauss, A.L. and Denzin, N.K. (eds), *Readings in Social Psychology* (Dryden Press, Fort Worth, 1975)

Davis, K. and Moore, W.E., 'Some principles of stratification', in Bendix, R. and Lipset, S. (eds), *Class, Status and Power* (Routledge & Kegan Paul, 1966)

Deem, R., *All Work and No Play* (Oxford University Press, 1986)

Delphy, C., 'Women in stratification studies', in Roberts, H. (ed.), *Doing Feminist Research* (Routledge, 1981)

Dennis, N., 'The popularity of the neighbourhood community idea', in Pahl, R.E. (ed.), *Readings in Urban Sociology* (Pergamon Press, 1968)

Djilas, M., *The New Class* (Thames and Hudson, 1959)

Dobash, R. and Russell, *Violence Against Wives* (Open Books, 1980)

Domhoff, G.W., *Who Rules America?* (Prentice Hall, 1967)

Donovan, J., *We Don't Buy Sickness, It Just Comes* (Gower, 1986)

Douglas, J.D., *The Social Meaning of Suicide* (Princeton, 1967)

Douglas, J.W.B., *The Home and the School* (MacGibbon and Kee, 1964)

Douglas, J.W.B., *All Our Future* (MacGibbon and Kee, 1971)

Duncombe, J. and Marsden, D., 'Women's triple shift', in *Sociology Review* (April 1995)

Durkheim, E., *The Rules of Sociological Method* (The Free Press, New York, 1938)

Durkheim, E., *The Elementary Forms of Religious Life* (Collier Books, 1961)

Durkheim, E., *Suicide: A Study in Sociology* (1897) (Routledge & Kegan Paul, 1970)

Durkheim, E. and Mauss, M., *Primitive Societies* (HarperCollins, 1972)

Dutton, B., *The Media* (Longman, 1986)

Eco, U., *The Role of the Reader* (Hutchinson, 1981)

Edgell, S., *Middle Class Couples* (Allen & Unwin, 1980)

Edwards, P.K. and Scullion, H., *The Social Organisation of Industrial Conflict. Control and Resistance in the Workplace* (Blackwell, 1982)

Eichler, M., *The Double Standard: A Feminist Critique of Feminist Social Science* (Croom Helm, 1980)

Elliot, F.R., *The Family: Change or Continuity?* (Macmillan, 1986)

Engels, F., *The Origin of the Family, Private Property and the State* (Lawrence & Wishart, 1972)

Erikson, K.J., *Wayward Puritans. A Study in the Sociology of Deviance* (J. Wiley & Sons, New York, 1966)

Etzioni, A. (ed.), *A Sociological Reader on Complex Organisations* (Holt, Reinhart and Winston, New York, 1975)

Etzioni, A., *The Parenting Deficit* (Demos, New York, 1993)

Evans-Pritchard, E., *Witchcraft, Oracles and Magic Among the Azande* (Clarendon Press, 1937)

Evesley, D. and Bonnerjea, L., 'Social change and indicators of diversity', in Rapoport, R.N. et al., *Families in Britain* (Routledge & Kegan Paul, 1982)

Fagin, L. and Little, M., *The Forsaken Families* (Penguin, 1984)

Fallows, J., *Breaking the News: How the Media Undermine American Democracy* (Pantheon, New York, 1996)

Faludi, S., *Backlash, The Undeclared War Against Women* (Chatto & Windus, 1992)

Feeley, D., 'The family', in Jenners, L. (ed.), *Feminism and Socialism* (Pathfinder Press, New York, 1972)

Fergusson, M., *Forever Feminine: Women's Magazines and the Cult of Femininity* (Heinemann, 1983)

Finch, J., *Married to the Job* (Allen & Unwin, 1983)

Firestone, S., *The Dialectics of Sex* (Paladin, 1972)

Fiske, J., *Understanding Popular Culture* (Unwin Hyman, 1989)

Fitzgerald, M., *Prisoners in Revolt* (Routledge & Kegan Paul, 1977)

Foster-Carter, A., *Developments in Sociology*, vol. II (Causeway, 1993)

Foucault, M., *Power/Knowledge: Selected Interviews and Other Writings* (Harvester Wheatsheaf, 1980)

Fox, R., *Kinship and Marriage* (Penguin, 1967)

Fox, N., 'Attachment of Kibbutz infants', *Child Development*, 46 (1977)

Frankenberg, R., *Communities in Britain* (Penguin, 1966)

Franklin, M., *Decline in Class Voting in Britain* (Oxford University Press, 1988)

Freidson, E., *Profession of Medicine* (Dodd Mead, New York, 1970)

Friedan, B., *The Feminine Mystique* (Penguin, 1965)

Friedman, M. and R., *Free to Choose* (Penguin, 1980)

Galbraith, J., *The Affluent Society* (Penguin, 1962)

Gans, H.J., *The Levittowners* (Allen & Unwin, 1967)

Gans, H.J., *The Urban Villagers: A Study of the Second Generation Italians in the West End of Boston* (Boston Center for Community Studies, 1959)

Garfinkel, H., *Studies in Ethnomethodology* (Prentice Hall, Englewood Cliffs, 1967)

Gaskill, G. and Smith, P., 'How young blacks see the police', in Moore, S., *Investigating Deviance* (Collins, 1991)

Gavron, H., *The Captive Wife* (Routledge & Kegan Paul, 1966)

Gellner, E., *Thought and Change* (Weidenfeld & Nicolson, 1965)

George, V. and Wilding, P., *Ideology and Social Welfare* (Routledge & Kegan Paul, 1985)

Gershuny, J., 'Changes in the domestic division of labour', in Abercrombie, N. and Warde, A. (eds), *Social Change in Contemporary Britain* (Polity Press, 1992)

Gibson, C., *Dissolving Wedlock* (Routledge, 1993)

Giddens, A., *The Consequences of Modernity* (Polity Press, 1990)

Giddens, A., 'Structuration theory: past, present and future', in Bryant, C. and Jary, D. (eds), *Giddens' Theory of Structuration: A Critical Appreciation* (Routledge, 1991)

Giddens, A., *Sociology* (Polity Press, 2nd edn, 1993)

Glass, D. et al., *Social Mobility in Britain* (Routledge & Kegan Paul, 1954)

Goffman, E., *The Presentation of Self in Everyday Life* (Penguin, 1956)

Goffman, E., *Encounters* (Penguin, 1961)

Goffman, E., *Stigma* (Prentice Hall, 1964)

Goffman, E., *Asylums* (Penguin, 1968)

Goldstein, H., 'Gender bias and test norms in educational selection', in Arnot, M. and Weiner, G., *Gender Under Scrutiny* (Hutchinson, 1987)

Goldthorpe, J., 'The current inflation: towards a sociological account', in Goldthorpe, J. and Hirsch, F. (eds), *The Political Economy of Inflation* (Martin Robertson, 1978)

Goldthorpe, J., *Social Mobility and Class Structure in Modern Britain* (The Nuffield Social Mobility Study) (Clarendon Press, 1980)

Goldthorpe, J. et al., *The Affluent Worker in the Class Structure* (Cambridge University Press, 1969)

Gomm, R. and Woods, P. (eds), *Educational Research in Action* (Paul Chapman/The Open University, 1993)

Gorz, A., *Farewell to the Working Class* (Pluto Press, 1982)

Gough, I., *The Political Economy of the Welfare State* (Macmillan, 1979)

Gough, K., 'Is the family universal? The Nayar case', in Bell, N.W. and Vogel, E.F. (eds), *A Modern Introduction to the Family* (Collier-Macmillan, 1959)

Gouldner, A., *Patterns of Industrial Bureaucracy* (The Free Press, New York, 1955)

Graham, H., *Women, Health and the Family* (Harvester Wheatsheaf, 1987)

Graham, H. and Oakley, A., 'Competing ideologies of reproduction', in H. Roberts (ed.), *Women, Health and Reproduction* (Routledge & Kegan Paul, 2nd edn, 1992)

Gramsci, A., *Selections from the Prison Notebooks* (Lawrence & Wishart, 1971)

Grant, W. and Marsh, D., *The Confederation of British Industry* (Hodder & Stoughton, 1977)

Grant, W., *Pressure Groups, Politics and Democracy in Britain* (Philip Allan, 1989)

Greer, G., *The Female Eunuch* (Paladin, 1970)

Grint, K., *The Sociology of Work* (Polity Press, 1991)

Habermas, J., *Legitimation Crisis* (Heinemann, 1973)

Hall, R.H., 'Professionalism and bureaucratisation', in *American Sociology Review* 33 (1968)

Hall, S. and Jefferson, T. (eds), *Resistance Through Rituals* (Hutchinson, 1976)

Hall, S. et al., *Policing the Crisis* (Macmillan, 1978)

Hall, S., *Hard Road to Renewal* (Verso, 1988)

Halloran, J.D., Elliott, P. and Murdock, G., *Demonstrations and Communication: A Case Study* (Penguin, 1970)

Halmos, P., *The Personal Service Society* (Constable, 1970)

Halsall, R. and Cockett, M., *Education and Training 14–19: Chaos or Coherence* (David Fulton, 1996)

Halsey, A.H., Heath, A. and Ridge, J.M., *Origins and Destinations* (Clarendon Press, 1980)

Ham, C., *Health Policy in Britain* (Macmillan, 1994)

Handy, C., *Understanding Organisations* (Penguin, 1989)

Hargreaves, D., Hester, S. and Meller, F.J., *Deviance in Classrooms* (Routledge & Kegan Paul, 1975)

Hargreaves, D., *Social Relations in the Secondary School* (Routledge & Kegan Paul, 1967)

Harris, C. et al., *Redundancy and Recession in South Wales* (Blackwell, 1987)

Harris, J. and Jarvis, P., *Counting to some Purpose* (Methodist Church Home Division, 1979)

Harris, N., *Of Bread and Guns* (Penguin, 1991)

Harrison, M., *Television News: Whose Bias?* (Policy Journals, 1985)

Hart, N., *When Marriage Fails* (Tavistock, 1976)

Hartman, P. and Husband, C., *Racism and the Mass Media* (Davis-Poynter, 1974)

Haskey, J., 'Social class and socio-economic differentials in divorce in England and Wales', in *Population Trends* (HMSO, 1994)

Haskey, J., 'Lone parenthood and demographic changes', in *Population Trends* (HMSO, 1991)

Hayek, F., *Road to Serfdom* (Routledge & Kegan Paul, 1976)

Heald, D., *Democracy and the New International Order* (IPPR, 1993)

Heath, A. and Britten, N., 'Women's jobs do make a difference', in *Sociology* 18 (1984)

Heath, A., Jowell, R. and Curtice, J., *How Britain Votes* (Pergamon Press, 1985)

Hebdidge, D., *Subculture, The Meaning of Style* (Methuen, 1979)

Henderson, P. and Francis, D., *Rural Action* (Pluto, 1993)

Heraud, B.J., *Sociology and Social Work: Perspectives and Problems* (Pergamon Press, 1970)

Hillery, G.A., 'Definitions of community', *Rural Sociology*, 20 (1955)

Hirschi, T., *Causes of Delinquency* (University of California Press, 1969)

Hobbes, T., *Leviathan* (Oxford University Press, 1909)

Hoggart, R., *Uses of Literacy* (Penguin, 1957)

Holdaway, S., *Crime and Deviance* (Collins Educational, 1991)

Hollowell, P., *The Lorry Driver* (Routledge & Kegan Paul, 1968)

Howitt, D., *Mass Media and Social Problems* (Pergamon Press, 1982)

Illich, I., *Deschooling Society* (Penguin, 1973)

Illich, I., *Medical Nemesis* (Marion Boyars, 1975)

Jensen, A., 'How can we boost IQ and scholastic achievement?', in *Harvard Educational Review* 29 (1969)

Johnson, M., 'That was your life', in Canver, V. and Liddiard, P. (eds), *An Ageing Population* (Hodder & Stoughton, 1978)

Johnson, N., *The Welfare State in Transition: The Theory and Practice of Welfare Pluralism* (Harvester Wheatsheaf, 1987)

Johnson, P., *Wake Up Britain: A Latterday Pamphlet* (Weidenfeld & Nicolson, 1994)

Jones, T. and Young, J., 'Crime, police and people', *New Society* (24 January 1986)

Jordan, B., 'Universal welfare provision creates a dependent population – the case against', *Social Studies Review* (P. Allan, November 1989)

Kamata, S., 'Diary of a Human Robot', Sunday Times, 17 April 1983

Katz, E. and Lazarsfeld, P.F., *Personal Influence* (The Free Press, New York, 1955)

Keddie, N., 'Classroom knowledge', in Young, M.F.D., *Tinker, Tailor, the Myth of Cultural Deprivation* (Penguin, 1973)

Kelly, A., 'The missing half: girls and science education', in *British Journal of Sociology of Education* 3 (1981)

Kennedy, I., 'Unmasking medicine' (Reith Lectures, 1980)

Kerr, C. and Siegel, A., 'The inter-industry propensity to strike', in Kornhauser, A. et al. (eds), *Industrial Conflict* (McGraw Hill, New York, 1954)

Kerr, C., *Industrialism and Industrial Man* (Penguin, 1973)

Kiernan, K. and Wicks, M. (eds), *Family Change and Future Policy* (Family Policy Studies Centre, 1990)

Kingdom, J., *Government and Politics in Britain* (Polity Press, 1992)

Klein, J., *Samples from English Cultures* (Routledge & Kegan Paul, 1965)

Knights, D. and Willmott, H. (eds), *Labour Process Theory* (Macmillan, 1986)

Knowles, J.H., *Doing Better and Feeling Worse* (W.W. Norton and Company Inc., New York, 1977)

Kuhn, T.S., 'Scientific paradigms', in Barnes, B., *Sociology of Science* (Penguin, 1972)

Kumar, K., *Prophecy and Progress: The Sociology of Industrial and Post-industrial Society* (Penguin, 1978)

Labov, W., 'The logic of non-standard English', in Young, M.F.D., *Tinker, Tailor, the Myth of Cultural Deprivation* (Penguin, 1973)

Laing, R.D., *The Divided Self* (Penguin, 1960)

Laing, R.D., *The Self and Others* (Penguin, 1971)

Laing, R.D., *The Politics of the Family* (Penguin, 1976)

Laing, R.D. and Esterson, A., *Sanity, Madness and the Family* (Penguin, 1970)

Laing, W., *Laing's Review of Private Health Care* (Laing and Buisson, 1990)

Lane, T. and Roberts, K., *A Strike at Pilkingtons* (Fontana, 1971)

Laurence, P.R. and Lorsch, J., *Organisation and Environment* (Harvard University Press, 1967)

Lawson, T. et al., *Sociology Reviewed* (Collins Educational, 1993)

Lawton, D., *Class, Culture and the Curriculum* (Routledge & Kegan Paul, 1975)

Layton-Henry, Z., *The Politics of Immigration* (Blackwell, 1992)

Le Grand, J., *The Strategy of Equality* (Allen & Unwin, 1982)

Le Grand, J. et al., *Privatisation and the Welfare State* (Unwin Hyman, 1989)

Lea, J. and Young, J., *What is to be Done about Law and Order* (Penguin, 1984)

Leach, E.R., *A Runaway World* (BBC Books, 1967)

Leavis, F.R., *Mass Civilization and Minority Culture* (Minority Press, 1930)

Lee, D. and Newby, H., *Community Studies* (Allen & Unwin, 1968)

Lee, D. and Newby, H., *The Problem of Sociology* (Hutchinson, 1983)

Lees, S., *Losing Out: Sexuality and Adolescent Girls* (Hutchinson, 1986)

Lemert, E.H., *Humans, Their Deviance, Social Problems and Social Control* (Prentice Hall, 2nd edn, 1972)

Leonard, D. and Hood Williams, J., *Families* (Macmillan, 1988)

Lewis, O., *The Children of Sanchez* (Random House, 1961)

Licht, B.G. and Dweck, C.S., 'Sex differences in achievement orientations', in Arnot, M. and Weiner, G., *Gender Under Scrutiny* (Hutchinson, 1987)

Lipset, S.M., Trow, M. and Coleman, J., *Union Democracy* (The Free Press, New York, 1956)

Litwak, E., 'Geographical mobility and extended family cohesion', in *American Sociological Review*, vol. 25 (1960)

Lively, J., *Democracy* (Blackwell, 1975)

Lobban, G., 'Data report of British reading schemes', in *Times Educational Supplement* (1 March 1974)

Lockwood, D., *The Blackcoated Worker* (Allen & Unwin, 1958)

Lukes, S., *Power, A Radical View* (Macmillan, 1974)

Lyon, D., 'Rethinking secularisation', *Review of Religious Research* (1985)

Lyon, D., *Post Modernity* (Open University Press, 1994)

Lyotard, J.F., *The Postmodern Condition* (Manchester University Press, 1984)

MacAnGhail, M., *Young, Gifted and Black* (Open University Press, 1988)

MacFarlane, A., 'Official statistics and women's health', in Roberts, H. (ed.), *Women's Health Counts* (Routledge, 1990)

Machiavelli, N., *The Prince* (Oxford University Press, 1921)

Malinowski, B., *Magic, Science and Religion and Other Essays* (Anchor Books, 1984)

Mangin, W., *Poverty and Politics in Cities of Latin America* (Sage, 1968)

Mann, M., *The Sources of Social Power*, vol. 2 (Cambridge University Press, 1993)

Mann, P.H., *An Approach to Urban Sociology* (Routledge & Kegan Paul, 1970)

Mannheim, K., *Ideology and Utopia* (Routledge & Kegan Paul, 1948)

Manning, N., 'What is a social problem?', in Loney, M., *The State or the Market* (Sage, 1987)

Manning, P., 'Consumption, production and popular culture' in *Sociology Review* (P. Allan, February 1993)

Marcuse, H., *One Dimensional Man* (Abacus, 1972)

Marshall, G., *In Search of the Spirit of Capitalism: Max Weber and the Protestant Ethic Thesis* (Hutchinson, 1982)

Marshall, G. et al., *Social Class in Modern Britain* (Unwin Hyman, 1988)

Marshall, G., 'The Protestant ethic', *Sociology Review* (P. Allan, September 1991)

Marsland, D., 'Universal welfare provision creates a dependent population – the case for', *Social Studies Review* (P. Allan, November 1989)

Martin, D., *A Sociology of English Religion* (Heinemann, 1967)

Martin, D., *The Religious and the Secular* (Routledge & Kegan Paul, 1969)

Martin, D. (1993), cited in Davies, R., 'Disabled by society', *Sociology Review* (April 1994)

Marx, G., 'Religion – opiate or inspiration of civil rights among Negroes', *American Sociological Review* 32 (1967)

Marx, K., *The Critique of Hegel's Philosophy of Law* (Lawrence & Wishart, 1959)

Marx, K., *The Communist Manifesto/Das Kapital* (Penguin, vol. 1 1970)

Marx, K., *The German Ideology* (1845) (Penguin, 1974)

Marx, K. and Engels, F., *The Communist Manifesto* (1848) in McLellan, D. (ed.), *Karl Marx, Selected Writings* (Oxford University Press, 1977)

Matza, D., *Delinquency and Drift* (J. Wiley & Sons, New York, 1964)

Maxwell Atkinson, J., *Discovering Suicide: Studies in the Organisation of Sudden Death* (Macmillan, 1978)

McGrew, A., 'A global society', in Hall, S. et al., *Modernity and its Futures* (Polity Press, 1992)

McKenzie, R.T. and Silver, A., 'The working class Tory in England' in Lipset, S. and Rokkan, S. (eds), *Party Systems and Voter Alignment* (The Free Press, New York, 1967)

McKeown, T., *The Role of Medicine* (Nuffield Provincial Hospitals Trust, 1979)

McNaught, A., *Health Action and Ethnic Minorities* (Bedford Square Press, 1987)

McNeill, P. and Townley, C., *Fundamentals of Sociology* (Hutchinson, 2nd edn, 1986)

McNeill, P., *Research Methods* (Tavistock, 1994)

McRobbie, A. and Garber, J., 'Working-class girls and the culture of femininity', in *Women Take Issue* (Centre for Contemporary Cultural Studies, 1978)

McRobbie, A., 'Jackie, an ideology of adolescent femininity', in Wantella, Whitney and Windall (eds), *Mass Communications Yearbook* (Sage Inc., Beverley Hills, 1983)

Mead, G. H., *Mind, Self and Society* (University of Chicago Press, 1934)

Medhurst, K. and Moyser, G., *Church and Politics in a Secular Age* (Routledge, 1988)

Mednick, S. et al., 'Biology and violence', in Wolfgang, M.E. and Weiner, N.A. (eds), *Criminal Violence* (Sage Publications, 1982)

Merton, R., *Social Theory and Social Structure* (The Free Press, New York, 1968)

Michels, R., *Political Parties* (The Free Press, New York, 1949)

Miles, R., *Racism* (Routledge, 1989)

Milgram, S., *Obedience to Authority* (Tavistock, 1974)

Miliband, R., *The State in Capitalist Society* (Weidenfeld & Nicolson, 1969)

Miliband, R., *Reinventing the Left* (Polity Press, 1994)

Millar, J. and Glendinning, C., *Women and Poverty in Britain* (Harvester Wheatsheaf, 1992)

Miller, W.B., 'Lower Class Culture as a Generating Milieu of Gang Delinquency', *Journal of Social Issues*, vol. 14 (1958)

Millett, K., *Sexual Politics* (Virago, 1969)

Mintzberg, H., *Structure in Fives: Designing Effective Organisations* (Prentice Hall, New Jersey, 1983)

Moir, A. and Jessel, D., *A Mind to Crime* (Michael Joseph, 1995)

Moore, S., *Investigating Deviance* (Collins, 1991)

Morgan, D., 'Gender', in Burgess, R. (ed.), *Key Variables in Social Investigation* (Routledge & Kegan Paul, 1986)

Morgan, D.H.J., 'The family', in Haralambos, M. (ed.), *Developments in Sociology*, vol. 7 (Causeway Press, 1990)

Morgan, M. et al., *Sociological Approaches to Health and Medicine* (Routledge, 1985)

Morley, D., *The Nationwide Audience* (British Film Institute, 1982)

Morris, J.N., 'Inequalities in health', in *The Lancet*, 336 (1990)

Mosca, G., *The Ruling Class* (McGraw Hill, New York, 1939)

Moser, C. and Kalton, J., *Survey Methods in Social Investigation* (Heinemann, 1971)

Moser, K. et al., 'Unemployment and mortality', *British Medical Journal*, 294 (1987)

Murdock, G.P., *Social Structure* (Macmillan, 1949)

Murray, C., *Losing Ground* (Basic Books, New York, 1984)

Murray, C., *The Emerging British Underclass* (IEA Health and Welfare Unit, 1990)

Navarro, V., *Medicine Under Capitalism* (Croom Helm, 1984)

Neibuhr, R. H., *The Social Sources of Denominationalism* (The World Publishing Company, New York, 1929)

Nettleton, S., *The Sociology of Health and Illness* (Polity Press, 1995)

Nicholl, J.P., 'Role of the private sector in elective surgery', *British Medical Journal*, 298 (1989)

Noyce, T. et al., 'Regional variations in the allocation of financial resources to the health service', in *The Lancet*, 1 (1974)

O'Donnell, M., *A New Introduction to Sociology* (Nelson, 3rd edn 1992)

Oakley, A., *Sex, Gender and Society* (Temple Smith, 1972)

Oakley, A., *Housewife* (Allen Lane, 1974)

Oakley, A., *The Sociology of Housework* (Martin Robertson, 1974)

Oakley, A. and MacFarlane, A., *Women Confined: Towards a Sociology of Childbirth* (Martin Robertson, 1980)

Oliver, M., *The Politics of Disablement* (Macmillan, 1990)

Oliver, M., *Understanding Disability* (Macmillan, 1996)

Oppenheim, C., *Poverty: The Facts* (Child Poverty Action Group, 1990)

Ortner, S. B., 'Is female to male as nature is to culture?', in Rosaldo, M. Z. and Lamphere, I. (eds), *Women, Culture and Society* (Stanford University Press, 1974)

Owens, J., 'Politics and unemployment – a return to full employment', *Social Studies Review* (P. Allan, January 1987)

Page, R., 'Social policy', in Haralambos, M., *Developments in Sociology*, vol. 9 (Causeway, 1993)

Pahl, J., *Divisions of Labour* (Blackwell, 1984)

Pahl, J., *Money and Marriage* (Macmillan, 1989)

Pahl, R. *Patterns of Urban Life* (Longman, 1965)

Pahl, R., *Divisions of Labour* (Blackwell, 1984)

Pareto, V., *A Treatise on General Sociology* (ed. A. Livingstone) (Dover Publications, New York, 1963)

Parker, G., *With Due Care and Attention* (Family Policy Studies Centre, 1985)

Parker, S. (ed.), *The Sociology of Industry* (Allen & Unwin, 1972)

Parsons, T., *The Social System* (Routledge & Kegan Paul, 1951)

Parsons, T., *Sociological Theory and Modern Society* (Collier-Macmillan, 1967)

Parsons, T. and Bales, R.F., *Family Socialisation and Interaction Process* (The Free Press, New York, 1955)

Pascall, G., *Social Policy – A Feminist Analysis* (Tavistock, 1986)

Patrick, J., *A Glasgow Gang Observed* (Eyre Methuen, 1973)

Pawson, R., 'Methodology', in Haralambos, M. (ed.), *Developments in Sociology*, vol. 5 (Causeway Press, 1989)

Payne, G., 'Community and community studies', *Sociology Review* (P. Allan, September 1994)

Peak, S. and Fisher, P. (eds), *The Media Guide* (Fourth Estate, published annually)

Pearce, F., *Crimes of the Powerful* (Pluto Press, 1976)

Perelman, L., *School's Out ...* (William Morrow, USA, 1992)

Pinker, R.,*The Idea of Welfare* (Heinemann, 1979)

Plant, R., *Community and Ideology* (Routledge & Kegan Paul, 1974)

Plato, *The Republic* (Dent, 1926)

Player, E., 'Women in crime in the city', in Downes, D., *Crime in the City* (Routledge, 1989)

Polanyi, M., *Personal Knowledge* (University of Chicago Press, 1958)

Pollack, O., *The Criminality of Women* (University of Pennsylvania Press, 1950)

Polsby, N.W., *Community Power and Political Theory* (Yale University Press, 1970)

Polsky, N., *Hustlers, Beats and Others* (Aldine, New York, 1967)

Popay, J. and Jones, G., 'Patterns of health and illness amongst lone parents', *Journal of Social Policy*, 19, 4 (1990)

Popper, K., *The Logic of Scientific Discovery* (Hutchinson, 1959)

Poulantzas, N., 'The problem of the capitalist state', in Urry and Wakeford (eds), *Power in Britain* (Heinemann, 1973)

Provenzo, E., *Video Kids: Making Sense of Nintendo* (Harvard University Press, 1991)

Pugh, D.S. and Hickson, D.J., *Writers on Organisations* (Penguin, 1995)

Pulzer, P., *Political Representation and Elections in Britain* (Allen & Unwin, 1967)

Ramon, S., *Beyond Community Care* (Pluto, 1990)

Redfield, R., *Tepoztlan* (University of Chicago Press, 1930)

Reed, M., *The Sociology of Management* (Harvester Wheatsheaf, 1989)

Reiche, P.L., 'Classroom use of a criminal activities checklist', *Teaching Sociology*, 3 (Sage, 1975)

Reid, I., *Social Class Differences in Modern Britain* (Fontana Press, 3rd edn, 1989)

Rex, J. and Moore, R., *Community and Conflict* (Institute of Race Relations/Oxford University Press, 1967)

Rex, J. and Tomlinson, S., *Colonial Immigrants in a British City* (Routledge & Kegan Paul, 1979)

Rex, R. and Moore, R., *Race, Community and Conflict* (Institute of Race Relations/Oxford University Press, 1967)

Robbins, T. and Anthony, D., 'New religious movements', *Annual Review of Sociology* (1978)

Roberts, H. (ed.), *Women, Health and Reproduction* (Routledge & Kegan Paul, 2nd edn, 1992)

Robertson, K., *Globalization* (Sage, 1992)

Rodinson, M., *Islam and Capitalism* (Penguin, 1977)

Rogers, C., *The Social Psychology of Schooling* (Routledge & Kegan Paul, 1982)

Rosen, H., *Language and Class* (Falling Wall Press, 3rd edn, 1974)

Rosenthal, R. and Jacobson, L., *Pygmalion in the Classroom* (Holt, Rinehart and Winston, Inc., 1968)

Rosser, C. and Harris, C., *The Family and Social Change* (Routledge & Kegan Paul, 1965)

Rostow, W. W., *The Stages of Economic Growth* (Cambridge University Press, 1960)

Rousseau, J., *A Dissertation on the Origin and Foundation of Inequality of Mankind* (1755) (Dent, Everyman's Library, 1952)

Rowntree, B.S., *Poverty: A Study of Town Life* (Macmillan, 1902)

Rowntree, B.S., *Poverty and Progress: A Second Social Survey of York* (Longman, 1941)

Russon, S.A., *Women and the Law: The Uses of Images of Femininity in the Courts* (Research project, City of Birmingham Polytechnic, 1984)

Rutter, M., *Maternal Deprivation Reassessed* (Penguin, 1972)

Rutter, M. et al., *Fifteen Thousand Hours: Secondary Schools and the Effects on Children* (Open Books, 1979)

Sabel, C., *Work and Politics: The Division of Labour in Industry* (Cambridge University Press, 1982)

Sahlins, M.D., *Stone Age Economics* (Tavistock, 1972)

Salaman, G., *Work Organisations: Resistance and Control* (Longman, 1979)

Saunders, P., *Social Class and Stratification* (Routledge, 1990)

de Saussure, F., *Course in General Linguistics* (Fontana, 1974)

Scheff, T., *Being Mentally Ill* (Aldine, Chicago, 1966)

Schlesinger, P., *Putting Reality Together: BBC News* (Constable, 1985)

Schofield, M., *The Sexual Behaviour of Young People* (Penguin, 1972)

Schutz, A., *The Phenomenology of the Social World* (Heinemann, 1972; first published 1932)

Scott, J., 'The British upper class', in Coates, D. et al., *A Socialist Anatomy of Britain* (Polity Press, 1985)

Scott, R., 'Professionals in bureaucracies: areas of conflict', in Volmer, H.M. and Mills, D.M. (eds), *Professionalism* (Prentice Hall, 1966)

Scraton, D. et al., *Law, Order and the Authoritarian State* (Open University Press, 1987)

Scruton, R., *Sexual Desires: A Philosophical Investigation* (Phoenix, 1986)

Seabrook, J., *The Neighbourhood* (Pluto, 1984)

Seers, D., 'The meaning of development', in Lekmann, D. (ed.), *Development Theory* (Frank Cass, 1979)

Selfe, P., *Work Out Sociology* (Macmillan, 1993)

Selznick, P., *TVA and the Grass Roots* (Harper Torch Books, New York, 1949)

Sewell, T.A., *Black Tribunes: Black Political Participation in Britain* (Lawrence & Wishart, 1993)

Shaw, C. and McKay, H., *Juvenile Delinquency and Urban Areas* (University of Chicago Press, 1942)

Shiner, L., *The Concept of Secularisation in Empirical Research* (Penguin, 1971)

Silverman, D., *The Theory of Organisations* (Heinemann, 1970)

Simmel, G., 'The metropolis and mental life', in Wolff, K. (ed.), *The Sociology of George Simmel* (The Free Press, New York, 1950)

Simmel, G., *Conflict and the Loss of Group Affiliation* (The Free Press, 1995)

Simpkin, M., *Trapped Within Welfare* (Macmillan, 1979)

Sklair, S., *Sociology of the Global System* (Harvester Wheatsheaf, 1991)

Skull, A., *Decarceration: Community Treatment and the Deviant – A Radical View* (Polity Press, 1985)

Sly, F., 'Ethnic groups and the labour market', in *Employment Gazette* (HMSO, 1994)

Smelser, N., *Social Change in the Industrial Revolution* (Routledge & Kegan Paul, 1959)

Smith, A., *The Wealth of Nations* (J.M. Dent, 1910)

Smith, C., *Work, Employment and Society* (Routledge, 1989)

Sorokin, P., *Sociological Theories of Today* (The Free Press, New York, 1966)

Spender, D., *Invisible Women: The Schooling Scandal* (Women's Press, 1983)

Stacey, M. et al., *Tradition and Change: A Study of Banbury* (Oxford University Press, 1956)

Stacey, M., 'The myth of community studies', *British Journal of Sociology*, 20, 2 (1969)

Stansworth, P. and Giddens, A., *Elites and Power in British Society* (Cambridge University Press, 1974)

Stanworth, M., *Gender and Schooling* (Hutchinson, 1983)

Stanworth, M., 'Women and social class analysis: a reply to Goldthorpe', in *Sociology* 18 (1984)

Strinati, D., *Popular Culture* (Routledge, 1995)

Sudnow, D., *Passing On* (Prentice Hall, Englewood Cliffs, 1967)

Sutherland, E. H. and Cressey, D. R., *Criminology* (J.B. Lippincott Co., Philadelphia, 10th edn, 1978)

Szasz, T., *The Myth of Mental Illness* (Hoeber-Harper, New York, 1961)

Taylor, F.W., *Scientific Management* (Harper & Row, 1947)

Taylor, G. et al., *A Tale of Two Cities* (Routledge, 1996)

Taylor, I., Walton, F. and Young, J., *The New Criminology* (Routledge & Kegan Paul, 1973)

Taylor, L., *In the Underworld* (Unwin Paperbacks, 1984)

Tester, K., 'The shopping mall', in Haralambos, M. (ed.), *Developments in Sociology* (Causeway Press, 1995)

Thackrah, R., *Policing the Nineties. In Whose Interest?* (Pavis Publications, 1994)

Thompson, I., *Religion* (Longman, 1986)

Thompson, J.D., *Organisations in Action* (McGraw Hill, New York, 1967)

Thorne, B., *Feminist Rethinking of the Family: An Overview* (Longman, New York, 1982)

Titmuss, R.M., *Commitments to Welfare* (Allen & Unwin, 1968)

Tomlinson, S., *Ethnic Minorities in British Schools* (Heinemann, 1983)

Tonnies, F., *Community and Association* (Routledge & Kegan Paul, 1955)

Townsend, P., *Poverty in the United Kingdom* (Penguin, 1979)

Townsend, P. and Abel-Smith, B., *The Poor and the Poorest* (G. Bell & Sons, 1965)

Townsend, P. and Davidson, N., 'The Black Report', in Townsend, P., Davidson, N. and Whitehead, M. (eds), *Inequalities in Health* (Penguin, 1982)

Townsend, P. et al., *Health and Deprivation: Inequality and the North* (Croom Helm, 1987)

Townsend, P., Corrigan, P. and Kowarzik, U., *Poverty and Labour in London* (Low Pay Unit, 1987)

Troeltsch, E., *The Social Teachings of the Christian Churches* (1931) (University of Chicago Press, 1981)

Trowler, P., *Active Sociology* (Bell and Hyman, 1987)

Troyna, B., *Public Awareness and the Media: A Study of Reporting Race* (Commission for Racial Equality, 1981)

Tuchman, G., *The Symbolic Annihilation of Women in the Media* (Oxford University Press, 1977)

Tuchman, G. et al., *Hearth and Home: Images of Women in the Media* (Oxford University Press, 1978)

Tuckett, D., *Meetings Between Experts* (Tavistock, 1985)

Tunstall, J., *The Fishermen* (Routledge & Kegan Paul, 1965)

Turner, R.H., 'Sponsored and contest mobility and the school system', in *American Sociological Review*, vol. 25 (1960)

Urry, J. and Wakeford, J. (eds), *Power in Britain* (Heinemann, 1968)

Volmer, K. and Mills, C.W., *Professionalisation* (Prentice Hall, Englewood Cliffs, 1966)

Voysey, M., *A Constant Burden* (Routledge & Kegan Paul, 1975)

Wadsworth, M. et al., *Health and Sickness* (Tavistock, 1971)

Walker, A., 'Community care: from consensus to conflict', in Bornat, J. et al. (eds), *Community Care: A Reader* (Macmillan, 1993)

Wallerstein, I., 'Culture is a world system', in Featherstone, M. (ed.), *Global Culture* (Sage, 1990)

Walliman, I. et al., 'Misreading Weber ...', *Sociology*, vol. 14, no. 2 (1980)

Wallis, R., 'The sociology of new religions', *Social Studies Review* (P. Allan, September 1985)

Walsh, P. et al., 'Gender and voting', *Sociology Review* (P. Allan, November 1991)

Warren, B., *Imperialism* (Verso, 1989)

Weber, M., 'Bureaucracy', in Gerth, H.H. and Mills, C.W. (eds), *From Max Weber* (Routledge & Kegan Paul, 1948)

Weber, M., *The Protestant Ethic and the Spirit of Capitalism* (Charles Scribner's Sons, New York, 1958)

Weber, M., *Economy and Society: An Outline of Interpretive Sociology* (University of California Press, 1978)

Weiner, G. (ed.), *Just a Bunch of Girls* (Hutchinson, 1988)

West, D.J. and Farrington, D.P., *Who Becomes Delinquent?* (Heinemann, 1973)

Westergaard, J. and Resler, H., *Class in Capitalist Society* (Penguin, 1975)

White, D.M., 'The gatekeeper: a case study in the selection of news', in *Journalism Quarterly*, 27 (1950)

White, D., *Families* (Falmer, 1992)

Whitehead, M., 'The health divide', in Townsend, P. et al., *Inequalities in Health* (Penguin, 1982)

Wilby, P., 'Habermas and the language of the modern states', *New Society* (22 March 1979)

Wilensky, H.L., 'Work, careers and social integration', in Burns, T. (ed.), *Industrial Man* (Penguin, 1969)

Wilensky, H.L., *The Welfare State and Equality* (University of California Press, 1975)

Wilkins, L., *Social Deviance* (Tavistock, 1964)

Wilkinson, H., *No Turning Back, Generations and Genderquake* (Demos, 1994)

Williams, J. et al., *Hooligans Abroad* (Routledge & Kegan Paul, 1984)

Williams, R., *Keywords: A Vocabulary of Culture and Society* (Fontana, 1984)

Williamson, J., *Decoding Advertisements* (Boyars, 1978)

Willis, P., *Learning to Labour* (Saxon House, 1977)

Willmott, P., 'Urban kinship past and present', *Social Studies Review* (P. Allan, November 1988)

Willmott, P. and Thomas, D., *Community in Social Policy* (Policy Studies Institute, 1984)

Willmott, P. and Young, M., *Family and Class in a London Suburb* (Routledge & Kegan Paul, 1960)

Willmott, P. and Young, M., *The Symmetrical Family* (Institute for Community Studies, 1975)

Wilson, B., *Religion in a Secular Society* (C.A. Watts, London, 1966)

Wilson, B., 'The Anglican Church and its decline', *New Society* (5 December 1974)

Wilson, J.Q., *Thinking about Crime* (Random House, 1977)

Wing, J.K. and Brown, G.W., *Institutionalism and Schizophrenia* (Cambridge University Press, 1970)

Winkler, K., 'Consumerism in health care: beyond the supermarket model', *Policy and Politics*, 15, 1 (1987)

Wirth, L., 'Urbanisation as a way of life', *American Journal of Sociology*, 44 (1938)

Wolf, N., *The Beauty Myth* (Vintage, 1990)

Wollstonecraft, M., *A Vindication of Women's Rights* (1972)

Wood, S., *The Degradation of Work, Skill, Deskilling and the Labour Process* (Hutchinson, 1982)

Wootton, B., *Social Science and Social Pathology* (Allen & Unwin, 1959)

Worsley, P., *New Introductory Sociology* (Penguin, 1990)

Wright, E.O., *Class, Crisis and the State* (New Left Books, 1978)

Wright Mills, C., *The Power Elite* (Oxford University Press, 1956)

Wright Mills, C., *The Sociological Imagination* (Penguin, 1970)

Young, J., 'The role of the police as amplifiers of deviancy, negotiators of reality and translators of fantasy' in Cohen, S. (ed.), *Images of Deviancy* (Penguin, 1971)

Young, M. and Willmott, P., *Family and Kinship in East London* (Routledge & Kegan Paul, 1957)

Young, M. and Willmott, P., *Family and Class in a London Suburb* (New English Library, 1971)

Young, M. et al., *Knowledge and Control* (Macmillan, 1971)

Young, M. and Willmott, P., *The Symmetrical Family* (Penguin, 1975)

Zimblast, A. (ed.), *Case Studies on the Labour Process* (Monthly Review Press, 1979)

Zola, I., 'Medicine as an institution of social control', *The Sociological Review*, 20, 4 (1972)

Zweig, F., *The Worker in an Affluent Society* (Heinemann, 1961)

Index